Barcode in Back

MW01122026

1

Reading Carol Bolt

edited by
Cynthia Zimmerman

Playwrights Canada Press
Toronto • Canada

PLAYWRIGHTS CANADA PRESS
The Canadian Drama Publisher
215 Spadina Ave., Suite 230, Toronto, ON Canada M5T 2C7
phone 416.703.0013   fax 416.408.3402
orders@playwrightscanada.com • www.playwrightscanada.com

The publisher acknowledges the support of the Canadian taxpayers through
the Government of Canada Book Publishing Industry Development Program,
the Canada Council for the Arts, the Ontario Arts Council,
and the Ontario Media Development Corporation.

Cover photo by Norm Betts – *Sunday Sun.* 11 August 1974
Typesetting: JLArt
Cover Design: JLArt with C. Zimmerman

Library and Archives Canada Cataloguing in Publication

Bolt, Carol, 1941–2000
Reading Carol Bolt / by Carol Bolt ; edited by Cynthia Zimmerman. -- 1st ed.

Plays.
ISBN 978-0-88754-807-9

I. Zimmerman, Cynthia   II. Title.

PS8553.O48R38 2009   C812'.54   C2009-905615-1

First Edition: August 2010
Printed and bound in Canada by Hignell Book Printing, Winnipeg.

Dedicated to Carol Bolt's family,
especially David, Alex, Stephanie, Charlie, and Clare.

TABLE of CONTENTS

Preface

Carol Bolt: 1941–2000

A reading of Carol Bolt's new satire, *Lives of the Poets*, was scheduled for Monday, December 11, 2000, at University of Toronto's Hart House Theatre. The reading, arranged by the Graduate Centre for the Study of Drama, was keenly anticipated. Suddenly the event was cancelled and the venue changed. Instead, the Factory Theatre held a public memorial. This well-loved woman, Carol Bolt, prolific playwright and proud theatre advocate, had died of liver cancer at the age of fifty-nine.

"A Tribute to Carol Bolt: In Celebration of her Life" was organized by Factory Theatre's artistic director, Ken Gass, friend and past Playwrights Union president Paul Ledoux, Carol Bolt's husband David, and others. I remember the lobby full of quickly collected posters, video clips, and memorabilia. There were photos of Bolt onstage, photos and selected quotations by her in the program. The house was full and attentive as fellow artists paid their respects, remembered her, honoured her. There were brief speeches, excerpts read from several plays, letters and tributes read by Nancy Beatty. The tributes and letters were particularly poignant. They reminded us of Bolt's engaging personality, her humour, her dedication; they acknowledged her generous contributions and her significant role in this whole enterprise called Canadian theatre. And because Bolt hated being bored in the theatre, the organizers made sure she would not have been. They brought it in at fifty-four minutes.

Carol Bolt was a tireless advocate, a great mentor, a tough-minded head of endless committees and caucuses, a wonderful playwright, and a bighearted, genuine buddy. She would be sorely missed. We all knew that. I did not know then, but I do know now, that ten years later many would feel insufficient attention had been paid. This collection of her works, her words, and laudatory statements about her is brought to you (and to future readers) as testimonial. This woman, Carol Bolt, deserves our applause.

The work on this book began when Angela Rebeiro was publisher of Playwrights Canada Press. I am indebted to her for her encouragement, commitment, and sage advice. She believed that this anthology should celebrate not only Bolt's playwriting, but also her arts advocacy, pioneering efforts, and central role in the founding and shepherding of many established arts organizations. Many remain crucial to the theatre community to this day, particularly Playwrights Canada Press and the Playwrights Guild of Canada, but also others. This idea determined the shape of *Reading Carol Bolt*. The first section is comprised of all of Bolt's major plays, several plays for young audiences, and a sample from what I think is her best writing for radio. In the Afterword section, four fellow playwrights tell of her enduring importance to them as individuals, and as members of the Canadian theatre community.

It is a pleasure to thank Angela Rebeiro, David Bolt, Annie Gibson, and Jodi Armstrong. Without their support this project would simply not have happened. I also wish to thank some of the many others who gave an assist along the way: I owe thanks to Keith Hart and Roy Harris of CBC Radio Archives; Théo Martin and Dan Somers, Reference Archivists at Library and Archives Canada (where the Carol Bolt fonds are housed); Bev Buckie, Reference Archivist at Guelph McLaughlin Archives; and Tim Borlase of the Labrador Creative Arts Festival. Bolt's family and friends were most generous, sharing information and fond memories: Alex Bolt, Dave Carley, Sally Clark, John Coulbourn, Ken Gass, Lynda Hill, Martin Kinch, Glenda MacFarlane, Richard Rose, and Larry Zacharko. To this list must be added those whose thoughts are included in Afterwords: Rex Deverell, Florence Gibson, Claudia Dey (who dedicated *The Gwendolyn Poems* to her mentor, Carol Bolt), and Paul Ledoux.

Finally, I must give special thanks to my research assistants, Jason Buccheri, who helped gather information at the start, and Jessica Huber, my indefatigable graduate research assistant who saw the project to its end and never seemed to tire of ferreting out another biographical detail. Her persistence as a research worker and her commitment to Carol Bolt's legacy were a delight.

Rereading Carol Bolt

The point is that biography is not just about the subject. It is about all of us.

Every life has a great deal to do with timing, but particularly the artistic life.

—Rosemary Sullivan "Writing Lives"

Carol Bolt's story begins in Winnipeg. Born Carol Johnson on 25 August 1941, she was the only child of a school teacher/librarian and a miner/logger. Her father's family came from the north of Sweden. He was a rough-edged labouring man and union agitator. Carol said he was a pioneer of sorts "who did a lot of things but mostly went off into the bush and chopped down trees" (James 17). Her mother was descended from United Empire Loyalist English "gentle folk." An odd marriage perhaps, says David Bolt, but the combination produced Carol. What the family shared was involvement in amateur theatre.

She spent her early years in various mining towns across the country: Wandago Mines, Ontario; McReary, Manitoba; Pioneer and Hudson Hope, British Columbia; to name a few. The family settled in Vancouver long enough for Carol to get her BA in English Literature from UBC, graduating in 1961. She then lived in England for a while before returning to Canada. In 1963, while working as a market researcher in Montreal, she and a few friends started a small theatre, The Wesley Players, on St. Luc Street. It closed soon after when it failed to meet fire regulations. She moved to Toronto in 1964 and started to work as a prop-maker and stage manager. While stage managing for an amateur production of Christopher Fry's *The Lady's Not for Burning,* she met actor David Bolt. They married in 1969 and had one child, Alex. Apparently, when Alex was an infant, his mother would bring him to rehearsals in a cardboard box. Martin Kinch says baby Alex was considered the Toronto Free Theatre mascot.

Although Bolt had written plays as an undergraduate, had a trio of one-acts (*One Plus One Plus One*) produced by an amateur group at the Toronto Central Library in 1966, and had the play *Daganawida* produced by George Luscombe at Toronto Workshop Productions in 1970, her career as a professional playwright did not really begin until a few years later. It began with *Buffalo Jump.*

Buffalo Jump started out as *Next Year Country,* a documentary revue on the Great Depression. Commissioned by Ken Kramer of Regina's Globe Theatre, it was staged in 1971. The following year Carol reworked it with Theatre Passe Muraille and Paul Thompson. The new title, *Buffalo Jump,* made a direct parallel between the Plains Indians's method of hunting buffalo, by stampeding them over a cliff, and the treatment of the desperate unemployed by the Conservative government of R.B. Bennett. Both versions of the play were based on an actual event, the On-to-Ottawa-Trek of 1935 when some two thousand unemployed men, mostly single, staged strikes in the relief camps in British Columbia and then crossed the country in search of justice. *Next Year Country* was closely documentary; *Buffalo Jump* was more theatrical and entertaining—less concerned with "faithfulness to history and its factual base" (Zimmerman, *Playwriting*, 35). According to Bolt,

> Paul Thompson turned it into a circus. We had a huge cast and wonderful cartoon sets by John Boyle. There were songs and dances and funny stories and we didn't really go deeply into the politics of the event. It was more of a comic strip, perhaps not so much as my later play about Duplessis, *Maurice*, but it was very episodic and highly coloured.
>
> In [*Buffalo Jump*] we had one show-stopping number after another. (Lister, 147, 152)

Buffalo Jump mixes actual data with fictional vignettes; songs, mime, and political cartoons with marches and speeches; and comic incidents with serious political concerns. The leader of the strikers, Red Evans (modelled on the historical figures Red Walsh and Slim Evans), is an ideal working-class hero: dedicated, articulate, and brave, but also fun-loving and unpredictable. Set against the unyielding bullish figure of R.B. Bennett, Evans and Bennett summarize the essential conflict: the idealistic struggle for social justice defeated by blind, contemptuous authority.

Except for the concluding scenes of the play—specifically, the bleak ending—Bolt plays down the real desperation of the situation. Her aim was epic and romance: to transform the journey into a mythic quest undertaken by larger-than-life characters. As she put it,

> Myth is more appealing than fact. It postulates that heroism is possible, that people can be noble and effective and change things. Maybe that's why I'm interested in myth. I think that what we were doing in *Buffalo Jump* was making those characters tragic heroes. (Souchotte, 8)

The central characters of the Bolt plays which followed, *Gabe* (February 1973) and *Red Emma* (February 1974), also believe that "heroism is possible," that noble individual actions can change things. But both these plays will be more serious treatments of the social issues they introduce.

The Passe Muraille production of *Buffalo Jump* was very much a collective creation. The conversion from *Next Year Country* to *Buffalo Jump* meant an almost total re-invention, with actors improvising new scenes and Bolt writing from the improvisations. According to Bolt, she had come in with a scenario but the script details were done on the spot. Using the actors as creative resources, as writers as well as performers, was the *modus vivendi* of the Passe Muraille collectives. Although Bolt was the writer on another Passe Muraille collective, *Pauline* (March 1973), she came to want more artistic control. Her subsequent plays, *Gabe* and *Red Emma*, would be produced by Toronto Free Theatre, which Bolt came to feel was her "spiritual home": "Those plays were written for a company too and had a sensibility that everyone involved in the theatre understood" (Rudakoff, 178).

The "sensibility" Bolt refers to is the sensibility of the times. When *Buffalo Jump* was playing at Toronto's Theatre Passe Muraille in 1972, alternate theatre was in the middle of its golden years. The 1971–72 season in Toronto saw some fifty productions of original Canadian plays and the first real hits. That was the season of Herschel Hardin's *Esker Mike and His Wife, Agiluk*; George F. Walker's *Bagdad Saloon* at the Factory Theatre Lab; the collectives *The Doukhobors*, *The Farm Show* and *1837: The Farmer's Revolt*, all directed by Paul Thompson at Theatre Passe Muraille; David Freeman's *Creeps* and David French's *Leaving Home* at the Tarragon; John Palmer's *The End* and Kinch's *Me?* at the Toronto Free, to name a few. The artists were part of an unprecedented situation in the history of English-Canadian theatre; indigenous Canadian theatre was finally happening:

> Whatever their initial impulses, the alternative theatres found themselves in the forefront of a popular nationalist movement. In the theatre the issues of post-colonial cultural independence were particularly visible and, deliberately, or not, theatres forced into a nationalist posture by the lack of good Canadian plays and the apparent preference for British plays and directors in the regional theatres found themselves typed as radical. (Filewod, 20)

According to Martin Kinch, one of the founders of the Toronto Free Theatre, "we were in the right place at the right time. We had a centre, and a purpose":

> As a group, it possessed within itself ideal conditions for fostering a new theatre: communality of interest in essentially dramatic issues, strong desire for live experience and a corresponding distrust of artifice and the synthetic…, a need to "come together," and a deep alienation from official culture. And culturally, this group in Canada was severely disenfranchised. One could not ask for better conditions. (Kinch, 5)

Kinch said it was a good time for directors: lacking established playwrights and set scripts, directors were at the centre of the play-making process. For the same reason it was an unusual opportunity for actors, a time when they could be intimately involved in the process of a new play's creation and development. It was a wonderful time for emerging playwrights, especially writers like Carol Bolt for whom a lively and supportive environment committed to producing together seemed to charge her own creative energies. All of this was possible, in good measure, because this was the time of the Local Initiatives Program (LIP) and Opportunities for Youth (OFY) grants. Since grant size was determined by the number of employees, Bolt could write a play like *Buffalo Jump* with thirteen characters and have the kind of time a collective creation needed. Because rehearsal period was not limited to three weeks, one could take the time to develop a new script, improvise, rewrite, and revise. It was out of this kind of collective commitment that the Passe Muraille production of *Buffalo Jump* emerged.

> I can't forget what it was like when the theatre first started here, when we had the institutionalized employment of LIP grants. The LIP program was set up to provide employment so we were encouraged to write great,

sprawling epics with huge casts because then you could employ more people. It's easier to write great, sprawling epics with huge casts because every time the action bogs down you can bring on another troop of dancing girls.... (Zimmerman, *Work*, 273)

Buffalo Jump initiated a period of incredible productivity for Bolt. In fact, Urjo Kareda wrote in 1974,

When, decades hence, "The Collected Works of Carol Bolt" come to be assembled, the volumes will probably be measured by the running mile.

This is an exceptionally prolific playwright; three of her works have already been seen in Toronto this month and a fourth, *Maurice*, has just opened. (Kareda "New Political Play...")

For the next couple of years, her productivity was indeed amazing. The same year as *Buffalo Jump*, she had two productions at Young People's Theatre (*My Best Friend is Twelve Feet High* in July 1972, and *Cyclone Jack* the following November); in 1973, *Gabe* was at the Toronto Free Theatre in February, *Pauline* at Passe Muraille in March, and *Tangleflags* at Young People's Theatre in September. In 1974 there was *Red Emma* in February (Toronto Free Theatre), *The Bluebird* the same month (St. Lawrence Centre), followed by *Maurice* (Young People's Theatre), *Blue* (Young People's Theatre), and *Shelter* (Firehall Theatre). There is an anecdote about Bolt's tenacious determination and resourcefulness: in the midst of mayhem, when things were not going smoothly and the situation was getting very tense, Bolt would go wash her hair and then return rejuvenated, ready for another round of revisions. She said washing her hair helped her think.

Between 1970 and 1975 Bolt also wrote a number of plays for children. During this period she was affiliated with Young People's Theatre and worked in close collaboration with her director, either Ray Whelan or Tim Bond. These plays—*Cyclone Jack*, *Tangleflags*, *Maurice*, and *Finding Bumble* (1975), among others—also explore Canadian history. For example, *Cyclone Jack* presents the life story, including the final humiliation, of the Indian marathon runner, Tom Longboat. Presenting social issues relevant for young people, *Tangleflags* encourages tolerance for different nationalities; in *Finding Bumble*, according to the brochure, "A film star and an ex-astronaut help their young audience choose a course for a world with limited resources but unlimited creative potential." The plays contain the Bolt medley: song and dance numbers, rapid scene changes, fast-paced action, mime, parade, and Canadian content in a lively and engaging combination. Her writing for Young People's Theatre was very much "of a piece" with the writing she was doing for adults. Moreover, both stages were providing the kind of encouraging atmosphere in which she thrived:

Tim Bond and I both wanted to do very high-tech kinds of kids' shows, working within the extreme limits of the form where you had to pack everything into a Volkswagen bus, perform on the floor of a high-school gym, without any lighting. We wanted to do a show-business

> experience…. I think the sense of freedom probably came as much from
> LIP grants… as anything else. (Zimmerman, *Playwriting*, 43)

Gabe was on at the Toronto Free in February 1973, one year after *Buffalo Jump* at Passe Muraille. In *Gabe*, as in *Buffalo Jump*, myth-making is central to plot and characterization. Two contemporary small-town Saskatchewan Métis, Gabriel and Louis, have idealized their namesakes: Louis Riel, who led the rebellion in 1885, and his general, Gabriel Dumont. Gabriel and Louis are just out of jail and on parole. Abject and aimless drifters, they want to make something important happen, as did their forefathers. But all they manage is to talk about it. Louis is back in jail before the play ends and Gabe, despairing of meaningful support, goes back into the bush alone, hopefully to rediscover his own native resources. Gabe has found some self-respect and his pride. A dreamer, he is not yet able to take significant action or take charge of his destiny.

With *Red Emma*, Bolt creates an even more complicated idealist; she also writes her first stage hit. The original production of *Red Emma* met with wide critical acclaim. First staged in 1974 at the Toronto Free Theatre, directed by Martin Kinch, it would be televised on CBC and, years later, become an opera commissioned by the Canadian Opera Company (through their Composer-in-Residence program). Gary Kulesha, who wrote the music for the opera while Bolt did the libretto, said *Red Emma* was a "natural" for opera with its enlarged characters, its portrait of the early years of the volatile Russian anarchist movement, and its fiery, charismatic young woman at the centre. As Urjo Kareda wrote, "*Emma* beautifully suggests the almost dangerous urgency of feelings within the heart of anarchy" and "the kind of passionate, fierce, honest, and determined woman who is drawn to anarchy as a source of emotional expression" (Anon "Queen," 13). Bolt herself was very clear about what she wanted:

> I wanted that play to be a homage to her personality, not to the struggle
> for an eight-hour workday, which was the main political issue she was
> involved in at that age. She fell in love with different people on page 1,
> 3, and 5 of her autobiography, and that was what mattered. (Lister, 150)

Bolt is not simply retelling history. Rather, she is giving us her Emma's very romantic and enlarged view of herself.

Red Emma has as its source the real life of the Russian-born immigrant Emma Goldman (1869–1940) who arrived in North America in 1885. The link to Canada, a minor one, is that in 1939, when several of her Italian friends were arrested for having subversive literature in their possession, she came to Toronto where she died of a stroke in February 1940. The play was written on Martin Kinch's suggestion, after he had discovered Goldman's autobiography. Reminiscing recently about the experience with Bolt, that is, his directing of *Red Emma*, he recalled her ability to quickly grasp and deliver what was at the heart of each scene, how rapidly she wrote, how clear she was about what she wanted, and how she was always in rehearsal, constantly rewriting. Bolt just loved rehearsals; they were the best part, she said: "I have seen [my plays] grow so much in rehearsal… that's a time I really look forward to. I take what I have into rehearsal and then it becomes a different thing!" (CBC Radio: "Authors").

Kinch said Bolt was writing for the Toronto Free company and to the strengths of particular actors: Chapelle Jaffe as Emma, David Bolt as Johann Most, the aging theorist of the movement, Nick Mancuso as Emma's lover, Alexander Berkman. He added that he believed the production gained something special by their working together: that Bolt was writing about "coming into your own" as a woman and as a political being in a sexist society. He was directing a play about an anarchist culture and its apotheosis in a significant terrorist act. The result was that *Red Emma* was splendidly and boldly both those things. Bolt dedicated the publication of *Red Emma* "[T]o M.K.: The finest mind in Canadian Theatre."

The plot of *Red Emma* centres on the early years, five years after Emma's arrival in New York in 1890. It tells of her meeting with anarchist comrades—most young fellow émigrés, but also Johann Most—and of the assassination attempt on the life of the industrialist, Henry Clay Frick. This act leads to the trial and imprisonment of Emma's lover, Alexander Berkman. The play is clearly political in its subject matter: the activities of a famous young anarchist, union fighter, and suffragette. However, since Bolt was herself more interested in the drama of Goldman's life than in her politics, the motivating force of the play is again that of romantic idealism.

> The people I'm interested in writing about, with the significant exception of those in *One Night Stand*, want to change the world. I'm really interested in the psychology of that attitude.
>
> I wish it were possible to change the world, but what I see when I look at the characters, Emma Goldman, for example, is not a "Hardy Boy" kind of character who can isolate what's wrong and then fix it. I see a complex woman who goes beyond what is reasonable in her quest. All my seekers have a flaw, like… Emma's romanticism. (Rudakoff, 181)

Bolt's Emma is an irrepressible idealist, an energetic and flamboyant romantic whose passionate intensity in love and politics entangles her, and others, in a series of adventures. Her peers find her zealousness and urgency contagious; her hopefulness, her ardent belief in "freedom, the right to self-expression. Everyone's right to beautiful, radiant things" (207) is the engaging stuff of young dreams. Her capacity for being joyously in love, an idealizing tendency (whether the target is the movement or an individual), inspires her high-minded phrases, charges her daring adventures, and, despite setbacks, lets her continue to believe that "dreamers can build castles" (207). However, *Red Emma* is not only about political naïveté and youthful enthusiasm; it is also a play about personal growth. Initially prepared to recite lines Most wrote for her, to surrender to authority within the movement while refusing its validity in the outside world, Emma moves to an independent position and a feminist perspective. She becomes a true revolutionary spirit.

Although Bolt scripted *Red Emma* herself, the play bears the imprint of the collective-creation process: quick scene shifts; marches, speeches, and direct audience address; realistic character portrayals alongside stereotypes and caricatures; minimal props and a large cast of characters. Significantly, *Red Emma* is Bolt's first play with a strong, fully-developed central character, her first with a female protagonist. But after *Red Emma*, she moved away from reinterpreting historical material. Written the same year as *Red Emma*, *Shelter: a Comedy* (November 1975) represents a new direction in her work. It is pure fiction, set in the present, includes no music, and best suits a realistic production style.

As a woman and as a politically conscious woman who considered herself a feminist, Bolt was well aware of women's issues long before they started to appear in her plays. Emma Goldman is her first woman character who grows to embody feminist ideals. *Shelter* brings on stage an all-female cast. This was a deliberate strategy. As Bolt said, "The women in *Buffalo Jump* and *Gabe* were paper thin and not very interesting and I was avoiding use of my own insights.... So I began quite consciously to create characters who were closer to me: women, or people who don't have those historical personae draped around them...." She became interested, she said, in "how women relate to each other" and how women's identity "depended upon their association with men... [the] Eva Peron Syndrome" (Zimmerman, *Playwriting*, 43). Bolt was criticized by some feminists who did not like how the women were portrayed, their evident flaws. "I don't like writing plays about gods and goddesses," Bolt retorted (Lister, 152).

But no one could argue with her next play, *One Night Stand*—it was not only a smash hit, it was a brilliant piece of theatre! *One Night Stand* marked a watershed. The circumstances of the early seventies had given Bolt the freedom to experiment with form, to play with styles and ideas. What Kinch calls the themes of the sixties—the concern for individual freedom, the yearning for community, plus the nationalist desire to rewrite Canadian history—are all characteristic of her early work. Specifically, the creating of community, often by a group organizing to effect social change, and the leader's role in this, is central to *Buffalo Jump, Gabe, Red Emma,* and *Shelter*. The importance of a team effort also describes Bolt's creative method at this point. Her own approach to the making of theatre was intensely collaborative. However, when the economic climate changed, there was less time for "play." So, at the same time as the theatres were experiencing an abrupt austerity, Bolt was moving into smaller cast plays.

The mid-seventies slump in the Canadian economy began a period of recession and retrenchment for the alternative theatres. The OFY and LIP grants were among the first to be eliminated; Canada Council funds were frozen, with no regard for spiralling inflation and the increased number of grant applications. The consequence for the struggling alternative theatres (many of which had overextended themselves during the affluent early seventies) was serious retrenchment. Naturally, the financial problems of the theatres influenced what kind of plays could be written. There was no point writing a play that theatres could not afford to produce. An inexpensive two-hander like *One Night Stand* (1977) was perfect.

One Night Stand has proved Bolt's most popular and most commercial adult piece. The spare comedy-thriller has received over a hundred productions since its opening. A finalist for the 1977 Chalmers Award, its film version—the CBC adaptation which used the same lead actors, directed by Allan King and Eric Steiner—won four Canadian film awards in 1978, including the award for best TV drama. Bolt claimed that its success is mainly due to its being a popular genre, that people like it when they know what to expect. But John Fraser, who said "It's a real winner," talked about its "shocking conclusion that has been carefully and meticulously mapped out" ("*One Night Stand*"). Martin Knelman wrote that the film version is a "rarity—a work of intelligence and feeling that is also a slick and gripping piece of mass entertainment" ("One Night Standout," 10).

With *One Night Stand* Bolt had deliberately set out to write a thriller. It was a technical exercise in structure. For her, the hide-a-bed sofa, and how to use it, became a particular focus: "The writing of *One Night Stand* was in one way the result of trying to work out how the body got into the hide-a-bed sofa." She added the character Sharon to the program "so that people looking at the program could say, oh well, Daisy's going to get rescued; this person, Sharon, is going to show up and everything will be all right" (Zimmerman, *Playwriting*, 48–49).

Disconsolate because neither her married lover nor her best friend arrives for her birthday celebration, Daisy heads for a downtown bar to pick up a quick good time. When the play begins she is opening the door to her fancy high-rise apartment; with her is Rafe, an appealing drifter who is carrying a knapsack and a guitar case. Thus begins another Bolt adventure.

At one point Bolt said she thought the play was really about loneliness and vulnerability. Her characters are both lonely and feeling stranded. Daisy's situation is essentially temporary: a lively, straightforward, and nice girl from Winnipeg, she is new to the city and her few friends have let her down. However, her romantic hopefulness, her naïveté, and her low self-esteem are crucial to the plot. Rafe is very complicated. Played by Brent Carver in the premiere production as well as in the film, he was totally mesmerizing. Volatile and unpredictable, with a frenetic energy that swings in a moment from tenderness to menace, Rafe is a dangerous man. But initially neither the audience nor open-hearted Daisy knows that. His imaginative and playful delay tactics, one game after another, are both amusing and highly theatrical. These quick manoeuvres, his rapid mood changes, and his constant lying keep Daisy, and us, guessing. The proximity of excitement and danger, plus the ingenious surprise ending, help explain the success of this tightly constructed thriller. The psychological complexity of these protagonists is impressive, especially the portrait of Rafe, such a sad and endearing psychopath who gets himself into terrible accidents. Like Daisy with her illusions of adventure and romance, Rafe imagines heroic exploits and desperately wants to escape his life. In this intense and intelligent play, not even Rafe could anticipate what would happen. The drama in *One Night Stand* is predicated on psychology.

This collection includes Bolt's original version of *One Night Stand*. A revised version was first produced at Victoria's Belfry Theatre in November 2000, entitled *One Night Stand: Una Aventura*. Bolt had been approached by Stephanie Jones and Jason

Cadieux of the Essential Players who asked her to update *One Night Stand*, which she agreed to do. In his foreword to the revised script, David Bolt mentions that Rafe becomes a Latino instead of a country and western wannabe, "though he is just as phony there."[1] Other alterations used to bring the play into the '90s are essentially superficial: cellphones, AIDS awareness, topical references, and so on. It is the same play; its themes are still relevant. Nonetheless, *One Night Stand: Una Aventura*, directed by Michael McLaughlin, was not treated well by the reviewers in Victoria, nor was it when the same production appeared, now directed by Sasha Wentges, at Toronto's Theatre Passe Muraille several months later. Reviewers from both cities argued that the actors and, even more, the direction, failed to meet the challenges of the genre and the script.[2]

After the popular success of the original *One Night Stand*, the fate of Bolt's next major play, *Escape Entertainment*, was a shock. *Escape Entertainment* began as a kind of reworking of *Desperados*, a play which had opened in October 1977. As Bolt commented,

> It's the same play essentially. And not just because *Desperados* is also about the film industry... they're both about people who think they want to change the world but who know the world will pay them $40,000 a year if they leave it alone. It's an interesting dilemma for me to explore. The first time I did it, I was very angry about the issue. I think that's basically why *Desperados* didn't work—I don't think it did work. *Escape Entertainment* has a little more distance in it. (Zimmerman, *Playwriting*, 57)

Originally workshopped as *Deadline* by Factory Theatre Lab in 1977, *Escape Entertainment* was produced at the Tarragon in January of 1981. It still did not have enough "distance" for the critics; they hated it. Opening night reviews from all three Toronto papers were savage. Some patrons at intermission had said to her, "Well, I'll say one thing, you've got guts!" Next morning when the reviews came out, she knew better what they meant. The production took a curve: previews were well attended, audience dipped seriously when the papers came out, and then in the last weeks they were playing to sold-out houses. "It was a show that, every night, someone would yell 'bravo!' Partly that was because they'd read the reviews and wanted to make a statement of their own," according to Bolt. Nonetheless, the work was not remounted for many years, until the Dark Horse Theatre Company of Vancouver performed it in January 1988. Bolt updated the 1988 version but, again, *Escape Entertainment* did not fare well. One reviewer described the unconvincing, "unrelenting bitch [who was] getting such a beating by the script" (Entz); another accused the play of hammering home an "outdated subject" (Groberman).

Escape Entertainment is a comedy about the Americanization of the Canadian film industry. In an interview Bolt announced with pleasure that,

> ...we've even figured out a happy ending. It took us, oh maybe eighteen tries. The actors got really fed up, but we did it, got a happy ending, and

that's a real accomplishment, you know, a real break with our Canadian playwriting tradition. (Corbeil, "Carol Bolt")

The play satirizes not only the doctoring of scripts to cater to the American market, but also the way in which New York standards of excellence—supposedly "international"—were being applied to Canadian work. This was a level of criticism that the Canadian theatre community was feeling very agitated about at the time. In the play, it is embodied in the journalist Laurel, a portrait obviously based on Gina Mallet, the theatre critic for *The Toronto Star* from 1976 to 1984. Mallet, who had come to Toronto from New York, had publicly stated that she greatly enjoyed lambasting the "parochial vision of directors and playwrights and bureaucrats" (Zimmerman, *Playwriting*, 60). In the play, the bitchy Laurel, who considers herself a "big town person in a small town place" and audaciously says, "you need me. To keep you honest" (307), goes through an as-you-like-it transformation. She falls madly in love and, head over heels, decides to assist the film production. This conversion via romance was Bolt's cheeky way to get a happy ending. But it was more than that to Bolt:

> [I]t was something about the act of criticism that I wanted to say. Pancho gives Laurel a little talk about how it's better to work with Baz and to create something that wasn't there before, that it's better to build than to just cut things up. Maybe it's not more valuable to society: he doesn't say that. He just says he thinks that it gives him personally more joy. (Zimmerman, *Work*, 271)

Bolt underlined the importance of this to her in an interview when she said, "I also want to be known as the writer who wrote *Escape Entertainment*" (Rudakoff, 185).

The play met a chorus of abuse. *The Globe and Mail*, citing "facile dialogue and barn-door satirical targets," was the most moderate (Conlogue, "Bolt Film"). The *Toronto Sun* reviewer was indignant: "Only a writer of insufferable conceit and indomitable confidence could submit such gibble-gabble to a producer" (Porter). The most extreme was the review in the *Toronto Star*. According to Mallet, the journalist who had "apparently annoyed author Bolt by deprecating Canadian theatre… seemed to be the only reason for the play's existence." In her opinion,

> *Escape Entertainment* lacks construction, wit, style, and has not so much as a shadow of an idea…. A novice playreader would have no difficulty spotting a dud. But presumably the fact that it is Canadian enhanced its failing in the eyes of its producers, and indeed director. (Mallet, "Play demands")

Clearly the critics were outraged and retaliated, despite the fact that all theatre professionals are expected to take damaging reviews in their stride, and despite the fact that for Canadian audiences cultural autonomy is an issue of importance. As Bolt said, "I don't mind people saying that they think my plays are bad, but this one ranks with *Winter Offensive* as one of the plays that has gotten the worst reviews in the history of Canadian theatre" (Rudakoff, 184).

The same year as *Escape Entertainment*, 1981, Bolt had several summer shows produced, but neither *Love or Money* nor *Love of Life* made a difference. After the jolt of the *Escape Entertainment* experience, Bolt decided to put her energy elsewhere. "It's no fun," she said, "being shafted week after week. I just didn't want to be there anymore" (Author interview, August 1988). The grand slam is not an uncommon event for a professional playwright, but neither is a subsequent shift in career goals. During the next seven to eight years she did a number of related projects—like the script for the 1985 Dora Mavor Moore Awards; the 1986 teachers' manual, *Drama in the Classroom*; Theatre on the Move's January 1987 school production of *Icetime* (based on the story of Justine Blainey, the teenage girl who fought for the right to play hockey), which won the Chalmers Canadian Children's Play Award for 1988; and the adaptation of Brian Swinne's *The Universe is a Green Dragon* (1988). But essentially Bolt had stopped writing for the stage.

By 1981 she had already written television adaptations of three of her plays plus several other pieces; by 1983–84 she was regularly writing for series like *Fraggle Rock*, *The Edison Twins*, and *The Raccoons*. During the same period, she was also writing radio drama and her commitment to that medium kept growing: in 1988 alone she completed five shows. The creative process was quite different than it was for her stage work. Bolt would deliver a completed script and then subsequent dealings would be almost entirely by telephone, since her producers were out west. Moreover, radio offered new opportunities and new limitations, both of which proved challenging. First of all, radio focuses on words and on sound: these generate the mental images. Second, because radio is so intimate, it invites reflective kinds of plays, plays which fluidly interweave inner and outer worlds, hidden thoughts and spoken words, voice and music.

Consequently, although exploring psychological themes is not a major feature of her stage work, radio provided a kind of natural opportunity. As well as being moral inquiries and meditations on serious social drama, both *Yellow Ribbons* and *Compañeras* contain important psychological themes (repression, denial, hysteria, false memory syndrome). *Compañeras* includes Robo the frightened clown, a chattering alter ego to the protagonist's surface calm. Each of the radio plays I have selected has a real event or real person for its source. For example, the award-winning *Yellow Ribbons*, a play about the investigation into the sudden disappearance of a twelve-year-old girl, is Bolt's spin on a haunting event that occurred in Toronto in the summer of 1986. It is also a reaction to a vocal group called the Victims of Child-Abuse Laws whose members, usually men, charge that their daughters are manipulated into becoming accusers by the estranged wives who are fighting for custody. Karen Ridd of *Compañeras* was the Canadian peace worker who was in the headlines in 1987. She was in a prison cell in El Salvador and refused to leave until her co-worker was also released. The basis in reality is particularly evident in Bolt's several series of plays about Canadians in Hollywood. I have included her introduction to *Two Cowboys and a Lady*, aired on CBC Radio in July of 1988.

Not surprisingly, many of the main characters in the radio dramas are dreamers with a heightened sense of possibility (like the Canadians who would be Hollywood stars), or young, idealistic leader types who want to make the world a better place, like Karen Ridd. Bolt's radio work was going very well. However, even as she was launching her *Canadians in Hollywood* series (which eventually became six one-hour dramas), Bolt expressed her hope for a return to the stage:

> There's something really powerful about the stage. It's quite an amazing experience to sit in an audience during a production of a play you've written and watch people react. The stage is where I started and it's where I always want to return. (Prentice)

While she was working on the operatic version of *Red Emma*, produced by the Canadian Opera Company in 1995, Bolt was also writing *Famous*, originally titled *Waiting for Sandy*.[3] She worked on the manuscript for a long time and did many drafts. This play, she hoped, could herald her return.

With *Famous* she started with a daring topical subject. Then she wrote an intense claustrophobic two-hander, not unlike *One Night Stand* with its frenetic, disturbing central character and its shocking conclusion. Others had spoken of *One Night Stand* as a portrait of urban alienation and loneliness, but Bolt always said "It's NOT a think piece." In contrast, with *Famous* she knew she was taking on a number of really serious subjects, including making theatre entertainment of material some would find offensive. It was only a couple of years since the murder conviction. She worried about that.

Famous (produced November 1997) was inspired by the infamous Paul Bernardo/Karla Homolka case, a case which filled the newspapers in 1987 and continued to do so well past Paul Bernardo's trial and conviction in September 1995. When the Bernardo–Homolka case began, the "Scarborough Rapist," the perpetrator of a string of sexual assaults, had not yet been identified as Paul Bernardo. In 1993 he was arrested and charged with these rapes as well as abduction, forcible confinement, and two murders. In Bolt's *Famous*, the co-accused "Sandy" (the surrogate for "Bobby's" wife "Karla") is in court, awaiting trial. Sheila, a black, American television journalist, has come to St. Catharine's to interview Sandy and Sandy's best friend, Kit. Sheila says,

> You know when I knew that I wanted this story? I did the research. I saw you on some stupid *News at Seven*. You were protecting Sandy. You were shielding Sandy from some camera. You were crying, Kit... (531)

Publicly Bolt claimed that her questioning about the case began in 1993:

> I was interested in examining the reaction to something horrific. A very common reaction to murders like this is [to believe] that they are committed by a loner, someone who is not like us. So I began to wonder, "who is like us?" Karla and Paul were a popular couple. They had many friends. And I started to wonder what those people were like and did

they think there was any possibility that Karla was innocent? Where did the complicity start? (Wagner, "Something horrific")

Carol was fascinated by all the uninformed speculation, by the magnetic pull to the unwholesome; she wanted to explore this fraught emotional terrain. And partly, she was drawn to engaging that rarely declared part of the real artist's work. As Joyce Carol Oates expressed it, "One of the little understood responsibilities of the artist is to bear witness—in almost a religious sense—to certain things."[4]

The issue of complicity, even the extreme idea of psychological merger, is central to Bolt's character Kit who says, "But I think I've done everything Sandy's done, haven't I? ...And anyway, she's sorry. Sandy's sorry. She's full of remorse. Really, Sheila. She would be, wouldn't she?" (531). Which means only that Kit would be. The journalist, who is the audience surrogate, also acknowledges a degree of complicity due to her voyeuristic interest in the details of the crimes and the psychological machinations of the perpetrators. Also, she has come here committed to taping an interview. Sandy and Kit are to be her "show." Ultimately, her complicity is that she is here to "reward" the crime, to bring the prospect of celebrity to Kit. Possibly Kit will become "famous for friendship" (493) if Sheila's documentary is successful. And Sheila, it seems, is another of Bolt's naive optimists, like Emma and others. For example, claiming to have spoken to Sheila's co-worker, Kit charges:

KIT   Tommy says that you're idealistic.

SHEILA *(as if it were an insult)* I am not "idealistic."

KIT   Tommy says you are. It's because you're so innocent, right? About television. He says that's why he loves you, because you think you're going to change the world...

        He says he and Boyd know. That the world pays you more if you leave it alone. (500)

These are familiar Bolt lines.[5] However, the reporter—as witness, facilitator, and instigator—remains an underwritten character. Kit, in contrast, is complicated and fascinating. She repeatedly calls herself a "bimbette," but it becomes apparent she only seems "so mindless that it's scary" (491). As Kit and the reporter create the show together (the documentary but also the current performance), there is an ongoing and intense power struggle between them, especially in Act II.

In *Famous* Bolt pursues her question—"what are those people like?"—and so conjures the best friend, Kit. She also engages other intriguing related issues: the dynamics of hero worship, angles on complicity, and sophisticated questions about the psychodynamics of sociopathic lawlessness. On the topic of lawlessness, it is Kit who astutely utters the banal truth: "Because it isn't lawless if you're doing it. Because everything you do, you make excuses for" (532). And, of course, central to the play's meaning as well as its structure is the ever-present video camera and the taping process. The constant awareness of the camera (by the characters and by the audience) is a visual reminder of the actual tapes from the Bernardo–Homolka trials. *Famous* also points to dangerous manifestations of our narcissistic culture and media culpability in encouraging or reinforcing anti-social behaviour. "But would you have that gun, Kit?" asks Sheila, "If I didn't have this camera?" (535).

Famous is a heady mix. It did not do well at the box office and met a cold, often hostile, reception from most critics. [6] It is instructive to compare this reaction to the one that met Lynn Crosbie's novel, *Paul's Case: The Kingston Letters* (Toronto: Insomniac Press, 1997), which came out the same year as Bolt's play was premiered. Both works are fictional imaginative explorations into aspects of the same case. Shelley Scott concludes in her book that the reason for the outrage was "the unbearable nature of the subject matter at the heart" of these works. Creative artists are not, she suggests, given the same freedom to speculate and imagine as journalists (39). Or perhaps *Famous* came out too soon; perhaps Bolt needed to maintain an even greater distance from the actual? Or it may be that onstage conjuring simply could not match the emotional charge of the offstage horrors. Perhaps for the audience to grant the author "permission" to summon such dark scenes, not long gone, viewers need to receive a sizeable payoff, sufficient insight delivered? Nonetheless, *Famous* is a bold, brave work which theatricalizes disturbing, compelling issues. I do believe that had Bolt had time to continue her work on it, the play would have realized its potential. *Famous* is worthy of more attention, and so I have included it in this anthology.

\ \ • / /

In Bolt's radio play *Compañeras*, the protagonist Karen Ridd introduces herself and her alter ego, the clown Robo, by saying: "Robo and I are clowns from Winnipeg.... We were raised in the United Church, the NDP. We grew up thinking it was possible to change the world" (456). This optimistic belief that individuals can make a significant difference is fundamental to the central characters in the majority of her works, as we have seen. However, it is not the success of the endeavour that matters most to Bolt: "what I want to create, in contemporary terms, is that kind of character: the adventurer, the seeker, the idealist who strives for the heroic possibility" (Zimmerman, *Playwriting*, 54). Striving for the heroic possibility requires an enlarged, enhanced sense of self, or at least an ardent hopefulness. Oftentimes the protagonists, like Karen Ridd, or Red Emma, or Jory of *Shelter*, are idealists who want to be part of something with large meaning. Other protagonists connect to the film industry (even Rafe in *One Night Stand*, a very troubled dreamer, takes on a persona borrowed from the movies and Kit, in *Famous*, is always watching the camera) and through that medium pursue an idealized sense of self. While Bolt's later plays are not as preoccupied with Canadian history and identity, the character type remains. Whether male or female, whether historical or pure invention, what intrigues Bolt is not simply the goal, but the pursuit, the myth-making of that personality type. In life as in art, she was interested in leaders, in strong, take-charge kinds of people who had a belief system which energized and could sustain them. She was not naive about this. As she said in interview when talking about Emma Goldman, "I always appear to write about... the Fascism of the Left, when people get so absorbed in a vision that the end justifies the means" (Rudakoff, 187). Martin Kinch believes that something of the strong-willed idealist that is Emma Goldman is also part of Carol Bolt; that Emma's final lines express Bolt's hopefulness about the role of art, beleaguered though she often was:

> I believe in freedom, the right to self expression.
> Everyone's right to beautiful, radiant things.
>
> …
>
> I know I can show you wonders
> I can paint the flags I fly
> I know dreamers can build castles
> I know castles can have banners
> I know dreams are going to flash across the sky.
>
> …
>
> I know I will do my living
> In my future and not your past
> There are certain stirring speeches
> There are drumbeats every morning
> And the chance that things will start to move too fast.
>
> …
>
> There are no countries
> There are no kings
> Only the people and all they can wish for
> All of the beautiful radiant things. (207) [7]

Of course, if you want to be an activist and arts advocate in this country, as Bolt was, you have to be something of an idealist and a dreamer.

In spite of serious disappointments in her life and career, Bolt hung on to this hopefulness. In her last play, *Lives of the Poets*, which was scheduled for a reading at Hart House on the date that became her memorial, she offers a comic take on the whole struggling Canadian theatre scene. A group of nationally-known poets have assembled in a small, northern Ontario town for the annual CanLit Day. A reading and a book launch have been scheduled. Unfortunately, a blizzard traps them all in the local library: they have no light, no heat, and no audience. Some individuals express dismay over their own unimportance and how little their work seems to matter. But instead of despairing over their obvious marginalization and neglect, the group begins to rally. They have no audience, but they have each other and determination: they will not give up CanLit Day! *Lives of the Poets* is an unfinished work but Bolt's notes direct us to expect a party. The group will make music together; they will celebrate each others' work. Everyone gets involved in staging a performance poem. As the curtain falls, the onstage candles grow brighter.

In this arena, what Bolt was writing about and what she was doing for the theatre community were entirely compatible. To divide things, as I have done here for organizational reasons, into her art and her activism, is a false division. She was never more obviously a playwright than when she was working for the theatre community, and she was never more obviously political than when she was writing for the stage. She had a strong, clear sense of what had to be done and what was important. She had the moral courage which required trusting her own experience in the world, and her own intuition about how it all worked. It was this deep core belief which allowed her to be so convinced and so convincing, such a fine fighter. And it was her playfulness, her instinctive theatricality and sense of colour, her enthusiastic embrace of everything connected to the making of theatre, which led to her best plays. Enjoy *Reading Carol Bolt.*

Notes

1   David Bolt's foreword to the publication of the revised script has been included in this collection.

2   It needs to be slick, fast-paced, with sudden changes of tone—like the quicksilver move from tender to scary. This production was not. See for example, "*One Night Stand* turns into theatrical terror" by Colin Plant, Martlet (University of Victoria's Independent Newspaper) 9 November 2000.

3   *Famous* had a number of iterations and changes of title, including *Waiting for Sandy, Strange but Beautiful,* and *Being Sandy.* An excerpt from the first version, *Waiting for Sandy,* a monologue by Kit, appears in *Taking the Stage: Selections from Plays by Canadian Women* (1994). Bolt read this excerpt when the book was launched.

4   Joyce Carol Oates, "The Wand of the Enchanter," *The New York Review of Books,* 20 December 2007: 64.

5   See, for example, the Bolt interview in *The Work,* Wallace and Zimmerman, eds. p.271 and *Compañeras* (451).

6   A collection of these reviews are presented in Shelley Scott's book, *The Violent Woman* (see Bolt bibliography).

7   Thea Gill read Emma's last song at Alex Bolt's wedding to Stephanie Anderson, 20 July 2002.

Bolt on Bolt

[W]hat I want to do is create, in contemporary terms, that kind of character: the adventurer, the seeker, the idealist who strives for the heroic possibility.

(Zimmerman, *Playwriting*, 54)

I'm a political writer and I want to change people's minds about issues. I prefer to think idealistically. ...I always appear to write about... the Fascism of the Left, when people get so absorbed in a vision that the end justifies the means.

(Rudakoff, 186–87)

I don't find *Red Emma* a searing political statement; you have, I think, a play about very young people who are standing up and saying, I will do this to change the world, and I'll die for it if necessary. If you produce it acknowledging that they're saying outrageous things, then they don't seem outrageous; you see where they're coming from. But if you approach it in the more realistic vein, then you have to realize they're advocating terrorism. And I don't think that's a reasonable reaction. I think *Red Emma* is a play about people who are very young and have all these ideals which are corrupted. I don't think that assassination is a reasonable way of handling political disenchantments. But I think that I should be allowed to show that on the stage.

(Zimmerman, *Work*, 269)

In a small theatre you might have a hundred people every night and that's all you're talking to. Mainly you're preaching to the converted and it can be a hot house. It'll be more exciting maybe to go into the larger arena. Now we want new people to fill the smaller arena theatres. That's probably the most difficult thing. It's hard to find new people...

(Poole)

I write about the things I am interested in exploring, and I want to make entertaining plays. I think it's my responsibility to make this work in theatrical terms.

(Lister, 150)

I hate those films. I hate those slow, sad films. I hate it when nobody wins. I hate it when the dream dies, when that's the message, that the dream dies. I hate it when it isn't possible. Whatever you want, it isn't possible.
Because it is. It's possible.

(Pancho in *Escape Entertainment*)

Seeing your work come to life before your eyes is what's best about being a playwright.

(James, 16)

The joys and dangers of discovery make improvised drama exciting. No one has to "make it new." It is new.

(Bolt, *Drama*, 8)

I think you can't write a play about how awful people are. You have to write a play about how you and the audience could get yourself into this spiritual or economic bind, this problem.

(Zimmerman, Work, 271)

It seemed to me that it was something about the act of criticism that I wanted to say. [In *Escape Entertainment*] Pancho gives Laurel a little talk about how it's better to work with Baz and to create something that wasn't there before, that it's better to build than to just cut things up. Maybe it's not more valuable to society: he doesn't say that. He just says he thinks that it gives him personally more joy.

(Zimmerman, Work, 271)

I'm not officially connected with any movement, but I'm aware of women's issues, more and more. I do consider myself a feminist but I generally get bad reviews in feminist newspapers.

(Poole)

Sharon Pollock once said in an interview we were doing together that, in a way, we were both really lucky because when we started writing, theatres could produce our plays and get both a Canadian and a woman in their season in one shot! So we were a minority, but it didn't necessarily work against us.

(Rudakoff, 188)

What I would really like to do as an artist is live in Canada and work anywhere in the world.... For example, if I go to New York to live, I become a New Yorker, and stop being what I am today. I don't mind being an expatriate as a person, but I don't want to be an expatriate writer.

(MacNiven)

Where am I going? I want to write plays here in Toronto. I want to put this society on stage. I think it's interesting. I think it's very amusing. I want to report it.

(Zimmerman, Work, 274)

[In the early seventies] the women's roles were mostly the type where they would bring drinks to the men on stage, while the men pretended to be Che Guevara.

(Rudakoff, 177)

[A book on the history of theatre in Toronto] tells us Toronto's new theatres were started by men, run by men, passed from man to man. It's interesting that it also provides us with considerable evidence about how and why that came to be.... Is that a gender issue? All I know is, it's hard to be left out of your own history.

(Bolt, "Anger," 10)

Playwrights in Profile

CAROL BOLT

Plays · Plays · Plays

Playwrights Co·op

CYCLONE
JACK

Cyclone Jack was commissioned and first produced by Young People's Theatre in November 1972, with the following company:

Richard Kelley	Tom Longboat
David Woito	Charlie Petch
Richard Gishler	Tom Flanagan, Announcer, Emerson Coatsworth
Stan Lesk	Chuck Ashley from the West End Y, Tom Shipman, Dorando
Janet Amos	Lauretta Maracle, etc.

Music by Paul Vigna
Directed by Timothy Bond
Production design by Doug Robinson

(In the original production, the cameo role of Tim O'Rourke was created by Paul Vigna.)

\ \ • / /

Cyclone Jack subsequently toured Ontario from January to May 1973. Produced by Young People's Theatre, sponsored by Prologue to the Performing Arts, with the following company:

David Woito	Tom Longboat
Miles McNamara	Charlie Petch
Martin Bragg	Tom Flanagan, Announcer, Emerson Coatsworth
Stan Lesk	Chuck Ashley from the West End Y, Tom Shipman, Dorando
Doris Cowan	Lauretta Maracle, etc.

Music by Paul Vigna
Directed by Timothy Bond
Production design by Doug Robinson

CHARACTERS

VOICE
CHARLIE PETCH
CHUCK ASHLEY
TOM LONGBOAT
ANNOUNCER
TOM SHIPMAN
APRIL
LADY FAN
TOM FLANAGAN
SECRETARY
LAURETIA MARACLE
EMERSON COATSWORTH
DORANDO

Cyclone Jack

VOICE

On your mark. Get set. *(a gunshot)*
He's running like joy, like the joy of the wind in his face.
And the beat of his heart and his feet feels it's setting the pace.
And his mind reaching out to what seems like a whole other space.
Reaching for, gasping for air, when it just isn't there
Aching, breaking, shaking, so why does he care
If he goes twice as fast, he might be getting somewhere.

> *TOM Longboat wins the Caledonia Marathon, followed across the finish line by CHARLIE Petch and the rest of the cast. There is a huge cheer.*

Ah, vi vi vi
Vi vi vum
Let's get a rat-trap
Bigger'n a cat-trap
Vum vum vum
Vum vum vum
Cannibal cannibal
Bowlegged bah!
West End! West End!
Rah! Rah! Rah!

CHARLIE

Running twenty-five miles is running far enough to put yourself into another world. Until you get your second breath. Until that isn't enough. Your third breath. Till your body is foggy with pain but your mind is perfectly clear.

Tom Longboat won the 1907 Caledonia Marathon, but he had some trouble on the way. Two Toronto gamblers drove right into him in their carriage. They said their horses went crazy. They forced him right off the road, but he won anyway.

ASHLEY	Congratulations, Tom. Now we can go down to Boston. You can run for Canada in the Boston Marathon.
TOM	Just as soon go back to Brantford.
ASHLEY	Charlie Petch from Hamilton wants to congratulate you, Tom. Good sportsmanship. He'll be going to Boston too.
CHARLIE	Congratulations, Mr. Longboat.
ASHLEY	You don't have to call him Mr. Longboat.
TOM	You can call me Cyclone Jack.

An amazing song and dance number.

Cyclone Jack was Tom Longboat
Tom was only nineteen
His one big sin
He didn't run to win
No man is a running machine

CHORUS *Repeat first two lines of verse.*

Said we wanted a runner
Was a marathon star
When he was twenty-one
We made him race the sun
But he didn't get very far

Repeat first two lines of verse.

Long as Tom wins races
He can do us no wrong
Since he takes first place
In every race
We're all singing Longboat's song

Repeat first two lines of verse.

What to do with a hero
A man like Cyclone Jack
When he was twenty-four
We sent him off to war
We didn't think he'd come back no more

Repeat first two lines of verse.

Tom came home from the trenches
Found his widow re-wed
When he was twenty-five
We brought him back alive
He might as well have been dead

Repeat first two lines of verse.

Tom was finished running
Just plain finished as well
We couldn't celebrate
A has-been at twenty-eight
Not much there that we could sell

Repeat first two lines of verse.

No one wanted a loser
Tom was down on his luck
When he was thirty-five
We let him drive
A big Toronto garbage truck
Just one place for a loser
Working on a garbage truck.

At the end of this song, we find ourselves on a train to Boston.

ASHLEY And I want you to train. Train? Well, you can't train on a train, Tom. But when we get back to the Y, you're a sportsman, you have to keep training. Early to bed and early to rise. You should be running twenty-five miles, three, four times a week.

TOM I've always been a runner. I've never trained before.

ASHLEY Ha ha! Always kidding.

TOM Ran from the Iroquois reservation at Brantford, all the way to Toronto and the West End Y. All the training I ever did.

ASHLEY talks with the physicality of an athletic coach. He pokes TOM a lot to make his point.

ASHLEY Discipline. Courage. Determination.

CHARLIE *(sings)*
Long way from Brantford to Boston
Riding on the miles of railroad track
And on the way we lost Tom Longboat
We found Cyclone Jack
Called him an Indian Iron Man
Called him an Indian Running Machine
Took him off the Brantford Reservation
To show him sights he'd never seen.

Tom was proud of his people
Of men who could run like deer
Said I'm not the fastest Onondaga marathoner
I'm the only Onondaga here.

Tom was young when they took him to the city
Showed him all the pretty ladies. Gave him a big cigar

	It's no place for a marathon runner Sitting up sleeping in a railway car.
ASHLEY	Spunk. Grit. That's what makes this country great. That's what made my country great, anyway. I'm an American.... Look, Tom, look... out the window! The Stars and Stripes. Oh say does that Star Spangled Banner still wave o'er the land of the free and home of the brave. That's an inspiration. That's a wonderful sight. Take your hat off, Tom, it's a mark of respect. Take your hat off! *(And TOM does. But with no enthusiasm.)* You feel tired?
TOM	I can't sleep before a race.
ASHLEY	Sleepy! I knew you'd say that. Lights out. No cigars. You've got a race to win in the morning. Doesn't that look good. I got us a lower berth. We have to relax. Relax, Tom. Relax! Relax! We'll have your arms flinging out, like this. Your legs all tensing up and jumping out like this. Call that muscle spasm. You remember our race strategy? We hold back at the start, let somebody else set the pace.
TOM	Charlie Petch.
ASHLEY	We can catch Petch in the stretch, Tom. We can show him that the north side of Hamilton is nothing like the west end of Toronto.
TOM	There are four or five runners in Brantford. All of them faster than me.
ASHLEY	When we pass him... he won't be any good to anybody after that.... Charlie Petch, he'll be eating nails, he'll be so mad when you pass him...
TOM	I run as fast as I have to to win.
ASHLEY	That's what I mean. That's strategy. Heh, heh, heh... oof! Tom... look, Tom.... You've got your elbow in my ribs.
TOM	I can't sleep before a race.
ASHLEY	Well, that's why I got a lower berth. Lots of room on your side. Ooof!
TOM	Sorry.
ASHLEY	Heh. Heh. That's all right, Tom.
TOM	It's a muscle spasm.
ASHLEY	Oof!
TOM	I feel too strong for sleeping. You can get like that.

The last thrust to the ribs and ASHLEY rolls out of bed.

ASHLEY

Heh, heh, heh, you're always kidding, Tom. Don't worry about a thing. I'll just curl up here in the aisle.

TOM

(sings)
Marathon runner, you're going to wait for the sun
Marathon runner, you're going to wait for the sun
You've got all night long to sit through
Then you've got all day long to run

Twenty-five miles, that's too long to run without crying
Twenty-five miles, that's too long to run without crying
The nights you feel too strong to sleep
Why do you think you're dying?

You got to feel it, all alone all through the night
You got to feel it, all alone all through the night
Reaching out for one more aching mile
Just waiting for the light.

And a vamp.

Waiting for the race to start
Waiting with the pounding of my heart
Beat, beat, beat from my head to my feet
I'm waiting for the sun.

ASHLEY

(ASHLEY wakes up.) Big race today. How do we feel this morning. Good day for the race… *(Leaving the Boston train we find ourselves at the track.)*

ANNOUNCER

Good day for the race, ladies and gentlemen. April 19, 1907. Runners from all over America here for the annual Boston Marathon and some friends from Canada…

SHIPMAN

(off) Where's my shoes?

LADY FAN

Who's that?

ANNOUNCER

Taking his position now, Charlie Petch from Hamilton, continuing Hamilton's great tradition of marathon runners. *(cheers for CHARLIE)*

SHIPMAN

(enters) Anybody seen my shoes.

LADY FAN

Who is it?

CHARLIE

Tom Shipman, being from Montreal. We forgot his shoes.

SHIPMAN

I can't run without my shoes.

CHARLIE

You weren't going to run very fast anyway, Shipman.

ANNOUNCER	The record for this course is two hours, twenty-nine minutes, twenty-three and three-fifth seconds, over the twenty-five mile distance.
LADY FAN	There goes Charlie. Charlie Petch.
SHIPMAN	*(off)* Going to make it one, two, Charlie? Petch is set for second place.
ANNOUNCER	Charlie Petch is in this race to win.
LADY FAN	I'd run twenty-five miles for Charlie Petch. He's only eighteen.
ANNOUNCER	Charlie Petch, at the age of eighteen, running against the running machine.

TOM enters to huge cheers. The fickle LADY FAN is particularly impressed.

And here's the favourite, Tom Longboat.

Gunshot.

And they're off.

CHARLIE takes an early lead.

TOM	After you, Charlie.

LADY FAN promenades through runners, walking an imaginary dog.

LADY FAN	This is my little dog, Tom. I call him Tom because he's an on-on-doggo. That means he's the fastest.
CHARLIE	Nobody starts out to run twenty-five miles unless they think they can do it. Do it faster. I don't run twenty-five miles for nothing. I can win it. I can't even see him. He's too far behind me now.
LADY FAN	*(sings)* Charlie Petch looks like a wreck He has two left feet . But that Indian from Brantford He's the man to beat He's just like Indian summer You wonder where he's gone The Onondaga runner At the Boston Marathon Charlie Petch is out of breath Dragging down the track But the hero here in Boston He's called Cyclone Jack He's just like Indian summer You wonder where he's gone

The Onondaga runner
At the Boston Marathon.

> *TOM is taking off his sweater.... ASHLEY runs up beside him,*
> *or drives a car or a bicycle.*

ASHLEY

Throw it here, Tom. Throw it here, Tom. I'll catch it. Give me your sweater. That's what I'm here for. I'll catch it.

> *TOM throws and ASHLEY misses the catch.*

Never mind, Tom. I'll get it. That's what I'm here for.

> *TOM runs back, picks up the sweater, and tosses it to him.*
> *Hopefully it hits him in the face.*

Thanks, Tom.

CHARLIE

(exhaustion) Where is he? Where is he?

> *TOM pulls up beside CHARLIE.*

TOM

You look tired, Charlie. Going to make it over the hill? Over the hill already. Your shoelace is untied. Petchie, Petchie, you can't catch me. Come on, Charlie, there's the finish line. Want to make it one, two?

> *TOM makes a last dash ahead to cross the finish line, followed*
> *by CHARLIE who comes nineteenth. As TOM passes the finish*
> *line, he is draped in a Canadian flag and mobbed by a lady*
> *from the Y, Emerson COATSWORTH, and ASHLEY.*

CHARLIE

He won. He doesn't race. He doesn't train, but he wins. I trained all winter for this race. I ran around Hamilton Bay with fourteen-pound weights on my shoes. But I place nineteenth. Now we're going back to Toronto for a ceremony at the city hall. He'll get all the medals. He'll make all the speeches.

> *A song bridge.*

Long as Tom wins races
He can do us no wrong
And since he takes first place
In every race
We're all singing Longboat's song
Long as Tom wins races
He can do us no wrong.

> *COATSWORTH discovers the podium at Toronto City Hall.*

COATSWORTH

Five minutes off the record for the Boston Marathon. The amazing time of two hours, twenty-four minutes, twenty and four-fifths seconds. *(large cheer)* The old record, of course, was also held by a Canadian, Mr. J.J. Caffrey from Hamilton, and we have here with us Charlie Petch from Hamilton *(large cheers)* who came nineteenth.

> *Large groan of disappointment.*

TOM   *(to ASHLEY)* See this. I beat them. I don't have to do it your way anymore.

Take your hat off, Ashley.

ASHLEY   Always joking, always joking.

TOM   Take your hat off, Ashley.

ASHLEY   That's not good sportsmanship.

TOM   Take your hat off, Ashley.

ASHLEY   If you win or lose…

TOM   I won.

ASHLEY   He's just joking, Mr. Mayor, Mr. Coatsworth, sir.

COATSWORTH
             As mayor of the City of Toronto…

ASHLEY   Emerson Coatsworth is talking, Tom…

> *TOM shouts with laughter.*

Quiet!

COATSWORTH
             This is a proud day for all of us. I know the citizens of Toronto are going to give these boys a fine welcome. We have medals to present. We have a scholarship for Tom Longboat. These boys don't want money or meals. They want you to cheer their victory. Hip hip hooray. Hip hip hooray. Hip hip hooray. Now here's Tom Longboat, to say a few words.

> *Cheers from everyone.*

Keep it short, Tom.

TOM   I thank you very kindly, Mr. Mayor.

> *A long pause. TOM beams, laughs. Everyone is uncomfortable. Except for TOM and except for CHARLIE PETCH, who sees his chance as the pause continues. And continues. And continues. At last.*

CHARLIE   Citizens of Toronto. I thank you for this great reception on this, our return from our great effort in Boston. I cannot say too much for the way Mr. Longboat won the race. We tried to make it first and second but he wouldn't. Again, I thank you and remain, yours truly, Charlie Petch.

A song.

At City Hall
The whole soul control routine.
Charlie Petch
Knows what I mean.
We'll dance, dance, dance, dance, dance
If you want to do it then you got to get into it.

Indian Chief
Man with a thousand faces
Party like this
What you get for winning races
Comedy team
Yeah Yeah Yeah Yeah
He's a running machine.

Dance, dance, dance, dance, dance, dance, dance
If you want to do it then you got to get into it.

ASHLEY COATSWORTH Goodbye Tom.

       Goodbye Tom.

ASHLEY COATSWORTH Don't do anything I wouldn't do.

       Does he?

ASHLEY COATSWORTH Keep away from the firewater, eh, Tom.

       Does he?

ASHLEY COATSWORTH Keep away from the firewater, eh, Tom.

       Where there is smoke, there must be firewater.

ASHLEY Be a good boy, Tom.

TOM Yeah.

    TOM is shaking the hand of the lady from the Y.

COATSWORTH

    Let him go, April.

    But TOM persists until CHARLIE pulls him off.

TOM Some people call me Wildfire, but you can call me Cyclone Jack.

CHARLIE	They aren't used to cyclones at the Y, Tom. They don't even have a storm cellar. *(CHARLIE hustles TOM off.)*
APRIL	He drinks whiskey.
ASHLEY	Well, he doesn't know what to do with himself in the city.
APRIL	He meets with gamblers.
ASHLEY	You don't understand, ma'am. Tom doesn't like the city. He's like a kid when he's by himself. I'm with him all the time.
APRIL	Except when he's with Tom Flanagan and Tim O'Rourke. They are gamblers.
ASHLEY	They're sportsmen, ma'am.
APRIL	They like to bet on sports.
ASHLEY	He's a strange kind of boy. I mean, he's not at ease in the city, not at all.
APRIL	He is not the sort of boy we need at the YMCA. He'll have to go.
ASHLEY	He trains here. He doesn't smoke his cigars here. He doesn't drink his whiskey here. He needs me to manage him, ma'am. You're going to drive him right into the arms of his gambler friends. Like Flanagan. Straight to the Grand Central Hotel.

Raucous and rowdy cheering followed by a song and dance, led by FLANAGAN.

FLANAGAN & OTHERS

My name is Tom Flanagan
O'Rourke and I
Are managers of the Grand Central Hotel
It's a haven for gentlemen
A hostel for sportsmen
For the man who is dapper and snappy and swell.

Are you the Tom Flanagan who keeps this hotel
Are you the same Flanagan they speak of so well
Are you the Tom Flanagan who's Tom Longboat's manager
Your man, again, Flanagan.
You're doing so well.

For fun and for frolic
For feasting and froth
The place that the vice squad quite often forgets
The whiskey is watered
The barmaid is beautiful
The boys in the backroom are placing their bets.

For rambling for roving
For football and sporting
For drinking rye whiskey as fast as you will
In all your days roving
There's none quite so jovial
As Flanagan of the Grand Central Hotel.

FLANAGAN   I have an appointment. I think I'm late.

He knocks on the desk.

Would this be the Canadian Olympic Committee?

SECRETARY   And who shall I say is calling?

FLANAGAN   Flanagan. Tom Longboat's new manager.

SECRETARY   His manager. Oh. We can't see you. No.

FLANAGAN   We're discussing my runner's status in the Olympics.

SECRETARY   Well, no. This is the Olympic Committee. We deal with amateur sports. Only.

FLANAGAN   The boy is a natural runner. He loves to run. *Amo amas amat* amateur. From the Latin, to love.

SECRETARY   Well, no. Mr. Longboat has run in county fairs all over Ontario. For money.

FLANAGAN   An amateur never runs for money. Well, not unless it's offered to him.

SECRETARY   Mr. Flanagan! You take him from town to town with bands and carriages and silk hats. That is not sport. That is a freak show.

FLANAGAN   He loves to run. He hardly has time to manage his cigar store.

SECRETARY   Well, no… the Olympic Committee is watching you, Mr. Flanagan…

FLANAGAN   We only bought him the cigar store, so he could afford to run.

SECRETARY   He does not manage a cigar store. It is our information he has smoked all the cigars.

FLANAGAN   He does it for the love of it, and if the Olympic Committee stops him from running, the people of Canada are going to rise up in arms and have your nose for breakfast.

SECRETARY   Well, no. The Olympics are for amateurs. The Italian, Dorando, an Olympian. The American, Hayes, an Olympian. Longboat is a professional.

FLANAGAN   The people want to see him run.

FLANAGAN fires a gun which begins the Olympic Marathon. DORANDO and TOM race.

SECRETARY When you think of the marathon runner, you think of the Olympics, don't you? The torch coming into the stadium. The runner carrying the torch. Tom Longboat is a paid professional...

FLANAGAN His prize money?

SECRETARY Yes.

FLANAGAN He gave it away. Every penny of it. Money means nothing to Tom Longboat. He simply loves to run.

SECRETARY Longboat's friends corrupt him.

FLANAGAN Every last dollar to a worthy cause. Distressed naval widows.

SECRETARY Bets are being placed on the Olympic games!

FLANAGAN The Humane Society. The Conservative Party of Canada.

SECRETARY Tom Longboat is notorious. Silk hats. Card sharks. Pool halls.

FLANAGAN Well, he's a sure thing, ma'am. Have you ever seen him run?

There he is. TOM Longboat!

SECRETARY Well, he does seem innocent enough in himself.

FLANAGAN Some men will bet on anything.

SECRETARY He's smiling. What a nice boy.

FLANAGAN I've known men who'll bet you the sun won't rise tomorrow. It's a sickness with them.

SECRETARY He breaks into a grin and... well, it's like the sun, smiling.

FLANAGAN And you can't blame them. Because Longboat is in the Olympics. That's a sure thing.

LONGBOAT collapses. As the finish line for the 1908 Olympics is arranged, DORANDO staggers into the stadium. Lots of cheering. DORANDO seems dazed. He is headed in the wrong direction, on the verge of collapse. He is pulled across the finish line.

(to TOM) You dropped out. After twenty-one miles.

SECRETARY They say he just spun around and then dropped senseless.

CHARLIE Dorando took three hours something. Tom can do better than that.

FLANAGAN *(to TOM)* I'm not in this for my health, you know.

CHARLIE *(to SECRETARY)* They say Dorando was drugged.

FLANAGAN	*(to TOM)* Do you know what pays for your room at the Grand Central Hotel? All the cigars you can smoke? Money. Do you know where the money comes from? Winning races.
CHARLIE	Is he hurt?
SECRETARY	He just fell. As if someone shot him.
FLANAGAN	Nobody pays to watch you get tired of running, Tom.
CHARLIE	Tom doesn't get tired of running.
FLANAGAN	*(to TOM)* I don't need a loser.
CHARLIE	*(to FLANAGAN)* You had money on the marathon. So did a lot of other people. They paid you to make sure he didn't finish.
SECRETARY	Dropped senseless.
CHARLIE	Bribery.
FLANAGAN	Not Tom.
TOM	*(to FLANAGAN)* WHERE WAS YOUR MONEY?
FLANAGAN	Don't be silly.
TOM	Who did you bet on?
CHARLIE	I want you to know I think it's disgraceful, Mr. Flanagan.
FLANAGAN	He can beat Dorando.
CHARLIE	But he didn't.
FLANAGAN	He'll race Dorando, anybody.
CHARLIE	Tom Longboat is the greatest runner in the world.
FLANAGAN	That's right! Tom Longboat is the greatest runner in the world!
CHARLIE	But it's four years to the next Olympics, Mr. Flanagan.
FLANAGAN	SO?
CHARLIE	So he's going to spend the next four years running around Hamilton Bay. That's not running the best in the world.
FLANAGAN	He won't be wasting his time racing amateurs. Tom's a professional now. Well he'll be a family man. Responsibility. Tom's going to be married, Charlie.
CHARLIE	Getting married?
FLANAGAN	To the lovely Lauretta Maracle.
LAURETTA	*(sings)* Indian Girl in a mission school Watching all the boys race horses Trying not to think they're crazy They think they can fly

See the boy against the horse
Run for miles and win, of course
Lazy boy in a mission school
Running, running, running by
City streets will hurt your feet
If you're flying high
Lazy boy in a mission school
Running, running, running by.

TOM is about to smoke a cigar.

TOM	Don't tell me, Lauretta. You're going to tell me I should be in training. For Madison Square Garden.
LAURETTA	I'm going to tell you I bought a new hat. A New York hat.
TOM	That I should drink my milk and learn my catechism…
LAURETTA	That you shouldn't hang around with gamblers.
TOM	That it doesn't matter if I win or lose, as long as I win.
LAURETTA	Flanagan runs you, Tom. I don't.
FLANAGAN	Well, if it isn't the two lovebirds. Discussing Tom's training for the big race tonight, I have no doubt. Well, talk is fine and love is fine, but it doesn't win races at all, at all.
LAURETTA	*(as FLANAGAN waves TOM out)* Will he win? Against Dorando?
FLANAGAN	He hasn't trained properly. After you're married, we'll change that, of course.
LAURETTA	Did you bet much money on him?

FLANAGAN begins to dress LAURETTA up in carnival-like Indian gear—feathers and beads.

FLANAGAN	No.
LAURETTA	Did you bet against him? On Dorando?
FLANAGAN	Lauretta. What do you take me for?
LAURETTA	Tom's manager, Flanagan.
FLANAGAN	This is just the beginning. We'll have other races. I'm booking a rematch with Dorando on New Year's Day, another race the week after that…
LAURETTA	Will he finish this race?
FLANAGAN	He's finished if he doesn't. War paint?
LAURETTA	Leave me alone. You make me look ridiculous.

FLANAGAN puts on his own headdress.

FLANAGAN	That ain't the half of it, Lauretta.

LAURETTA	We're a joke to you, aren't we? Like dancing bears.
FLANAGAN	*(applying his own war paint)* We're going into Madison Square Garden to watch Tom race. And we aren't going to win. So we're going to put on a show for them. So they'll come and see us again. I've got a box right down in front. Could you do a war dance if the race slows down, Lauretta?
LAURETTA	I'm going to war, Flanagan.
FLANAGAN	You're no help at all. There's Dorando. Boo! Boo! Boo!
DORANDO	Twenty thousand people here to watch me beat Tom Longboat. Fifteen thousand of them are smoking cigars. The air is dirty, heavy. Enough trouble breathing without thinking about the air. I was first across the finish line in the 1908 Olympics. I was so confused. I was running in the wrong direction.
	I'm afraid of this race.
TOM	Let you out of the old folks home this afternoon, Dorando? You got your wheelchair waiting in the wings?

> *A gunshot. The race begins. A song.*

He's running like joy, like the joy of the wind in his face
And the beat of his heart and his feet feels it's setting the pace
And his mind reaching out to what seems like a whole other space.

Reaching for, gasping for air, when it just isn't there
Aching, breaking, shaking, so why does he care?
If he goes twice as fast, he might be getting somewhere.

> *At the finish DORANDO collapses. TOM watches him fall. He looks like he doesn't know what happens next. He tries to help DORANDO to his feet. Cheers build.*

FLANAGAN	Call him, Lauretta.
LAURETTA	Tom! Tom! *(And TOM finishes the race, running toward LAURETTA.)*
FLANAGAN	Come on, Tom, come on, Tom. *(as TOM breasts the tape)*
	We won, Lauretta, we won!
LAURETTA	Tom won't have to race in January.
FLANAGAN	But Dorando will want to.
LAURETTA	It's too soon. You can't race him every week.
FLANAGAN	Madison Square Garden. Filled with people. They're like wild Indians. They'd come to see him race tomorrow.
LAURETTA	To see him collapse. Like Dorando.

FLANAGAN	They'd fight for tickets.
LAURETTA	You dress me up like a fool. You run him to death.
FLANAGAN	We got a good thing going here, Lauretta.
LAURETTA	Tom beat Dorando. He's the fastest. He doesn't have to prove anything.
FLANAGAN	The money, Lauretta.
LAURETTA	He won't race.
FLANAGAN	He's a professional. Lauretta. That's his job.
LAURETTA	He won't race.
FLANAGAN	Of course we'll race. How long do you think this is going to last?
LAURETTA	Where's Tom? *(TOM is with DORANDO. At his bedside, in fact.)*
TOM	How are you, Dorando?
DORANDO	Not bad. Look, the doctors say I strained my heart. What do they know? I feel fine.
TOM	Flanagan says we'll run again.
DORANDO	Sure. It's all arranged. I'll be fine.
TOM	Do they drug you, Dorando?
DORANDO	Look, if my brother comes in, don't talk about my heart. He's crazy, my brother.
TOM	Do you want to race again?
DORANDO	Well, we have to, don't we?
TOM	Why?
DORANDO	We don't have very long, do we? We have to race while we can.
TOM	Why?
DORANDO	Because there's nowhere else to go and we have to get there fast.
TOM	Because you love it.
DORANDO	For the money, Tom. While we can.
TOM	I don't think I race for the money.
DORANDO	Sure you do.
TOM	I don't race at all. I just run.
DORANDO	You're crazy.
TOM	All right.
DORANDO	I'm older than you are. I don't have as long to race. You can sit around drinking, give away your medals, all I know is in four or

five years, you'll be where I am. They'll say *you* strained *your* heart. You'll be worn out and Flanagan will sell you off. Or maybe he'll be long gone, Flanagan, because he'll get out before they drug you up like a workhorse to race. This is the top money. That's the kind of money that Flanagan wants.

TOM	Flanagan has nothing to do with me.
DORANDO	He owns you.
TOM	Back in Brantford, we used to run faster, longer than horses. I guess that's crazy. It was fun, though.
DORANDO	You're twenty-one years old. You've got maybe five years, maybe not that long. Get what you can while you can Tom, Flanagan will.
TOM	Ever hear of Cyclone Jack?
DORANDO	Oh sure. He's Flanagan's Racing Machine.
TOM	Cyclone Jack is nothing to do with Flanagan. But he runs, Dorando. It's beautiful to run like that.
DORANDO	Flanagan will burn you out. Ask him how long it will take.
CHARLIE	Mr. Flanagan, they say Tom's been missing for two days now.
FLANAGAN	Missing?
CHARLIE	What's wrong with him?
FLANAGAN	How's your own running going, Charlie?
CHARLIE	Is he drinking?
FLANAGAN	Still in shape? You used to be pretty good. I've had my eye on you, Charlie.
CHARLIE	I'm just an amateur, Mr. Flanagan.
FLANAGAN	Can't keep a good man down?
CHARLIE	Tom's down.
FLANAGAN	Well, Tom likes a drink now and then, Charlie. You know how it is. He's fast but there are times you want something to depend on. You've always been very dependable, Charlie.
CHARLIE	I can't run like Tom does, Mr. Flanagan.
FLANAGAN	You're nothing like Tom, Charlie. That's the joy of it, isn't it? You're not a drunken Indian.
TOM	I've been to see Dorando.
FLANAGAN	Now listen, Tom. I've got enough trouble with you winning races when you're not supposed to have a chance, losing races when you're a sure thing, without chasing around the dirtiest taverns in New York.

TOM	You weren't chasing me.
FLANAGAN	No. I wasn't. I don't have the time.
TOM	You aren't a runner.
FLANAGAN	And neither are you. You're some kind of freak who wins races. If the wind is in the right direction. If the bars are closed.
CHARLIE	He's been to see Dorando, Mr. Flanagan…
TOM	Dorando is a runner.
FLANAGAN	Some kind of brotherhood, is it? You and Dorando understand each other? You and Dorando and Charlie Petch. You're all runners and I don't belong.
TOM	That's right.
FLANAGAN	Look, Tom, you'd be far better off listening to me than some broken down fugitive from a squirrel cage who hardly knows enough to put one foot in front of the other.
TOM	Do you mean Dorando?
FLANAGAN	Yes, I mean Dorando. Dorando the dummy.
TOM	They say he strained his heart.
FLANAGAN	That's too bad.
TOM	Well?
FLANAGAN	I said that's too bad. Dorando's past it.
TOM	When will I be past it?
FLANAGAN	You're always joking, aren't you? How old are you?
TOM	That's right.
FLANAGAN	You're twenty-one years old.
TOM	That's right.
FLANAGAN	That's right, that's right. What do you mean, that's right.
TOM	Four or five years left, Flanagan. Running for the big money maybe not that long. You better start window-shopping. You'll need another runner.
FLANAGAN	Tom! Tom! Tom. Tom. Tom. Tom. Tom. You're only twenty-one years old. You'll be married in two weeks. Your whole life ahead of you and you are the fastest man in the world. Look, about your wedding. I have a surprise for you.
TOM	What?
FLANAGAN	Guess.

TOM begins to laugh. Anything will make him laugh. This mood continues to the end of the play.

A hint. It's about your wedding reception. *(No reply except more laughter.)* Guess where we're having the reception? I guess you thought we were having the reception at the Grand Central Hotel. No, sir, Tom. Massey Hall, Massey Hall, Tom. We're going to put on a wonderful show. I'm arranging it. We've got it all ready. Just a minute. A preview.

CHARLIE	Why do you let him do it?
TOM	He lets me run.
CHARLIE	He uses you. He sells you up and down the country.
TOM	He lets me run.
CHARLIE	He runs you.
TOM	What does it matter where I'm running? If I'm running in the reservation at Brantford. If I'm running at Madison Square Garden. What's the difference? I love it, Charlie.
CHARLIE	We think you're a fool. We thought you were drunk somewhere.
TOM	He likes to have someone to blame.
CHARLIE	And he asked me to race for him. To take over.
TOM	Well, Flanagan's a phony, Charlie.
CHARLIE	He's worse than that.
TOM	Sure. He's a fraud, he's a fake, he's a snake oil salesman.
CHARLIE	A liar and a cheat.
TOM	He's a two-faced, doubling-dealing…
CHARLIE	Mealy-mouthed…
TOM	Flim-flam, flash…
TOM & CHARLIE	Four-flusher *(They laugh.)*
TOM	Want to go to Flanagan's party, Charlie? At Massey Hall? Come on. It'll be fun. *(TOM exists to find LAURETTA.)*
CHARLIE	Massey Hall. Cyclone Jack's wedding party, held at Massey Hall. *(LAURETTA and TOM enter in as much of a procession as can be arranged.)*
LAURETTA	There must be a thousand people here.
TOM	Sure there are. Well, thanks for coming. *(There follows a hymn of praise.)*

A song.

Oh we admire him greatly
He's bigger than the Alps
He went to Boston lately
And took a hundred scalps
O make his bonnet regal
With feathers in a flock
He's swifter than the eagle
On far-flung tomahawk
Oh let the brass band thunder
And fill his heart with wonder
And all his nation under
The startled April dome!
On Onondaga swifter than the swan
Onondaga Onondaga Onondaga on!

His steady eye was glistening
As he went fleeting by
And his great heart was listening
For one great battle cry
He certainly did bully
He justified us fully
He's an injun horse and woolly and hard to curry comb
Ye housetops put your flags on
Folks get your good glad rags on
But don't put juicy jags on
To welcome Longboat home.

They call the deer a racer
I'd put it out of breath
The she-wolf, I'd outpace her
And hound her down to death...

    A bugle call "Reveille," FLANAGAN outfits TOM for battle,
    bracing him at attention. He might have a broom for a gun.

FLANAGAN   Tom's going overseas now, aren't you Tom? Fight the Hun in
World War I. Don't stop the party. Tom wants you to enjoy
yourself, don't you Tom?

    LAURETTA takes a flying leap into somebody's arms as the song
    begins again.

Back from the far off warpath
I many blankets bring
My feet have trod the star-path
My moccasins have wings
Let hill and plain and valley

With all your people rally
To cheer your dusky ally
Back to his native land.

> *This song should be staged as exuberantly as the original wedding reception when tumbling acts and female impersonators entertained. When the song is over, TOM finds himself alone in one area of the stage. There are a lot of streamers, confetti on the floor left over from the party. TOM begins to sweep up the debris with this broom.*

> *There is a reprise of two verses from the song "Cyclone Jack."*

> *All but TOM sing.*

Tom has finished running
Just plain finished as well
We couldn't celebrate
A has-been twenty-eight
Not much there that we could sell
Tom was finished running
Just plain finished as well

> *CHARLIE approaches TOM.*

CHARLIE Tom?

TOM Hi Charlie.

CHARLIE What are you doing here.

TOM I'm working Charlie. This is my job.

CHARLIE What ever happened to Cyclone Jack?

> *TOM smiles. He shakes CHARLIE's hand.*

> *All but TOM sing.*

No one wanted a loser
Tom was down on his luck
When he was thirty-five
We let him drive
A big Toronto garbage truck
Just one place for a loser
Working on a garbage truck.

> *The end.*

A documentary implies that the value of the piece rests in its faithfulness to history and its factual base. I would like to think that the value of my plays lies in their theatricality and their entertainment qualities. I think they're "true," but history is really only their starting point. What I'm trying for in all of the things I'm doing now is an epic kind of adventure or romance form.

(Zimmerman, *Work* 268)

BUFFALO JUMP

The original version of *Buffalo Jump*, under the title *Next Year Country*, was staged by the Globe Theatre, Regina in 1971, directed by Ken Kramer. This revised and rewritten version of the play was first produced by Theatre Passe Muraille, Toronto, June 1972, with the following company:

Anne Anglin	Alice Millar, Dorothy, Mrs. Mountjoy, etc.
Larry Benedict	Nick Sawchuck, Bible Bill Aberhardt, etc.
Michael Bennett	Ed Staple, Sun Reporter, Mayor of Golden, etc.
Peter Boretski	Red Evans, Garth McRae, etc.
Brenda Darling	Marjorie, Mrs. Merriweather, etc.
Howie Cooper	Peter Lowe, Merle Piston, etc.
Richard Farrell	R.B. Bennett, George Bridges, the Wandering Cook, etc.
Alan Jones	Horvath, Fellow Worker Neilson, Stuart "Paddy" O'Neill, etc.
Gordon May	John Cosgrove, Constable Beaumont, etc.
Miles Potter	Norman Lesker, Richard Martin, etc.
John Smith	Mickey, Wilf Carter, Gerry McGeer, Doc Savage, Sam East, etc.

Directed by Paul Thompson
Set design by John Boyle
Costumes by Gale Garnett

Characters

ALICE MILLAR
R.B. BENNETT
SUN REPORTER
FARMER
LESTER
HOWARD
FATHER
JOSEPH
HORVATH
NICK SAWCHUCK
ED STAPLE
MICKEY
NORMAN LESKER
PETER LOWE
GEORGE BRIDGES
JOHN COSGROVE
RED EVANS
FREE STATE
STRAITS SETTLEMENT
BALDWIN
CHATTERJEE
RUNCIMAN
STUART "PADDY" O'NEILL
WILF CARTER
GARTH
DOROTHY
MARJORIE
DOC SAVAGE
GERRY MCGEER
PREACHER

DELIVERY BOY
ANNOUNCER
MERLE PISTON
CONSTABLE R.D. BEAUMONT
FELLOW WORKER NEILSON
WORKER
WOMAN
GARTH McRAE
MRS. MOUNTJOY
TELEGRAPH BOY
MRS. MERRIWEATHER
WANDERING COOK
TOWN
FAVOURITE SON
STRIKERS
MAYOR OF GOLDEN
BIBLE BILL ABERHARDT
LADY POET
TEACHER
RANCHER
MacILRAITH
BOY
CCF'ER
MARCHER
CONVENER
McCAULEY
RICHARD MARTIN
SAM EAST
POLICEMAN

Buffalo Jump

ACT ONE

An election rally in Estevan, Saskatchewan. ALICE Millar, secretary to R.B. BENNETT sings.

ALICE

God save our gracious king
Long live our noble king
God save the king
Send him victorious
Happy and glorious
Long to reign over us
God save the king.

After this introduction, R.B. BENNETT appears. The cast, scattered as deeply as practical through the audience, reacts to BENNETT's speech. Some are for, some against. All are vocal.

BENNETT

My friends in Estevan, in the warp and woof of the Canadian cloth which is our fine British heritage, our immigrants are the embroidery on our sleeves. We want to roll up those sleeves and get to work.

Our country... our country, Canada, plunged into the depth of a great economic depression by unconscionable perversions of our great capitalistic system... by profiteers and speculators unchecked in nine years of Liberal Party mismanagement...

Mr. King and his Liberal Government are not concerned with the spectre of unemployment which stalks our land.

There are 175,000 men unemployed in this country today. 175,000 families with no captain at the helm. 175,000 frail craft awash in this sea of economic misfortune. Mr. King's message to this fleet is, and I quote from his record in Hansard, April 3, 1930, "I would not give them a five-cent piece!" Men and women of Canada, Mr. King's words are a small-craft warning.

Mr. King says to the men and women of Canada—and again I quote from his parliamentary record: "I might be prepared to go to a certain length, possibly, in meeting one or two of the Western provinces that have progressive premiers at the heads of their governments, but I would not give a single cent to any Tory government."

Shame! Betrayal!

We pledge ourselves to stop your betrayal in Ottawa. Nine years of betrayal! It didn't take Judas that long.

We pledge ourselves to foster and support a plan for greater Empire trade. We will set sail for the bright horizons of full employment under that proud banner, the Union Jack; that same standard, ladies and gentlemen, under which our brave fighting men fought and died in the Great War. With that kind of spirit, that kind of sacrifice, the spirit which is symbolized so perfectly in our brave ensign, we will reach port!

I speak for the Conservative Party in Canada. I sail under that standard and the course I steer is the course of the Conservative Party of Canada.

Ask yourselves, why is the ship of state foundering? Why is it awash? Why is this country so beset by economic storms that its present government in Ottawa can do no more than huddle in the cove of political patronage? Mr. King is not a sailor. The Houses of Parliament are not a naval academy.

I am a sailor.

At this moment, I think that the Dominion of Canada is faced with the greatest crisis of its history. We have the crew; we need the captain. We need the platform of the Conservative Party of Canada. We want to blast our way into the markets of the world.

We want Action! Action! Action!

From the tumultuous cheering that follows and at another part of the stage comes a radio announcer's election flash.

REPORTER   Beep. Beep. Beep. Beep. Beep Beep. Flash. The results of the 1930 federal election are: Progressive and other parties, twenty seats. Liberal Party, eighty-seven seats; Conservative Party, one hundred and thirty-eight seats. The Conservative Party led by R.B. Bennett has elected one hundred thirty-eight seats and will form the next government.

The cast may still be making its way through the audience to the stage.

Everybody sings.

CHORUS
Looks to me we should all agree
What we need for the people is the farm relief
Looks to me we should all agree
What we need for the people is the farm relief.

SOLO
Grasshoppers eating up all my grain
Dust blowing round, ain't got no rain
We got good people and it's their belief
What we need for the people is farm relief.

CHORUS
Looks to me we should all agree
What we need for the people is the farm relief
Looks to me we should all agree
What we need for the people is the farm relief.

During the chorus, two of the company move into position to play the following scene. One of them holds a rope knotted into a lariat.

FARMER
Well, most of what I planted last spring has blown all the way down to Montana and most of the topsoil followed it down. Kind of strange the way a dust storm comes up.

The rope begins to swing and continues faster and faster, creating the sound of wind.

You look up and the sun is kind of hazing over, the wind is whipping up, everything on the farm, except the mortgage, is just blowing past you, out of sight…

The cowboy throws the rope over the FARMER's shoulders. For the rest of the scene, he circles him, slowly, keeping him at the end of the rope, getting him more and more entangled in the rope and finally bringing him to his knees.

Well, the best thing to do when that happens is to get your neckerchief up over your mouth and nose, or get inside, but sometimes you can't do that because you're on your way into town for food or you're getting the kids from school.

The FARMER sinks to the floor in a coughing, choking fit as the rope wraps him tighter and tighter. At last, the cowboy drops the rope. The FARMER looks up, brightens.

But this is good country, though. My daddy got fifteen good crops out of this land and I figure everything's going to be all right, just as soon as all this blows over.

CHORUS	Looks to me we should all agree What we need for the people is the farm relief Looks to me we should all agree What we need for the people is the farm relief.
SOLO	Children all ragged and they got no shoes And all we got is the farm relief blues Us poor people got to work and fret Cause the doggone farm relief hasn't helped yet.
CHORUS	Looks to me we should all agree What we need for the people is the farm relief Looks to me we should all agree What we need for the people is the farm relief.

During the chorus, two of the company move into positions to play the following scene.

LESTER	I've been working on it, Howard, I know the farm hasn't been doing very well these last two years, but I've been doing some reading…
HOWARD	I've given you two extensions already, Lester.
LESTER	Yes, but I can make something out of it this year. I can get a crop out of her. That's good land, Howard, you know it…
HOWARD	Took over three farms in your section just last week. All of them useless.
LESTER	You're not going to take my farm?
HOWARD	I've got your file right here, Lester…
LESTER	I need another extension, Howard.
HOWARD	I got a letter in here from the head office in Montreal, they want to know why I gave you those first two extensions…
LESTER	Goddamn it, Howard, that farm's all I've got.
HOWARD	I got no answer for them…
LESTER	I don't know anybody in Montreal. I know you, Howard. Goddamn it, you can't take my farm.
HOWARD	Goddamn it, there's nothing else I can do. I just want you to know, Lester, you're going this week and I'm going next week, this bank's got nothing but equity in land that's worth nothing…
LESTER	You're going to take my farm?
HOWARD	I'm sorry, Lester, I just can't help you.

LESTER	All right. All right. If that's the way you want it…. If that's the way you want it, I guess I'm just going to have to beg you. *(He sinks to his knees.)* Sweet Jesus, don't take my farm!
CHORUS	Looks to me we should all agree What we need for the people is the farm relief Looks to me we should all agree What we need for the people is the farm relief.
SOLO	Freight rates too high and the market's too low We ask for credit and they will say no All start working at the break of day But we got no wheat so we got no pay.
CHORUS	Looks to me we should all agree What we need for the people is the farm relief Looks to me we should all agree What we need for the people is the farm relief.
	During the chorus, JOSEPH moves out of the group to begin packing. As the chorus ends, his FATHER approaches him.
FATHER	Joseph, I know we're going to be able to plant that bottom land, down by the slough. And if we send the livestock to pasture in Manitoba, if we send the cattle, then we'll have enough feed for old Tom. We couldn't send him, the horses don't do well away from home, but with the cattle gone, there'd be enough feed to get him fattened up, get him strong enough for spring plowing…
	During this speech, he enters JOSEPH's room, notices and realizes that his son is leaving. He decides not to mention it, to continue with his plans, but at last he trails off.
JOSEPH	I can't tell you anything about farming, Pa. You taught me, but I can't stay here any longer, that's all.
FATHER	Where are you going?
JOSEPH	Up north of P.A. There's crops there and there's timber.
FATHER	You're not a lumberjack.
JOSEPH	I can be.
FATHER	You can work your own land. You're not somebody's hired hand, Joseph, all this land is yours. Your mother and I spent all our lives building up this farm.
JOSEPH	You don't have a farm, Pa. You haven't had a crop for three years.
FATHER	Next year, things will be…
JOSEPH	I'm getting out of next year country.
FATHER	You're all I got left, Joseph.

JOSEPH	You don't need an extra hand, for that bottom land. Pa. I don't want to spend a year mending fences. I'm going to make some money, I'm going to save enough to come back and put this farm back on its feet, run it the way it should be run... *(JOSEPH realizes his own dreams are weak.)* I'm sorry, Pa. *(He puts his hand on his FATHER's shoulder.)*
CHORUS	Looks to me we should all agree What we need for the people is the farm relief Looks to me we should all agree What we need for the people is the farm relief.
FATHER	Sitting here watching my farm blow away Maybe it's in Ottawa, I can't say If you get there before I do And there ain't no dust storms, I'll come too.
CHORUS	Looks to me we should all agree What we need for the people is the farm relief Looks to me we should all agree What we need for the people is the farm relief.
	On HORVATH'S speech, which is heard from the back or side of the auditorium, the farm relief grouping changes into Mara Lake Relief Camp.
HORVATH	Okay, boys, I want you to take that rock and pound the shit out of it. I want to see gravel! *Everyone in the work camp has heard this speech before. They can sing along. NORMAN has discovered the task for the day is moving boulders from A to B. Everyone else is sitting around.*
NICK	Going to tell us times are getting better, Norman!
ED	He already said that.
MICKEY	That's the rock we shifted yesterday. He's moving it back where we got it.
NORMAN	This is a different rock.
PETER	*(to MICKEY)* I got a letter from my mother.
MICKEY	Oh, good. That's good. So what, kid?
PETER	If I don't give you the buck I owe you right now, I can send her three dollars.
HORVATH	*(approaching)* All right, boys, you finished assing around?
BRIDGES	Oh, jeez, it's Horvath.
ED	Keep your drawers on, Bridges.

MICKEY	*(to PETER)* You're playing poker with your little old lady's money?
PETER	You dealt me in.
HORVATH	I want you to try a little harder for me, boys. I want you hustling.
COSGROVE	Government paying you twenty cents a day. Let's show them they're getting their money's worth.
HORVATH	Let's just do that.
	All of the men begin to move rock with varying degrees of enthusiasm. In addition, COSGROVE baits HORVATH with a lot of enthusiasm.
MICKEY	Listen kid, you don't play poker with your mother's money. You got to have money to lose. Give me my buck.
COSGROVE	I hear R.B. Bennett's coming out to the camps.
HORVATH	What?
ALL	He's unemployed!
COSGROVE	He's sure not doing much.
MICKEY	I wonder what that fine young lady's doing right now. What time is it in Fort William anyway? I guess it's about three hours from now…
HORVATH	Some people in Ottawa…
COSGROVE	Are a hell of a lot fatter than most people here.
HORVATH	Some people in Ottawa say that relief camps are just a breeding ground for political unrest.
COSGROVE	Just a hotbed.
MICKEY	So I guess she's helping her mother with one of those fine dinners.
ED	*(to MICKEY)* Standing around doing bugger all.
MICKEY	When I want a job buggered up, I'll ask you in to bugger around.
BRIDGES	That's buggered it.
HORVATH	*(to COSGROVE)* I don't want any trouble.
NICK	Horvath, you got this camp running like a railway watch.
HORVATH	If we do have any trouble, we can bring the bulls in.
COSGROVE	Yes, sirree.
NORMAN	There's a science to it.
BRIDGES	To what?
NORMAN	Lugging boulders.
NICK	Hoo-bloody-rah.

HORVATH	This camp's set up so certain young men can do an honest day's work for their keep… and a certain small stipend.
COSGROVE	Twenty cents a day. Why don't you say. Because it's slave labour.
HORVATH	Certain others in the pay of foreign governments are bound to take advantage.
PETER	*(to HORVATH)* My mother says she hopes I'm getting lots of exercise.
COSGROVE	*(to HORVATH)* You keep looking for communists. This relief camp is the best thing that's happened to Communism since Karl Marx.
HORVATH	You don't like it, you can get out.
MICKEY	I like it fine, Horvath. I haven't had such a good time since the Oddfellows took me to the circus.
HORVATH	I got other crews to check on.
	Red EVANS has arrived. He is watching the proceedings.
COSGROVE	You want to see a communist agitator. Horvath? A real one?
HORVATH	*(to another crew, off)* You men, there. You're building a roadbed, not a fucking monument.
COSGROVE	You want to find out what it is you're so afraid of?
HORVATH	*(leaving)* Come on, come on. You've left your daddy's farm, my friends. You're here to work.
EVANS	*(handing out leaflets to the men)* My name's Red Evans. I'm a travelling salesman.
MICKEY	*(looking at his leaflet)* You've come to the wrong place.
EVANS	I sell young Canadian men to Moscow. It's all for the glory of the hammer, the sickle, and the international communist conspiracy.
NORMAN	*(He and MICKEY leave the group.)* I knew it.
EVANS	There's a story in this month's issue of your camp paper. Says you men are complaining about the food in this camp.
NICK	Just the ones who like to eat.
EVANS	You know what the government says about that? The food's fine, boys. You got Cream of Wheat for breakfast, hot cakes, and syrup.
NORMAN	Just like home.
MICKEY	It's pig slop.
EVANS	You boys are troublemakers.
MICKEY	We're in trouble, you Bolshevik bastard.

EVANS	*(ignoring MICKEY)* You're in trouble. You know why you're in trouble? If you've got grievances, if you want to organize, you can't do it, you're one man, you're a troublemaker, the government brings in the bulls. Your friend Cosgrove here tells me you had the town bulls in here last week…
BRIDGES	Breaking up a poker game.
ED	Mickey there went haywire.
NICK	Ain't the way I heard it.
ED	Just a jackknife carpenter, fucked and far from home.
MICKEY	I was drunk.
PETER	Man's got a right to be drunk.
MICKEY	I was really drunk.
NICK	On twenty cents a day?
NORMAN	Sawchuck, you're crazy, come on…
COSGROVE	Red Evans came all the way up here from Princeton, least you can do is listen to him, honest to pete…
EVANS	You men know about the Relief Camp Worker's Union. We're working for you. We've been working in Vancouver all winter. We've been going into camps to find out what you want, we've been talking to people who are willing to listen to you. You want a decent wage, you want work that means something. There are people in Vancouver who understand that.
NORMAN	Yeah, Reds.
BRIDGES	I don't know…
EVANS	They're your people. They're like your folks back home. We got a family in Vancouver that's going to work for you. For decent wages, for a chance to build something that means something. This is rich country, boys, we're all part of it. We're going to give you a chance to be part of it again.
NICK	You boys happy here? You like sweating your balls off for twenty cents a day?
PETER	No!
NORMAN	Nick…!
MICKEY	The thing I hate about all this union shit is all the stupid questions.
BRIDGES	What else is there!
MICKEY	That's another stupid question.

EVANS	The government wants to keep you in these camps, boys. They want you where you can't find out what your friends are doing, they want to force you into slave labour in a godforsaken corner of God's country where the people of Canada can forget what's happening to you.
PETER	He's right. Goddamn it, he's right.
NICK	Sure he's right. I'm fed up to here.
EVANS	The defence department tells you it's not going to listen to you. The people of Canada, that's your friends and your families, they'll listen. We're going to the people.
BRIDGES	How?
ED	Where?
EVANS	We're going to Vancouver.
NICK	I'm going to Vancouver.
NORMAN	*(to NICK, as he carries him back to the rock pile)* You're not going anywhere, you crazy bastard.
MICKEY	Last time I was in Vancouver, the railway bulls beat my head in.
EVANS	We're going on strike.
PETER	I'm going to Vancouver.
EVANS	Attaboy! It's April 2nd, right? You got paid yesterday. Twenty cents a day for a month. Your friends in Vancouver are going to help you along. There's nothing to stop us, we're going to move.
NICK	*(lugging NORMAN back)* I'm walking out of here and you're coming with me.
MICKEY	I'm not listening to this shit.
COSGROVE	What about your shit?
MICKEY	I eat it. That's been going on for years.
NORMAN	*(pushing NICK back)* Sawchuck, there is something gone wrong with your head!
BRIDGES	This could get us in a lot of trouble…
COSGROVE	This guy's the best friend you're ever going to have…
MICKEY	You go to Vancouver with him, you're going to march down the street in front of him, give the cops something to shoot at.
EVANS	We're going to Vancouver.
NICK	*(to NORMAN)* There's nothing wrong with me, my friend, I've just been here too long. Are you coming with me, Ed?

ED	Sure, why not. I said I was.
MICKEY	Stupid bastard.
EVANS	Fifty cents an hour. Work that's important.
MICKEY	No one's going to listen to you. Nothing's going to happen.
BRIDGES	Nothing's happening here.
NICK	We'll go to Vancouver. We'll win this one for Mickey. We'll tell them all about the boys we left behind.
MICKEY	Fuck you.

COSGROVE is organizing everyone who is going. He has a real live wire in PETER Lowe.

COSGROVE	All right, why are we going to Vancouver? *(no reply)* That's right… work. What else do we want?
PETER	Money! Money!
COSGROVE	That's right, wages! You're a real live wire, aren't you Peter?
PETER	Wait till my mother hears about this.
COSGROVE	*(making a chant, which the others join)* We want work and wages. We want. Work and wages. We want. Work and wages.

NORMAN, watching the departing group, throws his hat to the floor in frustration.

NORMAN	Ah. Jeez, Nick!

Someone in the group hits the first note of "Land of Hope and Glory." The group, joined by MICKEY and NORMAN, wheel into a kind of cadet chorus line, their caps under their arms. They sing:

Land of hope and glory
Mother of the free
How shall we extol thee
Who are born of thee
Wider still and wider
Shall thy bounds be set
God who made thee mighty
Makes thee mightier yet
God who made thee mighty
Make thee mightier yet.

R.B. BENNETT enters the Imperial Conference. "Land of Hope and Glory" is his favourite song so the choir hums the chorus through again. During the hum, BENNETT begins to speak.

BENNETT   It is a proud day for Canada, for in its capital city are gathered delegates from throughout the Empire, empowered to speak for one quarter of the earth's population and instructed to co-operate in delivering a plan by which this great empire may continue its leadership among nations.

I cast my mind back to the beginning of this conference and the dedication service in the Memorial Chapel here in the Houses of Parliament. That chamber commemorates Canada's part in the Great War. The names of sixty-eight thousand of her glorious dead are recorded within those walls. They are only a part of the vast army of our Imperial dead. When that altar was dedicated, in 1927, the then-Premier of England, who was present then, as now, made a striking address. He quoted Socrates before his judges: "Now we go our ways. I to die and you to live. But which is better. God only knows."

Now we are sure it is better to live. *(to the choir)* Thank you, boys.

They file off.

Who could see the brilliant assemblage gathered here in Ottawa without flushing, swelling with pride? This company of noble men of splendid purpose is a fresh breeze in the storm of economic ills which sweeps and eddies over all the nations. These fresh breezes will lead us to a cloudless day, smooth sailing, fair winds. The great brotherhood of nations which is the Commonwealth will breathe freely, bask in the sun. The Dominions...

The rest of the cast, representing Commonwealth delegates, begins to harass BENNETT and interrupts his speech.

FREE STATE   The Dominions and the Irish Free State.

BENNETT   The Dominions, tied to the mother country by the sterling and sovereign examples of brotherhood, our sacred trust, the British Commonwealth of Nations...

FREE STATE   The Irish Free State will not bargain with the British oppressor. We object.

BENNETT   We shall see Jerusalem, the Scripture has it. Truly the light is sweet and a pleasant thing it is for the eyes to behold the sun, the scripture has it. For lo, the winter is past, the rain is over and gone, the flowers appear on the earth and the time of the singing of birds is come, the scripture has it.

STRAITS SETTLEMENT
     Straits Settlement objects to scriptural references on behalf of our Muslim minority.

BENNETT	We meet in days when the machinery of world commerce is out of gear. International finance has broken down. But we meet in the knowledge that the tools we need to start those wheels moving again are in our hands. I speak of the retention of preferential tariffs.
BALDWIN	I had thought that we would lower tariffs.
BENNETT	Oh, I speak of new preferential tariffs in some areas and I speak of the extension of the free list so that members of the Commonwealth can blast their ways into the markets of the world. Our Commonwealth ties are an obligation and a sacred trust. Britain buys too much wheat from Russia. She buys from Soviet sources. Twenty-one percent of her wheat, thirty-two percent of her soft sawn woods, and thirty-four percent of her pit props.
BALDWIN	Russian prices are lower.
BENNETT	(*takes harassment and criticism very poorly*) The question of world trade is a very complicated one. If there were only one view, this conference would not be necessary. I think we can agree, however, that there is only one correct view, one course to steer which will give a stronger, clearer impulse to the life of the whole world. I will try to explain it to you, but you won't understand, even if you understood.
CHATTERJEE	Our basic difficulty was Mr. Bennett's personality.
RUNCIMAN	He has the manners of a Chicago policeman and the temperament of a film star.

> *They leave. During Mr. BENNETT's recitation, the stage is cleared of everything except his faithful secretary, ALICE Millar.*

BENNETT	In the words of Kipling, that great Empire poet: If you can talk with crowds and keep your virtue Or walk with kings, nor lose the common touch If neither foes nor loving friends can hurt you If all men count with you, but none too much If you can fill the unforgiving minute With sixty seconds worth of distance run Yours is the earth and everything that's in it And—what is more—you'll be a man, my son.

> *In another area of the stage, COSGROVE is addressing his boys, who are scattered thorough the audience.*

COSGROVE	You boys are probably wondering why we're marching so much. It's because we look good. We could stay in the union halls, playing cards all day. But there wouldn't be any point to it. When

we're marching around Vancouver, people can see us, they'll keep thinking on why we're here.

Just one thing we can do is learn to march a little better. And the reason for that is probably some people think we've got no pride in ourselves, we're beaten. And if we're marching and it's orderly, we'll look proud. There's a thousand of us down here in Vancouver now, that's going to look pretty impressive. We're asking for work and wages so let's let people know we deserve them.

Okay, let's do some practising.

The boys struggle up, although PETER Lowe is still enthusiastic.

Sure… Peter, looks good. Doc, Nick, Norman… good to see you, Norman. Garth looks cockeyed but there's nothing we can do about that.

Okay. By the left. Quick march! That's good, that looks good, boys. Mr. Hold-the-Fort, give us a song.

The men sing.

CHORUS   Hold the fort for we are coming
Union men be strong
Side by side we battle onward
Victory will come
We meet today in freedom's cause
And raise our voices high
We join our hands in union strong
To battle or to die

Repeat chorus.

Look my comrades see the union
Banners waving high
Reinforcements now appearing
Victory is nigh.

By the end of the song, the tempo has been slowed down to a painful halt. At random intervals through the song, the marching formation is frozen, one man steps out of the group and we listen to his "mind track." For example:

PETER   Cosgrove, I kind of like all this marching and the people waving back at us, but I got a letter from my mother and I don't know if she's going to be so happy because she thought I was looking for work down here, Cosgrove and I…

O'NEILL	…Going to listen. They can't help it. Fifteen hundred men down here and all yelling "Work and Wages!" And the people are all yelling back…
BRIDGES	Never going to remember the words of that damn song. "See our banner still approaching" …how the hell does it go?
ED	…don't know about these fellows but I got a stone in my shoe. But apart from that everything's wonderful, sure, only problem is we're marching and my left foot keeps hitting the god-fearing, blue-assed ground…

On another stage area, a spotlight, definitely a special, comes up on WILF Carter.

WILF	Hi folks, I'm Wilf Carter.

I know you all remember the men who made the Calgary Stampede great, names like Herman Linder, Clem Gardner, Pete Knight. They were all roping experts and bronco-busting champions.

As long as we remember those men, and as long as the golden poppies are blooming round the shores of Lake Louise, I'm proud to be a Canadian and I'm going to sing a little song:

The trail to that last happy roundup
Is narrow and steep so they say
But the broad one that leads to perdition
Is posted and blazed all the way
It's roll on, little doggies roll on
Roll on, little doggies, keep rolling along
Roll on, little doggies, roll on
Roll on, little doggies, roll on

Yodel.

Roll, little doggies, roll
Roll you little doggies keep rolling along
Roll, little doggies, roll,
It's roll, little doggies, roll.

And the lights fade down.

COSGROVE	*(from the back of the hall)* Company dismissed!

Loud cheers. NORMAN, NICK, ED, and GARTH race for the stage.

NORMAN	We got four hours off.
ED	Four hours. No meetings, no marching, no boxcars.

NORMAN	Jesus, look at that. That guy's got a dozen or more relief camp sweaters sitting in that window. Those deadheads are selling their sweaters.
ED	They'll freeze their asses off.
NORMAN	Wonder who thought of that.
NICK	Smell the ocean.
	The ocean smells more like the docks today. NICK, NORMAN, and ED don't mind. GARTH is not so sure.
ED	What are we going to do?
GARTH	We're going up to Pender Street. Chinatown. Good place for a good time if you know the right places. Fan-tan games. Opium dens. Won ton duck.
ED	All we've got are meal vouchers.
GARTH	Tong wars.
ED	Say, you think they'd take meal vouchers?
GARTH	By Jesus, I got a relief camp sweater, there's a fellow in that store back there going to want it for his collection.
NICK	You can't do that, Garth.
GARTH	Get me enough for a couple of beer.
NORMAN	You can't do that, Garth. Hang around a beer parlour.
NICK	Make us all look bad.
GARTH	I was talking to Evans…
ED	Sure you were.
GARTH	He asked me to be a group leader. Said I had natural ability.
NICK	Oh, sure.
GARTH	As a matter of fact, I told Evans he's got this trek organized all wrong. We're acting too quiet. What we want to do is raise a little hell.
ED	What did he say to that?
GARTH	I told him that in my experience, many of your enquiring minds in town will congregate in your hotel beverage room. I told him I'd be willing to take our message to those folks.
NICK	What did he say to that?
GARTH	You're a cattleman, he says to me. That's right, I says, and we know what that means. Takes something to head spooked cattle in a

thunderstorm, break a bronco. You're a veteran, he says to me, you've seen battle.

NICK   Thought you were tying your shoelace just as the army left.

GARTH   I'm a veteran. I was wounded. I'm a pensioner.

ED   You know what I'd like? There'd be a girl, walking down the street here. A really pretty young girl, maybe still in high school and we'd stop to talk to her and we'd walk down to the ocean with her and just look out over the water and we'd talk…

NORMAN   And maybe she'd have a friend.

NICK   You go down to the waterfront here, the longshoremen have just walked out.

GARTH   Never found myself a really pretty girl. All my women built more for speed than for style.

NICK   We should be on that picket line.

NORMAN   Jesus, Nick, we're in Vancouver.

NICK   I know, and there's a walkout.

ED   We've only got four hours off.

NORMAN   Look, I followed you down here from the camps, right? I haven't been past Vancouver railway yards and the relief camp office unless I'm marching in a line…

NICK   We've got no money, we've got no place to go. Let's do something useful. Get in a little excitement.

NORMAN   No.

NICK   No?

NORMAN   You heard me.

NICK   What do you mean, no?

NORMAN   I've been in the camps with you. I've been marching around Vancouver with you. And now I've got four hours off.

NICK   And we can go down to the docks…

NORMAN   Red said we should have some fun.

NICK   Okay, let's go and break the bank at Monte Carlo.

ED   I was stoking wheat last summer. I ended up in Winnipeg. I was walking down Lombard Street, past the YWCA…

NICK   *(He is somewhat more sophisticated.)* The YWCA, Jesus!

NORMAN   Church. Girls go to church.

ED	There was this girl. I guess I wasn't watching where I was going and I bumped right into her. She was carrying a lot of parcels and I knocked them all over the street.
NICK	You are so stupid, Ed…
ED	But she didn't mind. I helped her pick up the parcels, she was laughing…

Two girls who have been watching the boys laugh. There is a standoff. The girls are pretending they are not watching the boys, the boys are trying to decide what to do

	Jesus, look at that.
NORMAN	*(to NICK)* Now, that's Vancouver.
ED	What are they doing standing around the street corner?
NORMAN	They're waiting for a streetcar.
ED	Say something.
NORMAN	You say something, Nick.
NICK	Tell her you want to carry her packages.

NICK pushes NORMAN over to the girls. He is nonplussed.

NORMAN	You girls go to church?
NICK	Oh, Jesus.

The girls giggle. MARJORIE, who takes a while to windup, pushes DOROTHY forward.

DOROTHY	You're from the relief camps, aren't you?
NORMAN	Yes, I'm a Methodist.
DOROTHY	You're wearing a sweater just like all the other fellows we see walking…
NORMAN	I mean, we're from the relief camps.
MARJORIE	*(to DOROTHY)* I told you.
DOROTHY	You're out on strike.
NORMAN	Well, we're down here in Vancouver. I guess you girls know Vancouver…
ED	*(who has edged over to join the group)* What is there to do in this town… we've got four hours off.
NORMAN	Where does this streetcar go, for example.
DOROTHY	East on Hastings past the exhibition grounds.
NORMAN	Oh good, the exhibition grounds. That's probably something to see.

DOROTHY	We're going home.
NORMAN	Oh?

There is another standoff. The girls turn away but the boys are still standing there. DOROTHY finally takes pity on them.

DOROTHY	What's it like in the relief camps?
MARJORIE	My father says you boys are doing a fine, brave thing. He says that only the people are going to set this country back on its feet, and it's time that the people got together to protest and organize. My father voted for Angus McInnis in the last election and he says the days of the two old parties are past.
DOROTHY	What's it like in the relief camps?
NORMAN	It's rough.
MARJORIE	My father says it's just like a forced labour camp. My father says the government set them up so all the young men would be out of the cities, so that the capitalists could just make people believe that times weren't as bad as they are. My father says the capitalists are expecting armed insurrection and riots in the streets and they should be, the way they're exploiting the people. My father says there is no wealth, wealth is just a way of dividing people against each other in the class war. Wealth is just a product of our labour.
GARTH	Say, that little girl is making me thirsty.
DOROTHY	Who's that?
ED	Oh, that's Garth McRae.
NORMAN	Garth says he has a meeting with Red Evans. See you later, Garth.
GARTH	Say, I first came out West with the railway. I opened up the territory. *(No response from the boys.)* Ended up hanging around a bunch of green kids. Acting coltish. *(still nothing)* Well, hold the fort, boys.

GARTH leaves.

DOROTHY	Is Mr. McRae one of your organizers?
NICK	*(to DOROTHY)* No, Norman here, he's the organizer.
DOROTHY	Have you been in politics long, Mr…?
NORMAN	Politics?
MARJORIE	He's from the relief camps, dodo. He's devoted himself to the class struggle.
NORMAN	Yes.
NICK	His whole life is the worker's cause.

NORMAN	Work and wages.
NICK	He wants to go down to the docks, join the longshoremen's walkout.
DOROTHY	I think that's wonderful.
NORMAN	But we don't have to do that now.
DOROTHY	Oh, no, we wouldn't want to keep you.
NORMAN	Oh, no, it isn't that, no, you could help us.
ED	You could walk down to the docks with us.
DOROTHY	*(to ED)* We couldn't do that.
ED	Why not?
DOROTHY	We'd be in your way. You don't want girls along, I mean what would happen if there were strikebreakers and trouble and riots in the streets. Then where would you be, I mean if we were with you…
NORMAN	You could tell us more about Vancouver… about the political situation…. What I always say is, if you're working for something, you've got to know what you're working for, I mean, working with, you've got to know the ins and outs of the whole situation, what I mean is, maybe we could talk.

> *During MARJORIE's speech, at "It's time for action…," the set-up for the Hudson Bay Riot begins. It is done very noisily by RCMP officers.*

MARJORIE	My father says the time for talk is past. It's time for action and he and my mother and I are all going to the big rally in Stanley Park and my mother's lodge is going to form a big heart on the hill and the heart is going to be all mothers…
DOC SAVAGE	Okay, fellows, there's a riot at the Hudson Bay store. Everybody get back to their divisions!
MARJORIE	And they're going to hold a banner and the banner will say "Mothers Support the Relief Camp Marchers." I think that's beautiful and I'm going to help paint the banner.

> *The Hudson Bay riot includes confrontations between strikers and police, a lot of noise and confusion, and the striker's snake dance—they move quickly, arms linked together, weaving back and forth to avoid making a target for police.*
>
> *GARTH breaks out of the "snake" and the riot freezes.*

GARTH We were now marching past the Hudson Bay store. Someone cries out "There's no guards at the Bay," so the whole column of men just turned left and into the store.

This is Division Number 3 and they're a bunch of smart talkers. One of the young fellows is standing on a chair, making a speech and all the girls are gawking at him. A girl screams. There's a whole regiment of police barring the doors to the store and we're inside with them. Fearful. They all line up against one wall. I'm standing looking down the aisle between the glove counter and the stationery. There's a battalion of police down there with billies.

Our boys, they're youngsters for the most part, are standing there like boulders. The police haven't even started moving yet.

> *GARTH runs back into the snake which maneuvers for a five count or so before he breaks out again.*

They start to move.

Well, I waded right in, of course.

Yes, sir, I've always thought fast on my feet. Cowboy Jack Monaghan and I were always regular hellers for brawling.

Two of them come at me. They're both big. I go for the biggest one, put him out of action while I've got the advantage of surprise.

One. Two. He's down. I plowed him. A powerhouse.

His friend has got me behind. I run at the counter with him still holding on. I throw him over my shoulder. Do that with a twist in the shoulder muscles, here, used to call that the Winnipeg piledriver in my fighting days. He comes up at me again and I rassle him down. *(snake)* One of the big fellows picked me up then, threw me right through the air at the wall.

Now that made me mad. When I get mad. The fighting gets serious.

There was glass breaking. I was standing there and one of the boys runs at the bulls. Bounced right off and into a display case. He came out of it with the glass still crashing, cuts all over him and blood running into the eyes.

> *Snake. Which continues until a shot is fired.*

McGEER His Majesty the King charges and commands all persons assembled here immediately to disperse and peacefully to depart to their habitations or to their lawful business upon the pain of being found guilty of an offence for which, upon conviction, they may be sentenced to imprisonment for life.

McGEER   God save the King.

I'm the mayor of Vancouver, Gerry McGeer. I've been forced to read the Riot Act because of extensive property damage to the streets, here in Victory Square and especially in the Hudson Bay store.

As the strikers trail off in one direction, a spotlight comes up on PETER Lowe.

PETER   We walk around the streets at night to kill time, so we can sleep in late the next day. By doing so, we exist on two meals a day.

What do we see while putting in the hours? What do we think about?

We see a great many people going to shows, to this and that. Young couples, who seem to be enjoying themselves, well-dressed and acting as if the world isn't so bad after all. People who have homes and kids and all the rest of it. People who seem to have faith in the future.

We think that something is wrong. We can't do as they do. We must go around lonely and dejected. No home life to enjoy, shut off from all social existence. No laughter in our hours. No hope in our young lives.

We see wonderful things in the stores. Food! Clothes! Books! And shiny cars line the streets. But none such for us. Outside looking in! Or in jail looking out. Are we criminals, unwanted by society? Are we lunatics who are to be shunned? What's wrong with us?

We think of marriage and homes, just like others have. Can't even have a friend or two! Shunned like lepers of early times, we are left to our fate. Slave camps, jail, or else the salt chuck.

Because we have the guts to fight for our inherited rights we are put in jail. Called Reds and a lot of other meaningless names.

We see… we think. We see red… and we think Red. Can you blame us? Would you like to have us lie down like a bunch of spineless whelps and be contended as slaves? Is that all our grandfathers toiled for? Canada… young nation… letting her youth go to hell! We who should be the pride of the nation are the derelicts! The curse!

I leave it to you. Where do we go from here?

Where we go is to an area of the stage where all the lights available are banged up as quickly as possible while any set-up necessary continues. The pace of the next scene is frantic. Strikers are in and out all the time for new cans and tags.

ED	I'll put his chair here, Red.
EVANS	Thanks, Staple.
DOC SAVAGE	Table coming through.
EVANS	Move it right in there. *(When the table, chairs, etc., are set, the telephone rings.)* Hello…. Yes, Red Evans here. Tell them not to worry about getting arrested… *(DOROTHY and MARJORIE enter, chattering.)* Quiet, girls, quiet please. I'm on the telephone. Yes, if one of them gets arrested we'll send two more out in his place. Right. Goodbye.
DOROTHY	Well, Mr. Evans, we're ready for anything.
MARJORIE	I've got ten pencils sharpened.
DOROTHY	And I've got a chart made. It goes up to four thousand dollars.
	BRIDGES enters. EVANS and the girls applaud. It is a small ceremony for the first striker to return to the tag day office. The telephone rings and EVANS answers it.
BRIDGES	Say, this is tough. People kept moving me from in front of the stores.
MARJORIE	You're the first!
BRIDGES	Move on. Down the street, they'd say. You can't sell tags here.
MARJORIE	You're the first!
BRIDGES	Yeah, well some of them paid me to move.
	NICK enters at a run.
NICK	Am I the first?
MARJORIE	No.
NICK	Oh.
MARJORIE	But you're the second.
NICK	Oh.
PREACHER	Is this the relief camp worker's tag day office?
REPORTER	I'd like to talk to Mr. Red Evans?
PREACHER	*(to REPORTER)* Mr. Evans. This is fine work you're doing. This is what Christ meant when he said help your neighbour.
DOC SAVAGE	I just can't do this anymore, Red. I've been out for three hours and I only collected two cents.
NORMAN	How are we doing?
DOROTHY	We've got six hundred dollars already.
NICK	*(exits)* I was the second!

DOROTHY	Hey, second, you forgot your tags!
DOC SAVAGE	I'll just sit down over here.
PREACHER	(to REPORTER) I'm from the Holy Pentecostal Tabernacle. Have you been born again?
REPORTER	I'm from the *Vancouver Sun*.
EVANS	The *Vancouver Sun*. Who said that?
PREACHER	(to EVANS) I'd like to offer up a small prayer for the success of this tag day.... Oh, Lord, our Heavenly Father...

> *EVANS and the REPORTER make their escape as the prayer continues.*

REPORTER	How is the tag day progressing, Mr. Evans?
PETER	(enthusiastic) How are we doing?
DOROTHY	We've got eight hundred dollars already.

> *The telephone rings. DOC answers it.*

DOC SAVAGE	Sorry, wrong number.
BRIDGES	How are we doing?
DOROTHY	We've got one thousand dollars already.
MARJORIE	(very excited) One thousand dollars! One thousand dollars!

> *She kisses PETER Lowe in her excitement. The PREACHER approaches DOC SAVAGE who is peeling a banana.*

PREACHER	I noticed your head was bowed, my son. Have you been born again?
REPORTER	How about a picture, Mr. Evans?

> *EVANS poses against the table but just as the REPORTER lines up his shot the telephone rings and EVANS turns to answer it.*

EVANS	Two men arrested in Burnaby? Two men arrested in Burnaby? Two men arrested in Burnaby? (NORMAN has entered. To NORMAN.) Get three guys downstairs and get out to Burnaby right now.
NORMAN	Right away, Red.
PREACHER	(to NORMAN as he leaves) I'm from the Holy Pentecostal Tabernacle. We'd like to see all of you boys down there on Sunday.
REPORTER	The picture, Mr. Evans?
DOC SAVAGE	(blocking the shot) It was awful out there, Red. Three hours. Two cents. I'm not cut out for this kind of work.
EVANS	(to DOC) Why don't you make yourself useful. (The telephone rings.) Why don't you answer the telephone?

DOC SAVAGE	*(to telephone)* Hello. That's right. Steak and eggs to go.
	DOC drops the banana peel.
REPORTER	I'm ready for the picture now.
	EVANS steps toward the photographer and slips on the banana peel. Consternation.
EVANS	Who put that banana peel on the floor?
DOC SAVAGE	It came in through the window. Someone is throwing banana peels in through the window.
DOROTHY	I guess we have enemies.
PETER	*(who enters with a banana)* Hey, someone just brought in four whole stalks of bananas. Says they're a donation from the Safeway store.
EVANS	Don't touch them!
BEAUMONT	Police Constable R.D. Beaumont. What's going on here, some kind of tag day?
DOROTHY	We've got twelve hundred dollars already.
	There is a small celebration. MARJORIE hugs anyone handy.
BEAUMONT	Have to have a permit for that kind of thing.
EVANS	Tag day. Tag day? No, this is a donation from the Sunday school of the… of the…
PREACHER	Holy Pentecostal Tabernacle. My name is Reverend Peterson. Have you been born again?
BEAUMONT	*(to PREACHER)* It's Saturday.
PREACHER	Getting to heaven is a week-long job.
DOC SAVAGE	Care to buy a tag, officer?
BEAUMONT	Ah, hah. Who's in charge here?
DOC SAVAGE	*(pointing)* Red Evans.
EVANS	*(pointing past BEAUMONT to the door)* That's Red Evans there. 1914 hero. 1935 bum.
	BEAUMONT turns to investigate as NICK re-enters the office.
NICK	I was the second guy in Vancouver to get his can filled.
PETER	*(entering)* Say, will someone get those bananas out of the hallway? They're blocking the stairs.
EVANS	Don't touch them.
	PETER exits.

BEAUMONT	I'll get to the bottom of this.
DOC SAVAGE	Officer, I think you should know, there are certain subversive elements out to stop us. Someone is throwing banana peels through the window.
DELIVERY BOY	
	I got two eggs for delivery here.
DOC SAVAGE	Steak and eggs!
DELIVERY BOY	
	And the manager of the Safeway store would like to know if you've seen two guys in funny caps run by here with stolen stalks of bananas.
	BEAUMONT is holding a banana peel as evidence of subversives. He waves it at the DELIVERY BOY who follows him out.
BEAUMONT	All right. I'm leaving now, but I'm coming back here with a warrant.
REPORTER	*(to EVANS)* The picture, Mr. Evans.
DOC SAVAGE	These aren't even fried eggs.
EVANS	*(He has sat on one.)* Who put those eggs on this table?
DOC SAVAGE	Must be those subversives, Red. Infiltrators. And I'm going to find them.
EVANS	Well, go and find them.
DOC SAVAGE	Right. No, I'll wait here till they come to me.
NICK	*(enters)* I was the second guy in here and here I am back again.
PETER	*(to DOC)* Say, what are you doing here.
DOC SAVAGE	Shut up! I'm busy.
NICK	*(effectively blocking the REPORTER's last try at a candid shot)* I was the second guy in Vancouver to get his can filled.
REPORTER	That was the last of my film, Mr. Evans.
PETER	Last time I saw him, he was drinking beer in the Hotel Fitzroy.
PREACHER	What?
REPORTER	What?
EVANS	Roy has fits. Hold his head, Marjorie, there's a good girl.
BEAUMONT	All right. I've got a picture of Red Evans here and I've got a warrant for his arrest.

EVANS	Let me see that. Yes, that's Red Evans all right. *(to REPORTER)* Here's your picture, my friend, on your way.
REPORTER	Gee, thanks a lot, Mr…
EVANS	*(sings)* Hold the fort for we are coming.
PREACHER	That's a fine old gospel tune, Mr. Evans.
BEAUMONT	*(to EVANS)* You're Red Evans.
DOC SAVAGE	That's right.
EVANS	That's right. *(meaning DOC)* He's Red Evans.
BEAUMONT	I'll get to the bottom of this.
DOC SAVAGE	When are we going to Ottawa, Red?
EVANS	*(describing actor playing DOC)* You've got his description, haven't you? He's tall, skinny, dark curly hair.
DOROTHY	We've got more than four thousand dollars Mr. Evans. We've gone off the chart.
	There is a large celebration, cheering, hugging. BEAUMONT is carried away but recovers.
BEAUMONT	*(to DOC)* Why do they call you Red?
DOC SAVAGE	You must be one of those subversives.
BEAUMONT	You're a dangerous Communist agitator.
DOC SAVAGE	What's that banana doing in your holster?
	DOC makes his escape for as much of a chase as is practical. The PREACHER follows.
PREACHER	That boy is having a fit.
BEAUMONT	You come back here.
DOC SAVAGE	Let me go.
PREACHER	Out, Satan, out.
DOC SAVAGE	When you realize the mistake you're making, you're going to have egg all over your face.
DOROTHY	We've got more than five thousand dollars.
EVANS	Five thousand dollars. All that money. It's Saturday. The banks are closed.
DOROTHY	I called the police station. They're sending a guard over.
	The telephone rings.
EVANS	Yes, that's right chief, we have five thousand dollars. Just a minute. *(to BEAUMONT)* It's for you.

BEAUMONT	*(to telephone)* I got him. Chief. I got the dangerous communist agitator.
DOC SAVAGE	*(to PREACHER)* Let me go.
BEAUMONT	*(to PREACHER)* Excuse me, sir. That man's a dangerous communist agitator.
PREACHER	Out Satan, out.
BEAUMONT	*(to telephone)* Yes, Chief. Yes, Chief. Yes, Chief. Yes, Chief, Yes, Chief. *(He hangs up.)* The Chief says we're going to store your money in the station over the weekend.
EVANS	Moscow gold.
BEAUMONT	All right. We're all going down to the station.
NICK	*(racing on)* I was the second banana in the can to get his Vancouver filled.

Blackout. In the back, cowboy whoops. During the ANNOUNCER's speech, the contest between calf and cowboy is enacted in slow motion.

ANNOUNCER	Good afternoon ladies and gentlemen, and welcome to the first event of the afternoon at the Calgary Stampede. This is the calf-roping contest and our first contestant today is Mr. Merle Piston. Merle hails from Fir Siding, Alberta, and I know all his hometown folks are going to give this cowboy a big hand. Merle's in the chute. There's the horn. The calf is out of the chute. That's a fast little doggie and Merle might have some trouble there. He's got his rope up. It's a good throw and the calf is down, that little doggie is down. Merle's dismounting now, seems to have his foot caught in the stirrup… that'll slow his time a little. No, he's all right, he's over at the calf. That's one leg. Two. That's three. That's a pretty good time for Merle. We're waiting for the official clock on it, but let's have a big hand for Merle, folks.

Fade on large applause from the rest of the cast in the audience and MERLE waving his hat around in triumph. In this new black, the sound of a gavel on a table. Lights come up on a strikers meeting as DOC SAVAGE calls for order.

DOC SAVAGE	All right, fellow workers, we will now hear from Fellow Worker Neilson with the Treasurer's report.
NEILSON	The treasury stands at $211.82. That represents an expenditure, since yesterday, of one hundred and fifty dollars for room vouchers for one thousand men and two meal vouchers for one thousand men at fifteen cents each. $3.58 for shoe repair.

There has been a rumbling of voices in the back.

WORKER	Who the hell gets their shoes repaired?
NEILSON	… and six dollars worth of streetcar tickets. This expenditure is balanced by donations received. Sixty-eight dollars from Canadian Daughters Lodge 347 Bake Sale and Box Social. Three hundred dollars from the Lumberman's Union.
	The Sergeant at Arms, COSGROVE, is attempting to raise cheers, out of the general rumble of dissatisfaction.
COSGROVE	Let's hear it for the Lumbermen. Yeahhh.
NEILSON	Fifteen dollars from the Young Communist League. A dollar fifty Anonymous donation… $22.13 Wesleyan Methodist Church.
EVANS	Move to accept the Treasurer's Report as read. Do I have a second?
WORKER	Second.
DOC SAVAGE	All in favour.
	Aye's very weak. General conversation from the cast in the audience.
	Opposed? Carried. We'll hear from Comrade Staple of the Recreation Committee.
ED	We've got thirty-four tickets to *Beggars in Ermine*, fellows. That's on at the Orpheum on Granville Street, it has Lionel Atwill in it… it's about "a man who loses his legs in a railway accident, loses his wife and child in an influenza epidemic, loses his money in the Wall Street Crash, and still manages to come back." We're all going to meet for the two o'clock show tomorrow afternoon. These tickets were kindly donated by Colonel R.H. Armitage.
EVANS	Move a vote of thanks to Colonel Armitage.
DOC SAVAGE	Do we have a second?
	No second from the floor.
COSGROVE	I'll second it.
	From the audience, the following audible dialogue.
NICK	I hear they got work in the Okanagan.
NORMAN	How you going to get to the Okanagan? One step into the railway yards and the picket committee's going to bust your head in.
COSGROVE	*(trying to quiet the house)* Nice talk. Nice talk there.
DOC SAVAGE	We'll hear from Fellow Worker Bridges of the Billeting Committee.
BRIDGES	Fellow Workers, we have a complaint from the Ukrainian Labour Temple, where some of you guys are staying, about smoking in bed. Some of you boys have been smoking in bed, and some of the

blankets have got holes burned in them. There is also the possibility of a more serious fire.

In the audience, the following dialogue.

NORMAN	What did he say?
PETER	I can't hear him, I got a cigarette in my ear.
COSGROVE	Quiet down, guys.
BRIDGES	I'd like to move that smoking in bed be prohibited.
DOC SAVAGE	All in favour?
NORMAN	I've been smoking in bed since I was twelve years old.
EVANS	We've got discussion on this point.
DOC SAVAGE	Speak to the motion, please.
PETER	I don't give a damn about the motion. I'm smoking in bed if I feel like it.
DOC SAVAGE	*(COSGROVE, EVANS, BRIDGES, and DOC SAVAGE vote "Aye.")* Opposed. *(Everyone else votes "No.")* Carried. We will hear from the Picket Committee.
PETER	The hell with it.
COSGROVE	Thank you, Fellow Worker Chairman Savage. Fellow Workers, the boys on strike duty in the Longshoreman's Union have given me a message for you. They want a little company tomorrow. I'd say they were anticipating trouble with the bulls but I wouldn't want the police here with us today to think we weren't going to give them all a warm welcome…
BRIDGES	*(in the audience)* I don't know. All I know is I'm tired of marching around Vancouver.
DOC SAVAGE	That comrade at the back is out of order.
COSGROVE	I'm putting out a call for volunteers.
O'NEILL	Marching around Vancouver, going to goddamn revival meetings. We want work and wages…
COSGROVE	Volunteers for picket duty with the Longshoremen. Here's a volunteer.

But it isn't. It is NICK who wants to make a speech about his growing disillusionment.

NICK	I don't know how the rest of you feel. I know I'm fed up. We've had tag days. We've been marching around the city, singing. We've all talked to everybody we could find. We took over the museum, we took over the department stores. Somebody's talking about

taking over the North Van ferry and sailing back and forth all day. That's as far as we've got and it looks like it's as far as we're going to get.

> *From the audience: "Damn right," "We're all fed up!" etc.*

DOC SAVAGE
: You are out of order, Fellow Worker.

NICK
: Fellow Worker Chairman, I don't give a good goddamn.

DOC SAVAGE
: The Sergeant at Arms will take Fellow Worker Sawchuck back to his section.

NICK
: Nobody strong-arms me. I came down here to talk about…

> *Very loud support from the floor, as COSGROVE moves in on NICK. "Leave him alone," etc. EVANS takes over.*

EVANS
: Let him talk. *(Nothing happens. Everyone looks at EVANS.)* Go ahead, Nick.

NICK
: Well, I've been with you since we walked out of Mara Lake Camp. You were talking about work and wages. Sure I want work and wages and I don't mind asking for them. I do mind being sold down the river by another bunch of talkers. If that's what's happening.

NORMAN
: *(coming up to the platform)* Damn right.

EVANS
: Fellow Worker Sawchuck here has a point.

NORMAN
: Damn right.

> *EVANS whips the meeting to a new frenzy in the next section and wins them back to the cause.*

EVANS
: We've been here in Vancouver for two months. We've talked to Jeremiah Jesus McGeer, we've talked to the Premier of British Columbia. They know we're here, boys. They don't care. They tell us we're the responsibility of the Dominion government. They want to play political football. Many of us are thinking we could spend the rest of our lives marching up and down Granville Street. Not the Promised Land, is it?

NORMAN
: Came down here to get some action.

EVANS
: What do you think we should do about it?

NORMAN
: Nick's telling you. You're not doing anything but marching us around. That's bugger all.

EVANS
: This is a democratic association. This is the Relief Camp Worker's Union. We work together…. We need your help…

NORMAN
: We've been helping you for two months.

ED
: You can count me out of it.

EVANS	Solidarity…
ED	Stuff your solidarity up your ass.
EVANS	How are we going to get work and wages?
NORMAN	That's for you to tell us.
ED	Another bright idea like coming to Vancouver.
EVANS	There's a suggestion from the floor.
	Fellow Worker Peter Lowe has a suggestion. Get him, Cosgrove.
ED	Where is he?
O'NEILL	Who's Peter Lowe?

COSGROVE leads PETER Lowe to the front of the audience. He looks to EVANS for his cue.

PETER	Well, I say, on to Ottawa.
DOC SAVAGE	State your proposal as a motion, Peter Lowe.
EVANS	Moved that the Relief Camp Workers proceed to Ottawa by CNR and CPR freight to put their proposals before the Prime Minister of Canada.
PETER	R.B. Bennett!
COSGROVE	On to Ottawa!

Over general shouts of "On to Ottawa!" "Sure, now we're talking," etc., a WOMAN enters with a guitar. She takes over the striker's meeting area. They do not notice her. They proceed during her song to construct the train and mount it. The song is straightforward.

WOMAN

He was just a boy chasing gophers
Teasing the dogs and the mule
He used to ride our old plow horse
Before his first day of school

Where is my boy tonight?
Oh, where is my boy tonight
I miss him so 'cause I love him you know
Where is my boy tonight

Filled with the lust of a rover
Sunshiny weather or rain
Happy-go-lucky he rambles
Riding the rods of a train

No destination concerns him
His transient companions unknown

> Some mother's boy is a wanderer
> Off in the wide world alone.

A train bell and a loud cheer as the train leaves Vancouver. Everyone is waving goodbye. The train picks up speed. Train noise continues softly under each "mind track."

NORMAN	A thousand guys. All hanging on to one train and all with one idea. On to Ottawa!
ED	See the people back along the siding getting smaller and smaller. And you turn around and there's the mountains, right in front of you. We'll be in Ottawa before we know it.
O'NEILL	10:10 Seaboard Freight. It's like riding a pony through the Cypress Hills. It's like watching a storm come up.
PETER	I am so excited. I am so excited. I am so excited.
GARTH	I've been to Rio de Janeiro. I've been through the Panama Canal. But I never been to Ottawa.
DOC SAVAGE	When I get to Ottawa, I'm going to ask R.B. Bennett for a cup of coffee and a good used car.
NICK	If I can just get over to the side of this boxcar before we pass this river. We must be going fifty-five miles an hour. We'll be in Ottawa before tomorrow.
BRIDGES	When R.B. Bennett sees us marching down the street in Ottawa, he won't know what to do. He'll crap his drawers. He'll have to give us work and wages. Fifty cents an hour. We'll be millionaires!

Everyone cheers and the lights go black.

ACT TWO

In the blackout, the sound of the train, which slows to a halt as the lights come up full. The strikers are cold, tired, hungry, sleeping in shifts, and holding each other onto the top of the boxcar. COSGROVE is the first man off the train.

PETER	Where are we?
COSGROVE	Kamloops?
PETER	Where are the girls of Kamloops?
ED	Where is everybody?
COSGROVE	You guys stay on the train till I give you the signal. *(A bell rings.)* Okay, boys, get down now. I'll be back in a minute.
DOC SAVAGE	Sawchuck, you're sitting on my foot.
NICK	Yeah, well it kept you on the train all night, didn't it?
PETER	I'm cold.
DOC SAVAGE	Nope, you're feverish, kid. You better stay here while we go into town. Maybe we'll bring you back some of that good Kamloops grub.
GARTH	Feed a cold and starve a fever.
ED	Are they going to feed us?
NORMAN	They have to feed us.
COSGROVE	Good news, fellows. We're all going down to the Orange Lodge. They got something for us down there.
O'NEILL	My foot's asleep. Both my feet.
COSGROVE	Okay, somebody help Paddy down. He jumps off and he's going to break both his legs. Okay, boys, form up. Forward march.
DOC SAVAGE	We don't have to march, Cosgrove. There's nobody watching.
PETER	Where are they?
NORMAN	Let's wake them up a little.
ED	Hold the fort for we are coming Union men be strong Side by side we battle…

At "battle" there is a jagged effect, rather like a bad jump-cut in a film. The men are berating an imaginary janitor at the Orange Lodge.

NORMAN	What do you mean there's no food?

O'NEILL	There's supposed to be food here.
COSGROVE	Look, my information says…
NORMAN	Come on, Nick…
NICK	Norman?
NORMAN	We can do better on our own. Come on.
NICK	We can't, Norman…
ED	We've been on that train ten hours.
DOC SAVAGE	Oh, shit.
PETER	Well, I'm not moving till they feed me. Come on, you guys.
COSGROVE	Sure.
BRIDGES	I can't move.
PETER	Sure. If we stay here, they'll have to feed us.

They all sit down, huddling close to each other and miserable. After a moment of very miserable silence, PETER starts to giggle.

ED	What are you laughing at?
NORMAN	Somebody shut that guy up.

PETER falls over NORMAN, still giggling, and NORMAN starts giggling in spite of himself.

PETER	I can hear my stomach growling.
DOC SAVAGE	Oh, Jesus.
PETER	It's saying "steak and onions."
NORMAN	Apple pie and ice cream.

All the boys begin to laugh, they are listening to each other's stomachs, hearing all about their favourite foods.

DOC SAVAGE	Steak and onions, steak and eggs.
O'NEILL	R.B. Bennett with an apple in his mouth.

They ad lib, the laughter building to a peak, and the boys rolling around the floor like bears. EVANS enters. He is too preoccupied to notice.

EVANS	All right, boys, I've got two more divisions to talk to, so I want to make this short.
PETER	Where's the food, Red?
EVANS	(*Finally realizing the tone of the group, he tries a bad joke, which fails.*) Well, there isn't any.
ED	We've been ten hours on that train.

PETER	What do you mean?
DOC SAVAGE	You said there'd be food.
EVANS	Look, I've got twenty-four CCF ladies at work right now. They're going to make up a thousand sandwiches as fast as they can.
O'NEILL	*(petulant)* What kind of sandwiches?
PETER	That's not even one sandwich each, Red.
EVANS	I'm sorry, boys, something went wrong. It's the best we can do.
COSGROVE	Look Red, I can't tell these boys one thing and lead them all over town and another thing happens. You can't run a division that way. You told me there was going to be food here.
EVANS	I'm sorry, John. The wires crossed, that's all.
NORMAN	Come on, Nick. Let's go.
EVANS	Wait a minute.
NORMAN	I'm not going to starve to death for you.
EVANS	Who's starving?
NORMAN	I'm not going to make it to Ottawa with one sandwich in my belly and neither is anybody else.
NICK	Easy, Norm…
EVANS	You're a little hungry, Norm. You're not starving.
NORMAN	We can do better on our own.
EVANS	And when you get to Ottawa? R.B. Bennett's going to meet your train, I guess.
NORMAN	We're not going to get to Ottawa on one sandwich a day.
EVANS	We're going to do better for you. I promise you that.
NORMAN	You already promised…
EVANS	But when we get to Ottawa, who is it going to be able to talk from the gut? R.B. Bennett. Iron Heel Bennett with an apple in his mouth? Or guys who've been hungry? I thought you were hungry to get to Ottawa.
NORMAN	Yeah, sure. Sure I am.
EVANS	Okay. Things will be better at the next stop. I promise you.
BRIDGES	What's the next stop?
EVANS	Golden.

> *EVANS exits. MRS. MOUNTJOY walks into the scene, with her chair and her knitting. The Golden Men's Choir sings, infinitely*

harmonically, and except where indicated, all of the this next section is sung.

CHORUS   Golden. Golden. Golden, B.C.

MRS. MOUNTJOY

> Knit one, purl one
> Slip the knit stitch over
> Knit one, purl two
> Finish off the shoulder
> Coal and oil prices may soar
> We may well have need of more
> But we will weather any weather
> In our very woolly sweaters
> Knit one, purl one
> Slip the knit stitch over
> Knit one, purl two
> Finish off the shoulder.

There is a knock at the door.

TELEGRAPH BOY

> *(spoken)* I have a telegram for Mrs. Mountjoy.

MRS. MOUNTJOY

> *(sings)* Yes?

TELEGRAPH BOY

> *(spoken)* May I sing it to you? *(She nods. He sings.)*
> This singing telegram which is signed Red
> Tells you two thousand men have to be fed
> The road to Ottawa is hard and long
> We'll be in Golden at dawn.

MRS. MOUNTJOY

> *(sings)* Thank you.
> Red Evans always loved a joke
> Back in our old school-days
> But now I fear he's very serious
> And means no delays.
> What to do? Two thousand men.
> A problem very real.
> I have it.
> The women of the WA very well may save the day
> Mr. Merriweather's wife might provide a clue
> For he wields a butcher knife which might make up
> A stew!
> A stew! A stew! Might provide the clue!

A stew! A stew! (*She picks up her telephone.*) Ring.
Might provide the clue! Ring!

MRS. MERRIWEATHER

(*Answers her telephone. Sings.*) Hello?

MRS. MOUNTJOY

Hello, dear, I have news for you.
I just received a telegram.

MRS. MERRIWEATHER

A telegram? Who died?

MRS. MOUNTJOY

And two thousand men from the relief camps
Will arrive in Golden tomorrow.

MRS. MERRIWEATHER

Two thousand men?

MRS. MOUNTJOY

We'll have to feed them.

MRS. MERRIWEATHER

What's that again?

MRS. MOUNTJOY

We'll have to greet them warmly.

MRS. MERRIWEATHER

I can't believe this news I hear.

> There is a knock at the door. It is the Wandering COOK who is
> clearing his throat.

MRS. MOUNTJOY

It's true, I fear. One moment, dear.

COOK   I am a cook. I am a cook. I am a cook.

> He steps downstage for his aria.

I am a wandering cook and for work I look
So if you've got cooking that must be done
Look to me for I'm the one.

> Figaro's aria from "Barber of Seville."

Make spaghetti, macaroni, rigatoni and spumoni, ravioli,
cacciatore, pasta fasul.
Pasta fazool, pasta fasul, pasta fasul, pasta fasul!

MRS. MOUNTJOY

(*with the telephone*) Listen to this, my dear.

COOK   Make spaghetti, macaroni, rigatoni and spumoni, ravioli,
                  cacciatore, pasta fazool!

MRS. MOUNTJOY
                  What do you think of that, my dear. Oh! She hung up.

COOK   She hung up?

MRS. MOUNTJOY
                  Tell me good cook, could you make for us a beef…

COOK   Stroganoff?

MRS. MOUNTJOY
                  Stew?

COOK   Stew? Ahrrgh! *Chi a la donna e mobile!*

                  MRS. MOUNTJOY runs in fright.

                  My spaghetti. My macaroni. Mamma mia.
                  What can I do?
                  With all my dishes, so delicious
                  This crazy lady, all she wants is stew!

MRS. MOUNTJOY
                  People of Golden, arise! Open your doors! Open your windows!

MRS. MERRIWEATHER
                  Open your hearts!

MRS. MOUNTJOY
                  Two thousand men from the British Columbia Relief Camps are
                  on their way to our fair village.

MRS. MERRIWEATHER
                  It's true. It's true.

REPORTER   Just a conservative moment!
                  I have just heard an ugly rumour
                  Rearing its ugly head
                  Our little town of Golden is about to be invaded
                  By a raggle taggle mob of malcontents.

TOWNSPEOPLE
                  Malcontents? Malcontents?

REPORTER   Yes, Malcontents.

FAVOURITE SON
                  You couldn't mean the workers?

REPORTER   Ha! You call them workers?
                  What is their leader's name?

ALL   *(barbershop harmony)* Red Evans!

REPORTER   Aha! Bolsheviks! Communists.
                 Bolshevik communist dupes!
                 They'll rend and tear, destroy our town.
                 You poor people don't know what you're doing.
                 They'll leave our little town a smoking ruin.

MRS. MOUNTJOY
                 Nonsense!

                 I have known Red Evans since he was a boy.
                 I know him to be a righteous man...

STRIKERS   *(approaching to the tune of the Anvil Chorus)*
                 Hold the fort for we are coming
                 Union men be strong
                 Side by side we battle onward
                 Victory will come.

ALL   *(barbershop)* Welcome! Welcome! Welcome!

STRIKERS   *(same tune)*
                 We are tired, we are hungry
                 Won't you help us, please?

TOWNSPEOPLE
                 (same barbershop harmonics)
                 Welcome! Welcome! Welcome!

MAYOR   Welcomèd be! Welcomèd be! Welcomèd be!
                 As Mayor of the village of Golden
                 I greet you with open arms
                 With infinite love and compassion
                 And virtues old fashion... èd.
                 We have prepared food for you.

STRIKER ONE   Food?

STRIKER TWO   Food?

TOWN   *(barbershop)* Yes, food!

MAYOR   *(as they exit)* Members of the Ladies Aid have laid the table in the
                 sylvan glade.

REPORTER   *(the last to leave)*
                 I fear it is too late for Golden
                 But one battle does not make a war
                 I think I will hie me away to Ottawa
                 To inform the Prime Minister
                 Mr. R.B. Bennett.
                 That we got big trouble.

> *Exits. All lights hang up in the sylvan glade where the townspeople are laughing.*

TOWN Ha ha ha ha ha ha ha ha!

MRS. MOUNTJOY
Won't you have some beef stew with cabbage, beets, and celery too?

MAYOR We have salads for you.
Macaroni salad, Russian salad
Jelly salad and toss-èd salad.

TOWNSMAN You must have some cauliflower, radishes, and rhubarb.

SON And something I've prepared especially for you to wash it down.
Some buttermilk!

COOK And won't you try our fresh homemade bread with creamery butter.

MRS. MERRIWEATHER
Chocolate cake and strawberry shortcake, homemade ice cream, apple pie…

SON *(beginning a chorus which everyone joins)*
They're eating! They're eating. They're really, really eating.
They eating! They're eating! They're really, really, eating!

STRIKER ONE Golden days in Golden
Open hearts of Gold.

STRIKER TWO This is hospitality
That keeps away the cold.

STRIKER ONE We love it here, we love you
Love your cabbage, love your stew.

STRIKER TWO Oh, never end this golden day
We wish that we could stay.

> *But in the distance, there are heard the first few notes of "Hold the Fort." All action stops. They are repeated.*

STRIKERS *(to the tune of the Anvil Chorus)*
That's Red Evans, he's our leader
He recalls our duty
On to Ottawa because
We search for truth and beauty.
Thank you very much for all you've done
We feel much stronger
Now our cause is calling and we cannot stay
here longer.

"Hold the Fort" is played as a polka as the strikers dance onto the train. The FAVOURITE SON says goodbye to his parents, etc. The lights come up on a cabinet meeting in Ottawa.

BENNETT The Minister of Trade and Commerce, Mr. Harry Stevens, has resigned from the Cabinet.

I have accepted his resignation.

Certain findings of the Royal Commission on Price Spreads, which Mr. Stevens chaired, twisted out of context and unfortunately sensationalized by the gutter press, have caused a great deal of embarrassment to good friends, good Canadians, loyal supporters of this party. I refer in particular to Sir James Flavelle of Simpsons department store.

Certain statements in Mr. Stevens's preliminary findings could give the impression that Simpsons department store exploited labour in the garment trade. Mr. Stevens would have the country believe that Simpsons department store is a sweatshop.

I try to understand what kind of a man could betray his leader and his party in such a manner. That man has done me irreparable personal harm.

Judge not lest you be judged, the Scripture has it. I have read six verses of scripture every day of my life. I do not judge. I try to understand a man's betrayal.

I am a man. I seek and reach out as all men seek and reach out, for understanding. I do not understand betrayal.

I have a man's feelings. I feel pleasure in simple things. I feel great joy in work. I have friends and a man's trust in his friends. I might have thought that Harry Stevens was my friend.

Oh, I have my faults. It might be said that I am impatient, quick to anger. Anger is a fault but it is understandable. Anger is a human reaction to deceit, denial, as Peter forsook his Lord, as Judas sold his Lord for silver, willful, headstrong, arrogant self-interest. Mutinous, treasonable betrayal!

Lights down in Ottawa and up on the entrance to the spiral tunnel.

DOC SAVAGE That's the spiral tunnel up ahead. That's the long one, the big fellow.

ED Well, I'm not afraid a bit.

DOC SAVAGE Nothing to be afraid of. Unless you're afraid of the dark.

Stage goes to half-light.

ED	Yeah, it's kind of dark in here.
DOC SAVAGE	Wait till you can't see the end.
ED	How long does it take?
DOC SAVAGE	Twenty minutes.
ED	Smokey.

Everyone else on the train is choking, coughing, holding their caps up over their faces.

DOC SAVAGE	Put your handkerchief over your face. Usually, just a couple of guys on the train, they get off, climb up and meet the tunnel where it comes out.
ED	We're going to die in here.
DOC SAVAGE	No, we aren't.
ED	I'm getting off.
DOC SAVAGE	No, you aren't.
ED	I can't breathe. I'll meet the train at the top.
DOC SAVAGE	You've got to climb outside. You're inside a fucking mountain, for Christ's sake.

ED screams. He keeps screaming and struggling for the edge of the boxcar. DOC SAVAGE holds him down. DOC SAVAGE's speech will probably not be heard except when ED runs out of breath momentarily.

Look Staple, look Ed, don't think about it. Think about something else. I ever tell you when I was being a tour guide on Lake of the Woods? That's a fine life. Running those little boats all around. Nothing out there but you and the water and islands. They probably have forty thousand islands in Lake of the Woods and every one is beautiful.

ED	Let go of me. I'm getting off.
DOC SAVAGE	Get people coming down from Winnipeg, looking like the city worries them and that lake makes them look alive again. Night comes down, you can hear loons calling out across the water. Blueberries. You never tasted blueberries like that, Ed. Look Ed. There's a light up ahead.

Blackout on the train and lights up quickly on another area of the stage where the Prophetic Bible Hour Ladies Choir is singing something like "I Like the Christian Life," or "Turn Your Radio On." During the song, the train is dismantled.

Bible Bill ABERHARDT is standing by and when the song is over, he speaks.

ABERHARDT Thank you, ladies.

Fellow Christians, our bible study tonight is a story that each and every one of us heard first at our mother's knee. I would like to talk to you about the exodus of the Israelites from the land of Egypt, and I would like to draw your attention to the similarities between their experiences in the desert and our life today in the province of Alberta.

There is a famine in the land. And the question that the Israelites asked of Moses and the question that the people of Alberta are asking today is, "What are we going to do about our famine in our land?"

The Israelites went to the land of the Canaanites and the Hittites and the Amorites…

WORKER Work and wages!

ABERHARDT And the Perizzites. And the Hivites and the Jesusites which was the land of milk and honey. With Moses as their leader. Some of the people of Alberta are asking where are our leaders today and I can tell you where your leaders are today. Your leaders are among us. Look about you. There are many whose religion is still intact. There are honest men among you.

Fellow Christians, you have a responsibility and it is your responsibility to exercise that responsibility. Your responsibility is to gather together today for me one hundred honest men.

For when we know the names of one hundred honest men, we will know the names of one hundred honest men. To lead us.

I know you will sit down after this broadcast and talk it over with your family, which man in your community will you choose?

I'd like to offer up a short prayer for guidance in our choice. Oh Lord, our Heavenly Father please guide us, amen.

Why do I ask you to send me the names of one hundred honest men? Because only a man who is fundamentally honest will be able to lead us out of the Land of Canaan…

WORKER Work and wages!

ABERHARDT And into the land of economic democracy.

Do you doubt that this is possible? I suppose that one day many years ago, a man held up a little piece of paper, a stamp, and said that when attached to a letter it would carry that letter all around the world. Many doubted the truth of his statement but he had a vision and that vision has become a reality.

It's just like the circulation of the blood. The blood passes down the arm, through the body and into the leg, through the leg to the foot and back up the leg, down the other leg to the foot, back up to the arm and the head and the brain, down the other arm, back through the heart and the lungs to the foot, and every time the blood passes through the heart and the lungs it receives another twenty five dollars per month from the Social Credit government.

And that is why, ladies and gentlemen, this same blood can pass all the way through the province of Alberta today and through the rest of Canada tomorrow.

> *The marching begins once more. Most of the cast will be citizens of Calgary, watching the parade, but some sense of mass should be achieved by the remaining strikers.*

WOMAN	Hold it, it's a Kodak.... Reminds me of Harry marching back home with his regiment from the war. But there's more of them and they're just boys, aren't they…
LADY POET	…Better than the boys in Calgary. Sometimes I don't think the boys around here are interested in anything more than the Massey-Harris tractors. I don't think these boys would be like that. That dark-haired one, he looks very sensitive. I'll bet he's read *Anthony Adverse*.
TEACHER	All right, class. I want you to take out your history books and read chapter three silently. You aren't here to gape out the window. You're here to study and to learn.
WOMAN	They're going down to the stadium. Maybe Harry wouldn't mind if we took the Ford and drove by later in the afternoon…
RANCHER	What are these goddamned Communists…
WOMAN	Harry's not much for strangers but he's one for western hospitality.
RANCHER	'Scuse me, ma'am.
LADY POET	And his eyes would mist over and he'd turn away. He'd say, "Ma'am, I guess you recall the words of the poet…"
MacILRAITH	What are these goddamned Bolsheviks doing in Calgary? This is R.B. Bennett country.
WOMAN	So many of them.
LADY POET	"I would not love thee half so much loved I not honour more."

WOMAN	Harry laughs at me but sometimes I wish I'd been a man. I wish I could fly a plane. I wish I were an aviatrix. I wish I were marching.
WOULD-BE STRIKER	
	On to Ottawa. Work and wages. Vancouver to Ottawa. Edmonton to Ottawa.
TEACHER	I don't care what your father thinks of R.B. Bennett, Elizabeth. We're studying Henry VIII. Who can tell me the names of Henry VIII's six wives.
LADY POET	"It is a far, far better thing that I do now than ever I have done before."
BOY	What are these fellows doing marching down Fourth Street, Mr. MacIlraith?
MacILRAITH	Why aren't you in school, boy?
RANCHER	Way I look at it, nobody owed these boys a living. This is a big country. There's lots of work for those that want it and my taxes are not going to go to supporting a bunch of no-good, lazy, Bolshevik good-for-nothings, all foreigners anyway, should be shipped back where they came from…. If one of them came out to my ranch…
CCF'ER	Way I look at it these boys have the right idea. The whole country's gone crazy and these boys know it.
TEACHER	That's right. Anne of Cleves… Anne…
LADY POET	"He was born with a gift for laughter and a sense that the world was mad."
WOMAN	Amelia Earhart, for example…
MARCHER	This parade goes on for much longer I'm going to lose my liberal sympathies.
WOULD-BE MARCHER	
	Go to it, boys!
BOY	Go to it, boys!
CCF'ER	Go to it, boys!
WOMAN	If I were an aviatrix, I'd be up there in my Tiger Moth, flying circles around you. I'd be towing a sign saying "On to Ottawa."
RANCHER	One of them came out to my ranch, guess I'd have to tell him that there wasn't any work.
LADY POET	"Ho, ho, ho, he laughed madly."
RANCHER	My ranch isn't doing so well at that. Maybe they got the right idea.
BOY	Work and wages!

CCF'ER	On to Ottawa!
WOULD-BE MARCHER	
	Talk to Bennett. Tell him what it's like.
RANCHER	Go to it, boys!
WOMAN	We will go down to the stadium. I'll tell Harry we have to do what we can.
TEACHER	There's one more, class. Anne of Cleves. Anne....
LADY POET	"Cannon to the right of them, Cannon to the left of them..."
TEACHER	I don't know what it was. It was a parade of some kind. You aren't in school to watch parades!

Blackout. Lights come up on the arena at the Calgary Stampede.

ANNOUNCER Good afternoon, ladies and gentlemen, and welcome to Dominion Day at the Calgary Stampede. The first event this afternoon is the Brahma Bull Riding and the bull in the chute is R.B. Bennett. Bennett has proven to be the toughest bull to ride at this meet, so it should be an exciting contest. Bennett has been purchased by an English syndicate and at the end of the meet will be retired.

Attempting to ride Bennett today is Red Evans. Red hails from Drumheller by way of Vancouver and Toronto and I know we all wish him the best of luck. Red's an old hand with the bulls so we could have some interesting results here this afternoon.

There goes the horn. They're out of the chute. Red is holding on but this Bennett is a lot of bull. He's a tough one, ladies and gentlemen, but Red's a fighter. Oh no, he's through, Bennett's turning back at him, ladies and gentlemen. Get out there, Red. Get moving...

Lights fade as the rodeo clown, COSGROVE, leads Bennett away from EVANS. Lights up on another small area of the stage, a park in Regina.

NORMAN	This is real nice.
ED	The last time I was home, there was a big, huge party. Everyone in the district. I danced so long I had to take my shoes off. Then I danced so long after that I wore my socks right through.
NICK	We aren't home yet.
NORMAN	Close enough.
NICK	Regina? Doesn't take very much to make you happy.
NORMAN	I think Mr. and Mrs. Dougherty, they remind me of my folks.

NICK	They aren't your folks.
NORMAN	They invited me home for supper. You should have come with me, Nick.
NICK	Sure.
ED	What did you have for supper.
NORMAN	Mr. Dougherty makes wine in his cellar. They're Catholics, but they're real nice people.
NICK	I'm glad you like it here.
NORMAN	After supper, we listened to the radio. Those programs they have on the radio are quite funny.
ED	What did you have for supper?
NORMAN	And I told them a little bit about the strike. They were very interested.
NICK	Real night on the town.
NORMAN	Well, it must have been getting on for ten o'clock so Mrs. Dougherty made some tea and they all went to bed and I came back here and played poker with Cunningham.
NICK	I'm glad you're so happy here because R.B. Bennett says Regina's as far as we get.
ED	What did you have for supper.
NORMAN	I told you this morning. When we were lining up for sandwiches.
ED	Tell me again.
NICK	Did you hear me?
NORMAN	Sure. I heard that story too, Nick. But he can't do that. We're going to Ottawa. There's two thousand guys…
NICK	Any trains with more than four cars are rerouted through Saskatoon.
NORMAN	Come on!
NICK	They say they're going to set up a special camp at Dundurn, an internment camp.
NORMAN	I met a guy from Dundurn, came down to join the trek. There's guys from Edmonton, Calgary, Swift Current have joined us…
ED	There's two thousand guys in Winnipeg just waiting till we get there.
NICK	We aren't going to get there.
NORMAN	Sure we are.

GARTH	What we need is military tactics.
NORMAN	Mrs. Dougherty is going to make a quilt.
NICK	You're goofy, Norman.
NORMAN	The quilt will have the relief camp marchers going to Ottawa. Every worker will be carrying something that represents his trade. They'll all be looking off into the distance…
ED	Hey, maybe she could embroider "Hold the Fort" all around the edge.
NICK	You're both goofy.
NORMAN	There's too many guys. Not even R.B. Bennett can stop two thousand working people who know what they want and how they're going to get it.
NICK	As long as all they want is homemade cookies.
NORMAN	*(to ED)* You want to play some softball?
ED	Sure. Come on, Garth.
NICK	Look there's going to be trouble.
NORMAN	Oh, sure.
NICK	There are Mounties everywhere. Marching up and down. There are Mounties pretending that they're strikers.
ED	Sure. Me, for example.
NICK	How long were we supposed to be here?
NORMAN	Three days.
ED	Evans has everything organized. He'll tell us when to move.
NICK	How long have we been here?
NORMAN	I don't know.
NICK	Five days!
ED	*(to NORMAN)* Are you a Mountie or a striker?
NORMAN	Oh no, Mr. Mountie, don't shoot. I'm just a poor working boy on the way to see the Prime Minister.
NICK	Right. We said we were going to Ottawa. We can't just stop here because the weather's fine. Look, the people here have been good to us, maybe they could get some cars and trucks together, drive us to Winnipeg. We can hop the freights from there.
GARTH	Ranger tactics. Good for work in the field. When we go to meetings, expecting trouble. First of all we go out in the woods and we each catch a skunk.

NICK	That's a great idea.
GARTH	We put all the skunks in gunnysacks and we take them along to the meetings. When the police come in, we let the little creatures out of the sacks.
NICK	He's cock-eyed.
GARTH	I've seen battle.
NICK	Won the Great War single-handed.
ED	War of 1812.
NICK	I could get to Ottawa.
NORMAN	I'm going over to Dougherty's. Come on, Ed. They said maybe I could spend the night.
ED	Dougherty's probably working for the Mounties.
NICK	I could get to Ottawa by myself, if I didn't have to drag you three everywhere. I'd get right into R.B. Bennett's office.
GARTH	Sure.
NICK	And he'd make me General Manager of the Eddy Match Company.
GARTH	You wouldn't want to do that, would you, son?
NICK	What?
GARTH	You wouldn't want to go anywhere if we weren't following behind you.

CONVENOR enters.

CONVENOR   (to audience) Thank you for coming to our picnic which is in honour of the eight-man delegation now on their way to Ottawa to talk with our Prime Minister, R.B. Bennett. We hope that you will take this opportunity to get to know some of the young strikers.

> *The STRIKERS should begin circulating through the audience at this point, perhaps passing out song sheets, food, or just making conversation.*

We hope you all have your song sheets. We hope you remembered to bring your box lunches. I would like to thank Mrs. Amy Gelford for making the ribbons which identify our picnic officials. I would like to thank Mrs. Maisy Gilbert for leading us in that lovely prayer for the success of the Strikers Committee. I would like to thank Mrs. Alice Friedrich for her work with the Box Lunch Committee and of course a special vote of thanks goes to Miss Elizabeth Meadowcroft for her dramatic reading of the inspirational poem "No Port in a Storm." Miss Meadowcroft was once especially singled out by our Governor General, the Earl of Bessborough, at a drama festival in Guelph, Ontario. I have a few announcements. Will the Regina Boys Band please meet at the east door. Will the contestants for the egg and spoon race please register with Mr. Richards? He is wearing a blue and yellow striped ribbon.

> *The music begins. The cast will dance "The Butterfly" or maybe a schotisse, after which the house lights should come on. There will be an open polka, cast members inviting the audience. If possible, the floor where the audience sits should have some open space so that those who don't want to dance on stage can still dance. In this section, if the budget is available, strikers who don't get dancing partners can continue to hand out food. The polka ends when demand seems to warrant it. A last waltz clears stragglers off the stage. While the confrontation is being set up, COSGROVE sings.*

COSGROVE
All along the water tank
Waiting for the train
A thousand miles away from home
Sleeping in the rain
I walked up to a railway bull
To give him a line of talk
He said if you have money
I'll see that you don't walk
I haven't got a nickel
Not a penny to my score
Get off, get off, you railroad bum
He slammed the boxcar door.

Yodel-ay-ee. Yodel-ay-ee-o

They put me off in Moose Jaw
That's a town I dearly love
Wide open spaces all around me
The moon and stars shine up above
I've seen enough of soup lines
I'm tired of union halls
I'm on my way from Montreal
I'm going back to Ocean Falls.
Yodel-ay-ee. Yodel-ay-ee-o.

> *Mr. BENNETT ushers the STRIKERS into his office.*

BENNETT   We will get your names first, commencing on the left. Your name?

EVANS   Arthur H. Evans.

BENNETT   You used to be in Alberta, if I remember right?

EVANS	I have been in various parts.
BENNETT	You were in Drumheller in my time?
EVANS	Yes.
BENNETT	Where is your home?
EVANS	Vancouver, BC.

COSGROVE enters, late.

BENNETT	And your name?
COSGROVE	John Cosgrove.
BENNETT	Where is your home?
COSGROVE	In British Columbia at the present time.
BENNETT	And the next?
O'NEILL	Stuart O'Neill, Vancouver.
BENNETT	And your name.
DOC SAVAGE	Robert Savage.
BENNETT	Where is your home, Mr. Savage?
DOC SAVAGE	Vancouver.
BENNETT	And your name?
MARTIN	Richard Martin, Vancouver.
BENNETT	And the next?
McCAULEY	Mike McCauley, Vancouver.
BENNETT	And the next?
NEILSON	Peter Neilson, Vancouver.
BENNETT	Does that comprise the delegation?
EVANS	Yes sir.
BENNETT	Well now, who speaks for you?
EVANS	I have been elected as spokesman.
BENNETT	Yes, Mr. Evans, we shall be glad to hear you.
EVANS	We have a set of six points with respect to the relief camps.

EVANS continues:

In the first place, the relief camp situation in British Columbia presents an absolutely hopeless outlook for the men in these camps, for the youth. Some of them in British Columbia have not in three years been inside the four walls of a home.

We find conditions have only been improved through organization. When committees have attempted to function, the members have been blacklisted. What it really amounts to is blacklisted into starvation.

Our organization, the Worker's Unity League...

BENNETT	What is the name of the league?
EVANS	The Worker's Unity League, called a conference since blacklisting had increased.

One case is that of McCauley. He was distributing literature in the camps on the Princeton Road, working-class literature.

BENNETT	Communist literature.
EVANS	Not necessarily Communist literature.
BENNETT	But it was Communist literature.
EVANS	I say it was the Relief Camp Worker's Journal which is not a Communist journal. He was savagely attacked in the evening by a representative of the Department of National Defence and by the provincial police. After two o'clock in the morning he was taken out of bed...
BENNETT	In other words, he got into a fight with a policeman.
EVANS	In other words, he was dragged out of bed at two o'clock.
BENNETT	Before he went to bed he got into a fight with a policeman!
EVANS	That is not correct.
BENNETT	What is it, then? He got into a fight with the provincial police?
EVANS	He did not. He was lying in his bed.

On the basis of grievances like these, a walkout was approved.

Our first demand is for work with wages, a minimum of fifty cents per hour for unskilled labour, union wages for skilled workmen. The present cost of maintenance of the relief camps is forty-five dollars per month per man. The cost of this demand would mean sixty dollars a month and the workers would buy their own board and all their clothing.

Our second demand is that all relief projects be covered by the Workmen's Compensation Act.

Our next demand is for recognition of camp committees. The rules of the Department of National Defence regarding complaints say that superintendents and foremen will discuss complaints with individuals. But when this has been attempted, the man has been blacklisted and chased out of camp.

Our next demand is that all relief camps be taken out of the Department of National Defence, with no military regulations. This is one of our central demands.

Our next demand is for a genuine system of social and economic insurance.

Our next demand is that the workers in the camps be guaranteed the democratic right to vote. They have been denied the right to vote on the grounds that they have no habitation and that they are being provided for by the government.

BENNETT	How old are you, Mr. Evans?
EVANS	Forty-six.
BENNETT	How old are you, Mr. Cosgrove?
COSGROVE	Thirty-five.
BENNETT	How old are you, Mr. Savage?
DOC SAVAGE	Twenty-three.
BENNETT	Where were you born?
DOC SAVAGE	Birkenhead, England.
BENNETT	Where were you born, Mr. Cosgrove?
COSGROVE	Rothesay, Scotland.
BENNETT	Where were you born, Mr. Evans?
EVANS	I was born in Toronto, Ontario.
BENNETT	You were born in Toronto, you say.
EVANS	I am sure of it, and several of my family; my father was born there. We have been in this country something like one hundred and twelve years.
BENNETT	And how old are you, Mr. O'Neill?
O'NEILL	Thirty-six.
BENNETT	Where were you born?
O'NEILL	Newfoundland.
BENNETT	And the next.
MARTIN	I was born in London, England.
BENNETT	How old are you?
MARTIN	Thirty-one.
BENNETT	Does anybody else desire to make any observations?

COSGROVE	I am going to speak on the Compensation Act. Being first-aid man in the camps, I have seen many accidents take place. In one case, in particular, Case 346 at Yale, BC, fell seventy-five feet down a mountainside. He had a gash in his head six inches long and suffered twenty-one days with slight concussion of the brain. For twelve days he had no doctor. I had to doctor him.
MARTIN	We are ready to talk business on the six demands.
BENNETT	We have listened with much interest to what you men have had to say. With the exception of one of you, who has a record we will not discuss, you were born outside of Canada, and in the country from which you come, I was told the other day there are one million men who have no work and never will have. With respect to single unemployed men who have drifted into the province of British Columbia, we said we would provide one, food, two, shelter, three, clothing for such unemployed persons.

We have given you good food, good shelter, and good clothing.

There was no compulsion and no discipline. The Department of National Defence operated these camps because they had the equipment, tents, and they had the personnel.

It was felt that if the men went into camps and did some work or chores they might be better off than receiving merely relief, and that they would get some exercise and keep themselves fit. For that they received the twenty cents as a gratuity paid by the state.

Agitators went into these camps, agitators representing a form of government that we will not tolerate in Canada, agitators representing Communism which we will stamp out in this country with the help of the people of Canada.

The Unity League is not unknown to us. We are fully seized of all the circumstances in connection with the operations of the Unity League. We know from necessity where its agents are. They endeavour by force, if necessary, to destroy the institutions of this country.

Leaving Vancouver, you illegally trespassed upon railway property, endangering human life.

You reached Regina. At Regina, your numbers are now camped.

Now you ask for work. At one place it was for relief. At another place it is for work and wages. You have not shown much anxiety to get work. It is the one thing you do not want. What you want is this adventure in the hope that the organization which you are promoting in Canada may be able to overrun government and break down the forces that represent law and order.

You talk of the Workmen's Compensation Act. Every case in which a man has been injured has been investigated by the authorities. The case to which Mr. Cosgrove referred of a man falling is something which may happen to any man anywhere and may more easily happen climbing on a freight train than most places I know.

I do ask you young men, at your age, whether or not you think you are playing the part of good citizens when we are supplying you with the conditions of home, because you are homeless men. Now you suddenly say: We are going to violate laws and march to Ottawa. March to Ottawa for what purpose. What purpose?

EVANS	The purpose is to demand from you this program of work and wages.
	You referred to us as not wanting work. Give us work and see whether we will work. This is an insidious attempt to propagandize in the press on your part. Anybody who professes to be premier and uses such despicable tactics is not fit to be premier of a Hottentot village.
BENNETT	I come from Alberta. I remember when you embezzled the funds of your union and were sent to the penitentiary.
EVANS	You're a liar. I was arrested for fraudulently converting these funds to feed the starving. I say you are a liar if you say I embezzled.
BENNETT	I know your record in the penitentiary at New Westminster, your record in the penitentiary elsewhere.
EVANS	I was never in a penitentiary at New Westminster. You don't know what you are talking about.
BENNETT	Where was it.
EVANS	I know your…
BENNETT	You are here deluding a number of young men.
EVANS	I have stated that I used the funds for hungry people instead of sending them to Indianapolis to a bunch of pot-bellied business agents.
BENNETT	I was referring to the second time you were sent to the penitentiary.
EVANS	Where was the second time? I was never sent a second time to a penitentiary.
BENNETT	Jail.
EVANS	Under Section 98 for leading miners in a strike.
O'NEILL	You have accused us of all kinds of things…

BENNETT	Nobody has told you the facts and I am trying…
O'NEILL	I have ridden in boxcars in France and I sat in a trench and nobody called me a foreigner then.
COSGROVE	I take exception to any personal attack on this delegation and will not…
BENNETT	Sit down, Mr. Cosgrove.
COSGROVE	I will not.
BENNETT	Then you will be removed.
EVANS	Then the entire delegation will be removed.
COSGROVE	I will when I have said this. I fought in the war as a boy fifteen years old. I have the interests of this country as much at heart as you have.
BENNETT	You cannot take the government by the throat and demand that anything that pleases your sweet will be done…
O'NEILL	Two thousand men in Regina…
BENNETT	Who put them in that state of mind?
O'NEILL	You did!
EVANS	I propose we do not interject anymore. We will take the rest of what he has to say to the workers and citizens of Canada.
BENNETT	That is your privilege so long as you keep within the law and the minute you step beyond it, Mr. Evans, you will land where you once were.
	You were asking for work with wages, and a minimum of fifty cents per hour for unskilled labour. So far as that is possible, it is being carried on from one end of Canada to the other. When you suggest in your first demand that these camps be turned into work and wages, that is an impossible situation so far as the Dominion government is concerned.
	Your second demand. No.
	Your third demand. Impossible.
O'NEILL	You could have told us all this by wire.
BENNETT	I'm going on with this memorandum.
	In your fourth demand, you ask for no military control or training in the relief camps. There never has been. It was never suggested there should be.
EVANS	Military rules are published in every camp.
BENNETT	I am familiar with them.

EVANS	You are not.
O'NEILL	There was military training.
BENNETT	Never under the authority of the Department of National Defence.
O'NEILL	What about Point Grey Camp?
BENNETT	That is not a camp where military discipline is maintained.
O'NEILL	You don't seem to know. They wear a uniform and carry rifles… there are boys in Vancouver… they are on strike with us now.
BENNETT	They are not doing that under the direction of the government.
NEILSON	I am an old soldier, familiar with all forms of government…
BENNETT	The government thanks you. Demand number five: no. Demand number six: no.
	That is all that can be said. I want to warn you once more, if you persist in violating the laws of Canada, you must accept full responsibility for your conduct.
EVANS	And you also.
BENNETT	I am prepared for that.
EVANS	So are we.
BENNETT	In order that there may be no misunderstanding, you might make known to all those who are with you that they will be able to go back to their camps, and that as work develops on highways or on any other public undertakings, they will have the opportunity to work, but that a continuance of illegal trespassing upon the property of the railways involving the interruption of mails, the loss of life, and injury to property will not be tolerated. I have nothing more to say.
	Good morning, gentlemen, we have been glad to listen to you.
	Red EVANS joins Sam EAST at another part of the platform. During EAST's appeal, the Ottawa set is struck. Any representation of police are placed at the theatre's exit door. This change can be as noisy as need be. Members of the cast in police uniforms begin to range through the back of the theatre, talking loudly, discussing tactics for cleaning the area. Probably just before EAST's appeal for funds, police drag him and EVANS from the platform.
EAST	My name is Sam East. I have a pastorate here in Regina. I've seen a lot of the boys from the trek in our church. When the Ottawa delegation came back empty-handed, so to speak, a lot of the local people agreed to drive the boys to the Manitoba border. We

thought the march to Ottawa should continue. We arranged a truck cavalcade with the co-operation of the Minister of Highways here in Saskatchewan.

We got a mile and a half out of town.

We were stopped by RCMP federal police, wearing their hats, with riding crops and pistols.

I told them we had the permission of the provincial government to move on that highway.

I was arrested.

They say that any aid to the strikers is illegal under Section 98 of the Criminal Code. "Anyone who assists persons who are in unlawful association or assembly, in the way of transportation, use of buildings, food, and so on, is guilty of an offense."

The strikers are not in unlawful assembly. I was arrested so federal police could take me off the highway.

Unlawful assembly? Sure. Most of the boys are over on the other side of town watching a softball game right now.

I'm glad to see so many Reginans at this rally. We're going to ask you for money to help the strikers. We want to show the RCMP what we think of Section 98.

> *As the police move in, two STRIKERS at the door to the theatre begin to shout.*

STRIKER ONE   You can't do that, he's a preacher.

STRIKER TWO   Oh, God.

> *There are gunshots, sound of breaking glass, screams. All from the back of the theatre if that is possible. There should be a definite sound threat at the exit or exits. EVANS is tussling with a Mountie, or Mounties, on the stage.*

> *Slowly, the police move down to the front of the theatre. The STRIKERS are calling: "They're shooting at us. They're moving in with horses. They can't do this," etc. The police at the front of the theatre have batons. They strike them rhythmically against their palms. The house lights come up.*

POLICEMAN   All right, folks, we're going to clear this area.

POLICEMAN   We've had a little trouble here.

POLICEMAN   There's nothing more to see.

POLICEMAN   Help us along.

POLICEMAN   You're all going home.

POLICEMEN ad lib additional dialogue. At the door of the theatre, as the audience files out, the STRIKERS are handcuffed to policemen. They tell their own stories of what happened after the riot. All the charges were dropped at the trial the next year, they went to their homes or back to the camps which were disbanded the next year, they went to Spain, they fought in the Second World War, they were arrested for vagrancy, they bought a gas station, whatever.

The end.

NOTE on the PLAY TITLE

Plains Indians used to hunt buffalo by stampeding them over a cliff. That was called a "buffalo jump."

CHRONOLOGY of EVENTS

October 1929	Sudden price slumps on the Toronto and Montreal Stock Exchange, and on the Winnipeg Grain Exchange, heralded the arrival in Canada of the Great Depression and the end of the "Roaring Twenties."
July 28, 1930	The Liberal government of Mackenzie King severely defeated in a federal election by the Conservative Party of R.B. Bennett.
October 1932	A nationwide system of Relief Camps established by the Bennett government for single, homeless, and unemployed men.
March 10, 1935	At a Relief Camp Workers' Union meeting in Kamloops, Relief Camp strike planned for April to protest conditions of employment which at that time consisted of food, housing, and payment of twenty cents a day.
April 4, 1935	Beginning of Relief Camp strike.
April 5, 1935	Opening of federally appointed MacDonald Commission hearings into Relief Camp conditions.
April 10, 1935	Strikers congregating in Vancouver refused relief by the city.
April 13, 1935	Strikers' Tag Day in Vancouver, over five thousand dollars collected.
April 23, 1935	Riot involving strikers and police at Hudson's Bay Company store in Vancouver. Mayor Gerry McGeer forced to read the Riot Act.
May 18, 1935	Seizure of Vancouver City Museum by strikers; relief finally granted by the city.
May 29, 1935	Vote taken to begin a mass trek by freight train to Ottawa.
June 3, 1935	Departure from Vancouver of the On to Ottawa Trek.
June 4, 1935	Arrival of Trek in Kamloops.
June 6, 1935	Arrival of Trek in Golden.
June 8, 1935	Arrival of Trek in Calgary.
June 11, 1935	RCMP Assistant Commissioner in Regina instructed that Trek was to be forcibly stopped in that city.
June 14, 1935	Arrival of Trek in Regina.

June 18, 1935	After negotiations with federal ministers, departure of an eight-man delegation to Ottawa, to present the strikers' six main demands to Prime Minister Bennett.
June 22, 1935	Meeting of delegation to Regina; almost two thousand men camped in Regina, rations exhausted, despite the help of a Citizen's Committee formed to aid the trekkers.
July 1, 1935	Dominion Day rally in Market Square; the Regina Riot.
July 4, 1935	Departure of trekkers from Regina.
October, 1935	After a heavily fought election campaign, the Bennett government was defeated in a Liberal landslide victory, returning Mackenzie King to power on a platform that included a commitment to close the Relief Camps.
September 1936	Last of the Relief Camps closed, by which time many of the participants in the trek were on their way to fight in the International Brigades in the Spanish Civil War.

GABE

Gabe was first produced by Toronto Free Theatre on February 14, 1973, with the following company:

Peter Jobin	Gabe
Sol Rubinek	Louis
Brenda Donaghue	Rosie
Chapelle Jaffe	Vonne
Don MacQuarrie	Henry

Directed by Robert Handforth
Set design by Peter Jobin
Costumes by Miro Kinch

CHARACTERS

LOUIS
HENRY
VONNE
GABE
ROSIE

GABE

ACT ONE

The action flows freely, without blackouts, between three areas: The Tahiti Room of the Empress Hotel, Jackson's Service Station, and an exterior area which is presumably located behind the hotel.

The music for the songs should be improvised to suit the tastes and voices of the company. The effect should be of extemporaneous composition.

The Tahiti Room of the Empress Hotel.

LOUIS and HENRY

(*sing*) I got drunk that Friday night
I was pissed north by northeast
There's laws against a one-man war
They should have told me that before
They sent for the police.

I know the Lord loves his soldiers
God loves his soldiers
God loves his soldiers
The Bible tells me so.

I got drunk that Friday night
I got crazy drunk again
Sure I was going to give them hell
Like the crazy bastard Louis Riel
And then the fuzz walked in.

LOUIS   My friends, Gabriel Dumont has persuaded Louis Riel to come from Montana and live among us for a while. This is a great day for the Métis nation. What he did before, Monsieur Riel can do again.

VONNE   Did your friend talk like that in jail, Gabe?

GABE   Better.

VONNE   Best thing I seen in Batoche since the Carling salesman.

LOUIS   *(showing off)* Louis Riel! Was the maddest, smartest, bravest Métis bastard ever wrote his own treaty. Ever fought for the rights of his people. For their land. Fought for representation. For his people and for their children. And the white man. The fucking Canadian, listened to him. We didn't listen.

HENRY is distributing goodies, getting in the way.

VONNE   Sit down, Henry.

HENRY   I got beernuts, and a pepperoni sausage. I got sour cream and onion potato chips. That the kind you like?

VONNE   Shut up, Henry.

LOUIS discovers everyone listening to him. He tails off and dives for his beer bottle.

LOUIS   He was talking about Medicare, health insurance, social security.... Riel was.... The white government's got all that and the Métis got welfare. Got charity and handouts. You know. For being fool enough.... Getting... thirsty.

VONNE covers for him.

VONNE   Last time you saw Rosie, Gabe, she was running around with a bread bag on a string, trying to fly it like a kite.

GABE   *(watching LOUIS)* I guess so.

VONNE   Last time you saw me it was in this hotel. It was upstairs. You were treating yourself.

GABE   *(to LOUIS)* Tell them Louis.

LOUIS   And an Indian agent took some government people into a settlement up north... saw all the people living in shacks by the side of a lake... went back to Regina and planned a community for them. Sent a construction crew in to build a row of little white cottages.... Built them right in the middle of a swamp.

VONNE   *(to GABE)* Your friend is a good talker.

GABE   Heard him argue black is white. He should have been a priest.

LOUIS   People still living in the shacks by the lake... cottages buckling, sinking into muskeg.... Goddamn it, what the hell. I lost my train of thought.

VONNE   How the Indians got screwed.

LOUIS   That's right!

VONNE   How the Métis got screwed.

LOUIS   That's right!

VONNE   Makes a good story sometimes. And sometimes not, of course...

GABE	Tell her, Louis…
VONNE	How I got screwed, for instance. Very close to dull.
HENRY	We don't have to talk about that, Vonne.
VONNE	It's a party, Henry. Have yourself some fun.

HENRY screams wildly like a rodeo cowboy, heaves himself to his feet, picks up his chair, and throws it against the wall. In fact he need not do precisely that, but whatever he does, it will be a physical act of more than considerable force.

HENRY	Welcome! Home! Gabie! I want to make a speech.
VONNE	No use looking foolish, Henry.
HENRY	And I will make a speech. Because I remember, Gabe. Three years ago. Right here in the beer parlour of the Empress Hotel, and I showed him a white man could match him drink for drink.
GABE	Cost you twenty dollars.
HENRY	Cost me forty-five, goddamn it.
LOUIS	By Christ, you know how to have a party.
HENRY	And your friend too. Louis. Welcome to the goddamn Empress Hotel. Welcome to the goddamn Tahiti Room. I'm buying. Drink to Louis.
VONNE	I'll drink to that.
GABE	Louis…
LOUIS	I'll have Gabe's beer if he's not going to use it.
GABE	Louis…
ROSIE	Tell them yourself, Gabe.
GABE	I spent seven years of my life with the priests, five years with the police, and the last three years with Louis. Louis was the only one who taught me anything.
ROSIE	He smells of beer.
GABE	Yeah, well, he's better when he's sober.
ROSIE	He's like my father. Norbert and Louis. Drunks.
GABE	Tell her what we're going to do, Louis.
LOUIS	I'm going to have another beer.
GABE	Sure. And then what?
LOUIS	We'll drink. We'll talk…
GABE	And when we stop talking.
LOUIS	I never stop talking.

GABE	There's more to do than talking.
LOUIS	Gabe's beating drum for me. Going to set me up as a circuit preacher. Going from place to place. Gathering people together…. Going to tell them all about Louis…
HENRY	Riel…
LOUIS	…the one who led the old North-West Rebellion in 1885. And his general, of course, Dumont.
GABE	Don't joke about it.
LOUIS	Dumont, of course, he was the hero. He was the fellow could have made it happen. Went to war against paddle-wheeling steamboats and the brand new Gatling gun. Outnumbered. And he treated the Canadian army like he was hunting it for game.
GABE	And he didn't make it happen.
LOUIS	Yeah. Well, he listened to Riel too long, I guess. Crazy Louis. Watching visions, talking crazy.
GABE	What's so crazy about Louis Riel?
VONNE	Give Gabe a beer.
GABE	I don't want a beer.
VONNE	Sure you do. Get him a beer, Rosie.
GABE	I'm talking to Louis.
LOUIS	And Louis has five years of drinking to catch up on. Last time I was really drunk was the night I went to jail. Whole of the Queen's Beer Parlour tried to raise bail for me, but it didn't seem like such a good idea when they got the money on the table. Drank it up instead. Can't say I wouldn't have done the same.
GABE	Louis Riel was going to save the world. Is that crazy?
LOUIS	Yeah.
GABE	Louis Riel didn't spend much time in the Empress Hotel spinning stories with a halfwit and a broken-down rodeo rider.
HENRY	Who are you calling a halfwit?
GABE	Shut up, Henry.
HENRY	He's only kidding. He always jokes around like that.
LOUIS	*(a little dangerous)* Who are you calling a broken-down rodeo rider.
ROSIE	He's a straight speaker, Gabie. But he's hard to take sometimes.
LOUIS	He's saying, I talk about being out of jail when I'm in jail, and I talk about being in jail when I'm out. There's a lot of truth in that. Makes you think.

HENRY	Never had any sense, Gabie.
VONNE	Probably stole every car for forty miles around at least once.
HENRY	Never did anything with them except run them through fences.
VONNE	Probably broke down every fence for forty miles around at least once.
HENRY	I remember my brother got right sick of it. Putting up fences so that Gabe could knock them down.
GABE	You got very little else to remember, Henry. Save what your brother thought and what I did.
HENRY	He thought he'd teach him a lesson, and when the hotel closed one night he and some of his boys were waiting outside and Gabe came out sure enough and took off and Charles and his boys took off…
GABE	I heard all Henry's stories. Fifty times.
HENRY	And Gabe was tearing across the open country like the world was flat. But when he got to our section, he drove right up to a gate and opened it. Drove through. Got out. Closed the gate again. Well, Charles had to laugh…
ROSIE	Will you be like them? When you're older?
GABE	How?
ROSIE	You know… sitting around every night, getting crazy drunk.
GABE	Why you asking?
ROSIE	Why are you growing your hair so long?
GABE	Rosie is growing up, smartass.
ROSIE	Well, she's growing up.
GABE	You got plans for me? You and your drunken friends?
ROSIE	Why are your pants so tight?
	VONNE gooses him.
GABE	Fuck off, Vonne! Fuck off, everybody!
LOUIS	Gabe is going to have himself a little trouble readjusting.
GABE	Not planning to.
LOUIS	Straight out of jail, back home where there's pretty girls and beer. That's an adjustment. Your parole office will tell you about that.
GABE	Girls and beer got nothing to do with it.
LOUIS	That's where you're wrong. That's where a man of experience has got it all over the young fellows.
GABE	I did enough thinking these three years to know who I am.

LOUIS	Reading classic comic books, true west adventures, and the junior encyclopedia.
GABE	Listening to you.
LOUIS	There's your first mistake.
GABE	I don't switch on and off…
VONNE	Have a drink, Gabe.
GABE	…like a cheap hotel neon sign.
LOUIS	It's a party, isn't it? Take Rosie off somewhere and keep her warm.
GABE	Rosie and I got other things to do.
HENRY	Not Rosie.
GABE	*(to HENRY)* You, shut up!
HENRY	She's been waiting for you.
GABE	You'd stop pimping her and just get stupid drunk, I'd be happier.
HENRY	*(takes ROSIE's arm)* She likes to dance, Rosie does.
GABE	Leave her alone.
VONNE	Gabe's haywire.
GABE	I told you, hands off, Henry.
VONNE	*(to LOUIS)* Time to get under the table. Want to come?
HENRY	The girls are better in the dark and nothing else has changed, right, Gabe?
GABE	It's beer. Vonne throwing her ass around. Rosie on her back. There's nothing else for you.
VONNE	What's wrong with that?
HENRY	I'm dancing with Rosie.
GABE	You got no call to touch her.
HENRY	Try and stop me.
GABE	Going to get your brother in?
HENRY	I don't need old Charles. Not to work you over.
GABE	Step right up, Henry.
HENRY	Who you pushing?
VONNE	*(to LOUIS)* Last time he tried to break down the wall with him.
GABE	I'm not joking, Vonne.

ROSIE	You bring your friend home. Louis. Ask us to meet him. Have a party. First thing you know you got Henry laid out on the floor. Nothing funny about that.
VONNE	What's your friend going to think of us?
GABE	Who cares?
VONNE	You do, Gabie.
ROSIE	Sure you do.
LOUIS	You're a scrappy bastard, aren't you?
GABE	I don't take his kind of shit.
LOUIS	Keeps things lively.
GABE	I don't take any shit.
LOUIS	Give it out but you don't take it.
GABE	Meaning?
LOUIS	Tell Henry you aren't going to beat him, Gabe.
GABE	You got the brains of a rabbit, Henry. People with more sense have to keep telling you how to behave.
HENRY	You aren't known for sense.
GABE	Ask Louis then. Ask the big talker. He's got horse sense, common sense, savvy like your goddamn big brother Charles.... You aren't going to find him up shit creek without a paddle and if you ask him he will tell you to sit there, to keep drinking, and stay out of my way...
HENRY	You don't know your ass from your elbow.
GABE	You're an animal. There's nothing in your head but fucking and eating and drinking and sleeping.
VONNE	So what?
HENRY	What's wrong with Gabe?
GABE	Tell him, Louis. Where we're going. Why he's moving on.
LOUIS	I talk about being out of jail when I'm in jail and being in jail when I'm out.
GABE	Will you shove that crap?
LOUIS	And jail is going to change a person.
GABE	Not me.
LOUIS	Me for instance. They took an idle, good-for-nothing half-breed and they taught me a trade.
GABE	I haven't changed.

LOUIS	Taught me how to make car licence plates.
GABE	Useful.
LOUIS	I'm a machinist.
GABE	You're a drunken, jailbird half-breed.
LOUIS	Give him a beer.
HENRY	The thing about Gabie is, he's got to be yelling all the time.
LOUIS	Lively, goddamn it. Used to yell myself.
GABE	Why does the whole town come out and start drinking with you? Why are you the hero? Because you talk so fine. Like you talked to me. Day after day. I'm a prisoner because I'm a Métis. I'm a political prisoner from the lost Métis nation.
LOUIS	You're a good listener.
GABE	You've stopped talking.
LOUIS	The beer is talking.
GABE	Goddamn it, Louis. We might as well be where we're supposed to be, sucking a tit at the parole office. Talk is shit, Louis. Nothing is happening.
VONNE	And we'll drink to the Métis nation.
GABE	You aren't a political prisoner.
LOUIS	Drink to Louis Riel.
GABE	You went to jail because you got pissed, you put your fist through a store window, and you beat up a mounted policeman.
VONNE	Where Gabe got polluted and hot-wired a car.
GABE	Break and enter. Assault and battery. Auto theft.
LOUIS	You got to wonder why every young Indian, every young half-breed at P.A. got drunk enough once in his life to think he could drive some farmer's truck through a tree.
GABE	I'm wondering what you're going to do about it.
LOUIS	Help you look for Louis Riel. Come on. Where is the bastard. Time he bought a round.
GABE	I'm not looking, Louis. I am here. At Batoche.
LOUIS	Getting bigger and bigger and badder and badder…
GABE	Bravest, toughest, smartest…
LOUIS	Indian cowboys. Win both ways.
GABE	Why not?

LOUIS	Dance-hall girls. Prairie sunsets.
GABE	Seen it all.
LOUIS	Sell tickets to you.
GABE	Three fifty. Five dollars. Hell.
LOUIS	Northern lights. Gopher holes. Big black hats. Cinemascope.
GABE	Goddamn right, you son-of-a-bitch.
LOUIS	Three more hours in the Empress Hotel, you'll be larger than life.
GABE	I don't need the Empress Hotel.
LOUIS	By Jesus, I don't think you do.
HENRY	Gabe wants some excitement.
LOUIS	Why not?
GABE	Why not?
HENRY	You want to go through town raising hell.
GABE	Damn right.
HENRY	You've done that before, boy.
GABE	Don't call me boy.
HENRY	Gabie boy is playing he's a man.

GABE knocks HENRY out of his seat. He laughs.

GABE   Oh, those are fighting words, Henry. I heard nothing like that from you since you were fourteen. You called my mother a whore then sicced old Charles on me.

HENRY   I didn't say I wanted to fight.

GABE   I heard what you said.

HENRY   I didn't mean nothing with it.

GABE   Well, you don't have to worry, Henry, because I've been reformed and revised and rehabilitated. I'm an unabridged, unaggressive pacifist, Henry. I been born again, I seen the light. That's the Canadian prison system for you, Henry. They take a no-good half-breed roughneck and they put him in the chapel every Sunday, since there's nowhere else to go, and I saw God, Henry. God is where Vonne is going to take you, if she stops laughing long enough. Glory be to the Father and to the Son and to the Holy Ghost, Henry. God told me that I shouldn't fight you, no matter how goddamn stupid you were. *(He makes the sign of the cross on HENRY's forehead, using his beer as holy water.)* Let's pray together, Henry.

He pours the rest of the beer over HENRY's head.

HENRY	Leave go of me.
GABE	What do we want down here on our knees, Henry? We're looking for God. And if we find the bugger, we'll ask him for what you want most in the whole world. What's that, Henry? Another round of Molson Ex, good friends standing by you, Vonne, where you can get her easy enough. That's for you, Henry. And I want Louis Riel who fought at Batoche when that was somewhere to be.
VONNE	And what does Louis Riel want?
GABE	Métis rights!

GABE walks away from HENRY who tries to make a joke of it.

HENRY	Gabe was always good at stories. Hah. We'd be tracking things through the bush. Gabe saying he could live in the bush for six months without his rifle, without his pocketknife, Gabie making snowshoes…
GABE	I remember I tied you up in your barn and left you, Henry. I guess Charles got you free.
HENRY	He needs some help. *(pause)* Charles.
GABE	The whole family's in a bad way, my friend.
HENRY	At the gas station. *(to LOUIS)* He needs a machinist. *(to GABE)* And a pump jockey.
GABE	Your brother runs a one-man garage.
HENRY	He wants to expand.
GABE	He's losing more money than a dirt farmer now. Only way he can expand is to hire me and Louis. Because a half-breed gets minimum wage to do the mule work.
HENRY	He's got some things he wants fixed up. Couple of weeks work anyway.
GABE	And you put him up to it. Didn't you, Henry?
HENRY	He wants to expand. Charles.
GABE	Gets pretty lonely out there on the highway. Nothing to do but jerk yourself off. Henry's always liked me. Followed me around. Since we were boys.
HENRY	You're not working, Gabe.
GABE	No.
HENRY	Don't know how much opportunity you think there is around here…
GABE	A man wants to work, not afraid of getting dirty, he can dig in, put down roots, make a good life for himself, isn't that true?
HENRY	Not around here, Gabe.

GABE	Doesn't worry me. I expect any day now, some big record company executive is going to drive through here in a yellow Lincoln convertible, going to discover me singing by the side of the road and make me a star.
VONNE	Why don't you try pumping gas? If big cars impress you.
GABE	You're very understanding.
VONNE	Rosie's working. In the hotel dining room.
GABE	I don't give a good goddamn.
ROSIE	Gabie won't give a good goddamn about half the time. The other half he doesn't give a fuck.
HENRY	Norbert's land is up for taxes.
GABE	Leave me, Henry.
HENRY	So you can't work for him, I mean.
GABE	I know what you mean.
HENRY	If Charles wrote a letter. To the parole office. Said you turned down a job.
GABE	You make me real tired, Henry.
LOUIS	Heard about a high-steel gang in Cedar Rapids. You hear about that, Vonne? Danger pay. Only good Indian's the one that's falling from the forty-ninth floor.
HENRY	I'd like it. If you took the job. There's things to do. There's more than I can handle.
GABE	That's enough.
LOUIS	Easy, Gabe.
GABE	You ever stop to think that what a man can buy for two fifty an hour isn't much of a challenge…. Try a little harder.
HENRY	That's good money, Gabie, around here…
GABE	How much do you make?
HENRY	I got responsibilities.
GABE	You will have if you take us on.
HENRY	It's a start, isn't it? And nobody is going to pay you for living off the bush, are they?
GABE	The thing is, Henry, you got to realize, you're not buying a "pump jockey," you're buying a friend. Two friends. What's that worth, Henry?
HENRY	Working at the gas station could be a hell of a lot better than going back to jail.

GABE	But you aren't talking like a friend.
LOUIS	What they're building in Cedar Rapids…
GABE	You're talking like a soul-saving, do-gooder social worker. Taking trouble, making work for two worthless half-breeds on parole.
LOUIS	It's the tallest, highest, biggest, baddest insurance company in the world. Wouldn't that be something. Working up there, right against the sky?
HENRY	Going to jail is what is going to happen if the parole board finds you turning down work.

LOUIS has been trying to keep GABE off HENRY's throat. HENRY doesn't seem to realize he's talking too much. LOUIS gives him up as a lost cause and lets GABE loose.

GABE	You want your boots licked? You want your ass kissed? You want me to take this fucking job? What do you want me to do first?
LOUIS	He's saying he needs time to think.
VONNE	Ha.
GABE	Think! You know what I think…?
LOUIS	Shut up, Gabe!
GABE	Stoney Mountain is one kind of jail. Jackson's Super Shell Service Station is another kind of jail. Stoney Mountain costs you more and I think if you're planning on keeping me in jail, it's going to cost you.
ROSIE	I start at two.

She gets up. GABE grabs her arm.

GABE	Rosie always had ambitions. Waiting tables…
ROSIE	Washing dishes…
GABE	Whatever. Respectable. Not so rewarding as Vonne there, turning tricks, but it's steady. Isn't that right.
ROSIE	It's real dull, Gabe.

She exits.

GABE	Then stay here, honey.
VONNE	*(calling after her)* It's the beer talking, Rosie.
GABE	I'm not drinking. Louis, he's the drunken no-good. I'm the smartass punk.
HENRY	Rosie wants you to take the job.
GABE	She knows where she can stuff it.

VONNE	Louis doesn't need your job, Henry. He's going to work in high-steel construction.
LOUIS	Right across the border as if it wasn't there. Vonne's coming with me.
GABE	And you can shut up about Cedar Rapids.
VONNE	When I get to Cedar Rapids, I'm going to start all over as a call girl.
GABE	I'll kill you, Louis.
LOUIS	We're going to build our own high-steel project right here in Batoche.
GABE	Damn right.
LOUIS	Going to transmit from the top of it. To our Métis brothers.
GABE	That's right.
LOUIS	Going to generate the power. Going to stay here in Batoche. Going to get a job stake together.
VONNE	(*with wonder*) Gabie's taking Henry's job.
HENRY	I just want to help, Gabe.
GABE	I don't need your help.
HENRY	Well, sure you do…
GABE	Why Henry?
HENRY	Should be thanking me and Charles…
GABE	Why Henry?
HENRY	Like I said, there's not much work around here.
GABE	Why, Henry?
HENRY	And you're half-breeds, aren't you?
GABE	You know what he wants, Louis? Take that coil of rope and pipe it up to the ceiling. Like *Astounding Tales*. Like some Hindu mystical medicine man. Climb up the rope and disappear. That would be an Indian rope trick with some point to it.
HENRY	I want you to come and work for me.
GABE	Wouldn't it be easy if we just disappeared. Turn white for him, Louis.
HENRY	I just want you to go to work.
GABE	Jesus, Henry, you are really something.
HENRY	It's the night shift. I run the station at night.
GABE	Sure you do, Henry. Sitting up all night with nothing to do, that's about as far as your abilities stretch. But now you got two half-breeds on parole. So you can sit out on that highway with two half-breeds working for you.

HENRY	I don't hold a grudge, Gabe.
GABE	I read comic books…
HENRY	Well, hell, so do I!
GABE	…with heroes who can turn into rubber, into plastic. Bulletproof guys. People can fly.
HENRY	We write the comic books, you know. You're not so goddamn smart. Goddamn white man writes the goddamn comic books.

> *HENRY leaves and GABE shouts after him, before storming out in the opposite direction.*

GABE	…Mounties with sled dogs just as smart as they are. These are the guys I know about. You want me invisible, you're going to put up with this invisible bastard, laughing at you. You can't see him, but he's there.
VONNE	Watching Gabie is exhausting.
LOUIS	He'll take Henry's job.
VONNE	So I see.
LOUIS	So don't worry about him. If you want to make him feel better just tell him how Louis Riel told Sir John A. MacDonald that he was the pope of the fucking new world.
VONNE	Is that all?
LOUIS	Tell him how Gabriel Dumont took some spent cartridges and a silver arrow out in the bush. Then he captured three regiments of the Canadian Army, including the Prince Albert volunteers. I made that one up.
VONNE	Gabriel Dumont trained the birds off the trees. Charmed the birds and the bees.
LOUIS	And the loaves and the fishes. Christ, he's better than church.

> *In the parking lot or field behind the hotel, GABE sings to himself. ROSIE enters during the song.*

GABE	*(sings)* I gave my girlfriend a transistor radio She cuts me off all day I gave my girlfriend a transistor radio She cuts me off all day I got a girlfriend who's wired to the sound Of a country and western deejay.
	I took my girlfriend out in the country I meant to find us some hay I took my girlfriend out in the country

> I meant to find us some hay
> Her batteries went dead and she heard what I said
> I said let's go to bed
> She laid shit on my head.
>
> I give you a transistor radio
> I did not count the cost
> I got you a transistor radio
> I did not count the cost
> We can both plug in so let's begin
> But we got our wires crossed.

ROSIE   Thought you were up on your soapbox.

GABE   Passing through, Rosie. Wouldn't want to bore you.

ROSIE   Everyone for forty miles around thinks you and I are going to settle down. Except you.

GABE   Rosie reading movie magazines and true confessions. Amédée Forget falling down drunk all over you and you're watching the ceiling with bubble gum music in your head.

ROSIE   You don't know what I'm thinking.

GABE   Sure I do. You think I'm something. You think I'm getting out of Batoche and I'm going to take you with me. You think you're going to have a house with one bedroom for us and one for the girls and one for the boys. And those little boys and girls are going to get tucked up in their little white sheets. And you and I are going to be screwing around all night. On black satin sheets. They sell those in the movie magazines, don't they?

ROSIE   *(laughing)* Doesn't have to be black.

GABE   And I'll be so tired I'll hardly make it down to somebody else's service station. You got very romantic ideas, Rosie.

ROSIE   You been talking to Kenny Mitchell.

GABE   They been talking to me, sweet little girl, but that's not what they're saying. Kenny says you damn near froze his ass to the dashboard of McQuarrie's pickup truck.

ROSIE   I damn near killed him.

GABE   So he told me.

ROSIE   Because I had no more vouchers for panty hose and how am I going to explain that to the Welfare.

GABE   Yeah, I heard that.

ROSIE   Gabe?

GABE	What?
ROSIE	Did you ask Kenny about me?
GABE	Yes.
ROSIE	Were you mad?
GABE	Why would I be mad?
ROSIE	Why did you ask him?
GABE	What am I supposed to do? I come back here, first thing I understand is Norbert's daughter, Rosie, is all set up for me, not that anybody except Rosie thinks that's a good idea. So all of them are making sure I hear about Kenny Mitchell and the long cold winter when there's nothing else to do.
ROSIE	You know a lot of girls.
GABE	I've been in jail for three years, Rosie. I got political instead.
ROSIE	You used to know a lot of girls.
GABE	Yeah.
ROSIE	When you went to jail, that was because of a woman.
GABE	Like I said, you got very romantic ideas.
ROSIE	You got drunk because those two cowboys beat up a girl you knew.
GABE	I don't need an excuse to get drunk.
ROSIE	But you had one.
GABE	I love women. I love talking and women and everything that takes all your mind and your time. Everything except Jackson's gas station, which is not a consuming interest.
ROSIE	Are you leaving?
GABE	Nothing going around here.
ROSIE	Louis is here.
GABE	Talking in the beer parlour.
ROSIE	You like talking
GABE	More than you can fathom, is it?
ROSIE	Maybe.
GABE	Talking when it takes all my mind. Talking when I care about it. Just talking, I get tired. Why not? I've been talking crazy since I got here and now I'm sitting here like my father's beside me and a hundred ghosts, making some kind of holy agreement with them. I won't talk again. What's the use of talking. What else is there to do?
ROSIE	Did you miss me? While you were gone?

GABE	You're a pretty girl, Rosie.
ROSIE	Did you miss me?
GABE	No.
ROSIE	Crazy bastard.
GABE	I don't need people.
ROSIE	Save for Louis.
GABE	And I don't need him for damn sure. Not when he's sitting around like you and Henry Jackson. Living in some happy time when I lead you and Vonne and Henry out of the wilderness
ROSIE	Crazy bastard.
GABE	I don't need the wilderness. I'd rather steal cars, Rosie. Or set fires.
ROSIE	For your Métis brothers.
GABE	It could be.
ROSIE	Why don't you go to Regina and sit in the lobby of the Parliament Buildings. Why don't you sit on top of the Parliament Buildings? You look like you got a steeple up your ass.
	ROSIE walks into the area representing Jackson's Service Station as HENRY and VONNE enter.
HENRY	Now, I want you girls to hide. No. You're not both getting behind that gas pump. You're sticking out, girls. Quiet, they're coming. Quit giggling, Vonne. *(as he turns up his radio)* Giggle over that, goddamn it.
	LOUIS joins GABE.
LOUIS	Henry Jackson has a new transistor radio.
GABE	He has a credit rating.
LOUIS	Because he works for his brother and his brother's gas station puts four men to work. Man with that kind of business is the foundation of the community.
GABE	How's business, Henry?
LOUIS	Who's that giggling?
GABE	What's Vonne doing behind the gas pump?
HENRY	Got a visitor dropped by to see you.
VONNE	Two visitors.
HENRY	You aren't visiting, Ee-vonne. You make this place feel homey.
GABE	Rosie. Oh, Christ.
ROSIE	Keeps things lively.

LOUIS	Better late than never, Henry. Here's the graveyard shift.
GABE	*(to ROSIE)* You got nothing better to do than hang around a grease pit?
ROSIE	Dishwashing. Beer drinking.
GABE	Why are you following me around all the time? Want me to teach you how to pump gas? Want to crawl under a car with me.
ROSIE	How about a grease job?

HENRY is following LOUIS, brandishing a sheaf of paper.

HENRY	I've been working on some plans. Renovations.

LOUIS takes one sheet of paper and glances at it. The rest of the papers escape him and drift to the floor.

LOUIS	Let's see them, Henry.
HENRY	Got the idea out of *Popular Mechanics*. Where's the one I want here…

GABE has picked up a piece of the paper and glances at it idly.

GABE	Jesus, Henry, this looks more like a cathouse than a gas station.
HENRY	*(to LOUIS)* That's the front view. That's from the side road. Shows the new outbuilding. That's like a floor plan. From up above.
LOUIS	You been working on this all day?
HENRY	All week.
LOUIS	Think the trade will justify it?
HENRY	Sure it will.
GABE	Why don't you stand here and copy down the licence numbers, all the cars that go by. Be a more practical project.
HENRY	*(to LOUIS)* See this is the sales room like a before picture and this is the after…. Must have dropped the after.
LOUIS	A lot of work gone into those plans.
HENRY	*(eagerly)* Once I started, couldn't stop. See, here's the partition here now. Got to move the map rack.
GABE	Something obscene about the way you draw a gas pump.
LOUIS	Once Gabe starts, he just can't stop.
VONNE	Rosie came down here to see you, Gabe.
GABE	If she thinks I've got anything like these gas pumps, she's in for a surprise.
LOUIS	Gabie's got his sleeves rolled up. Let's get to work.

HENRY	I thought we could have a party. Well, sure because we don't get much business on the weekend. Vonne helped me plan it, didn't you, Vonne? There's music. And I bought some whiskey.
VONNE	I'm drinking this whiskey.
HENRY	Well, there's more. Sure. Because Friday night everyone stays in town, you see, and there might not be a car out here from one end of the shift to the other. Not unless we ask them to deliver Chinese food. Ha. (*But no one seems to think that's funny and no one wants Chinese food either.*) Well, I'd like to make a toast. Like to welcome you, Gabe, and also Louis, to Jackson's Service Station.

VONNE and ROSIE cheer.

VONNE	Says what he means and he means what he says.
ROSIE	And he's buying again.
VONNE	Ray. Ray. Ray.
HENRY	What do you think of that?

Pause.

LOUIS	(*finally*) It's kind of you, Henry. Isn't it, Gabe?
GABE	You're a prince, Henry,
HENRY	Now it wasn't all my idea. No. It was Vonne, too. Wanted to make sure you got the right kind of welcome, didn't you, Vonne?
VONNE	(*growing unaccountably shy*) The thing about Henry's radio, it has this plug here, you can stick it in your ear.

She does, and starts to dance.

HENRY	I told her, Vonne, a gas station, it doesn't seem to be much for a party atmosphere and she told me that it was having your friends around you made a party, even if all you were doing was passing a bottle around in a circle at the side of the road.
GABE	All we are doing, Henry.
LOUIS	(*to HENRY, but for GABE's benefit*) Nights like this with your friends around you. Makes it all worthwhile.
HENRY	(*to LOUIS*) Something I wanted to talk to you about.
LOUIS	What?
HENRY	You and Vonne should get together.
GABE	Vonne's all wired up to your transistor radio.
ROSIE	Shut up, Gabe.
HENRY	(*to LOUIS*) You should ask her to dance or something.

GABE	She's dancing. She don't need encouragement.
HENRY	*(to LOUIS)* Go on. Ask her.
LOUIS	No, I couldn't do that.
HENRY	Go on. She likes you.
GABE	Oh, Christ.
LOUIS	I thought you and Vonne…
HENRY	She likes you.
GABE	Oh, Christ.
LOUIS	*(to HENRY)* You think so?
GABE	I think this whole goddamn thing is crazy. *(to LOUIS)* Where do you think you're going?
LOUIS	Dance with Vonne.
GABE	She's a three-fifty ticket or a big wide smile. You know that, Louis.
LOUIS	Fuck off!
GABE	Well, I had enough of your party, Henry…
LOUIS	Vonne?
GABE	Vonne is bouncing up and down, saying she likes country music when it's just her pants are hot.
LOUIS	*(to HENRY)* She's not listening.
GABE	*(to HENRY)* And the whiskey's rotgut.
HENRY	Well, there's more. Hell.
GABE	And Rosie's watching me as if that passed the time.
LOUIS	*(to himself)* Well, why not then?
GABE	Because it's embarrassing, Louis.
LOUIS	*(to VONNE)* Vonne, well, I thought…
VONNE	*(jumping in)* What?
LOUIS	*(awkward)* I'm beginning to like you. When's your birthday. Ha.

GABE sings. LOUIS and VONNE dance.

GABE	*(sings)* I met a man who said to me The Métis nation's proud and free And you and me can show them what to be I felt the glory, seen the light But I end up here every night Eating shit and bored out of my tree.

I should have known it wasn't true
In fact I guess I know I knew
I knew that I had heard his con before
He's a rodeo rider who forgot his horse
And he don't have much to do of course
Save for jumping on and off a two-bit whore.

> *HENRY loves the song. He sings the second verse again. GABE cuffs*
> *him hard enough to knock him over.*

GABE You're so stupid, Henry.

HENRY You're kidding, aren't you?

GABE What do you think?

HENRY Haywire smartass bastard.

ROSIE Just leave him.

HENRY Gone too far.

LOUIS Leave him, Henry.

GABE What she wants you to do, Louis, is tear the goddamn radio off her ear, rip her blouse open. Back her up against a wall somewhere so Henry can watch.

LOUIS Leave me, Gabe.

HENRY He wants a fight, he's asking for it.

LOUIS No, he isn't.

HENRY I'll fight him for you.

VONNE *(with transistor radio)* Take this, Henry. Stick it in your ear.

LOUIS He wants a few speeches. A few fine thoughts.

GABE More than that.

LOUIS Gabe's very bright. Managed to go through eight years of church school without finding that out. Used to ask questions and the answers weren't in the books. Got his knuckles rapped.

GABE Beat me for it.

LOUIS Out of school with nothing to do but get in trouble. Finally made three years worth of trouble. Met me. I'm a rodeo hero, used to putting on a great amount of style. Gabe was listening… he had too much time to think… you remember what I told you?

GABE I'll kill you, Louis.

LOUIS I told him things he could be proud of. How the Indians lived before the whites came and about their ideas of property, how property was held in common. And I told him what I thought that private ownership did to people. That some people had and others had not. And that set-up can get kind of like a jail outside a jail, so pretty soon people can be born and live and die, having not, and their children the same. I gave him a lot of attention. He misses it. He's jealous, Vonne. Don't notice him.

GABE   You bastard!

LOUIS   I've been in jail a lot and I talk a lot in jail to pass the time. Because the conversation is not so stimulating in the ordinary way.

GABE   You come out of P.A. just to lie here dying.

LOUIS   You think you've got the answers now. You want to be a circuit-riding preacher and you want me to carry your cross.

GABE   I do, yes.

LOUIS   I've done the circuit breaking wild horses. I've had it.

GABE   What's the use of talking?

LOUIS   I think I made more money than you'll ever see. All off the rodeos. And I spent it all living higher than you'll ever want to... than I hope you'll ever want to. Almost killed myself spending it. I got myself drunk as a skunk on very old special brandy, drove my great big yellow convertible off a bridge into the mighty Saskatchewan River. Got out of hospital to find my luck was gone. Well, the big car was gone. I was still as big and brave as hell but I didn't win anymore. Ended up as a rodeo clown, running for a barrel. Quite a figure of fun. The money was not so good. The drinking was bad. So I stopped it. I got no intention of starting over. What do you think of that?

GABE   I think you're talking fine again. Talking poetry. Talking pretty. Talking shit.

LOUIS   It's not so much what you say, it's how you say it and if you say it so it sounds good enough, there's people going to believe it. You should leave off telling stories. Since you end up lying to yourself. You should try and learn a trade.

        GABE picks up HENRY's whiskey bottle.

GABE   You know what I think? I think I can finish this bottle in one swallow. Want to bet, Louis? Watch me.

LOUIS   No need to go that far.

ROSIE   Gabie drinks like a kid.

        GABE drains the bottle. The others watch.

GABE   By Christ, you're all looking at me like I was a bomb. Exploding. By Jesus. I see why you do it, Louis. Why you're drinking all the time.

LOUIS	Not your style.
GABE	You don't know my style.
LOUIS	You're not a drinker.
GABE	Henry will listen to you. Vonne will listen to you. Because they are shitheads. They got nothing else to do.
VONNE	Vonne is drinking.
GABE	So am I, Vonne.
	He takes VONNE's bottle.
VONNE	Just shove it up your ass, Gabe.
LOUIS	Leave it!
GABE	Leave me!
LOUIS	Goddamn kid! All right!
	LOUIS leaves.
GABE	Watch me, Rosie. I can finish this one too.
ROSIE	*(exits)* I've seen that done, Gabe.
GABE	You've seen nothing.
HENRY	Yippee, Gabie!
VONNE	Shut up, Henry.
HENRY	You see that? That's the second bottle he's got there. Isn't that something?
VONNE	Thought you were going to beat him for me.
HENRY	By Jesus, I wouldn't go near him. I seen him crazy drunk before.
VONNE	You can wait till he falls over and kick him a little.
HENRY	I seen him drunk but I never seen him so drunk as he's getting right now.
VONNE	Maybe he'll rush the gas station, Henry. Maybe you should plan on holding him off.
HENRY	Where's he gone? Where is he?
	In fact GABE has wandered off with the remains of the bottle.
VONNE	Right behind you.
HENRY	What? Shit, Vonne, no, he isn't. Say…
VONNE	What?

HENRY	You remember what happened when Charles got hold of that dog of Gabe's, used to follow him round. That orange dog. The one that pissed in Charles's hat that time.
VONNE	Goodbye, Henry.
HENRY	Vonne?

HENRY trails out after VONNE as GABE and ROSIE enter through the hotel to the exterior area at the rear of the hotel.

ROSIE	Henry doesn't know what you're talking about.
GABE	When?
ROSIE	When you tell him how stupid he is. If he did know, he'd kill you.
GABE	Henry's a white man with mush in his head. He thinks that makes him a full-scale Indian.
ROSIE	So do you.
GABE	Sure.
ROSIE	You think it's special being Indian. Sure there's a whole government department set up for you, but they're white, they don't know what they're doing. They don't understand you at all. They don't know how drunk you can get and they don't know how stupid you can be.
GABE	And you think just because a couple of nuns taught you how to run an adding machine, you're going to be a guiding light for the checkout girls at an IGA store in Saskatoon.
ROSIE	*(laughs)* I do not.
GABE	Shit, Rosie, next thing you'll be telling me you want to go to teacher's college.

This ROSIE finds terribly funny. GABE is not amused.

ROSIE	Next thing I'll say I want to be a nun.
GABE	Sure. You want out of here and you want me to take you out. I'm a half-breed. I've got white blood and it shows, doesn't it? I don't look greasy, do I? Catch me in a dim light, I might not be Indian at all.
ROSIE	You play the part real well.
GABE	Meaning?
ROSIE	You act like you're the band chief looking for the last buffalo.
GABE	I know what I am.
ROSIE	What are you cleaning that gun for?
GABE	It's my gun. It should be clean.

ROSIE	You're on parole.
GABE	I'm going hunting.
ROSIE	You're on parole. You work at Jackson's Gas Station.
GABE	Jesus, you do. You sound like a little white schoolteacher, you know that.
ROSIE	I don't…
GABE	I'm sick of it. I'm sick of Jackson's Gas Station and I'm sick of you following me around and I'm going out in the bush. I'm going to stay there till I got some peace again and Jackson's not going to do anything about it. The parole board's not going to send me back. Because I'm just another crazy Indian. They locked up all the crazy Indians, they'd have no place to build hockey rinks.

As GABE exits, the lights come up on Jackson's Service Station. HENRY, VONNE, and LOUIS enter. ROSIE joins them.

HENRY	Well, if he's going off, I'll tell you one thing. I'm not holding his job open for him. We got to get them renovations finished. Yes, sir, first person who comes out here, looking for work, the job's theirs if they want it. If they're qualified.
LOUIS	Gabe's got the qualifications.
HENRY	Well, he's handy.
ROSIE	He used to stay with us young kids when my mother and father went off. Drinking. Two, three days at a time. One time it was three weeks, but I was older then and I think that was after… no, that was the same summer Gabie went haywire. His mother thought she was something. She kept her looks. She looked like Gabie's sister, last time I remember her. He don't know who his father was.
HENRY	He's too wild.
ROSIE	I don't remember him like that. I remember him telling the little kids stories, comic book stories, but he'd make them up and I was the oldest girl.
HENRY	He only stayed around you because his ma was off to Regina, wearing silver slippers. You'd be better off with me, Rosie, if I'd have you.
VONNE	She don't want you, Henry. You're simple.
HENRY	Gabe won't have her. The thing about that bastard is he's got women flying over him, taking leaps at him. That Kennedy's wife thinks he's a hell of a stud. She's been driving their Chevy six miles down here so Gabe can top off the gas tank, she'll make it six miles back. Give Rosie a drink, Louis.

LOUIS passes ROSIE the bottle.

LOUIS	It's okay, Henry's got another twenty-sixer in the truck.
HENRY	He ever tell you how he came to steal that car? That was another woman. He hardly knew her. There was a fight outside the beer parlour. Two greasers pulled her into the car.
VONNE	We want to stop talking about Gabe all the time.
HENRY	Two Mounties standing there laughing. Gabe took off after them. He's got a mind of his own but he was totalled and he totalled the car, of course.
VONNE	You will understand, Henry, that Louis and I got better things to do.
HENRY	Well, sure. Keeps things lively.
VONNE	Isn't that right, Louis?
LOUIS	I guess I told him up to thirty, forty times, all about the North-West Rebellion, all about the rodeo.
VONNE	Isn't that right, Louis. You and I are going to have ourselves a time.
LOUIS	God loves his soldiers.
VONNE	Sure he does, honey.
LOUIS	Dumont was a general.
VONNE	What's going on?
LOUIS	*(to ROSIE)* Did he say where he was going?
ROSIE	To the bush.
LOUIS	Gabe can take care of himself.
ROSIE	He can't stay out of trouble.
VONNE	Sure. He's probably off somewhere right now, shooting a hole through his foot.
ROSIE	I remember Gabie came by one night. Tapping on the window. There was frost in his hair.
LOUIS	Gabe got me to come up here to Batoche with him. He said, it's my town Louis. You can take it over. They'll name it after you.
HENRY	Charles used to beat him up a lot.
ROSIE	Lets have a party.
VONNE	We're having a party.
ROSIE	Get the other bottle.
VONNE	Plenty there still.

ROSIE drains the bottle she's holding.

ROSIE	Get it, Henry.
HENRY	Sure. Why not?
LOUIS	He'll tell you I did the talking. Ha. That's one of his stories.
ROSIE	Frost in his hair. Pushing snow down my back.
HENRY	I guess he could kill Charles now, if he wanted.
ROSIE	It's no good, is it?
LOUIS	Got a mind of his own.
ROSIE	He's supposed to be your friend. He didn't even tell you he was going. Sometimes I could kill him, Louis.
LOUIS	Gone as far as that.
ROSIE	He's gone off because he thinks nobody tells him what to do. Thing is, everyone tells him what to do. He just does the opposite.
LOUIS	He's like you.

A blare of music, loud and tinny, badly amplified. HENRY returns with another bottle of whiskey.

VONNE	And I think we should have a party.
HENRY	You like that? I got a loudspeaker wired into the radio in the truck.
ROSIE	He doesn't care about me, does he?
HENRY	*Popular Mechanics.*
LOUIS	Sure he does. And we care about you. Little Rosie. Sweet little girl. We care about you a lot.
VONNE	Turn off that radio.
ROSIE	I want to dance.
LOUIS	Sure.
HENRY	Dance with her, Louis.
LOUIS	Well, all right then. Well, watch me.
ROSIE	Dance with me. Watch me. Fuck him.
VONNE	Turn off that radio. Turn off that fucking radio.

ROSIE dances, joined by LOUIS. The music and the dance peak. HENRY watches, very intent.

ROSIE	I don't care about Gabe.
LOUIS	It's okay, honey. It's all right.
VONNE	I didn't come out here to watch you two climbing all over each other.

HENRY   The thing is, Louis, I noticed Wednesday is always a little slow. You got to wait till Friday, if it's a payday Friday, to see any traffic at all on this road. I mean, I figure we could knock off for a while, Louis, what do you think. Not up to Gabe to have all the fun, is it? Louis? What do you say? Louis?

    Blackout.

ACT TWO

Lights up on ROSIE and GABE.

ROSIE   So I went to confession. I had Father Paul and he's been looking at you and me sideways ever since you came back. So I surprised him. He pretended he couldn't stop coughing.

GABE   Why did you go to confession?

ROSIE   You have to if you want to take communion.

GABE   Why do you want to take communion?

ROSIE   I don't.

GABE   You're like me, aren't you?

ROSIE   No.

GABE   Sure you are. Whole town watching your middle for signs of my kid and you end up laying out for all-talk-no-action Louis. Just for the shock of it. Rosie, honey, there's something real wrong with your head.

ROSIE   Passes the time.

GABE   Louis taken with you now?

ROSIE   He was drunk.

GABE   Yeah, well, he's always drunk.

ROSIE   I don't even think he remembers.

GABE   Drunk as a skunk in the cab of another pickup truck and him talking all the whole time while your head is banging on the dashboard. Little Rosie. I guess he told you it was poetry.

ROSIE   Yeah, well, I didn't believe him.

GABE   Why not?

ROSIE   It isn't poetry, is it?

GABE   Poor Rosie.

ROSIE   Why poor Rosie? What do you know?

GABE   I know it's better in bed for one thing.

ROSIE   You know street tramps in Regina!

GABE   I don't like my women so lonely there's nothing else for them to do.

ROSIE   Your women?

GABE   I had women when you were wishing I'd come by and catch frogs with you, Rosie.

ROSIE   You think you know everything.

GABE   Damn near.

ROSIE   You don't know so much because you make it all up. Your women. You
                got all your women dressed in silver paper in your head. Speaking
                French.

GABE   You going to ask me what happened when I was out in the bush?

ROSIE   No.

GABE   You peddling your ass around, you think that's all that happened?

ROSIE   I didn't peddle…

GABE   It's a big country, Rosie. Come on.

ROSIE   No.

GABE   I'm going to tell you. Didn't have a drink for two weeks. That's to
                satisfy the schoolteacher in you that wants me settled down. That's not
                the interesting part. I made a fast.

ROSIE   You mean you went hungry.

GABE   I lived off that bush when I was younger and stupider than you'll ever
                be…. I mean I didn't eat for two days, almost three… just to clear my
                mind.

ROSIE   What mind?

GABE   There it is. I'm not eating. I haven't spoken for about a week. I'm
                forcing myself to stay awake, just to see what will happen. This is the
                third day. The sun is coming up.

                A long pause.

ROSIE   What happened?

GABE   I passed out from the weakness. I woke up, my arm was gone right up
                to the shoulder, down the throat of a hungry looking wolverine.

ROSIE   What happened?

GABE   What happens when you fast, you wouldn't know this, being purely
                interested in physical pleasures, you have visions. You go right off your
                skull. The sun came up over the lake. The lake was on fire. There's a
                voice inside my head, but it's everywhere. Realest thing I ever heard.
                "Gabe, this is what you're going to do, I'll lay it out for you. This is
                your destiny." I knew it wasn't me talking then. Destiny is not a word
                I'd use.

ROSIE   Then what happened?

GABE   Voice kept going.

ROSIE   What did it say?

GABE   I don't know. I was laughing too hard.

ROSIE	Because I guess you think you're very funny.
GABE	No, it's true. The whole story. You know what I mean?
ROSIE	No.
GABE	You care?
ROSIE	No.
GABE	You know the only thing that worries me, Rosie? Sometimes I think I'm crazy. My father was some wandering white maniac. With an axe. Sure. He had fits, Rosie. Didn't know what was happening to him.
ROSIE	Norbert's crazy.
GABE	You aren't like Norbert, Rosie. You know it.
ROSIE	My old man is crazier than you could ever think up.
GABE	I'm trying to tell you that I don't know what I'm going to do next. Half the time. That I feel crazy, Rosie. Half the time. And the only thing that I can say about what is going to happen… I mean, happen to me… it's going to be wild, Rosie, it's going to be crazy.
ROSIE	I feel like that.
GABE	There are words in my head, if I say them, I can't understand why there isn't somebody there to answer back. And sometimes I think I know all the answers. Got the questions and the answers all my own in one head. You can see how crazy that is.
ROSIE	All the things in your head, Gabe, they already happened.
GABE	I guess so.
ROSIE	That's why you think they're so big.
GABE	Sure. Dumont and Riel made it happen. Right? Almost made it happen. And all I do is come back to Batoche.
ROSIE	Louis will be glad you're back.
GABE	Sure. Well, next time, I'll give you a little warning. Take you both with me. Take three things with me. Rosie. Louis. And a hunting knife. What will you take, Rosie?
ROSIE	Black satin sheets.
GABE	What else?
ROSIE	Why are you taking Louis?
GABE	All right. Going out in the bush with two things. Rosie and a hunting knife.
ROSIE	You can take him if you want to.

GABE	Oh, sure. I can go out in the bush with Louis. With Henry. All the white men of the world. All the losers of the world. I could guide them through the wilderness.
ROSIE	You like Louis.
GABE	Or I could do it by myself. I can't depend on Louis all my life, now can I?

Some of which is overheard by LOUIS and VONNE who enter from the Tahiti Room.

LOUIS	There's something we have to settle, Gabe.
GABE	There's something I want to finish telling you, Rosie. What happened when I was out in the bush. I followed Norbert's excuse for a trapline, mainly. Laughable. When I was young, I lived off Norbert's traps sometimes. He used to have it together. Christ. Well, it's one more thing I'm going to have to learn to do for myself. Right?
VONNE	Louis went hunting on the weekend.
GABE	What did you get, Louis?
LOUIS	Nothing.
VONNE	Rabbit.
LOUIS	Nothing.
VONNE	Bought three rounds at the Empress Hotel on the strength of them.
LOUIS	You know what happened while you were gone.
GABE	Empress sold a lot of beer.
LOUIS	At the gas station.
GABE	Trade was not substantial.

LOUIS delivers his next speech as a set piece, a formal apology. It seems to be the protocol of another time. The puncturing of LOUIS's posture satisfies GABE, he is willing to make peace but finds he's gone too far.

LOUIS	Want you to know, Gabe, that it wouldn't have happened. No. I don't know what to say. I feel kind of bad. I guess I stepped out of line but I don't know what to say about it. Is that all right?
GABE	What do you mean?
LOUIS	Me and Rosie.
GABE	Christ, Louis. Rosie didn't mind.

Pause. LOUIS explodes.

LOUIS	Saskatchewan does not amount to much.

GABE	Uncivilized.
LOUIS	There's other places I could be.
GABE	Well, sure.
LOUIS	Going to Cedar Rapids.
GABE	That's fine, Louis.
LOUIS	Don't believe me, do you?
GABE	Sure I do. Sure. It sounds like a good plan.
LOUIS	You don't think I'm going, do you? You think I'm shit. You think I'm going to stick around this asshole town with your name all over it. Watching you hell around like helling around was going out of style. Like there was a future in it. I've raised more hell than you'll even get a chance to dream about.
GABE	Going to get Henry to sell me a car he's got down at the station. Going to take advantage of his good nature, since he knows what a tough bastard I am. Going to say I'll give him fifty dollars for it, since it ain't worth ten.
LOUIS	I don't suppose you want a beer. You don't see the value of it. You're too good for beer drinking.
GABE	I don't need it.
LOUIS	I need a beer to stomach you.
	LOUIS exits.
GABE	Hey, Louis…
VONNE	Prick.
GABE	Hey, Vonne…
ROSIE	You think you want Henry's car.
GABE	I'll work it over, get it running, get into it, and drive until it falls apart. See where we are then. Take a deep breath and dive right in.
ROSIE	You don't have fifty dollars.
GABE	You don't understand finance.
ROSIE	You don't understand Louis.
GABE	Lost my train of thought.
ROSIE	Your train of thought! You do the talking. You tell the stories.
GABE	I'm not talking to you if you're not talking sense, Rosie. What's wrong with Vonne?
VONNE	Fuck off!

GABE Misses me. Don't worry, honey. Rosie and I is not significant. Won't change a thing. Vonne and I will climb a lot of steps together.

ROSIE Your pants are too tight and your hair is too long. There is nothing in your stupid head but you. You want Louis to be one thing. You want me to be one thing.

GABE I want excitement. There's a lot finer things in the world than Henry Jackson with his hands in his pockets. Than Batoche. Than a prairie fire.

VONNE You can leave Henry out of your discussions.

GABE Henry.

VONNE You can stop making fun of him.

GABE I love women. Sometimes I get the feeling that's about all you can count on to surprise you. Be just as pure and fine as the fire on the lake.

VONNE You can fuck off. You and your fine fucking talk about big talkers and white men with turnips for brains.

GABE Louis not talking to you?

VONNE He's another one.

GABE You got Louis all wrong. He'll be back. He and I have plans.

ROSIE Liar.

GABE Sure. We're going to Cedar Rapids.

ROSIE Stop laughing at him.

GABE Well, we're getting out of here for damn sure. Him and I get along.

ROSIE Like you and I get along like a prairie fire.

GABE I'm going to talk to Louis.

ROSIE No you aren't.

VONNE No more.

GABE (to ROSIE) Who says?

ROSIE I do.

VONNE I do.

GABE (to ROSIE) Like to see you stop me.

ROSIE You'll go through that door over my dead body.

GABE Have to do better than that.

ROSIE Try and pass me.

   ROSIE kicks, aiming for GABE's groin.

GABE	You stay above the belt, Rosie. Jesus, you don't know where to start.
ROSIE	I do what I like.
GABE	Yippee, Rosie!
ROSIE	If you're going to Cedar Rapids, I'm going with you. Louis driving your fifty-dollar car. And you in the back seat with me, keeping quiet.
GABE	Can't help liking you.
VONNE	You're staying off of Louis's back.
ROSIE	*(as their fight continues)* Crazy bastard! You and Louis get along, sure you do. If he is playing your rules. If you win. You got nothing going for you but wild, crazy talk and there isn't anyone can understand it. Isn't anyone would care if you did make any sense. I want you out of here! You aren't leaving, Gabe!

> ROSIE *frantically rushes* GABE. VONNE *joins in, and the fight continues through the following dialogue.*

VONNE	Just one reason he wants to go to Cedar Rapids. Get some quiet drinking done.
GABE	Now just a minute, Vonne.
VONNE	And he can't do that when you're around.
GABE	I'm not fighting the both of you girls.
VONNE	You're too young and stupid for him, Gabie. He remembers what that's like. He drinks beer about it. He remembers what it's like and he don't need you to remind him.
GABE	I want to explain to you about the victory at Duck Lake.
VONNE	Suck Duck Lake.
GABE	When Dumont had twenty-five men on horseback and a few men on foot and Crozier had one hundred soldiers, the Prince Albert volunteers, with cannon.
VONNE	You can leave him in peace.
ROSIE	You can stay here. You can go. You can make up your mind.
GABE	See Dumont's brother, Isidore, went out to meet Crozier's men. He was waving a white blanket.
ROSIE	White blankets. Sure.
GABE	And Crozier, rather than thinking that he wanted to parlay, figured Dumont was trying to outflank him.
VONNE	Rather have Louis falling blind drunk…
GABE	So he shot Isidore…

VONNE	…falling blind drunk than have you at the best of times.
GABE	Shot Isidore dead, goddamn it.
VONNE	I got him, Rosie.
GABE	Well, the Métis did outflank the government men. The government couldn't do anything right. They racked up their cannon. They loaded the shell in before the powder so they couldn't get the shell out.
ROSIE	I don't have to stay here.
GABE	The Canadians said the Métis fired the first shot. Well, that was a lie.
ROSIE	I don't have to stay here. I don't have to listen to you.
VONNE	We don't.
ROSIE	Crazy bastard.
VONNE	Come on, Rosie.
ROSIE	Crazy Bastard.
	They exit.
GABE	Crozier claimed heavy casualties on Dumont's side. Eighty men. Well, that was a lie. Maybe there were eight men in the neighbourhood heard the shots. And come to see what was going on. But by the time they got there, the Canadians was long gone. Nothing to see but Louis Riel riding up and down waving a big silver cross.
	GABE has had much the worse of his battle with the girls. He is flat out, exhausted. LOUIS enters from the bar.
LOUIS	*(amused)* You all right?
GABE	My hand's bleeding, that's all.
LOUIS	Can you get up?
GABE	I can do anything! Anything! Can't I? My ears are ringing. Look at that. Blood. Amazing, isn't it? Reminds me of the time I locked the keys inside an old car I had. I was drinking then. So I said, "We can fix that," and I put my fist through the window and I got the keys and my hand was bleeding and my arm, like it is now.
LOUIS	Your hand's not bleeding.
GABE	It's bloody.
LOUIS	It's your nose.
GABE	It's my head.
LOUIS	Sit down. Take it easy.
GABE	You're all right, aren't you? Not a mark on you. Not much of a fighter, are you?

LOUIS	Got a beer in my hand.
GABE	I'll join you.
LOUIS	First long step to being like me and Norbert. Fucked up traplines, pickled eggs, shuffle board. Draught beer politics at the Empress Hotel.
GABE	I got my own temperance league.
LOUIS	So I've seen. Got your own code of ethics. Coat of arms. Got your own newspaper. Print your own news. Make every goddamned night at a goddamned half-assed gas station into goddamned opening day at the goddamn Calgary Stampede.
GABE	So Rosie told me.
LOUIS	She's got a way with words.
GABE	Spellbinder.
LOUIS	You've got a good friend in Rosie.
GABE	I appreciate her interest.
LOUIS	Rosie sees where you're going.
GABE	More than I do.
LOUIS	Well, some are better at it.
GABE	It's kind of funny. I tell you I'm moving in with Rosie and I tell her I'm going to Cedar Rapids with you. And what I'm really going to do is stay in Batoche. End up killing some simple-minded white man like Henry Jackson in a barroom fight that gets out of hand.

GABE and LOUIS enter Jackson's Service Station where HENRY is sitting around with VONNE and ROSIE.

HENRY	You know, I always had trouble thinking of things to say to people until I read this magazine with some good advice. Talk about what you know about, it said, and if there's one thing I know about, it's cars. Well, happens that is something that just about everybody is interested in. Cars. So a good thing to do instead of standing around looking stupid, is to turn to the next fellow. Ask him what kind of car he drives. First time I tried it, the fellow drove a Chevy and he had a lot of trouble with the carburetor.
GABE	I'd like you to sell me that Ford you got out back.
HENRY	Seemed like he'd keep getting dirt in the fuel line.
GABE	Want to buy that Ford, Henry.
HENRY	Oh, I couldn't do that.
GABE	Why not.
HENRY	Well, it isn't worth much, Gabe. No. You wouldn't want to buy it.

LOUIS	He can get it running.
GABE	Hell, Henry. I won't lie to you. I got it running.
HENRY	Ford out back?
GABE	Sure.
HENRY	That's something, isn't it?
GABE	All the nights out here on the highway when I should have been watching you drink yourself stupid.
HENRY	That old Ford.
GABE	Fifty dollars.
HENRY	What do you want with that old Ford?
GABE	Well, the first thing we're going to do is paint it up like a medicine show.
LOUIS	That's because he's hell for style.
GABE	The second thing I'm going to do is take a leaf from your book, Henry…
HENRY	Yes?
GABE	Going to wire the whole vehicle for sound.
HENRY	Got a tip for you there.
GABE	There'll be speakers built in the doors. Under the floorboards. Inside the upholstery like a voice in your pillow.
LOUIS	We will broadcast from that car.
GABE	That car is going to be powered by sound, Henry.
HENRY	Needs an FM radio.
GABE	And then I'm going to jump parole and drive.
HENRY	Where are you going?
GABE	Where we going, Louis?
HENRY	Is Louis going?
GABE	We're all going.
HENRY	Who?
GABE	We're all going.
HENRY	Me?
GABE	Where we going, Henry?
HENRY	Well. Me. Well. Don't mind if I do.

GABE	You look to be the kind of man who wants to see the ocean. That's where we'll go, Henry. Stopping only in Cedar Rapids, Iowa, where Louis and I, since we're sure-footed, have a keen sense of balance… we'll be working in high-steel construction for a while.
HENRY	All of us?
GABE	And Rosie and Vonne are going. Keep that back seat homey. *(The girls are playing cards and GABE includes them in the story.)* The girls are going to dress up like gypsies. Tell fortunes. That's how we'll paint the car, Henry. Like a gypsy tea room.
VONNE	Rosie and Vonne heard enough of your bullshit.
ROSIE	We're staying right here.
GABE	Not when you hear about it. Bought the car for you. Have the doors painted yellow. Close to gold. With your name on. Rosie. That's a name. Curling all up over the door, looks like it's alive. And Ee-Vonne. Spell it with a Y.
VONNE	Want to tell Gabie's fortune, Rosie?
LOUIS	Gabe. Will. Make. It. Work. From the antenna on the tower in Batoche, Saskatchewan, Gabe will broadcast on an assigned frequency of sixty thousand kilohertz at a dangerous altitude with power of millions of watts. As he completes his broadcast day, good night and good morning.
ROSIE	Gabie is a tall, dark stranger. Thinks he came from across the sea somewhere. In a boat. To rescue somebody. Looks like a white man with a Bible in his hand. Standing right in front of the sun with a fierce-looking, stupid-looking smile.
	She pushes the cards she has laid out together and looks up for his reaction.
GABE	Jesus, Rosie.
VONNE	Want to go to the ocean with him?
ROSIE	I want to go to bed with him.
VONNE	I want to go to Regina. Think he'll get that far?
GABE	Take you where you want to go. Seen the error of my ways.
ROSIE	I heard that before.
GABE	Don't get anywhere by fighting you, do I? You're tough, Rosie. Beat me to the floor.
ROSIE	Because I'm sick of stories.
GABE	Ride the river with you. Sure. Vonne, too. Tough little broads.
ROSIE	All in your head. Crazy stories. What you need is an axe.

GABE	I need to fly, Rosie.
ROSIE	I don't care.
GABE	You can fly.
ROSIE	Sure I can.
GABE	Come on then.

He picks her up and spins her around.

VONNE	And we'll paint on the front of it. "Gabie's Crazy Ford." Louis can be president.
LOUIS	Not for long.
VONNE	Sure you can.
LOUIS	I'm tired, Vonne. I'm here for the ride.
VONNE	We'll go to Regina. Sure. Why not?
ROSIE	We'll eat in restaurants and sleep in hotels. Ride around in big cars, blowing smoke in people's faces.
VONNE	Remember Gabie's mother. She looked like his sister. We'll be like that.
ROSIE	We'll walk into this Chinese Restaurant, with red carpets and white napkins and bamboo screens.
GABE	Goddamn right.
ROSIE	And everyone there will be eating something different. And everyone, when they see us come in, they'll yell. They'll ask us over to their table. Want to feed us with their fingers. All the best parts.
VONNE	And it won't be a screwing hotel like the Empress. Where the sheets get thin. An honest-to-God, stay overnight hotel. With suitcases. Okay, Louis?
LOUIS	I'll keep going as long as I last. If I last that long.
GABE	Going to Regina, Louis.
LOUIS	Going to stop for a minute.
VONNE	*(to ROSIE)* What are you going to wear?
ROSIE	To the restaurant?
VONNE	I'm going to wear whatever I like.
ROSIE	I'm going to wear black. Every day. And a dress with a train.
GABE	Hey, Louis…
LOUIS	Leave me, Gabe. Let me watch.

GABE   Come on, Louis. You'll tell them. Remember. You met me when I was
         a punk kid in the Prince Albert pen. Singing songs about Gabriel
         Dumont.

         GABE sings and LOUIS claps.

         (sings) Back at Batoche where we started from
         There's times that life gets wearisome
         The wind's too cold and the air's too dry
         And there's telephone wires across the sky
         There's nothing to do but drink and fight
         And watch the hockey of a Saturday night.

         What the white man taught the Métis
         Told them virtue was its own reward
         Now they're waving at their Saviour
         Louis Riel in a fifty-dollar Ford.

         *During this, LOUIS and GABE, followed by HENRY, leave the
         gas station for the Empress Hotel's famous Tahiti Room. HENRY
         is puzzled but eager to take part in whatever fun is going on.*

HENRY   Something I want to talk to you about.

GABE   We're coming to your part, Henry. Just sit patient.

HENRY   Something we have to discuss.

GABE   *(sings)* It might be Henry Jackson's dream
         To score for the Toronto team
         But me, I'm leaving this hotel
         Going to find Dumont and Louis Riel
         Dumont shot and Louis scored
         Keeps a man from getting bored.

         What the white man taught the Métis
         Told them virtue was its own reward
         Now they're waving at their Saviour
         Louis Riel in his fifty-dollar Ford.

HENRY   *(clapping along)* Ha!

GABE   You see the beauty of it, Henry. Because you have always wanted to see
         the ocean and Louis always wanted to see Cedar Rapids. Rosie always
         wanted to tell fortunes.

HENRY   Can't sell you the car, Gabe.

LOUIS   Doesn't make any difference, Henry…

HENRY   Gabe?

LOUIS   It's a joke. It's a story. Gabe is flying. He don't need a car.

HENRY   I can't sell you the car, Gabe.

GABE	*(a little dangerous)* Sure you can.
HENRY	You don't have any money.
GABE	So what?
HENRY	So you can't buy the car.
GABE	Money, Henry? You can take it out in trade.
HENRY	What I mean is…
GABE	I thought you could get the supplies together. The provisions. You got a logical mind.
HENRY	I mean I was talking to Charles.
GABE	Charles ain't coming.
HENRY	The thing is Charles was looking to see a certain amount of improvements…
GABE	Charles has got no sense of fun.
HENRY	…around the place. He got some whitewash I was going to show you. I told him how busy we been.
GABE	No special talents. No fun. No place for him.
HENRY	Charles figures you're out of a job.
GABE	I see.
HENRY	So I can't sell you the car, Gabe.
GABE	Well, shit.
HENRY	Well, I tried to explain to him…
GABE	Well, I wouldn't worry, Henry. Kind of funny when you look at it right. See the joke, Louis?
HENRY	I wouldn't want to spoil your plans.
GABE	Won't change a thing.
HENRY	I wouldn't want to stop the trip.
GABE	Can't depend on you all my life. And your good nature. Have to depend on myself, don't I, Henry?
HENRY	Sure. There's other cars, eh. Gabe?
GABE	Look on the bright side.
HENRY	Sure, that's right.
GABE	Take the good with the bad.
HENRY	Take the bitter with the batter.
GABE	Which ocean do you want to see?

HENRY	Me?
GABE	Cedar Rapids is as close to the middle as makes no difference. Won't matter which way we go after that.
HENRY	Well, the thing is, like I said about the car. What Charles said…
GABE	Going swimming.
HENRY	I can't swim, Gabe.
GABE	I'll teach you.
HENRY	You don't have to do that…
GABE	I'm glad to do it, Henry. Friendship.
	HENRY laughs, uncomfortably.
HENRY	The reason I like drinking with you is you're both hellish, fine fellows. Hard drinkers. Good company. I like you. There's only one trouble with you, that's you're not responsible. I mean Gabe here, Louis, because you got a head on your shoulders. But Gabie, you never know that he isn't going to take off some place just because he feels like it. Now I can understand that in a young fellow. Feel like taking off myself sometimes. But you can't run a gas station that way. No sir.
GABE	Your brother's gas station isn't really running, Henry. It's just sitting there, looking kind of sad.
HENRY	Could make something out of that place. Good location.
GABE	Yeah, it's peaceful. Don't get a lot of traffic.
HENRY	If I had help I could depend on.
GABE	Buy me a drink, Henry.
LOUIS	You don't want to do that.
HENRY	Gabe goes crazy when he's drinking.
GABE	I'm going to get drunk, really drunk. I'm going to beat him unconscious. I'm going to steal his fucking car.
HENRY	I'm trying to talk sense to you, Gabie.
GABE	I'm going to let Henry buy the first round.
HENRY	You tell him, Louis. How he's acting foolish.
LOUIS	You're acting foolish, Gabe.
GABE	Oh yeah?
LOUIS	You're sitting around drinking with a broken-down rodeo rider and a halfwit.
GABE	Nice talk.
HENRY	Who are you calling a halfwit?

GABE	Who's the broken-down rodeo rider, more to the point?
HENRY	Who are you calling a halfwit?
GABE	I got no quarrel with you, Louis.
LOUIS	Why not?
GABE	Get me my own big yellow car some day. Drive it through the biggest towns in Saskatchewan. Sure. Making speeches from the back seat. Have people falling back in amazement, never having heard speaking like it before. It'll all be true, see. No word of a lie. Talking Métis rights. Singing Métis rights. Get a little fiddle breakdown, we'll have everyone back on their feet. Dancing on behind me.
HENRY	Who's calling who a halfwit?
LOUIS	It's me calling you. You can take it as a compliment.
HENRY	I take exception.
GABE	Shut up, Henry.
HENRY	No man's going to say that to me.
GABE	We always say it, Henry. You keep coming back for more. You like the attention.
HENRY	No drunken, lazy, no-good, dirty Indian's going to say it, that's for damn sure.
GABE	Leave him, Louis. He's a sick little bastard.

LOUIS has HENRY and he's beating him brutally. GABE tries to separate them.

Leave him go, Louis, goddamn it. You'll kill him. He's drunk, that's all. Rest of the week he follows you around like a dog. Goddamn it, you'll kill him. I don't understand you.

> *LOUIS has beaten HENRY very badly. He stretches back for one last punch or kick. Wonders why he is bothering and drops HENRY to the ground. He takes HENRY's cigarettes out of his pocket and lights one. GABE watches him. HENRY pulls himself together and out of the bar.*

HENRY	Goddamn fucking Louis Riel cowboy movie.
GABE	You're goddamn crazy, Louis. Don't let him bother you. Jesus, I would have beat him if I thought you wanted it done. He knows me.
LOUIS	He's worthless.
GABE	Sure he is. And that's why he's here, goddamn it. Why he wants to be like me. Just like me. Like you. And that's why he's going crawling home to Charles right now and Charles is going to send you back to jail so fast…

HENRY	*(as he leaves)* You know what they did to Louis Riel. They hanged the son of a bitch.
GABE	What are you doing, Louis?
LOUIS	I'm going to go to jail.
GABE	You go to jail, it's your own fucking fault.
LOUIS	I'm going to jail and you're not.
GABE	You're crazy, Louis.
LOUIS	I see Gabriel Dumont. He is afflicted and ashamed. He does not look at me. He looks to his future. His present. He is an outlaw. He has nothing and he blames me for it.
GABE	Okay, Sure. We'll go. We'll steal a car and drive. You want to? I've done it before.
LOUIS	The Canadians must punish before they can forgive. I will allow them to punish me again.
GABE	That's shit. That's Riel talking again.
LOUIS	Riel said: "There will be a trial. I will speak there. I will use it as a platform to talk of Métis rights. The Canadians will listen. There will be an investigation in Parliament. All the grievances, my people's grievances, will be exposed. I will fulfill my mission. I will speak…"

LOUIS exits as VONNE enters with ROSIE. VONNE is very angry.

VONNE	I hate Henry for being so stupid. I hate Henry's goddamn big brother Charles. I hate Louis for wasting his time with either of them. Louis beats Henry up. Louis goes back to jail, so what good does that do? You're always beating Henry up.
GABE	But he doesn't take me serious.
VONNE	And Louis goes to jail for it.
GABE	Parole.
VONNE	Parole.
GABE	Parole violation.
VONNE	Is that all you can say, parole violation? Because what is Louis supposed to do? Let Henry hire him and fire him and call him dirt. He's supposed to let you beat Henry up because you're not serious about it. You beating Henry, that doesn't count. Keeps things lively. No one holds a grudge about it. No one holds a goddamn grudge and Henry's little brain just goes on rattling around in Henry's big, thick head while Louis bangs his head against a wall. Parole violation. Parole violation. Parole violation.
GABE	I don't know what to say, Vonne. Is that all right?

ROSIE	Talk to Henry for her.
GABE	Oh, Rosie, honey…
ROSIE	Charles put him up to it.
GABE	So what?
ROSIE	Henry doesn't know anything.
GABE	Poor old Henry.
ROSIE	Do it.
GABE	What if I beat him up again? I could kill him.
ROSIE	You won't.
GABE	How do you know?
ROSIE	It will all strike you funny. At the last minute. You'll be laughing too hard.
GABE	I'd like to go out in the bush again. For a while. No, really. Because I love it. Because the welfare department doesn't take me serious, that's for damn sure. And I could get Norbert's traps together. Christ, that would be a Christian act of mercy.
ROSIE	Shut up, Gabe.
GABE	I'm just telling you.
ROSIE	You're making excuses.
GABE	I got no excuse, Rosie. I love the bush and I can't take Jackson's Gas Station serious. I think it looks stupid out there on the highway all by itself. When I'm working there… when I'm working for Charles, I feel like a rodeo clown…
ROSIE	Well you aren't.
GABE	Shit, I'm a half-breed pump jockey. I'm a disaster. I'm better in the bush. Shit, Rosie, every time I come out of the bush and I'm still together, Charles and Henry, they see they're the clowns.
ROSIE	Charles and Henry never think about the bush.
GABE	I'm a comic-book hero, Rosie.
ROSIE	I guess so.
GABE	You don't want to go. Do you? You don't like the bush.
ROSIE	I don't like mosquitoes. I like it in the fall.
GABE	Little white lies.
ROSIE	You could be an outlaw. In the woods. Nobody would see you again. Ever. Just tell stories about you.
GABE	You see too many movies.

ROSIE	Why not?
GABE	You could go to Regina. You and Vonne. Every night they'd turn the gaslight on. The big glass chandelier. And you'd come in, down the stairs, eating a flower. Everybody standing around the bottom of the stairs, clapping their fists together.
ROSIE	I don't know. I don't think so.
GABE	You got very romantic ideas.
ROSIE	Will you talk to Henry?
GABE	Jesus, Rosie, I said I would.

> HENRY enters as ROSIE exits. GABE watches him. Nothing is going on, although when he notices GABE, HENRY pretends to be busy.

HENRY	What are you doing here?
GABE	Come to say goodbye to you.
HENRY	That's a stupid thing to do.
GABE	Because Louis beat you when I should have done it? Come on, Henry, I don't hold a grudge.
HENRY	The thing about you is you got no sense of responsibility. You or Louis. None of you.
GABE	I'm going off in the woods, Henry.
HENRY	You aren't going anywhere. You're on parole. Like Louis was.
GABE	Going to see how long I last. On my own. No supplies. No pack. No gun.
HENRY	Parole. That's a responsibility. That's an obligation. Parole. That's a promise. You wouldn't give that a second thought. None of you.
GABE	Us half-breeds are very wily in the woods.
HENRY	You half-breeds aren't responsible.
GABE	We're very close to nature.
HENRY	You drink too much.
GABE	When I was a kid, I ran away from the correctional institute. I lived off the land till the breakup. Only year I never got in trouble. Not till spring. Then they finally got it together, came and got me.
HENRY	Last winter. Over at the Empress. Two half-breeds, a woman and a man, Charles told me. Over there spending their welfare cheques. They left their kids out in their broken-down old car with the heat off. The kids fell asleep. Those two were so drunk they drove all the way home, forgot about the kids, left them in the car all night. They froze

to death, the kids. That's half-breeds drinking for you. Or maybe they were Indians.

GABE   Even if you knew anything about hunting, fishing, trapping, anything about the land and how to use it, you'd be dead in the bush, Henry. You're a city man, Henry. You can't live by yourself.

HENRY   Even if you didn't drink, you'd still have no sense of responsibility.

GABE   You win, Henry.

HENRY   I'm not afraid of you. Or crazy Louis.

GABE   Who?

HENRY   Crazy Louis.

GABE   Louis wasn't crazy.

HENRY   Sure he was.

GABE   I wouldn't say that.

HENRY   Well, it's true. Beat me up and where did it get him. Back in the Prince Albert pen. Sure. Good place for him. Bang-his-head-against-the-bars crazy. Ha.

GABE   Nothing crazy about beating you. Wouldn't want you to think that.

HENRY   You'd never get away with it.

GABE   I wouldn't beat you, Henry.

HENRY   No.

GABE   All of us half-breeds are very sociable.

HENRY   Yeah.

GABE   True?

HENRY   Hell, I know that.

GABE   Sure. We know how to have a party.

HENRY   Well, you're right there.

GABE   Friendly. Give you the shirt off my back. You want it?

HENRY   Well, I got a shirt like it.

GABE   And I don't have to beat you, Henry. Because all of us half-breeds, we're hunters. We got special knowledge. Of the future. When my hand moves like this, that means something's going to happen. Or when there's a twitch in my neck. Here.

HENRY   Like the time you told me that the spring flood was going to knock the bridge out and I told Charles and he didn't believe me. So he drove into town and stranded himself. Had to stay overnight.

GABE   That's right.

HENRY	Wonderful thing.
GABE	Sure. I can see things you can't see. Like Louis Riel. Riding out of Montana. Saw a tree on the hill. And he said to Dumont. That's a tree, isn't it? I thought it was a gallows. With me hanging from it.
HENRY	You and Louis Riel. I heard that before.
GABE	I can see you beaten.
HENRY	What?
GABE	It's a vision. I can see you lying there on the floor, looking like something out of one of those comic books. Not the ones with the people. The animal books. Where the stupid-looking cat gets rolled out and hung up to dry.
HENRY	Rolled out?
GABE	Lying there, Henry. Looking stupid.
HENRY	Where?
GABE	I guess someone's finally done it right. Someone's finally kicked your teeth down your throat.
HENRY	You?
GABE	Not me. You got to understand I'm not threatening you, Henry. I think it's comical. I think it's kind of sad in a way.
HENRY	I don't know what you're talking about.
GABE	Because you're stupid, Henry. Because you're not afraid of me. Or Louis. Because you think we're crazy. You don't have the brains of a rabbit, Henry.

> *GABE walks off into a spectacular prairie sunset.*
>
> *Fade to black.*
>
> *The end.*

I don't write living room drama.... I don't put those realistic kinds of domestic scenes on the stage. I write elaborate romances!
(Lister 152)

I wish that it were possible to change the world, but what I see when I look at the characters, Emma Goldman, for example, is not a "Hardy Boy" kind of character who can isolate what's wrong and then fix it. I see a complex woman who goes beyond what is reasonable in her quest. All my seekers have a flaw, like Bethune's egotism, or Emma's romanticism. (Rudakoff 181)

I think Emma Goldman is a wonderful character. We want to do another play about her.... I don't think I would like to live in a world that didn't include people like Emma Goldman.... She was an irrepressible idealist. (Zimmerman, *Work* 267)

Red

Emma

Queen of the Anarchists

To M.K.

The finest mind in Canadian theatre

WHO is EMMA GOLDMAN?*

Who is Emma Goldman? J. Edgar Hoover called her "the most dangerous woman in the world."

I first wrote about Emma Goldman more than twenty years ago. My play was called *Red Emma: Queen of the Anarchists,* since it followed only a part of this remarkable woman's story.

The play was inspired by Emma's autobiography, *Living My Life.* In this document, the mature Emma Goldman shows us a young Emma larger than life: a young woman in love with life, in love with New York, in love with her friends—all her friends, who are, because she loves them, the brightest and the best. She's in love with the idea of political change, the possibility of political change. She says, "I believe in freedom, the right to self-expression—everyone's right to beautiful, radiant things."

The mature Emma gives young Emma extravagant adventures. She tells us a dubious story about young Emma's attempt to sell her body to buy the pistol her lover Sasha needs for his attempt on the life of Henry Clay Frick. She tells us young Emma horsewhips another lover, Johann Most, at a public place.

Are these stories true? For me, they're romantic, larger than life, attractive, and also dangerous. In *Living My Life,* the mature Emma shows us young people who are willing to attempt assassination in order to change the world.

In the opera *Red Emma,* Emma asks us to ask if we want to change the world or if, like her friend Fedya, we're content to discover "the world will reward those who accept things as they are."

Carol Bolt
Toronto, 1995

* Excerpt from Canadian Opera Company program (Toronto: du Maurier Theatre Centre, 1995).

Red Emma: Queen of the Anarchists, was first performed at the Toronto Free Theatre, February 5, 1974, with the following company:

Chapelle Jaffe	Emma Goldman
Diane D'Aquila	Helen Minkin
Nick Mancuso	Alexander Berkman (Sasha)
Jim Henshaw	Fedya
William Webster	Henry Clay Frick
Miles Potter	Kreiderman
A.J. Henderson	Parks
David Bolt	Johann Most (Hannes)
Phil Schreibman	Piano Player

Directed by Martin Kinch
Designed by Miro Kinch
Music composed by Phillip Schreibman

\ \ • / /

The Canadian Opera Company presented the opera World Premiere at the du Maurier Theatre Centre, Harbourfront Centre, Toronto, November 28, 29, December 1, 2 & 3, 1995 with the following company:

Artistic Director	Richard Bradshaw
General Manager	Elaine Calder

*Anita Krause, Sonya Gosse	Emma	*Anita Krause (Nov 28, Dec 1, 3)
*Nathalie Paulin, Rayanne Dupuis	Helen	Sonya Gosse (Nov 29, Dec 2)
Dan Chamandy	Fedya	Nathalie Paulin (Nov 28, Dec 1, 3)
Igor Emelianov	Sasha	Rayanne Dupuis (Nov 29, Dec 2)
Matthew Lord	Johann Most	
Marcos Pujol	Kreiderman	
Bruce Schaef	Parks	
Robert Milne	Henry Clay Frick	

Directed by David William
Set & Costumes Designed by Teresa Przybylski
Lighting Designed by John A. Munro
Choreographed by Donna Feore
Music by Gary Kulesha
Conducted by Gary Wedow
Libretto by Carol Bolt

CHARACTERS

HELEN
ALEXANDER BERKMAN (aka SASHA)
EMMA
FEDYA
KREIDERMAN
PARKS
FRICK
JOHANN MOST

Red Emma

Queen of the Anarchists

ACT ONE

In the original production, a two-level set made it possible to switch quickly from scene to scene. There was a table on the lower level which was used for Sach's Café, the Freiheit office, and the anarchists' commune. On the upper level there was a speaker's podium.

Sach's Café. 1890.

HELEN (*sings*) I was young at Sach's Café
I drank my coffee black
You could find me talking politics
At a table in the back
All my friends were beautiful
All the talk was good
The rooms were always smoky
And I never understood
Half the things I found I said
Half the thoughts inside my head
Half the books I said I read
Why the coffee tasted sweet

This is the song of Sach's Café
This is the song of years I've lost
This is the song of happy times
This is the song of the holocaust

I was young at Sach's Café
The coffee tasted sweet
You could find me talking politics
I never had to eat
All my friends were crazy drunk

All their lies were true
The answers seemed so easy
The things I had to do
How my work would be begun
How I had to race the sun
How the well-known West was won
Why I couldn't speak.

> *Sach's Café is attended by PARKS, a Pinkerton man disguised as a waiter. EMMA and HELEN are sitting together over a glass of tea. HELEN is hoping to pick up some boys. BERKMAN and FEDYA enter. FEDYA sits at the far end of their table. BERKMAN paces.*

BERKMAN   I want two steaks and two coffees…. Make that a pot of coffee and a three-pound steak! Fried potatoes. String beans. Lots of butter on the beans.

EMMA   Who is he?

HELEN   Alexander Berkman.

EMMA   You know the one I mean?

HELEN   His friend is an artist. Fedya. They call them the "twins" because they are always together.

EMMA   Berkman is the tall one.

HELEN   Hello, Fedya.

BERKMAN   I want sliced tomato on the side. And dill pickle.

EMMA   Does Alexander Berkman always jump around like that?

BERKMAN   *(to the waiter)* I want all of that, comrade. As soon as you can.

HELEN   He eats more than anyone else. He drinks more than anyone else. He jumps around more than anyone else.

EMMA   And he's going to eat standing up?

HELEN   I don't know, Emma.

EMMA   It makes me nervous watching him.

HELEN   You don't look nervous.

BERKMAN   You are Emma Goldman.

> *HELEN slides over to FEDYA's end of the table, leaving EMMA a clear field. EMMA doesn't notice. She is watching BERKMAN.*

HELEN   Hello, Fedya.

BERKMAN   You are Emma Goldman. You just came to New York. The only man in New York you knew was Solatoroff and you went to his address, but Solatoroff moves twice a week and all the janitor knew was he'd gone to Montgomery Street. And you, Emma Goldman, went to every house on Montgomery Street until you found him. You found Solatoroff. You found Sach's Café. You found one of the famous Minkin sisters. Which one? Is it Helen.

HELEN   Yes.

BERKMAN   And now you find Alexander Berkman. An extravagant spirit to match your extravagant eyes.

EMMA   How old are you?

BERKMAN   I'm eighteen. *(He lights a match and holds it up to her face.)* You are all of nineteen and I want to watch you closely.

         EMMA blows out the match.

EMMA   Children burn themselves so easily.

BERKMAN   I'm a revolutionary. I love fire. Your comrade Solatoroff will tell you that.

FEDYA   He wouldn't let you near her.

BERKMAN   Emma is not bound to Solatoroff.

EMMA   Emma is not bound to any man.

         There is a pause. EMMA and BERKMAN are delighted with each other. EMMA chuckles. BERKMAN chuckles. HELEN is pleased things are going so well.

HELEN   Shall we have another glass of tea, Emma?

BERKMAN   I am making a speech this evening. About revolution. You will come and hear me.

HELEN   We are going to hear Solatoroff.

FEDYA   He teaches anarchy to night school classes.

BERKMAN   You will hear me instead. Take the Minkin sister if you will. Come on.

HELEN   What is Sasha's topic, Fedya?

BERKMAN   I will speak on propaganda of the deed, I think.

FEDYA   You will introduce the main speaker.

BERKMAN   Johann Most is not the main speaker, Fedya…

         Pronounce MOST to rhyme with cost, not strictly correct but less confusing in English.

EMMA   Johann Most? Tonight?

BERKMAN   …We are all equals. We are comrades in anarchy.

FEDYA	Tell Most he's equal. If you can get him off the grandstand.
EMMA	I came to New York to hear Johann Most.
BERKMAN	You will hear me as well.
EMMA	Because in Rochester, I read his newspaper. He is revolution.
BERKMAN	Most will send me to Rochester this month. On a speaking tour.
EMMA	Do you know him very well?
BERKMAN	Of course I do.
EMMA	I read everything he says.
FEDYA	You are a victim of publicity.
EMMA	I know him.
FEDYA	*(flamboyantly)* A long black coat, a big black hat, a big black bomb. They draw him in cartoons in Rochester. They call him the devil and make him the symbol of anarchy.
EMMA	He is the lifeblood of anarchy.
BERKMAN	You are nineteen. You are very impressionable.
EMMA	I am twenty.

He pulls her to her feet.

BERKMAN	Come with me. Are you coming?
EMMA	I'm older than you are.
BERKMAN	You have a lot to teach me, I suppose.
EMMA	You have a lot to learn.
HELEN	Are you going to hear Johann Most, Fedya?
FEDYA	Yes, there's a free lunch.

They exit. PARKS enters to clear the table and follow them out with the bill. Henry Clay FRICK enters, on the upper level, followed by KREIDERMAN, who has a portfolio of correspondence.

KREIDERMAN	You speak to the Unity Club at ten, Mr. Frick. I have given the press copies of the text of your remarks. You lunch with Mr. Andrew Carnegie and he will want these figures. These letters are requests for proxies in the matter of the stock options. These letters are answers to requests for funds, solicitations, letters of sympathy and condolence…

PARKS enters bustling. He is carrying a newspaper which he hands to KREIDERMAN officiously.

PARKS | There is a cartoon. On the editorial page. Mr. Frick is shown grinding the faces of the poor in the mud.

KREIDERMAN | Mr. Frick doesn't want to see that kind of trash, Mr. Parks.

FRICK | Find out who owns that newspaper and buy it.

FRICK exits.

KREIDERMAN | You heard Mr. Frick, Mr. Parks. Who owns that newspaper?

PARKS | It's a German newspaper, sir. From New York. How do you say "owner" in German?

KREIDERMAN and PARKS exit. BERKMAN enters and mounts the podium to introduce Johann MOST. He is carrying the banner of anarchy—a red flag is more exciting than the correct black. During his speech EMMA, HELEN, and FEDYA enter on the lower level, also with flags.

BERKMAN | Johann Most began his work as a revolutionary pamphleteer and a member of the Reichstag. He was persecuted for his opinions. He was exiled from his native Germany. In England he was imprisoned because he supported the assassination of Alexander II. His newspaper *Freiheit* was suppressed. Johann Most, brave spirit, now a free voice in America. I am proud to introduce him.

MOST enters, pausing only briefly to shake BERKMAN's hand and show BERKMAN is his protege. He is an electric speaker.

MOST | We will see the world change. We are dedicated and determined men. We are men who know that a bloodless revolution is no revolution at all. We are men who understand the power of the individual act of violence. The Attentat! We can tear out the throat of tyranny.

We will change the world. That is why we act. If our violence brings our death then we will be anarchy's martyrs.

Anarchy has martyrs now.

In 1886, all across the country, workers demanded the eight-hour day. In Chicago, at the McCormick Harvester Company, a workers' meeting was attacked by police. Men and women were beaten. Several were killed. To protest the outrage, the workers met in Haymarket Square. A quiet, orderly meeting. Carter Harrison, the mayor of Chicago, said that. A quiet, orderly meeting. It was clouding over. A light rain began. Very few remained to hear the last speakers. The police attacked again.

EMMA's following interjections into MOST's text should be like a litany. We should get the impression that she feels this story deeply and that MOST becomes aware of her presence at the meeting because of the depth of her feeling.

EMMA Captain Ward, accompanied by a strong force of police, suddenly appeared on the square. The police fell upon the people, clubbing them unmercifully.

MOST There was a bomb. A bomb was thrown, killing a number of police officers and wounding many others. No one knew who threw the bomb but orders were immediately issued for the arrest of every prominent anarchist in Chicago.

EMMA The bourgeois of Chicago asked for blood...

MOST The police began a campaign of terror which ended when five men were sentenced to die by hanging...

EMMA Albert Parsons, August Spies, Louis Lingg...

MOST Five men innocent of crime and in no way connected with it...

EMMA Adolph Fischer... George Engel...

MOST Five martyrs. Albert Parsons. August Spies. Louis Lingg. Adolph Fischer. George Engel.

EMMA August Spies knew he was a martyr. He knew that ordinary people could see farther than vicious attacks in the press. Ordinary men and women were not as blind as the justice in American courts. August Spies answered his death sentence in these words: "Our silence will speak louder than the voices that you strangle today." The eleventh of November. A five-mile line of workers followed the martyrs to their graves.

All sing, waving banners.

November Eleven
The Haymarket Martyrs
Were strangled and silenced
But we can be free
Their voices were ringing
In moments of silence

The martyrs are singing to me
Five men dead
They've made us strong
Fifty thousand sing their song

November Eleven
Means we have our martyrs
Their voices are ringing
And we can be free
The silence is singing

The martyrs speak wonders
The voices mean freedom to me.

> *At the end of the song MOST approaches EMMA. BERKMAN is trying to get her attention but EMMA's concentration is totally on MOST.*

MOST	Do you speak English?
EMMA	Me?
MOST	I'll lend you some books. Not English. You read German?
EMMA	Yes, I do.
MOST	You want to learn about anarchy.
EMMA	More than anything. Of course I do.
MOST	*(gently mocking)* More than anything. Of course I do.
EMMA	It's my first day in New York. I came to New York to hear you speak.
MOST	I'm enchanted by your enthusiasm.
EMMA	About the Haymarket Martyrs. It was those events. In Chicago. They awakened my political conscience.
MOST	*(amused)* Really?
EMMA	Yes.
MOST	I'm sorry. I don't mean to be patronizing.
EMMA	Oh, you aren't.
MOST	No?
EMMA	I came to New York to meet you.
MOST	We'll drink to that. Shall we? We will go to Sach's Café. We will order Liebfraumilch.
BERKMAN	Emma…
EMMA	Here is your comrade Alexander Berkman.
MOST	Berkman is zealous, dedicated. We have work for him to do.
EMMA	He said you will send him to Rochester. To speak. That's where I'm from.
MOST	Give the girl her shawl, Berkman, and drop her hand, if you permit?

> *MOST and EMMA exit.*

HELEN	As Johann Most tells us, man does not need authority, law, or government to keep him virtuous.

FEDYA	*(to BERKMAN)* Did you ask about the tour?
BERKMAN	No.
HELEN	I find his remarks instructive and illuminating. And uplifting. He is a man of extraordinary vision, is he not?
FEDYA	If Anna Minkin sees Most's vision then it must be large and clear.
HELEN	I'm Helen. As you know.
FEDYA	Anna is the one who follows Sasha around. You're the one who follows me.
HELEN	He isn't serious. Is he, Sasha?
BERKMAN	Fedya is never serious. Most is always serious. What is your friend Emma like?
	Exit BERKMAN, FEDYA, HELEN. KREIDERMAN enters, disguised as a drunk to establish Sach's Café. MOST and EMMA enter.
MOST	Liebfraumilch!
	PARKS appears with a bottle.
EMMA	I've never tasted wine before.
MOST	*(amused)* I'm sure you haven't.
EMMA	Except the kind my mother made for Passover.
MOST	Your name is Emma, isn't it?
EMMA	Yes it is.
MOST	And you are from Rochester?
EMMA	Yes.
MOST	You will promise not to tell me about your mother's wine, Emma.
EMMA	I don't want to bore you. I don't want to talk about myself. I want to learn about anarchy.
MOST	Prosit, my young, naive lady.
EMMA	I've read everything you ever wrote. *(MOST drains his glass and pours another.)* Everything they printed in Rochester, I mean. *(MOST drains his glass and pours another.)* Do you acknowledge the thought of William Godwin at all?
MOST	Another bottle please.
	He pours himself another drink and takes a deep breath. He finds EMMA's intensity overpowering. Both EMMA and MOST drink a lot in this scene. By its end, they are drunk.

EMMA	Because you say "a bloodless revolution is no revolution at all." Which is what Godwin says, although of course he is not lead to your conclusion.
MOST	What is needed here is to lighten the atmosphere somehow. Perhaps if I ordered still another bottle of wine and spilled it all over the front of my shirt.
EMMA	I don't understand.
MOST	You are Russian?
EMMA	Yes.
MOST	Perhaps if I threw the wine glasses against the wall. Drink up. Well try it.
EMMA	Drink up?
MOST	Toss it back. Like this.
EMMA	Like this?

> *EMMA tries to throw the glass against the wall but MOST catches her wrist.*

MOST	You are very charming, my dear. Please excuse the clumsy compliment.
EMMA	You were talking about anarchy. I didn't want to interrupt.
MOST	Anarchy. Of course. Anarchy.
EMMA	Yes.
MOST	You want to learn about anarchy?
EMMA	Yes.
MOST	Well, I'm the one to teach you, am I not?
EMMA	As I said.
MOST	I am the master anarchist. Known in Rochester.
EMMA	Yes, you are.
MOST	The path of anarchism is steep and painful. Do you believe that? Do you have a sense of humour, my very young lady? You will need it as an anarchist. Steep and painful. Many have attempted to climb it and fallen back. The price is exacting. Few men will pay it, few women can pay it…
EMMA	There are women here in New York…
MOST	Stupid women.
EMMA	Women who work for anarchism…
MOST	I don't believe women have revolutionary zeal. Do you?

EMMA	Of course I do.
MOST	Your friend Helen Minkin is looking for a husband.
EMMA	Now you're joking. Now you're patronizing…
MOST	Of course she is. She's a young girl. She goes to meetings only to find out who will take her home from meetings. Stupid.
EMMA	Helen Minkin is my comrade.
MOST	You hunt together?
EMMA	I do not hunt.
MOST	No, of course not. You dedicate your life to the cause.
EMMA	I do. Yes.
MOST	To anarchy.
EMMA	I do, Yes.
MOST	Parsons. Spies. Lingg. Fischer. Engel. They are the men you walk with?
EMMA	They are my martyrs.
MOST	Emma speaks ardently.
EMMA	Now you're laughing at me.
MOST	I have need of ardent friendship.
	Pause.
EMMA	No you don't. Not me.
MOST	Of course, you.
EMMA	You're joking.
MOST	Why would I joke?
EMMA	I know thousands of people read everything you write. They follow you from one meeting to another just to hear you speak…
MOST	Perhaps you will be my student. You can speak ardently. I can teach you to speak well.
EMMA	You mean to speak in public?
MOST	You say you must work for the cause.
EMMA	I'm very nervous. I wouldn't know what to say.
MOST	I can tell you what to say.
EMMA	You're joking, aren't you?
MOST	No.

EMMA	You want me to speak about the cause… as Alexander Berkman does…
MOST	You will listen to me.
EMMA	… I amuse you.
MOST	You make me happy. That's all. Are you drunk?
EMMA	Now you're laughing at me. Are you drunk?
MOST	I'm very serious. I'm happy. You make it possible for me to make plans. Drink up.
EMMA	(drinking her glass) Like this?
MOST	Where will we go now?
EMMA	Everywhere. All over New York.
MOST	This is my first happy evening in a long while.
EMMA	Because I came to New York with hope that I could hear you speak. And we've met so soon. We drink wine together.
MOST	Do you hear me, Emma? It is the first time in years I have been happy.

> They exit. KREIDERMAN and PARKS compare notes.

PARKS	Did you hear what they said?
KREIDERMAN	No, I didn't. They were speaking Russian.
PARKS	Is Liebfraumilch a Russian word?

> KREIDERMAN and PARKS clear the table and exit.
> BERKMAN and FEDYA enter on the upper level. By the
> time they reach the lower level it is the Freiheit office.

BERKMAN	Labourers arise! The bosses have you in chains. Do you like that, Fedya?
FEDYA	It sounds familiar.
BERKMAN	It's the English translation of my new essay. Here. Look. Fifty copies.
FEDYA	It sounds like your last essay.
BERKMAN	My last essay was about nihilism and the Attentat.
FEDYA	Labourers arise! The bosses have you in chains. I've heard it before.
BERKMAN	The first statement was something of a personal reminiscence. I recalled my nihilist uncle Maxim hanged by the Cossacks. This is more of a political diatribe.
FEDYA	Maybe you should find a new translator.

BERKMAN	You don't like it? "Labourers arise!" Perhaps "Workers arise!" Is that correct in English?
EMMA	*(enters)* Workers arise! That's very stirring.
FEDYA	At least Emma hasn't heard it.
BERKMAN	If you help me mail my broadsheet, Emma, I'll show you New York. I'll take you to the Battery.
EMMA	I've been to the Battery.
BERKMAN	You have?
EMMA	Johann Most took me. To escape the heat.
BERKMAN	Staten Island then.
EMMA	I've been there.
BERKMAN	With Most.
EMMA	Yes.
BERKMAN	Where else have you been? With Most?
EMMA	To Sach's.
BERKMAN	Most has no right to squander money. To go to expensive restaurants…
EMMA	It was Sach's…
BERKMAN	To drink expensive wines. He is spending money contributed for the movement. He is accountable. I'll tell him myself.

He starts to exit. EMMA stops him.

EMMA	No you won't.
BERKMAN	You are very young in the movement. You know nothing about revolutionary ethics. You can't tell revolutionary right from revolutionary wrong.
EMMA	And you can?
BERKMAN	Of course I can.
EMMA	You are eighteen years old, Alexander Berkman…
BERKMAN	Experience doesn't make an anarchist. Commitment makes an anarchist. You tell that to Johann Most. No. I'll tell him myself.
EMMA	No you won't.
BERKMAN	He'll see his error. He'll thank me for it.
EMMA	I will not have Most hurt.
BERKMAN	I will educate him.

FEDYA is busy destroying BERKMAN's pamphlets by folding them into different shapes.

FEDYA	Ha.
EMMA	We are having a private conversation, Fedya.
BERKMAN	No we aren't.
EMMA	I am.
FEDYA	What is her concern for Most?
EMMA	I am having a private conversation.
BERKMAN	*(ignoring her)* He is her teacher. He is the King of the Anarchists.
EMMA	You treat women very badly, don't you? A woman is never your comrade. A woman is always your child.
FEDYA	Does she see a lot of Most?
EMMA	And if I do, I'm wrong, I suppose?
BERKMAN	At the offices of *Freiheit.* Then at Sach's…
FEDYA	With Most.
BERKMAN	Of course with Most.
FEDYA	Practising anarchy.
BERKMAN	Disguising themselves with false black beards.
FEDYA	Rehearsing the lurk and the skulk.
BERKMAN	Emma wishes to appear in an anarchist cartoon.
FEDYA	Most alone and only Most.
EMMA	I find him remarkable.
FEDYA	He's remarkably fond of taking young girls to the *Freiheit* office. He lends them books.
EMMA	Get out of here, Fedya.
BERKMAN	Emma is not interested in Most as a man.
FEDYA	You hope.

BERKMAN is too young to want his obvious feeling for EMMA broadcast publicly. He is annoyed.

BERKMAN	Fedya is not a good anarchist. He isn't serious enough. He is a bourgeois.
FEDYA	I'm an artist.
BERKMAN	You are not a worker.
FEDYA	I am a drone. You are a worker and I am a drone. Buzz, buzz…

He begins to tear up a broadsheet.

BERKMAN	You annoy me, Fedya.
FEDYA	That's too bad.
BERKMAN	Anarchy is our only concern. The Cause.
FEDYA	You bore me, Sasha.
BERKMAN	Anarchy is our only concern. The Cause. Isn't that so, Emma?
EMMA	You're joking.
BERKMAN	I sound like I'm joking. Because I'm cheerful. I have never been so serious. Emma loves anarchy. As I do.
EMMA	I love other things.
BERKMAN	I don't.
EMMA	Of course you do.
BERKMAN	I don't.
EMMA	You must.
BERKMAN	Why?
EMMA	You must love flowers or going to the theatre or music or dancing.
BERKMAN	I don't.
EMMA	You love to eat.
BERKMAN	No.
EMMA	You do, Sasha. You eat like a horse.
BERKMAN	You think you have me? You think you've found me in a contradiction. No. Because I eat ravenously but I never notice what I eat. I could eat anything. And I must eat something…
FEDYA	You eat a lot, Sasha.
BERKMAN	I eat a lot because I care so much. About anarchy.
FEDYA	I go to the theatre a lot because I care so much. About anarchy.
BERKMAN	Fedya is something of a fake.
FEDYA	Because I don't talk politics? Emma is tired of politics.
BERKMAN	Emma? Tired? Talking?
FEDYA	Look Emma. I have a present for you.
EMMA	What is it, Fedya?
	It is whatever fantastic device FEDYA can fashion from SASHA's broadsheet, e.g., a cocked bat, a palm tree.
BERKMAN	It is my essay. My latest essay…

EMMA	It's very beautiful…
BERKMAN	It is destruction of serious thought. It is useless frivolity.
FEDYA	Feeding Emma's spirit isn't frivolous.
BERKMAN	You are wasteful, Fedya.
FEDYA	You like it, don't you, Emma?
EMMA	Yes, of course I do.
BERKMAN	You're an incurable bourgeois. You're a mindless parasite, Fedya.
FEDYA	No.
BERKMAN	Emma doesn't want it.
FEDYA	Yes she does.
BERKMAN	Of course she doesn't.
FEDYA	You don't know Emma. You know nothing about her.
BERKMAN	What I know about Emma has nothing to do with your wastefulness. Materials. Time. Money. It isn't even your money. You take money from your parents.
FEDYA	And they are revisionist, reactionary, middle-class.
BERKMAN	That's right. Yes.
FEDYA	I give you the money. Don't I? I give it all to you.
BERKMAN	And I spend it on anarchy, don't I? Every cent. What's wrong with that?
FEDYA	You are single-minded.
BERKMAN	Of course I am. I'm proud of it.
FEDYA	You are narrow.
BERKMAN	Yes! Yes! I am!
FEDYA	Love everything, Emma.
BERKMAN	Don't listen to him, Emma.
FEDYA	Love anarchy and everything else.
BERKMAN	You can't escape. There is no escape from the revolution.
EMMA	*(exploding)* Boom.
FEDYA	*(for fun)* Boom! Boom!
BERKMAN	*(annoyed, exploding)* Boom! Boom! Boom!

> *The anarchist kids bounce around booming out each other.*
> *FRICK enters, followed by KREIDERMAN and PARKS. FRICK*
> *is instructing his men how to get ahead.*

FRICK	America is the land of opportunity, if you can see the opportunity. Take your irons from the fire. Strike while your iron is hot. Do you know what I'm talking about, Kreiderman?
KREIDERMAN	Yes, sir.
PARKS	I'd like to talk about this strike, sir. At the Homestead Steel Mills.
KREIDERMAN	It isn't a strike, Mr. Parks. It's a walkout.
FRICK	You feel some sympathy for the men at Homestead?
PARKS	They don't make much money, sir.
KREIDERMAN	Ho. Ho. He's only joking, Mr. Frick.
FRICK	Some men have. Some men have not. But the haves have a responsibility. The haves help the have-nots. That is social justice.

Exit FRICK.

PARKS	He makes it sound easy, doesn't he, Kreiderman?
KREIDERMAN	Because he's a great man, Mr. Parks.

Exit KREIDERMAN and PARKS. Enter EMMA, followed by HELEN. They are in the Freiheit office.

EMMA	I was standing at the gates to the Triangle Factory, shaking this collection box. Listen, Helen, if you worked for the Triangle wouldn't that sound cheer you up? Even if you couldn't afford a penny to drop in the slot? Wouldn't you feel better knowing all these pennies were going to the cause?
HELEN	You love Johann Most?
EMMA	He loves me, Helen. I idolize him.
HELEN	And Sasha?
EMMA	Of course I love Sasha.
HELEN	And Fedya?
EMMA	Yes, I told you. Yes, Fedya, too.
HELEN	Fedya isn't anything like Sasha and Sasha isn't anything like Johann Most.
EMMA	I cannot get the lid off this cash box.
HELEN	That must be why you can love them. All. Both intensely and sincerely.
EMMA	Intensely, yes. Sincerely, yes. Will you open this?
HELEN	All at the same time.
EMMA	You analyze too much, Helen. Your approach is too intellectual.
HELEN	The subject interests me.

EMMA	I'm counting, Helen. I can't talk.
HELEN	If we went down to Sach's right now. And if you met someone as different from those three as they are from each other…
EMMA	I don't want to go to Sach's.
HELEN	But if you did. I'm curious. That would make four. Why not four?
EMMA	I feel restless.
HELEN	Let's go to Sach's.
EMMA	I feel homeless.
HELEN	Why not five? Why not six? Why not seven?
EMMA	We'll move in together. We'll be comrades. Fedya. Sasha. Helen. Emma.
HELEN	You're changing the subject, Emma.
EMMA	You sound like my aunt and uncle. When I came to New York from Rochester, I arrived at their gallery, they have a photographic gallery and they said I must stay with them, they must give me their spare room. "Where else would you go, a young woman alone in New York?"… Well, of course I had to get away. I went to Solatoroff. I visited with the Minkin sisters. I lived with my comrades Sasha and Fedya. You'll come with us, Helen?
HELEN	Who is us?
EMMA	Sasha and Fedya will come. Of course they will. Will you?
HELEN	I don't know.
EMMA	Of course you will. Your father is worse than my uncle. My aunt and uncle are nothing more than dull. I was in danger of nothing but falling asleep in my plate at their very dull dinners. Your father is a violent man.

This is true, but HELEN does not like to hear it.

HELEN	Emma, you exaggerate.
EMMA	He beats you. Doesn't he beat you?
HELEN	I don't wish to talk about it.
EMMA	I'm your saviour, Helen. I give you an excuse to leave your father.
HELEN	Anna won't leave.
EMMA	Leave Anna. Your father is erotically fond of Anna.
HELEN	Emma.
EMMA	But he hates you, oddly enough.
HELEN	I don't want to discuss it, Emma!

EMMA	You mustn't think I speak frankly to hurt you.
HELEN	You do hurt me.
EMMA	It's because we're friends. We're comrades. We'll live together and work together. Come with us, Helen?
HELEN	I don't know.
EMMA	Do you love anarchy?
HELEN	Why is it that anarchists are always asking me if I love anarchy? I am always at meetings everlasting. I do nothing but listen to speeches. Of course I love anarchy. *(She bangs the cash box on the table to make her point.)* And I've cut my hand on this box.
EMMA	I'm just asking.
HELEN	You ask too much sometimes.
EMMA	In Rochester, I followed the case of the Haymarket Martyrs in the newspapers. I went to hear Johanna Griei speak. After the meeting, she called me up to the platform. She told me that she'd watched my face as she spoke. She thought I must know the martyrs. I seemed to feel their tragedy so deeply. I said: "Unfortunately I do not know the men, but I do feel the case with every fibre and when I heard you speak it seemed to me as if I knew them."
HELEN	You recite very dramatically, Emma.
EMMA	Do you know what she said to me?
HELEN	Something inspirational.
EMMA	She put her hand on my shoulder. "I have a feeling that you will know them better as you will learn their ideal and that you will make their cause your own."

> *Alexander BERKMAN enters to hear this last. FEDYA is with him.*

BERKMAN	I hope you do.
EMMA	I have, Sasha.
BERKMAN	Imperfectly.
HELEN	Look, Sasha. I cut my hand on the collection box.
EMMA	Look, Sasha, I dedicate my life to anarchy.
BERKMAN	I am committed. You are romantic.
EMMA	Johann Most doesn't think me romantic.
BERKMAN	Johann Most doesn't think of you at all, Emma. He is a very busy man.
EMMA	He is sending me to Rochester.

BERKMAN	To Rochester?
HELEN	But Sasha was supposed to go…. Oh…
BERKMAN	It doesn't matter.
EMMA	I'm sorry, Sasha. I always speak too fast.
BERKMAN	No. I'm glad you told me. Johanna Most will have his own reasons, of course.
FEDYA	He wants her in bed.
BERKMAN	Fedya!
FEDYA	It's true.
BERKMAN	I don't want to hear about it, Fedya!
EMMA	I'll kill you, Fedya!

EMMA is furious. She begins to chase FEDYA around the table.

FEDYA	Look, Helen's finger is bleeding. Let me help you, Helen.
HELEN	It's all right.
FEDYA	You look faint, Helen. *(He picks her up and begins to carry her out of the room. To EMMA, as he exits.)* You shouldn't strike a man with a woman in his arms.

EMMA is speechless with rage. Alexander BERKMAN tries to comfort her.

BERKMAN	Fedya is a moral cripple.

MOST has entered to watch this romping. He shouts. BERKMAN and EMMA make a fast exit.

MOST	I cannot work in this confusion. Everything is chaos and I cannot work in chaos. My library is upside down. I find my own work… I find *The Science of Revolutionary Warfare* filed between Bakunin and Kropotkin. I cannot find my notes on the cloakmakers' strike. Emma! Emma! Emma!
EMMA	*(re-enters)* Yes?
MOST	What have I written about the cloakmaker's strike?
EMMA	I don't know, Most.
MOST	And where have I written it?
EMMA	I don't know.
MOST	I can't work in this confusion.
EMMA	I don't blame you.
MOST	You will do me a kindness, Emma. You will pick up after me. Bring me peace and order.

EMMA	Me?
MOST	You will give me time for my work.
EMMA	You're much neater than I am.
MOST	Everything is chaos and I cannot work in chaos.
EMMA	You will clean it up.
MOST	You will clean it up.
EMMA	You have an orderly nature.
MOST	*(who has already begun to square things off)* That's true.
EMMA	And you know where everything goes.
MOST	*(picking something up)* I want to ask you something.
EMMA	Ask me?

MOST uses picking things up to cover his confusion.

MOST	Do my looks frighten you?
EMMA	No, of course not.
MOST	I am disfigured, am I not? The beard doesn't disguise it. I look like a man who eats children.
EMMA	I never think of it.
MOST	Of course you do.
EMMA	Really.
MOST	My jaw. It's deformed.
EMMA	I don't think so.
MOST	Well, look at it.
EMMA	I see it, Hannes.
MOST	It is deformed.
EMMA	I see everything about you. You conceal nothing.
MOST	You think that?
EMMA	Yes, I do.
MOST	You don't notice my face... you say you don't and I believe you... *(A pause. MOST will not be denied his theatrical story.)* I know what it looks like, however, if you do not. It's come near to driving me to kill myself. Yes, "really." Before I was old enough to grow this moustache. And once in prison when they shaved my beard. My face is frightening.
EMMA	I don't notice your face. Or if I do, it seems beautiful. Really.

MOST	I used to love the theatre. Schiller. I loved Schiller. William Tell. I became obsessed with the idea that I could go on the stage, play those tragedies. I went so far as to apply to a theatre manager.
EMMA	And you acted?
MOST	He said I looked like a clown. Yes, because of my face. A clown to play Schiller. Schiller as a Punch and Judy show. Don't cry. Are you crying?
	Of course she isn't crying.
EMMA	Yes I am.
MOST	I've been married twice. The marriages were failures. Since I met you I've thought of that. I have a new obsession. I thought if you need me…
EMMA	I cannot go to Rochester, Most.
MOST	I was not talking about Rochester…
EMMA	I don't know the issues. I'm not ready…
MOST	We don't have to talk about Rochester now…
EMMA	Alexander Berkman has prepared himself for that tour. Most… he knows the problems…
MOST	And I will not talk about Alexander Berkman!
EMMA	He understands the struggle for the eight-hour day.
MOST	We are against that struggle. We don't have to understand it.
EMMA	I could stay here in New York. I could work on the cloakmakers' strike
MOST	If you are my student, Emma…. If you follow me, you can do anything. Do you believe that?
EMMA	I can do anything.
MOST	Be bold. Be arrogant. I am sure you will be brave.
	They exit. KREIDERMAN and PARKS enter, bumping into FEDYA and HELEN who carry picket signs about the cloakmakers printed in Cyrillic characters. FEDYA and HELEN picket with some dignity.
KREIDERMAN	You people are violating a public ordinance the moment that your protest blocks the public right of way.
PARKS	Get a job!
KREIDERMAN	You live in a democracy now. That gives you the right of free speech. It does not give you the right to obstruct traffic.
PARKS	Get a job!

KREIDERMAN	This is a public thoroughfare. I mean to see that people continue to move along this street.
PARKS	Get a job!
KREIDERMAN	I think they have work, Parks. I think they are protesting the conditions in their various factories.
FRICK	*(enters)* What's going on here?
KREIDERMAN	Anarchist street meeting, sir.
PARKS	Go back where you came from.
KREIDERMAN	Bolsheviks and their dupes, agitating against the free enterprise system.
PARKS	You people are asking for it.
KREIDERMAN	Foreigners, sir.
PARKS	That's right.
KREIDERMAN	Russkies and Krauts. Ivan and Hansel.
PARKS	Ask for it and you're going to get it.
FRICK	Can I get through?
PARKS	If you don't like it, stand up and fight for what you do like.
KREIDERMAN	See what you can do, Parks.

PARKS flourishes a bullwhip.

FRICK	You move on unarmed men and women with a bullwhip?
KREIDERMAN	There's no use talking to them, sir. We can't understand a word they say.
FRICK	Your enthusiasm is astonishing.
PARKS	Move along there. You heard me. I said move along, get moving. Make way for Mr. Frick…. That means you as well. Move along, get moving…
FRICK	Give me your whip, Parks.
PARKS	Beg your pardon, sir?
KREIDERMAN	Give Mr. Frick your whip, Mr. Parks.
FRICK	This isn't Mother Russia. We do not horsewhip the peasants in New York.
PARKS	Talking their language, sir.
FRICK	Teach them our language.

Exit FRICK.

PARKS	*(to FEDYA)* See that line. Step over that line. I dare you. Come on and get what's coming to you.
KREIDERMAN	Henry Clay Frick is a fine man. He's a captain of industry.
PARKS	*(to FEDYA)* I'm not going to waste my breath asking you twice, you godless, murdering Bolshevik. I dare you. Step over that line.
KREIDERMAN	He's probably meeting Mr. Andrew Carnegie, the philanthropist who owns the Homestead Steel Mills. But he still has time to give us his advice.
PARKS	All right, you yellow-bellied, yellow-livered Red, if you aren't going to step over here, I'm going over there to get you.
KREIDERMAN	*(sharply)* Parks!
PARKS	Yes, sir.
KREIDERMAN	Teach them our language.

> *FEDYA turns to see what KREIDERMAN is saying. KREIDERMAN escorts HELEN offstage. PARKS clips FEDYA behind the ear and beats him down to the ground. MOST enters to deliver a speech to the audience.*

MOST	Know your enemy. It is capitalism. It is the capitalistic system. Capitalism denies your humanity. Capitalism's greatest achievement, capitalism's crowning glory, is the assembly line. The assembly line binds a man, a free man, to a machine. For up to fourteen hours a day the man serves the machine and the machine creates material wealth. The man serves the system and the system cages the man. We know that men are free. We know we can act. It is you who must act. We will act to free our brothers. It is the individual act of a free man that is creative. It is by the individual acts of free men that we progress. Attentat!

> *PARKS aims his foot for one last kick. Blackout.*

> *Lights up on HELEN, wrapped in a blanket, sitting at the table in the anarchists' commune. EMMA enters, very happy.*

EMMA	Good morning, Helen.
HELEN	Don't say anything. Don't say anything more.
EMMA	We are free and the morning is bright.
HELEN	You are free. I am tired.
EMMA	You look tired.
HELEN	Yes, I am.
EMMA	You didn't sleep well.
HELEN	Not at all.

EMMA	*(glorious)* Neither did I.
HELEN	I know that.
EMMA	We woke you. We kept you up. Is that what you're trying to tell me?
HELEN	I'll take a leaf from your book, Emma. I'll confess something to you. When I am lying in a very narrow bed somewhat cold and almost damp, I am not amused by whispers and chuckles, by heavy breathing and theatrical groans, I am not amused by carols of joy from the room next door. You know when the sun rose this morning, Emma, I think you woke Sasha to tell him about it, do you remember? I did not share your happiness.
EMMA	We disturbed you.
HELEN	It is jealousy. I admit it. I see that I am weak and mean. Mean and weak, oh God. I see why you do it, Emma. I see why you flay yourself with every emotion that flickers through your eyes. This is marvellous. Oh God, she said, she tore her hair, she tore open her waist. She fainted.
	FEDYA enters, shirtless, wrapped in another blanket. There is a large bruise on his chest.
	Look, Fedya. I have learned from Emma. Self-expression. I have freed my emotions. I am playing at being Emma and I have shut her up. I have finally shut her up.
FEDYA	I see that.
EMMA	What's the matter with Helen?
FEDYA	What did you say to her?
EMMA	I said, "Good morning, Helen."
FEDYA	Your enthusiasm is infectious.
BERKMAN	*(enters, looking the worse for wear)* Good morning all.
HELEN	Dance with me, Sasha.
BERKMAN	I want four cups of coffee and a long rest.
HELEN	Dance with me, Sasha. While the dawn comes silently. Till the sun streams in the window and warms us. I can see the dawn on your skin, Sasha.
BERKMAN	You told her.
EMMA	Me? She overheard.
FEDYA	We overheard.
EMMA	You want some toast, Sasha?

FEDYA	The neighbourhood overhead, I suppose. Emma is not discreet.
EMMA	I'm really hungry this morning.
FEDYA	How about you, Sasha?
BERKMAN	What do you mean?
FEDYA	Are you really hungry this morning?
BERKMAN	You insinuate.
FEDYA	I ask about your appetite.
BERKMAN	I'm getting out of here.
FEDYA	Eh, Dushenka?
HELEN	Oh, Dushenka! Dance with me, Dushenka!
FEDYA	Kiss me, Dushenka. Because tomorrow I go to Rochester.
HELEN	Will you miss me while I am in Rochester, Dushenka?
BERKMAN	Where's my hat? Where's my scarf?
EMMA	Be a good sport, Sasha.
BERKMAN	Where are my boots?
FEDYA	Be a good sport, Dushenka. Helen and I, we are both good sports.
EMMA	Come on, dance. We'll all dance.
BERKMAN	Sure we'll dance. And Emma will practise public speaking. As she did last night. So when she goes to Rochester, she'll make sure she's heard.
HELEN	Dushenka! Dushenka! Dushenka!
EMMA	Wait a minute, Sasha, I'll go with you.
BERKMAN	No.
EMMA	I don't mind. I'll just get my coat.
	They exit in opposite directions.
HELEN	Johann Most is a man of some sensitivity, Fedya, is he not?
FEDYA	I'm going back to bed.
HELEN	*(following him)* He'll see Emma for what she is. He'll see how silly she is.
	They exit. Enter FRICK, KREIDERMAN, and PARKS. *KREIDERMAN and PARKS are in ludicrous disguises.*
FRICK	I hope you men are here with open minds.
PARKS	Yes, sir.

KREIDERMAN	Interesting to hear the other side. See the other fellow's point of view.
PARKS	Yes, sir.
KREIDERMAN	We like to be reasonable. That's our training. We're Pinkerton men.

> *EMMA enters and mounts the speaker's podium. She seems to begin to speak although we don't hear anything.*

PARKS	What did she say?
FRICK	Fellow workers.
PARKS	Speaking some foreign language.
KREIDERMAN	She's speaking German.
PARKS	That's what I said.
FRICK	She's talking about the struggle for the eight-hour day.
PARKS	Do you understand German, sir?
KREIDERMAN	Mr. Frick has travelled extensively. In Europe.
PARKS	Does he understand German, I'm asking him.
FRICK	Yes. I do.
PARKS	Do you understand what she's saying, sir?
KREIDERMAN	It's in German, isn't it?
PARKS	That's what I'm asking him.
FRICK	She's talking about the struggle for the eight-hour day.
KREIDERMAN	Make a note of that, Parks.
PARKS	*(to KREIDERMAN)* Is it subversive, sir?

> *They join applause which seems to be going on about them.*

KREIDERMAN	What's all the cheering for? I don't understand a word she's saying.
PARKS	Bunch of foreigners here. They all speak German.
KREIDERMAN	*(to FRICK)* Is it subversive, sir?

> *Lights up full on EMMA.*

EMMA	In the past, we've asked you to fight with us for the eight-hour day. Now I've come to ask you to stop that fight. We have something bigger to do. We must work together to destroy the capitalist system.
	Here in Rochester, we have been concerned with the eight-hour day. In Pennsylvania, at the Homestead Steel Mills, the workers ask for higher wages and the right to organize.

Sometimes we see no further than our own small concerns. We can't understand that as long as Andrew Carnegie owns the product of our labour, as long as Henry Clay Frick works for Andrew Carnegie, and we work for Henry Clay Frick, it doesn't matter how long we work or how much we are paid.

KREIDERMAN and PARKS cheer at the sound of these familiar names. Henry Clay FRICK tries to silence them.

As long as Andrew Carnegie owns us, the world is horribly wrong. We must change the world.

FRICK and the Pinkerton men are unmoved.

Until we own the factories, our work will be drudgery. When we own the factories, our work will be joy. All of us work fourteen, sixteen hours every day for the cause. We have dedicated our life to the cause and the work is our joy. We have no concern for personal comfort. We will work as long as we must. We will not stop working until we reach our goal.

KREIDERMAN and PARKS cheer, carried away by oratory and occasion. FRICK waves his hand in the air.

FRICK	Excuse me… my friends don't understand your point.
EMMA	*(to FRICK)* Are you factory workers?
FRICK	I wonder if politicians ever think that their talk directs our lives. I wonder if you know how easy it is for you to talk of abandoning the struggle for the eight-hour day. Those who work each day for ten hours or twelve hours or fourteen hours. Those who have spent their lives in a mill and want nothing but a few hours every day in peace. They will be glad to talk philosophy with you.
EMMA	Do you work in a mill?
FRICK	It doesn't matter.
EMMA	Who are you.
FRICK	It doesn't matter who I am if I'm telling you the truth.
EMMA	I tell you the truth.
PARKS	Kreiderman?
KREIDERMAN	What, Parks?
PARKS	You think she's one of those suffragettes?

PARKS and KREIDERMAN are giggling and leering.

EMMA	What about your friends. What about you? How do you feel? You are working men. I'm talking to you.
FRICK	You will excuse my friends.

PARKS	Hey, Cookie… *(as EMMA turns toward him)* Not you, hard tack.
FRICK	They are going back to work. Come, Parks. Kreiderman.
EMMA	I explain myself so badly. My English is poor. But you speak German, perhaps you could explain…

> *They exit. EMMA follows. BERKMAN, HELEN, and FEDYA prepare to welcome EMMA home. They enter and the scene becomes the Freiheit office.*

BERKMAN	Do you have the banner?
HELEN	Do you think Emma will like that banner? What if she sees the other side?
BERKMAN	The other side is "Remember the Haymarket Martyrs."
HELEN	It seems impersonal.
FEDYA	Sasha would say it's a fine revolutionary sentiment.
BERKMAN	Sasha would say it isn't enough.

> *EMMA enters, very downcast, in time to hear this last.*

EMMA	No, of course not.
FEDYA	Welcome home, Emma.
BERKMAN	We came to make sure Johann Most put headlines in his newspaper. "Emma… The Girl… Comes Home."
EMMA	Words aren't enough. Words are never enough. Words are meaningless.
FEDYA	You're a success, Emma. A huge success.
HELEN	Everybody cheering. All the crowds.
EMMA	It was awful, Sasha.
BERKMAN	Fedya has composed a song on the condition that Helen and I will sing it. I indulge myself.
EMMA	I am very ignorant.

> *They sing a capella.*

Welcome Emma, queen of the Anarchists
Had you been gone much longer
We might have slashed our wrists.

FEDYA	Sasha has allowed me to buy you flowers. Here it is.

> *He presents EMMA with a bushy potted plant.*

BERKMAN	I chose the flower for you, Emma.
EMMA	Johann wants to talk to me.

BERKMAN	Fedya says it is a good, sturdy plant. I see it is practical. I want it to be more than that.
FEDYA	Johann Wurst wants to talk to you. That's his name. Johann Sausage.
BERKMAN	Take your flower.

MOST enters carrying violets.

BERKMAN	What is that?
MOST	Violets.
BERKMAN	It is the middle of winter, Emma, and he gives you violets.
MOST	You see she has taken the violets and you are left holding that colourful tree.
BERKMAN	Thousands of people out of work and hungry and he gives you violets.
MOST	Alexander Berkman does not have a generous spirit.
BERKMAN	I do not indulge myself at the expense of others.
MOST	You attack me. That is an indulgence.
BERKMAN	Violets are stupid. Useless. Extravagant.
MOST	You resent Emma's success.
BERKMAN	I do not.
MOST	That is why you are angry. That is why you attack me.
BERKMAN	I attack you because you are wrong.
MOST	You see yourself as a spokesman for anarchy.
BERKMAN	And I am.
MOST	Your dreary philosophy is anarchy.
BERKMAN	My philosophy is clearly reasoned. It is sane and humanistic.
MOST	You have no imagination.
BERKMAN	Of course I do not take theatrical poses.
MOST	You do make rules for anarchists, however.
BERKMAN	I do not dramatize myself until I'm a figure of fun.
MOST	Anarchy is a living force above your rules.
BERKMAN	I do not see myself as a character in a cheap melodrama.
MOST	I see myself in Schiller tragedies, Berkman. I see you as a political puppet.

BERKMAN	Violets. Cheap theatrics. You are an old man dreaming of romances on the barricades. Emma will not play in your romance.
MOST	And here is the tragic Anna Minkin.
HELEN	I'm Helen. Minkin.
MOST	So you are.
HELEN	Anna is my sister.
MOST	It was seeing you with Berkman. Berkman and Anna Minkin. They are inseparable I had understood.
BERKMAN	Emma says that she must talk to you.
MOST	Then no doubt you will leave Emma here to talk.
BERKMAN	If she wishes.
MOST	And you will return to Anna Minkin. Since you are so seldom apart.
BERKMAN	We did not come here to discuss where I go or what I do.
MOST	Certainly not. Because here we discuss anarchy. We dedicate our lives to anarchy. We are not self-seeking young men chasing silly young women.
BERKMAN	I will ask you to be brief, Emma.
MOST	I will ask you to leave my office.
BERKMAN	Who?
MOST	As she has told you, Emma and I have business to discuss.
BERKMAN	But not alone.
MOST	Yes.
BERKMAN	She'll come with me.
EMMA	No, Sasha.
BERKMAN	Yes, you will.
EMMA	I won't.
BERKMAN	Yes, you will.
EMMA	I won't.
BERKMAN	I think Johann Most believes that man does not need law or government or authority because he feels man has some special strength.
MOST	That's correct.
BERKMAN	There are others and I count myself among them, who want individual autonomy because man is inherently good. You pervert

every principle of revolution. You lead the revolution because you want the power. You want to be an anarchist king. Come Fedya, Helen.

> *They exit.*

MOST	I have brought you flowers. Violets.
EMMA	I want to tell you about the tour.
MOST	I know about the tour. Do you like them?
EMMA	What happened in Rochester…
MOST	You were eloquent in Rochester…
EMMA	It went very badly.
MOST	You were entertaining in Buffalo. In Cleveland you entered an entirely new arena. Anarchy became a popular attraction.
EMMA	That's what you printed in *Freiheit*. Do you want to know what I felt?
MOST	Of course I do. Another time.
EMMA	Now.
MOST	We have been apart for two weeks, Emma.
EMMA	You were wrong, Most.
MOST	Agreed. We will not be apart again.
EMMA	About the struggle for the eight-hour day.
MOST	I don't want to talk about the eight-hour day.
EMMA	I do.
MOST	Don't be silly, Emma.
EMMA	I will not be treated like a silly woman. You sent me out to speak for you like a trained dog. I've made a fool of myself. I didn't speak for myself, I said your words. I've said pretentious, pompous things. There are men who work fourteen hours a day. I spoke to them. One man came up after my lecture, Johann. Grey-headed, his hands shook. He had spent his life on a factory assembly line, Johann, and I learned more from his simple words than from all your books. You care only for the symmetry of your world. You only want your philosophy secure.
MOST	Viper.
EMMA	If you worked in a factory fourteen hours a day…
MOST	Snake!
EMMA	Breathing foul air, cramped in a space beside a machine.

MOST	I taught you everything!
EMMA	I'm only telling you what I feel.
MOST	You've betrayed me.
EMMA	I speak for you but I will not say your words.
MOST	You're like everybody else. I would rather cut you out of my heart altogether than have you as a lukewarm friend… who is not with me, is against me! I would not have it otherwise. I gave you my mystery and you ate it!
EMMA	I think for myself! I speak for myself! Johann!

MOST storms out. FEDYA enters, since he has been listening at the door.

FEDYA	Johann Wurst has eaten his violets.
EMMA	Fedya…
FEDYA	Are you all right?
EMMA	Yes.
FEDYA	You look like you're going to cry.
EMMA	I'm not crying.

But she is. FEDYA holds her.

FEDYA	If I were going to paint you…
EMMA	Will you paint me?
FEDYA	I am not a painter, Emma. I do crayon enlargements for a commercial artist. I do advertising.
EMMA	If you paint me, will it be a nude?
FEDYA	No.
EMMA	Why not?
FEDYA	You're ready to pose in the nude, I suppose?
EMMA	Of course.
FEDYA	If I paint you, Emma, you will not look like a statue in a public park.
EMMA	Why not?
FEDYA	I am an artist.
EMMA	There is nothing wrong with nudity.
FEDYA	I love you, Emma. I take your nudity seriously. I take your tears seriously but you aren't crying anymore. Sometimes I wish you

were vulnerable, Emma. Sometimes I wish you were mysterious. Do you know what that means?

EMMA   *(nonplussed)* Are you a pre-Raphaelite?

FEDYA   Do I look like a pre-Raphaelite?

EMMA   Well, I don't know what a pre-Raphaelite looks like.

FEDYA   You'll be all right, won't you? You'll be in a union hall tomorrow, organizing somebody. You're very strong and healthy.

HELEN and BERKMAN enter to join in the song and dance.

The cloakmakers' bosses
Say their striking workers
Should not have the right
To fight to be free
The cloakmakers' bosses
Depend on our labour
They cannot continue
Without you and me

If helping our sisters
Is what you would like
Come to the dance
For the cloakmakers' strike.

EMMA climbs on a table to speak. She is more confident and more convincing than before.

EMMA   Women's emancipation? How much independence is gained if the narrowness and lack of freedom of the home is exchanged for the narrowness and lack of freedom of the factory, sweat shops, department store, or office.

Why should I join a union? I am going to get married and have a home. Have you not been taught from infancy to look upon that as your ultimate calling? You learn soon enough that the home, though not as large a prison as the factory, has more solid doors and bars.

The song continues.

The Cloakmakers' Union
As strong as its members
And strong as its members
Means like you and me
And fighting together
Means winning our battles
So our lives will be
What we want them to be

If helping our sisters
Is what you would like
Come to the dance for
The cloakmaker's strike.

EMMA   Woman's development, her freedom, her independence must
come from and through herself. First by asserting herself as a
personality, and not as a sex commodity. Second by refusing the
right to anyone over her body, by refusing to bear children unless
she wants them, by refusing to be a servant to God, the state,
society and husband, the family. By making her life simpler,
but deeper and richer. That is, by trying to learn the meaning
and substance of life in all its complexities, by freeing herself from
the fear of public opinion and public condemnation. Only that
will set woman free, will make her a force hitherto unknown in
the world, a force of real love, for peace, for harmony—a force of
divine fire, of life-giving, a creator of free men and women.

The song continues.

The Cloakmakers' Union
Is standing together
The bosses will listen
The bosses will see
That we stand united
Our voices are strong
And the Cloakmakers' Union
Will make us all free

If helping your sisters
Is what you would like
Come to the dance for
The cloakmakers' strike.

Blackout.

ACT TWO

A small table has been added to the upper level. The speaker's podium has been moved to the lower level.

KREIDERMAN discovers PARKS working in FRICK's office on the upper level. He gives him a Cossack hat.

KREIDERMAN Mr. Frick is appearing tonight in *The Assassination of Alexander II.*

PARKS Yes, sir.

KREIDERMAN At the Philadelphia Light Opera Society. It's a benefit performance for charity.

PARKS Yes, sir.

KREIDERMAN You're playing a Cossack.

PARKS But sir, I can't do that. I couldn't appear on the stage.

KREIDERMAN You will do it. There is a spectacular effect in the assassination scene. The Czar's sleigh pulled by his famous team of matched greys has been blown apart by the bomb of the conspirator Rysakov. The Czar steps from the carriage. Thank God you're all right, sir, says the Cossack.

PARKS *(sings)* Thank God you're all right, sir.

KREIDERMAN Yes, I'm all right, thank God, sings the Czar. The conspirator Grevevitsky steps from the crowd. His hands above his head. It's too soon to thank God, he sings. He walks right up to the Czar and drops his bomb directly between them. Boom! The Czar's right leg is blown off. Above his waist his body is an unrecognizable mass of blood.

KREIDERMAN exits. FRICK enters dressed as Czar Alexander II.

FRICK *(sings)* Emperor of all the Russias
Ruler of a mighty nation
Statesman Judge and King and Czar
Working for emancipation
All reforms come from the Czar
Reforms come from above.
That way though the serfs are free
And Russia lives in liberty
Russia still will always be
The Russia that we love
BUT
Though everyone sings praises
And advisors may applaud

Remember it is hard to be
An instrument of God.

> *FRICK and PARKS exit to huge rounds of applause. FEDYA, HELEN, and EMMA enter the anarchists' commune.*

FEDYA
I am going to paint an epic canvas. The Imperial Family. Czar Alexander II as he freed the serfs. Helen will pose as the Empress.... Here Helen, hold this. Pretend it's a Fabergé egg.

EMMA
The Czar and the Empress will be shown as little people in the background of the canvas. They will be overwhelmed by the tide of events. In the foreground, there will be a serf, free and noble. I will pose for that figure.

FEDYA
Alexander frees the serfs. It will be a series.

HELEN
What will I wear, Fedya?

EMMA
There will be a wind. It will blow my hair back. There will be an aura of golden light around my face.

> *BERKMAN enters. He is not amused.*

BERKMAN
And behind you here will be a line of dancing workers.

HELEN
Come and stand beside me, Sasha. Be in Fedya's picture.

BERKMAN
There are some books that I should have.

HELEN
Come and be Alexander II.

BERKMAN
(horrified) Alexander II?

HELEN
Alexander frees the serfs. It's history.

FEDYA
It's an advertising campaign.

BERKMAN
You are a traitor to our class, Fedya.

FEDYA
It's a public service. To sell sardines.

BERKMAN
Alexander II freed the serfs because he feared the will of the people. He was a spineless worm. My uncle Maxim hanged the Cossacks. That's history.

EMMA
Sasha and Fedya arrive in New York. Friendless. Without money. They huddle together in a doorway as the wind whistles. As the snow blows. That's history.

BERKMAN
I will not tax you with this stupidity, Emma. I try not to criticize, although we are so different.

EMMA
Because I want freedom, the right to self-expression, everybody's right to be beautiful, radiant things.

BERKMAN
I live austerely. With my philosophy. You do not. You like to romp.

EMMA
To what?

BERKMAN	To romp. You know. Your sense of fun.
EMMA	How is Anna Minkin, Sasha?
HELEN	Sasha and Anna are living together.
EMMA	All right! I know!
FEDYA	Emma… calm yourself.
EMMA	I'm sorry. I scream at you. I turn on my closest companion. It is an emotional indulgence. Forgive me, Helen. It is not your fault if Sasha lives with your silly sister.
HELEN	Anna is a very quiet woman.
EMMA	Sasha needs peace. Of course.
HELEN	They speak of having a family.
EMMA	Anna speaks.
HELEN	And Sasha. He wants children. He wants peace.

> *EMMA now begins to build to a hysterical scene. HELEN, FEDYA, and BERKMAN have seen it all before, hundreds of times. They are bored. BERKMAN reads. FEDYA sketches HELEN.*

EMMA	I can never have children.
FEDYA	Emma…
EMMA	I can never have children. I suffer. Sometimes I suffer unbearable pain. When I first came to New York, I discussed my complaint with Solataroff who took me to a doctor.
BERKMAN	Emma, you dramatize yourself again.
EMMA	The specialist urged an operation. He was surprised that I had been able to stand my condition so long. He said I would never be free from pain. I would never experience full sexual release, unless I submitted to the operation.
HELEN	Heaven forbid that your sexual release should not be full.
EMMA	He said I could never bear children. I love children madly.
FEDYA	You'll make yourself sick, Emma.
EMMA	I love babies passionately but I remember my own childhood. My father wanted a boy. The pig woman had brought me instead, he told me. The pig woman had cheated him. Perhaps if I were very sick, perhaps if I were dying he would be kind.
FEDYA	You're raving, Emma.

EMMA	No child of mine will be unwanted. No child of mine will be unloved. I won't have a child. I will live for my ideal. I will suffer for my ideal. I will not have the operation.
FEDYA	She's going to faint.
HELEN	She's always going to faint.

EMMA faints. FEDYA and BERKMAN catch her.

FEDYA	Help me with her, Sasha.
EMMA	Fedya and I are lovers, Sasha.
FEDYA	She's raving.
EMMA	It's true, isn't it?
BERKMAN	It's true, isn't it?
FEDYA	Of course it's true. But she doesn't know what she's saying, Sasha.
BERKMAN	Emma, listen to me. The catechism of the Russian Revolution says the revolutionary must give up his home, his parents, his lover, his children, everything. I agree with that absolutely. But I do love you. I wanted you to know that.

FEDYA has tried to ease EMMA back to the table. BERKMAN leans over to kiss EMMA. She's enthusiastic. FEDYA tries to extricate himself from their embrace.

HELEN	She has fooled you again. All she has to do is scream and faint.
EMMA	Helen, you must calm yourself.
HELEN	Of course you and Fedya are only boys. You cannot help your immaturity. A man of more experience, of more intelligence, a man like Johann Most would not be taken in.
BERKMAN	Johann Most? Johann Most has had her name carved on his chest.
HELEN	You are very stupid, Sasha, if you think Most concerns himself with a silly girl.
BERKMAN	He has made a career of it.
HELEN	You show how small you are when you mock him.
FEDYA	Why is Helen so concerned with Most?
HELEN	I love him.
FEDYA	Go and make some popcorn, Helen.
HELEN	I love Most.
FEDYA	Stay home tonight, Helen. Rest. Drink plenty of liquid.
HELEN	I love him.
EMMA	I knew it.

HELEN	You knew it! Of course, you know everything!
FEDYA	What is Sasha doing?
EMMA	Helen…
HELEN	Perhaps one thing you do not know…. I can make Johann Most happy if you cannot…
EMMA	I have offended you, Helen. I see that. I know how you feel.
HELEN	You do not.
FEDYA	What are you doing, Sasha?
BERKMAN	I'm moving this table.
EMMA	I can tell you about Hannes, Helen…
HELEN	I will go to hear him. I will go anywhere he speaks. I will follow him from one engagement to another.
EMMA	You're very foolish, Helen.
HELEN	You think you're very clever and you think I'm very stupid and you think I don't know what you think.
FEDYA	This is our table.
BERKMAN	I need it for my work.

BERKMAN and FEDYA carry the table out. It's necessary to clear the lower stage area for the trial scene.

EMMA	Be quiet, Sasha.
HELEN	You think no one understands anything but you… you understand everything, you love everything, you have everything.
EMMA	I will go to Hannes because I know him better than you do. You are wrong to think he is mature, Helen. He is very impressionable. He is weak with women.

EMMA exits.

HELEN	I don't want your help. I don't want your help. I don't want your help! She thinks she can do anything. She can save me. She can save the world. She can scream louder than I can.

HELEN exits. Enter FRICK, KREIDERMAN, and PARKS on the upper level.

PARKS	What are you going to tell the union at Homestead, Mr. Frick?
FRICK	Union?
KREIDERMAN	Mr. Frick doesn't recognize the union, Mr. Parks.
FRICK	I won't negotiate, I'll propose a twenty-two percent wage cut throughout the mill. I'll put that on their bargaining table.

PARKS	What will they say to that, sir?
FRICK	I don't sit at their bargaining table, Parks. I don't know what they say and I don't care.

They exit. Enter MOST and EMMA.

EMMA	Helen Minkin says she loves you.
MOST	Helen is available. I know that, of course.
EMMA	Tell me what you feel for her.
MOST	Nothing.
EMMA	She loves you.
MOST	I think Helen's passion is largely sexual.
EMMA	I don't see the difference.
MOST	Love isn't sex. Sex isn't love.
EMMA	They are inseparable.
MOST	Not in Helen's case.
EMMA	For any woman.
MOST	She thinks she loves me. I am sure any other man would do as well.
EMMA	Helen is not often in hysterics.
MOST	Is she not?
EMMA	You are either cruel or stupid.
MOST	Have her try that arrogant Russian Jew.
EMMA	Who?
MOST	Your friend. Your young fool.
EMMA	I am a Russian Jew, Most.
MOST	I said arrogant. He is arrogant.
EMMA	He is inspired.
MOST	He tells me about evolutionary ethics.
EMMA	Why not?
MOST	He knows nothing of life. He bores me.
EMMA	Many things bore you. It's why you bore me sometimes.
MOST	And he offends me.
EMMA	You are talking rubbish.
MOST	You will have to choose between us.

EMMA	There's no choice for me in an idiot who thinks all women are fools.
MOST	I think Helen is a fool.
EMMA	Who dares to say he wants me all to himself. Who treats me like an object he can own.
MOST	Choose Berkman then.
EMMA	Of course I will.
MOST	Choose your beautiful, mindless boy.
EMMA	Choose my arrogant Russian Jew.
MOST	Yes.
EMMA	Sasha knows women and he knows you.
MOST	Sasha! Who is Sasha? Children!
EMMA	He says you're no longer an anarchist. He says you're a posturing cripple.
MOST	Calling names.
EMMA	He is right.
MOST	AAAAhhh!

MOST screams and falls at her feet.

EMMA	Most? Most?

EMMA is very tentative. Very embarrassed. FRICK appears.

FRICK	Get up! Get up!
EMMA	Get up, Most.
FRICK	That looks like very "disorderly" conduct.
EMMA	Will you go away? Will you mind your own business?
FRICK	An old man and a young girl "making love" in the street? Someone should call a policeman.
EMMA	What do you want a policeman for?
FRICK	To maintain order.
EMMA	Get up, Most.
MOST	No, I won't.
FRICK	Officer?

PARKS appears.

EMMA	(to MOST) If they recognize you. They're police. If they know who you are…

MOST	The King of the Anarchists dying of love in the streets of New York.
FRICK	Excuse me, officer…
MOST	Excuse me, officer. Take me to prison. I'll go back to Blackwell's Island. It is the Inquisition brought to American soil.
EMMA	Excuse me, officer, my father has had a sudden attack of dizziness.
FRICK	Are you trying to tell a New York policeman that man is your father?
EMMA	Why not?
FRICK	He won't believe that. Will you?
PARKS	No, sir.
EMMA	My father is very ill. If you could run for a doctor.
FRICK	What your father should do is give the policeman five dollars. I would. In the unlikely event that the policeman had found me "grovelling" in the street with a child. "Disturbing the peace," so to speak.
MOST	Bribery.
FRICK	As I said. Five dollars.
MOST	I won't pay bribes. Take me.
EMMA	I'll give you five dollars.
MOST	I'm not her father. Believe me. I am her lover. She is rejecting me.
EMMA	Here. Take the money. Pay him. I'll take my father home.
MOST	I'm not your father.
FRICK	If he is her father, he has unhealthy passions. Perhaps ten dollars.
EMMA	Come on, Most.
FRICK	What do you think, officer? Shall we make sure the aged gentleman reaches his home safely?
PARKS	Perhaps fifteen dollars.
FRICK	Twenty?
PARKS	Twenty-five.
	The bids escalate as they exit. FEDYA enters and sings "The Song of the Homestead Strike." During his song, BERKMAN and EMMA enter.
FEDYA	*(sings)* Henry Clay Frick hated unions with passion The Steelworkers' Union worked militantly

Frick said to his boss, Mr. Andrew Carnegie
Go off to Scotland and leave it to me

Widows and orphans evicted and tricked
At the hands of the villainous Henry Clay Frick

Henry Clay Frick told the strikers at Homestead
He'd see them dead rather than bargain again
Six of them died on the banks of the river
Shot without cause by his Pinkerton men

Widows and orphans evicted and tricked
At the hands of the villainous Henry Clay Frick

Pinkertons hired to guard Homestead Steel Mills
Strikebreakers hired to help keep things hot
Pinkertons fired on unarmed steel workers
A nine-year-old boy was the first man shot

Widows and orphans evicted and tricked
At the hands of the villainous Henry Clay Frick.

BERKMAN	I must go to Homestead.
FEDYA	Alexander Berkman fights the forces of oppression.
BERKMAN	Henry Clay Frick is a cold-blooded murderer. He's responsible for the deaths. He must take the consequences.
FEDYA	There are no consequences.
BERKMAN	There will be.
FEDYA	He owns the police.
BERKMAN	That is why, in anarchism, we speak of the individual act. Read Most. Read *Science of Revolutionary Warfare.*
FEDYA	Don't quote Most to me. You aren't even speaking to him.
BERKMAN	He taught all of us. He told me what to do.
FEDYA	You're crazy, Sasha.
BERKMAN	I will act against Frick.
FEDYA	No you won't. You're crazy.
BERKMAN	I want to accomplish an act of significance.
FEDYA	Well, you won't.
BERKMAN	I will assassinate Henry Clay Frick.
FEDYA	I knew you were going to say that. I knew you were crazy.
BERKMAN	It is an Attentat.

FEDYA	You think if you kill Frick, that all across the country people will rise up and throw off the laws and the systems that make them slaves.
BERKMAN	Propaganda of the deed.
FEDYA	Well, they won't. Nothing will happen. Except Frick will be dead and you will be dead. No one will listen, Sasha. If you kill Frick, they will kill you.
BERKMAN	I know that. I must act.
FEDYA	No.
EMMA	We are anarchists, Fedya.
FEDYA	We are friends.
BERKMAN	Insufferable bourgeois.
FEDYA	Don't call me names.
BERKMAN	Mindless capitalist lackey.
FEDYA	I'm trying to talk sense to you.
BERKMAN	Sentimental reactionary coward.
FEDYA	You are dangerous.
BERKMAN	A political assassination.
FEDYA	You're out of your mind.
EMMA	I'll help you, Sasha.
BERKMAN	I'll make a bomb. With a time regulator.
FEDYA	Now you're talking like Most.
BERKMAN	I know that.
FEDYA	Individual act of violence. Attentat. *The Science of Revolutionary Warfare.* Chapter Four, "Blowing up a Capitalist."
BERKMAN	So I can kill Frick and save myself. Because I'll kill him, I'll be captured, no, I'll give myself up. And of course, I'll be condemned to death. But I'll speak in court before I die. I'll speak in court and I'll kill myself.
EMMA	And the people will know you aren't a criminal.
BERKMAN	The people will know I'm an idealist.
FEDYA	*(sings reprise)* He knows he must find a significant act He makes the decision with terrible calm Consider the case of Henry Clay Frick The murderer dies by an anarchist's bomb

Widows and orphans evicted and tricked
At the hands of the villainous Henry Clay Frick.

At the end of the song, BERKMAN is working over his bombs.

BERKMAN	I don't want you here, Emma.
EMMA	Why not?
BERKMAN	Because I am testing the bomb, of course. Because I must see its effect. I have two bombs and I set this one off to learn how I may best use the other.
EMMA	Right. We must see its effect.
BERKMAN	I'll tell you about it.
EMMA	After the events in Chicago, Louis Lingg blew himself up with his own bomb and on the wall, in his own blood, he wrote "Long live anarchy." As he died.
BERKMAN	Get out of here.
EMMA	You have the bomb in the sand pit. Let me watch.
BERKMAN	Go find Fedya.
EMMA	There. I lit the fuse.

BERKMAN pulls her away from the bomb.

BERKMAN	Get down. *(as FEDYA enters)* Watch out, Fedya. We have lit the fuse.

FEDYA falls flat. BERKMAN pushes EMMA down and falls on top of her. A pause until the bomb's fuse fizzles out.

FEDYA	The bomb is silent. It is useful for clandestine work.
BERKMAN	Very funny.
FEDYA	Henry Clay Frick won't know he's been killed.
EMMA	What happened? What went wrong?
BERKMAN	The dynamite was too damp. The directions were wrong.... I don't know.
FEDYA	It didn't go off. All right. It's over.
EMMA	What about the other bomb?
BERKMAN	It won't work either.
EMMA	Why not? Of course it will.
BERKMAN	I went to some trouble to make them exactly the same.
EMMA	It won't go off?
BERKMAN	I have another plan. I need a gun. I need the money to get a gun.

EMMA	Go to Johann Most.
BERKMAN	He won't help us.
EMMA	He will. He'll help me.
BERKMAN	I need a gun. I need a suit of clothes so I can present myself at Frick's office.
FEDYA	I won't help you.
EMMA	I can get the money, Sasha. We can go to Homestead.
FEDYA	You aren't going, Emma.
EMMA	I could be the first one in Frick's office. I could say I was skilled at the typewriter. I could carry a small handbag to conceal the gun.
BERKMAN	You aren't going.
FEDYA	Emma isn't crazy enough to go. Sasha is the one who thinks he can walk in and murder a man.

       Exit FEDYA.

EMMA	Of course I'm going.
BERKMAN	I don't have time to argue with you, Emma.
EMMA	I don't want to argue. I believe in this act, absolutely. I want to go to Homestead and I will go.
BERKMAN	We do not go to Homestead because we "want" to go. Each of us has responsibility. You will get the money for me. Get Johann Most. I'll talk to him. Go Emma. Please. Go now.

       EMMA exits. BERKMAN is left alone on the lower level. Enter
       KREIDERMAN and FRICK on the upper level.

FRICK	I didn't ask for strikebreakers, Kreiderman. I asked for police.
KREIDERMAN	The Pinkerton Detective Agency, sir…
FRICK	I wanted order. And we had a war.
KREIDERMAN	It was the strikers, sir. Look, sir, we were trying to land in barges from across the Monongahela, but those people had a homemade cannon, sir. They had fire bombs. They wanted to blow those barges out of the water, sir, so one of our men opened fire and then he…
FRICK	I suppose your man was mad with fear.
KREIDERMAN	Yes, sir.
FRICK	That one man, Kreiderman. Who lost his head. Since he was mad with fear. He and his single police special killed one nine-year-old boy and five strikers. In pitch darkness from a barge in the middle

of the Monongahela River. And the barge was being shelled.
I think you said.

KREIDERMAN Yes, sir.

FRICK I suppose there's no chance I would talk to this man. I suppose he's now employed with a Wild West Show.

KREIDERMAN There were other men began to fire, sir. It got confusing. Men from Pinkertons were killed.

FRICK I know that, Kreiderman. It's a bloody massacre. There are seventy-five dead now and eight thousand soldiers attacking my steel mill.

Exit FRICK and KREIDERMAN. Enter EMMA and MOST.

MOST What do you want from me?

EMMA I want you to help us. To help Sasha.

MOST What kind of help?

EMMA Money, Hannes, for friendship. As old friends.

MOST I don't live in the past.

EMMA For anarchy. For the cause.

MOST Your companion is drunk with his particular cause, is he not? He feels he is some sort of messiah. The arrogant Jew will go to Homestead and save us all from the forces of oppression. I beseech you, Emma. I beg you to give up this plan. You see him. You see how his mind works. He is a brainless romantic.

EMMA You'll drink wine with me. When I first came to New York, you took me to Sach's, you ordered wine. Liebfraumilch. The first wine I had ever tasted. You said, "Prosit, my young naive lady."

MOST You are asking me a favour, Emma. Don't remind me of my past mistakes.

EMMA I was naive.

MOST So was I.

EMMA You change drinking wine. I've often noticed it.

MOST You want me drunk.

EMMA No, of course not.

MOST You want me to make a fool of myself.

EMMA No, Hannes.

MOST You want money for your lover, Alexander Berkman, so you want me to tell you how much I love you.

EMMA	I want to talk to you. For friendship.
MOST	I will say it, I love you.
EMMA	Hannes…
MOST	That means nothing to you, of course. You care about your "work."
EMMA	I care about social justice.
MOST	You delude yourself, Emma. You love attention. You love your life with famous men.
EMMA	Famous men?
MOST	I am the King of the Anarchists. Berkman is a unique personality.
EMMA	I am Emma Goldman.
MOST	How convenient. You have your own fame.
EMMA	We are planning an Attentat.
MOST	You are Berkman's mistress. He sends you out to beg money for his schemes.

MOST exits. EMMA sings.

EMMA

If the world were fair and fine
I could be a heroine
I could fight the battles
I could win
It's second place in every race
With rules against the way I ran
But reading Russian novels
Reading Russian novels
I find out I can
Be brave and noble, fine and sure
Self-sacrificing, pure.

Sonja
In *Crime and Punishment*
Became a prostitute
To help her family
Sonja
Agreed to pay that price
Could make that sacrifice
So why not me?

If the world were fair and fine
Lightning flashes in the sky
I would change the world
And I would fly

But flying with the wings of man
The victory is bittersweet
Reading Dostoevsky
Reading Dostoevsky
Going on the street
I know I have a heart of gold
I know I'm bought and sold.

> *FRICK enters. EMMA strikes a provocative pose. She is*
> *endearingly naive.*

EMMA	Would you like a good time?
FRICK	With you?
EMMA	Well, yes, of course with me.
FRICK	Would you like me to buy you a drink?
EMMA	All right.
FRICK	At Sach's? The anarchists' café?
EMMA	Not there.
FRICK	A young reactionary.
EMMA	Somewhere else. We can walk…
FRICK	You don't do this very often.
EMMA	You haven't seen me.
FRICK	I haven't seen you because you haven't been here.
EMMA	I have a natural talent for it.
FRICK	Perhaps.
EMMA	How much I know shouldn't concern you. If I'm willing.
FRICK	I do not give lessons.
EMMA	I know what I'm doing. I know why I'm here. Try me.
FRICK	You look very sweet, my dear. I'm sure you made your dress yourself.
EMMA	And the price is right.
FRICK	Of course it is.
EMMA	If price is a consideration.
FRICK	I don't believe you've done this before. You are a seamstress. Some kind of dressmaker. You found yourself short of money so you've gone on the street.
EMMA	I am a courtesan.
FRICK	This is your first night on the street.

EMMA	Don't concern yourself with my experience. I'm very experienced.
FRICK	How much money do you need?
EMMA	Ten dollars.
FRICK	Here. Take it.
EMMA	*(a delaying tactic)* You don't want to argue? Over the price?
FRICK	I don't want to discuss it at all.
EMMA	Of course not.
FRICK	You're a professional.
EMMA	Of course.
FRICK	I want you to take the money and go home.
EMMA	Of course… go home?
FRICK	I will walk you to your door, young lady, to make sure you are not accosted in this neighbourhood.
EMMA	Thank you.
FRICK	Tell me, young lady, why do you need ten dollars?
EMMA	I have to buy a pistol.
FRICK	*(urbane)* Oh? And why do you need a pistol?

> *They exit. BERKMAN enters to be met by KREIDERMAN and PARKS, who enter from the opposite side.*

BERKMAN	I want to see Henry Clay Frick.
KREIDERMAN	Whom can I say is calling.
BERKMAN	What?
PARKS	Do you have a card?
BERKMAN	What? Oh, yes, I do.
PARKS	You sell insurance?
KREIDERMAN	That says employment. He's from an employment agency.
BERKMAN	I want to see Henry Clay Frick.
KREIDERMAN	We understand that Mr…. I can't read your name.
PARKS	It's Berkman.
KREIDERMAN	But does Mr. Frick want to see you?
BERKMAN	*(He draws his gun.)* I want to see your hands up.
KREIDERMAN	Who are you?
BERKMAN	*(very nervous)* I want to see your hands up…. I want to see your hands flat on the table…

KREIDERMAN	(*very nervous*) But you want to see Mr. Frick. One of us will have to get Mr. Frick.
BERKMAN	Don't move.
KREIDERMAN	Stay calm. Keep calm. Calm yourself.

> *FRICK enters. He is the only one who seems calm.*

FRICK	(*behind BERKMAN*) Who are you.
BERKMAN	(*wheeling to face him*) I want to see your hands up…. I want your hands flat on the table.
FRICK	(*to KREIDERMAN and PARKS who are moving in*) Get him out of here.
BERKMAN	(*dodging wildly*) Get back. Get them out of here. Get your hands up. I'm going to shoot. I warned you.
KREIDERMAN	(*frightened*) How far would you get, friend?
PARKS	Put the gun down, friend.
KREIDERMAN	This mill is under armed guard.
PARKS	You wouldn't get out of this office.
KREIDERMAN	You'd never get away with it.

> *FRICK is impatient. He moves towards BERKMAN.*
> *BERKMAN fires wildly. FRICK falls.*

PARKS	(*grabbing him*) Mr. Frick…. You've shot Mr. Frick.

> *PARKS tries to pull BERKMAN away. BERKMAN is trying to*
> *stab FRICK's legs.*

KREIDERMAN	(*with FRICK*) Are you all right, Mr. Frick?

> *KREIDERMAN helps FRICK offstage. PARKS pulls BERKMAN*
> *downstage.*

BERKMAN	You can let go of me, I am not a criminal. I will explain myself.
PARKS	Not on your life, friend. You stay here till the guard gets back.
BERKMAN	This was not a criminal act. This was a political assassination…
PARKS	Sure it was. You might have killed the guy…
BERKMAN	I've lost my glasses.
PARKS	There's more than that coming to you.
BERKMAN	Can you take my statement?
PARKS	Jesus, statement!
BERKMAN	Will you take this down, please. I want a record of my explanation.
PARKS	You'll hear it in court, friend.

EMMA and FEDYA enter the courtroom.

EMMA   Does it say in the newspapers they'll allow Sasha to have visitors?

FEDYA   It says in the newspapers he is a mad dog. Visiting doesn't seem to be an issue.

EMMA   They must let his family see him.

FEDYA   If he had a family.

EMMA   I can be his sister.

FEDYA   Perhaps.

EMMA   Like Louis Lingg's friend. When Lingg was confined, his friend visited him in prison. They embraced and with the kiss, Lingg received a capsule of nitroglycerine. I could make a capsule and take it to Sasha. Sasha will want to commit suicide.

FEDYA   Sasha?

EMMA   I don't know why he hasn't killed himself already.

FEDYA   Sasha?

EMMA   He has tried to kill Frick and Frick is still alive. He has been captured by the forces of reaction. His protest is over.

FEDYA   Maybe he's waiting till the newspapers publish his statement.

EMMA   It could be a posthumous statement.

FEDYA   I was joking, Emma.

EMMA   You don't think he wants to live merely to see his statement in the filthy capitalist press.

FEDYA   I don't think he wants to commit suicide.

EMMA   Why not?

FEDYA   Would you?

EMMA   Of course I would. And Sasha would. Any of us would die for what we believe in.

FEDYA   If we had to.

BERKMAN   I have a letter from Emma and Fedya. It is bitter. They say that because Frick did not die, the moral effect of the act will be less. There will not be so much propaganda value. They actually presume to reproach me with my failure to suicide. How am I to kill myself? By banging my head against the bars of my cell? By what right do they reproach me? By the right of revolutionary ethics, I suppose and they are correct. Emma the girl, Fedya the twin. Emma and Fedya will have to forgive me. I did not think that I could live in prison, but I find I must.

KREIDERMAN enters, as JUDGE. PARKS escorts BERKMAN
to the podium/witness stand on the lower level.

KREIDERMAN   Is it true that the prisoner wishes to conduct his own defence?

BERKMAN   Yes sir.

KREIDERMAN   *(to PARKS)* He will need an interpreter.

PARKS   Yes sir.

BERKMAN   I...

PARKS   I...

BERKMAN   ...address myself to the people.

PARKS   ...make a speech to all.

BERKMAN   Some may wonder why I have declined a legal defense.

PARKS   Some may think funny I say no to lawyer.

BERKMAN   My reasons are two-fold.

PARKS   I say two things.

BERKMAN   In the first place...

PARKS   One thing.

BERKMAN   I am an Anarchist.

PARKS   I am an Anarchist.

BERKMAN   I do not believe in man-made law designed to enslave and oppress humanity.

PARKS   I say no lawyer can make up laws made up to tie up and sit down on men.

BERKMAN   Secondly...

PARKS   I say two things.

BERKMAN   ...an extraordinary phenomenon like an Attentat cannot be measured by the narrow standards of legality.

PARKS   A funny thing like an Attentat is not like law.

BERKMAN   It requires a view of the social background to be understood...

PARKS   It depends where you come from. What you think.

BERKMAN   The translation is inadequate.

KREIDERMAN   We speak English in this court.

BERKMAN   My English is very poor. But it's good enough to know he's not saying what I'm saying.

EMMA   *(to FEDYA)* I have to speak to Johann Most. He can help us.

KREIDERMAN	Silence in the court.
FEDYA	If he wanted to help he would be here.
KREIDERMAN	There is a disruption in the court.
EMMA	We have to ask him, Fedya. We have to try. Come on.

They exit.

BERKMAN	I have a statement. It's impossible to understand my act against Frick unless you hear the statement.
PARKS	We don't want to know why you did it. We want to see if you did it.
KREIDERMAN	Whatever it is that he's saying, we've heard enough of it.
BERKMAN	The removal of a tyrant is not merely justifiable, it is the highest duty of every true revolutionist. Human life is sacred and inviolate. But the killing of a tyrant, of an enemy of the people, is in no way to be considered the taking of a life. In truth, murder and Attentat are to me opposite terms. To remove a tyrant is an act of liberation, the giving of life and opportunity to an oppressed people.
KREIDERMAN	Alexander Berkman. You have been found guilty of the attempted murder of Henry Clay Frick. And the attempted murder of Harry Parks. Of trespassing three times on the property of the Homestead Steel Mills and of trespassing in the office of Henry Clay Frick. I sentence you to twenty-one years in the Western Penitentiary at Pennsylvania.

They exit. HELEN enters, followed by EMMA and FEDYA.

EMMA	I must speak to Johann.
HELEN	He isn't here.
EMMA	I must ask him to help Sasha. They are railroading Sasha into prison.
HELEN	Yes.
EMMA	Have you heard about it, Helen? Sasha in prison. It's dreadful.
HELEN	Go away, Emma.
EMMA	Johann will help us.
HELEN	Go and ask him then.
EMMA	He was our teacher. Of course he'll help.
HELEN	I suppose Sasha thinks that terrorism is part of Hannes's philosophy.
FEDYA	Sasha made his bomb from Hannes's book.

HELEN	You ignore him except when you need him. You make fun of him behind his back. Fedya calls him Johann Sausage, isn't that right?
FEDYA	Sasha's bomb didn't go off. Either Sasha can't make bombs or Johann can't write books.
HELEN	I don't care what you say anymore. You can't hurt me, Fedya. Because I'm content.
FEDYA	Because you're smug.
EMMA	We are all anarchists together, are we not? We help each other.
HELEN	I've told you Emma, Johann isn't here.

> *MOST enters and begins to speak to a public meeting. FEDYA and EMMA become part of his audience. HELEN joins him on the platform.*

MOST	The capitalist press cries out against the anarchist. They want our blood. Why? Because someone has made an attempt on the life of Henry Clay Frick. Alexander Berkman waves our banner and hides behind the name of anarchy but he is an inept, self-seeking bungler, with too much faith in a master plan that was ill-timed, ill-formed…
EMMA	I demand proof of your insinuations against Alexander Berkman.
MOST	This is a public meeting.
EMMA	Proof.
MOST	These people haven't come here to watch Emma Goldman in temperamental display.
EMMA	They haven't come here to listen to lies.
MOST	I am an anarchist. Alexander Berkman has attempted a murder. He claims that I inspired him…
EMMA	Attentat!
MOST	A fool calls me a murderer.
FEDYA	I call you a sausage.
MOST	Berkman was my student. You were all my students. Berkman doesn't learn very well. A young man with a toy pistol and more concern for himself than the workers' problems. Berkman has failed to do anything but find himself the centre of attention.
EMMA	His intention was serious.
MOST	He is a child.
EMMA	It was not a toy gun.
MOST	It was not the gun for the job.

EMMA	It was a cheap revolver. He had no money. Did you give him money? Did you help him at all.
MOST	Of course not.
EMMA	Attentat!
MOST	The Attentat is the act which captures the imagination of men and women everywhere. It makes everyone brave. It makes revolution possible. Has Berkman done this?
FEDYA	Have you?
MOST	Talk to the strikers at Homestead. Berkman tried to "save" those men but they do not understand him. They do not sympathize. They think Frick cheated him in business, perhaps. I have been in prison because of the things I believe in. Berkman makes my philosophy ludicrous.
FEDYA	Berkman is in prison now.
MOST	I denounce him as a self-seeking fool.
EMMA	I call you a coward and a traitor, Johann.
MOST	As you will.
EMMA	You taught me. You called for acts of violence. Sasha is the one of us who moved against the injustice of Homestead. Sasha acts and you deny everything. Every principle you hold important, you deny.
MOST	You are hysterical.
EMMA	When I met you, you asked me for an ardent friendship. Now you call it hysteria.
MOST	It is hysteria.
EMMA	You do not act. You are impotent.
MOST	I do not think of anarchy as some kind of springtime sexual rite.
FEDYA	Johann Wurst. Johann Sausage.
MOST	Berkman's mistress attacks me in the columns of my own newspaper. Because I talk about his stupidity. Because I tell the truth. Berkman was arrogant, opportunistic.
EMMA	Stop it, Johann!
MOST	Egotistical, pretentious.
EMMA	Stop it!
MOST	Self-indulgent.

> EMMA *takes off her belt. She rushes at MOST. The belt comes down on his back.*

EMMA	Be bold. Be arrogant. I am sure you will be brave.
MOST	Emma!
EMMA	Who is not with me is against me!
MOST	Emma!
EMMA	I think for myself. I speak for myself, Johann!

> *EMMA is exhausted. There is a long pause. Though it may not be possible to arrange exits, EMMA and FEDYA are alone.*

FEDYA	Anarchy is a glorious political theory. We have proved it doesn't work.
EMMA	No.
FEDYA	We said an act against a tyrant would begin the revolution. We found we were wrong. We said that man was pure and fine…
EMMA	Man is pure and fine.
FEDYA	You are.
EMMA	I believe in freedom, the right to self-expression. Everyone's right to beautiful, radiant things.
FEDYA	You are pure and fine and gullible.
EMMA	*(sings)* I know I can show you wonders

    I can paint the flags I fly
    I know dreamers can build castles
    I know castles can have banners
    I know dreams are going to flash across the sky

    There are no countries
    There are no kings
    Only the people and all they can wish for
    All of the beautiful radiant things.

    I know I will do my living
    In my future not your past
    There are certain stirring speeches
    There are drumbeats every morning
    And the chance that things will start to move too fast.

    There are no countries
    There are no kings
    Only the people and all they can wish for
    All of the beautiful radiant things.

> *Blackout.*
>
> *The end.*

ONE NIGHT STAND

One Night Stand: Una Aventura
Forword

Carol Bolt intended *One Night Stand* to be an unashamed thriller, a departure from her other work. It was a remarkable success, with the run selling out almost immediately and a film version planned within weeks. In the following years it received well over a hundred productions.

As time went by the script gradually fell out of fashion (as both comedies and thrillers are wont to do) and Carol resigned herself to wondering, on occasion, what might be done to take it from the '70s to the '90s.

It turns out that two young people were also wondering the same thing and in March 2000, Stephanie Jones and Jason Cadieux of the Essential Players approached Carol to revise it. With director Sasha Wentges added to the team, the revised version began to take shape.

There are some significant changes in the new version: Rafe is transformed from Country and Western to the Latin scene, though he is just as phony there. As for structure, I remember Carol heaving a big sigh one afternoon and declaring that "the second act finally works."

The first production of the new version was in its last week of rehearsal when Carol was diagnosed with fatal liver cancer. She died on November 28, 2000. It is always possible that she would have made further changes but my impression is that that she regarded this text as final.

In the Belfry production, and the following one at Theatre Passe Muraille directed by Sasha Wentges, there were some flamboyant stage effects which seemed part of the new version. But I have opted to keep those to a minimum here, trusting that new directors will be as real or surreal as they like.

David Bolt
May 2002

The revised version of One Night Stand *is available in the Second Scene Editions imprint from Playwrights Canada Press. The script that appears in this volume is the version as performed in 1977.*

One Night Stand was first performed at the Tarragon Theatre, Toronto, in April 1977 with the following company.

Chapelle Jaffe   Daisy
Brent Carver   Rafe
Carole Strypchuk   Sharon

Directed by Eric Steiner
Design by Shawn Kerwin
Lighting by Bjarne Christensen
Sound by Jack Ralph

\ \ • / /

The film version of *One Night Stand,* produced by Allan King and the CBC, directed by Allan King and Eric Steiner, starring Chapelle Jaffe and Brent Carver, was produced in 1978.

\ \ • / /

The revised version of *One Night Stand: Una Aventura,* premiered in November 2000 at the Belfry Theatre, Victoria, co-produced with the Essential Players, with the following company:

Stephanie Joncs   Daisy
Jason Cadieux   Rafe
Connie McConnell   Sharon
Patricia Leger   Riva

Directed by Michael McLauglin
Assistant Director: Sasha Wentges
Set/Costumes by Kate King
Lighting by Brian Pincott
Stage Manager: Meredith MacDonald

Special thanks to Maureen A. Dool who created the part of Riva.

CHARACTERS

RAFE
DAISY
SHARON

One Night Stand

ACT ONE

A high-rise apartment. No one home. Light coming in the balcony window from the buildings across the street. There is someone in the hall, opening the door with a key. This is hard to hear because there is music blasting from the apartment next door. As the door to the hallway opens, the music blares louder.

It's DAISY's apartment. She is a little high, glad the music is as loud as it is. She dances into the apartment. RAFE hangs back in the corridor. He has never been here before. In fact, he has never been to an apartment building which seemed to promise such high times. DAISY turns on the lights, pulls him into the apartment, closes the door behind them, and bolts it. The music is still too loud to encourage conversation. DAISY dances instead. RAFE looks around while she dances off with his jacket.

He is carrying a guitar case and a knapsack. He opens the guitar case and takes out his guitar. DAISY thinks she's going to have a private concert. She bangs on her neighbour's wall. Hard. The music becomes sub-audible.

RAFE plays guitar like a good ol' boy from east Texas. He need not be very good. Even if he were good, DAISY would hate it. She isn't comfortable west of Bathurst Street.

RAFE   *(sings)* I said I liked the way you looked
I said I liked your style
And I sat right down beside you
Bought a drink and watched you smile
I told you I picked a guitar with
A country 'n western band
But I didn't want another one night stand.

    RAFE begins to yodel. He knows DAISY hates it.

	I wrote that song. I'm a composer.
DAISY	I guess.
RAFE	But I've got a lot of other songs here…. They're sort of audition tapes.
	He produces cassettes from his knapsack.
DAISY	You've got your whole wardrobe. You've got your whole repertoire. I picked you up and you may move in for the next six months.
RAFE	And you'll be trapped up here with a fugitive from the Grand Ol' Opry. Don't worry. I only came up here so you could sew the sequins on my shirt.
DAISY	I think you should take your shirt off.
RAFE	You're kidding.
DAISY	Who me?
RAFE	You want me with my shirt off?
DAISY	Sure.
RAFE	Well, sure, okay.
	He starts to unbutton his shirt.
DAISY	I want to see if you've got a tattoo someplace that says "mother."
	RAFE stops unbuttoning his shirt.
RAFE	You were kidding.
	DAISY nods.
	You've got a real good sense of humour.
DAISY	It's an act, isn't it? You're all country boy and flannel shirts and aw shucks…
RAFE	What do you want me to be?
	DAISY laughs.
	Why did you let me pick you up if you thought I was a phony?
DAISY	I picked you up.
RAFE	Why?
	He kisses her.
	Is that why? Really?
DAISY	I think so.
	The telephone rings. DAISY wants to answer it.
RAFE	When are you going to know for sure?
DAISY	The telephone…

RAFE	You don't care about the telephone. *(as she picks it up)* You know, I wrote a really boring song about it. About waiting for the phone to ring.
DAISY	*(on the phone)* Hello…. Oh, hello, Mother.
RAFE	Oh sure.
DAISY	*(on the phone)* No, thanks very much for calling. No, thanks very much.
RAFE	Does your mother call you at eleven-thirty every night? Is that to check up on the guy you brought home?
DAISY	*(on the phone)* Well, yes, but I don't have time to talk to you right now. Well, yes, because there are some people here…. Well, yes, it's sort of a party…
RAFE	Where?
DAISY	*(on the phone)* Just some friends, Mother.
RAFE	Where?
DAISY	*(on the phone)* No really, thanks very much for calling but I have to get back to the party, that's all…. Say hi to him from me too…. Say hi to Auntie Vi…. Say hi to Tippy and Edward…. Goodbye. *(hangs up)* You see. That was long distance.
RAFE	It was your mother.
DAISY	So?
RAFE	I bet she would have called back.
DAISY	Everybody calls back.
RAFE	How would you know? You pick up the phone every time it rings.
DAISY	She wanted to wish me happy birthday, that's all.
	Beat.
RAFE	Is it your birthday?
DAISY	So my mother tells me. I guess she would know.
RAFE	Happy birthday, Daisy.
DAISY	*(flat)* Thanks.
RAFE	Where's your party?
DAISY	Oh come on.
RAFE	The one you told your mother about. Where are all your friends? Where's the cake, where's the presents?
DAISY	I hate cake.
RAFE	Nobody hates cake.

DAISY	I do. I'm a vegetarian.
RAFE	Since when are cakes made out of meat.
DAISY	Sugar. Sugar. They are made out of refined sugar...
RAFE	How come you go out picking up strangers on your birthday? Hey, Daisy? Hey, babe?
DAISY	Because I'm adventurous.

> *RAFE lights one of the candles sitting on the coffee table.*

RAFE	Do you want an adventure?

> *He hands the candle to DAISY.*

Make a wish.

> *DAISY blows the candle out. A beat.*

DAISY	I got that candle in Majorca.
RAFE	Oh yeah.
DAISY	*(picking up another one)* And I got this one in Port-au-Prince.
RAFE	You're sentimental. You remind me of my sister.
DAISY	I'm not sentimental.
RAFE	I'm going to throw a birthday party for you. So you can feel young again. We'll have balloons and crêpe paper streamers and funny hats. Have you got any balloons?
DAISY	I don't care about birthdays. I'm grown up now.
RAFE	Have you got any crêpe paper?
DAISY	No.
RAFE	Here. I made you a funny hat.

> *He has made a cocked hat out of newspaper. He drops it on her head.*

DAISY	The last time I had a hat like this, I had cake on my face.

> *She tries it out in one of her mirrors, tries to make it more sophisticated.*

RAFE	Going to make you a cake.
DAISY	No!
RAFE	Do you have any eggs?
DAISY	Stay out of that refrigerator.

> *But RAFE has opened the refrigerator. He whoops.*

RAFE	*(with the cake)* Hey, Daisy, I don't have to make a cake.... Look. Because the good birthday cake tooth fairy has put this chocolate layer

cake in that refrigerator and it says "Happy Birthday Daisy" on the top…. What do you think about that?

DAISY   It's my cake.

RAFE   I see that.

DAISY   Okay… now you know.

RAFE   Know what?

DAISY   Now you can have your big laugh.

RAFE   I wouldn't laugh at you.

DAISY   No?

RAFE   You know it's been scientifically discovered that people who make jokes about other people are very unsure of themselves.

DAISY   Who discovered that, Albert Einstein?

RAFE   That's why stand-up comics are unhappy.

DAISY   Oh sure.

RAFE   Stand-up comics have the highest suicide rate of any occupational group.

DAISY   Oh sure.

RAFE   That's true.

DAISY   Oh sure. You see them lining up to jump off the CN Tower.

RAFE   You argue about everything, don't you?

DAISY   I mean, people don't kill themselves because they have a sense of humour.

RAFE   The last person I know committed suicide was a girl I went to school with. We used to call her Laugh-A-Minute Appleton.

DAISY   What do they call you?

       Beat.

RAFE   How come you have this big cake, Daisy?

DAISY   For my big party. What do you think.

RAFE   There can still be a party. You don't have to be so mad about it.

DAISY   I mean a dinner party. I mean my stupid friend, Sharon, she was supposed to bring her stupid boyfriend, Eddie…

RAFE   Who were you supposed to bring?

DAISY   No one.

RAFE   Who?

DAISY   Look, that's another story.

RAFE   What's his name?

DAISY   *(with some finality)* Nick.

RAFE   *(arranges an imaginary table)* Sharon. And Eddie. And Daisy. And Nick… where's Nick?

DAISY   I've known Sharon for years. We went to Daniel Mac High School together. In Winnipeg, if you really want the sad, dull tale. And after she finished high school, she bought a bus ticket to Los Angeles. She said she was the only girl from Daniel Mac High School ever to do that, and the first person she met in Los Angeles married her and brought her back to Winnipeg every Ukrainian Christmas, but she really hated him. But it turns out he knew a guy who knew a guy at William Morris and she got a job, she finally did, in the national tour of Disney on Parade. It was just like you read about in the movie magazines except that she didn't get into the movies. She danced the part of Dewey Duck for eighteen months with a big papier-mâché duck head on her head… can you imagine anything that stupid? I mean, Sharon and I used to take dancing lessons together. From Rita Melnick. She was a June Taylor Dancer before she moved to Winnipeg.

         Beat.

         I could always dance better than Sharon could, but I never had the guts.

RAFE   I thought you picked me up. I thought that was gutsy.

DAISY   You picked me up.

RAFE   I think you're gutsy. I think you're very brave.

DAISY   Sharon thinks I'm a pushover. She quit the show the second time she toured through Buffalo. She took a Greyhound bus to Toronto and moved in with me.

RAFE   When are you expecting Sharon?

DAISY   And I am a pushover. I let her stay. For three weeks in a bachelor apartment. I might have let her stay forever but she met Eddie…. Eddie plays hockey, believe it or not. I mean, really he sells insurance but he and the other salesmen play hockey every week and pretend they're Bobby Clark. It's like a beer commercial.

RAFE   Is Sharon staying with Eddie?

DAISY   You know why she told me we were friends? When we were kids? Because I had every Nancy Drew book ever written. Too bad for me she's such a slow reader.

RAFE   Is Sharon going to walk in on us?

DAISY	I'm glad she met Eddie, even if I sit around till nine-thirty looking at a dinner that's supposed to be served at eight and a stupid-looking chocolate cake. And I'm glad Nicky got a chance to phone me and tell me he had to work late. Because what I really wanted tonight was an overpriced drink in a cheap bar and a chance to meet new people.
RAFE	I'm sorry.
DAISY	I'll bet.
RAFE	Really. I like you, Daisy.
DAISY	Sharon said I should have got the job with Disney on Parade. She said I looked more like a duck than she did.
RAFE	I can quack like a duck.
DAISY	Oh sure.
RAFE	Quack quack.
DAISY	I needed that.
RAFE	You try it.
DAISY	Don't be stupid.
RAFE	Quack quack.
DAISY	You're quacking in my ear.
RAFE	Quack quack. Let me see your imitation of a duck. Come on.
DAISY	Quack quack.
RAFE	(*encouraging*) Quack quack.
DAISY	Quack quack.
RAFE	(*moving cushions*) This is a hide-a-bed sofa, isn't it?
	The telephone rings.
	Oh no!
DAISY	I can answer it.
RAFE	After the mating call of the eiderdown goose.
DAISY	(*picking up the phone*) Hello, Sharon… oh, goodbye Sharon.
RAFE	Don't hang up.
	He stops DAISY before she can cradle the receiver.
	Tell her you have some people over.
DAISY	(*plays along*) I'm glad you called earlier, Sharon. I'm sorry I was out.
RAFE	Tell her you're having the party anyway.
DAISY	It's too bad you didn't call before dinner. To say you couldn't come…

RAFE	I'll make party noises. I'll get my guitar. *(gets guitar)*
DAISY	You did not forget it was my birthday, Sharon. You were born on July 20 and I was born on March 20.
RAFE	Not everyone has a composer at their party.
DAISY	That's a friend of mine. He's a composer. He's playing his guitar.
RAFE	*(sings)* That Sharon is a real bitch, isn't she?
DAISY	*(on the phone)* What do you mean, "ha"? There are lots of people here, Sharon. I can hardly hear what you're saying.
RAFE	*(takes the phone)* Let me talk to her.
DAISY	*(knocks on table)* Just a minute, Sharon. There's someone at the door.
RAFE	*(on the phone)* There are lots of people here, Sharon. I can't hear what you're saying.... What do you mean, "ha"? Are you calling me a liar, listen nobody calls me a liar. Who are you, you think I'm such a phony?
DAISY	*(discovers tape recorder)* Here are some people at my party and I don't know how to turn them on.
	She takes tape recorder back to RAFE, expecting to continue the game.
RAFE	*(on the phone)* Who are you, you phony bitch?
	RAFE's anger has escalated quickly enough to be puzzling. DAISY tries to pull the phone away.
DAISY	Let me talk to her.
RAFE	Nobody's going to make a liar out of me. We're going to have a party.
DAISY	*(on the phone)* I guess he had a little too much to drink, Sharon.
RAFE	*(opens door to apartment hallway)* I'm going to get some people.
DAISY	*(on the phone)* Wait a minute.... Rafe, where are you going?
RAFE	Going to ask your neighbours to your party.
DAISY	I don't know my neighbours. I hate my neighbours.
RAFE	That's not neighbourly. *(exits)*
DAISY	*(on the phone)* What do you mean "who's my friend"? ...He does not sound crazy, Sharon. We are having a party, that's all... I don't know where Nicky is and I don't care.
	A shriek of delight from RIVA next door is heard.
	No, he isn't here.... I do have other friends.... What do you mean "who"?

Someone bangs on the wall, "Shave and a haircut." DAISY bangs back "Two bits."

He isn't crazy, he's a musician.... He's a singer. No, he doesn't want to sing you something. He doesn't even want to talk to you. He can't talk to you because he isn't here right now, he's next door. He just banged on the wall. Stop laughing, Sharon.... Listen, there's a tape of him, if you want to hear him sing, you can listen to that for a while.

A knock on the door is heard. RAFE had closed it behind him.

Wait a minute Sharon...

DAISY puts the tape recorder next to the phone and turns up the volume.

How's that, Sharon? Can you hear that all right?

RAFE (*outside door*) Daisy?

A knock at the door is heard. On the tape, RAFE sings: "I said I liked the way you looked," and the song continues under.

DAISY And he's at the door, too. Just a minute, Sharon. I have to answer the door.

A burst of laughter from RIVA as DAISY opens the door.

Rafe? Rafe?

The song on the tape ends. Applause and a girl's laughter. There is no one at the door. DAISY leaves the door open and goes back to the phone.

He was at the door, Sharon, but he got tired of waiting while I talked to you. I don't want to talk to you anymore.

I've got better things to do. What girl on the tape? There isn't any girl on the tape.

The girl on the tape laughs again. It sounds like a seduction.

Goodbye, Sharon.

DAISY hangs up. The tape continues with soft murmurs, rustling, everything but bed springs creaking. DAISY is listening intently to the tape as RAFE enters from the hallway.

RAFE The girl next door says she does know you. She met you in the laundromat. Her name is Riva, do you remember?

DAISY ignores him, engrossed in the tape. There is a laugh from RIVA next door which sounds through the wall, as all RIVA's sounds do.

Another minute and she was going to let me climb over here by her balcony railing. You know how close your balcony is to Riva's balcony?

> *He demonstrates with his hands.*

DAISY   Yes, I do.

RAFE   Have you ever been in her apartment? She has mirrors on the ceiling. She upholstered the floor and she has John Wayne posters all over the walls. She and this weird guy are sitting around rubbing oil all over him, so she said they weren't dressed for a party.

> *Very loud disco music begins in RIVA's apartment. It drowns out DAISY's voice.*

DAISY   Who is the girl on the tape?

RAFE   What?

> *DAISY goes over, pounds on the wall. Someone pounds back. The volume of sound is lowered. RAFE turns his tape recorder off.*

DAISY   Who is the girl on the tape?

RAFE   What girl?

> *DAISY stares him down.*

She's a fan, I guess.

DAISY   Oh sure.

RAFE   I didn't know her very well.

DAISY   You were making love to her. You have a tape recording where you're making love to her.

RAFE   I didn't get a chance to turn if off.

DAISY   I noticed.

RAFE   Look, you didn't think I was raised in a locker room somewhere.... You figured I knew some girls.

> *RIVA shrieks.*

Riva really screams a lot, doesn't she?

DAISY   I don't care about your girls...

RAFE   Maybe she's in some kind of trouble... she's screaming.

DAISY   Shrieking.

RAFE   She is screaming and you don't even care.

DAISY   Can't you tell the difference between a scream and a shriek? They are in bed together. Or she's swinging from the shower rail. It's showtime.

RAFE   Is it the Jack the Ripper Show?

DAISY   No.

RAFE	There's a pretty big, weird-looking guy in there with her. He told me he sold exploding cigars and dribble glasses.
	Random bumps from next door.
	Maybe we should call the police?
DAISY	Who?
RAFE	For next door. Listen.
DAISY	*(because the music continues)* I've heard all her records already.
RAFE	Maybe she's getting strangled. Or smothered.
DAISY	I've heard her scream too. She screams in the laundromat. She screams when her wash turns to rinse cycle.
RAFE	I guess you don't want to get involved.
DAISY	You're kidding.
RAFE	You're isolated. You're alone.
DAISY	Some people do not mind being isolated and alone, you know. Some people like privacy.
	There is a cry of "olé" from next door.
	You see, he didn't strangle her.
RAFE	Yet.
	The crack of a whip from next door.
	Maybe I should go back in there, check the situation out.
DAISY	If I were swinging from the shower rail, I wouldn't thank you for the interruption.
RAFE	I'm going.
	DAISY bars the door.
DAISY	You're embarrassing me.
	The telephone rings. RAFE picks it up.
RAFE	*(on the phone)* Hello…. Can I tell her who's calling? …It's Nicky.
	He dangles the phone in front of her. She grabs for it. He is kind enough to know she'd like to talk to NICKY alone. He speaks while exiting.
	Here I come, Riva. I'm riding to the rescue like Tyrone Power in *Captain from Castile.*
DAISY	*(on the phone)* Hello, Nicky…. He's just a guy, Nicky…. I don't know, I just met him. That's right, it's my birthday and I went out and picked up a guy…. Well, I did call you first, Nicky, but they told me you

weren't working late at the office so I wondered where it was you were working late…. That's right. You got it. I don't trust you.

> *DAISY hangs up. And bursts into tears. A knock on the door.*

RAFE *(outside)* Hey, Daisy, I locked myself out.

> *The telephone rings. DAISY reaches for it.*

DAISY *(on the phone)* Hello…. I don't care if you're sorry, Nicky. I don't care if I should have told you when my birthday was. Is it so hard to remember a birthday? I know your birthday. You were at my party last year, weren't you? It did not conflict with your wife's subscription concert series…. I am not crying.

> *DAISY slams the phone down again. RAFE enters behind DAISY, through the balcony doors. He is wearing a rubber Ronald Reagan mask. DAISY hangs up the phone, he reaches down and takes if off the hook. She sees the hand before she's really realized he's there. She looks up at him. She screams.*

RAFE Guess who.

DAISY What are you doing on my balcony?

RAFE It's okay. It's only me. Rafe. The guy with Riva sells these wholesale.

DAISY *(looking for it)* Valium.

RAFE I scared you. You don't trust me.

DAISY I don't trust anybody.

RAFE You know what you have on your balcony? I bet you forgot about it. There's a dead Christmas tree out there.

DAISY Who cares?

RAFE *(produces tree without needles on stand)* I bet they told you that you couldn't have a tree. Because of their fire insurance rates or something. But that didn't stop you. You smuggled it in…

DAISY I'm a real rebel.

RAFE And here it is March and you haven't had the guts to smuggle it out again.

DAISY I'm impulsive.

RAFE You know what I think we should do? Since we don't have any crepe paper? We should decorate the tree for your birthday.

DAISY Over my dead body.

RAFE Why? Do you think it's sacrilegious?

DAISY   Will you stop pretending you're so goddamn cute? Can we please remember that I picked you up, that's all. We are not supposed to be decorating a Christmas tree.

RAFE   Look Daisy...

He hangs the Ronald Reagan mask on top of the tree. She laughs. He takes off his St. Christopher medal and hangs it on the tree. She takes off her bracelets and throws them toward the tree, aiming for one of the branches. He takes off his boots and puts them under the tree. So does she. He takes off his belt and hangs it on the tree. She takes the flower out of her hair and hangs it on the tree. The whole scene becomes progressively giddier and more Rabelaisian. There seems to be nothing left to do but move the coffee table and pull out the hide-a-bed sofa. They are a little embarrassed by the finality of it all. They jump into bed enthusiastically to show they aren't embarrassed. RAFE kisses her. DAISY laughs.

DAISY   Do you want to turn your tape recorder on?

RAFE   What?

DAISY   Do you want to turn your tape recorder on?

RAFE   *(rolls away from her)* What do you mean?

DAISY   We could try for the Top Ten.

She laughs longer. He has his back to her. She reaches out to touch him.

RAFE   Why are you all messed up with a married man?

DAISY   I beg your pardon?

RAFE   Nicky.

DAISY   I don't care about Nicky.

RAFE   He's married, isn't he?

DAISY   That is none of your business.

RAFE   I mean, if you're supposed to be so mature. Is that supposed to be adult behaviour?

DAISY   Well, kids don't do it.

RAFE   Let's talk.

DAISY   I don't want to talk.

RAFE   Let's try to get to know each other. Let's be friends.

DAISY   I don't want to be friends.

RAFE   Do your friends have to pay at the door?

DAISY   What do you mean?

RAFE	Do you have to have a reason for being friends with people? Do you have to get something from all your friends?
DAISY	No.
RAFE	I am not the kind of guy who thinks that just because a fairly beautiful chick who is anyway five years older than me picks me up in a disco and brings me home to her high-rise apartment; I am not the kind of guy who thinks that means we're going to climb into bed with each other right away or anything. I mean, I know we have to get to know each other. We have to be honest with each other.
DAISY	Ha.
RAFE	I mean if I wanted to sit around with a complete stranger I could have gone to the bus depot, right?
DAISY	Right!
RAFE	I mean, for example, what do you do?
DAISY	Who cares?
RAFE	I can guess people's occupations. The other day I guessed a guy who was a chocolate dipper. You're going to be easy.
DAISY	I would be if you gave me half a chance.
RAFE	You work in a bank.
DAISY	I beg your pardon.
RAFE	Am I right? Do you know how I knew?
DAISY	Why did you guess I worked in a bank?
RAFE	I'm magic.
DAISY	There is nothing duller than banking, is there? Why did you take one look at me and think that I worked in a bank?
RAFE	I do too.
DAISY	What?
RAFE	Takes one to know one.
DAISY	Ha.
RAFE	I'm a loan officer.
DAISY	What bank do you work for?
RAFE	Guess.
DAISY	You know if your bank manager saw you walking around dressed like that, he'd tell you to get a job with a finance company.
RAFE	Would I lie to you?
DAISY	You don't even have a bank account.

RAFE
I'm perfectly presentable. I have a whole collection of Herb Alpert records. I have an attaché case with my initials on it. I have some Canada Savings Bonds and a 1976 Datsun and a really great future. The only difference between us is you were born in Winnipeg and I was born in Kapuskasing.

DAISY wishes they were in bed. She reaches for him. He pulls away.

Does it make you feel safe to think I'm just like you are?

DAISY
You and your plaid flannel shirt and your guitar case and your jeans are too damn tight you know. You were standing there, arguing with the bouncer and I hustled you out onto the street.

RAFE
Because you're adventurous.

DAISY
And you're nervous.

RAFE
Me?

DAISY
What do I have to do to get to bed with you? Make an audition tape?

RAFE
(reaching for his glass) What's in this drink anyway?

DAISY
It's a margarita. Margarita is Daisy in French.

RAFE
How do you make a drink like that?

DAISY
It's tequila and lime juice and you rub salt around the edge of the glass.

RAFE
Is that right?

DAISY
I learned to make it last year in Mexico. In San Miguel de Allende. That's the artists' colony.

RAFE
Here I am with a margarita in a high-rise apartment that looks like Mary Tyler More slept here.

DAISY
What is that supposed to mean?

RAFE
You remind me of my sister.

DAISY
I do not.

RAFE
Her name is Marguerita. That's Daisy in French.

DAISY
Cut it out.

RAFE
My sister is French. So am I.

DAISY
Oh sure.

RAFE
So am I.

DAISY
Your name isn't French.

RAFE
My name is Raoul but no one can spell it. I mean, I can't spell it, you know what I mean? But you know what Raoul is in English? Ralph. I mean, would you have picked me up if my name was Ralph?

DAISY	I would have picked you up if your name was Rover. But you don't seem to understand that.
RAFE	What I try to tell my sister is there's more to life than sex.
DAISY	In Kapuskasing?
RAFE	There is adventure.
DAISY	I don't remember what sex is like. It's been so long that I've forgotten.
RAFE	You think making jokes is adventurous. You think if you go somewhere you've never been before.... If you wake up in the morning and you don't know who with, that's an adventure.
DAISY	Yes. I do.
RAFE	It is low-level adventure. It is low life.
DAISY	What do you want me to do? Discover insulin?
RAFE	I want you to talk to me. I want you to listen to me.
DAISY	I don't want you to think that picking up strange guys and taking them to bed is the only thing I do. Sex is not the only thing in my life, but it is the only thing right now, that's all. I'm very single-minded.
RAFE	Did you ever see *Captain from Castile*?
DAISY	No.
RAFE	Did you see *Son of Ali Baba* with Piper Laurie and Tony Curtis in it? Or the one where they squeezed Tony Curtis's eye like it was a grape?
DAISY	No.
RAFE	What I need to do is ride to the rescue, am I right? The strange prince of the desert drugs the young virgin he met at the foreign exchange counter and drags her off on his camel. And she gets sand in her hair.... And she gets sand between her teeth. And there is sand at the back of her throat...
DAISY	Why?
RAFE	Because she's trying to get away.
DAISY	Why?
RAFE	Because she's heard about the initiation rite. I mean the loathsome initiation rite that inspired the phrase "a fate worse than death."
DAISY	Do you think it's a fate worse than death?
RAFE	I need to get you away from your birthday parties and your bank job. You know why you're in that bank job? Because your friend is the bank manager. Isn't that so? What's his name? Nicky?
DAISY	Nick.

RAFE	Yeah. Who ever heard of a bank manager named Nicky.
DAISY	How did you know that?
RAFE	I'm going to rescue you. I'm going to tear these sheets in strips and throw you over my shoulder and climb down over the balcony just like in the movies.
DAISY	How did you know about Nicky?
RAFE	Except we're on the seventeenth floor.
DAISY	How do you know everything I'm going to say before I'm going to say it?
RAFE	Because I heard it before. Because Joan Crawford was in it. Joan Crawford always liked married guys.
DAISY	The worst part about married guys is they're so grateful. Or that's the worse part about Nicky, anyway.
RAFE	I bet he's boring.
DAISY	He does almost everything right.
RAFE	I bet he told you he could get you into an IBM training course. So your future would be secure. I bet he told you he would call you every time the symphony concert had an intermission.
DAISY	We don't argue all the time, anyway.
RAFE	Is that all you want?
DAISY	Like I argue with you.
RAFE	Is that all you want, not to argue?
DAISY	And he makes me feel elegant.
RAFE	You are elegant, Daisy.
DAISY	He makes me feel like…. Look, I don't know, he bought me this dress…
RAFE	It's a pretty dress.
DAISY	It's a wonderful dress. It's a dream of a dress. Because he's married already, he's got enough of real life.
RAFE	You are a beautiful, elegant lady, Daisy.
DAISY	Then why do you make me feel smartass?
	Beat.
RAFE	I don't want to fight with you.
DAISY	Okay.
RAFE	So what do you want me to do?

> *DAISY turns down the sheet on his side of the bed.*

Is that all?

> *RAFE brings her her drink. He lies down beside her. He still feels uncomfortable. He takes a sip from the drink and makes a horrible face.*

Is this supposed to be a margarita?

DAISY   Yes.

RAFE   Do you call this a margarita?

DAISY   Yes.

RAFE   Let me mix you a margarita.

> *He jumps out of bed to demonstrate.*

Do you know how to do it? You take a jigger full of tequila and you pour it over crushed ice.... You fill the glass up with lime juice and then you rub salt around the edge of the glass.

DAISY   Where did you learn to do that?

RAFE   I used to be a bartender.

DAISY   Oh sure.

RAFE   That's how I got out of Kapuskasing. That's how I worked my way through school. I was sitting in the Holiday Motor Inn beverage room in Kapuskasing, listening to this bad Toronto rock band named Dark Victory. Do you know why they were called Dark Victory? They were all blind, but that wasn't the worst part. The worse part was they were tone deaf too.

I said to myself, look at those guys. They are terrible but they do not have to live in Kapuskasing eighty percent of the time.

I was cleaning under my fingernails with a paper match and I saw on the matchbook cover, "Learn a Trade." So I sent off for the free aptitude test and I found out I should be a bartender. I was sixteen years old. Now you probably know, at that time you had to be twenty-one years old to be a bartender. But I had to get out of Kapuskasing, you see. Because it's the bush, you know, and you can cry all you want to about getting back to the land, but the land is very nutsy when you come right down to it. I don't know if you have ever come right down to it, but you know, you can be out in the bush and the nutsy thing is there is nothing going on out there. Nothing.

There are a lot of people who will try to tell you that nothing is peaceful, but don't let them kid you because it's noisy. I mean, there is the wind in the trees all the time. It's windy and that is only one example. A country stream is a picture of bucolic simplicity to most people who do not have to sit beside it, hearing it.

Kachunga. Kachunga. Kachunga. The water rushing over pebbles. Dzzzzzzzzzzzzzzzzzzz. The wind in the grass. Of course, there is no wonder that the noise in the country is so omnipresent because of all the stuff going on. Nature. Nature is very busy, of course. There are so many things growing and eating and changing into chlorophyll that it makes the Yonge Street strip look like the core of downtown Detroit.

Have you ever been to Detroit? It can be very quiet there. Just as quiet sometimes as the middle of the northern woods, but you always know the next sound you hear is going to tear your guts out…. Have you ever been to Detroit?

DAISY	No.
RAFE	I was born in Detroit. That's why you think I'm weird. I'm an American.
DAISY	I thought you said you came from Kapuskasing.
RAFE	Kap.
DAISY	What?
RAFE	No one from Kapuskasing calls it Kapuskasing. They all call it the Kap.
DAISY	I don't care where you come from.
RAFE	That's right. What difference does it make? Detroit. Kapuskasing. What are they? Maybe five hundred miles apart? I mean, if you were looking at a map of the globe and somebody tried to explain the difference between Detroit and Kapuskasing, you wouldn't even have time to listen, would you? Who the hell cares where I come from as long as I go away.
DAISY	What is it you really do?
RAFE	For work you mean?
DAISY	Yes.
RAFE	I don't work. I'm looking for work. I just got out of prison.
DAISY	Why were you in prison?
RAFE	I murdered a girl.
DAISY	*(backing away)* Now wait a minute.
RAFE	What's the matter?
DAISY	You're kidding, aren't you? *(backs away)*
RAFE	You come here and sit beside me…. Come on…
DAISY	No.

RAFE	Why are we chasing each other around the room? ...Nervous, aren't you? Is it because you're a vegetarian? Do health foods make you nervous?
DAISY	Who is it you murdered.
RAFE	Is that why you're scared?
DAISY	You told me you murdered a girl. Who was she?
RAFE	Look, I'm sorry.
DAISY	Some fairly beautiful chick you picked up in a bar one night?
RAFE	Did you believe me?
DAISY	Stay away from me.
RAFE	Look, I'm sorry, Daisy...
DAISY	Get out of here, okay?
RAFE	Daisy, look, I said I was sorry...
DAISY	I don't care if you're sorry.
RAFE	I didn't kill anybody.
DAISY	You said you did.

She reaches for the phone.

RAFE	Who do you want to call? Sharon? Will that make you feel more secure? Is this her phone number? Is it Eddie's number written on the phone book?
DAISY	Give me the phone book.
RAFE	*(as she dials)* Why would I kill anybody? No, really. Why would I kill a girl? Look, it's because you were coming on to me, right? All about how to mix drinks and what kind of music. And how I should get myself a good job in a bank. Look, I think you're a very nice girl. You're a beautiful girl. And you're very warm...
DAISY	*(on the phone)* Hello, Sharon...
RAFE	You really called her.... The girl who thinks you look like a duck?
DAISY	*(on the phone)* Can you get over here? Fast?
RAFE	You're going to hate yourself if you tell her what I think you're going to say.

He takes the phone.

DAISY	Give me that phone.
RAFE	*(on the phone)* Hello, Sharon.... Hi, it's Rafe.... How come you haven't heard about me when I know so much about you? I do.... I know you danced with Disney on Parade.

DAISY	Let me talk to her.
RAFE	(*on the phone*) Quack quack, eh Sharon?
DAISY	Give me that phone.
RAFE	(*on the phone*) No, she can't talk to you right now. She's, you know…. She's in the shower.
DAISY	Rafe…
RAFE	(*on the phone*) This is a really nice apartment you have here, Sharon.
DAISY	Give it to me.
RAFE	(*on the phone*) Daisy wanted to know what time you thought you'd get back to this nice apartment.
DAISY	(*trying to get the phone*) …Right now…
RAFE	Oh, Daisy is going to be glad to hear that, Sharon. She'll see you in the morning.

>   *DAISY screams.*

	Wait a minute. I think Daisy turned the water off. Yeah, here she is…. She wants to talk to you.
DAISY	(*taking phone*) Sharon? You have to come home right away.
RAFE	Come on, Daisy.
DAISY	(*on the phone*) I am here. Alone. In this apartment with a very weird guy, Sharon.
RAFE	Me?
DAISY	He *does not* sound nice.
RAFE	The trouble with bankers is they never have a sense of humour.
DAISY	(*on the phone*) I am going to tell him to go. As soon as I get off the phone. But what if he won't go.
RAFE	She thinks I'm weird.
DAISY	(*on the phone*) I am not in the shower. I did not just get out of the shower. He told you that. He is weird, Sharon. He lies all the time.
RAFE	I lie? Oh sure. I don't go around pretending I was born in San Miguel de Allende.
DAISY	(*on the phone*) You can bring Eddie. And Eddie can bring his hockey stick.
RAFE	You are a very nervous, very strange lady, you know that, Daisy?
DAISY	(*on the phone*) I don't care how long it takes to get here.
RAFE	I'm going, all right?

DAISY   (*on the phone*) What do you mean what's the use of coming back? Because I need you, Sharon. This weird guy could murder me.

RAFE   Oh sure. Oh brother. That does it.

DAISY   (*on the phone*) I know I could be dead before you got here, Sharon. That's exactly the point.

RAFE   (*struggling with locks on the door*) You're the kind of loony lady who locks herself in with an axe murderer.

DAISY   (*on the phone*) How am I supposed to call the cops, Sharon? I am talking to you on the phone.

RAFE   (*at the door*) Goodbye, okay?

DAISY   (*on the phone*) Wait a minute, Sharon. I think he's leaving.

RAFE   The trouble with people who work in banks, they're much too imaginative. (*exits*)

DAISY   (*on the phone*) He's gone. Oh wow! Sharon, he's gone. He just wound himself up and slammed out of the apartment.

>   *A shriek of laughter from next door.*

I am not hysterical. I am perfectly calm. That is Riva screaming in the background.... I don't know, maybe she opened her refrigerator and the little light went on.

>   *RIVA laughs.*

That's right. I picked him up.... I did not pick him up because I was angry with you. I don't care that you weren't at my birthday party.... Well, fortunately, it doesn't matter what you think. Fortunately, you can crawl back into bed with your friend Eddie and no further thought of me.... No, I'm fine, Sharon.... I wouldn't want you to drive half an hour all the way in from Scarborough just because I'm hysterical. Goodbye, Sharon.

>   *She hangs up the telephone. There is a tap on the window behind her. She turns to see RAFE wearing a Dracula mask and an evening cape that could belong to no one but RIVA. DAISY screams. RAFE waves. She turns back to the phone and starts dialling rapidly as RAFE enters the room behind her.*

RAFE   Don't scream, Daisy.... You're always on the phone, aren't you?

>   *DAISY fumbles the phone and starts to dial again.*

I'm going, all right? Do you want me to go? I forgot my guitar, that's all. And my tape recorder. And I came back for my shoes. Look, a guy walking around without shoes at this time of night is going to get picked up by the cops. It's March, Daisy. You're supposed to wear shoes in March.

DAISY	*(on the phone)* I'll give you cops.
RAFE	Are you calling the cops? Are you crazy or something?

DAISY screams.

Stop screaming!

DAISY	Stay away from me.
RAFE	What am I doing on the seventeenth floor of a high-rise apartment with a crazy screaming lady who thinks I murder girls.
DAISY	You told me you murder girls.
RAFE	Did you believe me when I said I came from Kapuskasing?
DAISY	Yes!
RAFE	Ha! Did you believe me when I said I came from Detroit? Did you believe me when I said I worked in a bank?
DAISY	What am I supposed to believe?
RAFE	Why aren't your neighbours beating down the door? You're screaming like I killed you and nothing happens.

A shriek from the apartment next door.

You don't care about Riva next door, so she doesn't care about you.

DAISY	You're so exhausting.
RAFE	*(shouting)* Where are all you people? Daisy was screaming! She could have been dying in here and you all want to pretend it's a K-tel commercial. *(still louder)* In memory of Kitty Genovese!
DAISY	The people downstairs have called the police.
RAFE	Not a chance.
DAISY	You don't know. I spilled a bag of brown rice once and they called the police. They hear everything.

RAFE yells like Tarzan.

RAFE	Ah-eee-ahhhhhh!
DAISY	What's going on?
RAFE	Did they hear that?

RIVA did. She calls "Ah-ee-ahhhh!" like Tarzan back. RAFE tackles DAISY and throws her down on the couch.

Would they hear if I swung through the trees with you?

DAISY screams. The people next door scream in reply and pound on the wall. RAFE gets up off DAISY.

Okay, I'll call the police.

RAFE reaches the phone and dials.

DAISY   What?

RAFE   If you're so nervous, you won't even talk to me.

DAISY   Now what?

RAFE   If calling the police is going to make you feel better, I'll call them and they'll come over and you can tell them why you can't stop screaming.

DAISY   Oh sure. You'll call the police.

RAFE   *(on the phone)* Hello, police…

He hands her the phone.

DAISY   *(on the phone)* Is this the police? *(to RAFE)* You weren't kidding. *(to phone)* There is a guy here who just told me he murdered a girl…. Why do you want to know my name, I'm not the one who…. I don't know if I know his name, because he lies all the time…. No, I haven't been drinking…. Look, I haven't been drinking very much. *(to RAFE)* He wants me to say my address.

RAFE   Go ahead.

DAISY   They'll come up here if I tell them where I live.

RAFE   You're the one who's scared, Daisy.

DAISY   *(on the phone)* Look, I live on Yonge Street. But I have to move my house because there's a car coming.

DAISY hangs up.

RAFE   Why did you do that.

DAISY laughs.

The cops can't help you if they don't know where you are.

DAISY   I feel so stupid.

RAFE   You still want me to go?

DAISY   I do. Of course I do.

RAFE   Okay.

He starts to get his things together. DAISY is miserable..

RAFE   Pass me that tape recorder first, okay?

DAISY   Why?

RAFE   What do you mean "why"? No wonder you don't trust me. You don't trust anybody. If Pope John Paul came in here and asked you to hand him the tape recorder, you'd say "Why?" I want to play a tape, that's all.

DAISY   Is it you singing?

RAFE	Indulge me.
DAISY	What is it?
RAFE	And right after this, I'm leaving for Lima, Peru.
DAISY	What's on tape?
RAFE	*(turns on tape recorder)* It's a birthday present.
DAISY	On tape?
RAFE	Shhhhhh!

The tape beings. RAFE is singing on the tape.

Happy birthday, baby
That's all I've got to say
I called you to make sure you had
A happy birthday day
I know that we've been fighting
And I know I've been unkind
But I called you on your birthday
Just because you're on my mind.

RAFE turns the tape off with some satisfaction. He is proud of that song.

I made that tape for a girl who was glad it was her birthday, you know what I mean?

DAISY	It's a very stupid song.
RAFE	No, it isn't.
DAISY	I hate country 'n western music. Well, I hate it when they sing through their nose.
RAFE	You think I sing through my nose? Oh brother.
DAISY	You're about as Nashville as smoked salmon.
RAFE	What do you want me to be?

She reaches for him.

DAISY	Rafe…
RAFE	Why don't you kick me out if you think I'm such a phony?
DAISY	You're not a phony.
RAFE	Is that right?
DAISY	Phony is not the word

He kisses her. She kisses him.

RAFE	Is that right? Really.
DAISY	Yes.

RAFE　　　　But what is the word? What's the good word, Daisy?

> *The word is "crazy" but DAISY doesn't care. RAFE is ecstatic. He breaks away from her. He is bouncing off the walls, collecting candles, arranging them on the coffee table.*

DAISY　　　Rafe…

RAFE　　　　Come on, Daisy, it's your birthday. What are you saving all these candles for?

DAISY　　　It better be better with candles.

RAFE　　　　We're going to celebrate, okay?

DAISY　　　We're going to bed together, that's all. What's it supposed to be, "Great Moments from the Twentieth Century"?

RAFE　　　　You have no sense of occasion.

DAISY　　　This *is* going to be worth waiting for? Isn't it?

> *RAFE is lighting candles. He seems entranced by the flames.*

Because many great moments from the twentieth century turned out to be real turkeys.

> *DAISY sweeps regally into the bathroom. Her exit is ruined because she has to come back out to turn on the light.*

Oh sure.

> *RAFE seems puzzled by her defection.*

RAFE　　　　Daisy?

> *He knocks on the bathroom door.*

Daisy?

> *He rattles the doorknob.*

You locked yourself in.

> *He races around the room collecting the telephone book, telephone. He finds Eddie's number on the phone book cover, dials it.*

(*on the phone*) Hello, Eddie…. Listen my name is Tyrone Power and I'm trying to rescue a friend of yours.

> *DAISY throws open the bathroom door and arranges herself in the doorway wearing a slip. RAFE is too preoccupied to notice, but she looks stunning.*

(*on the phone*) I don't care if I woke you, fella, because she locked herself in the bathroom and the last girl I know did that was taking sleeping pills.

DAISY　　　Let me talk to him.

	She takes the phone away.
RAFE	*(overjoyed)* Daisy?
DAISY	*(on the phone)* Hello, Eddie…. No, I'm all right.
	RAFE takes the phone back.
RAFE	Let me talk to him.
DAISY	Rafe…
RAFE	*(on the phone)* Eddie…. Let me talk to Sharon…. Well, roll her over and hand her the phone because I want to tell her her friend, her best friend, does not look like a duck…
	DAISY laughs.
	(on the phone) What do you mean I'm crazy?
	He laughs and hangs up the phone.
	She's coming over.
DAISY	Sharon?
RAFE	She'll take Eddie's car unless he kills her first.
DAISY	She was fighting with Eddie.
RAFE	He was fighting with her.
DAISY	I'm the one who's going to get killed.
RAFE	Maybe she is a friend of yours.
DAISY	*(on the phone)* Hello, Eddie…. He hung up on me.
RAFE	So she's on her way.
DAISY	She's going to tear my throat out.
RAFE	We'll turn off the lights and pretend we aren't home.
DAISY	Sharon is going to kill me.
	RAFE is putting out candles with his fingertips, playing dangerous-looking games with flames. DAISY laughs. She helps him extinguish candles. It becomes something of a competition in daring and style.
RAFE	Hey, do you want to marry me?
	DAISY laughs.
	You think that's funny?
DAISY	Yes.
RAFE	Why?
	DAISY laughs. He must be kidding.
	Why do you think that's funny?

DAISY wonders.

Let's get married, okay.

He takes a ring off DAISY's finger and puts it on his own.

DAISY   Rafe…

RAFE   Tyrone Power married Jean Peters.

DAISY   Do you want it like the movies?

RAFE grins at her. Of course he does.

In slow motion or what?

The room is lit by birthday candles.

RAFE   Happy birthday, Daisy.

He kisses her.

Blow out the candles, okay. Make a wish.

He moves her head so she's facing the birthday cake. There is something frightening about the way he holds her neck. DAISY decides it's an accident. She blows the candles out. The room is lit by moonlight. RAFE carries her to bed like Clark Gable carried Vivian Leigh in "Gone with the Wind." RIVA puts on yet another disco record which segues into intermission music. Fade-out moonlight.

End of Act One.

ACT TWO

As the lights come up, DAISY is singing in the bathroom. RAFE is accompanying her on the guitar. He has tied one of DAISY's straight-backed chairs to the bathroom door with his belt. DAISY will be able to open the door a little, but she won't be able to get into the room.

DAISY   *(sings)* I said I liked the way you looked.
I said I liked your style.

RAFE   Hey Daisy...

DAISY   *(sings)* And I sat right down beside you
Bought a drink and watched you smile

RAFE   Hey, Daisy... do you know how often they fly to Lima, Peru?

DAISY   *(sings)* You told me you picked a guitar
With a country 'n western band

RAFE   Should we phone Air Peru? Would they tell us?

DAISY   *(sings)* But I didn't want another one night stand.

RAFE   You can put airplane tickets on a credit card, can't you? Hey, Daisy... where's your credit card?

RAFE is searching through her closets. He finds her wallet in her coat pocket, or in her purse if she has one.

DAISY   The door won't open.

She rattles the handle, RAFE stuffs her wallet in his pocket.

RAFE   Hey, Daisy, Nicky's on the phone.

This is patently untrue.

DAISY   How did you lock the door on that side? There isn't any lock.

RAFE   I told him you're running off with me. I told him you're going to be a bandit queen, is that okay?

DAISY   Let me out of here.

RAFE   Is it okay? What I told Nicky?

He opens the door.

DAISY   No, it isn't okay.

RAFE hands her the phone.

RAFE   Call him back. Go on. That's his number. You wrote it down there right under Eddie's.

DAISY   He didn't call, did he? Why would Nicky call me at four in the morning?

RAFE   I called him.

DAISY   What?

RAFE   I said listen, this is just like on daytime TV. Here is Daisy in love with her boss…

DAISY   What did he say?

RAFE   But Daisy isn't on TV. Daisy is real.

DAISY   What did he say?

RAFE   It was like on TV. His wife answered.

>   *DAISY moans.*

I said is this Mrs. Nicky and she said who's this. You know, some of your friends aren't very friendly.

DAISY   We aren't friends. Why should we be friends?

RAFE   I said you'd been locked in the bathroom for half an hour with a blow dryer and a bottle of Vitabath but she didn't care. She wanted to tell me what time it was, that's all. I said who cares. She said at the tone the time will be four thirty-eight and ten seconds, beep. At the tone the time will be four thirty-eight and twenty seconds, beep. At the tone the time will be…

DAISY   Rafe…

RAFE   I said you were locked in there…. I told her about Laugh-A-Minute Appleton. And the sleeping pills. I told her to wake Nicky. She hung up on me.

DAISY   I have to work on Monday.

RAFE   No, you don't.

DAISY   With Nicky. And he hates to fight with his wife.

>   *RAFE is ranging around the apartment opening drawers and cupboards.*

RAFE   Where do you keep your Christmas stuff?

DAISY   I am going to have to fight with Nicky. I am going to have to fight with Sharon. You poured her Vitabath all over me.

>   *RAFE discovers a box of Christmas lights and tinsel.*

RAFE   Never mind, I found it.

DAISY   Sharon is going to come in here and demand her Vitabath.

>   *RAFE is decorating the Christmas tree.*

RAFE   Tell her to smell you.

DAISY   Sharon is a very selfish person.

RAFE	Tell her to take one last deep breath.
DAISY	Where is she anyway?
RAFE	I don't care, Daisy. Look at the Christmas tree.
DAISY	It doesn't take an hour and a half to drive in from Scarborough.

RAFE plugs in the Christmas tree lights.

	Why is Sharon crawling in from Scarborough? Why did you lock me in the bathroom?
RAFE	Daisy, you are locked into all sorts of things.
DAISY	Why?
RAFE	It's safe in there, isn't it? It's secure. It's a minimal sort of environment, but a space you can understand. Thoroughly. It's like a bank job.
DAISY	Why?
RAFE	You know why you're working in that bank? So you can suffer every day. Keep your guilty secret from the tellers in the trust department. Daisy loves Nicky but nobody must ever know.
DAISY	Everybody knows.
RAFE	I wrote a song about it.
DAISY	Sure. You locked me in the bathroom and you wrote me a song.
RAFE	Don't you want a song about your birthday cake and your dancing lessons and your Valium…
DAISY	Rafe…
RAFE	And your *TV Guide* and your married lover and your future…
DAISY	Shut up, Rafe.
RAFE	*(sings)* Daisy I think I'm crazy I think I'm crazy I think I'm crazy I think I'm crazy I think I'm crazy I think I'm crazy I think I'm crazy

And he continues to sing. There is no doubt RAFE is prepared to go on all night. He sings like a madman until he's sure DAISY is speechless, then he sings to her gently.

	I think I'm crazy over you.
DAISY	Rafe…
RAFE	I didn't call Nicky.

DAISY	I knew it.
RAFE	But I think you should call him. Okay? Tell him who we are and where we're going? Come on, Daisy. Phone him up and tell his wife what time it is.
	DAISY reaches for the phone.
DAISY	I'll disguise my voice, okay?
	RAFE picks her up and spins her around.
RAFE	This is the first day of the rest of our lives.
DAISY	Who told you that, Marshall McLuhan?
	RAFE pulls DAISY out on the balcony.
RAFE	Look over that way. The sun's going to rise in an hour and a half.
DAISY	Look down there.
RAFE	Look up, Daisy. Come on. We're supposed to stare off to the future. We're idealistic.
DAISY	There's a cop car in the parking lot.
RAFE	You're paranoid.
DAISY	Someone must have called them. Because of the noise.
RAFE	They're going next door. They're going to the tenth floor where someone else was murdered.
DAISY	They're going to come up here. Say it was the people downstairs who called. They know my apartment number. These cops are going to come up here and knock on the door and they'll want to come in and they'll want us to tell them what's wrong.
RAFE	Tell them nothing is wrong.
DAISY	I can't go to the door dressed like this. They'll think we're in bed.
RAFE	It's four in the morning, Daisy. You're supposed to be in bed.
DAISY	But they know I screamed. They know, you know, that I don't know you.
RAFE	*(gives up)* Get dressed.... Go on, get dressed and save your reputation.
DAISY	I don't want to get dressed.
RAFE	We won't go to the door.
DAISY	They'll think I'm dead.
RAFE	Are you crazy?
DAISY	I was screaming. If I don't answer the door, they'll think I'm dead.
RAFE	You think cops break down doors just because it's quiet inside?

DAISY	If they thought I was getting killed…
RAFE	We'll turn the lights out.

He goes. The room is lit by moonlight.

DAISY	They'll want us to answer, Rafe.
RAFE	Look, the cops will come up here. They'll knock on the door. We'll stay still inside and nothing will happen. They'll knock, they'll go away. They'll ask the people downstairs exactly what happened and we'll be laughing.

A knock on the door.

DAISY	That's them.
RAFE	Shhhhhh…

Pause. DAISY giggles.

Shhhhhh!

DAISY	*(whisper)* They won't believe it. They won't believe everything is quiet and we've gone to sleep.
RAFE	*(whisper)* They want to go catch crooks, Daisy. Catch crooks or have coffee.
DAISY	*(whisper)* Isn't it against the law to scream all night for no reason? Isn't that disturbing the peace?
RAFE	Shhhhhh!
DAISY	I mean, I could get evicted, couldn't I?

Anther knock at the door. DAISY giggles.

RAFE	Shhh!
DAISY	Maybe it's Sharon.
RAFE	Does Sharon ride around in a cop car?
DAISY	Maybe I was wrong about the cop car. Because the light is different down there, you know, the parking lot has those weird arc lights. How am I supposed to recognize a cop car?
RAFE	It isn't Sharon.
DAISY	How do you know?
RAFE	I can recognize a cop car from underneath it.

Another knock.

DAISY	This is stupid. When somebody knocks, you answer the door, don't you?

She moves for the door. RAFE dives for her and catches her.

RAFE	When somebody knocks, you lie there quite still in the dark.
DAISY	Let me go.
RAFE	It isn't Sharon at the door. She called back, you know, while you were in the shower. I explained. I told her not to come.... I tried to get you to the phone, but you didn't answer. You know. The shower was running. Kachunga. Kachunga. Kachunga.... Sharon reminds me of a friend of mine, Andy. He's a con man.... You know how he gets girls to go to bed with him?

Whatever efforts DAISY makes to get away, RAFE meets, with as little force as possible.

He tells them sad stories of how he needs them, he can't get along without them. He told one girl he had to go to New York to rescue his kid brother. The kid brother had actually killed somebody in the streets of New York, but Andy knew he could talk the kid into giving himself up to the police. He'll say anything. He lies all the time. And the girl believed him. She gave him her credit card to book the airline ticket.

He takes her wallet out of his pocket and hands it to her.

DAISY	You lie all the time.
RAFE	Not as much as Andy.
DAISY	You're a real rat, aren't you?
RAFE	I wish I weren't.
DAISY	Oh sure.
RAFE	I wish every story I told you was true. I wish everything didn't have to change into garbage at midnight.
DAISY	Rafe...
RAFE	I wish I didn't have to go back to Andy. He cons me. I try to con him. I wish I could stay here with you until all the planes had left for New York.
DAISY	You lie all the time.
RAFE	The thing about you, Daisy, is I can believe everything that you say.
DAISY	Let me go then.
RAFE	What?
DAISY	You trust me. I'm like your sister.
RAFE	*(rolling away from her)* Sure. Okay.
DAISY	And we'll sit here, in the dark, perfectly quietly. And we'll wait for the cops to go away.

They have been sitting under the Christmas tree, its lights providing the only illumination in the room. RAFE turns out the Christmas tree lights.

RAFE   It's boring. Isn't it?

DAISY starts for the door in the dark. RAFE follows her, catches her as she tries to unlock the door. She screams. He switches the light on.

Trust, Daisy. Friendship. Do you know who your friends are? Because the cops have gone away.

He opens the door to show her the hallway. DAISY looks out into the hall.

DAISY   *(sotto voce)* The cops are waiting at the elevator.

RAFE   Call them. Call Riva in from next door and she can chaperone. But if we have the cops in here. And Riva. And Sharon. And John Wayne next door. There won't be any room for us, Daisy. I mean the springs, they won't take it.

DAISY finds herself locking the door against SHARON's entrance.

DAISY   I would hate it if Sharon were here.

RAFE   Sharon told me her side of the Disney on Parade story. How you never shut up about dancing around for eighteen months with a duck head on her head. How you tell every new guy she meets about the time she made the dog food commercial…

DAISY   She did phone.

RAFE   She left you in my hands.

DAISY   What?

RAFE   She said she was sure I could handle it. She was going to turn around and drive back to bed with Eddie.

DAISY   Why should I believe you?

RAFE   You think I'm a con man. No, I told you. My friend Andy is a con man. If you want to watch a beautiful con, you want to call Andy.

DAISY   There isn't any Andy, is there?

RAFE   That would be convenient.

DAISY   I mean, you're Andy.

RAFE   That would wrap everything up very neatly. You could call it *Three Faces of Rafe* and Joanne Woodward could be in the movie.

DAISY   Look…

RAFE   I'm like Andy. Except he is so into the con, you know, he can't do anything else, so some people might say he was sicker than I was.

	I mean, Andy is what they call impotent, and I make love like an Arthur Murray dance teacher.
DAISY	I guess.
RAFE	I make love like Genghis Khan and the Mongol hordes.
DAISY	I'm not going to argue with you.
RAFE	I make love like it was tax deductible.
DAISY	You're all right. Look, you don't have to worry about it.
RAFE	I'm not worried. I'm very secure. Because I'm a computer programmer. And that's security, isn't it? It's better than a bank clerk. Because we'll only have banks as long as we have our present economic system. But we'll always have computers. We might have computers longer than we have people.
DAISY	What do you do? Really.
RAFE	I look for work.
DAISY	Of course. You don't work.
RAFE	I go down to Canada Manpower and I tell all those little girls with their Honours BA in English and psychology, I say, what do you have for me, I don't play guitar very well, I do not have a useful trade and I cannot talk to the latest computers because I do not have recent computer experience.
DAISY	And then what happens.
RAFE	They say why is it you do not have recent computer experience and I tell them because I was in prison.
DAISY	We're supposed to be friends.
RAFE	We are friends, Daisy, and I was in prison.

He waits until she nods.

And the girls at Canada Manpower say oh why were you in prison and I say homicide. And then they blink at me for a while. You know how Canada Manpower finds a job for an ex-con axe murderer? Very carefully.

DAISY	Rafe…
RAFE	They sent me out to a gas station on the Danforth. Can you figure why a computer programmer who also happens to be an ex-murderer should end up pumping gas?
DAISY	I want to get dressed.

She crosses to her closet to change into jeans and a T-shirt.

RAFE	After I go to Canada Manpower then I come home and watch TV. That is my main occupation, if you like. I watch all the game shows. I like to watch people winning Jacuzzi whirlpool baths.
DAISY	You have to ruin everything.
RAFE	What's the matter?
DAISY	Oh shut up.
RAFE	You know why you're mad?
DAISY	I'm not mad. Mad is not the word.
RAFE	Yes you are. I do that to people. My friend Andy says I am a self-punishing criminal. Every time I con somebody I feel so bad I come back and let Andy con me.
DAISY	Shut up about Andy.
RAFE	Daisy… do you ever think about suicide?
DAISY	No.
RAFE	Me neither. I could never commit suicide. I don't like to think about the quiet. I go crazy when I think of you locked up in the bathroom. When I think you might have killed yourself.
DAISY	I don't want to talk about how crazy you are, is that all right?
RAFE	Someone else will have to do it. Someone else will have to kill me.
DAISY	Is that supposed to be funny?
RAFE	I'm sorry. I shouldn't joke.
DAISY	Shut up about it.
RAFE	I'm sorry.
DAISY	I'm not very good with mental illness. I think people with head colds are self-indulgent.
RAFE	I'm sorry, Daisy…. Look, I know people who make love are not necessarily friends, but I like you, Daisy. I liked you before…. I liked you before and I like you after…
DAISY	Stop smiling at me.
RAFE	You know what people say when I smile?
DAISY	You look like someone's kid brother.
RAFE	They say I can't be all bad.
DAISY	I don't care what you are.
RAFE	Yes you do.
DAISY	I'm a bandit queen, remember.

RAFE	And you aren't afraid of me. Even if you should be.
DAISY	Don't be stupid.
RAFE	We get along. We like each other. We're like family, aren't we, Daisy?
DAISY	Yes.
RAFE	So I'm going to call the cops.
DAISY	What?
RAFE	I want to take care of you, Daisy. I feel responsible for you.

DAISY speaks as RAFE is dialing the phone.

DAISY	I guess you know that number off by heart by now.
RAFE	It's the emergency number.
DAISY	I'm sure they'll think it's an emergency.
RAFE	A family quarrel can be a serious thing.
DAISY	Call them. Sure. Cops love to go up and down in elevators.
RAFE	*(on the phone)* Hello, police…. There is a girl in trouble here, she lives in apartment 1720 and the apartment is up here at Yonge and St. Clair…. What's the address?

DAISY takes the phone away.

DAISY	You got the apartment number wrong.
RAFE	I get everything wrong.
DAISY	*(on the phone)* Hello, police?
RAFE	I wanted you to feel secure, Daisy, that's all. I wanted to protect you.
DAISY	There is no one on the phone.
RAFE	What difference does it make? You were going to tell them not to come.
DAISY	*(with a dangling cord)* This telephone is dead. This telephone is not connected to the wall.
RAFE	Who do you want to phone now?
DAISY	*(about the phone)* Why?
RAFE	Let's go out to the airport…. No, what time is it, let's go back to bed.
DAISY	I want to know why you pulled my telephone out of the wall.
RAFE	Me?
DAISY	*(tracing the phone cord)* Look at it.
RAFE	I didn't tear your telephone out of the wall, Daisy.
DAISY	Yes. You. Did.

RAFE   I don't have to tell you anything about your telephone. Look, the only person you ever talk to is Sharon, right? You don't need a telephone to talk to Sharon because you and Sharon are exactly the same person...

DAISY   You said you talked to Sharon.

RAFE   No, I didn't.

DAISY   On this telephone...

RAFE   I didn't tell you she called. I don't tell you every thought that flickers through my mind. I didn't tell you about the time I had scarlet fever when I was eight years old. I didn't tell you about Sharon calling...

DAISY   But you know what Sharon said to you, but you didn't talk to Sharon.

RAFE   All right. So she called me. We had a long talk. She told me all about you. She told me your middle name. Corinne. Daisy Corinne.

DAISY   The phone is disconnected.

RAFE   She called me. You can ask her.

RAFE is digging around in the unmade sofa bed. He pulls out the body of a girl. He pulls away the bedclothes she's tangled in.

DAISY   Sharon!

RAFE   Be quiet, Daisy... be quiet okay? You know what you should do, you should pretend you're Faye Dunaway and I'm Warren Beatty and I just told you I robbed banks.

DAISY   Please...

RAFE   Look, I want you to know you're the one, sure you are. I mean, it was you made me see how stupid I was sitting around looking at a matchbook saying "Learn a Trade." I mean, it was you who told me all about San Miguel de Allende and made me realize that Andy was trying to suck me dry...

DAISY   Look, please...

RAFE   It's going to be okay, isn't it. Daisy? We aren't playing games anymore, are we? We aren't going back to square one where I tell you I killed somebody and you get scared.

DAISY   You did kill somebody.

RAFE   You don't believe that, do you?

DAISY   Sharon...

RAFE   The trouble with modern life is that people don't trust, do they? Paranoia. You know, if you go out on the street, you're more likely to get killed by a car than you are to get murdered.

DAISY   Out...

RAFE	What's the matter, Daisy?
DAISY	I'm getting out of here, right now.
RAFE	Where are you going?
DAISY	I'm going to call Eddie. I'm going to call Nicky.
RAFE	*(holding out the phone)* Call him.
DAISY	The phone doesn't work.
RAFE	Try it. Come on. I'll dial the number for you.

DAISY throws the phone at him and dodges for the door.

I told you, Daisy. You could get killed out there.

He blocks her way. She runs for the bathroom.

You know you could get killed out there. That's why you locked the door, remember.

DAISY comes out of the bathroom with the only weapon at hand— a curling iron. She decides that was stupid and breaks the bathroom mirror with the curling iron. She then threatens RAFE with a shard of glass.

DAISY	Get away from that door.
RAFE	You are going to cut yourself.... Your hand is bleeding, look at your hand.

He catches her wrist, forces her to drop the glass.

Look at your hand, Daisy.... Look I can fix it. I can use this towel, can't I? Does it hurt? Are you okay? What's the matter?

He bandages her hand as tenderly as possible.

You don't understand about Sharon, is that it?... That Sharon is a real bitch, isn't she?

He turns on the tape recorder.

SHARON	*(on tape)* Where's Daisy?
DAISY	*(live)* That's Sharon.
RAFE	*(on tape)* She's in the bathroom. She says she's putting on her nails.
SHARON	*(on tape)* You really make yourself at home, don't you?
RAFE	*(live)* She said your mother knew her mother. She said she was like your family...
DAISY	*(runs for the balcony door)* Riva! Riva!
RAFE	*(follows her)* Riva! Riva! Come on over. Daisy wants us all to get acquainted.

He catches her in an ambiguous embrace, waves to RIVA, carries her back into the room.

I mean, she wanted to stay here, Sharon did…. She wouldn't leave, she kicked her shoes off.

RAFE sets up SHARON's body like a ventriloquist's dummy, as if SHARON were saying her lines.

SHARON *(on tape)* Here's your hat and what's your hurry. As Daisy's dad would say.

RAFE *(on tape)* What?

SHARON *(on tape)* Goodbye…. Look, I'm going to bed. I'm not driving back to Scarborough at four in the morning.

RAFE *(on tape)* Hey, I'm recording you.

SHARON *(on tape)* What?

RAFE *(on tape)* I've got every word you're saying right here on tape.

DAISY screams—that's live sound. The tape recorder is still running. The tape contains scuffles, pounding, screams, the sound RAFE describes.

RAFE *(live)* That's when she screamed. And I kept her away from the bathroom door. But she was pounding on the wall…. And you started pounding back…

DAISY No, please…

RAFE *(describing sounds on tape)* And she thought she could run to the kitchen. She's looking through the drawers in there…. She has a knife now…

DAISY runs towards the kitchen and rummages through the drawers.

SHARON *(on tape)* Keep away from me. Keep away from me.

RAFE *(live)* I got rid of the rest of the cutlery.

DAISY drops an empty drawer on the floor.

I hid it in the refrigerator. In the vegetable crisper.

DAISY tears open the refrigerator, rummages through the vegetables.

DAISY You didn't. There are no knives here.

RAFE I fooled you.

DAISY Where are they?

RAFE I lied.

DAISY throws vegetables at him in frustration. He throws pillows at her, caught up in the game.

(describing sound on tape) That's Sharon when she tripped over the telephone cord. And she dropped the knife. And I was there with her by that time. And I kicked the knife away. Right under the hide-a-bed sofa.

DAISY dives for the floor, rummaging around under the sofa.

DAISY There is a knife here. Sharon's knife…

She produces it.

RAFE *(enjoying the chase)* This is like the duelling scene in *Captain from Castile*.… Remember Tyrone Power and the guy from the Inquisition?

RAFE picks up one of the bedsheets to use as a cloak. They fight across the bed and back behind the sofa. RAFE trips on the pillows on the floor and crawls forward.

And then he escaped to the New World, Daisy…. To the Aztec Empire. Do they have Aztecs in Peru?

RAFE has arranged one of the pillows under his sheet as a shield. DAISY rushes forward to stab him and he pretends to die.

That's the way she stabbed him in *Captain from Castile*, Daisy…

He staggers back toward her, "dies" behind the hide-a-bed.

Rosebud.

DAISY Sharon… Sharon… Sharon…

She pulls herself together enough to want to try to reach the door. Behind her, RAFE's body comes to life, producing the pillow with a knife stuck in it.

RAFE Like in the movies, Daisy. Don't you want to be in the movies?

He sticks the knife in SHARON's hand.

Look. Tony Perkins's mother.

DAISY screams.

Don't you want to be a bandit queen?

DAISY Please, Rafe…

RAFE Do you want to kill me? Really?

DAISY can't answer.

Please, Daisy.

DAISY What?

RAFE Where did I put the rest of the stuff? The rest of the knives?

The knives are in his knapsack. He empties them on the floor.

Take one. Look, Daisy, you just found this prowler, right. This thug. I could be walking off with your silverware. I could be Alan Ladd in *This Gun for Hire*. You're scared, aren't you? You would be scared if you thought I was Alan Ladd?

DAISY   Rafe...

RAFE   *(his last Alan Ladd imitation)* You won't gut me. You don't have the guts.

> *He rushes her. She stabs him. Once. Twice. Three times. She tries to stop the blood. He is dying. The tape recorder is still running. On tape, the act begins again.*

DAISY   *(on tape, sings)* I said I liked the way you looked
I said I liked your style

RAFE   *(on tape)* Hey, Daisy...

DAISY   *(on tape, sings)* And I sat right down beside you
Bought a drink and watched you smile

RAFE   *(on tape)* Hey, Daisy... do you know how often they fly to Lima, Peru?

DAISY   *(on tape, sings)* You told me you picked a guitar
With a country 'n western band

RAFE   *(on tape)* Should we phone Air Peru? Would they tell us?

DAISY   *(on tape, sings)* But I didn't want another

One night stand...

> *Fadeout.*
>
> *The end.*

ESCAPE ENTERTAINMENT

Escape Entertainment was first produced at the Tarragon Theatre in Toronto, in January 1981, with the following company:

R.H. Thomson   Pancho
Peter Jobin   Matt
Katy Michael McGlynn   Laurel

Directed by Timothy Bond
Designed by Michael Eagan
Lighting by Lynne Hyde

CHARACTERS

CLAPPERBOARD GUY
PANCHO
AD
MATT
LAUREL
DENNIS

NOTES

Ukrainian dialogue:
Dobrhey-dhen cohanna, Bazoochkoo.   Hey Baz, Bazzie.
Meh dhi-stall-eh feellm nah-zhad.   We got the picture back.
Nah-rash-tea.   It works.
Shilakh trah-fid yiah teh-beh lew-blue.   I love you, Baz.
Mattuooshkoo.   Mattie.

Filmmaking terms:
CCA	Capital Costs Allowance
CFDC	Canadian Film Development Corporation
eighty-six	cancel, remove, delete
overcall	an amount of money a producer agrees to supply if and when production costs go over budget

Escape Entertainment

ACT ONE

The set shows us the sound stage of a low-budget action picture. We are behind the main interior. We see trestle tables with a coffee machine and trays of stale doughnuts. We see two directors' chairs. We see a wardrobe rack with sixteen identical Hawaiian shirts. There are two telephones. They should be touchtone. PANCHO makes a lot of calls. The lights go out. A film is projected on the back of the movie's interior flats.

THE FILM

Water. Glistening in the sun. A clapperboard appears in the frame, announcing the particulars of the shoot. The picture is called Man with a Gun. *The producer: Panaba Productions. The director: PANCHO Potter. It is Scene 116. Take 3.*

CLAPPERBOARD GUY
  (voice-over) Man with a Gun. Scene 116. Take three.

PANCHO *(voice-over)* Cue the flame-thrower.

AD *(voice-over)* Flame-thrower standing by.

PANCHO *(voice-over)* Cue the fireboat.

AD *(voice-over)* Fireboat standing by.

PANCHO *(voice-over)* Cue the helicopter.

AD *(voice-over)* Standing by.

PANCHO *(voice-over)* Action.

  Nothing happens. The sunlight glistens on the water.

  (voice-over) I said "Action." Where is he?

AD *(voice-over)* Cue Matt.

PANCHO	*(voice-over)* Cue Matt?
	Hubbub off: "Where's Matt?" "Where is he?" *(etcetera)*
	(voice-over) I have been trying to get this shot since six a.m. this morning and now you say, "Cue Matt"?
	Excited hubbub off: "Hey, here he is!" "Where?" "Look at him." *(etcetera)*
AD	*(voice-over)* He's unconscious.
PANCHO	*(voice-over)* What?
AD	*(voice-over)* I don't think he's breathing.
	The screen goes blank. PANCHO turns the lights on. He is very angry.
PANCHO	Thanks, Matt.
	MATT is sitting in his directors' chair. His name is on the back.
MATT	Don't worry.
PANCHO	Thanks very much.
MATT	Hey, Pancho…
PANCHO	No, really, I have a fireboat. I have a helicopter. The light is right for the first time in two weeks and I have you in intensive care.
MATT	You know who else was in intensive care?
PANCHO	*(short)* Yes.
MATT	One of your investors. Garretson.
PANCHO	*(short)* I know that.
MATT	I guess you asked him for the overcall.
PANCHO	*(short)* Garretson had a heart attack.
MATT	Hey, Pancho…
PANCHO	Are you making jokes about a heart attack?
MATT	I'm not joking.
PANCHO	My investor's heart attack?
MATT	Hey, I'm serious.
PANCHO	That's good. Because it's serious. Because we're trying to make a movie here. Because I've been up for three days, trying to get the rewrites, trying to sweat the rewrites out of Baz. Because I haven't seen Nadja in three days. The last time I saw her was when we tried to shoot the love scene.
MATT	I like Nadja.

PANCHO	And she couldn't stop sneezing.
MATT	Hey, how does that feel?
PANCHO	And her eyes were streaming, and she was popping antihistamines.
MATT	How does it feel, Pancho? When it's your lady, I mean…
PANCHO	She has hay fever!
MATT	When it's my love scene?
PANCHO	She has hay fever. Baz has writer's block. Garretson's on oxygen. And I haven't slept for three days. Then there's you. Then you OD. I don't need it, Matt. Do you know what I need? I need sleep. I need twenty thousand dollars worth of palm trees, by ten a.m. tomorrow morning.
MATT	Hey, I know.
PANCHO	That's serious.
MATT	Hey, I know it's serious. Hey, I OD'd, didn't I?
PANCHO	You always OD.
MATT	You know why?
PANCHO	It's what you do in California. When you don't feel like jogging.
MATT	Hey, Pancho…
PANCHO	Let me tell you something, Matt…
MATT	You said Laurel would be here…
PANCHO	There are better ways to handle stress.
MATT	You know how it is between Laurel and me. I mean was, you know how it was. I love her, Pancho…. We were married for two years, Pancho. So what do I say to her?
PANCHO	It's publicity, Matt… it's what you're doing now, your future plans…
MATT	What future plans?
PANCHO	Tell her your Roger Korman stories. Tell her about your Silver Bear.
MATT	Pancho…
PANCHO	*On the Highway*. Berlin Film Festival. Best film. Best director. Best performance…
MATT	She knows about my Silver Bear. She slugged me with it.
PANCHO	You know the first time I saw that film. It was my birthday, Matt, and I cut my seminar in film aesthetics. *On the Highway*. I sat through it three times. I was late for my party. That was 1968. I was twenty-one years old.
MATT	Where's the Scotch?

PANCHO	No, Matt.
MATT	I want a Scotch.
PANCHO	Stick to pineapple juice.
MATT	You think I'm afraid?
PANCHO	It's organic, Matt. Try it.
MATT	You think I'm afraid to talk to Laurel?
PANCHO	Scotch is toxic for you. Toxic.
MATT	I'm not afraid. I talk to her. I call her.
PANCHO	You're nervous.
MATT	Before I came up here, I called her.
PANCHO	You know what I do when I'm nervous? Beside pineapple juice?
MATT	I used to call her all the time. I called her from the Cayman Islands.
PANCHO	Yoga breathing.
MATT	I called her from Vera Cruz, the last time they dried me out.
PANCHO	Yoga breathing. Watch me.

He demonstrates. MATT ignores him.

MATT	I disguise my voice because she doesn't want to talk to me, but I guess I call her maybe three times a week, from wherever I am. Sometimes more. Sometimes I send her stuff. Sometimes I wake up in the middle of the night, and I say, "Hey, I bet Laurel would like a pizza."

The telephone rings.

	You can charge pizza, did you know that?
PANCHO	*(on the phone)* Hello…
MATT	You can charge pizza long distance if you talk fast enough.
PANCHO	*(on the phone)* I need those palm trees, Deedee.
MATT	I wrote a poem for her once. There was a young lady named Laurel…
PANCHO	*(on the phone)* Tomorrow.
MATT	That's cute, huh?
PANCHO	*(on the phone)* Do it, Deedee.
MATT	I had that iced on a chocolate chip cookie.
PANCHO	*(on the phone)* Do it. For me.
MATT	I send her telegrams.
PANCHO	*(persuasive)* You just do what you do. You know what you do. You're good, Deedee. I think you're good.

MATT	You know what I sent her at Christmas?
PANCHO	Goodbye, Deedee.
	He sends affectionate kisses winging towards her as he hangs up. The telephone rings again.
MATT	Twenty-four red roses.
PANCHO	*(on the phone)* Hello. *(He punches another line, trying to find his call.)*
MATT	Twenty-four red roses.
PANCHO	Hello.
MATT	Two dozen.
PANCHO	Dennis.
MATT	You know what I put on the card?
PANCHO	*(on the phone)* We have to shoot tomorrow, Dennis.
MATT	With love and compassion.
PANCHO	I know what day it is. I know it's Saturday.
MATT	That's good, huh? "With love and compassion."
PANCHO	And I know what it costs. But we have to start to shoot the car chase. We have to start to get the car chase in the can.
MATT	Hey Pancho?
PANCHO	*(on the phone)* It is not going to snow, Dennis. I don't care what the weather office said.
MATT	Do you think she liked it?
PANCHO	It won't snow. Trust me. *(He hangs up. He has dialed the second phone.)*
MATT	Hey, Pancho…
PANCHO	*(on the phone)* Oh, hello, Markie, is your daddy there?
MATT	You think she liked the roses? Laurel, I mean?
PANCHO	*(on the phone)* Oh, hello Mr. Ellis.
MATT	Hey, Pancho?
PANCHO	Just a minute, Mr. Ellis. *(He covers the mouthpiece and hisses.)* This is Mr. Ellis.
MATT	Who?
PANCHO	How is Mr. Garretson tonight, sir? Have you talked to him?
MATT	Who is on the phone, Pancho?
PANCHO	Have you talked to the hospital?
MATT	Is it for me?

PANCHO	Yes, I understand that, sir. I talked to his doctor, sir.
MATT	Is it the doctor?
PANCHO	You tell him, sir, we hope he's feeling better.
MATT	I feel fine.
PANCHO	And when he's feeling better, if he could look at the new budget breakdown…
MATT	Let me talk to him.
PANCHO	About the five hundred thousand dollars overcall, sir.
MATT	Hey, Doc…
PANCHO	It's the lawyer, Matt. It's Garretson's lawyer.
MATT	You tell him I'm fine.
PANCHO	*(on the phone)* No, everything's fine, sir.
MATT	I OD'd, that's all.
PANCHO	*(on the phone)* We want to refinance, that's all.
MATT	I stopped breathing, that's all.
PANCHO	*(on the phone)* Because this picture… there's something about this picture…
MATT	I was nervous, that's all…
PANCHO	*(on the phone)* There's a lot of interest…
MATT	…because of Laurel…
PANCHO	*(on the hone)* Media interest…
MATT	I can't talk to her, Pancho…
PANCHO	You tell Mr. Garretson to read the paper next week, sir.
MATT	No, Pancho…
PANCHO	*(on the phone)* The morning paper, sir.
MATT	No, Pancho…
PANCHO	*(on the phone)* Goodbye, sir. *(He hangs up.)*
MATT	No. No. No. No. No. No.
PANCHO	No what?
MATT	I can't do your interview. I can't talk to Laurel.
PANCHO	Don't be stupid.
MATT	I told you.
PANCHO	You told me that you call her all the time.

MATT	If I disguise my voice.
PANCHO	Look Matt…
MATT	She hangs up if she knows it's me.
PANCHO	She what?
MATT	So I call her, but I say it's a wrong number. Or I listen and she says, "Who's there?" I just listen to her that's all. I mean, I'm in Vera Cruz…
	The telephone rings.
	And she's up here, saying "Hello."
PANCHO	*(on the phone)* Hello.
MATT	Sometimes I say that I'm someone she knows. But I've got a cold…
PANCHO	*(on the phone)* Look, I can't talk to you right now.
MATT	And all I have to do is tell her things she wants to hear.
PANCHO	*(on the phone)* I'll put you on hold, okay?
MATT	If I read her my bad reviews. She likes to hear my bad reviews.
PANCHO	Look, Matt…
MATT	Right now I'm offering her a job.
PANCHO	I beg your pardon?
MATT	I know this girl, she works for *Women's Wear Daily*. And I hung around her office long enough to steal some letterhead. Then I wrote to her. To Laurel. And I offered her a job. And I call her about it.
PANCHO	We can't talk about this right now.
MATT	I love her, Pancho.
PANCHO	Later…
MATT	I want to talk to her, that's all. But I don't want her talking to me.
PANCHO	Later, Matt.
MATT	You can understand that, can't you, Pancho? Why I can't do your interview.
PANCHO	Yes, Matt. You can. It's in your contract.
MATT	What am I supposed to say to her? If she's sitting right there and she knows who I am? We were married for two years, Pancho. Do you know what we've said to each other already? In court? Under oath?
PANCHO	Tell her everything is fine.
MATT	Will that work?

PANCHO	Don't worry, Matt. Davina will be there. That's what she's supposed to do. She's there to help you. She knows all the stuff you're supposed to say.
MATT	Then she should do the interview.
PANCHO	She's the press agent, Matt. And she said she'd phone before she left and she's on the phone right now...
MATT	No. Pancho.
PANCHO	Everything is fine, Matt. You love it here, you love the picture, the story, the crew. The crew is very solid, very professional. Good crew, good picture, good solid entertainment values. On time. Under budget.
MATT	You want me to tell her about the palm trees?
PANCHO	Forget the palm trees.
MATT	You want me to tell her about the rewrites?
PANCHO	Did you hear me?
MATT	You want me to tell her about Garretson?
PANCHO	Everything is fine, Matt.
	LAUREL has entered to hear as much of this as seems convenient.
LAUREL	May I quote you on that?
MATT	Laurel!
PANCHO	What's she doing here?
MATT	You look great.
PANCHO	What's she doing here without Davina?
MATT	You look pretty. Doesn't she look pretty?
PANCHO	*(on the phone)* She's here, Davina.
MATT	Hey, sit down. Can I get you a drink?
LAUREL	Scotch.
MATT	Hey, I know what you drink. Hey, Laurel...
PANCHO	*(on the phone)* So why are you there?
MATT	*(to LAUREL)* Hey, you haven't changed...
LAUREL	Yes. I have.
MATT	*(to PANCHO)* Hey, I love this girl. Did I tell you? I love this girl.... Hey, Laurel. It's been a long time. It's been too long, hasn't it?
LAUREL	Since when?
MATT	Since we... you know.... Hey, Laurel... we lived together for almost three years, you know that?

LAUREL	It seems longer.
MATT	*(to PANCHO)* We had this beach house. In the bedroom, there was one wall, it was twenty feet of glass. We could lie there, we could see right across the Pacific Ocean if we dropped enough acid.
PANCHO	*(on the phone)* You're fired, Davina. *(He hangs up.)*
MATT	Couldn't we? Laurel? Couldn't we see across the ocean? Hey, you remember that?
LAUREL	I hate California.
PANCHO	*(to LAUREL)* Hi there, look come on in…. Look, sit down…
MATT	*(to PANCHO)* You know where I met her? You know where I met this girl?
LAUREL	*(to PANCHO)* You're Pancho, aren't you?
MATT	*(to PANCHO)* In New York.
LAUREL	*(to PANCHO)* I lost your press agent.
MATT	*(to PANCHO)* She was New York.
LAUREL	*(to PANCHO)* But I guess you'll pour the drinks.
MATT	*(to LAUREL)* It was a party. At Hap's. You remember, Laurel. It was James Fenimore Cooper's birthday.
LAUREL	Matt remembers. He was wearing his Stetson.

> *PANCHO is wearing a Stetson. She makes him feel uncomfortable.*

MATT	That's right.
LAUREL	And his suede pants.
MATT	And my squirrel rifle.
LAUREL	Matt was one of those people who dressed like west Texas to eat pizza.

> *She directs that at PANCHO to make him more uncomfortable.*

PANCHO	Is that right?
LAUREL	He kept telling people how the West was won. He kept telling people they couldn't win Newark…

> *The telephone rings.*

So Hap told him to go read *The Pathfinder.*

MATT	I said I was *The Pathfinder.*
PANCHO	*(on the phone)* Hello…
LAUREL	And you shot out the bulbs in his Tiffany lamps.
MATT	Hap's gay, you know.

PANCHO	*(on the phone)* I fired her, Nadja…
MATT	And he'd look stupid, if he still had Tiffany lamps. He'd look like a discount steak house.
PANCHO	*(on the phone)* I know that…
LAUREL	*(to PANCHO)* He terrorized everybody.
MATT	They didn't mind.
LAUREL	*(to PANCHO)* He chased people into the sauna.
PANCHO	*(on the phone)* I know she's a single parent.
MATT	*(to LAUREL)* People like being scared.
LAUREL	They do not.
MATT	It gives them something to talk about.
LAUREL	Do you know what we talked about?
MATT	Me.
LAUREL	Yes. We said you passed out.
PANCHO	*(on the phone)* Look, Nadj…
MATT	You liked it. Being scared…
PANCHO	*(on the phone)* I can't do this alone, but I'm out here alone…
MATT	You liked it. That's why you went home with me.
LAUREL	Somebody had to.
MATT	I scared the pants off you.
PANCHO	*(on the phone)* Nadja…
MATT	Didn't I? Didn't you go home with me?
PANCHO	*(on the phone)* Don't, Nadja…
MATT	You walked me home. You walked in the door. You took off your clothes.
LAUREL	You had ruined my clothes.
MATT	I knew you an hour, you were wearing my track suit.
LAUREL	I spent forty-five minutes in a sauna, I remind you.
MATT	You were twenty-two years old. Two weeks in New York. And you'd never been shot at before. By a movie star, I mean.
LAUREL	And I went home with you. And Hap lent you his Chrysler.
PANCHO	*(on the phone)* You think I enjoy it.
MATT	And that was only James Fenimore Cooper's birthday.
PANCHO	*(on the phone)* You think I enjoy it? Firing people?

MATT	Hey, Laurel, remember the Orange Bowl?
LAUREL	(*sounds vindictive*) I'm glad I get to write this story.
PANCHO	(*on the phone*) I can't talk about it, Nadja. I can't talk to you right now.
LAUREL	(*to PANCHO*) Matt is colourful, isn't he? He's always good copy.
MATT	Hey, thanks…
LAUREL	Matt Payne, Jr. Aging B-movie beefsteak.
MATT	Hey, Laurel…
LAUREL	Do you know what I said about his last film? *Tomburu?*
MATT	Pancho doesn't care about *Tomburu*.
LAUREL	I said it was "maudlin, cheap, trite smut."
MATT	Yeah, but Laurel…
LAUREL	What's your picture like, Mr. Potter?
MATT	This one's different, Laurel.
LAUREL	Really?
PANCHO	Do you have the press kit? I should get the press kit.
LAUREL	Why is this one different, Matt?
	MATT calls PANCHO back.
MATT	I like it, don't I, Pancho? We like it.
PANCHO	We like it.
MATT	We're very excited about this project.
LAUREL	Why?
MATT	Well, it's exciting.
LAUREL	Why?
MATT	You know all about that stuff, Laurel. You write how I like it here, my favourite restaurant… you write the crew is very solid. Good crew, good director… good script, good friends…
LAUREL	You closed down last week.
PANCHO	We what?
LAUREL	And he disappeared. No one knew where he was.
MATT	It was twenty-four-hour flu.
LAUREL	It was overproof bourbon.
MATT	I don't drink anymore.
LAUREL	Tell me more.

MATT	I drink pineapple juice.
LAUREL	Don't we all?
MATT	It's in the press kit, isn't it? Did you read what it said in the press kit?
LAUREL	Do you know what they're saying downtown?
MATT	Where's the press kit?
LAUREL	*(to PANCHO)* They say he threw your chief investor in his swimming pool.
MATT	I threw his wife in.
PANCHO	I don't think you can print that.
LAUREL	They say he set fire to his Winnebago.
MATT	We were fooling around.
PANCHO	I don't think you can print that.
LAUREL	Why is it that every time I talk to you people, everything is fine…
MATT	Hey, Laurel…
LAUREL	…before we see the picture…
MATT	I am not you people…
LAUREL	You like it here, the crew is solid.
MATT	I am Matt.
LAUREL	And six months later when the turkey's on the table, that's when you notice the egg on your face. That's when we hear the leading lady was allergic to you.
PANCHO	Wait a minute…
MATT	Nadja's nervous.
PANCHO	I don't think you can print that.
MATT	Pancho makes her nervous.
PANCHO	That's the kind of story.
MATT	It's the yoga breathing.
PANCHO	That is gossip. That is irresponsible fabrication.
LAUREL	My source also tells me the script is in trouble.
PANCHO	Who is it?
LAUREL	The writer.

        Pause.

He says it's a nightmare. He says he's been up for three days. And he's working on rewrites he can't even read.

MATT	Baz can read.
PANCHO	*(to LAUREL)* I don't believe you.
MATT	Even I can read, Pancho.
PANCHO	No, I don't believe her, about Baz. It's his script. He wouldn't talk like that.
LAUREL	He was drunk.
PANCHO	Do you know how long it took to put this thing together?
LAUREL	That's why he was drunk.
PANCHO	And he doesn't drink.
LAUREL	Neither does Matt.
MATT	Right.
PANCHO	He shouldn't drink. He gets crazy when he drinks.

PANCHO heads for the phones.

LAUREL	We noticed that.
PANCHO	We who?
LAUREL	At Bemelmans. You know Bemelmans, don't you? You know the mirror that they used to have behind the bar?
PANCHO	No, Baz…
LAUREL	He said he'd pay for it. He kept pulling money out of his pockets. He said it was your money and he didn't want your money anyway.
PANCHO	*(dialling)* I have to find him.
LAUREL	He says he wrote a story set in Montreal, but you changed it to Miami. He wrote about separatists, and you changed that to Cuban refugees. He said Matt was supposed to be a PQ Member of Parliament…
PANCHO	*(on the phone)* Hello, Baz…
LAUREL	But now he's a CIA agent.
PANCHO	*(on the phone)* Wrong number. *(He hangs up. He dials again.)*
LAUREL	He says he doesn't feel like a writer. He feels more like he's got the lead in some weird porno film.
PANCHO	*(on the phone)* Where is he?
LAUREL	Because he hasn't slept for three days. Because he's been up for three days with you on his back. Because everything you want him to do is either banal or bizarre.
PANCHO	Have him call me. *(He hangs up. He dials again.)*
LAUREL	Well, Matt…

MATT	Huh?
LAUREL	I guess you got yourself another winner.
PANCHO	*(on the phone)* Hello, Nadj…
LAUREL	I don't know how you do it. You must tell me how you do it.
PANCHO	*(on the phone)* Look, I'm out on the set. Look, I have to find Baz.
LAUREL	How do you do it? How do you pick them?
MATT	Hey, Laurel…
LAUREL	Three points for tacky. Six points for tasteless. And it's shot in Toronto. That's Bingo!
MATT	Go easy, okay?
PANCHO	*(on the phone)* Will you phone around, Nadj?
MATT	It's important to him.
PANCHO	*(on the phone)* Will you try to find him? It's important.
MATT	He's been working on it for two years.
LAUREL	They should give him two years. He should get two years for making it.
PANCHO	*(on the phone)* Tell him we have to talk. About the script.
MATT	Where's the Scotch?
PANCHO	*(on the phone)* More. We have to talk more.
LAUREL	*(to MATT)* Naughty, naughty.
MATT	Huh?
LAUREL	You don't drink, do you? You said you didn't drink.
MATT	Get off my case.
LAUREL	*(to MATT)* You drink pineapple juice. So what's that in your hand?
	MATT studies LAUREL. LAUREL smiles at MATT.
PANCHO	*(on the phone)* I'll be home. In forty minutes.
MATT	This is Scotch, Laurel.
LAUREL	Yes, I know.
MATT	It's for you.
	MATT refills her glass.
PANCHO	*(on the phone)* Look, just find him, okay? Look, I'll see you, okay?
	PANCHO hangs up. He starts for his coat.
LAUREL	*(to MATT)* Is that why you quit drinking?
PANCHO	Where's my script?

LAUREL	*(to MATT)* Because your hand shakes while you pour?
MATT	It doesn't shake.
LAUREL	You want to bet?
PANCHO	Look, I'm going to have to leave you, eh? I have to get back to town.
MATT	*(to LAUREL)* My hand's not shaking.

MATT pulls a gun.

PANCHO	What?
MATT	You think my hand is shaking?
PANCHO	No, Matt…
MATT	I'll show you if my hand is shaking. Sit down, Pancho. Watch this, Laurel. What do you want me to shoot at? What do I shoot?
PANCHO	Matt…
MATT	Freeze.

MATT aims the gun at PANCHO. PANCHO freezes.

LAUREL	You know what I think you should do, Matt? I think you should shoot the cigarette out of my mouth.
PANCHO	Give me the gun.
MATT	I want to show her, that's all.
LAUREL	That would be cute. That would look good in print.
PANCHO	Will you two calm down?
LAUREL	I could get a photographer.
PANCHO	Will you cut that out?
LAUREL	For a story like that?
PANCHO	Do you want him to shoot you?
LAUREL	He can do it if his hands aren't shaking.
MATT	Don't, Laurel…
LAUREL	He does all his own stunts, you know.
PANCHO	No, Matt.
LAUREL	It's all part of the act. His daddy taught him. You know his father, the living legend.

MATT shoots. PANCHO deflects his arm upward.

Don't try this stunt at home now, boys and girls.

PANCHO	Are you crazy?

LAUREL	Matt Payne, Jr. is a sharpshooter. And he trained many years for this trick.
PANCHO	*(to MATT)* You shot her.
LAUREL	You think I believed him?
PANCHO	You stood there and asked him to shoot you.
LAUREL	It's a fake gun.
PANCHO	No, it isn't.
LAUREL	Where did you get it, anyway? From your prop man? Where did he get it? At Woolworth's?
PANCHO	You load it with blanks or you load it with bullets.
MATT	Hey Laurel…
PANCHO	You don't fool around with guns.
MATT	It isn't from Woolworth's.
PANCHO	How do you open this, Matt?

> *MATT takes the gun.*

MATT	It's a .38 Smith and Wesson.
LAUREL	Matt's such a liar, isn't he?

> *MATT aims the gun at a can of pineapple juice. He fires. PANCHO inspects the damage.*

You fired that at me.

MATT	I didn't hit you.
LAUREL	That's a .38 Smith and Wesson.
MATT	I wouldn't hurt you, Laurel.
LAUREL	It's a gun. It's a real gun.
MATT	You said my hand was shaking.
LAUREL	You pulled the trigger. You pointed the gun at me and pulled the trigger.
MATT	I was kidding around.
LAUREL	You could have killed me.
MATT	Like the last time, remember? Remember the Ali-Spinks fight?
LAUREL	*(to PANCHO)* Did you see that? He could have killed me.
PANCHO	Wait a minute…

LAUREL	I'm glad I get to write this story. This is better than your story. How did you put it? How you like the script, you like the crew, you like the Courtyard Café…
PANCHO	You told him to do it.
LAUREL	You tell me about it.
PANCHO	You dared him to do it.
LAUREL	Oh, sure.
PANCHO	You stood there. You dared him to pull the trigger.
LAUREL	Sure. Blame me. Blame the victim. That's typical, isn't it? That's the same kind of woolly mind that's trying to tell me he's under budget.
PANCHO	Wait a minute…
LAUREL	You go ahead, Mr. Potter. You go back to the city and sort out your script. Matt and I will sit down together and talk about old times, won't we, Matt?
MATT	Hey, Pancho…
PANCHO	Wait a minute…
MATT	*(confidential, to PANCHO)* Could you, you know, could you find something else to do?
PANCHO	Could I what?
MATT	I can handle her.
PANCHO	You must be joking.
MATT	She wants to be alone. She means with me.
PANCHO	She wants to chop you up for dog food.
MATT	She sounds tough.
PANCHO	She is tough.
MATT	You know why she does that? She's insecure. You know what she's doing, she's coming on at me.
PANCHO	You're kidding.
MATT	I know her, Pancho. We were married for two years. I love her, Pancho.
PANCHO	She wants her story, that's all.
LAUREL	You think I charged a forty-dollar cab fare for a story?
MATT	There's a press kit in the office. If I had a press kit then I'd know the stuff…
PANCHO	Matt…
MATT	The stuff that you want me to say, like where I was born.

PANCHO	I want to be here, Matt. I have to be here. For the interview.
MATT	I'll do your interview, if you give me ten minutes with her. I want to talk to her, that's all. I love her, Pancho.
LAUREL	I think they went thatta way.
MATT	The press kit…
PANCHO	You don't have to answer. If she asks you something, there's no one going to make you answer.
LAUREL	I'll read him his rights while you're gone.
PANCHO	I'll be back.

> *PANCHO exits.*

LAUREL	I'm sure he'll be back.
MATT	Hey, Laurel…
LAUREL	They always come back, don't they? Especially if they can't think of an exit line.
MATT	Hey, Laurel, we've got ten minutes.
LAUREL	Is that what his script is like?
MATT	You don't care about the script.
LAUREL	Do you say things like that? "I'll be back." Is it like *Tomburu* where you hear the talking drums?
MATT	Hey, I liked that review. Your *Tomburu* review. Hey, I cut it out, I've got it in my scrapbook.
LAUREL	But you like the script for this picture, too, don't you? You like *Man with a Gun.*
MATT	The script is good.
LAUREL	I'm sure.
MATT	It was good when I first read it.
LAUREL	That doesn't count.
MATT	Before they got at him. The guys with the money. Before they started talking box office. Talking bankable star.
LAUREL	Are you a bankable star?
MATT	Hey, Laurel…
LAUREL	Matt Payne, Jr.?
MATT	Hey, Laurel, you know how it is…
LAUREL	You know why they hired you?
MATT	But I like the script. Really.

LAUREL	You were all they could afford.
MATT	But it isn't my image, that's all.
LAUREL	Please, Matt…
MATT	I mean, I don't read as French-Canadian. I mean, that's why they put in a car chase. That's why they beefed up the fight scenes.
LAUREL	And where was the cowboy? While all this went on?
MATT	He's a good kid, Laurel.
LAUREL	While they shot his story full of holes.
MATT	He's a nice guy.
LAUREL	And you know how nice guys finish? With exit lines like "I'll be back." With pictures starring Matt Payne, Jr.
MATT	I think it could be good.
LAUREL	I'm sure.
MATT	He wants it to be good.
LAUREL	I know the type. I bet he wants world peace.
MATT	He wants to make a good picture.
LAUREL	Good luck.
MATT	We talk about it.
LAUREL	He made a good picture the first time out. And he let it die. He showed it at a film festival in Kamloops.
MATT	They think faster than he does, that's all.
LAUREL	They think meaner than he does. They think dirtier. They think in net instead of gross. And he's a good kid, he's a nice guy, so he lets them. Lets them walk all over his film. Lets them walk away with his film. And he is standing back to do the decent thing. He is standing there looking stupid. You know something? I don't care about nice guys, Matt. Nice guys make me sick.
MATT	It could be the Scotch.
LAUREL	And this Scotch makes me sick.
MATT	But it's okay. It's government issue. (*He shows her the bottle.*)
LAUREL	(*with loathing*) LCBO.
MATT	Maybe it's good for you, or something.
LAUREL	Only in Canada.
MATT	And that's why the government wants you to drink it. Maybe they add vitamins.

LAUREL	I hate it here, Matt.
MATT	It's okay.
LAUREL	I don't want it "okay."
MATT	Hey, Laurel…
LAUREL	You know why this Scotch tastes so bad, you know why your film doesn't work. It's deliberate. They set out to be second-rate, you know. They don't make Scotch as well, they don't make cars as well. They don't make films as well….
MATT	Hey, Laurel…
LAUREL	Well, do they?
MATT	Hey, Laurel. I've made bad pictures all over the world.
LAUREL	You know the only thing they're good at? Bad-mouthing. Bitching. Small-time, small-town meanness, acts of petty malice. They don't like me, you know, you know why?
MATT	Hey, they like you…
LAUREL	Because I try to set standards…
MATT	Hey, I like you…
LAUREL	Because I try to suggest there is something more than mediocrity…
MATT	Where?
LAUREL	The world is full of nuts, you know. This town is full of nuts, anyway.
MATT	What's wrong with that?
LAUREL	Every time I say things could be better. Work could be better. Every time I write a review, then it starts. They call me up. They send stuff over that I didn't order.
MATT	Hey, Laurel…
LAUREL	I get pizza. I get obscene poems iced on chocolate chip cookies.
MATT	Wait a minute…
LAUREL	They breathe at me on the phone, Matt…
MATT	They who?
LAUREL	You know what they sent me for Christmas? Twenty-four red roses.
MATT	You like roses.
LAUREL	You know what it said on the card? "With love and compassion." Who do they think they are? Who do they think I am?
MATT	Where's my pineapple juice? *(He sucks on it moodily.)*
LAUREL	So I'm going to New York.

MATT	You are what?
LAUREL	I will work in New York, that's all. I love New York, Matt. If you want to do your best work, you work with the best people… and you know where you find the best people? In New York.
MATT	Wait a minute…
LAUREL	Like Hap…. Look, he wrote me a letter… *(She digs it out of her shoulder bag.)*
MATT	No. Laurel…
LAUREL	And he calls me from Nassau. At first the money wasn't right…
MATT	Oh, no…
LAUREL	But he called me Sunday and I said, "Wait a minute. I hate it here." I was standing on my balcony. It is on the lake. It's dark out there. It is black. It is empty. And I thought: You don't have to be here. You could be in Hap's apartment. You could be in New York.
MATT	Are you kidding?
LAUREL	You could be looking down on Central Park West. Instead of Lake Ontario. I hate it. I hate the smell of it. I hate to look at it. You know what the beach is like? Well, there isn't any beach, but if there were, it wouldn't be covered with sand. There'd be ale-wives. Dead fish on the beach.
MATT	They have dead fish in New York.
LAUREL	They have everything in New York.
MATT	They have dirty phone calls, too. You think you won't get dirty phone calls?
LAUREL	They'll be creative dirty phone calls.
MATT	You'll get shot at. In New York.
LAUREL	I'll pretend I'm a war correspondent.
MATT	I mean, it's tough, that's all. I mean you know what they said about my last picture. About *Tomburu*. They said it was maudlin, cheap, trite smut.
LAUREL	I said that.
MATT	Maudlin, cheap, trite smut. That's the way they talk in New York.
LAUREL	That's the way I talk.
MATT	So maybe you shouldn't go back there, you know…
LAUREL	Are you kidding?
MATT	Maybe you should say "stuff their job."

LAUREL	Don't be silly.
MATT	Maybe you should stay here. Where it's safe.
LAUREL	It isn't safe. It's boring.
MATT	It's peaceful, Laurel. What is wrong with that. Huh? I mean, look at cloistered nuns, do you think they have cable TV in there? No, It's dull in there, but they're happy. I'm saying you can be bored and happy at the same time, do you hear what I'm saying? I mean, nuns don't moan around and yell, "What's happening?"
LAUREL	You know what's happening here?
MATT	Look for spiritual values.
LAUREL	In Toronto?
MATT	New York was eight years ago, Laurel.
LAUREL	What difference does that make?
MATT	Look, it's harder now. Look, you know why I asked you to marry me?
LAUREL	I don't care, Matt.
MATT	Because you looked lonely. At Hap's. Because I asked you to dance and you knocked over a Tiffany lamp. Because Hap laughed at you.
LAUREL	He did not.
MATT	I mean, who cares. About Tiffany lamps. So we showed him, didn't we? You have to show them you don't care…
LAUREL	Matt…
MATT	You're not tough enough for New York, that's all.
LAUREL	I was tough enough to live with you.
MATT	Look, I want to explain…
LAUREL	For three years. Your bike pictures. Your good old boys. Your ex-wives, your new girls. Your attempted suicide.
MATT	That was Father's Day, that's all.
LAUREL	And I walk in and you've got a gun to your head.
MATT	And my kids hung up on me. And my dad hung up on me.
LAUREL	I think I can handle New York now, that's all. I can handle Hap.
MATT	No, Laurel…
LAUREL	You know what I told my editor? When I quit?
MATT	You what?
LAUREL	I told him what he could do with his job and his paper and his two-bit hick town. And I'm going out in style.

MATT	I could go out in style.
LAUREL	You know what I want all next week? Every day. A Laurel Hayes exclusive. And on Saturday I want the front page of the entertainment section.
MATT	We can get the front page.

MATT has the gun. He put it to his head. LAUREL turns to discover him.

LAUREL	"How to Make Schlock Movies in Toronto." *(She sees him.)* Is that loaded?

LAUREL jumps for MATT. They wrestle with the gun.

MATT	You know how I felt? On Father's Day?
LAUREL	Put that gun down.
MATT	People kept hanging up. Was it something I said? I thought there must be something I can say.
LAUREL	You're crazy…
MATT	No one knows what I'm saying.
LAUREL	Please, Matt.
MATT	I wish I could tell you, Laurel. I wish I could say what I want to say, but I can't talk anymore.

The gun goes off. MATT slumps to the ground. PANCHO enters.

PANCHO	Now what?
LAUREL	I didn't hit him!
PANCHO	Matt!
LAUREL	I couldn't have.
PANCHO	Are you all right, Matt?
LAUREL	I shot that way. It hit this wall. Here.

There is no apparent damage to the wall. LAUREL wonders why. She turns back to PANCHO who is checking out MATT's body.

PANCHO	He's drunk.
LAUREL	He couldn't be.

PANCHO sniffs MATT's glass.

PANCHO	There is Scotch in his pineapple juice.
LAUREL	You think I got him drunk?
PANCHO	Hey, Matt? *(He tries to wake him up.)*
LAUREL	You think I got him drunk to get the story?

PANCHO	Will you give me the gun?
LAUREL	I wouldn't have. I wouldn't have to…
PANCHO	May I have the gun, please…
LAUREL	Look, I know the story. It's the same old story. He's drunk. Sure, I made him get drunk. Sure I forced him to do it. Because I said something to him, because I reminded him of something, because I pushed him, because I left him, because I hang up when he calls me, then they call me from Emergency. Sure, it's my fault. Blame the victim. That's the same kind of stupid thinking…
PANCHO	I didn't say it was your fault.
LAUREL	That's good. Because it wasn't. My fault.
PANCHO	Come on, Matt…
LAUREL	*(a little late)* Is he all right?
PANCHO	He's breathing, anyway.
LAUREL	Is there anything that I can…
PANCHO	You can go home and write your story…
LAUREL	…I could help, I…
PANCHO	…since you know the story…
LAUREL	It helps if he keeps moving.
PANCHO	Yes, I know.
LAUREL	If there's coffee…
PANCHO	I've done it before.

PANCHO *tries to pick MATT up. MATT slips out of his grasp and thumps to the floor.*

Pancho Potter, paramedic.

LAUREL	Wait. There's Scotch in this coffee.
PANCHO	Come on, Matt. Let's take a little walk, let's keep moving.

PANCHO *picks MATT up. The telephone rings. PANCHO wants to answer it.*

LAUREL	And there's Scotch in the milk.
PANCHO	*(to MATT)* Let's keep walking. Come on. Let's keep walking.
LAUREL	Water. I'll get some water.
MATT	The phone's ringing.
PANCHO	Who said that?
MATT	*(delighted)* Hey, Pancho…

PANCHO	Did you pretend to pass out?
LAUREL	*(on the phone)* Hello…
MATT	Ah, Pancho, we're friends, eh?
LAUREL	*(on the phone)* No, he's still here. He hasn't left yet.
PANCHO	Did you pretend to pass out? So I'd think you passed out?
LAUREL	*(on the phone)* Just a minute…
MATT	I like you, Pancho. *(He grabs his neck with drunken affection.)*
PANCHO	Let me go.
LAUREL	It's your wife. On the phone. She wants to speak to you.

> *PANCHO reaches for the phone. MATT grabs him sentimentally.*

MATT	You're all nice kids, you know that? I like you. *(He gives PANCHO a drunken kiss.)*
LAUREL	He can't come to the phone.
MATT	And I want to help you. With your picture. Because you care about your picture. Your picture means something, doesn't it?
PANCHO	Matt…
MATT	Tell me what it means.
LAUREL	*(on the phone)* I'll tell him.
MATT	Will you do that? Do you promise?
LAUREL	*(on the phone)* All right. I'll tell him.

> *LAUREL hangs up as PANCHO reaches the phone.*

MATT	*(to PANCHO)* Like the scene we're going to shoot tomorrow. I could help you, if I knew what it meant. If I knew what you wanted. I'm an actor. I could do it different ways. I could say, "Follow that car" or I could say, "Follow that car." You see the difference?
LAUREL	Your wife says Baz is drunk, too.
PANCHO	Fine.
MATT	*(a new reading)* Follow that car.
PANCHO	That's all I need. That's fine. *(He is dialing the phone.)*
LAUREL	He's sitting at the kitchen table.
MATT	Follow that car.
LAUREL	He keeps saying: "I can't do it alone. I can't do it alone."
MATT	Follow that car.
LAUREL	She says the housekeeper is in tears.

MATT	Follow that car.
	MATT smiles. He falls asleep. He should still be visible on stage. PANCHO has dialed the phone.
LAUREL	She says Baz is crying.
PANCHO	*(on the phone)* Hello, Nadj…. Don't, Nadj…. Don't okay?… Look, I'll be there, okay? Forty minutes, okay? *(He hangs up.)*
LAUREL	She was crying too, wasn't she?
PANCHO	She cries at card tricks.
LAUREL	She and Baz are sitting there… at your kitchen table…
PANCHO	They're like that. They're emotional.
LAUREL	And you're not? *(She sees PANCHO is.)*
PANCHO	They're Ukrainian.
LAUREL	Are you? Ukrainian?
PANCHO	I am tired, okay? Let's call it quits, okay. And I'll drag Matt here back to his hotel, you'll file your story, sure, why not? The Matt Payne, Jr. Story. With everyone in it in tears or unconscious.
LAUREL	Is this the press kit?
PANCHO	You don't need the press kit.
LAUREL	Hey…
	PANCHO has taken it away from her. He throws it in the trash can.
PANCHO	Because you know it all, isn't that right? It's all maudlin, cheap, trite smut, isn't that right?
LAUREL	I don't know the whole story.
PANCHO	And you aren't going to know the whole story.
LAUREL	Want to bet?
PANCHO	What do you want me to do?
LAUREL	It's over, isn't it?
PANCHO	Should I call you a cab?
LAUREL	That's sad, isn't it? That's typical, isn't it?
PANCHO	Wait, I'll call you a cab.
LAUREL	That's Canadian, isn't it?
PANCHO	What?
LAUREL	I thought if you were second-rate, you had to try harder.
PANCHO	What did you say?

LAUREL	I would try harder. If I had a film I wanted to make. If I wanted to make a film, I would bleed to death for it.
PANCHO	*(hands her the phone)* Would you go and bleed?
LAUREL	*(hangs up the phone)* I would mortgage my house.
PANCHO	I have mortgaged my house.
LAUREL	I would sell my children at Yonge and Bloor.
PANCHO	You don't have children.
LAUREL	You have two. Children.
PANCHO	Is that a Laurel Hayes exclusive?
LAUREL	And a wife who's in your film, but she doesn't like your film.
PANCHO	Go away.
LAUREL	What would happen if I liked your film, if I wrote I liked your film. On the front page of the weekend entertainment section.
PANCHO	Is that what you want?
LAUREL	What would happen?
PANCHO	There's a problem. You don't like my film.
LAUREL	You convince me I should. If you think I should. Why should I like your film, Mr. Potter?
PANCHO	Go away.
LAUREL	I'm open-minded.
PANCHO	Yes, I'm sure.
LAUREL	But I don't know much about you, do I? I don't even know your real name.
PANCHO	My name is Pancho.
LAUREL	No, I'm serious.
PANCHO	P.A.N.C.H.O.
LAUREL	Really. I'm curious.
PANCHO	My friends call me Pancho.
LAUREL	It's interesting. You're interesting.
PANCHO	What are you going to call me?
LAUREL	I mean, how does a grown man from Winnipeg, Manitoba, end up in a cowboy hat and boots. How does he have the nerve to get people to call him Pancho?
PANCHO	My mother called me Pancho.

LAUREL	Oh, I'm sure.
PANCHO	Because I used to like westerns. She never saw me, I was always at the movies.
LAUREL	That's charming, isn't it? You're charming, aren't you?
PANCHO	And I was a kind of a fat kid.
LAUREL	Which figures.
PANCHO	What do you mean?
LAUREL	You heard me.
PANCHO	You think I'm fat. I'm not fat. *(He isn't.)*
LAUREL	You are soft.
PANCHO	No. Think again.
LAUREL	Your work is soft.
PANCHO	What did you say?
LAUREL	I saw your first film. *Dominion Day.*
PANCHO	I won six awards with that film.
LAUREL	They were Canadian awards.
PANCHO	Cheap shot.
LAUREL	And here's your new film. *Man with a Gun.* And you've got a hack actor who's been getting fat making spaghetti westerns.
PANCHO	You talk a lot about who's fat.
LAUREL	I say what I think.
PANCHO	I think you're coming on to me.
LAUREL	I beg your pardon?
PANCHO	Matt says that's how you do it. Come on to people.
LAUREL	What?
PANCHO	You go for the throat. The weakness. You tell them they're fat and you don't like their films.
LAUREL	I didn't say I didn't like your films.
PANCHO	You said *Dominion Day* was uncommercial.
LAUREL	When they sang Slavic wedding songs, yes.
PANCHO	And you say this one is a sellout.
LAUREL	A what?
PANCHO	*(He's sensitive about the word "sellout.")* You haven't even seen it and you say it's a sellout.

LAUREL	It doesn't matter what I say…
PANCHO	You got it.
LAUREL	It's what your housekeeper says. It's what your friend the writer says. It's what your wife…
PANCHO	You don't know what they…
LAUREL	They are sitting at your kitchen table saying, "What happened… whatever happened…"
PANCHO	I'm glad. I'm glad it happened.
LAUREL	"Whatever happened to Pancho Potter's Perfect Picture?"

Pause. LAUREL knows the way BAZ and NADJA talk.

PANCHO	Look, anyone can have a perfect "picture." We had one for years, every frame the way we wanted it. Every picture, every image, every line of dialogue. We had that film running through our brains for years, I can still see it, but it wasn't real.
LAUREL	You think this is real?
PANCHO	What do you do? To get a film out of your head. What do you do if you want to do more than dream about it? You talk about it. I used to talk about it all the time. I took it to parties. I took it to bed.
LAUREL	With who?
PANCHO	With Nadja, mostly. She knew, you know, what I was trying to say. And after a while, almost everybody else, they looked at me a little oddly, you know. As if I had a dead bird around my neck.
LAUREL	Did you write her a part?
PANCHO	No. Baz wrote her a part. I talked it, I told you. I tried to sell it. Dressed up downtown with the lawyers and the bankers.
LAUREL	And you look good dressed up.
PANCHO	Good enough
LAUREL	Sure, why not?
PANCHO	Because Garretson called. He had a package. He had two million dollars and some cheap advice.
LAUREL	And that was it.
PANCHO	And I talked him up to three.
LAUREL	You what?
PANCHO	You know how I did it? I said "I need three million dollars, Mr. Garretson." And he said, "Kid." He calls me "kid." "Grow up, kid. You're not a kid anymore, kid, and you can't go around making films because you like them." But he's the kid… he's like a kid. All the time

he's smiling and his lawyer's writing cheques. Grow up. Do you know what that means? To him? To Garretson? It's easy. Be practical, that's all. Look at the budget, look at the balance sheet, look at the box office. Grow up. So you can make films for overgrown kids with popcorn for brains. So you can take care of overgrown kids like Matt.

LAUREL   You bought the package.

PANCHO   Two years.

LAUREL   And you trashed your film. For palm trees and the CIA. For three million dollars…

PANCHO   And Matt.

LAUREL   Grow up. Sell out.

PANCHO   No, it's all right. No, Matt's okay.

LAUREL   You bought him and Garretson bought you.

PANCHO   No, I like him. Because he lives big, doesn't he? He lives larger than life. He makes grand gestures.

LAUREL   What's so grand about passing out.

PANCHO   You know what it is with Matt? He thinks he's the hero. Whatever the story is, whatever the scene is, he thinks he's the hero. And he firmly believes he can ride to the rescue. He still thinks that's possible. He's like the miner in my strike film. The Mounties stop the demonstration on Dominion Day. And they have guns, the strikers have sticks. The hero steps out of the crowd. There's a fire engine out there, in case they need the hoses. He climbs up on it. He tears open his shirt. He yells "Shoot me! Shoot me if you dare."

LAUREL   So they shoot him.

PANCHO   That's a grand gesture.

LAUREL   That's a stupid gesture.

PANCHO   That's how Matt lives. Do you know what Matt did for you?

LAUREL   Please. Don't ask.

PANCHO   You know what Matt's like. You know how he gets what he wants. We spent twenty thousand dollars dressing this interior and Matt hated it, so he got accident-prone. He made us rebuild it.

> *PANCHO is pushing open the back wall to expose the interior set. Wherever MATT has passed out, he is now masked by this flat.*

LAUREL   This is our place. This is our beach house.

> *LAUREL explores. PANCHO watches her. He points out places of interest.*

PANCHO	That's the balcony he said he'd jump off.... The glass doors you broke when you threw the hairdryer.
LAUREL	Look at all this...
PANCHO	The bar.
LAUREL	Look at it...
PANCHO	Take a drink. You drink Scotch, don't you?
LAUREL	All these records.
PANCHO	Golden oldies.
LAUREL	They're the same. They're our records.
PANCHO	Is the bed the same? *(It is. It's gaudy.)*
LAUREL	Oh, Matt...
PANCHO	*The Joy of Sex* within easy reach.
LAUREL	Here's his track suit.
PANCHO	You see what I mean?
LAUREL	I used to wear this.
PANCHO	I know.
LAUREL	I used to wear his track suit.
PANCHO	It's really something, isn't it? He's really something. It's a labour of love. You know what I think...
LAUREL	This is wrong.
PANCHO	It's Matt's version of the Taj Mahal.
LAUREL	This picture's wrong.
PANCHO	He built it for you.
LAUREL	This is supposed to be my wedding picture.
PANCHO	It's Nadja.
LAUREL	Wait a minute...
PANCHO	My wife in your wedding. She's playing you.
LAUREL	You can't...
PANCHO	She says she hates his work. She can't respect him because she hates his work. She thinks he's sold out. She thinks he's drinking too much because he knows he's sold out. She thinks he ODs on pills like I OD on film. She wants to leave him.
LAUREL	Stop it!

PANCHO   And he can't explain... he can't talk to her.... He loves her but that doesn't seem to make any difference...

LAUREL   Of course it doesn't make a difference.

PANCHO   He is losing his wife. He's right there for us, losing his wife. He's on the telephone... the only time they talk is on the telephone. And he doesn't know what to say, he can't talk to her.... He says, "Hey, it's okay, okay..." I'll be home, okay..." It's like a record he keeps playing over and over. He has to keep playing it over and over. He can't leave it alone. He is losing his wife.

LAUREL   It isn't true.

PANCHO   I beg your pardon?

LAUREL   What he told you. About me and him. About me.

PANCHO   He told me he loved you. He told me the first time he met you he asked you to dance. (*He puts a record on the stereo.*)

LAUREL   That's very cheap.

PANCHO   That's true. But it's true.

LAUREL   Will you turn that thing off?

PANCHO   You know your problem?

LAUREL   I hate that record.

PANCHO   You know what Matt says. You're insecure.

LAUREL   No. I'm not.

PANCHO   Matt's inarticulate.

LAUREL   You got it.

PANCHO   I know he's inarticulate, but he knows, doesn't he? That when I say he talks about you, then the first thing you think is you have to deny it. The first thing you think is I know all your guilty secrets.

LAUREL   I don't have any guilty secrets.

PANCHO   That's right. Because we know it all. How you leave the bathroom in the morning. What you looked like when you went to high school. Where you keep the handgun. With the socks.

          PANCHO has been carrying the gun since he took it from LAUREL. He puts it in the drawer on the set.

LAUREL   Now listen, cowboy...

PANCHO   Who cares, Laurel? Want to trade? I do not have a handgun. I spent high school at the movies, in confusion. I'm worse than you are in the bathroom...

LAUREL   I didn't buy *The Joy of Sex,* you know.

PANCHO	*(amused)* I beg your pardon?
LAUREL	It was Matt.
PANCHO	I didn't say…
LAUREL	I mean, he's the one who's insecure…
PANCHO	Sure. I see what you mean. You don't need *The Joy of Sex*.
LAUREL	That's right.
PANCHO	Why? Because you know it all already?
LAUREL	That's right.
PANCHO	And that's the way you'd do it. By the book. So you'd know what you were feeling since you knew what it was called.
LAUREL	What's wrong with that?
PANCHO	No wonder you married Matt.
LAUREL	What do you mean?
PANCHO	There's more to it, that's all.
LAUREL	More than what?
PANCHO	Than what it's called. Than you get from a how-to manual.

> *PANCHO is leafing through* The Joy of Sex. *LAUREL doesn't want to look.*

There's more than A fits into B…

LAUREL	You want to bet?
PANCHO	There's Matt.
LAUREL	Who needs it?
PANCHO	And five years later, he's building monuments to you…
LAUREL	On a soundstage in Kleinberg.
PANCHO	Five years later, he can still see it, every frame of it. Like a film in his head playing over and over. With the music.
LAUREL	I hate the music.
PANCHO	With the water out there.
LAUREL	There is no water out there.
PANCHO	Matt can see it. And the sunset. Five years later. He can see you on the balcony…

> *PANCHO turns off the lights on the set.*

…in the very chic Borkmann recliner…

He turns on one of the "sunset" lights to illuminate the cyclorama. It's blue.

...every evening.

He adds red.

...every sunset.

He adds the sun's disc.

Five years later, you're still there for him. Five years later he still sees you, even if the only time you ever speak is when he calls you in the middle of the night.

LAUREL   He doesn't call me.

PANCHO   We wrote a scene about it. For the picture. You know what I like about this picture. You know the one thing we've got left? The way Matt looks when he talks to you.

LAUREL   He doesn't talk to me.

PANCHO   He doesn't have to talk to you. He doesn't have to say anything. We can see it. I have got it on film. I love it, Laurel...

LAUREL   I don't know what you're talking about.

PANCHO   It's a love story. It's bent, it's wrong...

LAUREL   It's sentimental. It's maudlin.

PANCHO   It's sad, it's funny, but it's a love story. And it has grand gestures, big mistakes. Because here is a guy who talks about you like I talk about film.... Here is a guy who remembers the last time he danced with you... the music... which lights were on... *(He turns on the interior lights.)*

LAUREL   He's a psychopath.

PANCHO   He's a romantic.

LAUREL   Matt has a number of vivid and appalling fantasies. And so, I see, do you.

PANCHO   Why not?

LAUREL   While I have a letter from *Women's Wear Daily...*

PANCHO   I know.

LAUREL   Which is signed by Hap Kelly, Features Editor. In which he says he has been following my work. *(She produces the letter.)*

PANCHO   Is that it?

LAUREL   In which he quotes from my work. See. Here. I wrote, "Matt Payne, Jr. gives his usual cigar store Indian performance as a Great White Hunter."

PANCHO	And Matt wrote that letter.
LAUREL	What?
PANCHO	He knows this girl in the office. He stole the letterhead. He forged the signature.
LAUREL	He what?
PANCHO	I thought you knew.
LAUREL	He forged the signature?
PANCHO	How come you didn't know? How come your ex-husband phones you up three times a week and you don't even notice? How come you're limp enough to sit around at night getting drunk enough...
LAUREL	I do not get drunk.
PANCHO	You've drunk all my Scotch.
LAUREL	Your what?
PANCHO	You get so drunk that you don't even know who's calling you. He's your ex-husband and you can't even recognize his voice. You know why?
LAUREL	I don't need your advice.
PANCHO	You're insecure.
LAUREL	Wrong.
PANCHO	You don't like yourself, do you?
LAUREL	Wrong again.
PANCHO	And you have to keep drinking so you don't notice. And you have to keep on at other people.
LAUREL	I don't like other people.
PANCHO	Why not?
LAUREL	Because they lie. And they cheat. And they walk around in cowboy boots.
PANCHO	Who, me?
LAUREL	Why not you. You're trying to tell me Matt Payne, Jr. is a human being. You're trying to sell me the Taj Mahal.
PANCHO	I said he loves you.
LAUREL	But it isn't like the movies, is it? Not for him. He isn't going to do it for the Gipper.
PANCHO	Laurel...
LAUREL	Matt is crazy. His reels are all mixed up. He's in some horror film. He's last on the bill at some all-night drive-in movie. He is up there riding

to the rescue, but the paint is peeling off the screen. I know. I'm up there with him. Step right up, folks. See it. Live. Laurel Hayes meets Matt Payne, Jr. We ran for three years, you know that. Three years with the battle of the century. Every night. Every night another title fight, but we kept changing the title. *Love me or Leave Me, Lost Weekend, Indiscreet. Scream and Scream Again. Battle for the Planet of the Apes.* You know the worst part. The part I hated most. No matter what the title was, the story was the same. Boy meets girl. Boy loses girl. He loves me, he loves me not, he loves me, he loves me not. He loves me, he loves me. He loves me…. He loves me so that makes him the hero…. He loves me so I lose. I don't care if he loves me. I hate it that he loves me…

PANCHO   Look…

LAUREL   I can see him at the fade-out saying, "Love makes the world go wrong," and you give him all the angles and I'm not even in the picture…

PANCHO   Hey, Laurel…

LAUREL   I quit my job, you know. Because of his undying love.

       Pause.

PANCHO   Look, maybe you should be glad you quit your job.

LAUREL   Oh, sure.

PANCHO   Since you hated your job. Didn't you? Maybe Matt did you a favour.

LAUREL   Oh, sure.

PANCHO   Because you say you want to go to work in New York. Why not go? If you hate it here, since you say you hate it here. What do you need? You need a bus ticket, that's all.

LAUREL   Is that all.

PANCHO   Why not?

LAUREL   I'll go down to Bay and Dundas. And I'll look both ways before I cross the street. I'll buy my one-way ticket, watching out for strangers.

PANCHO   If you don't want to stay here…

LAUREL   I'll just skip down the yellow brick road.

PANCHO   You can't spend your life doing things that you hate.

LAUREL   Do you really believe that?

PANCHO   I believe you can do what you want.

       The phone rings.

       Exactly what you want.

LAUREL   The phone's ringing.

PANCHO   If you want it hard enough.

LAUREL   *(on the phone)* Hello.

PANCHO   If you work at it hard enough. You want to work in New York. I want to work on my film. What's going to stop us? Who's going to stop us?

LAUREL   It's Nadja.

> *PANCHO takes the phone.*

PANCHO   *(on the phone)* Hello.

LAUREL   She's crying again.

PANCHO   Look, don't cry okay. I'll be home, okay.

LAUREL   She isn't home.

PANCHO   What did you say?

LAUREL   She's left you.

PANCHO   *(on the phone)* Where are you? Nadj?

LAUREL   She's with your friend. What's his name. The writer.

PANCHO   Nadja…. Don't hang up on me. Look, you can't hang up on me.

> *She does. He hangs up. He dials the phone again. He stops. He hangs up again. LAUREL turns away to pour herself a drink. PANCHO leafs through his script, then he throws it in the trash can. LAUREL starts her record over from the beginning.*

LAUREL   Are you a romantic?

PANCHO   Would you leave me alone for a minute?

LAUREL   There are people who say that romance is a kind of escape.

PANCHO   Well, it isn't escape.

LAUREL   Why not?

> *LAUREL kicks off the interior lights. The sunset is still up. She and PANCHO are in silhouette.*

PANCHO   What are you doing?

LAUREL   Extravagant adventures. Mysterious events. Grand gestures.

PANCHO   Will you leave the lights alone?

> *PANCHO starts toward the switch boxes. LAUREL catches his arm as he passes.*

LAUREL   Big mistakes.

PANCHO   Look, lady…

LAUREL   Can you dance, cowboy?

> *She kisses him. Fade-out.*

ACT TWO

PANCHO is asleep. LAUREL is depressed. She is drinking the Scotch from the set. She pours herself another drink as PANCHO stretches and wakes.

PANCHO   That was fun.

LAUREL   Oh, yeah?

PANCHO   I had fun.

LAUREL   You are Little Mary Sunshine, aren't you?

PANCHO   It gets me through the night.

LAUREL   It was perverse. It was stupid. And illogical.

PANCHO   It's funny, but that never stops me.

LAUREL   And I want to tell you, this is not going to change the world, that's all.

PANCHO   I'm hungry.

PANCHO looks for food and rejects his options—stale doughnuts, dead pizza—the food on the set.

LAUREL   This is not you and me and the meaning of the universe.

PANCHO   You're kidding.

LAUREL   Because we went to bed together…

PANCHO   Is that what happens in New York?

LAUREL   You know why I went to bed with you?

PANCHO   When people go to bed together in New York, then the world changes?… Hey, no wonder you like it.

LAUREL   Leave me alone.

PANCHO   Here the only thing that happens is the earth moves.

PANCHO has wrapped himself in a blanket. He flashes at LAUREL. She isn't amused.

You don't have to drink your breakfast, you know.

LAUREL   I beg your pardon?

PANCHO   There's stuff in your kitchen. *(He rummages in cupboards offstage.)* Laurel, is this what you eat in New York?… *(He appears with an armload of junk food.)* Or is this California? You know what's in this junk? *(He reads the chemicals on the label. He throws the food offstage.)* Laurel? Are you crying?

LAUREL   No.

PANCHO	Look, don't cry, okay? I'm sorry, okay? Don't worry, there's stuff we can eat. In my office. You know what I've got in my office… granola… Laurel?… Look, do you want to take a shower or something? There are showers. If you go out… out there, past the dressing rooms and past the johns…
LAUREL	I do not want to talk about plumbing.
PANCHO	You know why you're sad?
LAUREL	I'm not sad.
PANCHO	Because of Matt.
LAUREL	Matt who?
PANCHO	It makes you sad. When you wake up with a stranger. If all you've been doing is getting even with a friend.
LAUREL	We aren't friends.
PANCHO	You are wearing his track suit.
LAUREL	I was cold.
PANCHO	You are playing his records.
LAUREL	Yes, I know I'm playing his records.
PANCHO	That's all I'm saying.
LAUREL	I'm sitting in a beach house that I left five years ago, that's what I'm saying. What do you think? How do you think I feel? It's exactly the same, it's creepy…. It's like meeting our double, you know what that means?
PANCHO	Laurel…
LAUREL	You're going to tell me he loves me. But all I can say is, I feel like a clone.
PANCHO	Hey, calm down, okay?
LAUREL	It is five years later and I am back in the same apartment and I haven't changed.
PANCHO	You can change.
LAUREL	Five years later. In the same bed with another stranger.
PANCHO	It's okay, okay.
LAUREL	You know who it was the last time? The pizza delivery boy.
PANCHO	Poor old Laurel.
LAUREL	And I don't get any choosier, do I?
PANCHO	She's so tough. She won't stop.

LAUREL	Five years later, it's a would-be cowboy. And all he wanted was the front page of the entertainment section…
PANCHO	Wait a minute….
LAUREL	Just so people would think he was making a film.
PANCHO	I am making a film.
LAUREL	Tell me more.
PANCHO	I was making a film.
LAUREL	You were making a tax writeoff.
PANCHO	Wrong.
LAUREL	That's why they make films in Canada, isn't it? To lose money?
PANCHO	Wrong again.
LAUREL	You won six film awards for your last film, didn't you? And nobody's seen it. How many people have seen it?
PANCHO	You've seen it.
LAUREL	At a free screening. At Harbourfront.
PANCHO	I'm not a distributor…
LAUREL	The distributors are American, isn't that right? So it's their fault, isn't that right? The Americans buy junk like *Man with a Gun*, so you make junk like *Man with a Gun*.
PANCHO	It isn't junk.
LAUREL	Maybe not. Maybe it's right up there in the Maple Leaf Hall of Fame. Right next to Chateau Gai Baby Duck.
PANCHO	Good point.
LAUREL	I have heard your sad stories so many times. Ever since I got here. About how we come up here and take you over. About how the Americans set your standards and buy your wheat and sell you franchises for Peter Pizza outlets. But you know why you've got me? And junk food? And *Starsky and Hutch*? Because you don't have the guts to do it yourself.
PANCHO	I've got better things to do than listen to this.
LAUREL	Like what?
PANCHO	Goodbye, okay.
LAUREL	Like what? Take a shower?
PANCHO	What is wrong with that?
LAUREL	You're one of those people who thinks that things will work out well, aren't you? You're one of those people who thinks all you need is a cold

shower and bowl of granola…. So you sit back with your government grants…

PANCHO	I beg your pardon…
LAUREL	And you tell us the story of Louis Riel.
PANCHO	I don't care about Louis Riel.
LAUREL	Then you'd better try a little harder, hadn't you?
PANCHO	Get out of here.
LAUREL	You'd better try for an international standard…
PANCHO	A New York standard.
LAUREL	That's what I said.
PANCHO	Your standard.
LAUREL	I'm from New York. I have worked in New York.
PANCHO	You're the journalist, aren't you?
LAUREL	You know who I am.
PANCHO	Matt has a scrapbook, you know. He has a collection of your work. So I've seen your work.
LAUREL	What is wrong with my work?
PANCHO	I think it's cheap, that's all.
LAUREL	I beg your pardon?
PANCHO	What was your first piece?
LAUREL	For *New West Magazine*
PANCHO	The piece on movie machismo.
LAUREL	*New West Magazine* is not cheap.
PANCHO	Then the piece on the biker pictures, then the piece on famous father syndrome. And then your reviews. And your lists of ten worst movies. I think you've built your whole career on the garbage heap you've made out of Matt's career and I think that's cheap, that's all, and that's all I want to say because I have to leave you now, thank you for a very nice evening, but it's six o'clock and I have a call at seventy-thirty. I have to meet my crew on location.
LAUREL	And you have to get your car chase in the can.
PANCHO	And I have to can my car chase, don't I?
LAUREL	Is this a Laurel Hayes exclusive?
PANCHO	I'm giving up, I'm closing down. I've eighty-sixed my picture. Yes, you're right.

LAUREL	May I quote you on that.
PANCHO	But I have to be there. You can see that. The crew is good. They've been good, they should know. There are things I should say. That's the right way to do it, isn't it? Isn't that the way they do it in New York?
LAUREL	Do you want a photographer?
PANCHO	Go away.
LAUREL	I could get a photographer.
PANCHO	Go on back to New York. If you like New York so much.
LAUREL	I love New York.
PANCHO	The people who brought you shopping bag ladies.
LAUREL	Cheap talk.
PANCHO	Garbage strikes. Audience participation crime.
LAUREL	I love New York. I don't care what you say.
PANCHO	Then go there. Go and live in the Dakota. And leave us alone.
LAUREL	You should be glad I'm here.
PANCHO	I beg your pardon?
LAUREL	I said you need me. To keep you honest. Because if I weren't here, you'd sit around congratulating yourself all day. We don't have busing. We don't have street crime. We don't have thugs kicking doors down.

MATT kicks a door down. He enters.

MATT	I woke up in the dark. It was dark out there.
LAUREL	Good morning, Matt.
MATT	So I kicked down the door.
PANCHO	That's excessive.
MATT	Hey, Laurel…
PANCHO	That's overkill, Matt. That's stupid. That's like getting up in the morning and invading Angola.
MATT	Something's funny here. Something's wrong with this picture.
PANCHO	The door was on the floor. *(He clears it.)*
MATT	Why is Laurel wearing my track suit?
LAUREL	Matt, it's not what you think.
MATT	Do you know what I think?
LAUREL	Look, Matt…

MATT	Why is she wearing my track suit, Pancho? And where is your shirt, Pancho?
LAUREL	I spilled my drink...
MATT	Let me get this straight...
PANCHO	She spilled her drink...
MATT	It's six o'clock in the morning and you spent the night spilling drinks on each other?
PANCHO	Wait a minute...
MATT	It's the same, isn't it? It's a time warp, isn't it? We've gone back to the Ali-Spinks fight.
PANCHO	I can explain...
MATT	Where's the pizza?
PANCHO	Matt...
MATT	Did he bring you a pizza?
PANCHO	I was tired, that's all. Look, three days without sleep. You know how it is when you're tired.
MATT	Where did you leave the pizza? Where did I leave the gun? *(He finds it in the drawer with the socks.)*
LAUREL	No, Matt...
PANCHO	Not again.
LAUREL	Will you stop him? Will you get the gun away from him? Will you put the gun down, Matt?
PANCHO	Shoot me.
MATT	Hey, Pancho...
PANCHO	Shoot me if you dare.
LAUREL	Will you cut that out?
PANCHO	He tears open his shirt. He jumps up on the fire truck.
	PANCHO does whatever seems convenient, using one of the Hawaiian shirts from the wardrobe rack. He will probably have to button the shirt up before he can rip it open.
LAUREL	Do you know what he did the last time? With the pizza delivery boy?
PANCHO	Matt won't shoot me. It isn't his image. *(Now he demonstrates the full glory of the scene.)* Shoot me! Shoot me if you dare!
	MATT is delighted. He throws PANCHO the gun so he can demonstrate.

MATT   There's a better way to do that, tear open your shirt. There's a way it looks good. *(He demonstrates.)* Shoot me! Shoot me if you dare!

> *PANCHO turns to put the gun away. MATT kicks the drawer shut on his hand.*

PANCHO   Matt!

MATT   Don't worry. We'll put blocks in the drawer, that won't hurt you. *(He sets up a fake punch.)* Hit me. Hit me here.

PANCHO   No, Matt…

MATT   *Wichita Kid.* 1972. Hit me here.

> *PANCHO throws a fake punch. MATT overreacts, falling backward like a comic-book villain; PANCHO reaches down to help him to his feet.*

PANCHO   Come on, Matt.

> *MATT kicks him backwards.*

MATT   *Hell Wheels.* 1976.

> *MATT kicks him. It's violent, but obviously fake.*

PANCHO   No, Matt.

MATT   *Outlaw Rider.* 1973.

PANCHO   Cut it out.

> *PANCHO pushes him off. Again, MATT overreacts. He's delighted.*

MATT   Keep rolling. Keep rolling. *(He grabs a bottle from the bar.)* This is from *Vengeance of Hercules.*

PANCHO   *(real fear)* Put the bottle down, Matt.

MATT   It's breakaway.

PANCHO   It isn't breakaway.

MATT   There must be a breakaway here someplace.

> *MATT is about to wreck PANCHO's bar, looking for a non-existent breakaway bottle. PANCHO pulls a non-existent gun.*

PANCHO   All right! Freeze!

> *MATT is overjoyed.*

MATT   *Hell's Outlaws.* 1969. *(He "dies.")*

PANCHO   Take it in the heart. *(He "fires" again.)*

MATT   *Hell's Rider.* 1976. *(He dies more extravagantly.)*

PANCHO   Take it in the forehead. *(He "fires" again.)*

MATT   *Hell's Angels' Beach Party.* 1975. *(The most extravagant death scene.)*

PANCHO	Okay, Matt…
MATT	Give me the boot. Give me the boot.

> *PANCHO is about to fake a kick. MATT twists his foot and flips him.*

	That was my biker period.
PANCHO	Okay, hot shot. Come at me with a gun.
MATT	*Fistful of Pesos.* 1977.

> *MATT approaches PANCHO with his non-existent gun. PANCHO flips him.*

PANCHO	Daniel Mac High School Junior Wrestling. 1963.

> *MATT is winded.*

MATT	Hey, Pancho…
PANCHO	*(concerned)* Are you okay?
MATT	No, I'm fine. What do you mean?
PANCHO	Did you land the wrong way?
MATT	You go out the door and into the chase. You go in the door and into the fight.
PANCHO	Hey, Matt…
MATT	That's what I do, you know. I go through the script, and if that's all I do, if I throw the punch or I get on the horse or I crash the car, I write N.A.R.
LAUREL	Why is he spelling?
MATT	No Acting Required.
PANCHO	Look, Matt…
MATT	That used to be enough, eh, Pancho…
PANCHO	It's all right.
MATT	That used to be all right. That used to look good.
PANCHO	You know what else looks good?
MATT	I'm tired.
PANCHO	The telephone. We'll do the telephone, okay?
MATT	No Acting Required.
PANCHO	You pick up the telephone, Matt… you dial the number… the phone is ringing…
MATT	Is this scene in my script?

PANCHO   Sit there, Matt. Be there, Matt. You don't have to say anything, you don't know what to say, there's nothing left to say, it's like me on the phone, you've seen me on the phone. I say, "Don't…" I say, "Please…" You just have to listen, Matt, listen that's all. *(He adjusts the lights. No more sunset.)* I'm rolling, Matt…. You pick up the telephone, you dial the number, my shot is moving, the phone is ringing…. Now, she picks up the phone… she says, "Hello"…. Listen, Matt…. "Hello"… a little panicky… she doesn't know who's there… "Hello"… it's like a cry for help…. Look over here, Matt.

PANCHO snaps his fingers so MATT is looking at LAUREL.

MATT   …Laurel?

PANCHO holds the shot for several beats before releasing MATT with a hand on his shoulder.

PANCHO   Good stuff.

LAUREL   Is that in your film?

PANCHO   When we're lucky.

LAUREL   And you talk about me.

PANCHO   Would you look at him?

PANCHO frames a shot, using LAUREL as the focus. She ignores him.

MATT   We can print that, eh, Pancho?

LAUREL   And you think I used him. You tell me I used him. But he's out there alone, you put him out there alone…

In fact, PANCHO is rubbing MATT's shoulders. Whatever. Their camaraderie makes LAUREL even angrier.

MATT   Are we going to shoot the car chase?

PANCHO   Yes.

LAUREL   You're closing down.

PANCHO   I can't.

LAUREL   You're giving up.

PANCHO   Not yet.

MATT   I've been thinking about the car chase.

PANCHO   You can do it.

MATT   You can't have a car chase in a Honda Civic.

PANCHO   Trust me, Matt.

MATT   It isn't my image.

PANCHO	I don't want your image, Matt…
LAUREL	What are you doing?
PANCHO	I can't take it seriously.
MATT	Hey, Pancho…
PANCHO	When you're the hero. It's like a comic book, it's funny, Matt…
MATT	Hey, Pancho.
PANCHO	But you trust me, okay? You'll look good. I'll make sure you look good.
LAUREL	This is folly.
PANCHO	This telephone is off the hook.
LAUREL	This is irresponsible, self-indulgent…
PANCHO	These telephones are off the hook.
LAUREL	I know.
PANCHO	These lines are all on hold.
LAUREL	Because the phones kept ringing.
PANCHO	Of course they were ringing. They're phones. That's what they do. Phones ring. I am trying to make a picture here.
LAUREL	Have you asked why?
PANCHO	*(on the phone)* Hello, Deedee…
LAUREL	Why bother?
PANCHO	*(on the phone)* It isn't snowing.
LAUREL	Who cares about your picture?
PANCHO	*(on the phone)* Tell Matt's limousine I've got him.
LAUREL	I don't care about your picture.
PANCHO	*(on the phone)* Goodbye, Deedee. *(He blows her kisses. He hangs up. He sets up his typewriter.)*
LAUREL	Deedee… is she pretty?
PANCHO	Yes.
LAUREL	I knew that. Somehow I knew that.
PANCHO	I have to type my short list. *(He does.)*
LAUREL	Deedee. You're AD is called Deedee.
PANCHO	What's that? Another Laurel Hayes exclusive?
LAUREL	It is a fluffy name, isn't it.
PANCHO	Stop the presses.

LAUREL	You know what I think? You are sleeping with her.
PANCHO	You know what Deedee tells me?
LAUREL	No.
PANCHO	She says I'm an easy lay.
LAUREL	You know what I'll tell you…
PANCHO	When I finish my short list.
LAUREL	You're finished.
PANCHO	Then I'm going to grab a shower.
LAUREL	You are going down for the third time.
PANCHO	I am going to shoot my car chase. I am going to get my overcall. I am going to gross twenty-five million. Domestic.
LAUREL	You delude yourself. You indulge yourself. You do what you want, but you don't know what you're doing. You don't know how to do it. You don't know entertainment values. You don't know soap operas, situation comedies, you don't know vaudeville, Broadway musicals…
PANCHO	You know what Baz says we should have? In my films?
LAUREL	Besides second-rate Americans?
PANCHO	He wants to write them. Pancho Potter's Perfect Pictures…
LAUREL	I know his type. I bet he wants world peace.
PANCHO	He says you have to set the people up, the place, the period, the point of view, the philosophy behind the film, the premise…
LAUREL	Yes, I'm sure.
PANCHO	And then he indicates the plot.
LAUREL	Will you stop!
PANCHO	He says there has to be a promise, you have to make a promise to the audience and they have to know what you're going to deliver and you have to deliver…
LAUREL	I have better things to do…
PANCHO	And there has to be poetry, there has to be passion…
LAUREL	I have better things to do than listen to this. (*She could put on her shoes.*)
PANCHO	There has to be politics, prophecy, isn't that right?
LAUREL	Are you kidding?
PANCHO	And there has to be pain.
LAUREL	They all begin with "P," that's all.

PANCHO	That's what I told him. And he threw his script at me.
LAUREL	What does that mean?
PANCHO	You're a writer.
LAUREL	What is that supposed to mean?
PANCHO	You explain it. I am going to grab a shower.
LAUREL	Who cares anyway?
PANCHO	I'll be back.
LAUREL	Who cares what they begin with?
MATT	Hey, Laurel…

MATT has not understood a word of this. Perhaps he has been asleep.

LAUREL	I don't care.
MATT	I do.
LAUREL	Shut up, Matt.
MATT	What begins with "P"?
LAUREL	Pretentious.
MATT	Hey, that's right.
LAUREL	Ponderous.
MATT	Hey…
LAUREL	Pompous. Pre-pubescent, plodding, puerile. Also phony.

Pause.

MATT	You know what?
LAUREL	Go away, Matt.
MATT	You can tell you're a writer.
LAUREL	Thank you.
MATT	Hey, you know all the words.
LAUREL	Yes, I do.
MATT	Hey, you remember what you said about *Tomburu*? You remember what you said about me?
LAUREL	Yes. Of course.
MATT	*(admiring)* Maudlin, cheap, trite smut.
LAUREL	I said Matt Payne, Jr.…
MATT	Hey, that's writing, you're a…

LAUREL	Son-of-a Matt Payne, Sr.
MATT	Hey…
LAUREL	Son-of-a-living legend.
MATT	Hey, Laurel…
LAUREL	So he lives like a comic book.
MATT	Hey, Laurel. Hey, we'll leave my father out of this.
LAUREL	Matt hates Father's Day…
MATT	Now that's not true.
LAUREL	Matt spends Father's Day at AA meetings…
MATT	Laurel…
LAUREL	Or he tries to get his father on the phone.
MATT	I warn you, Laurel…
LAUREL	It's strange, but they're estranged. Matt Payne, Sr.'s number is unlisted.
MATT	No!
LAUREL	So the son is on the phone…
MATT	He moved, that's all!
LAUREL	To his father's agent, trying to get his father's number. It's Father's Day, but he can't reach his father.
MATT	Because he moved…
LAUREL	He's sentimental, suicidal…
MATT	When I was in Morocco!
LAUREL	Matt Payne, Jr. is a gun nut.
MATT	Look, he'd talk to me.
LAUREL	Matt Payne, Jr. has a .38 Smith and Wesson. You know who taught him to shoot? His daddy taught him to shoot.
MATT	You think I'd shoot myself?
LAUREL	Why not?
MATT	I wouldn't shoot myself.
LAUREL	No such luck.
MATT	Hey, Laurel…
LAUREL	His psychiatrist says it's like a cry for help. Every time he tries to kill himself, he's just crying, "Help."
MATT	Hey, Laurel…

LAUREL	Help. It's Father's Day. Help. My father hung up on me. Help. My kids hung up on me. Help. I have to go to Panama to make a picture with absolutely no redeeming social value.
MATT	You know what I'd do. If I wanted to kill myself.
LAUREL	You don't want to kill yourself.
MATT	I would walk out to sea.
LAUREL	You're not that crazy.
MATT	I'd walk out to sea. Have you seen that before?
LAUREL	You want everyone else to be crazy. You want to drive everybody else crazy.
MATT	I'd walk out that door. I'd walk into the water.
LAUREL	There's no water out there, Matt.
MATT	I'll find it.

MATT exits. The phone rings. PANCHO enters.

PANCHO	Where's Matt?
LAUREL	*(on the phone)* Hello?

Car effects.

PANCHO	No, Matt…
LAUREL	*(on the phone)* Who is this?
PANCHO	May I please have my phone?
LAUREL	*(on the phone)* Who is this? I don't understand.
PANCHO	Will you give me my phone?
LAUREL	He's talking Russian.
PANCHO	*(on the other phone)* Hello, Deedee.
LAUREL	*(hangs up)* Wrong number.
PANCHO	*(on the phone)* We have a problem here.
LAUREL	I am wrapped up in telephone cord.
PANCHO	One, I need a limo.
LAUREL	Get me out of this, Pancho…
PANCHO	Two, we're going without Matt.
LAUREL	Wait a minute.
PANCHO	Get a stunt man. We'll use a stunt man.
LAUREL	Let me get this straight?
PANCHO	Goodbye, Deedee. *(He blows her kisses. He hangs up.)*

LAUREL	You are going to use a stunt man?
PANCHO	Yes.
LAUREL	Since you can't *use* Matt?
PANCHO	Wait a minute…
LAUREL	Since Matt is halfway into Kleinberg at the speed of sound. He could kill himself, you know. He could kill someone else.
PANCHO	I can't control him, Laurel.
LAUREL	Yes, I see that.
PANCHO	I do what I can.
LAUREL	I'm sure you do. I'm sure you boycott grapes. I'm sure you never eat Kraft cheese.
PANCHO	Now look, Kraft is now called Kraftco, so it isn't enough just to boycott Kraft, you have to look out for…
LAUREL	It isn't enough to do what you can.
PANCHO	I beg your pardon?
LAUREL	You don't try hard enough, do you? You try hard enough for nice guy, but nice guy isn't hard enough. It's all leftover cub scout stuff. You think all you have to do is think good thoughts…. All you have to do is one good deed a day…
PANCHO	You want a vitamin?

PANCHO is eating breakfast. LAUREL ignores him.

LAUREL	Or now that you're older, one good deal a day.
PANCHO	Wait a minute…
LAUREL	And you'll get your happy ending. Does your movie have a happy ending? Does Matt drive off into the sunset with the palm trees waving in the breeze?
PANCHO	The palm trees!
LAUREL	The music swells. The credits start to roll. The end.
PANCHO	I forgot about the palm trees..

PANCHO reaches for the phone. It rings.

LAUREL	You don't seem to notice.
PANCHO	*(on the phone)* Hello.
LAUREL	Matt's stolen your car.
PANCHO	*(on the phone)* I love you, Deedee!
LAUREL	You don't seem to notice.

PANCHO	*(on the phone)* I want the palm trees at Mount Sinai.
LAUREL	The last authentic happy ending was on a Ronald Reagan movie.
PANCHO	*(hangs up)* I got the palm trees.
LAUREL	And that's all you want.
PANCHO	It helps.
LAUREL	Your palm trees. Your granola.
PANCHO	It all helps.
LAUREL	It is seven o'clock in the morning. And you woke up with a stranger and your best friend is in bed with your wife somewhere and all you care about is palm trees!
PANCHO	Is that what you think?
LAUREL	I think Matt screwed you. I think we screwed each other.
PANCHO	You think Baz and Nadj…
LAUREL	I think they screwed each other.
PANCHO	You know where Baz and Nadj are now?
LAUREL	In bed.
PANCHO	He was best man at my wedding.
LAUREL	You can do the same for him.
PANCHO	You know what they did last night? Baz and Nadj?
LAUREL	Yes. I do. Of course I do.
PANCHO	They went for coffee.
LAUREL	You delude yourself.
PANCHO	I know them. I know Baz. So do you. He's a nice guy, isn't he? He's another nice guy. He's nicer than I am.
LAUREL	Oh, no one's that nice.
PANCHO	The trouble is, he loves her.
LAUREL	Sure!
PANCHO	Like you love New York. He has some perfect Nadja in his head like you have some golden city.
LAUREL	Just a minute…
PANCHO	So he wants to do it right. He wants to do the right thing. And that isn't easy. It isn't like dragging me to bed…
LAUREL	I beg your pardon?

PANCHO	So they sat in the Courtyard till it closed. Then they walked. They agonized. Baz is a writer. He has to agonize. I feel sorry for writers, don't you?
LAUREL	I beg your pardon.
PANCHO	Then they sat in the Fiesta till it closed. Then they walked. It was probably raining, but they walked for hours, there was cold rain dripping down their necks, but they kept walking.
LAUREL	Don't be stupid.
PANCHO	Now they're sitting in Fran's. And Baz just bought another package of Export A.
LAUREL	That's stupid.
PANCHO	He smokes too much. He drinks too much. You should have seen him at our wedding…. Have you ever seen a Ukrainian wedding? Nadja's dad had two twenty-sixers of rye in the middle of every table. And a bottle of Scotch and a bottle of vodka. And he and Baz sat at a table for two. They were drunk, they were singing, they were making up verses for this wedding song. And Baz got sadder and sadder and the verses got dirtier and funnier and Nadja's dad laughed till he cried and Baz was crying…
LAUREL	You're making this up.
PANCHO	You think so?
LAUREL	You made it up already. That's in your first film.
PANCHO	Baz wrote it.
LAUREL	It's a scene from the movie, that's all.
PANCHO	He's good at that, Baz. He took my wedding, he took all the pain… all his pain from my wedding and he put it in my film, do you know what I mean?
LAUREL	No, I don't.
PANCHO	And it isn't like you. When you rip Matt up…. When you rip Matt off…
LAUREL	I beg your pardon…
PANCHO	Because it changes. Because it isn't real life when's he's finished… There's something else there. There's something Baz wrote. There's something I can film.
LAUREL	I do not rip Matt off.
PANCHO	Look. I'm sorry…
LAUREL	You rip him off. You're ripping him off.

PANCHO	It's how you write it. It's where you start. As if you were the hero.
LAUREL	I am the critic.
PANCHO	That's what I mean.
LAUREL	I say what I think, that's all.
PANCHO	You're the one who knows what kind of smut it is. You're the one who's always right.
LAUREL	I beg your pardon...
PANCHO	You can cut it open, sure, you're good at that. You can cut to the bone. You can go for the heart. But what have you got when you're finished?
LAUREL	It depends what you had when you started.
PANCHO	You've got dead meat when you've finished.
LAUREL	Cheap shot.
PANCHO	But Baz gave me back my wedding. He gave me more than my wedding. It's the same, it looks the same, everybody is drunk, they're singing, the song gets louder and louder and the verses get dirtier and dirtier and the hero jumps on the table, just like Baz jumped on the table, but he isn't singing about what I did in high school. Do you know what he sings?
LAUREL	I don't care.
PANCHO	In a cavern, in a canyon Excavating Estevan Mining doesn't leave much time for Pondering the rights of man.
LAUREL	Is that dirty?
PANCHO	In some circles. In some circles the rights of man are seldom pondered. Self-interest is a prime concern. In your circles, for example.
LAUREL	You think I'm selfish? Me?
PANCHO	How do you do it? How do you do it? How do you keep your head together with no more personal philosophy than look out for number one?
LAUREL	I remind you, I am not the one who let a friend drive off to certain doom.
PANCHO	Yes, you are.
LAUREL	I have a personal philosophy.
PANCHO	Maybe you did, a long time ago. When you were young and bright and starving. Maybe you wanted truth and social justice. You wanted to

change the world, but you noticed the world would pay you forty thousand a year if you left it alone…

LAUREL   How much?

           Car effects.

           They don't pay me forty thousand…

PANCHO   *(dials the phone)* I can cancel the limo.

MATT   *(offstage)* Hey, Pancho…. Hey, Laurel…

LAUREL   Matt?

PANCHO   *(on the phone)* Has the driver left yet?

MATT   *(enters)* Hey, Laurel…

PANCHO   *(on the phone)* Eighty-six the limo, Dennis.

MATT   You got a story. In the paper.

LAUREL   Let me see that.

MATT   It's the front page.

PANCHO   Let me see that.

MATT   It's the front page of the entertainment section, anyway.

LAUREL   It's called "How to Make Schlock Movies in Toronto."

PANCHO   Yes. I see what it's called.

MATT   *(indicating)* That's a picture of me. It's from *Tomburu.*

PANCHO   *(to LAUREL)* When did you write this? You wrote this before you came out here, didn't you? One more time.

LAUREL   That's my job, you know. That's what I do.

PANCHO   You have trashed him one more time.

LAUREL   I write.

MATT   *(reads, with difficulty)* By Laurel Hayes.

PANCHO   And then you came out here. Why did you come out here?

MATT   *(reads)* Part One. Of a series.

PANCHO   You came out here…

LAUREL   Go away.

PANCHO   And you and I…. We had quite a nice time…. But you knew you wrote this.

LAUREL   Leave me alone.

PANCHO   So you stuck around to watch us read it.

LAUREL   So I got hammered.

PANCHO	*(reads)* Matt Payne, Jr., son-of-a-Matt Payne, Sr.
MATT	Huh?
PANCHO	*(reads)* He's a B-movie G-man who lives like a four-letter word.
MATT	Hey, Laurel…
PANCHO	Did you write this?
MATT	What was that
PANCHO	It says, "has-been, maybe never was." It says, "failure."
MATT	What did it say about my father? *(He takes the paper. He reads.)*
LAUREL	You've heard that before.

The telephone rings.

PANCHO	*(to MATT)* Are you okay?
MATT	I'm fine. I'm reading.
PANCHO	Leave it, Matt.
MATT	It's the phone. The phone's driving me crazy, that's all.
PANCHO	*(on the phone)* Hello…. Oh, hello, Mr. Garretson.
LAUREL	Mr. who?
PANCHO	How are you this morning, sir?
MATT	*(reads)* *Tomburu.* With its plastic rubber trees. With its rubber army ants.
LAUREL	Matt…
MATT	*(reads)* It made him a household word. Turkey.
LAUREL	You're not reading it all.
MATT	You want more?
LAUREL	You make it sound unbalanced.
PANCHO	*(on the phone)* You're up early, sir. I guess hospitals are like that.
MATT	You know who's unbalanced? *(He takes out his gun.)*
PANCHO	*(on the phone)* Oh, have you read it?
LAUREL	Is that loaded?
MATT	You know how I feel, Laurel. I feel depressed, Laurel.
LAUREL	That isn't loaded, is it?
PANCHO	*(on the phone)* Yes, sir, we've read it. We're just reading it now.
MATT	But it's okay, I'll be all right. *(He is toying with the gun.)*
PANCHO	*(on the phone)* It's quite a story.

MATT	You could have a better story. *(He fires at one of the liquor bottles in the bar. He knocks it backwards.)*
LAUREL	Pancho, help me!
PANCHO	I am on the phone right now.
MATT	If all you want is a story, Laurel.
LAUREL	No, Matt! Don't.
	LAUREL dives at MATT. They struggle. The gun goes off when pointed at LAUREL's stomach.
PANCHO	*(on the phone)* I'll have to put you on hold, Mr. Garretson.
LAUREL	He shot me. He shot me in the stomach. How?
PANCHO	It's okay. You're okay. We're okay. *(He goes back to the phone.)*
LAUREL	I don't feel anything.
MATT	That's to bad, Laurel. That's too bad you don't feel anything.
PANCHO	*(on the phone)* I'm here, sir.
MATT	*(to LAUREL)* Because I do. Because I feel something.
LAUREL	You didn't shoot me, did you?
MATT	So does Pancho. You know why I think it is? That you don't feel anything.
LAUREL	That gun is loaded with blanks, isn't it?
MATT	You've been working for that newspaper too long.
LAUREL	First you load it with bullets. Then you load it with blanks.
MATT	I don't have to use bullets. *(He aims his finger at the palm tree on the balcony, as if it were a gun.)* Bang!
	The top of the palm tree falls off.
LAUREL	How did you do that?
MATT	Movie magic. *(He takes a small transmitter out of his pocket. He blows a box of doughnuts off the prop table.)*
LAUREL	I'll kill you, Matt… *(She launches herself at him.)*
PANCHO	Hey, don't fight. Hey, it's all right.
LAUREL	No, it isn't.
PANCHO	Garretson's all right. He phoned. I just talked to him. He read your story. He loved your story… what you said about the picture.
LAUREL	I said it was trash.
PANCHO	Thank you.

LAUREL	I said it was schlock.
PANCHO	Garretson loves schlock movies. That's the only reason he's giving me five hundred thousand dollars.
LAUREL	He's giving you what?
PANCHO	He said I grew up.

The telephone rings.

LAUREL	Well, you haven't grown up.
MATT	Hey, Laurel…
LAUREL	Did you read my story? Cowboy?
MATT	It's a party, Laurel.
LAUREL	Did you read what I wrote about you?
PANCHO	*(on the phone)* Oh, hi, Nadja…
LAUREL	She's in the story.
PANCHO	*(on the phone)* Did you read it? I didn't read it.
LAUREL	In the sidebar. Look, I called it in last night. Look, the whole thing, the kitchen table, the telephone calls…
PANCHO	*(on the phone)* Hey, Nadj…
LAUREL	It has your real name in it.
PANCHO	*(on the phone)* Hey, thanks.
LAUREL	Baz told me. Your real name.
PANCHO	*(on the phone)* Hey, I love you, eh? Really.
LAUREL	Bill. Bill Potter.
MATT	He can't hear you, Laurel.
LAUREL	He can hear me.
MATT	He's talking to Nadja. She called him.
PANCHO	*(on the phone)* It's okay, Nadja. Really.
MATT	I knew she'd call him.
LAUREL	You what?
MATT	She would do the right thing, wouldn't she? So would Baz. If they read your story. If they thought Pancho needed them.
PANCHO	*(on the phone)* I love you, Nadj.
MATT	They'd be there. If he needed them.
LAUREL	Be where?
MATT	And I want to do the right thing. I mean, for you.

LAUREL   I beg your pardon?

MATT   Because you lost your job. I mean, I made you lose your job…. Because I care about you, Laurel. And I don't think you should go to New York. I don't think you're tough enough for New York.

LAUREL   Drop dead, Matt.

MATT   Pancho…

But PANCHO is talking to NADJA on the phone. The interior walls roll, the screen descends, masking MATT as PANCHO continues.

PANCHO   *(on the phone)* The shoot is down on Walmer Road, okay? You want to keep Ivan out of school?… Because we're going to shoot the car chase…. Look, the kids are going to love this car chase.

Blackout. A film is projected on the back wall of the set.

THE FILM

A clapperboard announces the particulars of the shoot. The title: Man with a Gun. *Etc. It is Scene 250. Take 16.*

CLAPPERBOARD GUY
Man with a Gun. Scene 250. Take 16.

PANCHO   *(voice-over)* Action.

Nothing happens. The film shows a car pulled up to the curb.

(voice-over) I said "Action." Matt.

Nothing happens.

(voice-over) All you have to do is run down here and get in the car. No, keep rolling. I said "Action."

There is the sound of a gunshot.

(voice-over) What's he doing? What's he doing with that gun? Not that car, Matt!

Sound effects of a motor running. Car screeches away, PANCHO screams.

(voice-over) No, Matt! Please!

The camera swings wildly looking for the action. Its viewfinder is blocked by people in the way, its focus is blurred.

Sound effects of an automobile crash.

(voice-over) Please! No!

The camera is moving, following PANCHO. We don't see anything but PANCHO's back, or sky or trees, until the camera is poked in the window of a car where MATT lies, apparently unconscious, apparently covered with blood.

A confusion of voices off. "Is he hurt?" "Is that blood?" "Is he dead."

PANCHO (*voice-over, clear as someone covers the lens*) No, his blood bag burst, that's all.

Take the sound out, Deedee.

DEEDEE complies. PANCHO watches the footage again. Morosely, MATT enters.

Close the door.

MATT Hey, Pancho… (*He turns on the light.*)

PANCHO Turn that light off.

MATT (*ignores him*) Are you okay?

PANCHO I'm watching rushes in here, Matt. I'm watching your rushes.

MATT Are you okay.

PANCHO Me?

MATT Because I wondered…

PANCHO No, I'm fine…

MATT Because you've got, what, maybe two hundred feet of film looped around up there and you've been watching it since they brought it back from the lab.

PANCHO It's all the film I've got, Matt.

MATT Hey, Pancho…

PANCHO I was making a picture called *Man with a Gun*. It was a simple story. It was a genre picture, an action picture. It had a car chase, what is wrong with that. From page eighty-six to page ninety-three, there was a car chase.

PANCHO goes over to check his script. He turns on another light. The film, which is still looping, is now washed out enough so it isn't distracting.

MATT No.

PANCHO A car chase. What is wrong with that?

MATT It isn't my image.

PANCHO That's a key scene. That's an important scene. That's the set-up for the whole resolution of the picture.

MATT See, I don't run away.

PANCHO A car chase. A simple car chase.

MATT I mean, I don't run away from a Volkswagen Rabbit. I don't run away from a Honda Civic.

PANCHO	I told you to trust me.
MATT	I tried.
PANCHO	You can trust me, Matt. You have to trust me.
MATT	No, Pancho.
PANCHO	Two years.
MATT	Ah, Pancho…
PANCHO	Two years of PQMP's, then the CFDC, the CCA, PR, CPA's. BMW's and BS. Do you know what I was like two years ago? I did not wear designer cowboy shirts for one thing. I did not owe the telephone company three thousand dollars. And I hadn't met you two years ago. And you hadn't stripped the transmission in my Trans Am.
MATT	I like your car.
PANCHO	And you hadn't stolen my heart. No, It's been worth it…. I think it's been worth it. I'm glad. I'm glad it happened.
MATT	I like you, Pancho.
PANCHO	Because I've got your rushes. Because I've run your rushes maybe three hundred times. And every time I run that garbage footage, I get closer to it. Every time I watch my film go down the tubes, it gets clearer.
Because I see the light, Matt. I've seen the light, Matt.
Look at that light. Look at that sky. It is slushy, isn't it?
Don't tell me it will print up brighter. Don't tell me to throw more light on it. It looks like slush.
Do you know what happens in light like that?
(ironic) Not much.
It isn't Carnival in Rio, that's for sure. It isn't springtime in Miami. We don't have bright white California sun. We can't put mariachi bands on Walmer Road…
Incredible.
You know what is credible in light like that? You know what I believe?
There is some plot, some huge plot, I am at the centre of a gigantic plot. Some sinister secret power wants a film, wants a very bad film. To use as a secret weapon. *Man with a Gun* will bore people to death and I'm responsible. Do you know how I feel in light like that? I feel responsible.
MATT	Hey, Pancho…
PANCHO	I feel despair, I feel self-doubt, I feel suspicion, paranoia…
MATT	You sound depressed…

PANCHO   But I also feel responsible, so there's a happy ending. There's a Canadian happy ending. Where my picture is a gross of guitar picks, but we learn something from it, we're all better people for it.

I hate those films. I hate those slow, sad films. I hate it when nobody wins. I hate it when the dream dies, when that's the message, that the dream dies. I hate it when it isn't possible. Whatever you want, it isn't possible.

Because it is. It's possible.

MATT   What's possible?

PANCHO   All right, what have we got. We've got you. You're the hero. *(He studies MATT a moment.)* I can't take that seriously.

MATT   It's the cars.

PANCHO   It's a cartoon, Matt. You are out there larger than life, you are walking around as if you knew the answers, as if all the answers beamed straight down from heaven like the desert sun, but the sun comes at you sideways in Toronto. It's oblique. The light's oblique.

You're the only person in the picture with a suntan, have you noticed? But we can use it. Well, we have to use it. If it looks like you don't belong here, then you don't belong here. You're an agent, sure why not? You work for the CIA, that's all right, that reads, but you're up here in Toronto. What are you doing in Toronto?

MATT shrugs.

That's right. You don't know what you're doing here? This is some kind of plot. It's some kind of weird American takeover.

LAUREL   Energy.

MATT   Hey, Laurel…

LAUREL turns on more lights. We have bright white comedy lighting. MATT blinks.

LAUREL   Baz says energy. It's some kind of plot. It's some kind of weird American takeover.

PANCHO   Baz?

LAUREL   You know what we did last night? After the rushes? We walked all the way up Bloor Street, in the rain, remember it was raining, and Baz explained, about the film, about how we can make it work, because we can make it work…

PANCHO   Who's we?

LAUREL   What?

PANCHO   Who said "we."

LAUREL is setting up her director's chair.

LAUREL   Are you a Canadian nationalist?

PANCHO   Look, Laurel…

LAUREL   That is so petty, Pancho. That is so provincial…

PANCHO   You're New York. You keep saying, "I'm New York…"

LAUREL   I am a landed immigrant.

MATT   *(reads the name on the chair back, with difficulty)* That says "Laurel."

LAUREL   Do you like it?

PANCHO   Wait a minute…

LAUREL   I just ironed on the letters…

PANCHO   Wait a minute, Laurel…

LAUREL   Because I can help you, Pancho… and Baz, I can help Baz, if he's writing for Matt…

PANCHO   What's going on?

LAUREL   Baz is good, you know, isn't he?

MATT   I like Baz.

LAUREL   I love Baz.

PANCHO   Wait a minute…

MATT   Hey, Laurel…

PANCHO   It's not that easy, Laurel…

LAUREL   Do you know what he did last night, after the rushes?

PANCHO   Do you know what he's like in the morning?

LAUREL   He wrote a scene. For Matt.

PANCHO   He what?

LAUREL   In a bar. Matt is sitting in a bar. In Bemelmans.

PANCHO   Baz is writing?

LAUREL   Matt is drunk. And he's trying to explain to someone that he works for the CIA…

PANCHO   Let me see those.

LAUREL has a bunch of menus or cocktail napkins. PANCHO reads them on the way to the phone and as he dials.

LAUREL   And no one believes him.

MATT   That's he's drunk?

LAUREL	No, about the plot. He's screaming at them. "We're going to take you over. We're going to take you over."
MATT	We're going to take you over. We're going to take you over…
PANCHO	*(on the phone)* Hello, Baz… *(He breaks into Ukrainian.) Dobrhey-dhen cohanna, Bazoochkoo.*
LAUREL	But no one takes him seriously. Everyone thinks it's a joke.
PANCHO	*(on the phone) Meh dhi-stall-eh feellm nah-zhad.*
LAUREL	And he throws his glass. He breaks the mirror behind the bar.
MATT	He's talking Russian.
PANCHO	*(on the phone)* We got the picture back. You gave me my picture back.
LAUREL	He throws his money out on the bar. He's crying, "I'll pay for it. I'll pay for it."
MATT	Why is he talking Russian?
LAUREL	Read this, Matt… *(She thrusts a menu at him.)* Baz is good, isn't he?
MATT	Bemelmans.
LAUREL	Read the ballpoint, Matt.
PANCHO	*(on the phone) Nah-rash-tea.* He's a cosmonaut.
MATT	Did he rewrite the car chase?
PANCHO	*(on the phone) Shilakh trah-fid yiah teh-beh lew-blue.*
MATT	Because you can't have a car chase with subcompact cars.
	PANCHO approaches MATT.
PANCHO	*Mattuooshkoo…*
MATT	Who?
PANCHO	You're an astronaut, Matt.
MATT	You're talking Russian.
PANCHO	You're an astronaut, ex-astronaut…
MATT	Where are we anyway?
PANCHO	And you burned out of the space program, but the CIA can use you…
MATT	Where are we, Pancho?
PANCHO	You are sitting in Bemelmans looking for Russians…
MATT	*(about the Russians)* Where?
PANCHO	No, you're up here in Toronto, Matt, and it's sad and seedy how you got here, how you used to be an astronaut…
MATT	Hey, Pancho…

PANCHO	But we aren't going to talk about what you used to be, Matt.... We're going to talk about you, being here, because you're the hero, Matt... you will read as the hero in the Honda Civic... and you don't have to jump on the horse or crash the car...
MATT	Hey, I like crashing cars.
LAUREL	He means you don't have to do anything...
PANCHO	No, Laurel...
LAUREL	Because it's Canada, where heroes can be harmless.
PANCHO	I mean it isn't a comic book, Matt. I mean, I'm not as sure as you are there are Russians down there, eating fettuccine alfredo...
MATT	Huh?
PANCHO	Look, it isn't good guys, bad guys, but I do know you'll look good. I can make you look good, you know that, don't you?
MATT	Hey Pancho...
PANCHO	You know that. You trust me.
	PANCHO and MATT embrace.
LAUREL	You are such a Boy Scout, Pancho.
PANCHO	I like him, that's all. I want him in my film.
MATT	He likes me, that's all.
LAUREL	You are so provincial, Pancho.
PANCHO	You think so?
LAUREL	Small time. Small town. Petty.
PANCHO	Because I like it here, is that provincial?
LAUREL	Yes.
PANCHO	Because I want to make films about it. What I like, what I hate, what I think is funny.
LAUREL	Films are international.
PANCHO	You know what I think is funny? You.
LAUREL	Me?
PANCHO	No, it's okay, okay. We can use it in the picture... I love it, Laurel.... You are sitting there in Bemelmans, you are drinking Manhattans, you are looking south, letting other people tell you what to think...
LAUREL	Now look, cowboy...
PANCHO	I love it Laurel. And you should be in love. We'll say you're in love.
LAUREL	I am in love.

MATT	You think I used to be an astronaut?
PANCHO	*(to LAUREL)* You want to be in pictures.
MATT	*(demonstrates)* Ten, nine…
PANCHO	Good stuff, Matt…

> *PANCHO has an arm around MATT. He reaches out for LAUREL.*

MATT	Eight, seven…
PANCHO	*(to LAUREL)* I could put you in pictures.
MATT	Six, five, four…
LAUREL	I am in your picture.
MATT	Three…
PANCHO	*(to LAUREL)* Trust me.
MATT	Two…
PANCHO	*(to LAUREL)* I'll make you look good.
MATT	One…
PANCHO	*(to LAUREL)* Will you trust me?
MATT	Blast off!

> *Blackout. The last film begins.*
> *THE FILM*

CLAPPERBOARD GUY
> *Man Without a Gun.* Scene 116. Take 1.
>
> *A palm tree fills the screen.*

PANCHO	*(voice-over)* Wait a minute? What's that?
DENNIS	*(voice-over)* That's the palm tree, Pancho.
PANCHO	*(voice-over)* Get it out of there.
DENNIS	*(voice-over)* But you told Deedee…
PANCHO	*(voice-over)* Eighty-six the palm tree, Dennis.

> *Chainsaw begins. Fade up on an up-tempo version of "Oh Canada" as the palm tree topples. The camera moves in on a Canadian flag which has been masked by the palm tree as production credits are superimposed over.*
>
> *The end.*

ICETIME

ABOUT *ICETIME*

This play is based on a true story.

I met Justine Blainey because she played lacrosse with my son Alex every summer. They were both thirteen when Justine went to court, just so she could play in the same hockey league Alex played in. I thought her adventure should be in a play.

I think Justine is a heroine.

But what is a heroine? Some people think heroines and heroes are the best and the bravest or the smartest and the slickest. In comic books and video games or on television, the heroines and heroes have super powers.

Justine isn't a superhero. When this story starts, she's a twelve-year-old girl and the important thing about her is not that she's smarter than anyone else, or prettier, or even that she plays the world's best hockey. She plays good hockey. She wants to play better hockey. She just wants to play the best hockey she can, for as long as she can.

Plays are about people with problems.

As soon as someone says, "Okay, you're right. You can have what you want. Go ahead." Then the story is over, isn't it?

Plays are about people who can't get what they want.

Sometimes, the most important thing about heroines and heroes is that they want things to be different. They have a quest. They want to climb the mountain or find the treasure or rescue somebody. But they can't. There is some kind of obstacle. It could be the weather, or the dragons, or their own fears.

Sometimes in comic books and video games or on television, it's easy to tell the dragon from the princess or the good guys from the bad guys, but I think Justine's story is more interesting when everyone seems to be partly right and when Justine herself has doubts or feels alone.

Everybody in Justine's story loves hockey. No one wants to stop girls playing hockey. Sometimes it seems the better the arguments against Justine's case, the more interesting her story is. Of course I'm glad Justine won her case, but I'm also glad I got a chance to find out why some people thought that they should try to stop her.

Plays are about journeys.

The people in plays start in one place and end in another. The play lets us watch them grow and change and become a little different.

By the end of this story the whole world has changed a little bit, for Justine and everybody else.

This is the story of a twelve-year-old girl who won the right to play hockey the way she wanted to, who won the same right for other girls and, more importantly, it's the story of a twelve-year-old girl who helped people think about things differently.

I remember the father of one of the boys on a team where Justine might have played. He was a man who thought the world did not need changing. He thought that things were running fairly smoothly, so he was not so sure that Justine's adventure was a good idea.

He asked his son what he thought and his son said, "Why not? If she can make the team, why shouldn't she play?"

The father was amazed. He told everyone this story. "I learned something from my son," he said, and although he seemed surprised, he also seemed pleased.

I hope Justine's story will make you think about how you can change the world.

Carol Bolt
January 1992

Icetime was commissioned by Theatre on the Move in September 1986. It was workshopped in December 1986, directed by Jim Biros.

It was first produced in January 1987 with the following company:

Briar Boake	Justine
J. Brian Macdonald	David
Alison Macleod	Bitsy
Ian Prinsloo	Jason

Directed by Michel Lefebvre
Music by Kathy Nosaty

Characters

JUSTINE
BITSY
DAVID
JASON
LAWYER
SPORTS DOC
NEWS 1 & 2

Icetime

JUSTINE, DAVID, and JASON are dressing for a hockey practice, while BITSY is practising figure skating. JASON might be a goalie.

JUSTINE My name is Justine Blainey. I love hockey. And all I want to do is play hockey, the best hockey I can.

BITSY Justine, hockey is sweaty.

JUSTINE And compulsory figures are boring.

BITSY But it's graceful, figure skating is graceful.

She demonstrates ungracefully.

JUSTINE I guess I don't care about graceful.

BITSY Figure skating is what girls do, Justine.

JASON and DAVID take shots on each other as JUSTINE explains.

JASON Come on, David. Try to deke me out.

JUSTINE It all started when we were six years old. And my brother David went off to play house league hockey every Saturday morning.

JASON Hey, David…

DAVID Hey, Jason…

JASON Try to score on me. Come on.

DAVID Okay.

He scores. Easily. JASON sprawls, trying to block the puck.

JASON *(as he picks himself up)* Hey, try it again. I wasn't ready.

JUSTINE I went off to learn figure skating. There I was every Saturday morning, tracing compulsory figures, until I realized something.

BITSY has tired of figure eights and drifted over to where the boys are practising.

BITSY	Hey, David…. Hey, Jason…
DAVID	Hey, Bitsy.
BITSY	I've come to watch your game, okay.
JUSTINE	Everyone else was watching hockey. I mean, my mother, my father. They didn't care about compulsory figures any more than I did.

DAVID scores on JASON again. BITSY cheers wildly.

BITSY	Give us a D. Give us an A. Give us a V. Give us an I. Give us a D.
JUSTINE	I think I decided I wanted some attention. So I told my mother that I wanted to play hockey.
DAVID	My dad says hockey is like life. You know, it's about winners and losers and getting out there and fighting. He says I like it because of the adrenalin. But why do I like the adrenalin?
JUSTINE	The coach says David thinks too much. It slows him down.
DAVID	I like the feeling you get skating out on new ice. I like the feeling you get just before the ref drops the puck. I like the feeling you get on a breakaway, when you know everything's right, it's going to work, when you're concentrating so hard that things that were colour go to black and white, and you can't even hear the crowd anymore.
JUSTINE	David wrote a poem about hockey once.
DAVID	It wasn't a poem.
JUSTINE	He was inspired by one of those big machines that clean the ice.
DAVID	It was an essay.
JUSTINE	A poetic essay. He calls it "The Zamboni."
DAVID	Forget about "The Zamboni."
JUSTINE	"The Zamboni" by David Blainey.
DAVID	I was six years old at the time, so you can forget about my poetry.
JUSTINE	This is him. My brother. The poet.
DAVID	This is my sister. Justine. She thinks she's funny.
JUSTINE	*(to audience)* My brother and I both play minor peewee because we were born in the same year…. But we aren't twins…. Look, don't ask me to explain, okay?
JASON	Hey, David, how come you and Justine were born in the same year, but you're not twins.
JUSTINE	*(to audience)* …Because it's boring to explain.
DAVID	*(to JASON)* Because Justine was born in January and I was born in December.

JUSTINE   Because when people find out, all they say is "Boy, your mother must have been busy that year."

JASON   Boy, your mother must have been busy that year.

> *JUSTINE moves in to score on JASON, who tries for a save but sprawls on the ice.*

JUSTINE   She shoots. She scores. Sorry Jason.

JASON   Okay, once more. Go ahead. I'm ready this time.

> *She does. And she scores again.*

JUSTINE   I like winning. I can't help it. Sometimes I think victory is winning a trophy in a contact sport.

JUSTINE and DAVID

> *(sing)* My dad says
> Life is just like hockey
> And I say "Hey, wouldn't that be great?"
> I mean if life were like playing a game
> And if somebody told you the rules
> You would know what to do
> You could be on the team
> You could go find some ice
> And just skate.
>
> I remember
> One game
> I was right on the point
> And I deked out this guy
> And I set up a shot
> It can be such a high
> When you know that you're hot
>
> I remember
> That game
> I was back of the net
> And I came round the side
> Took a shot at the goal
> It can be such a high
> It's as good as a win
> When you try
>
> So when my dad says
> Life is just like hockey
> I say "Hey, wouldn't that be great?"
> I mean if life were like playing a game
> And if somebody told you the rules
> You would know just what to do

> You could be on the team
> You could go find some ice
> And just skate.

BITSY enters to join JUSTINE.

BITSY   My mom says winning is a zero-sum situation.

JUSTINE   A what?

BITSY   For every winner, there's a loser, right. I mean, you can't have winners without losers, right? Winners minus losers equal zero. And zero plus zero is not exactly progress.

JUSTINE   But what if you're winning. And you keep winning.

BITSY   My mom says sports is just aggression.

JASON   What's wrong with that?

BITSY   She says we have sports and the stock market and the nuclear arms race and it's all the same thing.

JASON   What's wrong with that?

BITSY   Did you show your father your report card, Jason?

JASON blocks one of DAVID's shots. They congratulate each other with high fives.

DAVID   Hey, Jason…

JASON   Hey, David…

BITSY   Jason's father thinks report cards are mucho serious. It's as if they were NHL scores.

JASON   My father's going to kill me.

BITSY   I guess he's not the kind of guy to understand. How you failed everything but cooking. But what I want to know is how did you pass cooking?

JASON   Hey, anyone can cook, Bits. I've heard even girls can cook.

BITSY   Your dad *should* kill you, Jason. *I* should kill you, Jason.

She goes after him. He uses DAVID as a shield.

JASON   What are you and Justine going to do this winter, Bitsy? I mean, when David and I are playing hockey? You want my recipe for ginger snaps?

BITSY   Justine's playing hockey.

JASON   Justine's playing ringuette or something. And David and I tried out for the Metropolitan Toronto Hockey League.

JUSTINE   You tried out for the East Enders. So did I.

JASON   Tell Justine she can't play MTHL, David.

DAVID	Why can't she?
JASON	Because MTHL is serious stuff. And Justine isn't serious.
BITSY	And Jason isn't real.
DAVID	Justine's serious.
JASON	My dad says that hockey is like life, David. And life is serious. You know my dad still plays hockey with guys he used to play with in the MTHL. And one of them is his bank manager and one of them is his accountant…
BITSY	Have I seen them? Do they have a beer commercial?
JASON	You know when my dad used to play in the MTHL, he knew a guy whose little cousin played with Gretzky. Now Gretzky is serious. Do you think Justine is Gretzky?
DAVID	Justine isn't. I'm not. Neither is your father.
JASON	Justine doesn't *care* about hockey.
DAVID	Sure she does.
JASON	She likes to play, that's all.
DAVID	So why can't she? If she's good enough? If she can make the team?
JASON	Oh sure.
DAVID	And she'll make the team, don't worry.
JASON	Oh sure.
BITSY	You're jealous, Jason.
JASON	Me?
BITSY	Aren't you?
JASON	Me? Jealous? It's called Barbie Plays Hockey.
JUSTINE	Get him out of here, David.
JASON	Me? Jealous? Of Miss Sweatpants of 1986?
JUSTINE	Does he want to live?
DAVID	Let's get out of here, Jay.
JASON	I guess the girls have got important stuff to do, like fix their hair or something.
JUSTINE	I warn you, Jason…
	JASON hides behind DAVID.
JASON	Help, David…
JUSTINE	You're dead meat.

JASON	It's Barbie Goes Rambo.
JUSTINE	Go and count your chest hair, Jason.
	The boys retreat. BITSY does elaborate things with makeup.
BITSY	Don't you think hockey is kind of, you know, jock?
JUSTINE	Jock?
BITSY	Don't you think guys will think you're kind of, you know, weird?
JUSTINE	I'm not weird.
BITSY	But what if people thought you were, Justine?
JUSTINE	Then they'd be wrong, Bitsy.
BITSY	Don't you ever, kind of, you know, worry? About what people think?
JUSTINE	Why should I?
BITSY	Because other people are important, Justine. You have to live with other people.
JUSTINE	Bitsy, why do people call you Bitsy?
BITSY	Beg your pardon?
JUSTINE	Don't you worry sometimes? Because everybody always calls you Bitsy? Don't you think that could mean people don't think you're serious?
BITSY	But I'm not serious.
JUSTINE	Bitsy…
BITSY	Why would I be serious?
JUSTINE	Okay. So you're thirteen years old. But say you were twenty years old. Say you wanted to be something. A brain surgeon.
BITSY	Hey, if I were a brain surgeon I could operate on you.
JUSTINE	Who ever heard of a brain surgeon named Bitsy.
	BITSY studies her hair.
BITSY	Should I dye this part? Green? Should I get a mohawk?
JUSTINE	Cut it out.
BITSY	You ever hear of a brain surgeon with a mohawk?
JUSTINE	Please stop acting like an airhead.
BITSY	But Justine, I am an airhead.
JUSTINE	We're supposed to be friends, aren't we?
BITSY	Sure. Except you're mucho serious. And you want me to be mucho serious. And get involved in sports and school politics and extracurricular activities. What you don't understand is I want to

be an airhead. Because the last time I thought seriously about growing up, I thought how am I going to get to grow up, I mean without blowing up or glowing in the dark. So I thought, why bother. When all I want is a platinum credit card.

JUSTINE   I don't believe you.

BITSY   About what? About being blown up?

JUSTINE   I don't believe all you care about is money.

BITSY   And I don't believe all you want is more ice time. Justine, give me a break.

JUSTINE   It's not all I want. I tried out for the team, that's all. Because I thought I could make the team. And I want to play. Hockey. For as long as I can and as well as I can.

BITSY   You know, you should get a mohawk.

JUSTINE   Bitsy...

BITSY   (*sings*) Girls all know that
Girls just want to have fun
They want to go to the Virgin Islands
Lie at the pool
Drinking Shirley Temples
When the sun
Goes down
They'll get down to the
Serious party

JUSTINE   (*sings*) I like cabanas
I like computers
Chocolate cookies
Tom Cruise's hair
And Sidney Sheldon
And Benetton sweaters
And I think I'd like to travel
Everywhere

BITSY   (*sings*) Girls all know that
Girls just want to have fun
They want to go to the mall on Friday
Don't want to think what will happen Monday
When the sun goes down
They'll have fun
Coming up with something.

JUSTINE   (*sings*) I like Nina
In *The Seagull*
Have you ever read that play?

My ambition is to travel
Want to see the world some day
My ambition is to travel
Everywhere!

THEY   *(sing)* Girls all know that girls
Just want to have fun.

> *JASON and DAVID enter.*

DAVID   Hey, Justine. The tryout's going to start.

> *A number which becomes faster and faster paced as JUSTINE, DAVID, and JASON try out and BITSY blows whistles, throws pucks on the ice, whatever.*

ALL   *(sing)* You try out for a lot of teams
It always works the same
They put you through a lot of drills
They want to see your shooting skills
And then they say, "We've got your name
So don't call us. So we'll call you"
And so you know you're kind of through
Unless they ask you back
To their next tryout.

You try out for a lot of teams
It always works the same
They put you through a lot of drills
They want to see your shooting skills
They want to see how hard you try
How long you last before you die
And they say "We've got your name
So don't call us. So we'll call you"
And so you know you're kind of through
Unless they ask you back
To their next tryout.

Can you deke and can you pass
Can you think about the game
Can you speed skate, are you fast
You try to cut it, you try to last

You try out for a lot of teams
It always works the same
They put you through a lot of drills
They want to see your shooting skills
They want to see how hard you try
How long you last before you die
And so they say "We only want the best

We'll see if we want you"
And so you know you're kind of through
Unless they ask you back to their last tryout.

> *At the end of the tryout, JUSTINE, DAVID, and JASON collapse.*
> *BITSY hands letters to JUSTINE and DAVID.*

BITSY   Justine! David! You have letters from the MTHL.

> *JUSTINE and DAVID open the letters and cheer.*

DAVID   Justine! We made it!

JUSTINE   You made it! I made it!

> *The kids congratulate each other until BITSY notices that JASON*
> *has wandered away from the group.*

BITSY   Hey, guys… Jason didn't get a letter.

DAVID   I know how you feel, Jay.

JASON   Do you?

DAVID   I know how I felt, last year, the first time I tried out and the coach told me I didn't make it, and I felt like someone threw a football at my stomach. And I felt sick. And I felt like the whole world was lit with a sixty-watt bulb.

JASON   That's because you're a wimp, David.

DAVID   Look, I know why you're mad…

JUSTINE   Look, Jason, I'm sorry…

JASON   Go ahead, David. Play for MTHL. Justine and I don't care, do we, Justine?

DAVID   Justine's playing, Jason.

JASON   Want to bet?

DAVID   They want to sign both of us.

JASON   You want to bet?

JUSTINE   Ask Mr. Johnson, Jason. He's the coach.

JASON   Let me spell it out to you in words of one syllable.

BITSY   Ignore him. He's jealous.

DAVID   Bitsy, mind your own business.

BITSY   I forgot. You're talking hockey. Of which I know nothing. Please. Excuse me for living.

> *Exit BITSY.*

JASON   The East Enders is an MTHL team, David, isn't it? And MTHL is a boy's league, isn't it? Boys, guys, males, creatures of the opposite sex,

	I mean, opposite from girls. And Justine's a girl. I mean, oh brother, your sister.... Point of information... she's a girl.
DAVID	She's a girl who plays hockey.
JASON	Don't hold your breath.
DAVID	What are you trying to say?
JASON	My dad's on the board at the MTHL, that's all. And you know what he'll say if Justine gets signed? Put it this way, David. It won't be "congratulations."
JUSTINE	Why shouldn't they sign me?
DAVID	She made the team, Jason. So they have to sign her.
JASON	Do they?
DAVID	What do you mean, Jason?
JUSTINE	Jason, wait...
	DAVID follows JASON out. BITSY calls JUSTINE as she is about to follow. She is dressed as the OWHL official.
BITSY	Wait, Justine...
JUSTINE	What?
BITSY	I'd like to talk to you a minute? Do you have a minute?
JUSTINE	What's going on.
BITSY	Look, I'm sorry if I startled you, but I'm from the Ontario Women's Hockey League, and I was watching your tryout.... And I just wanted to say that you were terrific, I thought you looked good.
JUSTINE	Thank you.
BITSY	...And I wanted to say.... Look, you don't have to play for the East Enders, you know.
JUSTINE	But I want to play for the East Enders.
BITSY	Because you may not know, but we have a girls' hockey league. Here in Toronto.
JUSTINE	Yes, I know that.
BITSY	So you could play for us.
JUSTINE	Look, no offence...
BITSY	We have a team in Mississauga...
JUSTINE	Look, girls' hockey... it's just that the level of play's not the same.
BITSY	I don't know what you're trying to say.

JUSTINE	The East Enders practise two hours a week and your teams practise one hour a week. Isn't that right?
BITSY	But that gives you more time for yourself.
JUSTINE	But if you don't live in Mississauga, then you have to drive an hour to get to the arena. Then you have to drive to Kingston to find another team to play. Isn't that right?
BITSY	But we only played Kingston twice last year.
JUSTINE	You still spend more time in the car than you do on the ice.
BITSY	There's a lot more to hockey than ice time, Justine.
JUSTINE	Look, no offence…
BITSY	You think girls' hockey is inferior, don't you?
JUSTINE	I just want to play the best that I can.
BITSY	You think you'll get more practise time and more support and more competition if you play with the boys.
JUSTINE	I *know* I will.
BITSY	But how is girls' hockey ever going to be any good unless we all work to make it better?
JUSTINE	Look, no offence…
BITSY	I wish you'd help us, Justine. Because you might need our help someday.
	She puts on the mask and exits.
JUSTINE	Wait… what do you mean?
	DAVID enters with his equipment bag and a letter.
DAVID	There's a letter for you, Justine. From the MTHL. You want me to open it?
JUSTINE	I can open my own mail, David. Thanks just the same.
DAVID	How come they sent you a letter and they didn't send me a letter?
	JASON, on a skateboard, enters with BITSY.
JASON	David, haven't you heard? You aren't on the team anymore.
DAVID	Very funny.
JASON	I guess they want Justine to break it to you gently.
JUSTINE	*(is reading the letter)* They don't mean this.
JASON	Don't worry, Justine. He can take it.
JUSTINE	It isn't fair.
DAVID	Justine, what's wrong?

JASON	Don't worry, David. If you're not on the team. You'll have that much more time to play video games.
	JUSTINE has crumpled up the letter and thrown it to the floor. DAVID picks it up.
DAVID	*(reads letter)* What is this?
JUSTINE	*(is on the verge of tears)* It's simple, isn't it? It's in English, isn't it?
DAVID	I don't understand.
JUSTINE	They say I can't play for the MTHL.
DAVID	But they signed you.
JUSTINE	They say MTHL is a boys' hockey league and it's against the rules for me to play. They don't want me.
DAVID	Look, Justine… I know how you feel.
JUSTINE	No. You don't.
DAVID	Look, Justine…. Remember last year…
JUSTINE	Look, David, please… please don't tell me that you understand. Because I don't care right now. If you understand or not.
DAVID	Last year, I tried out, and I didn't make it, and I felt…
JUSTINE	Go and write a poem about last year, David.
DAVID	Sure. Fine. Okay. I'll do that. "Last Year My Sister was a Human." By David Blainey.
	Exit DAVID. BITSY approaches JUSTINE.
BITSY	Look, Justine…. You feel bad, I know you feel bad…
JUSTINE	Go away, Bitsy. Please…
BITSY	I want to help.
JUSTINE	I just want to be alone. Is that okay?
BITSY	Justine, you're my friend. And this is important to you.
JUSTINE	And you can't help. No one can help. Go listen to your Walkman.
BITSY	*(exits)* Sure. Fine. This is hockey, of course. Of which I know nothing.
	JASON sits on his skateboard. He sighs.
JASON	I can help.
JUSTINE	You must be kidding.
JASON	No, really. I didn't make the team either, remember.
JUSTINE	That was different, Jason.

JASON   Okay, I wasn't good enough to make the team. So that was different. But it wasn't any easier.

JUSTINE   *(sings)* It makes me mad that
The world runs like a boys' club.
With rules that say
The way that we should be
Not just the way I wear my hair
The colours of the clothes I wear
You want to tell me where to go

And what to do when I get there
It makes me angry
Thinking
All I have to do
Is look pretty in pink
I get so angry
Thinking
Nobody thinks I can think

JASON   *(sings)* It's too bad that
The world runs like a boys' club.
With rules that say
The way that we should be
I know the kind of clothes to wear
And I don't care about my hair
But I don't know which way to go
Or what to do when I get there

It makes me wonder
Sometimes
How I'll get to be
What they want me to be
Because I wonder
Sometimes
What kind of club would take me?

THEY   *(sing)* It makes us sad that
The world is like a boys' club
With rules that say we're
On different teams
Why should we do all the things they tell us to do
If finally we wake up one day
Still wondering
What happened to our dreams.

        BITSY enters as JUSTINE's lawyer. She hustles JASON out.

LAWYER   It's all right. We can handle this.

JASON	Hey, wait… what's going on?
LAWYER	Don't worry, Justine. You can play hockey. We'll make sure that you play hockey.
JUSTINE	Who are you?
LAWYER	Your lawyer.
JUSTINE	But I don't need a lawyer.
LAWYER	Want to bet?
JUSTINE	Look, this is silly. Why would I need a lawyer?
LAWYER	Because the other side will have them.
JUSTINE	What other side?
LAWYER	I remember the first time I walked into a courtroom…. And the judge said "Speak up. I'm not used to listening to women." But you don't have to be afraid, Justine. You just have to stand up and say what you believe in.
JUSTINE	You want me to stand up in court? You want me to speak?
LAWYER	Don't worry. Because under the Charter of Rights no one can discriminate because of sex. So that means no one can stop you playing hockey if you're good enough to make the team.

JASON enters as SPORTS DOCTOR with charts and graphs.

SPORTS DOC
    Unless they look at the evidence.

JUSTINE	Who's that?

JASON swears himself in.

SPORTS DOC
    I solemnly swear to tell the truth, the whole truth, and nothing but the truth.

JUSTINE	What's going on?

SPORTS DOC
    Of course, I think that girls are equal to boys, Your Honour, and women are equal to men, in fact, I think, they're probably superior. But I have here a picture of an adolescent girl hockey player…

He unrolls it.

And here is a picture of an adolescent boy hockey player.

He unrolls it. The boy hockey player is much larger.

JUSTINE	What difference does that make?

SPORTS DOC

> May it please the court, as we see there are definitely differences between boys and girls, especially after puberty. There are physiological differences in muscle strength and muscle mass which put the female player at a disadvantage.

JUSTINE   But I made the team.

> *JASON ignores JUSTINE. He unrolls another chart.*

SPORTS DOC

> In fact, as we see on this graph, the average female hockey player is five foot five inches and weighs one hundred and thirty-eight pounds and the average male hockey player is six foot one inch and weighs one hundred and eighty-eight pounds.... Now those are American figures but that's one hundred and thirty-eight centim...

JUSTINE   But I'm just as tall as David.

LAWYER   Call David Blainey.

SPORTS DOC

> Now there's a safety factor involved here.

> *DAVID enters. JUSTINE pulls him over in front of the SPORTS DOCTOR.*

JUSTINE   David...

DAVID   What's the matter, Justine?

SPORTS DOC

> It's our job to minimize risks for these young people, so putting the post-pubescent male and the post-pubescent female together, the female will be at a disadvantage, that's unhealthy.

JUSTINE   Show him... that I'm just as tall as you are...

DAVID   Wait a minute...

SPORTS DOC

> We think sports are supposed to be healthy.

DAVID   You're not taller than I am, Justine.

SPORTS DOC

> There is also the psychological factor.

JUSTINE   I didn't say I was taller than...

DAVID   You just grew faster, that's all...

SPORTS DOC   We have found when girls play on boys' teams, it changes them... it changes their character, it makes them more independent, more aggressive, so when they go back to play on girls' teams...

JUSTINE   Look, I just want to show him, I'm almost as tall...

DAVID   *(to JUSTINE)* You have to be right, don't you?

JUSTINE   But he said you were six foot one.

DAVID   Justine, you're embarrassing me.

SPORTS DOC
           Girls who play on boys' teams then can't fit in with the other girls.

DAVID   You're making me look like some kind of freak. I'm not a freak. You're
           the freak.

SPORTS DOC
           I rest my case.

           Exit.

JUSTINE   Is that true? What he said? What you said? I'm too independent, I'm
           too aggressive, I'm a freak.

DAVID   No, of course not.

JUSTINE   But you said it.

DAVID   I got mad, that's all. When you said I was short.

JUSTINE   David, I didn't say you were short. David, he said I was short.

DAVID   I guess everyone has to speak, that's all. Both sides. I guess that's what
           court's about.

JUSTINE   But I feel like I'm on trial, David. Why am I on trial?

DAVID   You aren't. No, Justine, really. It's more like you're on a breakaway.
           And you're way out in front of everyone else, so you're the one that
           everybody watches.

           *JASON and BITSY burst on the scene with cameras and lights, as the
           CWHO News team.*

NEWS 1   Lights. Can we please have more lights?

NEWS 2   Her nose is shining, Garth.

NEWS 1   Makeup. Can we have makeup, please. Oh, here it is.

           He passes it to NEWS TEAM 2.

NEWS 2   Close your eyes, dear. Your eyes need a little colour.

JUSTINE   What's going on?

NEWS 1   Now we need a little colour. Background. Whose idea was this, Justine?

JUSTINE   What do you mean?

NEWS 1   This hockey thing. You wanting to play hockey. Was it your mother?
           Does she believe in women's liberation?

JUSTINE   It was my idea.

NEWS 1	Sure it was.
JUSTINE	I was jealous of my brother.
NEWS 1	Do you believe in women's liberation?
NEWS 2	This will be cute.
NEWS 1	Say anything you want, Justine. Say something really outrageous. We want to make *The National*.
JUSTINE	I just want to play hockey.
NEWS 2	That's cute.
NEWS 1	I was hoping for cuter.
NEWS 2	No, it's fine, Garth, really. It's sincere, really. It's just she has too much eye makeup, because you know, if her nose was shining, she could do that shtick "I want to play hockey" and people would say it was cute. She has too much makeup, Garth.
	JUSTINE tries to fight her way out from under their attentions.
JUSTINE	Hey, what's going on?
NEWS 1	I think it's cuter with the makeup.
JUSTINE	What about what I think?
NEWS 1	*(ignores her)* It's a statement. You know. She paints her toenails, but she still wants to score.
NEWS 2	What colour toenail polish do you wear, Justine?
JUSTINE	Who cares?
NEWS 1	Everyone cares, Justine. You're on the front page.
JUSTINE	Front page? Me? Why?
NEWS 1	Because of your court case, of course.
DAVID	*(enters with JUSTINE's hockey bag)* Justine! You won!
NEWS 2	You see. You won.
JUSTINE	I what?
NEWS 1	You won.
NEWS 2	Girl takes on MTHL.
NEWS 1	Girl plays boys' hockey.
NEWS 2	Do you really wear toenail polish?
JUSTINE	David! I won!
DAVID	That's what I said.
JUSTINE	Oh David… that means I can play!

DAVID	Hey…. Yeah…. Hey…. Here's your shin pads.
NEWS 2	Garth, are you getting this?
JUSTINE	I can't find my gloves. Have you seen them, David?
NEWS 1	How about you, David? How does all this make you feel.
DAVID	What do you mean?
NEWS 1	Since your sister is getting all this attention. And you're looking for her gloves?
DAVID	I feel fine.
NEWS 1	That's the boy.
DAVID	Why wouldn't I feel fine?
NEWS 1	Because she's on television. And all you've got to do is carry her equipment bag.

> NEWS TEAM 2 sets JUSTINE up beside her for a stand-up interview.

NEWS 2	Justine Blainey, the young girl who recently won the historical court case which allows her to play hockey with the Metropolitan Toronto Hockey League, was delighted by the news of her victory today. Well, Justine, are you ready to play?
JUSTINE	David, have you got my equipment?
NEWS 1	(pushes DAVID on camera) David Blainey, Justine's brother says he finds it hard to get used to the idea of Justine as a role model.
DAVID	Justine isn't a role model.
NEWS 2	How does it make you feel, David, to know that there are thousands of young people all over the province who are going to look up to your sister? Because she knew what she wanted to do and she did it. Because she took on the adult world and she won. Because she's the first young woman on the East Enders Minor Peewee Hockey team. She reminds me of me. I was a role model. Remember Garth, when I did my first stand-up in the Argos dressing room?
DAVID	I don't think Justine wants to be a role model.
NEWS 2	I don't think she has much choice. Where is she?
JUSTINE	(sings) Wait a minute Is this where I want to be This is more than a joke It's like going for broke Is it too fast for me. Wait a minute Do I really have to be

On that clean sheet of ice
It's so cold, it's so bright
Is it too bright to see

It seems so lonely
When you're the only
Dreamer in the dream
When the ice is as bright
And the ice is as hard
As the eyes on the rest of the team

Wait a minute
This is where I want to be
Right out here in the light
It's so cold
It's so bright
But not too bright to see

If I want it
I can have it
There's a high note
I can reach it
Just watch me.

JASON enters.

JASON   My father says you shouldn't play. For the East Enders.

JUSTINE   Your father can't stop me.

JASON   Want to bet.

JUSTINE   Hasn't he heard about the court case? Didn't he read it in the papers?

JASON   My father doesn't blame you, Justine.

JUSTINE   Blame me for what?

JASON   All this going to court. This legal action. He says it was feminists.

JUSTINE   I just want to play hockey, Jason.

JASON   He says these people are taking advantage of you. They're using you. They want to keep sending you back to court when you haven't got a hope.

JUSTINE   But I won, Jason. And the court said I could play.

JASON   My dad says he has nothing against you personally. But, he says, if you play, other girls will want to play.

JUSTINE   What's wrong with that?

JASON   He says he'll fight you to the death on this.

JUSTINE   To the death?

JASON	He says it's a matter of life or death. It's a matter of principle. He says you could kill organized hockey as we know it.
JUSTINE	Excuse me, Jason, but I have a practice.
JASON	He says you step out on that ice and he'll disqualify your team.

BITSY enters, putting on her lawyer's robes.

LAWYER	Don't worry, Justine.
JUSTINE	It isn't fair.
LAWYER	We'll go to court again.
JUSTINE	We went to court. They lost. Now they're changing the rules.
LAWYER	People do that sometimes. When they're losing.
JUSTINE	You know, when they first told me I couldn't play hockey, I felt sick. I thought it was me. They didn't want me on their team. And now that I've thought about it, I still feel sick, because it's true, isn't it? It is me they don't want, no matter how many times they say it isn't personal. It's because I'm a girl. But they still don't want *me*.
LAWYER	Don't worry, Justine. Don't cry.
JUSTINE	I'm not crying. Not exactly.
LAWYER	We'll win the appeal.
JUSTINE	You think so? Really?
LAWYER	They don't have a case. They're just stalling.
JUSTINE	But how long can they stall?
LAWYER	They hope you'll give up. Are you going to give up?
JASON	Hey, Justine? Is she one of the feminists?
LAWYER	I beg your pardon?
JASON	I think you should leave Justine alone.
LAWYER	I beg your pardon?
JASON	My dad says you think you'll make your reputation, taking Justine to court...
LAWYER	And what do you think, Jason?
JASON	Justine just wants to play hockey, don't you, Justine?
JUSTINE	Yes, but...
JASON	Do you know what will happen if you take the MTHL to court? If you sue the East Enders? The club will collapse, Justine.
LAWYER	Don't believe him, Justine.
JUSTINE	I don't know.

JASON	You won't be able to play. Neither will anyone else. Isn't that more important than what *you* want?
JUSTINE	I don't know.
LAWYER	Don't believe him, Justine.
JUSTINE	I don't know, please, both of you, leave me alone.
LAWYER	*(exit)* Fight for your rights, Justine.
JASON	*(exit)* Remember your friends, Justine.
JUSTINE	*(sings)* Wait a minute Does it have to be this tough? If I've passed every test And I'm doing my best Is that still not enough?
	BITSY enters.
BITSY	What's the matter, Justine?
JUSTINE	I can't do it.
BITSY	Do what?
JUSTINE	Be everything everybody wants me to be. All at once.
BITSY	At least you're not Jason. Because his dad wants him to be a Supreme Court judge.
	JASON enters with DAVID and a new equipment bag.
JASON	Congratulate me, girls.
BITSY	And Jason can't even spell Supreme Court.
JASON	I have signed with an MTHL team. I'm a Jet.
JUSTINE	Jason, the Jets are jerks.
JASON	Justine, you're jealous.
JUSTINE	They're jerks. They play bozo gazoonie hockey. They're all brain donors.
JASON	You're speaking of my dad's old team.
JUSTINE	I don't care.
DAVID	Justine, calm down…
JUSTINE	It isn't fair, David.
DAVID	I know how you feel but…
BITSY	Why do you think it's supposed to be fair?
JUSTINE	Jason gets to play MTHL. Just because he's a guy. It isn't that he knows the plays. It isn't that he has the skills.

BITSY	Did you ever think what it would be like if boys could play on girls' teams?
JUSTINE	Bitsy, don't start.
BITSY	If they let boys on the gym team or the swim team. They'd take over. There wouldn't be a girls' team.
JUSTINE	Bitsy, please… we're supposed to be friends.
BITSY	Or what if all the girls who were any good played for the boys' teams? I guess the girls' teams would be even wimpier, wouldn't they?
JUSTINE	I just want to do my best.
BITSY	You think other girls don't?
JUSTINE	You don't.
BITSY	Thanks Justine.
JUSTINE	You don't care about anything.
BITSY	What you don't understand is, I try not to care. About whether it's fair or not. Because I look at my mother who is just as smart as my father and she was his secretary before he married her. And I look at my sister, she is somewhat smarter than the jerk she married, isn't she? But she quit school to put *him* through school. And I look at my father who has a new secretary and a new wife and condo in Ajax and my mom has custody and she works at the IGA when he forgets to send support.
JUSTINE	It doesn't have to be that way.
BITSY	Doesn't it?
JUSTINE	Bitsy…
BITSY	You have to learn not to care about stuff like that, Justine. And sit back. You can listen to my Walkman.

Exit BITSY, followed by JUSTINE.

JUSTINE	You can't just quit, Bitsy. I don't want to quit.
JASON	Do you think Justine is better than you are? At hockey?
DAVID	That is such a stupid question.
JASON	She's faster than you are.
DAVID	We're different.
JASON	She's stronger than you are. Does that bother you?
DAVID	Look, Jason, she grew faster than I did. That happens. People grow at different rates. People have growth spurts and some people mature faster than other people, that's all.

JASON	You know what my dad heard?
DAVID	I don't care.
JASON	He heard the only reason you got signed was because of Justine.
DAVID	Oh, sure.
JASON	Your coach wanted Justine and your mom said he'd have to take you.
DAVID	Justine isn't playing, Jason. They won't even let her on the ice.
JASON	They say your coach wanted the publicity.
DAVID	Publicity? That's crazy.
JASON	He wants his name in the papers, that's all. Since he hasn't got Justine. And he has to play you.
DAVID	Drop dead, Jason.
JASON	The Jets were talking about Justine. At the practice. I mean in the locker room. The Jets are split about whether she should play or not. But they all want to get her against the boards. Get it? Against the boards?
DAVID	Jason, I'm going to kill you.
JASON	You know what the Jets say when other guys say stuff like that?
DAVID	What?
JASON	Go ahead and try it.

DAVID attacks JASON. They wrestle. JUSTINE enters.

JUSTINE	David… Jason…
JASON	What's that supposed to be? A suplex?
JUSTINE	Let go of him, David. He's bigger than you are.
JASON	This is a hold that our other goalie taught me. Called a camel drop.

And JASON leaves DAVID flat.

DAVID	Okay, Jason, you win.
JASON	I won? I really won?
DAVID	Are you happy now?

But JASON sees DAVID is still lying there.

JASON	Hey, David, did I hurt you?
DAVID	I'm fine, Jason.
JASON	Look, I'm sorry if I hurt you.
JUSTINE	You shouldn't fight. Either of you.
DAVID	Never mind, Justine.

JUSTINE	Why do guys have to fight all the time? What are they trying to prove?
DAVID	What are you trying to prove?
JUSTINE	I beg your pardon?
DAVID	Why can't you be like everybody else?
JUSTINE	Meaning what?
DAVID	Meaning why do you have to play hockey?
JUSTINE	You play hockey.
DAVID	I mean, why can't you be like your friends and stay home and watch *Dynasty*. Like Bitsy.
JUSTINE	Bitsy doesn't watch *Dynasty*.
DAVID	Bitsy doesn't make waves.
JUSTINE	What are you trying to say?
DAVID	Bitsy doesn't have her name all over the front page and the national news and the locker room walls.
JUSTINE	You don't care about me at all, do you, David?
DAVID	I just got murdered for you, Justine.
JUSTINE	You don't care what I want or what I do. As long as no one notices.
DAVID	Everybody notices everything you do. And everybody thinks you're weird.
JUSTINE	You know what really bothers me. If you want something, really want something, you just assume you can do it. You can play hockey or take off for Mexico, or start a rock band or join the forest rangers.
DAVID	You don't want to join the forest rangers.
JUSTINE	But if I did, David…
DAVID	You'd look pretty silly running through the forest in high heels.
JUSTINE	That's so stupid, David.
	BITSY enters as JUSTINE's lawyer.
LAWYER	Are you ready, Justine?
JUSTINE	You're so childish.
LAWYER	We're going back to court.
JUSTINE	How come you can be so stupid, David, and you can still expect to get to be what you want to be? Can you explain that?
LAWYER	Justine…
JUSTINE	And if I want something, all I get to do is dream about it.

LAWYER	We have a plane to catch, Justine. We're going to Ottawa. To the Supreme Court. This is real.
JUSTINE	The Supreme Court?
DAVID	Justine's going to the Supreme Court?
JUSTINE	*(sings)* What I remember is Lions all over the place And the crest that they have on the Face of the one dollar bill In the rest of the space And a clock like the one that they have at our school At the side of the men dressed in red I remember that more than Just why we were there What it was that we said All I remember, It wasn't a comfortable space All the chairs were too hard There were lions all over the place And the clock was like school And the judges all had the same face What I remember is lions What I remember is lions What I remember is lions
JASON	Your honour, may it please the court, we'd like to introduce a few statistics.
	He unfolds a long computer printout.
JUSTINE	*(sings)* And there were lawyers There were all these lawyers…
JASON	Your honour, we would like to introduce our list of expert witnesses…
	Another printout.
JUSTINE	*(sings)* There they were the lawyers And their old school ties were tied
JASON	Your honour, I'd like to introduce our reasons for delaying these proceedings…
	An even longer printout.
JUSTINE	*(sings)* They talk to you They smile at you As if they might agree with you

It's only that they've been employed
By the other side

DAVID appears as JUDGE to announce the verdict.

DAVID Will Justine Blainey approach the bench?

JUSTINE approaches.

In the matter of Justine Blainey versus the Metropolitan Toronto Hockey League, the court finds that the Hockey League has discriminated against Justine Blainey in not allowing her to play.

BITSY *(as JUSTINE's LAWYER)* Justine, we won!

JUSTINE We won?

DAVID And the court orders that she be allowed to play forthwith.

BITSY You can play! They have to let you play!

JUSTINE They do?

JASON *(as HOCKEY LAWYER, exit)* This isn't over.

DAVID The court further orders that the Metropolitan Toronto Hockey League be ordered to pay such court costs as Justine Blainey may have accrued to date.

JUSTINE Does that mean you get paid?

BITSY It means *they* have to pay me.

DAVID And the Metropolitan Toronto Hockey League will pay such court costs as may accrue in future.

JUSTINE Wait a minute…

BITSY It's wonderful, Justine.

JUSTINE He said, "Such court costs as may accrue in future."

BITSY It means they have to pay. If they take us back to court.

JUSTINE But it's over isn't it?

LAWYER Not according to the MTHL.

JUSTINE But I can play, can't I?

Her LAWYER hesitates.

The Supreme Court said that I could play. Forthwith.

JASON enters.

JASON My father says the ruling is unfair.

JUSTINE But it's the *Supreme* Court, Jason.

JASON He says he's not a quitter and the MTHL shouldn't quit. He says they have to keep fighting. On principle.

JUSTINE	What principle?
JASON	He says the club has rules. He says you can't just change the rules in the middle of the game.
BITSY	(*as JUSTINE's LAWYER*) Justine, if they don't let you play, we can take them to court.
JUSTINE	Again?
LAWYER	We can petition the Human Right Commission.
JASON	My father says what about his rights? What about everyone else's rights?
JUSTINE	Why is it so important? Keeping me off the ice?
LAWYER	Don't worry, Justine. Because you'll win. In the end.
JUSTINE	But how long will it take?
LAWYER	They hope you'll give up. They're just stalling.
JUSTINE	But how long can they stall.
LAWYER	Do you want to quit?
JUSTINE	No.
LAWYER	Even if it takes years.
JUSTINE	No, of course not.
LAWYER	Even if you're too old to play when they let you play
JUSTINE	I think I'll always want to play some kind of hockey. I'll be an old bag playing hockey. I'll be a hockey-playing grandma…
LAWYER	Even if you can't play in the MTHL. Even if you can't play for the East Enders.
JUSTINE	But there'll be other girls who want to play.
LAWYER	Yes, there probably will.
JUSTINE	I'll bet there will be. So I can't quit, can I? Because we will win, won't we?
LAWYER	Yes, I hope so.
JUSTINE	We will win. If not this year, then next year. And if it isn't for me, it will be for somebody else.
DAVID	Hey, Justine. Two on one.
	DAVID passes the puck to JUSTINE, who dekes past JASON who sprawls trying to save it.
LAWYER	She shoots.
DAVID	She scores.

JUSTINE   Thanks, David.

JASON   Hey, look, try that again. I wasn't ready.

> *JUSTINE and DAVID sing, joined by BITSY and JASON.*

My dad said
Life is just like hockey
And I said
Hey, wouldn't that be great?
I mean if
Life were like playing a game
Then if
Somebody told you the rules
You would know what to do
You could be on the team
You could go find some ice
And just skate.

> *The end.*

Yellow Ribbons

Program title: Studio Theatre
Broadcast date: 27 December 1987
Episode title: *Yellow Ribbons*

David Ferry	Alan
Booth Savage	Danny
Pat Hamilton	Mrs. Morrison
Alana Shields	Della

Joanne Shellenberg,	
Karen Birthright,	
Marsha Moreau,	
Barbara Redpath,	
Tara Cherenoff,	
Maja Ardal,	
Elliot McIver,	
Linda Stephen	Child's Voice

Bruce Vavenut	Suspect
Francine Volker	Therapist
Roger Dunn	Psychiatrist

Executive Producer and Director in Toronto and Vancouver: John Juliani
Announcer: Vicki Gabereau
Production Assistant: Kate Nickerson
Production Assistant: Loretta Joyce
Audio Engineers: Glen McLoughlan and Gene Loverock
Sound effects: Joe Silva and Matt Willcott

CHARACTERS

AMY
ANNA
SHANNON
ALLAN
KERRY
POLICEMAN
MRS. MORRISON
ANNOUNCER
CHILD
DISPATCHER
DONNIE
TV ANNOUNCER
MOSELY
SUSPECT
GIRL
ARCHIE
DELLA
ROBBINS
ABIGAIL

Yellow Ribbons

Sound: Shopping mall ambience continues under.

Sound: Fountain with running water continues under.

AMY   Where is she?

ANNA   Trust Abby.

AMY   We said three-thirty by the fountain.

Sound: Clock strikes four.

ANNA   You think we should call her?

AMY   You think she's still home? It's four o'clock, Anna.

ANNA   You think we should call her mother or something?

AMY   Be real, Anna…. Please, we can't tell her mother.

ANNA   But where is she, Amy?

AMY   Look, you know her mother. Her mother would freak.

ANNA   It's four o'clock and she said three-thirty. And she said don't be late, and this whole deal is her idea…

AMY   Look, her mother is going to go crazy. Her mother will think she's been kidnapped, her mother will think she's been white-slaved. Her mother will think she's dead.

Sound: Young girl screams and continues under with scary music as young girl says "No, please… stay away from me, no please…" etc. With sounds of scuffle and small shrieks… the effect of a very cheap thriller.

ALLAN   Shannon… Shannon?

SHANNON   Just a minute, Dad…

ALLAN   Dinner's on the table.

SHANNON	Can I eat it in here?
ALLAN	(*closer*) Does your mother let you watch junk like that when you're with her?
SHANNON	It's homework, Dad.
ALLAN	It's cheap television. Where's your sister?
KERRY	Hi, Dad
ALLAN	Do you let your sister watch junk like that?
SHANNON	She's only five years old, Dad.
ALLAN	Yes, I think that's the point.

Sound: Girl shrieks on TV.

SHANNON	I have to finish this tonight. It's for media studies.
ALLAN	What is media studies?
SHANNON	Did you know the average child watches sixteen thousand hours of television before she's eighteen. Did you know the average prime-time hour of television has six point eight acts of violence.

Sound: Girl makes a blood-curdling scream on TV.

KERRY	Daddy, what's that man doing?
ALLAN	Shannon, where's the remote switch?
SHANNON	Dad, you don't understand...

Sound: Scream cut off mid-screech.

SHANNON	I was taping that, Dad.
ALLAN	Shannon, give me a break.
SHANNON	Now I'm going to fail media studies.
ALLAN	Shannon, tape *Nova*. Tape *Masterpiece Theatre*.
SHANNON	You don't understand.
ALLAN	I understand I have to get to work and you and Kerry have to eat and I have to drive you to your mom's.
SHANNON	Junk TV is real, Dad. It's out there. And everybody watches it. Hundreds of millions of people, Dad...
ALLAN	Shannon, look, I don't have time...
SHANNON	Thousands of millions of people, they're all watching junk at any given moment of the day. And you want me watching *Mr. Rogers*.
ALLAN	...I don't have time to talk media studies.
SHANNON	*Mr. Rogers* is unreal, Dad. Life's not like that.

ALLAN	Can you eat your spaghetti? Can we get out of here?
SHANNON	You should know about life, Dad. You're a policeman.
	Sound: Phones ringing under.
POLICEMAN	No, ma'am, I am taking you seriously, but I can't report your daughter as a missing person…
MRS. MORRISON	*(filter)* My daughter as been missing for almost four hours….
POLICEMAN	Your daughter is twelve years old, ma'am. And she went to a mall.
MRS. MORRISON	*(filter)* What's wrong with that?
POLICEMAN	Nothing, ma'am.
MRS. MORRISON	Are you accusing me of something?
POLICEMAN	Look, ma'am, I've got kids of my own.
MRS. MORRISON	I told her she could meet her friends. In broad daylight. To go to a movie.
POLICEMAN	Kids, ma'am, and shopping malls. I mean some of them live in shopping malls…. Look, ma'am, her friends, the ones who called you when your daughter didn't meet them. I'll bet they're still down at that mall. And she could be too.
	Sound: Mall ambience continues under.
ANNOUNCER	*(on PA)* Would Abby Morrison, age twelve, please report to mall security?
	Sound: Child screams.
	(on PA) Would Abby Morrison, age twelve, please report to mall security?
CHILD	*(cries)* Mommy!
AMY	Anna, why do they say that?
ANNA	Amy, what did I tell you?
CHILD	*(cries)* Mommy!
AMY	Why do they say Abby Morrison, age twelve. I mean, Abby knows how old she is.
ANNA	It's her mom. I told you. She thinks it's a federal case.
AMY	Okay, listen Anna, let's not tell, okay? About, you know, okay? You swear?

ANNA	About what?
AMY	Because we could get in trouble.
ANNA	But we have to tell, Amy. If Abby's in trouble. I mean, don't we?

Sound: Sirens.

DISPATCHER	Attention all cars. Abigail Morrison. Age Twelve. Brown eyes, brown hair, wearing blue shorts, pale blue T-shirt...

Sound: Sirens fade out.

ANNOUNCER	*(on PA)* Attention shoppers. A twelve-year-old girl is lost in the mall. Abigail Morrison is wearing blue shorts and a blue T-shirt. She has brown eyes and brown hair tied back in yellow ribbons.... Attention shoppers. A twelve-year-old girl is lost in the mall...

Sound: Phones ringing under.

ALLAN	So, what's up Donnie?
DONNIE	The usual.
ALLAN	The usual woman in tears at your desk?
DONNIE	The usual Friday night missing kid.
ALLAN	The one on the blower?
DONNIE	You heard it. Morrison. Her name is Abigail. Brown eyes. Brown hair tied back in yellow ribbons...
ALLAN	Have you talked to the mother?
DONNIE	I was waiting for you.
ALLAN	Mrs. Morrison...

MRS. MORRISON sobs.

DONNIE	We know you're upset, Mrs. Morrison...
ALLAN	Detective Dobbs and I are only trying to help.
MRS. MORRISON	Please.... I want to help... please...
ALLAN	Was Abigail in trouble, Mrs. Morrison? At home?
MRS. MORRISON	Abigail?
ALLAN	Mrs. Morrison, please...
MRS. MORRISON	There's nothing wrong with Abigail. She's missing, that's all. She's been kidnapped, that's all.
ALLAN	We understand your concern, Mrs. Morrison... but in our experience, most children of your daughter's age...

DONNIE	There's some family squabble.
ALLAN	Some small thing.
DONNIE	Some argument. Some quarrel.
ALLAN	And the child is angry…
MRS. MORRISON	Not Abigail.
DONNIE	The child thinks she's going to be punished.
MRS. MORRISON	Not Abigail.
DONNIE	Mrs. Morrison, these kids. I mean, I have kids of my own.
MRS. MORRISON	I'm sorry, Detective…. I don't know your name?
ALLAN	He's Detective Dobbs, ma'am. And I'm Detective Bradshaw.
MRS. MORRISON	You think Abigail's a runaway, Detective Dobbs?
DONNIE	I'm saying it's a possibility.
MRS. MORRISON	Has your daughter run away, Detective Dobbs?
ALLAN	His daughter is three years old, ma'am, but I have a ten-year-old.
MRS. MORRISON	You don't understand.
ALLAN	I tell her, "Practise your piano," she says, "Why?" I tell her, "Eat your ice cream," she says, "Why?"
MRS. MORRISON	Abigail isn't a runaway.
ALLAN	Teenagers, Mrs. Morrison…
DONNIE	Who knows with teenagers, Mrs. Morrison.
MRS. MORRISON	Abigail is twelve years old. She is a happy child. She is a normal child. And she's been missing from her home for almost ten hours.

Music: Cheap newscast music.

TV ANNOUNCER

No word yet on the twelve-year-old girl who has been missing from her home since yesterday…. And tonight Abigail Morrison's mother issued this emotional appeal.

MRS. MORRISON

I know that somewhere, someone is holding my daughter against her will. And I have to ask… I beg you… bring her back… please, bring my daughter back..

> *Sound: Phones ringing under.*

MOSELY   *(filter)* Hello…. Police?

ALLAN   This is the police, ma'am.

MOSELY   *(filter)* I have some information. About the little girl who's missing.

ALLAN   Yes, ma'am.

MOSELY   It's my next door neighbour. He's been acting strangely.

ALLAN   Yes, ma'am.

MOSELY   *(filter)* He watches the children in the schoolyard. We're across the street from a schoolyard. And he spends a lot of time out front, you know, gardening. He pretends he's gardening… but if he's so fond of gardening, I say, what about his backyard.

ALLAN   Ma'am?

MOSELY   I say his backyard's a disgrace.

ALLAN   Is there something specific you'd like to report, ma'am?

MOSELY   Yes, of course. It's the screams.

ALLAN   The screams?

MOSELY   I heard a young girl screaming late last night. It woke me up.

> *Sound: Girl screams. Continues under. Like the movie Shannon watched. The same, only different.*

SUSPECT Mrs. Mosely, right?

ALLAN   I beg your pardon?

GIRL   *(continues under)* No, please… stay back… get away… no…

SUSPECT Mrs. Mosely… my neighbour… the old biddy next door. I woke her up watching this video, so she called the cops.

> *Sound: Another scream from the video continues under.*

SUSPECT You seen enough of this?

ALLAN   You watch stuff like this at three in the morning?

SUSPECT Is there a law against that? Is this something I don't know? Is this something new? You can't watch videos after 2:59 a.m., is that it? Look, this is an art film, imported.

ALLAN   I'm sorry, sir…

SUSPECT It's that old lady who's the weird one. You ought to check her out, if you want something weird. Do you want something weird?

ALLAN	Sir, if you want to lay a complaint against your neighbour...
SUSPECT	What about those cats?
ALLAN	I beg your pardon?
SUSPECT	You know how many cats she has? She has forty-five cats. No, I'm kidding. I'm sorry. Forget it. She's fine. She's a wonderful neighbour. Look, am I complaining? She's the ideal neighbour, I mean, talk about Neighbourhood Watch...
ALLAN	Sir, we're sorry to bother you...
SUSPECT	No, I'm glad you're so alert.... No, really... because when they come for me, you'll be there, won't you? Because Mrs. Mosely will be dialing 999, or whatever you dial.
DONNIE	It's 911.
SUSPECT	Sure. Whatever. Mrs. Mosely knows, so what? So what if she thinks I murder children.
ALLAN	We aren't talking about murder, sir.
SUSPECT	Aren't you?
ALLAN	No, sir.
SUSPECT	You're talking about that girl that's missing, aren't you? And how long has it been now? She's been gone two days.
	Sound: Phones ringing under.
AMY	The thing about Abigail was... I mean is... she used to make things up.
ANNA	Amy means she does, she still makes things up, but you know, not big things.
ALLAN	You mean she'd make up little things.
ANNA	That's right.
ALLAN	What kind of little things?
AMY	Like, you know, she said she met this guy...
ANNA	And he said she'd be good in movies.
AMY	And then she said, she said she had some friends.
ANNA	And we'd all meet him in the mall.
ALLAN	So you went to the mall to meet this producer.
AMY	No, of course not.
ANNA	That's what she told us... like we told you...
ALLAN	Beg your pardon?

AMY	That's how Abigail was. I mean is.
ANNA	She used to make things up. I mean she does. She makes things up.
ALLAN	You think she made this up? About the movie producer?
AMY	Would I go to the mall to meet a movie producer dressed like this? I mean because this is how I was dressed?
ANNA	I mean, we didn't even have eyeliner on.
AMY	We were wearing shorts. We were wearing T-shirts. We were wearing scruffies.
ALLAN	But Abigail was wearing yellow ribbons.
AMY	Beg your pardon?
ALLAN	She had her hair tied back in yellow ribbons.
ANNA	She wanted an excuse, you know, to go to the mall. Because her mother didn't want her hanging out.
ALLAN	So you think she told her mother that she went to meet this guy…
AMY	Don't be stupid.
ANNA	Are you kidding?
AMY	Her mother wouldn't let her meet a guy like that.
ANNA	Are you kidding?
AMY	She told *us* she was going to meet this guy. She told her mother something else.
ANNA	She told her mother my mother was there or something.
AMY	She told her we were all going shopping for camp stuff or something.
ALLAN	She said you were going to a movie.
AMY	Whatever. Look, we told you.
ANNA	Abby made things up.
	Sound: Brakes shriek.
	Sound: Street ambience continues under.
ALLAN	Excuse me, sir. Can you tell us about your sign here?
CONMAN	Why?
ALLAN	It intrigues us, sir. It interests us, right, Donnie.
DONNIE	That's right, Al. We're intrigued.
CONMAN	Are you guys cops or what?

DONNIE	Are you in business or what?
ALLAN	Look, you've got a sign here, it says "Extras. Movie Casting." And we wonder what that means exactly.
CONMAN	It means Extras. Movie Casting. What do you think?
ALLAN	What do you think?
CONMAN	Are you trying to say there's something wrong with casting movies?
ALLAN	Show him the picture, Donnie.
DONNIE	Have you seen this girl?
CONMAN	Wait a minute…
DONNIE	He looks worried, Allan.
CONMAN	Wait a minute… that's the girl that's missing.
ALLAN	Have you seen her?
CONMAN	Look, what do you think, I don't know what you think? Look, what do you think, I'm stupid… look, I read the papers, I know why you're here.
ALLAN	Have you seen this girl?
CONMAN	Look, this is a scam. All this "extras, movie casting." I admit it. A scam. So what. What's the harm? I mean people think they're going to get in movies, so we sign them up. And then we try to sell them acting lessons. That's what this is about. That's all that's happening… look, please, give me a break, please, be serious, this is lucrative. Am I going to give all this up to meet twelve-year-old girls in some shopping mall, someplace…? What do you think?
ALLAN	We think she thought she was going to be in movies.
CONMAN	No, man…
ALLAN	Who else tells twelve-year-old girls they're going to be in movies.
	Sound: Pinball arcade.
ALLAN	Excuse me, sir.
DONNIE	Are you Mr. Archie Rainbow?
ALLAN	Mr. Archie Rainbow of Ramrod Video productions?
ARCHIE	Screw off, pig.
ALLAN	Mr. Archie Rainbow, producer of *Debbie Does Dartmouth*?
ARCHIE	You two got an appointment or what?
DONNIE	We were directed to you, Mr. Rainbow, by one of your colleagues.
ALLAN	He said you might assist in our inquiries.

ARCHIE	You tell my colleague I'm in a conference.
	Sound: Video fireworks.
DONNIE	Have you seen the girl in this picture, Mr. Rainbow?
ARCHIE	No, man.
ALLAN	Will you look at the girl in the picture, Mr. Rainbow?
	Sound: Video fireworks.
ARCHIE	I'm sorry, man, but I'm saving earth from alien invaders.
	Sound: ALLAN slams ARCHIE against the wall and his video game dies.
ALLAN	I'm sorry, Archie, but I guess earth's doomed.
ARCHIE	Hey, man, take it easy.
ALLAN	Look at the picture for us.
ARCHIE	Hey, man, she's just a kid.
ALLAN	You mean you don't have kids down here?
ARCHIE	I mean if I saw a kid like this down here, man, I'd send her right back to Scarberia.
ALLAN	You've got twelve-year-old kids on the street for you, haven't you?
ARCHIE	Me?
ALLAN	You've got twelve-year-old kids in hard porn.
ARCHIE	You've got the wrong idea, man.
ALLAN	Have we?
ARCHIE	Hey, look, I don't make porn, I make erotica.
ALLAN	You can't even spell erotica.
ARCHIE	I know twelve-year-olds spell trouble, man. I know you can get shot for less.
	Sound: Loud rock club ambience continues under.
AMY	Anna, is he cute or what?
ANNA	*(can't hear)* What?
AMY	He said I should be a model.
ANNA	What?
AMY	He said he booked models. For TV commercials.
ANNA	For TV? Really?
AMY	No, Anna, he just says stuff like that. Do you think I believed him? Am I stupid or what?

ANNA	I can't hear you, Amy.
AMY	Anna, phone your mom, okay, and say you're staying over at my place and I'll phone my mom and say I'm staying over at your place.
ANNA	You want to stay out all night? Tonight?
AMY	Not by myself, Anna. Not after what happened to Abby.
	Sound: Scream cut off.
	Sound: Fusillade of gunshots with car chase continues under.
DELLA	Allan… Allan, its two in the morning.
ALLAN	I know.
DELLA	What are you doing?
ALLAN	Nothing?
DELLA	What are you watching?
ALLAN	Nothing.
DELLA	Isn't that Shannon's homework?
ALLAN	Susan has to send her to that stupid school…
DELLA	Don't ask your second wife to criticize your first.
ALLAN	You know what this is. It's a video montage. For her grade five English class. She can't spell but she has thirty-two different violent deaths. All from prime time.
DELLA	Shannon's just like you.
ALLAN	I don't know what you mean.
DELLA	She takes her work so seriously.
ALLAN	You think this is serious.
	Sound: Music changes to Journal theme.
DELLA	She has everything on that tape, doesn't she?
ALLAN	From *The National* to *Masters of the Universe*.
DELLA	At least she isn't watching soaps.
ALLAN	You think that's funny? My daughter isn't even twelve years old and she's preoccupied with violent death and you think that's funny?
DELLA	Shannon says that children watch sixteen thousand hours worth of television before they're out of high school.
ALLAN	I heard that, Della, and I said, "So what."

DELLA	She says that watching television is second only to sleeping. As an occupation. Do you believe that?
ALLAN	I think that watching television is like sleeping, don't you?
DELLA	Except that you can't sleep.
ALLAN	Look, I'm fine.
DELLA	You've been sitting there, playing Shannon's tape. Running it back and forth.
ALLAN	Look, don't worry about me. Look, I'm fine.
DELLA	It's the case, isn't it? It's because you think that girl is dead. She's dead and you don't know where or why or how. You don't know what to do about it.

Sound: Phones ringing under.

ANNA	Look, the thing is, we were talking to some kids last night.
AMY	You know, about Abby.
ANNA	And they thought we should come down here to the station...
AMY	Is it always like this? I mean the station.
ANNA	Amy...
AMY	I mean, it's so grotty. I mean, I'm sorry, but look at this ashtray.
ANNA	It doesn't matter about his ashtray.
AMY	Did you really smoke all those cigarettes?
ALLAN	Did you girls have something that you wanted to report?
ANNA	The thing is there's something that we didn't tell you about Abby, but it's kind of embarrassing...
AMY	The thing is, we didn't know what to say exactly.
ANNA	It's about Abby and her father.

Sound: Siren.

MRS. MORRISON	I don't understand what you want... why you're here.
ALLAN	Because your daughter told her friends that she'd been sexually abused.
MRS. MORRISON	Her friends?
ALLAN	Mrs. Morrison... please.
MRS. MORRISON	You mean, Anna, don't you? And Amy. Preteens in spandex.

ALLAN	We have to check out the report, Mrs. Morrison...
MRS. MORRISON	But you don't understand, about Abby's friends... because some of those girls can be ferocious little liars.
ALLAN	So you don't know whether this report is true, ma'am.
MRS. MORRISON	Of course it's not true. Of course it's well-known that girls fantasize about things like this, isn't it?
ALLAN	If we could speak to Mr. Morrison?
MRS. MORRISON	It's normal, isn't it? That kind of fantasy? Read Freud.

Sound: Phones ring under.

ALLAN	I tell her her husband's abusing her daughter and she tells me to read Freud.
DONNIE	Have you read Freud?
ALLAN	Her daughter's missing. She's been missing for a week but Mom wants to think it's a fantasy.
DONNIE	Because I have read Freud. As it happens, I mean.
ALLAN	Oh yeah. Sure you have, Donnie.
DONNIE	Have you heard of the Oedipus complex?
ALLAN	You've read Freud and Spiderman.
DONNIE	Girls fantasize about their fathers...
ALLAN	Please...
DONNIE	They do, Al. That's accepted. Face it.
ALLAN	Donnie, she's gone. We don't know where she is. That isn't fantasy.
DONNIE	So she tells these stories about her dad, Al... and they're not true so she feels guilty...
ALLAN	Sure.
DONNIE	So she runs. Look, that could happen.
ALLAN	Why don't you save those cards for "blame the victim"?
DONNIE	That could happen. You know it could happen.
ALLAN	She's gone. And Mom is quoting Freud. And Dad's in Paris on a layover. His daughter's gone and he's in Paris. I mean, where would you be, Donnie? If your kid was missing?
DONNIE	Al, he works for an airline. They *sent* him to Paris.

ALLAN	He could be here. He could be on the street looking for her. He could be sitting by the phone, waiting for it to ring.
DONNIE	Except he had to go to Paris.
ALLAN	He has responsibilities right here, doesn't he?
DONNIE	Everybody's not like you, Al.
ALLAN	You know what I'm thinking? That it's like they say. That happy families are all the same. But unhappy families are different.

Sound: Phone rings out.

DELLA	*(calls)* Allan…
ALLAN	Kerry…
DELLA	Are you still on the phone? Look, your omelette is ready.
ALLAN	Kerry… Kerry… are you there, honey? Kerry?

KERRY giggles.

ALLAN	Kerry? It's Daddy, honey.

Sound: Phone dropped.

DELLA	What happened?
ALLAN	Kerry?
DELLA	You told her we'd take her to the zoo and she fainted?

Sound: Muffled giggles before phone picked up.

ALLAN	Look, Kerry… you know what Daddy wants to do tomorrow?
SUSAN	*(filter)* Sorry, Allan.
ALLAN	I was talking to Kerry, Susan.
SUSAN	She's not talking to you.
ALLAN	Put her back on the phone, Susan.
SUSAN	*(filter)* Look, you know how it is.
ALLAN	Put her back on the phone, please.
SUSAN	*(filter)* Allan, she is five years old. She has a short attention span. I think she's watching a potato chip commercial.
ALLAN	She's my daughter, Susan, and I…
SUSAN	*(off receiver)* Kerry, please, leave the cat alone, honey…
ALLAN	I want to talk to her. I have the right to talk to her.
SUSAN	*(Filter. Breezily, overly polite.)* One moment, Allan *(muffled)* Kerry, honey, Daddy wants to talk to you…. Kerry? It's Daddy…. On the phone… *(on phone)* Sorry, Allan, this could take some time.

ALLAN   Susan…

SUSAN   *(off mic)* Kerry, don't you want to talk to Daddy?… Kerry? Daddy wants to talk to you.

ALLAN   Forget it, Susan.

       Sound: Phone hung up in anger.

DELLA   Forget it, Allan.

ALLAN   Bitch.

DELLA   Don't let her get to you.

ALLAN   She has my daughter.

DELLA   She's her mother, Allan…

ALLAN   She is turning my daughter against me. She is poisoning my daughter.

DELLA   You can't be serious.

ALLAN   She won't let me talk to her, will she? You heard…

DELLA   Allan. Think. Kerry is five years old. She doesn't have much conversation. Face it, how long do you *want* to talk about her fingerpainting.

ALLAN   I want to talk to her.

DELLA   And you did talk. She told you. She is in her post-minimalist phase. Or whatever she said. So she went off to watch *The Friendly Giant*. Do kids still watch *The Friendly Giant*?

ALLAN   She was watching cartoons.

DELLA   What's wrong with that?

ALLAN   It is Saturday morning.

DELLA   Allan, you watched cartoons on Saturday morning. I watched cartoons on Saturday morning.

ALLAN   Her mother switches on the television automatically. Every Saturday morning…

DELLA   You think she should be in advanced French lessons?

ALLAN   She is watching the World Wrestling Federation. She is watching potato chip commercials.

DELLA   Never mind, Allan…

ALLAN   She'll grow up with popcorn for brains. Like her mother.

DELLA   She'll grow up like a media critic. Like you and Shannon.

       Sound: Afternoon TV sound continues under.

ALLAN	Shannon, turn that thing off.
SHANNON	But I have to watch *Days of Our Lives*.
ALLAN	No, you don't.
SHANNON	Dad... Simon holds Alice hostage and she suffers a heart attack. Frankie and Jennifer help Sasha get rid of Nick the pimp by calling Roman.
ALLAN	I don't care, Shannon.
SHANNON	*(explodes)* No, you don't. You don't care about anything...
ALLAN	Shannon...
SHANNON	You don't care about me.
ALLAN	Shannon, wait, come back here...
SHANNON	You care about yourself, that's all. You care about your stupid self and your stupid work and that's why Mom left you.

Sound: Door slams.

ALLAN	Shannon...

Sound: Phones ringing.

ANNA	Your work must be fascinating, Mr. Bradshaw.
AMY	And very stressful too. I guess that's why you smoke so much.
ALLAN	You didn't come down here to tell me to quit smoking.
AMY	No, this policeman picked us up on Yonge Street.
ANNA	He wanted to know what we were doing.
AMY	He wanted to send us home.
ANNA	He thought we were loitering, so we told him we came into town to see you.
AMY	Because we were helping you with your investigation.
ALLAN	You want me to drive you home now?
ANNA	We want to tell you about Abby.
AMY	The thing about Abby is, she drank.
ANNA	I mean, she drank a lot.
AMY	Look, it wasn't because she liked it.
ANNA	It was because she felt bad... you know, about her father.
AMY	And her father is a pilot.
ANNA	So they had these little airline bottles.
AMY	And we would pour them into Coke bottles.

ANNA	We would buy these big Coke bottles and pour the booze into them and carry them around all day.
AMY	Except it kind of made us sick.
ANNA	But it didn't make Abby sick.
AMY	So she kept doing it. And when her mom got suspicious about the little airline bottles, she started buying them. You know, getting kids to buy them.
ANNA	Because you know, we know kids.
AMY	We know kids who know kids who know people who'll do anything.

> *Sound: Phones out.*

> *Sound: Ambience shopping mall continues under.*

ALLAN	They know everyone these kids.
DELLA	Did you believe them?
ALLAN	They know dope dealers, they know hit men.
DELLA	They think they know it all, that's all.
ALLAN	I'm sorry. I don't want to talk about my work. Look, Susan used to hate it when I talked about my work.
DELLA	Never compare your first wife to your second wife.
ALLAN	After we were separated, she'd come down for inspections. She'd come tearing into the apartment. Into the bedroom where the kids slept and she'd find the sheets all on the floor. She would go tell her lawyer that the kids were sleeping without sheets. And they'd file a deposition that said I was neglectful…
DELLA	Forget it, Allan.
ALLAN	Me? Neglectful? You know all she cares about? *Santa Barbara.* Eden is kidnapped by Cain at gunpoint after her escape. Cruz comes to her rescue and shoots Cain.
DELLA	You've been reading Shannon's homework.
ALLAN	Susan watches that stuff. As if it were John Stuart Mill.
DELLA	Look, you don't read John Stuart Mill.
ALLAN	It's because she wants Kerry.
DELLA	She's Kerry's mother.
ALLAN	That's not the point.
DELLA	Do you want Kerry? How much time did you spend with her before?

ALLAN	That's not the point.
DELLA	When you and Susan were together.
ALLAN	I want to see her now. She's my kid, isn't she? She's my daughter and I want to see her and I have access. I have papers that say I have access.
DELLA	Where is she anyway?
ALLAN	I beg your pardon?
DELLA	Kerry... where is she?
ALLAN	She's over by the pet store. She's looking at the puppies.
DELLA	No, she isn't, Allan.
LOUDSPEAKER	
	Will Kerry Bradshaw please meet her father at the information desk in the concourse.... Will Kerry Bradshaw please meet her father at the information desk in the concourse?
ALLAN	Kerry, honey, are you all right?
KERRY	I'm fine. I met a man.
ALLAN	Kerry, sweetheart...
KERRY	A nice man. He gave me ice cream.
ALLAN	Kerry, honey.... Look, you know what Daddy told you...
DELLA	Kerry, honey, Daddy's told you not to talk to strangers.
KERRY	But you weren't there, Della.... And he knew where the lost children went.

Sound: Sirens.

ALLAN	What's going on?
POLICE ONE	Police officers.
ALLAN	What's wrong?
POLICE TWO	There's nothing wrong.
ALLAN	Where's Shannon? Shannon?
SHANNON	Dad?
POLICE ONE	We're responding to a complaint, sir.
ALLAN	Shannon? Are you all right?
SHANNON	Dad... Mom called...
ALLAN	So what? Who cares? Why, Shannon?
POLICE ONE	Your wife called your daughter, sir. She was concerned to find her alone.

ALLAN	She was concerned to what?
POLICE ONE	You did leave her alone.
ALLAN	It's eleven o'clock. In the morning.
POLICE ONE	You're daughter's ten years old, isn't she?
ALLAN	I went to the supermarket.
POLICE ONE	And the beer store, I see, sir.
ALLAN	And the beer store. Which is beside the supermarket.
POLICE ONE	It's against the law, sir…
ALLAN	Look, I know the law…
POLICE ONE	Then you know better than to leave a child under twelve unattended. While you go to the beer store.
ALLAN	I know the law, I'm a policeman.

Sound: Gunfire. Firing range ambience continues under.

DONNIE	Bull's eye. *(shot)* Bull's eye. *(shot)* Bull's eye. You know, some days you're an overachiever, aren't you, Al?
ALLAN	Some days it's like that.
DONNIE	You know why that is? Your wife is on your case again.
ALLAN	She's my ex-wife.
DONNIE	Am I right? What is it? Custody?
ALLAN	She is out of her mind.
DONNIE	My wife's the same.
ALLAN	Not a chance.
DONNIE	Maybe worse.
ALLAN	Really? Worse. You think so? You know where she was this weekend? You know why she let me have the kids? She was being reborn. She was reliving her birth experience. It seems that when she was born, she heard the doctor say, "She's a real little runt," and she's never gotten over that. So she goes out every weekend. She screams "I'm okay, you're okay" to the bunch of loony tunes she calls her group…
DONNIE	My wife spent the weekend with her lawyer.
ALLAN	Susan's sleeping with her lawyer.
DONNIE	My wife's charging me with child abuse.
ALLAN	I beg your pardon?
DONNIE	Beat that.

ALLAN	She's charging you with child abuse?
DONNIE	That's a ten, isn't it? That's Olympic-class bitch, isn't it?
ALLAN	What kind of child abuse?
DONNIE	You see. That's what it's like. I say I'm charged with child abuse and you believe it.
ALLAN	Look, Donnie…. I'm sorry…
DONNIE	You know, sometimes, I don't see those targets. I imagine she's standing there. I have her right in the middle of my sights and I aim right between her baby blue eyes.

> *Sound: Gunfire.*
>
> *Sound: Very civilized music. Philip Glass.*

ALLAN	He says he didn't do it.
DELLA	And you believe him?
ALLAN	He's my partner, Della.
DELLA	Look, I'm sorry, Allan…
ALLAN	He's my friend.
DELLA	And his wife has medical reports. And his daughter has nightmares.
ALLAN	Look, I know his wife. His wife's hysterical.
DELLA	*I* get hysterical. When I think about the way people think. About girls.
ALLAN	Della, please…
DELLA	Girls are sexual beings, aren't they? Isn't that what they say.
ALLAN	Della, don't get hysterical *now,* okay?
DELLA	Your grandmother was married when she was seventeen, wasn't she? And there are fifteen-year-olds who look seventeen. Hell, there are twelve-year-old girls, you can see them at the bus stop in the morning, and they're going on thirty-five, aren't they?
ALLAN	Della, what's going on?
DELLA	Girls are attractive. You've seen girls you've found attractive. Not children. A sixteen-year-old isn't a child.
ALLAN	Is it something I said? Am I missing something here?
DELLA	I forgot about it. For years. I remembered my happy childhood. My mother and I… we both pretended that it hadn't happened. Look, maybe it didn't happen. My mother knew. I knew she knew.

But she had to pretend she didn't know, didn't she? Because if she knew, she'd have to leave him.

ALLAN Della, look...

DELLA So I couldn't tell Mother what was happening. Because she wouldn't believe me. She couldn't believe me. But you believe me, don't you? You used to believe me.

ALLAN Of course I believe you.

DELLA It happened, didn't it? I didn't imagine it, did I?

ALLAN Look, your father was different.

DELLA How could I imagine a thing like that? That's sick.

ALLAN Della, don't. Look, I believe you. Please.

DELLA Look, maybe it didn't happen.

ALLAN I beg your pardon?

DELLA Look, I'm sorry... look, I don't believe in analysis, you know that.

ALLAN Della, what's wrong?

DELLA Freud... you know, Freud, he's such a crock.

ALLAN Della, calm down...

DELLA Except for repression.

ALLAN Della, please...

DELLA Repression, the unconscious, I believe in that, because I spent years not remembering. I spent years thinking that my dad was just a dad, like everybody else's dad. Like your friend Donnie says he is.

ALLAN Look, you don't understand, Della.

DELLA I understand.

ALLAN Donnie's wife... she wants custody, that's all.

DELLA Why shouldn't she have custody? If he abused his kids?

ALLAN Look, he didn't abuse his kids. Look, do you think he's some kind of monster?

DELLA Oh, Allan...

ALLAN Look, I know you've never liked him...

DELLA How do you tell? What do monsters look like? Have you ever met my father? Do you want to see his picture?

ALLAN Donnie is my partner, Della.

DELLA And you know him.

ALLAN	That's right.
DELLA	And he isn't a monster.
ALLAN	That's right.
DELLA	Are monsters like Abigail Morrison's father, is that it? When he comes back from Paris will he show you the hair that he has on the back of his hands?

Sound: Phones ring under.

ALLAN	Morrison knows. He knows what happened.
DONNIE	You don't know that.
ALLAN	Donnie, you saw him. You heard him. He knows. He knows something.
DONNIE	He says he never touched her.
ALLAN	And what do you want him to say? I confess?
DONNIE	I would like some sort of indication.
ALLAN	Indication?
DONNIE	Some sort of evidence.
ALLAN	She told her two friends what was going on, Donnie, didn't she?
DONNIE	You know what this reminds me of?
ALLAN	Those kids have seen him with a smoking gun, if you'll pardon my French.
DONNIE	It's a kangaroo court here, isn't it?
ALLAN	No, Donnie…
DONNIE	You should go down to work for Children's Aid, Al. On my case. You'd fit right in.
ALLAN	Look, Donnie…. Just because I think he's guilty…
DONNIE	You don't know…
ALLAN	…That doesn't mean I think you're guilty…
DONNIE	When a kid says something, then it doesn't matter what you say.

Sound: Clock ticking.

ROBBINS	Detective Dobbs's daughter made this drawing for us, Mr. Bradshaw.
ALLAN	Mrs. Robbins, I don't think I understand.
ROBBINS	I asked his daughter where her father touched her.
ALLAN	I don't see this as a drawing.

ROBBINS	Would you like me to interpret our findings for you?
ALLAN	The kid scrawled all over the paper.
ROBBINS	That's what's significant, you see.
ALLAN	Beg your pardon.
ROBBINS	It shows that the child has a lot of hostility.
ALLAN	It shows that the child has a green crayon.
ROBBINS	She was asked where her father touched her, and she scrawled all over the picture. She crumpled up the paper. She threw the drawing onto the floor.
ALLAN	You are talking about a child who is three years old.
ROBBINS	I am talking about a baby who describes oral sex with perfect clarity.
ALLAN	Detective Dobbs says his daughter is very suggestible.
ROBBINS	Yes, of course he does.
ALLAN	She tells this story in the morning. She denies it happened in the afternoon.
ROBBINS	Of course.
ALLAN	Don't you find that significant?
ROBBINS	Denial is normal. It's part of the process.
ALLAN	Do you know what you're saying?
ROBBINS	She's accusing her father, Mr. Bradshaw. Frankly, I would find it strange if she didn't deny it at some point.
ALLAN	Her father can't win, can he?
ROBBINS	I don't see any reason why he should.
ALLAN	She says he did this and you believe her.
ROBBINS	Children don't lie about things like this.
ALLAN	And she says he didn't do this and you still believe he did.
ROBBINS	We've gone into this case very thoroughly, Mr. Bradshaw…
ALLAN	What's this guy supposed to do?
ROBBINS	Your friend has been the subject of a comprehensive and professional evaluation.
ALLAN	Do you have any physical evidence?
ROBBINS	Physical evidence?
ALLAN	Of the alleged assault?

ROBBINS	Do you want us to wait till he injures the child? So you'll have evidence?
ALLAN	You're assuming he's guilty, of course. You've made up your mind that he abuses children. That's your professional opinion, isn't it? And there's nothing he can do about it, is there?
ROBBINS	He can obey the court order. He can stay away from her. He can see us in court.

Sound: Phones ring under.

ABIGAIL	*(home videotape sound quality continues under)* Okay, Dad… look at the camera… wave, do something… say something…. Dad, Mom's taping this and you're wasting tape… *(continues under)*
DONNIE	Abigail Morrison. With her father.
ALLAN	On videotape.
DONNIE	Does she seem frightened of him?

ABIGAIL laughs on tape.

Does she seem nervous? Or uncomfortable?

ALLAN	No.
DONNIE	Beg your pardon?
ALLAN	No, she doesn't.
DONNIE	You know why you want to think her father did it?
ALLAN	I don't want to think her father did it.
DONNIE	You do, Al. Because then you can believe she's still alive. You can think she's run off. You can go on showing her picture to people up and down Yonge Street.

ABIGAIL laughs on tape.

You don't want to think that it's some stranger, it's some nutcase. You don't want to think she's dead.

ALLAN	Will you turn that thing off?
DONNIE	Will you watch her with her father? Look, she's happy with him, Allan.
ALLAN	All right, I'll turn it off.

Sound: Videotape out. Phones continue under.

DONNIE	They have my kid on videotape.
ALLAN	Where's rewind on this thing?

Sound: Rewind continues under.

DONNIE	The social worker's talking to her. She has one of those dolls. They say they're anatomically correct.... I don't know about that, but I can tell you that their Daddy-doll makes me look sad.
	Sound: Rewind click.
ALLAN	Eject the tape for me, Donnie, will you?
DONNIE	I think *that's* child abuse. To give a kid a doll like that. What do you think?
ALLAN	I want to put the tape away.
DONNIE	So my daughter undresses the doll, she undresses all her dolls, what's wrong with that? They say that she's preoccupied with sex, but they're the ones who keep asking her about sex, isn't that right?
ALLAN	Take it easy, Donnie...
DONNIE	So the doll is undressed. So the social worker says, "Is that what Daddy did?" And my daughter picks up the doll by its privates and the social worker says, "Did you touch Daddy like that?" And the kid is obviously bored, she doesn't know what's going on, and she spins the doll over her head by its over-sized but anatomically correct parts and she says, "I'll show you what Daddy did." This is all on the tape, you can watch it on tape. She said, "Daddy plays Superman" and she throws the doll against the wall and laughs. She thinks it's a joke. They think its hostility. They think it's evidence and she thinks it's a joke.... I wish you could see that tape, Al, and I wish you'd watch this one.
	Sound: VCR on.
ABIGAIL	*(on tape continues under)* Okay Dad... look at the camera... wave, do something.... Dad, Mom's taping this and you're wasting tape.
DONNIE	She's there with her father. She's happy with her father. She loves her father...
ALLAN	Look, Donnie, I'm sorry...
DONNIE	You don't want to watch, do you? You don't want to see what's there.
	Sound: Videotape continues under with child's giggles and random shuffles.
ROBBINS	*(on tape)* Missy? Why are you undressing the Daddy-doll?... Missy? Is that what Daddy did?
ALLAN	How much more of this junk do you have?
ROBBINS	This isn't junk, Mr. Bradshaw.

ALLAN	You think this is evidence? You take a three-year-old and you grill her for almost two hours…
ROBBINS	I don't think I'm grilling her.
ALLAN	You want her to tell you that her father molested her.
ROBBINS	And she wants to tell me.
ALLAN	She's sure taking her time.
ROBBINS	Of course the child finds this kind of accusation difficult.
ALLAN	And so you help her.
ROBBINS	I support her, Mr. Bradshaw.
ALLAN	So you tell her that you know she wants to tell, she'll be a brave girl if she tells, Mommy wants her to tell.
ROBBINS	This isn't evidence, it's therapy.
ALLAN	Therapy!
ROBBINS	The child is a victim, Mr. Bradshaw.
ALLAN	You told the child to tell you she's a victim.
ROBBINS	I told her I believed her. I told her I support her. I think that's crucial. Acceptance of her statement, validation of her experience. That's crucial to the victim's psychological survival and that's the most important part of the therapeutic process…
ALLAN	You call it therapy.
ROBBINS	It is therapy.
ALLAN	But you use it for evidence, don't you?
ROBBINS	Are you involved in your partner's defence, Mr. Bradshaw?
	MISSY laughs on tape.
	(on tape) Missy? Missy? Is that the way that you touch Daddy? Is that what Daddy does?
ALLAN	Now this is where she throws the doll against the wall.
	Sound: On tape. Thud. Doll is thrown against the wall.
	On tape, MISSY laughs delightedly.
ROBBINS	*(on tape)* Missy…
MISSY	*(on tape, garbled)* Daddy's Superman.
ALLAN	What was that she said?
ROBBINS	She said, "Daddy's Superman."
ALLAN	You think that's evidence? What's that evidence of, Mrs. Robbins?

ROBBINS	You saw her throw her doll against the wall. Her father doll.
ALLAN	But she thinks he's Superman, Mrs. Robbins, doesn't she? She thinks he's flying.
ABIGAIL	*(on videotape)* Okay, Dad… look at the camera… wave, do something… say something…. Dad, Mom's taping this and you're wasting tape… *(continues under)*
DELLA	Allan…. Allan, do you know what time it is?
ALLAN	There's the monster, Della. Mr. Morrison with Abby.
DELLA	Allan, please come to bed.
ALLAN	There he is. On tape. As large as life. What do you think? Remind you of home?
DELLA	Is that supposed to be a joke?
ABIGAIL	*(laughs on tape)* Daddy, please…
ALLAN	I'm sorry, Della…. I'm tired, I don't know what I'm saying.
ABIGAIL	*(on tape, not frightened)* Daddy, don't please.
DELLA	He's tickling her. Did he do that a lot?
ALLAN	Is there something wrong with tickling, Della? Really?
DELLA	That's what my mother said. When I tried to talk about my father.
ALLAN	But Abby didn't tell her mother.
DELLA	Is that what her mother says? Do you believe her?

Sound: Videotape out.

MRS. MORRISON
Look, I have been through this with Abby's therapist.

ALLAN   With Abby's therapist?

MRS. MORRISON
He says there can be many reasons for this kind of accusation.

ALLAN   Like?

MRS. MORRISON
Like the child's wish for power, for seduction, conquest.

ALLAN   Did Mr. Morrison see this therapist as well?

MRS. MORRISON
This was not Mr. Morrison's problem, Mr. Bradshaw.

ALLAN   He wasn't concerned? When his daughter said he was molesting her?

MRS. MORRISON
This was Abigail's problem.

Sound: Piano. Tap-dance chorus line continues under.

DONNIE More videotapes.

ALLAN The new family album.

DONNIE Can you go back? On that shot of the audience?

ALLAN It's funny, isn't it? We have her on tape. She is there with her father. At her birthday. She is there at her tap-dance recital and we've watched it all, haven't we? To get to know her. To see who else is watching her. In the tape of the swim meet there's a guy with another camera. Is that him? Is he sitting back in some condo in Mississauga, right now, watching people taping him taping her? If he is, I don't know. I don't know anymore. I don't feel evil coming off the tape. I don't feel anything.

Sound: Phone rings. ALLAN picks it up.

ALLAN Bradshaw.

WOMAN'S VOICE *(filter)* Are you investigating the little girl's murder?

ALLAN Yes, ma'am.

WOMAN'S VOICE *(filter)* I have some information. You believe me, don't you?

ALLAN We'll follow up on your report, ma'am.

WOMAN'S VOICE *(filter)* It's a judgment of God, on those who have fallen into evil…

Sound: ALLAN hangs up.

DONNIE Allan?

ALLAN Thank you, ma'am.

DONNIE Allan, are you all right?

ALLAN God's wrath. That explains it. We'll have Morrison down here to say that God told him to do it.

DONNIE Morrison was down here.

ALLAN When?

DONNIE He volunteered to take some tests. You know, lie detector, those psychological things.

ALLAN Is he still Dr. Jekyll?

DONNIE The reports aren't back yet, Allan, wait, where are you going?

ALLAN I'm going to find Mr. Hyde.

Sound: Hospital ambience continues under.

PSYCHIATRIST

He's a normal man.

ALLAN   What does that mean?

PSYCHIATRIST

That I've talked to your suspect, detective. And I've administered a number of diagnostic tests. On the Projective Drawings, there is normal male identification.

ALLAN   What does that mean?

PSYCHIATRIST

On the Minnesota Multiphasic Personality Indicator, he's normal. On the Myers-Briggs Type Indicator, he's normal. On the revised Bender Gestalt…

ALLAN   He's normal.

PSYCHIATRIST

There is a fair degree of anxiety, but that would be normal for his circumstances.

ALLAN   You say he's normal.

PSYCHIATRIST

He's accused of murder, Mr. Bradshaw, so naturally he's anxious.

ALLAN   You say he's normal, but I have witnesses to say he's not.

PSYCHIATRIST

Detective Bradshaw…

ALLAN   I have two witnesses who tell me he abused his daughter.

PSYCHIATRIST

It's naive, Mr. Bradshaw, to think these children are telling you the truth.

ALLAN   It's what?

PSYCHIATRIST

It's psychiatrically naive.

ALLAN   Look, you'll have to forgive me.

PSYCHIATRIST

Do you have children, Mr. Bradshaw?

ALLAN   Yes, I do. As a matter of fact.

PSYCHIATRIST

Because it's common psychiatric knowledge that children of all ages fantasize, they engage in explicit and intensive sexual fantasies… many of which my seem perverse to the adults around them.

ALLAN   Does sexual abuse ever happen, do you think?

PSYCHIATRIST

I beg your pardon?

ALLAN   When does it stop being fantasy? What would it take to convince you that it really happened?

PSYCHIATRIST

I suppose you've been told that children don't lie about things like this. Perhaps they don't…

ALLAN   Perhaps?

PSYCHIATRIST

Far be it from me to be the first to call a young child a liar, Mr. Bradshaw, especially in court, but why don't we imagine they believe the abuse really happened. In the same way they believe in Santa Claus.

ALLAN   Do we have to find the body for you?

PSYCHIATRIST

Beg your pardon?

ALLAN   Before you admit the abuse could be real?

PSYCHIATRIST

Please read Freud, Mr. Bradshaw.

ALLAN   Look, I have read Freud, as it happens.

PSYCHIATRIST

I congratulate you.

ALLAN   You think policemen don't read Freud.

PSYCHIATRIST

If you've read Freud, you'll know what I'm saying.

ALLAN   You're saying they're making it up. And they don't even know that they're making it up. Because these three little girls want to sleep with their fathers, but they know they can't, so they imagine that your client is making moves on them.

PSYCHIATRIST

Have you ever heard of the Salem witch trials, Mr. Bradshaw?

ALLAN   I don't care about the Salem witch trials.

PSYCHIATRIST

But it's true, isn't it, that in Salem, little children testified that they saw women flying through the air on broomsticks.

ALLAN   I care about this girl. This missing girl.

PSYCHIATRIST

And these people were persecuted, prosecuted, punished.

ALLAN   The girl's in trouble, but what happens when she tries to tell us? Do we tell her it's a fantasy?

PSYCHIATRIST

It's true, isn't it, that some of these men and women were put to death on the testimony of children and it's generally accepted, is it not, that these men and women weren't witches, they didn't fly through the air on broomsticks. You don't really believe there are witches, Detective... or do you?

Sound: Phones ringing under.

MRS. MORRISON

Do you believe that Abigail is dead, Detective Bradshaw?

ALLAN   I don't know, Mrs. Morrison.

MRS. MORRISON

If she is dead, will she be in heaven?

ALLAN   Mrs. Morrison...

MRS. MORRISON

She was only twelve years old. But she wasn't perfect. She was willful...

ALLAN   Mrs. Morrison, please...

MRS. MORRISON

I've tried to think why it happened, you see, if it could have been some kind of judgment.

ALLAN   I don't think I believe in judgments, Mrs. Morrison...

MRS. MORRISON

But you don't know, do you?

ALLAN   I suppose not.

MRS. MORRISON

Sometimes I think I want to think she's dead, that's awful, isn't it?

ALLAN   Look, Mrs. Morrison...

MRS. MORRISON

I'm her mother and I want to think she's dead. Because he wouldn't have killed her, would he? I mean, whatever else he did, he wouldn't have killed her...

Sound: Police siren.

Sound: Car interior with cheerful country western song
continues under.

ALLAN I want him, Donnie.

DONNIE Then go get him, tiger.

ALLAN They say he's normal. He's testing in the normal range. They say he's anxious, that's all. They say that's normal, that he should be anxious. So I said what if he wasn't. What if they tested him and he wasn't anxious? Would that be normal? Would that mean he was innocent? He knew he was innocent and so he wasn't anxious?

DONNIE Hey Allan, take it easy...

ALLAN Or would it mean he was psychopathic? He knew he was guilty and he didn't care?

DONNIE Back off. Cool down.

ALLAN It's all very scientific, isn't it?

DONNIE Walk away from it. Really.

ALLAN He didn't do it. Because he's normal. They say he's normal, so he didn't do it. But who's normal, Donnie?

DONNIE You're asking me who's normal?

ALLAN They say he's conservative, consistent, and responsible. And stable, Donnie, this guy's stable...

DONNIE They say I beat my wife and abuse my kid.

ALLAN What happens with the guys they say aren't normal? What happens to the whackos, Donnie? Where are the whackos? The whackos are locked up somewhere, aren't they? Taking tests while under care. The whackos are the ones we've caught, aren't they? So what about the guys still out there?

DONNIE What about the women out there?

ALLAN Beg your pardon?

DONNIE I blame the battered women's shelters.

ALLAN I beg your pardon?

DONNIE These bimbos sit around these battered women's shelters, bitching. It starts there, that's where everything starts. That's where they get these ideas, from each other.

ALLAN What ideas?

DONNIE You wait till Susan starts with it. She'll tell you what her social worker says... what the other broads are saying...

ALLAN What is Brenda doing in a battered women's shelter?

DONNIE	Look, partner, you know how it is.
ALLAN	No, I don't.
DONNIE	I'm not doing anything that anyone else isn't doing. I'm not doing anything weird. I don't "abuse" my wife and kid, I don't call that "abuse."
ALLAN	What do you do, Donnie?
DONNIE	You know where all this comes from? I blame women's lib.
	Sound: Lakeshore. Water laps under.
DELLA	Allan? Are you all right?
ALLAN	I'm fine, Della.
DELLA	You're so quiet.
ALLAN	Do you want to talk?
DELLA	I want to help, Allan.
ALLAN	You know there was a body here last summer. Right here on the beach.
DELLA	Allan, please…
ALLAN	No, you wanted to talk. Let me tell you about it. Yellow ribbons. All around the site. They say, "Police Lines. Do Not Cross." And inside the lines, we sifted through sand. For evidence. In case our guy had dropped his credit card or his monogrammed handkerchief. In case he'd smoked a cigarette… we checked out cigarette butts, beer cans, garbage, looking for garbage…
DELLA	Please, don't…
ALLAN	She was eight years old.
DELLA	Allan, you're killing yourself.
ALLAN	Eight years old and he killed her. And he sat here, smoked a cigarette…. It was late June…. She died about nine o'clock… and he sat here, right here where we're sitting, and he smoked a cigarette and watched the sunset.
DELLA	He sat here?
ALLAN	They say cops are like crooks. Do you believe that?
DELLA	No, of course I don't.
ALLAN	No, really, Della. Think about it. Because, sometimes, I think it's true. Sometimes I'm looking at a crime scene and I can see it, the way it was, I can get inside the guy's head…. I sat here, Della, last year, and I watched the sunset, and I saw the body, lying there, beside me…

DELLA	We don't have to talk about your work.
ALLAN	You don't. I do.
DELLA	Not all the time.
ALLAN	I'm sorry, Della. I can't help it.
DELLA	There are so many other things in the world…
ALLAN	So many beautiful things, is that right?
DELLA	Allan, don't…
ALLAN	There are little girls with yellow ribbons in their hair. Little girls and yellow ribbons…. They're beautiful and I'm supposed to keep them safe. That girl down there on the beach. In the T-shirt that says Jennifer, you think she's safe.
DELLA	Allan, please…
ALLAN	She'd be easy.
DELLA	Please don't do this to yourself.
ALLAN	I could have her in the car within three minutes. You want to bet?
DELLA	Of course not.
ALLAN	What will it be? Her mother's sick or there's a puppy we've found.
DELLA	Allan, stop it.
ALLAN	Hey, Jennifer…
DELLA	Allan, stop it… are you crazy?

       Sound: Sirens.

       Sound: Knock on door.

DONNIE	Do you want me to tell her?
ALLAN	No, it's all right. I'll tell her.

       Sound: Door opens with security chain on.

MRS. MORRISON
       Yes…

ALLAN	Mrs. Morrison?

MRS. MORRISON
       Yes…

ALLAN	It's Allan Bradshaw, Mrs. Morrison. I'm working on Abigail's case.

       Sound: Security chain off.

MRS. MORRISON
       You've found her? Where is she?

ALLAN Mrs. Morrison…

MRS. MORRISON
Where is she? Why isn't she with you? What's wrong?

ALLAN We haven't confirmed that it's Abigail, Mrs. Morrison.

MRS. MORRISON
I don't understand

ALLAN We need someone to make an identification.

MRS. MORRISON
I don't know what you mean.

ALLAN Is Mr. Morrison at home? Could we speak to him, ma'am?

DONNIE Is there someone who could stay with you, Mrs. Morrison? Is there someone we could call.

MRS. MORRISON
No…

ALLAN Mrs. Morrison…

MRS. MORRISON
You think she's dead, don't you? You're telling me she's dead.

ALLAN Do you want us to call a neighbour, Mrs. Morrison?

MRS. MORRISON
I thought it would be over. You'd come to the door just like this and you'd say she was dead and it would all be over.

ALLAN Mrs. Morrison, we'd like to help you.

MRS. MORRISON
You don't think he did it, do you?

ALLAN You mean Mr. Morrison?

MRS. MORRISON
It isn't over. I thought it would be over.

ALLAN We'll keep working on your daughter's case, Mrs. Morrison. Till we find out what happened.

MRS. MORRISON
But it isn't over, is it? And it isn't going to be.

Sound: Police siren.

Finis.

Two Cowboys
and a Lady

Two Cowboys and a Lady begins a three-part story which features three Canadians in Hollywood. We bring you Yvonne De Carlo, famous for harem pants and wearing rhinestones in her navel. Walter Wanger called her the most beautiful girl in the world. We remind you of Rod Cameron. The studio publicity machines told us he wanted to be a Mountie, and maybe he did, but he ended up a contract player; one of those useful actors who appear in dozens and dozens and dozens of films, in Rod's case, mostly Westerns. And finally we recall Jay Silverheels: the Lone Ranger's faithful side-kick, Tonto. A lacrosse champion and Golden Gloves contender before he became an actor, he is probably the most talented of our three performers. He was also an Indian, the son of a full-blooded Mohawk chief, the publicity tells us. The stories take place from the late 1930s to the mid '50s, in the glorious days when there were real movies and real movie stars; before the advent of television changed the industry violently and forever.

There may be those who would say that Cameron and De Carlo and Silverheels aren't real movie stars and they may be right. It could be that Yvonne was too much like Dorothy Lamour. It could be that Rod was imitation Randolph Scott. And of course, Jay almost always played Indians and at this stage of Hollywood history, the cowboy was the starring role, the Indian played support. So these won't be plays about superstars. De Carlo and Cameron, Silverheels, they're working actors, they make B pictures, they do television when it's not fashionable to do television. They're ordinary people caught up in extraordinary circumstances: ordinary people, simple people, decent people, trying to live in Hollywood where Marilyn Monroe said, "They'll pay you ten thousand dollars for a kiss, and fifty cents for your soul." These plays were written during an ongoing debate on the values and virtues and dangers and drawbacks of free trade with the United States. Here are three young adventurers who set out to compete in the American market and who see no reason to fear. I wondered, as I wrote the plays, if I could learn anything from their journey. It's the middle of the depression. A shy ballet student from Vancouver, a six-foot four-inch sandhog born in Calgary, and a remarkable Indian athlete from Brantford, Ontario are on their way to Hollywood to seek their fortune.

Carol Bolt
(1998)

Program title: Stereo Theatre
Broadcast Date: 31 July 1988
Episode title: Part One of Canadians in Hollywood – *Two Cowboys and a Lady*

Tom Macbeth	Milan
Eric Schneider	Silverheels
Don MacKay	Brown
Norman Browning	Cameron
Angela Gann	Marie
Judith John	De Carlo (Yvonne)
Janet Hodgekinson	Felicia
Arty Shaw	Shaw
Joseph Scala	Brecht
Janey Woods Morris	Yvonne's Mother

Others heard in the play:
Owen Foreign
William Samples
Bill Butt
Paul Batton
Barney O'Sullivan
Marcy Goldberg
Wally Marsh

Produced and Directed in the Vancouver studio by Don Kowalchuk
Production Secretary: Loretta Joyce
Sound Engineer: Gene Loverock
Sound Effects by Joe Silva
Musical Director for the series: Brian Tate
Story Editor for the series: Tom Lacky

Characters

MILAN
SILVERHEELS, J. (aka HARRY SMITH)
CRAZED MAN
MARIE WINDSOR
BROWN
EMPLOYMENT OFFICER
CAMERON (RODERICK/ROD COX)
YVONNE DE CARLO (PEGGY ANN MIDDLETON)
MARIE MIDDLETON (PEGGY'S MOTHER)
WAITER
FELICIA
DANCE CAPTAIN
AUDIENCE
DRUNK
MAÎTRE D'
CLAPPER
DIRECTOR
ASSISTANT DIRECTOR
SHAW
BRECHT
FIREMEN

Two Cowboys and a Lady

PART ONE

Canadians in Hollywood

Sound: Distant roar of Madison Square Garden fight crowd continues under.

MILAN	How do you do it, Harry?
SILVERHEELS	Me? Do what?
MILAN	Stay so cool?
SILVERHEELS	You think I'm cool?
MILAN	Here we are in New York. All the way from Brantford, Ontario. All the way from the Six Nations Reserve, all the way to New York City.
SILVERHEELS	It seems further.
MILAN	And you're fighting in the Golden Gloves and I walk in the dressing room and you're stretched out on the bench, asleep.
SILVERHEELS	Look, I wasn't asleep.
MILAN	You know if it were me instead of you, I'd be unconscious.
SILVERHEELS	I was thinking, that's all.
MILAN	Thinking what?
SILVERHEELS	What's important.

Sound: Fight in progress continues under. We're at ringside.

CRAZED MAN	Hit him!
WINDSOR	Is this the kid you came to see, Joe?
BROWN	Harry Smith.
WINDSOR	This Indian kid? From Canada? You really think he can compete?

BROWN	I got money on him.
CRAZED MAN	Come on, you bum. Hit him again!
WINDSOR	I hate boxing.
BROWN	How can anyone hate boxing?
WINDSOR	I just think that it's too much like life. They keep hitting each other.
BROWN	Pretend it's a picture, Marie.
WINDSOR	Did we have to sit ringside?
BROWN	You like boxing in pictures.
WINDSOR	But in pictures, they show you how the poor kid is from the wrong side of the tracks and boxing's the way he gets out of the slums…
BROWN	Maybe that can be arranged, Marie.
WINDSOR	Oh, yeah?
BROWN	Look, this is the Golden Gloves, isn't it? And there are people here from Hollywood, from Vegas, aren't there? I mean, we're here, aren't we?
WINDSOR	You think this kid belongs to Hollywood.
	Sound: Crowd gasp. Fight action increases.
BROWN	This could be his big break.
	Sound: Crowd sigh.
WINDSOR	Except he's down.
BROWN	Get up, kid.
WINDSOR	He's getting beat.
BROWN	Come on! Get up! You can do it.
WINDSOR	I guess he's going back to Brantford. Canada.
	Sound: Cross-fade boxing match to:
	Sound: Clock ticking.
	Sound: Fly buzzes lazily, in and out, under.
EMPLOYMENT	Roderick Cox?
CAMERON	Yes, sir. That's me.
EMPLOYMENT	I don't think New York State Employment can help you, Mr. Cox.
CAMERON	Look, I need work. Look, times are tough.
EMPLOYMENT	I see it says here you're from Canada.

CAMERON	But I've got papers. I can work here in the States.
EMPLOYMENT	Yes, Mr. Cox, but…
CAMERON	I have been working. And I was laid off. I wasn't fired.
EMPLOYMENT	It says you've been a house painter and a taxi driver and a camp cook.
CAMERON	And a door-to-door salesman and a walking billboard.
EMPLOYMENT	You may think of all this as experience, of course…
CAMERON	You can see, I've been working for more than ten years. I've been working since I was twelve years old.
EMPLOYMENT	This is all unskilled labour, Mr. Cox.
CAMERON	I've been a mason.
EMPLOYMENT	Look, I have a suggestion. Look, why not go back to Canada?
CAMERON	Because I live here. Because my family lives here.
EMPLOYMENT	Times are tough, as you say. And we have our own hewers of wood and drawers of water.
CAMERON	I'll do anything.
EMPLOYMENT	Have you ever been a sandhog?
CAMERON	Sandhog?
EMPLOYMENT	A sandhog works in construction. Underground or underwater. Under compressed air.
CAMERON	*(is aware of danger)* Yes, I know what a sandhog does.
EMPLOYMENT	It's work. Take it or leave it. What other choice do you have?
	Sound: Rehearsal piano and class of tap dancers with a gay thirties kind of tune like "Sunny Side of the Street" which continues under.
DE CARLO	Mom, I can't play the Mandarin Gardens.
MARIE	Why not, Peggy Ann?
DE CARLO	Because it's the second biggest club on Pender Street.
MARIE	So what, Peggy Ann?
DE CARLO	I am sixteen years old, Mom.
MARIE	I know that.
DE CARLO	And the Mandarin Gardens has an all-star revue.
MARIE	Remember I'm your mother. So I know how old you are.
DE CARLO	The Mandarin Gardens books big names. Imported acts. From the United States.

MARIE	That's right.
DE CARLO	You know who played there last week?
MARIE	Peggy Ann, don't you see?
DE CARLO	Sally Brander.
MARIE	I said this was their chance. To discover the new Sally Brander.
DE CARLO	But, Mom…
MARIE	This could be their big break! They could give you your big break!
DE CARLO	You rush down here, Mom, and you pull me out of my tap dancing class…
MARIE	Because it's a whole week's booking and you've got featured billing. "Peggy Ann Middleton. Fresh from her successful LA–San Francisco tour."
DE CARLO	What LA–San Francisco tour?
MARIE	Three months ago. That counts as fresh.
DE CARLO	Mom, we went to LA to visit Aunt Jean.
MARIE	And we toured it, didn't we?
DE CARLO	You mean on the sightseeing bus?
MARIE	Peggy Ann, are you afraid to dance at the Mandarin Gardens?
DE CARLO	Mom, I'm sixteen years old.
MARIE	Are you afraid to take a chance? To make a stand? To go out there to say, "Look at me. See. I'm good! I'm just as good as your imported stars!" Are you afraid you can't compete with Sally Brander?
DE CARLO	Sally Brander gets her name in lights.
MARIE	But you could too.
DE CARLO	But Sally Brander has something to say in lights, Mom. Sally Brander is Miss American Beauty Rose and Miss Five Roses Flour. Sally Brander's been on calendars.
MARIE	I think she made half that stuff up, Peggy Ann.
DE CARLO	Mom, I haven't done anything.
MARIE	She just says things. For publicity.
DE CARLO	Sally Brander danced in Earl Carroll's *Vanities*.
MARIE	Don't you see? We could say you did too. In fact, I did say, sort of…
DE CARLO	Mother…

MARIE	Don't you remember, Peggy Ann, when we were in Los Angeles and we walked by Earl Carroll's *Vanities* and I saw your picture out in front?
DE CARLO	Mom, you imagined that.
MARIE	You were all dressed up. Like you were when you danced *Swan Lake*.
DE CARLO	Mom, I danced *Swan Lake* at the Oddfellows Concert. When I was nine years old.
MARIE	*(inspired)* You could start with *Swan Lake*. Then the music could change.
DE CARLO	*Swan Lake* at the Mandarin Gardens?
MARIE	You could say a little poem, to explain what was going on…
DE CARLO	A poem? At the Mandarin Gardens?
MARIE	*(declaims)* Stop! Don't applaud! Why watch *Swan Lake*? When Ruby Keeler takes the cake.

> Sound: *Nightclub ambience from MARIE's point of view.*

> Sound: *Swan Lake. A scratchy record which gets faster and faster.*

DE CARLO	Stop! Don't applaud! *(A beat as she realizes no one is applauding.)* Why watch *Swan Lake* when Ruby Keeler takes the cake?

> Sound: *DE CARLO starts a frantic tap dance to* Swan Lake *which continues under.*

> Sound: *MARIE applauds madly. The lonely sound of two hands clapping.*

MARIE	That's my daughter.
WAITER	*(bored)* That so?
MARIE	She writes her own material.
WAITER	That so?
MARIE	She's just back from her successful tour of Hollywood and San Francisco.
WAITER	That so?
MARIE	You don't believe me, do you? Wait, I'll show you the postcards.

> Sound: *MARIE burrows through her purse.*

You see, look. That's Fisherman's Wharf.

> Sound: *Mournful foghorn.*

> Sound: *Rain continues under.*

Remember when we went to Fisherman's Wharf, Peggy Ann? Remember how foggy it was?

Sound: Mournful foghorns.

Remember that supper club right by the ocean. And I saw your name up in lights out in front.

DE CARLO   Mom, you imagined that.

MARIE   And the foghorns kept sounding. As if they were trying to tell me something. Don't give up. Keep trying. I love foghorns.

Sound: Mournful foghorn.

I mean, I love American foghorns. American foghorns sound so much more cheerful.

DE CARLO   I thought I could do it. I let you persuade me I could to it. I could go out on the stage of the Mandarin Gardens and people would think I was just back from my successful California tour.

MARIE   Now, Peggy Ann…

DE CARLO   I was terrible, wasn't I?

MARIE   Now, Peggy Ann…

DE CARLO   Stop, don't applaud. Oh, God…

MARIE   Now there was one thing I will say that I didn't like.

DE CARLO   Me. I stunk.

MARIE   You just rushed off the stage, Peggy Ann.

DE CARLO   Because I was dying. I died out there, didn't I?

MARIE   You have to wait for your applause.

DE CARLO   *(groans)* Mom…

MARIE   I've told you that before, now, haven't I?

DE CARLO   Mom, there was no applause.

MARIE   I applauded.

DE CARLO   You applauded and everyone else turned around to watch. They watched you instead of me, Mom. They thought you were more entertaining. That's why I got fired. That's why I opened and closed the same night.

MARIE   Now you know what I think we should do, Peggy Ann.

DE CARLO   I think we should walk down to Hastings. And catch the streetcar. And we should go home. And I should do my math homework.

MARIE   I think we should go to LA.

DE CARLO   To LA?

MARIE	Now that you have professional experience.
DE CARLO	That's a joke, right?
MARIE	Los Angeles, Peggy Ann. California. The United States of America. We belong there.
DE CARLO	We just got back Mom. And we're broke.
MARIE	LA's the land of opportunity.
DE CARLO	Mom, I just started school…
MARIE	Now what difference does that make?
DE CARLO	And I just walked off stage at the Mandarin Gardens and nobody cared.
MARIE	What's the Mandarin Gardens, Peggy Ann?
DE CARLO	It's the second biggest club on Pender Street.
MARIE	And where is Pender Street? It's in Vancouver, isn't it? And where's Vancouver? Vancouver's in Canada. Is Canada the Land of Opportunity? Now, you answer me that.

Sound: Locker room continues under.

MILAN	Look at Harry. He's asleep again.
SILVERHEELS	I'm not asleep, Milan.
MILAN	We come all the way from Brantford, all the way to Hollywood. All to show all these Americans how to play lacrosse…
SILVERHEELS	I was thinking, that's all.
MILAN	I don't know how come you're so cool.
SILVERHEELS	You know, my grandfather said his grandfather played lacrosse. And there were two hundred men on each team. And they'd play for days. And it was as much like a war as it was like a game.

Sound: Lacrosse game continues under.

BROWN	Watch number twelve. He's the Indian kid. See, he's walking all over us.
WINDSOR	So why can't they play baseball?
BROWN	The kid's scored two goals.

Sound: Cheers.

WINDSOR	Isn't baseball more American?
BROWN	The kid scored a hat trick!
WINDSOR	If they played baseball, then people could tell what they were doing, am I right? I mean, they'd be pitching, catching, stealing bases. I mean what kind of game is lacrosse?

BROWN	Watch him run! The kid's good.
WINDSOR	Then what's he doing in this game we never heard of?
BROWN	It's a chance for guys like number twelve, Marie. Because he comes down to Hollywood, because I see him…. You see him…
WINDSOR	You said that last year at the Golden Gloves.
BROWN	The Golden Gloves?
MARIE	You remember that Indian kid?
BROWN	Number twelve is an Indian kid.
WINDSOR	And that guy was from Canada too, wasn't he?
BROWN	Marie! Number twelve! Look him up in your program!
WINDSOR	I spilled coffee on my program.
BROWN	Look, if that's the same kid, this could be his big break.
	Sound: Lacrosse game out suddenly.
	Sound: Clock ticks under.
	Sound: Fly buzzes a moment, continues under, then out.
FELICIA	It says here you're from Canada, Mr. Cox.
CAMERON	Yes, ma'am.
FELICIA	And it says here that you've been a house painter and a taxi driver and a camp cook…
CAMERON	Yes, ma'am.
FELICIA	And a door-to-door salesman and a walking billboard.
CAMERON	Yes, ma'am.
FELICIA	And a grocery delivery man. And a window washer and a ditch digger.
CAMERON	And a sandhog.
FELICIA	How old are you, Mr. Cox?
CAMERON	I was working as a sandhog in New York. That's why I came here. To LA. I heard there was work on the water project.
FELICIA	You were born in 1912. That makes you twenty-five years old. But you've had more than thirty jobs.
CAMERON	Look, times are tough. Look, on my last job, I was laid off. I wasn't fired.
FELICIA	You don't look like a sandhog, Mr. Cox.
CAMERON	Do I have to?

FELICIA	How tall are you anyway? Six-foot-four? And how would you describe your eyes? Steel blue?
CAMERON	Why should it matter how I look?
FELICIA	Can I ask your opinion of something, Mr. Cox? Do you think that I look like an employment office clerk?
CAMERON	Huh?
FELICIA	Maybe if I took my glasses off…. How do I look when I take my glasses off?
CAMERON	What's going on?
FELICIA	They have movies in Canada, don't they, Mr. Cox?
CAMERON	Of course, but…
FELICIA	And you've been to the movies?
CAMERON	Of course, but…
FELICIA	Then you know what you're supposed to say. You're supposed to say, "You're beautiful without your glasses."
CAMERON	Look, you look fine, but…
FELICIA	Look, I'm working here in the California State employment office, but that's not what I want to do. No more than you want to build the Hoover Dam, am I right?
CAMERON	I want to eat.
FELICIA	Can you ride, Mr. Cox?
CAMERON	You mean horses, don't you?
FELICIA	Have you ever been a cowboy?
CAMERON	I was a shepherd once. You see, it's down there after selling shoes.
FELICIA	Not real cowboys, Mr. Cox. This is Hollywood, remember. You can't ride the range on Sunset Boulevard.
CAMERON	Run that by me again.
FELICIA	I think you should be an actor, Mr. Cox. Except you can't be Mr. Cox, of course.
CAMERON	What do you mean?
FELICIA	Look, there is a Rod Cox. At RKO. And all he plays are crooked lawyers. And you aren't going to end up playing crooked lawyers. Not with those shoulders.
CAMERON	Look, Miss…
FELICIA	Rod is good. Rod is strong. We'll keep Rod, okay.
CAMERON	Who is "we"?

FELICIA	Pass me that phone book. Never mind, I'll get it myself.
	Sound: Pages phone book rustle.
CAMERON	Look, I just came in here to register for work, that's all.
FELICIA	Rod Allen. No, he's at Twentieth. Rod Blodgett, no you'd sound like a plumber. Rod Caban. No, that's silly…. Rod Cadorette, Rod Cake… Rod Cameron. *(savours it)* Rod Cameron. That's you, Rod. I know it's you.
CAMERON	Look, you don't even know me.
FELICIA	*(sigh)* Rod Cameron.
CAMERON	We just met when I walked in your office.
FELICIA	You don't know me either, do you? I mean, unless you read my name tag. Look, you don't have to call me Miss Snape. You can call me Felicia.
CAMERON	Look, Miss Snape…
FELICIA	Just think. You're going to be an actor.
CAMERON	Me?
FELICIA	And I'm going to be your agent. You know what I think we should do? Right now? We should empty my in-basket out on the floor.
	Sound: Fluttering papers.
CAMERON	Look, Miss Snape…
FELICIA	And then we'll walk right out of here. Together. To our new life!
	Sound: Squeal of brakes.
DE CARLO	Mom! Watch out!
MARIE	Look, Peggy Ann! Across the street! We're here!
DE CARLO	You almost got run down.
MARIE	*(swoon)* Earl Carroll's *Vanities!*
DE CARLO	Remember what you always told me?
MARIE	See the sign? I can see your name up there, Peggy Ann.
DE CARLO	Mom, please, you're imagining things.
MARIE	"Through these doors pass the most beautiful girls in the world." And we're here, Peggy Ann. And you're going through those doors.
	Sound: Car horns honk.
DE CARLO	Mom! The light changed.
MARIE	Through those doors goes my daughter. Peggy Ann Middleton. Doesn't that sound wonderful?

DE CARLO	Mom, we can go now.
MARIE	No, wait, Peggy Ann Middleton. It doesn't sound wonderful, does it?
DE CARLO	Mom, please…
MARIE	Peggy Ann Middleton. It sounds like you should have a babysitter, doesn't it?

Sound: Car horn.

DE CARLO	Can't we discuss this on the curb?
MARIE	You know I named you after Baby Peggy, so I would always have a Baby Peggy, but would Baby Peggy dance in Earl Carroll's *Vanities*?
DE CARLO	Maybe not, but…
MARIE	Baby Peggy just sounds short and cute, but you're not short and cute. I should have named you something taller, shouldn't I?
DE CARLO	It's okay, Mom.
MARIE	Something more exotic. More sophisticated. Like Yvonne.
DE CARLO	Yvonne?
MARIE	My middle name.
DE CARLO	It's my middle name too.
MARIE	And we can't call you Middleton, can we? I mean, Middleton. That sounds so average.
DE CARLO	Maybe we should just go home and think this through.
MARIE	No, Peggy, I'm your mother. You can use my middle name. You can use my *maiden* name.
DE CARLO	But Mom…
MARIE	Yvonne. You're Yvonne. Yvonne De Carlo. That's pretty, isn't it?
DE CARLO	You can't just change your name in the middle of Sunset Boulevard.
MARIE	Yvonne. It's glamorous. Exotic, isn't it?
DE CARLO	I guess so, Mom, but…
MARIE	Of course it's exotic. So come on, Yvonne, let's go.

Sound: Restaurant ambience continues under.

Sound: Champagne cork pops.

WINDSOR	Congratulations, kid.
SILVERHEELS	I can't believe it.
WINDSOR	Here you are in the Brown Derby.

SILVERHEELS	That's right.
WINDSOR	With half of the Six Nations Indian Lacrosse Team.
SILVERHEELS	It's the Canadian Lacrosse Team.
WINDSOR	And Joe E. Brown just told you he could put your name in lights.
SILVERHEELS	I can't believe it.
WINDSOR	Don't worry. He'll do it. Except you'll have to change your name, of course.
SILVERHEELS	I beg your pardon?
WINDSOR	Look, face it… Harry Smith. What kind of name is Harry Smith?
SILVERHEELS	Harry Smith is my name.
WINDSOR	Look, let's face it. So what?
SILVERHEELS	Look, Miss Windsor…
WINDSOR	I mean, you put Harry Smith up in lights, you'd be wasting the bulbs, am I right? Of course I'm right.
SILVERHEELS	I'm named after my father.
WINDSOR	Sure you are. And that's nice. But you can't say it's box office, can you?
SILVERHEELS	My father was Major Harry Smith, Miss Windsor. He was a war hero. He was the most decorated Indian soldier in World War I.
WINDSOR	*(seductive)* Let's drink to that.
	Sound: Champagne poured.
SILVERHEELS	I'm named after my grandfather too.
WINDSOR	And let's drink to that too.
	Sound: Champagne pours.
SILVERHEELS	My grandfather was a hereditary chief. And an orator.
WINDSOR	We're going to have to order more champagne.
SILVERHEELS	They called him "Three Rows of People." Because people gathered round him when he spoke.
WINDSOR	Now that's the kind of name *you* need.
SILVERHEELS	You can't just call yourself a name like that.
WINDSOR	You need an Indian name.
SILVERHEELS	Three Rows of People. That's the kind of name you have to earn.
WINDSOR	You want some more champagne?
SILVERHEELS	No, please…

Sound: Champagne poured.

WINDSOR	We'll find your name.
SILVERHEELS	No, please…
WINDSOR	Harry Crazy Horse. Or Harry Sitting Bull. It could be animal.
SILVERHEELS	Be what?
WINDSOR	It could be all about your body.
SILVERHEELS	Don't you think that we're moving too fast?
WINDSOR	Sure. But why not? This is Hollywood.
SILVERHEELS	Look, Miss Windsor, I don't know…. Look…
WINDSOR	If you don't move too fast, people see what you're doing. Think about it.
SILVERHEELS	Miss Windsor, please… you probably don't realize… but your hand is on my thigh.
WINDSOR	You know what I think we should do?
SILVERHEELS	I know you're trying to help, but…
WINDSOR	We should have some more champagne…
SILVERHEELS	Look, I don't drink much.

Sound: Champagne poured.

WINDSOR	We'll have another drink and make a list. All the names we can think of. All the animal names. All the names that sound like weather. Running Bear. Thunder Cloud.
SILVERHEELS	Please, I don't think so.
WINDSOR	You'll be the same person, you know. You'll just have another name, that's all. I mean, I haven't changed. Except for my eyelashes. And you won't change either. Honest. Trust me.

Sound: Telephone rings under.

SILVERHEELS	Go away…. Go away, please, you're making my head hurt.

Sound: Phone picked up.

(bleary) Go away!… *(unintelligible response)* No, I'm sorry wrong number. *(unintelligible)* Yes, I'm sure that there's no Mr. Silverheels here. Goodbye.

MILAN	Harry, wait…

Sound: Phone hung up.

SILVERHEELS	It was just a wrong number, Milan.
MILAN	Did they say Silverheels?

SILVERHEELS	We don't know anyone named Silverheels.
MILAN	But that's you, Harry.
SILVERHEELS	Who?
MILAN	You're Jay Silverheels.
SILVERHEELS	I'm who?

Sound: The phone rings and continues under.

MILAN	And people have been calling you all morning.
SILVERHEELS	Explain, Milan.
MILAN	Aren't you going to answer the phone?
SILVERHEELS	Milan, please tell me. What's going on?
MILAN	Don't you remember last night at the restaurant?
SILVERHEELS	*(light dawns)* Oh no…
MILAN	You told everybody how your mother called you Blue Jay. Because you talked all the time, like a blue jay.
SILVERHEELS	Oh, no.
MILAN	Then you told us that your grandfather called you Silverheels. Because you ran so fast.
SILVERHEELS	Milan, you should have stopped me.
MILAN	Why?
SILVERHEELS	I told them I was twelve years old. I told them my grandfather said that I ran like quicksilver…
MILAN	Sure, but what's wrong with that?
SILVERHEELS	Oh, no…
MILAN	It's all true, isn't it?
SILVERHEELS	Oh, no…. Oh, no…
MILAN	Your dad used to tell those stories. Your mom used to tell those stories.
SILVERHEELS	You know that's all they needed, don't you? That's all they wanted. I gave them what they wanted.
MILAN	Harry, what's going on?
SILVERHEELS	I was twelve years old and I ran like quicksilver. But now I'm twenty and my grandfather's dead and his name was Harry Smith and my name is Jay Silverheels.
MILAN	It sounds good. Jay Silverheels.
SILVERHEELS	You think so? Really?

MILAN	I told you that last night.
SILVERHEELS	*(groans)* It sounds like money in the bank.
MILAN	What's wrong with that?
SILVERHEELS	I feel rotten, Milan.
MILAN	I guess you drank too much champagne.
SILVERHEELS	I feel sick.
MILAN	You're hungover, that's all.
SILVERHEELS	I feel like a thief.
MILAN	You aren't a thief.
SILVERHEELS	I feel like I've sold something that wasn't mine to sell.
MILAN	That's crazy, Harry.
SILVERHEELS	I've sold my memories, haven't I? My family's stories. And just so my name would look better in lights.
MILAN	You just talked about your family, that's all.
SILVERHEELS	Is that all? Really?
MILAN	You've done that before. I've heard all those stories before.
SILVERHEELS	At home, Milan. In Brantford.
MILAN	Well, sure, but…
SILVERHEELS	With people I loved. With people who knew what I was saying.
MILAN	Well, sure, but…
SILVERHEELS	I gave away my name, Milan. Because a very pretty woman told me to. Because I'd make it faster with a new name. Make it where, Milan?
MILAN	To the top, I guess.
SILVERHEELS	I gave away my name, Milan. And what else is going to go before I get to where I'm going?

Sound: Rehearsal piano under as dancers tap feverishly and sing brassily.

The DANCERS sing "Give My Regards to Broadway."

DANCE CAPTAIN	
	No, no, no, no, no, no, no…
MARIE	What's wrong?

Sound: Rehearsal piano discords out.

MARIE	Was it Yvonne? Did she do something wrong?

DANCE CAPTAIN
You sing and you smile. Both at the same time. Is that so hard to remember?

CHORUS *(all together)* No, sir. Sing and smile, right. I can do that… etc.

MARIE Yvonne was smiling, wasn't she?

DANCE CAPTAIN
(to MARIE) Please, I'm trying to rehearse. *(to the dancers)* Can we take it again? From the top?

> *Sound: Rehearsal piano begins with new vigour and new tap dancing under.*

MARIE I mean Yvonne De Carlo, she's my daughter and she's good, isn't she? I mean, that's why you called her back, isn't it?

DANCE CAPTAIN
We called her back because Mr. Carroll wants to see her.

MARIE Mr. Carroll?

DANCE CAPTAIN
He thinks she might do.

MARIE Do?

DANCE CAPTAIN
But he needs to see her upper assets.

> *Sound: Rehearsal piano out.*

DE CARLO He needs to see my what?

MARIE Your breasts, Yvonne.

DE CARLO No, Mom.

MARIE Yvonne…

DE CARLO I can't

MARIE Now, it's perfectly natural.

DE CARLO It's perfectly natural to have breasts, Mom. It's not perfectly natural to show them to your boss.

MARIE But we've come all the way downtown. Three times. And I bought that new bathing suit for your audition.

DE CARLO I can't, Mom.

MARIE *(pleads)* Yvonne, please…

DE CARLO What would Grandma say?

MARIE Yvonne, think. Your grandma is a thousand miles away.

DE CARLO But she raised me.

MARIE	She's in a different country. She's in Canada. She's in another world.
DE CARLO	She raised you too, Mom. To do what was right.
MARIE	*(pleads)* Yvonne…
DE CARLO	Didn't she?
MARIE	All right. Okay, sure. Fine. Never mind. We'll do what's right.
DE CARLO	Thanks, Mom.
MARIE	We can go up the street.
DE CARLO	We can what?
MARIE	There's a club up the street. The Florentine Gardens. They have shows. They need show girls…
DE CARLO	Do they have nude auditions too?
MARIE	Please don't do anything that Grandma wouldn't like, Yvonne, but we don't want to waste the carfare, do we? Or your new bathing suit. Remember, it cost nearly three dollars and a half.
	Sound: Cash register.
	Sound: Department store ambience continues under.
CAMERON	Felicia, you're crazy.
FELICIA	*(delighted)* I know.
CAMERON	You just spent your last dime.
FELICIA	Don't look now, but I spent more than that.
CAMERON	No, Felicia…
FELICIA	I just kited a cheque.
CAMERON	No, Felicia that's fraud.
FELICIA	No, Rod, haven't you heard? If you want to make money, then you have to spend money. That's what John D. Rockefeller does.
CAMERON	John D. Rockefeller *has* money, Felicia…
FELICIA	Isn't this exciting?
CAMERON	It's illegal.
FELICIA	It's just like in the movies, isn't it?
CAMERON	You could spend six months in jail, Felicia…. For a pair of size twelve cowboy boots.
FELICIA	You remember that scene in the movies? Where the kids all decided that they'll put on the show in the barn. And then one of

them says, "This is just so crazy that it just might work." I love it, Rod, don't you? Don't you just love it?

CAMERON   I think we should take this stuff back.

FELICIA   Will you look at that shirt?

CAMERON   No, Felicia…

FELICIA   Do you know how you'd look in that shirt with the fringe on the yoke?

CAMERON   Look, I'd feel like a crook.

FELICIA   Look, don't worry. Look, It's going to be worth it. Because you'll be six foot six in these boots.

CAMERON   I don't know about those boots.

FELICIA   Trust me, Rod. And we'll have you riding the back lot at Universal before you can say "Head 'em off at the pass."

            Sound: Horses galloping. Indian war cries. Sounds like an old-fashioned movie chase continue under.

MILAN   *(conversation is conducted sotto voce)* There you go, Jay.

SILVERHEELS Where?

MILAN   Your screen debut. You're the one on the pinto.

SILVERHEELS Sorry, Milan, I missed it. I guess I must have blinked.

            Sound: Gunfire continues under.

MILAN   Don't worry, there you are again.

SILVERHEELS That's the posse, Milan.

MILAN   You played the posse in the afternoon, remember? When they passed out the white hats after lunch. Because they didn't want to pay for extra extras.

SILVERHEELS You know what my grandfather would say? If he saw this picture?

MILAN   Your grandfather's dead, Jay.

SILVERHEELS I know.

MILAN   He died when you were twelve years old.

SILVERHEELS But he raised me, Milan. So I know what he'd say. And so do you, don't you?

AUDIENCE   Shhhh!

SILVERHEELS Don't you?

MILAN   I guess.

AUDIENCE   Excuse me, please, we're trying to watch this picture.

SILVERHEELS	He'd say why are you acting the part of an Indian as if he were a savage? And why are you acting the part of a white man who only wants to kill you? He'd say, what are you doing, Jay?
AUDIENCE	What's that guy think he's doing? Making a speech?
SILVERHEELS	I suppose I am making a speech.
MILAN	Look, Jay, please…
AUDIENCE TWO	Down in front.
MILAN	We're disturbing people.
AUDIENCE	Shhhhhh!
SILVERHEELS	But I can't help thinking, Milan, about my grandfather. If he saw this picture, he'd say, do they pay you for this? Do they pay you to chase yourself around all afternoon? Do they pay you to say that everything you know about your people is a lie, that your people lie and cheat and lay back and never work and they don't understand the American Dream…

Sound: Changes from gunshots to war whoops.

AUDIENCE	What's going on?
SILVERHEELS	You may well ask.
AUDIENCE	I mean, I'm trying to watch this picture.
MILAN	Jay, let's go.
SILVERHEELS	It's only that I'm in this picture. And I'm asking why.
MILAN	Jay, please, before we're thrown out.
AUDIENCE	You're in pictures?
SILVERHEELS	There I am again. The one who's falling off the pinto.
AUDIENCE	You're in pictures? Really? Can I have your autograph?
AUDIENCE TWO	Down in front!
AUDIENCE	Write "To Eddie."
SILVERHEELS	Look, Eddie, you don't want my autograph.
AUDIENCE	Look, buddy, I'm a fan. Don't try to tell me what I want.
AUDIENCE TWO	Who is that, anyway?
AUDIENCE	It's some guy from the picture.
AUDIENCE THREE	What's going on?

AUDIENCE TWO
> It's some movie star.

AUDIENCE THREE
> Who is it? Gable?

AUDIENCE   Gable's in the theatre?

AUDIENCE TWO
> Gable?

AUDIENCE THREE
> Gable's in the theatre!

AUDIENCE TWO
> Where?

MILAN   Let's get out of here, Jay. There's going to be a riot.

AUDIENCE THREE
> That's him going up the aisle.

AUDIENCE TWO
> Mr. Gable…?

AUDIENCE   Mr. Gable…! Wait, come back! Want to see my Spencer Tracy imitation?

> *Sound: Siren.*

> *Sound: Street ambience continues under.*

SILVERHEELS   Why are we running?

MILAN   This way, Jay.

> *Sound: Brakes squeal.*

SILVERHEELS   You'll get us killed, Milan.

MILAN   And if they catch us, they'll kill us. They'll blame us for the riot.

SILVERHEELS   They thought I was Gable.

MILAN   Come on, Jay…

SILVERHEELS   Don't they know that I couldn't be Gable?

MILAN   Down this alley…. Duck.

> *Sound: Siren rises and fades away.*

SILVERHEELS   Don't they know the white men are the good guys and the Indians are the bad guys?

MILAN   *(sighs)* I think we made it.

SILVERHEELS   They don't even want real Indians.

MILAN   Never mind, Jay.

SILVERHEELS	All the Indians with dialogue are Mexican. Or Italian. Or Greek. They don't let Indians play Indians. Why not?
MILAN	You know why not.
SILVERHEELS	Because Indians can't say the lines, that's why. Because what Indian is going to be believable saying lines like "White man smoke-um pipe of peace."
MILAN	Look, Jay…. It's just the way things are.
SILVERHEELS	But why?
MILAN	You think we're going to change the world?
SILVERHEELS	Why not?
MILAN	Jay, how old are you? How old am I?
SILVERHEELS	If the world needs changing, why not?
MILAN	You think we're going to rewrite all the scripts. We're going to recast all the parts.
SILVERHEELS	Milan, I want to get us out of war paint, that's all. And turkey feathers. And breech clouts and bathing suits. Because we're people, aren't we?
MILAN	It's entertainment, Jay, that's all.
SILVERHEELS	We're real people, aren't we?
MILAN	It isn't serious.
SILVERHEELS	Wouldn't it be great, Milan, if we could be real people in our pictures? It we could be Indians walking down the street in shirts and ties like we are now. Indians on Sunset Boulevard. If we didn't have to get dressed up and shot up…
MILAN	It's all just fantasy. Like this kid here on this billboard in the harem pants.
SILVERHEELS	*(reads)* The Florentine Gardens presents Yvonne De Carlo.
MILAN	They say that she's "The Pearl of India."
SILVERHEELS	I'll bet.
MILAN	We get turkey feathers. She gets a G-string and two pasties. And she has to dance with a gorilla.
	Sound: Band fanfare.
ANNOUNCER	*(on stage)* And now the moment that you've all been waiting for, as our Florentine Gardens showgirls choose that one special partner for one special dance.
DRUNK	*(very drunk, but amiable)* Yvonne… do you mind if I call you Yvonne?

DE CARLO	The customer is always right.
DRUNK	Does that happen every night when you dance with the gorilla? When your G-string breaks, I mean?
DE CARLO	Now what do you think?
DRUNK	I think it's cute. I think you're cute. You know, I've always wondered. What's a G-string made of?
DE CARLO	Hands off, buddy.
	Sound: Scuffle and elastic snap.
DRUNK	They're pretty sturdy, aren't they? Just a joke.
DE CARLO	You're quite a joker.
SILVERHEELS	*(is watching from the bar)* First she dances with a gorilla, then she dances with a drunk.
MILAN	He paid the maître d' to dance with her, that's all.
SILVERHEELS	How much?
MILAN	Jay, wait…
SILVERHEELS	I just got paid, Milan. And you get ten percent.
MILAN	Look, it's not that…
SILVERHEELS	Then what?
MILAN	Remember who we are. And where we are, that's all.
SILVERHEELS	We're in America, aren't we? That's the land of the free and the home of the brave, isn't it?
MILAN	Jay, we're Indians.
SILVERHEELS	You think they won't let me dance with her? If they notice I'm Indian?
MILAN	Jay, don't be crazy.
SILVERHEELS	Milan, they promote me to posse, remember. Every afternoon.
MILAN	No, Jay, please…
SILVERHEELS	Got to put on my white hat and ride to the rescue.
MILAN	Come back, Jay, wait…
SILVERHEELS	*(moves to dance floor)* Excuse me, may I cut in?
MAÎTRE D'	*(arrives smoothly)* Excuse me, sir. The lady and the gentleman are dancing, I believe.
SILVERHEELS	Except the gentleman is drunk.
DRUNK	*(amiable)* Who me?

SILVERHEELS	The gentleman can hardly stand up.
DRUNK	Who me? Look, I'm not drunk.
SILVERHEELS	Don't let go of him, Miss.
DE CARLO	Me? I can't…
DRUNK	Look, I'm not drunk. I'm just a little tired, that's all.
	Sound: Crash as the drunk falls and slides to the floor.
	Sound: Night club patrons gasp. Music falters.
SILVERHEELS	Will you take my friend back to his table? Will this cover it?
	Sound: New paper money passed.
MAÎTRE D'	*(alacrity)* Yes, sir.
	Sound: Band plays with new enthusiasm.
SILVERHEELS	May I have this dance? Look, don't say yes unless you want to.
DE CARLO	*(flat)* No, don't worry, I'm enjoying it.
SILVERHEELS	You're kidding, aren't you?
DE CARLO	No, really. You're a wonderful dancer. You're light on your feet.
SILVERHEELS	Does that happen every night when you dance with a gorilla? When your G-string breaks, I mean?
DE CARLO	I thought you'd never ask.
SILVERHEELS	Because I was thinking, watching you, we have something in common…
DE CARLO	Yeah, I'll bet.
SILVERHEELS	You want to be an actress, don't you?
DE CARLO	Look, I am an actress.
SILVERHEELS	They tell me I'm an actor too. But every time I get to an audition, then they tell me to take off my shirt. And I do. And I tense this muscle when they tell me. Or I tense that muscle. To show off my chest.
DE CARLO	I don't know what you're trying to say.
SILVERHEELS	Sure you do. You get treated that way.
DE CARLO	Now, look, buddy…
SILVERHEELS	I think that maybe sometimes, women are like Indians…. I'm Indian…
DE CARLO	This is some kind of line, right?
SILVERHEELS	I'm Indian, so I'm not a real person, and you're a woman, so you're not a real person…

DE CARLO	You're moving in on me.
SILVERHEELS	I mean, I get to ride around with a tomahawk. You get thrown around by a gorilla.
DE CARLO	Look, don't worry about the gorilla.
SILVERHEELS	They dress me up like a savage. They dress you up like a tart.
DE CARLO	You know what the gorilla means? That I'm a featured act.
SILVERHEELS	When he rips your costume, do you find that funny?
DE CARLO	That was an accident.
SILVERHEELS	The bartender says it happens every night. And twice on Saturday. Is that true?
DE CARLO	It happened once. It was an accident. But it went over well. Look, I don't have to do it.
SILVERHEELS	But you have to dance with me? If I pay the maître d'?
DE CARLO	Look, I've met lots of people here. Contacts. I've met Orson Welles and Franchot Tone. And Artie Shaw. Look, this is temporary till I get my big break.
SILVERHEELS	You really want to be an actress?
DE CARLO	I *am* an actress.
SILVERHEELS	Then keep smiling while you're dancing.
DE CARLO	I'm smiling.
SILVERHEELS	Just keep smiling. And keep thinking is it worth it?
	Sound: Nightclub sound segues to one finger piano.
	DE CARLO sings "Try a Little Tenderness" tunelessly.
MARIE	Yvonne, you seem depressed.
DE CARLO	Who me?
MARIE	You always sing when you're depressed, now why is that?
DE CARLO	I'm practising, that's all.
MARIE	You're moping around the apartment. You should have come down to the diner with me. You know who came in? George Burns and Gracie Allen. Now he's a card. And so is she. They both asked about you.
DE CARLO	They did not.
MARIE	I said, "Remember my daughter, Mr. Burns," and he said, "Ah, yes, how is she?"
DE CARLO	Mom, please…

MARIE	We discussed your career. I said, "It's hard for a young girl, Mr. Burns, because there is so much temptation and Yvonne is only eighteen, and of course, she's still a virgin…"
DE CARLO	*(outrage)* Mom…!
MARIE	And George asked me to remind you that you don't have to sleep around to get ahead. Because talent counts too.
DE CARLO	Yes, I know that, Mom.
MARIE	And Gracie had some good advice, Yvonne, she said, "Tell her that a woman's virtue is her most valuable possession."
DE CARLO	Yes, I know that, Mom.
MARIE	And George had some more advice. He said, "Don't give up hope. Don't be depressed."
DE CARLO	Did you ask him why not?
MARIE	Look, Yvonne, a year ago, did you think you'd be a professional dancer? Featured? At the Florentine Gardens?
DE CARLO	Did I think I'd be dancing with visiting firemen? And gorillas?
MARIE	It's a start, Yvonne.
DE CARLO	Did you ever think that women aren't real people?
MARIE	Don't be silly.
DE CARLO	It's just sometimes I feel like I'm a costume, that's all. Like the dress I wear for "Bobalu."
MARIE	Now that's silly.
DE CARLO	That dress makes me look like I'm naked underneath. Even though I'm not.
MARIE	Now, Yvonne, that's a beautiful dress.
DE CARLO	I wear rhinestones and G-strings and flesh-coloured lace. I pretend I like drunks. Gorillas.
MARIE	But you meet so many people, don't you?
DE CARLO	Sure, Mom.
MARIE	You've met Franchot Tone. And Burgess Meredith. And I've met George Burns.
DE CARLO	Sure, Mom.
MARIE	You know George Burns is very interesting.
DE CARLO	Mom, please…
MARIE	He likes pepper. Lots of pepper. And Gracie always orders apple pie.

DE CARLO	I feel sick. Please don't talk about food.
MARIE	Oh, no, Yvonne…
DE CARLO	I think I'm going to throw up.
MARIE	Yvonne, you aren't…?
DE CARLO	No, I'm not pregnant, Mom. I'm still a virgin, Mom, remember…
MARIE	Because remember what I told you. And what George and Gracie told you.
DE CARLO	You know what they call me down at the club?
MARIE	You don't have to sleep around, Yvonne. Because talent counts too.
DE CARLO	They call me Icebox, Mom.
MARIE	Now that makes me feel better.
DE CARLO	They think I'm cold. I am cold. I feel cold.
MARIE	It's going to be all right, Yvonne. Believe me. I know it. I can feel it. It's like that morning last week when I saw your name in the cement outside Grauman's Chinese Theatre.
DE CARLO	Mom, you imagined that.

Sound: The phone rings and continues under.

MARIE	Just think. We're here in Hollywood. And every time the phone rings it could be anyone…. It could be Paramount Pictures, calling up to say they've found the part that you were born to play.
CLAPPER	*Harvard, Here I Come.* Scene thirty-four. Take six.

Sound: Clapper board.

DIRECTOR	Action!
DE CARLO	I really think a girl should show a front.
DIRECTOR	Cut!
ASST. DIRECTOR	Okay, Yvonne, we're going to take the scene again.
DE CARLO	Again?
ASST. DIRECTOR	Take seven.
DE CARLO	Is there something wrong?
DIRECTOR	Could we take Miss De Carlo's line again, please?
DE CARLO	Did I say it wrong?

ASST. DIRECTOR
> The reading's fine, babe, but just stick your chest out when you say it.

DE CARLO   What?

ASST. DIRECTOR
> Just stick your chest out more, do you know what I mean?

DE CARLO   For breath control?

DIRECTOR   I mean, "I think a girl should show a front." It's a joke. Don't you get it?

> *Sound: One-finger piano plays "You Oughta be in Pictures,"*
> *under.*

MARIE   And then George said, "Say good night, Gracie," right in the middle of the diner. And it was the middle of the afternoon.... Yvonne, it's a joke, get it?

DE CARLO   Yes, Mom.

MARIE   Yvonne, you seem depressed.

DE CARLO   Who me?

MARIE   It's about your picture, isn't it?

DE CARLO   What picture?

MARIE   You think nobody noticed *Harvard, Here I Come*, you think nobody noticed you, but don't worry, Yvonne...

DE CARLO   Me? I'm not worried.

MARIE   Because there'll be other pictures. There'll be other calls. You're meeting new people all the time.

DE CARLO   I'm meeting men, that's all.

MARIE   You're making contacts.

DE CARLO   They just want me in bed.

MARIE   What about Orson Welles?

DE CARLO   Orson Welles showed me his Japanese erotica.

MARIE   Tony Quinn. He seems nice.

DE CARLO   "Your body is so beautiful," he said. "You know, you should never wear clothes."

MARIE   What about Jimmy Stewart?

DE CARLO   Mom, forget it. Please.

MARIE   Jimmy Stewart isn't like that, is he?

DE CARLO   Jimmy Stewart didn't call back, either, Mom...

Sound: The telephone rings and continues under.

MARIE	There, you see.
DE CARLO	That isn't Jimmy Stewart, Mom.
MARIE	But it could be, couldn't it? Because this is Hollywood. It could be anyone, couldn't it?
DE CARLO	Jimmy Stewart doesn't care if I live or die.
MARIE	Go ahead, Yvonne. Answer it.

Sound: Phone picked up.

DE CARLO	Hello…
DRUNK	*(filter)* Hello, Yvonne, you won't remember me, but we met at the Florentine Gardens. I danced with you. I'm the one with the Hawaiian sunset on my tie…
DE CARLO	Look, I'm sorry…
DRUNK	I got your number from a friend of mine.
DE CARLO	I don't know you. I don't remember you.
DRUNK	My name's Charlie Gioe. They call me Cherry Nose, remember?
DE CARLO	No.
DRUNK	I got your name from Frank Nitti.
DE CARLO	I don't know Frank Nitti.
DRUNK	Sure you do. They call him The Enforcer.

Sound: House band at Florentine Gardens continues under. 1941 dirty dancing.

DE CARLO	I don't know them, Artie.
SHAW	Keep it that way, kid.
DE CARLO	But they call me up. Why? How do they get my number?
SHAW	These guys get what they want, that's all. Phone numbers. Ringside tables.
DE CARLO	You mean they're here? Now?
SHAW	There at table three.
DE CARLO	*(discover)* You man they're regulars?
SHAW	That's Paul "The Waiter" de Lucia with the Pink Lady. That's Frank "The Immune" Maritone with his shoulder holster so badly concealed. That's Willie Bioff who just waved at you.
DE CARLO	They're regulars. They're gangsters.

SHAW	They say when Bioff was moving in on pictures someone said he's killing the industry.
DE CARLO	I've danced with them. I've danced with gangsters.
SHAW	Bioff said, "If that will kill Grandma, then Grandma must die."
CAMERON	*(another part of the nightclub)* Felicia, you just waved at Willie Bioff.
FELICIA	Because he knows someone who knows someone who can lend us money.
CAMERON	Felicia…
FELICIA	It's someone in this new actor's union that he wants to start.
CAMERON	He's a gangster, Felicia.
FELICIA	Aren't we all? A little?
CAMERON	Felicia, he is going to jail for tax fraud.
FELICIA	He says the Screen Actors Guild is for fat cats, and maybe he's right. Because how much did you make last year?
CAMERON	Look, I owe you money. I know that.
FELICIA	He says actors starting out should have a better deal, that's all.
CAMERON	I owe you money. You owe Willie Bioff's friend.
FELICIA	Look, don't worry…
CAMERON	I wonder sometimes, what would have happened if I'd stayed in Canada.
FELICIA	I've got you up for *North West Mounted*.
CAMERON	I wanted to be a real Mountie, that's crazy, isn't it?
FELICIA	That's cute.
CAMERON	I wanted to join the Mounties, but my mother brought me down to New York…
FELICIA	I told *Photoplay* about the Mountie bit. And they thought it was cute too.
CAMERON	I could have been a real Mountie. But I ended up in a night club, waving at Willie Bioff.
FELICIA	Willie Bioff got the stagehands ten percent, Rod.
CAMERON	I end up wearing a Mountie uniform in *North West Mounted*. And watching Gary Cooper play a Texas Ranger who can help the Mounties out.
FELICIA	What's wrong with that?
CAMERON	Then I do screen tests. Other people's screen tests.

FELICIA	Look, it's work. At Universal.
CAMERON	I say old lines from old films to thirty different starlets every day. I say Lew Ayres's lines and no one even knows I'm there.
FELICIA	But you are there. You're in pictures.
CAMERON	Sometimes I stand there on the sound stage after everyone else has gone home. And I say the lines just for myself, as if the lights were on, as if the cameras were rolling. And I change the lines, too, so the Texas Rangers don't have to ride in to help the Mounties. You should see it, Felicia. That's real acting.

Sound: Dance band out.

DE CARLO	Don't pass out, Jordan. Think about America…. I can't…. Think about Madrid…. I can't.
MARIE	Yvonne?
DE CARLO	Think about Maria…. I could do that all right. No, you fool! You weren't kidding, Marie, about that talk of "now." Now they can't stop us, ever…. Yes, by damn!
MARIE	Yvonne, are you all right?
DE CARLO	I know it's harder for you, but now I am you also. If you go, I go, too. That's the only way I can go. You're me now. Surely you must feel that, Maria. Remember last night. Our time is now and it'll never end. You're me now and I am you.
MARIE	You sound depressed.
DE CARLO	Those are Gary Cooper's lines. When he's saying goodbye. In *For Whom the Bell Tolls*.
MARIE	Gary Cooper?
DE CARLO	He's talking to Maria. I would kill to play Maria.
MARIE	Well, why don't you?
DE CARLO	Never mind, Mother…
MARIE	Because they think the world of you at Paramount.
DE CARLO	Oh, sure.
MARIE	They signed you to a six-month contract, didn't they?
DE CARLO	To play harem girls, Mother.
MARIE	If you want to be in *For Whom the Bell Tolls*, you should ask. You should put yourself forward.
DE CARLO	I really think a girl should show a front.
MARIE	What did you say?

DE CARLO	I did ask. I asked Sam Wood. I said "Gee, Mr. Wood, is there a part for me?" He said, "No, Yvonne. I don't think Ernest Hemingway had you in mind when he wrote this novel."
MARIE	Well, what does he know? About Ernest Hemingway, I mean.
DE CARLO	I think they're friends, Mom.
MARIE	Well, what does Ernest Hemingway know. About pictures, I mean. He's probably star-struck. He probably wants a name, that's all. He probably believes all the things he hears about this Ingrid Berman.
DE CARLO	I wish I were dead.
MARIE	Now, Yvonne…
DE CARLO	What's the use, Mom. I'm twenty years old.
MARIE	Now, not quite…
DE CARLO	And I've been trying to get in pictures for three years now, haven't I? And I've had two speaking parts and one of them was "Cigarettes, sir?"
MARIE	Now, Yvonne, please, repeat after me…. "Every day in every way, I'm getting better and better."
DE CARLO	Please, Mom…
MARIE	Every day in every way, I'm getting better and better. Just say it. I say it. It works. Please, Yvonne.
DE CARLO	*(without spirit)* Every day in every way, I'm getting better and better.
MARIE	You're depressed, aren't you?
DE CARLO	Every day in every way, I'm getting better and better.
MARIE	Why don't we turn on the radio for George and Gracie. That will cheer you up.
	Sound: Radio turned on.
	Sound: Station changed, static wows in and out under.
ANNOUNCER	*(through static)* We interrupt this program to announce that the Japanese air force has launched an attack on Pearl Harbor…. *(clearer)* I repeat, the Japanese air force has launched an attack on our fleet at Pearl Harbor.
	Sound: Radio is turned off.
FELICIA	I suppose you'll want to rush off and sign up.
CAMERON	Don't you think I should?
FELICIA	Everybody says that it's their patriotic duty.

CAMERON	I guess I could have rushed off and signed up years ago. In Canada.
FELICIA	I don't know what you mean.
CAMERON	You know what Lew Ayres said about war, Felicia? In *All Quiet on the Western Front*?
FELICIA	Is Canada at war? Who with?
CAMERON	"I'll tell you how it should all be done. Whenever there's a war coming, you should rope off a big field and sell tickets. And on the big day you should take all the kings and cabinets and their generals, put them in the centre dressed in their underpants and let them fight it out with clubs."
ANNOUNCER	*(on radio)* We interrupt this program…
	Sound: Radio turned off.
MILAN	Well, I guess the party's over, Jay.
SILVERHEELS	You think so?
MILAN	All we have to decide is whose side are we on? What do you think? Are we Americans? Or are we Canadians?
SILVERHEELS	Or am I going to play Geronimo? At MGM.
MILAN	You're kidding, aren't you?
SILVERHEELS	Am I?
MILAN	You're going to stay here? In Hollywood? You hate Hollywood.
SILVERHEELS	You think I should go marching off to war instead?
MILAN	But, Jay…
SILVERHEELS	I don't think so.
MILAN	But why?
SILVERHEELS	Who wins a war, Milan?
	Sound: Big band '40s dance band under. Something jaunty and warlike, like "Over There."
DE CARLO	Congratulate me, Artie!
SHAW	Congratulations, Icebox. Why?
DE CARLO	It is my big break.
SHAW	Again?
DE CARLO	This time it's real. Because I'm dancing at the Hollywood Canteen. And it's wonderful. We do a show, then we dance with the boys, then we sign autographs.
SHAW	Say, that sounds like real war work.

DE CARLO	You know who runs it? Bette Davis. You know who was there last night? Hedy Lamarr.
SHAW	I used to like this town.
DE CARLO	I love this town.
SHAW	It used to be that it was sunny here. That's all. Just sunny. Dry. A little dull.
DE CARLO	Hey, I don't think it's dull.
SHAW	Now what have we got?
DE CARLO	I think it's glamorous.
SHAW	Now everybody's noticed there's a war on.
DE CARLO	But there is a war on.
SHAW	Everybody wants to get involved.
DE CARLO	What's wrong with that?
SHAW	You know when the war started, Icebox?
DE CARLO	You know when they bombed Pearl Harbor, you know what I was doing? I figured it out. I was washing my hair.
SHAW	Do you know what you were doing when Hitler came to power? Do you know what you were doing when they burned the Reichstag?
DE CARLO	I don't know what you mean.
SHAW	Forget it, Icebox.
DE CARLO	You know what Hedy said last night? She'll kiss any man who buys $25,000 worth of war bonds.
SHAW	Good old Hedy.
DE CARLO	And Lana Turner says she'll do it for $50,000.
SHAW	That's what I call patriotism.
DE CARLO	How much do you think I should charge?
SHAW	I think you should quit, Yvonne.
DE CARLO	Quit?
SHAW	Because you're in a rut, do you know what I mean?
DE CARLO	I can't quit.
SHAW	You should go back to Oshkosh or wherever you come from…
DE CARLO	I come from Vancouver.
SHAW	You see, that's what I'm saying.

DE CARLO	You know, when I was a kid, my mother used to bring me down to Los Angeles. Every year, she'd scrape the money together somehow. She'd drag me across the border from Vancouver. She'd say this was the land of opportunity…. You believe that, don't you?
SHAW	Yvonne…
DE CARLO	This *is* the land of opportunity.
SHAW	You're not in a rut, Yvonne…. At least in a rut you can move sideways. You're in a hole… the kind of hole where you can't move at all.
DE CARLO	Who me?
SHAW	You're not tough enough for Hollywood.
DE CARLO	Who me?
SHAW	Yvonne, please. Go home.
DE CARLO	But I love it here.
SHAW	Why, Yvonne?
DE CARLO	I remember on our second trip. I must have been fourteen years old. My mother was in the hospital and I was staying with my aunt, trying to keep out of my aunt's way. I hardly knew her. I guess I spent most days in the library reading Greek myths. I loved Greek myths. Reading astrology. I was experiencing great mental clarity, Artie. And one day when I was walking home, I felt as though I was outside the earthly plane in some way and I was getting a glimpse of some greater truth.
SHAW	You're not serious, are you?
DE CARLO	I didn't hear a voice. I'm not saying I heard voices. But I knew. I saw myself rising above the crowd. "You will one day become famous," I was told. "Your time will come."
SHAW	That's dumb, Yvonne.
DE CARLO	I don't think so.
SHAW	You're sitting in the Los Angeles Public Library. And you're reading astrology…
DE CARLO	I believe there's something larger than ourselves, that's all. Don't you?
SHAW	If there were something larger than ourselves, why would it spend its time giving career advice.
	Sound: Alarm clock under.
MARIE	Yvonne…

DE CARLO	Go away, Mother.
MARIE	Yvonne, wake up, it's your big day.
DE CARLO	Last night was my big night, Mom. At the Hollywood Canteen.
MARIE	But I worked the swing shift at the diner and I met a writer who was talking to a stunt man who was talking to a friend of Walter Wanger's...
DE CARLO	*(fully awake)* Walter Wanger?
MARIE	At Universal.
DE CARLO	Universal?
MARIE	He's casting the lead in his new feature. It's called *Salome, Where She Danced.*
DE CARLO	*Salome, Where She Danced.* That's beautiful.
MARIE	It's about this dance hall girl in the Wild West. And he wants a new face. An unknown.
DE CARLO	Mom, I'm unknown.
MARIE	And he's putting up this big publicity campaign to discover the girl.
DE CARLO	Mom, I'm here.
MARIE	First he looks for the girl. Then he finds her. Then he announces she's the Most Beautiful Girl in the World.
	Sound: DE CARLO climbing out of bed.
DE CARLO	What time is it? I have to see him.
MARIE	He wants someone who dances like Zorina, acts like Ingrid Bergman, and sings like Deanna Durbin.
DE CARLO	*(a little worried)* Oh, Mom...
MARIE	Don't worry, Yvonne, I told him you could handle it.
	Sound: Studio commissary continues under.
DE CARLO	Artie, look. On the front page of the *Hollywood Reporter.*
SHAW	"Allies Cross the Rhine."
DE CARLO	Not there. Look. Further down where it says "Contest Winner."
SHAW	"Most Beautiful Girl in the World," says Walter Wanger of Universal.
DE CARLO	Don't you see? It's all come true. The voice...
SHAW	Look, Yvonne...
DE CARLO	The voice that said I would be famous.

SHAW	I know you think you're Joan of Arc, but…
DE CARLO	Listen. It says, "Walter Wanger says he's found the most beautiful girl in the world." And that's me.
SHAW	Look, you can't take this stuff seriously.
DE CARLO	It says, "I discovered Miss De Carlo when a Royal Canadian Air Force Squadron first sent me her picture."
SHAW	He discovered you when you auditioned. Three times.
DE CARLO	"She's the sweetheart of the barracks up in Saskatoon."
SHAW	Because you sent your picture to your Cousin Kenny.
DE CARLO	I really think it's going to happen. I'm going to be famous. Really famous.
ASST. DIRECTOR	
	Quiet on the set.
CLAPPER	*Salmone, Where she Danced.* Scene six. Take one.
DIRECTOR	Action.
DE CARLO	*(acting)* It's a very bad likeness of me. Are my shoulders made of iron?
CAMERON	No, ma'am. I'd say they were made of sugar and butter.
DIRECTOR	Cut. Print it.
	Sound: Champagne cork pops. Champagne pours.
MARIE	To Universal Pictures!
DE CARLO	My co-star's named Rod Cameron, Mom.
MARIE	To Hollywood!
DE CARLO	He's from Canada too. From Calgary.
MARIE	To America!
DE CARLO	And Walter Wanger's wonderful. He told Billy Wilder I could sing and dance and everything. And Billy Wilder told Walter Reisch…
MARIE	Who's Walter Reisch?
DE CARLO	*(getting tipsy)* Reisch's a writer. And he wants me for the life of Rimsky-Korsakov.
MARIE	*(getting tipsy)* Who's she?
DE CARLO	He's a composer, Mom. He wrote "Scheherazade." And the picture's called *Song of Scheherazade.*
MARIE	I knew that.

DE CARLO	And I'm going to his house on Sunday. To discuss Rimsky-Korsakov. And eat strudel.
MARIE	*(with difficulty)* Strudel?
DE CARLO	Strudel's Austrian. And so is he. And every Sunday, he invites his friends for cake and conversation.
	Sound: Teacups under.
	I'm sorry, but I didn't get your name.
BRECHT	It's Brecht.
DE CARLO	Brecht?
BRECHT	Bertolt Brecht.
DE CARLO	Are you a writer too?
BRECHT	I write with difficulty, Fräulein.
DE CARLO	That's too bad.
BRECHT	I find it difficult, of course, to write the truth.
DE CARLO	*(a little shocked)* You do?
BRECHT	You don't?
DE CARLO	I don't know what you mean.
BRECHT	You don't find the truth difficult.
DE CARLO	I don't know what you mean.
BRECHT	It takes courage, does it not, to say the truth today, when it is everywhere suppressed?
DE CARLO	But not here in America.
BRECHT	It takes intelligence to recognize the truth when it is everywhere concealed.
DE CARLO	But not here in America.
BRECHT	It takes art to wield truth as a weapon.
DE CARLO	I don't know what you mean.
BRECHT	And of course it takes judgment to know in whose hands truth will be effective, and it takes cunning to spread the truth among those who can use it.
DE CARLO	Look, you and me, I don't think that we're on the same wavelength.
BRECHT	Do you not?
DE CARLO	I think we're talking about two different things.
BRECHT	So, you think the truth can be two different things?

DE CARLO	I think you're talking politics.
BRECHT	And is there something wrong with politics?
DE CARLO	Look, er, should I call you Bertolt?
BRECHT	We are both immigrants, I think.
DE CARLO	You'll have to excuse me, look, my politics…
BRECHT	I think I am from Germany. You are from Canada…
DE CARLO	Look, I don't want to fight with you…
BRECHT	I think I will relate to you a scenario I have invented, a scenario I call *The Bread King Learns Bread Baking*.
DE CARLO	The who, what?
BRECHT	It is an interesting idea, is it not? It will make what is called a major motion picture, don't you think?
DE CARLO	Look, my politics, I'm sorry, but my politics, I think America's the land of opportunity.
BRECHT	I speak about bread, Yvonne, because I really like bread, of course, and there is no real bread in the States, don't you find?
DE CARLO	I don't know what you mean.
BRECHT	Bread should be real, should it not?
DE CARLO	There is bread everywhere in the States.
BRECHT	Not real bread.
DE CARLO	Have you spent much time in an A&P lately?
BRECHT	You miss my point, Yvonne.
DE CARLO	They've got rye. They've got pumpernickel. And it's sliced.
BRECHT	Americans have no real need for real bread, because real bread cannot be sold in slices like the bread at your A&P. Americans are nomads. They change their jobs like boots, they build houses to last twenty years and they don't live in them even for that long, so that their hometowns are not really places at all. Where, for example, is your hometown?
DE CARLO	*(not poetically)* Vancouver.
BRECHT	When people speak of their hometowns, it always sounds like poetry.
DE CARLO	*(not poetically)* It's in British Columbia. In Canada.
BRECHT	Is it beautiful, your hometown? Will it still be there when you're finished your adventures?

DE CARLO	As a matter of fact, I went home last year. On a war bond tour. And Vancouver was the same, exactly the same.
BRECHT	Indeed.
DE CARLO	Except that I went over big, since I had made it in the States.
BRECHT	And is that how it should be, do you think?
DE CARLO	Don't you believe in the free enterprise system?
BRECHT	Do you think I should?
DE CARLO	Because that's why you've come here, isn't it? To Hollywood?
BRECHT	Because the streets are paved with gold?
DE CARLO	Because it's the land of opportunity, isn't it?
BRECHT	Let's drink to that, Yvonne. To Hollywood. Where the economic laws of Adam Smith have been suspended. By bribery. By corruption.

Sound: Sirens.

Sound: A huge fire continues under.

FIREMAN ONE	Watch out! That storefront's going to fall.
FIREMAN TWO	The fire's spreading to the jungle set.

Sound: Sirens rise and fade, continuing under.

DE CARLO	*(waking suddenly)* No! No!
MARIE	Yvonne, Yvonne, what's the matter?
DE CARLO	Oh Mom, I was dreaming. The sirens. I had a terrible nightmare.
MARIE	It's all right Yvonne, it's all right.
DE CARLO	Mom, what time is it?
MARIE	Ten to seven.
DE CARLO	But I have a call. You didn't wake me.
MARIE	Because the studio called.
DE CARLO	The studio? What's wrong?
MARIE	There's a fire on the lot, Yvonne…
DE CARLO	A fire?
MARIE	You can see it out the window. Over there. That red glow in the sky.
DE CARLO	How did it happen?

MARIE   No one knows, but the whole Western town is gone.

                   SOUND: Sirens are heard.

                   The end.

COMPAÑERAS

INTRODUCTION

Five years after the events of Karen's Ridd's story and four years after meeting her, I'm still inspired by what she did because it shows us change is possible. We can stand up for what we think is right. We can make a difference. It's a story that makes us all brave.

It's a wonderful story, so big with so many textures and colours, so hard to contain in a half-hour format, that I hope I can write about it again. The first draft of this play reached more than eighty pages. So much has been left out. Some of the scenes you didn't hear and won't read are:

The Story of Renaldo the Snake: When Karen is waiting to be questioned by the Treasury Police, refugees from the bombing wander in and out, visiting brothers and uncles and fathers, trailing household baggage. One shopping bag undulates. It is filled with Renaldo, a pet snake, and work stops while the young soldiers find an excuse to visit this marvel.

The Story of Marcella's Birthday Party: While Marcella celebrates her birthday, soldiers storm the Peace Brigades house, running over the roof, appearing at grilled windows, all wearing wool ski masks in spite of the heat. They tear the house apart looking for subversive material, but they miss the revolutionary poster because it's on the back of the bathroom door. Karen is ill with fever. Everything seems surreal. The young soldiers are charmed by the young Peace Brigades workers. They take off their ski masks. They eat cake, no longer terrible. They agree they will come back for tea one day.

The Story of the Fourth Woman: Daysi. Marcella. Karen. There is another woman in the story arrested with Karen and Marcella, who did not walk back into the prison, as Karen did. It would be interesting to explore her choice as well as Karen's.

The Stories of Peace Brigades: Working for Peace Brigades means starting cars which may be car bombed, answering doors for people whose lives have been threatened, standing watch all night in the union office of a newspaper because a bomb threat has been received. Peace Brigades work is filled with choices that make a difference. Karen stopped a kidnapping in progress at a demonstration simply by taking pictures of it.

The Stories of the People of El Salvador: Karen would tell you the story is not about her. It's about the people of El Salvador. Their struggle inspired everything she did and theirs is the real story.

The Stories of Robo the Clown: I am pleased to introduce you to Karen's clown, Robo, but I have not done him justice. Robo is actually a mute clown, but the challenge involved in radio mime was overwhelming.

Carol Bolt

Compañeras was commissioned by the Canadian Broadcasting Corporation for Studio '93, and first broadcast on the CBC Stereo network on March 12, 1993, with the following company:

Alison Sealy-Smith	Karen / Robo
Alisa Palmer	Daysi
Malika Mendez	Marcella
Guillermo Verdecchia	Consul / Soldier Two
Louis Di Bianco	Priest / Captain / Soldier Three
Robert Persichini	Soldier One

Produced and directed in Toronto by Baņuta Rubess
Original music by Ramiro Puerta
Casting consultant: Linda Grearson
Recording engineer: John Marynowicz
Sound effects by Joe Hill
Production assistant: Peggy Este
Script editor: Ann Jansen
Executive Producer of Studio '93: Bill Lane

Characters

KAREN, Karen Ridd
ROBO, Karen Ridd's clown and alter ego
DAYSI, A Salvadoran working for the Union of the Unemployed
MARCELLA, A Peace Brigades worker from Columbia
SOLDIER ONE, SOLDIER TWO, and SOLDIER THREE
PRIEST
CONGREGATION
CAPTAIN
CONSUL

Compañeras

Scene One: Hospital

Music. "Clown" theme.

Sound. Hospital ambience, up and continuing underneath.

KAREN   *(internal)* It happened this way. A young woman from Winnipeg, Manitoba, was working as a clown…

Sound: Clown noises, honks, and whistles.

(internal) She made videotapes for a hospital, to help children deal with treatments that they didn't understand…

ROBO   *Mechana…*

KAREN   Don't worry, Robo…

ROBO   *Mechana. Gros mechana. Nix mechana.* [Big machine. No way.]

Sound: Bells and whistles indicate ROBO is worried. They continue underneath.

KAREN   It's just a machine that takes pictures of your head.

ROBO   *Nix mein kopla.* [Not my head.]

KAREN   Please don't worry, Robo. It doesn't hurt and it can't tell what you're thinking.

ROBO   *Rayvee?* [Really?]

KAREN   Look at it, Robo. If you see what it is, it won't scare you.

ROBO   *Rayvee?*

KAREN   Electroencephalograph.

ROBO   *(discovers)* Selectoandparamet…

KAREN   Sure. That's close, Robo. Watch, see, I just put this on my head. It's like a hat.

ROBO	*(with enthusiastic noise making) Kopla topper ha ha ya ya.* [Robo wants the hat. It's funny.]
KAREN	*(internal, over)* My name is Karen Ridd. Robo is my alter ego. He is not a very smart clown, he's not a very brave clown, but clowns are anarchists, they're order-breakers, so in 1988, having taped his reactions to EEG's and fracture clinics, Robo and I decided on a new career.

Scene Two: Interior Dialogue

Sound: Enthusiastic bells and whistles, underneath.

KAREN	That's right, Robo…
ROBO	*Ha ha kopla topper. Mucho grosso kopla topper.* [Robo's new career is making bigger funny hats.]
KAREN	Robo and I decided to go to El Salvador…
	Music: Synthesized brakes applied heavily.
ROBO	*Robo kay?* [Robo who?]
KAREN	Because Robo and I are clowns from Winnipeg, of course…
ROBO	*El-sal-va-kay?*
KAREN	We were raised in the United Church, the NDP. We grew up thinking it was possible to change the world…
ROBO	*El-sal-va-far. El-sal-va-nix.*
	Sound: Horns and whistles as ROBO tries to get KAREN's attention, underneath.
KAREN	Robo and I have a strong sense of right and wrong, an even stronger suspicion that absolutes are dangerous…
ROBO	*Resta minim…* [Wait a minute…]
KAREN	Don't worry, Robo…
ROBO	*El Sal-va…*
	Sound: ROBO begins a two-tone European siren noise, "Ee ah, ee ah…," which continues underneath.
KAREN	It will be all right. Remember, clowns are healers.
ROBO	*(stops his siren imitation) Ee ah…. Rayvee?*
KAREN	Laughing is healing. Remember that it's the court jester who heals the king's mind.
ROBO	*Rayvee? Caramba!*
	Music: "El Salvador" theme.

Scene Three: Office of the Union of the Unemployed

Sound: Phones, typewriters, and the bustle of an office continue underneath.

ROBO	*(approaching a new language with energy and enthusiasm) Buenos dias…. Buenos dias…. Buenos dias…*
MARCELLA	*Buenos dias*, Karen.
KAREN	*(in good Anglo Spanish) Buenos dias.*
DAYSI	Does your friend realize, Marcella, it's the third time she's said "buenos dias" this morning. To me, I mean.
MARCELLA	Or perhaps the fourth time.
DAYSI	Please tell her she's amiable.
KAREN	*Muchas gracias.*
ROBO	*(enjoying the language, underneath the others, with reverb) Muchas gracias, muchas gracias…*
DAYSI	You and Marcella, you're both so polite. Is it because you're from the Peace Brigades?
KAREN	I'm sorry, I…
ROBO	*Habla inglés?*
DAYSI	Peace. Brigades. International. It's a strange concept, don't you think?
KAREN	A strange what?
ROBO	*(with a little reverb)* A strange kay?
DAYSI	Why is it you're here, Marcella?
MARCELLA	You know why.
DAYSI	Marcella has come all the way from Colombia and you have come from Canada. All to ensure that the police do not raid and the rhinoceros do not go on stampede.
ROBO	*(savouring the Spanish) El rinoceronte.*
KAREN	I'm sorry, my Spanish…
DAYSI	The Union of the Unemployed receives a bomb threat, so Peace Brigades sends in a witness. Because then, of course, if there is a bomb, it blows up a tall blond *gringa*, and it makes the North American newspapers and the government look bad and the people who support the government look bad…
KAREN	I don't understand…
ROBO	*(loves the strange word) El rinoceronte!*

DAYSI	And you are successful, please don't think I'm not grateful… there are no bombs, it's as if bombs did not exist, and there are no rhinoceros and of course it is so much easier to work when the rhinoceros are not stampeding. Am I speaking too fast for you?
MARCELLA	Yes, Daysi, and you know you are.
DAYSI	She doesn't have the words, your friend. I mean in Spanish. The situation is surreal, is it not? Do you appreciate the surreality?
KAREN	I'm sorry, I…
DAYSI	El Salvador. My country. You'll grow to love it if you spend much time here. Tell her, Marcella. You've been here six months now.
MARCELLA	*(with a Spanish accent)* Daysi's teaching you, Karen.
DAYSI	It is unbelievable. Nothing is believable, which gives everything a kind of magic, I suppose.
KAREN	Marcella, please tell her. If she could just speak more…
DAYSI	I live in a country where it seems it is necessary I'm protected from my countrymen. Because I want to do my job. I want to work here at the Union of the Unemployed. That is not a political act. I know, since I am not political. And usually, it is not an impossible act, but there are days when a tall, fair, stranger saviour stands blocking my file drawer. Will you ask her to move, Marcella…
KAREN	I'm sorry…
	Sound: File drawer opens, papers rustle underneath.
DAYSI	A tall, fair, uncomprehending stranger saviour. But polite.
	Sound: File drawer slams shut.
KAREN	I'm sorry, I…
DAYSI	Do you understand one-fifth of what I'm saying?
ROBO	*(savouring)* El Salvador.
KAREN	I know I'm not supposed to be your saviour.
DAYSI	Your Spanish must be better than your accent.
KAREN	I hope so.
MARCELLA	If I may present Daysi Alonzo…
DAYSI	Tell her we are more alike than I admit, Marcella. Tell her I like her shoes.

Scene Four: Market

Music: Lively band blaring on the radio.

Sound: Street market ambience, continues underneath.

DAYSI	Do you like these shoes?
KAREN	Of course.
ROBO	Gustarle? Zapatos?
DAYSI	Do you think I should buy them? Red shoes? I'll wear red shoes and you'll wear your pants with the orange dots and purple lozenges. We will both make a statement.
KAREN	Statement?
ROBO	*Zapatos rojos?*
DAYSI	Don't worry, it's not a political statement. For me a fashion statement will suffice.
KAREN	Will what?
DAYSI	As I told you, I'm not political.
KAREN	*(quoting the song "A Bicycle Built for Two.")* "Daisy, Daisy…"
ROBO	*(singing to the same tune)* Mar-gar-ita.
DAYSI	Wear high heels. And pink. And smile a lot. We are women, we are not taken seriously. We must make macho work, or be clowns, don't you think?
ROBO	*Pensar? Pensar?*
KAREN	I don't believe you.
DAYSI	Why don't you buy shoes like this, Karen? So we can go dancing?
KAREN	I don't believe you could ever stand back and wear high heels and not speak out…

Sound: ROBO blows a high-pitched whistle.

I don't believe that you don't care. Daysi, I'm serious.

DAYSI	Of course, since that's why you're here. Because things are serious.
KAREN	Do you have to make fun of me? All the time?
DAYSI	Karen, why don't you buy shoes like this? And I'll take you to La Puerta del Diablo.

Scene Five: La Puerta Del Diablo

Music: "La Puerta" theme, eerie and haunting.

Sound: Wind underneath.

ROBO   La Puerta del Diablo.

DAYSI   The Devil's Gate. My father tells stories of coming here for picnics as a child. But when I was a child it was much used as a body dump.

KAREN   I know.

DAYSI   It's beautiful, isn't it?

KAREN   I know about La Puerta del Diablo.

DAYSI   You can see for miles. You can see right over the city, except for the smog. Or would you call it mist?

KAREN   Daysi…

       Sound: ROBO makes his European siren sound, which continues underneath.

DAYSI   Mist sounds more magical, I think. And mist means you can't see the bodies, of course.

KAREN   You keep saying that you're not political

DAYSI   Mist. It's all you see, but the city is still there, of course. And you can't see the bodies, but the places where the bodies were… they're still there, of course. Remembering the bodies, it's not a political act. It's a human act, isn't it? To forget the bodies, that would be political.

KAREN   I'm sorry, my Spanish…

DAYSI   I think El Salvador is like your movie.

KAREN   My what?

ROBO   *Si. Muy cine.*

DAYSI   And you are the hero in this movie…

KAREN   I'm what?

ROBO   *Ser héroe.*

DAYSI   But you're the tallest, the blondest, you save me from bomb threats. What did you do before you decided to save me from bomb threats?

       Sound: KAREN laughs.

Why are you laughing? Karen?

Scene Six: Visa Office

Sound: A hot office, one typewriter clicks along slowly, a fly buzzes around. A rubber stamp.

SOLDIER ONE   You are Miss Karen Ridd… you are Canadian… and you wish to obtain an extension to a tourist visa.

KAREN   Yes, sir.

SOLDIER ONE   Might I ask why, Miss Ridd?

KAREN   I beg your pardon?

ROBO   *Por que? A que discutir?*

SOLDIER ONE   Are you working here in El Salvador, Miss Ridd?

KAREN   I'm sorry, my Spanish…

SOLDIER ONE   I ask you if you are employed.

ROBO   *Empleo… empleado por…*

KAREN   I'm trying to learn Spanish.

SOLDIER ONE   And if you were employed, what is it you would do, Miss Ridd?

KAREN   I'm sorry?

SOLDIER ONE   Your occupation? Your profession? When you are not a tourist, learning Spanish.

KAREN   I'm a clown.

Sound: ROBO laughs.

SOLDIER ONE   I beg your pardon?

Sound: ROBO laughs.

Sound: Goofy synthesized sound as time passes.

Scene Seven: Visa Office, Later

Sound: A balloon blowing up; it pops. A burst of male laughter, underneath.

SOLDIER ONE   Señorita Karen…

ROBO   *El balon rinoceronte.*

SOLDIER TWO   Señorita Karen, my balloon has broken…. If I could have another…

SOLDIER ONE   With my balloons, I've made a beagle.

ROBO   *El sabueso.*

SOLDIER ONE   Señorita, my beagle… do you like him?

Sound: A balloon pops.

SOLDIER TWO Señorita?

SOLDIER ONE You see, I've made him glasses. Little cardboard glasses just like mine.

SOLDIER TWO Señorita? Another balloon *por favor?*

Sound: ROBO laughs.

Sound: Goofy, synthesized sound fades.

Scene Eight: Street

Music: Menacing band plays on the radio.

Sound: Street ambience. A distant siren starts subliminally and slowly grows louder, underneath.

DAYSI Balloons! This scene will not be in your movie, I assure you.

ROBO *El perrito?*

KAREN *(amused)* They extended my visa.

ROBO *El rinoceronte.*

DAYSI We're not used to heroes carrying balloons, blowing up balloons, making sculptures of balloons.

ROBO *Ser héroe.*

KAREN I don't want to be a hero.

ROBO *Como no?*

SOLDIER ONE Excuse me, señorita…

SOLDIER TWO We must ask for your identification, señorita.

KAREN My name is Karen Ridd.

ROBO *Ser héroe.*

SOLDIER TWO Not you, *señorita.*

SOLDIER ONE You are free to go.

KAREN We have done nothing wrong. We are both free to go.

SOLDIER ONE Your friend will come with us.

SOLDIER TWO To answer questions.

KAREN Do you think so?

DAYSI Karen…

KAREN I don't think so. I think I will stay. To take pictures. Do you mind if I take pictures.

ROBO	*Sitzen photo. Ya. Ya.*
	Sound: Camera equipment being taken out.
DAYSI	Karen, please…
KAREN	Smile Daysi… say "Cheese." …No, I don't think that's what you say in Spanish.
ROBO	*Sitzen ha ha. Dicta fromagio.*
	Sound: Enthusiastic clown noisemakers, fading underneath.

Scene Nine: Office of the Union of the Unemployed

Sound: An office clock ticks, a typewriter stops. KAREN blows her nose to finish a good cry.

MARCELLA	*(with a Spanish accent)* She's all right, Karen.
ROBO	Olé Robo! Bravo bravo Robo!
MARCELLA	*(Spanish accent)* They questioned her, that's all.
KAREN	Was it my fault, Marcella?
MARCELLA	*(Spanish accent)* No, of course not!
ROBO	*Supra Robo!*
KAREN	But why Daysi?
MARCELLA	Karen…
KAREN	Because Daysi's not political. Except that she knows me…
MARCELLA	*(Spanish accent, fading underneath)* Karen, Daysi is political… everyone's political.

Scene Ten: Interior Monologues

Music: "Clown" theme, in a surreal prison continues underneath.

KAREN	*(internal)* Ten days later, Daysi disappeared. We had no trace of her, except for one red shoe that was left in the street. It was thirty-six hours until we heard she was alive, held in the women's prison.
	Sound: Distorted hubbub of the prison courtyard. Shrieks and laughter. Women's voices in Spanish, lots of swearing; continuing underneath.
	(internal) The women's prison was a mad house.
ROBO	*Señorita…*

KAREN	*(internal)* The mad can be clowns. Six hundred years ago there were mad clowns. *Buffon.* The wounded, the lepers, dwarves, who tiptoed round as if their feet were pretty…
ROBO	*Señorita….* You're so tall and fair….
KAREN	*(internal)* They tiptoe around, full of compliments, but there's nothing but hate in their eyes.
ROBO	Can I help you, *señorita?*
KAREN	*(internal)* I'm looking for Daysi Alonzo.
	Sound: ROBO shrieks with laughter.
	(internal) Gloria Daysi Alonzo Jaimes.
ROBO	*(babbling)* I am Daysi. I am she. I'm your friend, I'm your sister. What did you bring me? Are you taking me home, dear heart? Am I going home? *(babbling continues underneath)*
KAREN	*(internal)* Daysi saw me from across the courtyard.
	Sound: Prison ambience no longer distorted, but crisp and real.
	Music: "Clown" theme out.
ROBO	*(babbling)* Karen? Is that your name? Karen? My sister, my friend, my *compañera? (babbling continues underneath)*
KAREN	*(internal)* Daysi ran toward me, but before she took more than three steps, she fell. She couldn't get up. She'd been beaten, tortured. The young soldiers who questioned her had taken it in turns, to rape her, or kick her repeatedly in the spine.
DAYSI	I'm fine, Karen.
KAREN	Oh, Daysi…
DAYSI	I will be fine. I promise.
KAREN	Lean on me. Let me help.
DAYSI	The woman you were talking to… did you help her?
	Sound: Distant, crazy laughter from ROBO.
KAREN	Let me help you.
DAYSI	First they raped her. Vaginally. Then the commandant raped her anally and when he was done, he wiped his penis on her shirt.
ROBO	*(laughing and babbling, underneath.)* Ha ha Robo. Ha ha, *señor, muy bravo…*
	Music: "Clown" theme, disturbed, creeps back.
KAREN	I'm a clown.

Music: A clown explosion: the sound a clown makes when things are going very badly.

I am Robo, the clown who is proud of his manicure until he discovers that he has no hands.

Sound: A real explosion.

Clowns want to be loved. That may be all they want. And they are loved so they tend to think that things are simple.

Music: Barrel organ clown music cranked erratically, underneath.

Now I felt as if I had no hands. I felt as if I were no help. Daysi was in prison. El Salvador was changing. It had been a police state.

Sound: A siren begins to rise and fall, underneath.

It was now a state at war with its civilian population. There was a shoot-on-sight curfew, more raids, more disappearances.

Scene Eleven: Prison

Sound: Prison courtyard ambience, continues underneath.

ROBO	*(singing lustily to the tune of "A Bicycle Built for Two.")* Mar-gar-it-a. Esta peligrosa. No tengo miedo…
KAREN	Daysi, she won't let go of you.
DAYSI	I think it's because I taught her your song.
ROBO	*(singing)* No tengo miedo.
DAYSI	She takes it as a sign of friendship.
ROBO	*(singing)* All for the love of you…
DAYSI	She doesn't understand I'm leaving, do you, *compañera*?
ROBO	*(singing)* Daisy, Daisy…
DAYSI	You can help me say goodbye, Karen. You can give her a present…
ROBO	*(singing)* Daisy, Daisy…
DAYSI	You can blow up one of your balloons. You can make her a bird or a monkey… you'd like that, *compañera*, would you not?
ROBO	I'm half crazy…
DAYSI	Everybody likes balloons.
KAREN	Daysi…
ROBO	Daysi, Daysi…

DAYSI	But hurry, Karen, or we'll miss the bus. And I won't get back to work this afternoon.
KAREN	You aren't going back to work today.
DAYSI	Of course I am.
KAREN	That's crazy, Daysi…
DAYSI	No, it's simple. If I don't go, then it means they've won. And they haven't won. They can't think that they've won.
KAREN	Daysi, forget it. Please, you're not political, remember.
DAYSI	But Karen, to not work against them. I think that would be political.
KAREN	*(internal)* So we went back to work. We all went back to work. Six weeks later, the university was attacked again.

Scene Twelve: Church

Music: A sombre drum introduces the church service.

Sound: A microphone squeaks in a cavernous room, murmuring of the congregation, shuffling feet.

PRIEST	We are gathered with our martyrs. Father Ignacio Martin Baro.
CONGREGATION	
	Presente.
PRIEST	Father Segundo Montes.
CONGREGATION	
	Presente.
PRIEST	Father Ignacio Ellacuria.
CONGREGATION	
	Presente.
PRIEST	Father Amado Lopez.
CONGREGATION	
	Presente.
PRIEST	Father Juan Ronon Moreno.
CONGREGATION	
	Presente.
PRIEST	Father Joaquin Lopez y Lopez.
CONGREGATION	
	Presente.
PRIEST	Elba Julia Ramos.

CONGREGATION

Presente.

KAREN   (*internal, over*) Six Jesuit priests, their housekeeper and her daughter were murdered. In El Salvador a memorial service takes a certain form. The martyrs' names are read and the congregation responds "Presente."

> *Sound: The roll call of names and the response, "Presente," continues.*

(*internal*) It's a simple and beautiful statement, and of course, it's dangerous. You know you are in the company of the martyrs. You know you may join them.

Scene Thirteen: Church Sanctuary, Dawn

> *Sound: Birds chirp outside. People sleeping. Loud knocking on a huge church door, people waking up, disoriented, Spanish dialogue.*

KAREN   (*internal*) The air force had begun a bombing campaign against it's own civilians. Marcella and I were assigned to the Lutheran church, assisting refugees.

> *Sound: Louder knocking.*

SOLDIER TWO   (*through a distant loudspeaker*) Es la policía.

KAREN   (*internal*) Five hundred refugees at the church, seeking sanctuary.

> *Sound: A baby cries.*

MARCELLA   Karen... Karen... wake up?

ROBO   Nonononono...

KAREN   What time is it

ROBO   Nonononono...

MARCELLA   It's five a.m. Get dressed okay?

> *Sound: Breaking glass.*

ROBO   (*like a siren, frightened*) Nonononono...

MARCELLA   The police are here. And you can't get arrested in that T-shirt. Please, Karen. It says "Liberation Theology."

Scene Fourteen: Truck

Sound: Truck driving over rough terrain, underneath.

KAREN   *(internal)* We were handcuffed, blindfolded. We were thrown in the back of a truck.

SOLDIER ONE   Do you know where you're going, girls?

SOLDIER TWO   La Puerta del Diablo.

Music: The eerie theme of "La Puerta" creeps in.

ROBO   La Puerta del Diablo.

SOLDIER ONE   La Puerta del Diablo. Have you seen the view?

Sound: SOLDIERS laugh, underneath.

ROBO   *(babbling underneath)* La-puerta-del-diablo-la-puerta-del-diablo-la-puerta-del...

MARCELLA   *(whispers)* Karen? It's all right. We'll stay together for as long as we can.

ROBO   *(moans)* No no no no noo noo noo...

MARCELLA   We'll stay together. We'll leave together. We'll walk out together. From wherever it is that they take us.

ROBO   *No hablo español.*

KAREN   We'll stay together. Because we're *compañeras.*

Sound: The truck motor grows louder, drowning out nearly all other sound.

(internal) At Peace Brigades, we'd discussed what we'd do when picked up by police. Survival strategy. And I'd decided I would answer all their questions in as much detail as possible. The clown who says too much.

Music: "Clown" theme, very slow and stealthy.

Scene Fifteen: Interrogation Room

Sound: A cigar is lit. A clock ticks.

CAPTAIN   Your name is Karen Ridd.

KAREN   Karen Elizabeth Ridd. *(spelling her name)* K. A. R. E. N. E. L. I. Z. A. B. E. T. H. R. I. D. D. I was named for my father's grandmother. *(internal)* I would provide much too much information. I would look at every question metaphysically.

CAPTAIN   Perhaps you will tell us what you're doing in El Salvador...

KAREN	It happened this way… I know it sounds unlikely, but I was working as a clown. At a hospital. In Winnipeg. In Canada. With kids. I was Robo the Clown.
ROBO	El-sal-va— *(siren effect, continuing underneath)*
CAPTAIN	My question is why are you here. In El Salvador. Today.
KAREN	I'm trying to explain.
CAPTAIN	No, *señorita*, you are trying to fill in time. You're trying to entertain me.
KAREN	I'm sorry, my Spanish… *(apologizing continues)*
	(internal, over her apologizing) As survival strategy, the technique may be transparent but this doesn't mean it's not effective. The storyteller can control the story and the prisoner who maintains control is not truly and totally a prisoner.
CAPTAIN	I'm not so sure this information is important, *señorita*.
KAREN	*(internal)* The object is to tell these stories well, so the listener will allow them to continue.
ROBO	Winnipeg. W. I. N. N…
CAPTAIN	*Señorita*…
KAREN	*(internal)* Scheherazade. A woman, not a threat.
ROBO	Volleyball. V.O. L. L…
CAPTAIN	I'm not so sure we need to know so much. About volleyball. About Winnipeg.
KAREN	*(internal)* A strange thing you should know. I wasn't afraid.
ROBO	*Tengo miedo.*
KAREN	No, Robo… not really afraid. Not because I was brave, but because there wasn't time. I wasn't afraid. I wasn't alone. There was too much to think about. So many stories to tell. So many questions to answer.
CAPTAIN	*(angry)* We need to know your contacts in El Salvador. We need names of the people you work with.
KAREN	*(internal)* I knew that I'd be safer than Marcella. Because I'm tall and blond and she's small and dark. Because I'm North American and she's from Colombia.
	Sound: Paper ripped in half.
	Sound: ROBO gasps.
	(internal) I was safer. I was not immune.
CAPTAIN	The prisoner's statement is ingenuous.

KAREN	Is what?
ROBO	*Ingenuo. Candoroso.*
CAPTAIN	Do you think I'm naive?
KAREN	I'm sorry, my Spanish is imperfect.
ROBO	*Esta candoroso.*
CAPTAIN	You're in El Salvador to work with subversives, *señorita*, the FMLN…
KAREN	I'm in El Salvador to learn about the country, because I find it beautiful. I'm working for…
CAPTAIN	We know who you're working for.
KAREN	I am working for Peace Brigades Inter—
	Sound: A slap. KAREN cries out.
	Peace Brigades International which is non-violent, non-aligned—
	Sound: More slaps: one, two. KAREN gasps and cries out.
KAREN	*(internal)* Three hours of questions. And I am not beaten much…
CAPTAIN	I am frustrated, *señorita*, I'm afraid…
ROBO	*(underneath) No tengo miedo, no tengo miedo.*
CAPTAIN	It seems you've said so much, yet you've told me so little.
	Music: Stealthy "Clown" theme fades in.
KAREN	*(internal)* Five hours of questions. I am Scheherazade…
ROBO	*Ich bin ein Berliner, ein Winnipeger…*
CAPTAIN	My clerk begs your indulgence. Since he must write down everything you say.
KAREN	*(internal)* Six hours of questions. So many stories I can't tell. Survival strategy. I take to asking questions of my own.
CAPTAIN	You are trying to entertain me, *señorita*.
KAREN	Do you have a family?
ROBO	Am I like your daughter? Like your sister?
KAREN	*(internal)* I have an agenda. Survival strategy. I have something I can do so I am not afraid. I have something I can do. I still have power.
CAPTAIN	I have a daughter. She is eight years old. This week.
ROBO	I am eight years old this week.
KAREN	*(internal)* And I am so much safer than so many. Because I'm tall. And blond. And North American.

CAPTAIN	But I regret, *señorita*, we have no more time for pleasantries.
	Music: "Clown" theme pulls short, alarmed.
KAREN	We don't?
ROBO	*Como no?*
CAPTAIN	It seems your consul has arrived. To secure your release.

Scene Sixteen: Prison Hallway

Sound: Military escort marching, keys jangling, prisoners' muffled curses and sobs, all underneath.

| KAREN | *(internal)* On the way out of the cellblock, I saw Marcella. She was handcuffed, blindfolded, pushed face against the wall. Objectified. She wasn't a person. She was a prisoner. The image of a prisoner, nameless, faceless, forgotten…. I knew I couldn't leave her as if she were a poster, ignored on a wall… |

Scene Seventeen: Prison Office

Sound: Rubber stamp, pesky fly buzzes.

SOLDIER ONE	Her name is Karen Ridd?
CONSUL	That's right.
SOLDIER ONE	Her papers seem to be in order.
CONSUL	Thank you.
SOLDIER ONE	And she's released to your authority.
CONSUL	Yes.
KAREN	No.
SOLDIER ONE	I beg your pardon?
CONSUL	He's saying you're released to my authority. Because I'm your consul.
KAREN	I know that.
CONSUL	He's saying you're free.
KAREN	I can't leave.
SOLDIER ONE	*(with a Spanish accent)* Excuse me, *señorita*, but…
KAREN	I can't leave without my friend.
CONSUL	Of course you can.
KAREN	I'm sorry.

CONSUL	You realize, of course, that we've gone to some trouble to ensure your release, Miss Ridd.
	Music: "Colombian" theme, with a driving rhythm, begins underneath.
KAREN	I'm sorry
CONSUL	You realize, of course, it's twenty minutes until curfew.
SOLDIER ONE	You realize, of course, your friend has been released.
KAREN	No, I'm sorry. She hasn't.
CONSUL	Miss Ridd…
KAREN	I've seen her.
CONSUL	Miss Ridd, we have to leave before the curfew.
KAREN	I'm sorry.
CONSUL	Your friend will have to work with her own consul.
KAREN	My friend is handcuffed, blindfolded. She's alone and I can't leave her. *(internal)* It wasn't brave. I didn't feel brave, it wasn't hard to say I couldn't leave. It seemed the only thing to say, it seemed right, of course, and also, to be honest, I didn't think they'd let me stay.
CONSUL	Miss Ridd, I must warn you…
KAREN	*(internal)* I imagined the scene in the movie. The heroine protests the hero's fate.
CONSUL	You're being very foolish.
KAREN	*(internal)* She throws herself in front of the firing squad, she's dragged away…
	Sound: Briefcase snapped shut, chair pushed away.
CONSUL	I can't help you, Miss Ridd.
KAREN	Please…
CONSUL	I can't order you to come with me.
KAREN	But you do understand, don't you?
CONSUL	No, I don't.
KAREN	You understand loyalty. And camaraderie. You understand Marcella and I… we're *compañeras*.
CONSUL	I can guarantee your security now. If you come with me now.
KAREN	No. I can't.
	Music: "Colombian" theme ends with a flourish.

Sound: A rubber stamp.

SOLDIER ONE You will get what you want. We can give you what you want… if you choose to be in prison…

Scene Eighteen: Prison

Sound: Rattling bars. Hoots and jeers of young soldiers. "La quiero!" "Hey, gringa," air kisses, etc., underneath.

ROBO *(talking back, underneath)* Cojones grandes. La boca grande…

MARCELLA *(calling out)* Karen!

Sound: Handcuffs being unlocked, soldiers saunter by.

KAREN *(internal)* They put us in a room together. I was blindfolded again, but they took Marcella's handcuffs off and we joined hands. The young soldiers came by the room where we'd been put. To see the curiosity.

SOLDIER ONE Are these the girls who like us so much?

ROBO *Mucho macho!*

SOLDIER TWO Are you going to spend the night, girls?

SOLDIER ONE They're holding hands.

ROBO *Macho mucho!*

SOLDIER TWO Do they like us? Or do they like each other?

Sound: SOLDIER TWO laughs, but his laugh peters out.

Music: "Magic" theme, continuing underneath.

KAREN *(internal)* This is the magic. The soldiers became clowns. They wanted simple answers, or they wanted to be loved, perhaps, but something happened. Something changed. Something reached them.

SOLDIER TWO *Las putas…. Las huecas…*

SOLDIER ONE Leave them alone.

SOLDIER THREE

(with a Spanish accent) Si, deja las. Leave them alone. They're compañeras.

Music: A sweet crescendo, mingling of "Clown" and "El Salvador" themes, up and into next scene.

Scene Nineteen: Interior Monologue

Sound: siren and TV babble.

KAREN *(internal)* We were released at nine o'clock that evening. A military escort took us through the curfew. We went to the Hilton hotel where we watched CNN.

Sound: A clown explosion.

ROBO *Esta Robo brava con El Sal-va... (makes explosion sound)*

Sound: A real bomb drops in the distance.

KAREN *(internal)* We laughed a lot. We were clown CNN reporters as the news denied bombing we saw from our balcony.

ROBO *El. (explosion sound) Esta de ningun manera una explosion.*

Sound: TV and siren out. Roll call of martyrs begins and continues underneath.

KAREN *(internal)* I wanted to tell Daysi what had happened. How simple it had seemed to know what to do, both for me and for the soldiers who recaptured me.

ROBO *(singing to the tune of "A Bicycle Built for Two," underneath)* Mar-gar-ita.... *No tengas miedo...*

KAREN *(internal)* But we were asked to leave the country the next day. I came back to Canada, to write and talk about El Salvador.... Marcella went to Mexico. Where she works with a union.

Sound: Roll call of martyrs continuing underneath.

(internal) Daysi "disappeared" in December 1989. Her body was discovered six days later. She had been tortured for some time before she died. Daysi Alonzo Jaimes. *Presente.*

Sound: Sirens wail, then stop.

Music: Big drum goes on for a long time.

The end.

FAMOUS

Famous premiered on November 25, 1997 at the Tarragon Theatre Extra Space, with the following company:

Linda Prystawsk	Kit
Yanna McIntosh	Sheila

Directed by Pam Eddenden
Set and Costume Design by David Wootton
Sound Design by Rick Sacks
Stage Manager: Marla Friedman
Production Manager: Keith Freiter
Technical Director: David Horner

CHARACTERS

KIT
SHEILA

FAMOUS

ACT ONE

KIT lies on a deck chair by a pool under bright, white sunlight. She is wearing a string bikini and very dark glasses. She is wired to a Walkman. On a table beside her is a large container of yogurt and a large pitcher of orange juice. The whole place smells of suntan lotion.

There is a chain-link fence upstage, protecting the pool. It is covered by vines and foliage. From behind this fence, we hear the click of a camera shutter. Then another. Then another. Camera shutters continue under.

Camera flashes and shutters also from the house behind the audience. KIT addresses these cameras.

KIT   I hear you. You think I can't hear you? You and your cameras. You're not the only one who has a camera.

She takes a camcorder off a tripod. She aims it at the photographers—and the audience.

Do you like it? Getting your picture taken? You could be on TV. On the *Candida Grey Show*, right? Just as long as you sign their release.

She reverses the camera so it's pointing towards her, perhaps holding it between her feet or her knees. She leans in to address the camera directly.

Yes. I'm ready for my close-up now. *(KIT and the camera, a dance and seduction.)* "Kits Video Diary. Chapter 312." Where? Sandy's pool. And the photographers are back. Even though Sandy is in court, of course, which they must know.

She raps.

Since you all shot her going into court
You must have got her going into court

*She takes off her Walkman to try a new and even more seductive
song:*

She raps.

What is it you want to see?
I know what you want to see
More… right?

*She turns the volume up on a boom box, and begins to strut and pose
for the photographers.*

Yes. My name is Kit. And I'm your Sunshine Girl. I like health foods.
You want to see me drink my orange juice? Eat my yogurt? *(She drinks,
then licks her yogurt spoon.)* Yum. What? My favourite music? Well, I
like Mozart, because it makes you smarter—did you know that…? But
I like all kinds of music, you know. I like country, heavy metal, rap…

She turns up the volume.

She raps.

Am I a feminist? Forget it.
Feminism? Who can sweat it?
Guys will always be preliminary
to my work with battered women

*SHEILA, a young black woman, appears from the house with a
wheeled cart. The cart holds a TV set, trailing wires, and extension
cords. SHEILA is full of energy and dressed rather wonderfully.*

SHEILA	Okay! I'm back.
KIT	*(to the paparazzi)* No, really, I want to work with battered women.
SHEILA	I got Sandy's TV. And her VCR.
KIT	Hundreds of… thousands of battered women.
SHEILA	From the basement.
KIT	I could teach them a trade. Like lap dancing.

Paparazzi shutters increase.

SHEILA	What is it? More photographers?
KIT	Oh dear. My shoulder strap slipped off my shoulder. Mercy me. How did that happen?
SHEILA	Kit, don't…
KIT	What do you want to see? I know what you want to see…

*KIT is about to pull off one or another part of her bikini. SHEILA
grabs her and shields her body from the continuing action of the
cameras.*

SHEILA	It's okay. Let me handle it.
KIT	Tits and ass. Is that all they want? Tits and ass.

> *KIT sits on the deck chair. SHEILA moves lawn umbrellas, or whatever, to block the photographers' view.*

SHEILA	*(to paparazzi)* Get out. Out.
KIT	No, they want more. Like, "What is Sandy like?"
SHEILA	Out of here. Slime. You don't want her story.
KIT	"What's that like? Being Sandy's best friend?"
SHEILA	Sleazy weasels. No more pictures. Scum buckets.
KIT	"What's it like, Kit? How do you deal with it? When you're Sandy's best friend, and she's on trial for—"
SHEILA	It's all right. They're gone.
KIT	But they'll be back, won't they? They'll climb some tree. They'll find some better angle.
SHEILA	Yes, probably.

> *SHEILA turns off the boom box and prepares to tape.*

KIT	Until the trial's over, right? Until they get to pull the switch on her.
SHEILA	That's not going to happen.
KIT	I know that.
SHEILA	Because you don't pull switches, do you? Here in Canada?
KIT	Because Sandy's going to say what happened. Nothing happened. It's all Bobby's fault.

> *SHEILA focuses the camera on KIT.*

SHEILA	Is that true, Kit?
KIT	What time is it?
SHEILA	Do you think that's true? Really?
KIT	I know. It's time for *Candida*.
SHEILA	Forget *Candida*.
KIT	*(connecting cables)* We don't have to use this for our monitor.
SHEILA	But we should
KIT	Broadcast mode.
SHEILA	We should work on our show, Kit…
KIT	We should watch *Candida*. Because you like this one, right?

> *KIT turns on the TV. CANDIDA appears on the screen.*

CANDIDA   *(on screen)* Welcome back to *Candida*…

KIT   It's Sir somebody something.

SHEILA   Isaiah Berlin.

KIT   Because you won all those awards, right?

CANDIDA   *(on screen)* Today we are talking to "Mothers Whose Sons Are Gay Bar Strippers."

KIT   Right on.

SHEILA   This is not Sir Isaiah Berlin.

KIT   No, don't change it.

> *TROY, a clean-cut gay bar-stripper, in a sports jacket and a button-down shirt, gets up to do a bump and grind. The audience applauds, hoots, and whistles, led by TROY's MOM.*

TROY's MOM
> *(on screen, continues under)* Go, Troy! Go, Troy!

SHEILA   This is a rerun.

KIT   I know.

SHEILA   This is a Sweeps Week thing.

KIT   Is that Troy's mom? Really?

SHEILA   This needs a context.

KIT   Troy's cute.

> *KIT lies back on her lounge chair, replacing her sunglasses as TROY takes off his tie and drapes it around CANDIDA, to more hoots and applause.*

CANDIDA   *(on screen)* So, if you were Troy's mom, how would you feel about his lifestyle?

> *CANDIDA heads up through the audience for an answer.*

SHEILA   This show may seem cheap. It is cheap…

TROY's MOM
> *(on screen)* I've always been glad Troy has wanted to express himself.

SHEILA   "Mothers Whose Sons Are Gay Bar Strippers." Okay, it's on the edge. Okay, it's not high-concept. Okay, it's a joke.

CANDIDA   *(on screen)* We'll pause now in this edition of *Candida*: "Mothers Whose Sons Are Gay Bar Strippers," to bring you these messages…

> *SHEILA turns off the TV sound.*

SHEILA   Isaiah Berlin is dead, you know.

But he and Troy live on, together, forever, on *The Candida Grey Show*.

They're both good on TV, whatever that means. Isaiah Berlin, historian, philosopher. And Troy, the Sweeps Week thing.

In the Berlin interview, we talked about his essay—you know, his essay on Archilochus... no, you probably don't... "The Hedgehog and the Fox."

Because Archilochus wrote "The fox knows many things, but the hedgehog knows one big thing." And Sir Isaiah asked us to try to go beyond the literal meaning of those words. Beyond the image of the hedgehog in a spiky ball, the fox defeated.

Because he thought, taken figuratively, the words might expose one of the deepest differences between writers, between thinkers, between all of us.

The fox knows many things, but the hedgehog knows one big thing.

Taken figuratively.

What does that mean? I don't know, but I cried when I heard Isaiah Berlin was dead. Not because of my award—it was only an ACE award, I mean you get them for breathing, and they look like hockey pucks. And not because he had died. Not exactly. Because he was eighty-eight, which is not a sad time to die, exactly. But I cried.

I probably won't even hear when Troy dies. He may be dead already, and nobody knows, unless he's from a very tiny town and his very tiny hometown paper printed his obit: "Dancer Dies. Appeared on *Candida Grey Show*."

Fame. It's strange, isn't it.

(SHEILA notices KIT might be dead.) Hello? Earth calling Kit? *(pause)* You aren't listening, right? Are you still alive?

> *No response from KIT. SHEILA turns the TV sound up. Loud. It's a hard sell pitch for life insurance, which continues under. KIT takes off her sunglasses.*

KIT   Were you talking to me?

SHEILA   Did I interrupt something? *(turns sound off)* Of course. Your Mozart tapes again.

KIT   *(removes earphones)* You should try them.

SHEILA   "Kit's Video Diary. Chapter Eight."

KIT   Self improvement.

SHEILA   "Mozart Makes You Smarter."

KIT   Sheila, you know what I think sometimes? I think you don't like us.

SHEILA   You're kidding, right?

KIT	Me and Sandy. We like you. But you, you think we're trashy. You think all we think about is sunblock.
SHEILA	I am not your friend, Kit. I'm your videographer.
KIT	But I would like to ask you something…. Can I ask you something?
SHEILA	Hey, why not?
KIT	You know that guy you introduced us to? Last night? You know the white guy?
SHEILA	The who?
KIT	The guy you work with. Because Sandy and I were thinking, is he your boss? And Sandy thought he was, but I thought, I don't know.
SHEILA	The "white" guy.
KIT	You know, the guy who gets to go to court. The guy who's at the trial today. You know, what's his name? Tommy. I mean, are you more important, because you've been up here all week with us, getting to know us… me and Sandy…. Or is he more important, because he flies up, you know, at the last minute. And he goes to the trial?
SHEILA	It doesn't work like that.
KIT	He's there. Right now. At the trial.
SHEILA	It isn't who's important. Who's more important…
KIT	He's there.
SHEILA	Tommy and I work together.
KIT	He's there. With Sandy.
SHEILA	Tommy and I are friends, Kit. We've been friends for years.
KIT	He said he flew up here. First class.
SHEILA	He said what?
KIT	Is that true?
SHEILA	He didn't fly first class.
KIT	Would you pass me my sunblock?
	SHEILA does. KIT applies sunblock carefully.
SHEILA	I don't care who goes first class.
KIT	Tommy does.
SHEILA	No. I doubt that.
KIT	And maybe you're working together, but… but I'd watch my ass.
SHEILA	You don't quite understand…

KIT	I mean, you're at the bar, trying to get them to forget last call. And Tommy's on your case. "So, girls, is Sheila working out?" "So girls, are you getting along?"
SHEILA	I've known Tommy since high school.
KIT	"So girls, what's the girl talk? What are you telling Sheila you're not telling me? What's the story on the flashlight? What's the story on the sister?" But don't worry, Sheila…
SHEILA	Tommy got me this job. With Candida.
KIT	Sandy and I, we said how much we liked you. And Sandy said that you were simpatico. And he wasn't simpatico. She doesn't like him. I mean, I'm sorry. I guess, since you're "working together."
SHEILA	You don't think we're working together?
KIT	I mean, I like him. I think he's cute, but Sandy doesn't like him, so she plays this trick on him, okay? So she tells him that you told us that we had to sign some papers…
SHEILA	Our releases?
KIT	So he gets all excited, so he's fumbling for his briefcase, so he brings out all these papers, and Sandy pretends it's too dark to read them, and he says that's okay, he'll explain, and he explains: "This release is for *Candida*. This release is for your documentary." So, Sandy says, well, he didn't explain as well as you did, but she'll sign…
SHEILA	She signed? She signed the releases?
KIT	So, then she pretends she's a little looped, and she spills the sangria all over the table…
SHEILA	But she signed.
KIT	And Tommy's wiping off the pineapple and kiwi fruit, and telling her the sangria is all his fault, and then he sees what she signed: "U.R.A. Dickhead."
SHEILA	She didn't sign.
KIT	She signed "U.R.A. Dickhead."
SHEILA	Which I'll bet Tommy thought was really funny.
KIT	He swore at her.
SHEILA	He never jokes about releases.
KIT	She should have signed "I.M.A. C-word." That's what he told her.
SHEILA	Tommy takes his work seriously.
KIT	But that's disgusting, right? So that's why Sandy doesn't like him. So that's why she told him how she liked you.

SHEILA	Let me put this in context for you, Kit—
KIT	No, really, you came up here, and you brought your briefcase out, and showed her all your papers, and Sandy was a little looped…
SHEILA	I'm just as serious as Tommy.
KIT	But Sandy was so looped, she would have signed anything. But you told her what she was signing. You told her what "release" meant.
SHEILA	I'm much more serious, in fact.
KIT	That's not what Tommy thinks.
SHEILA	It's what he knows. Because his last three shows were based on my proposals.
KIT	No. Sheila. Really, please. Don't get me wrong. Tommy says Candida loves you. They all love you. Because you're so crazy. You go crazy over stories, you love stories. Tommy says that you're a sweetheart.
SHEILA	No.
KIT	You care. And you let people know that you care.
SHEILA	Tommy doesn't think that I'm a sweetheart.
KIT	But he said he was here now. He said we'd see. That he was a mean SOB. *(pause)* What's wrong, Sheila? *(pause)* Sheila? Are you crying?
SHEILA	*(is she crying?)* Tommy thinks I'm a poseur. And I am… I am a poetaster.
KIT	Are you okay? No, really…
SHEILA	He thinks I think I can work in TV, I can make it an art. But he knows it's a game. And it is a game. It's a game for him. And he takes it so seriously. Wheeling, dealing, winning. Pro-ball. And he says I've been playing around. He says I'm an amateur.
KIT	You've been working. No, really.
SHEILA	I should have tape by now. For *Candida*. That's what Tommy said. "Where's your tape?"
KIT	You've taped us.
SHEILA	Let me put this in context for you—
KIT	You've got lots of tape. Of Sandy. Of me. And Sandy asks me what I think is important. And then I ask Sandy.
SHEILA	What I've got—
KIT	Can you play me those tapes again? Can I see the one where we're like rap stars?
SHEILA	Candida wants—

KIT	Our release. Right. I know.
SHEILA	She wants sound bites. She wants mainstream. She wants Fox. What I've got, you and Sandy, all your numbers—I know there's a story there…
KIT	And that's our documentary, right?
SHEILA	And Candida may love it too, but she'll point out… it isn't Fox.
KIT	I can do Fox.
SHEILA	We can both do Fox. Anytime.

SHEILA slots a tape in the VCR, and punches it up. KIT appears on the screen.

SHEILA	But you remember this, Kit?
KIT	*(on video)* "Kit's Video Diary, Chapter One." In my opinion, it's all Bobby's fault.

The KIT on video freezes, frightened, like a deer in headlights. SHEILA, on the video, is side coaching, not very audibly, as SHEILA, live, prods KIT, live.

SHEILA	Kit? What is Bobby's fault? Kit?

SHEILA sets up the camera. KIT pouts.

KIT	Sandy's going to testify? Now the trial has started. It was Bobby's fault. What happened?
SHEILA	What's she going to say, Kit?
KIT	She will testify.
SHEILA	Tell me what happened.
KIT	Nothing happened.
SHEILA	Three girls are dead, Kit…
KIT	Sheila? If we sign your release? Does that mean we won't get paid?
SHEILA	Why is it Bobby's fault?
KIT	Why won't you pay us? Why not? Sheila? Then we'd go on TV, and we'd say…

Pause.

SHEILA	Say what?
KIT	We'd say whatever you wanted us to say.
SHEILA	I don't want you to say what I want you to say.
KIT	Why not? Sheila? Then we'd go on TV and be famous.
SHEILA	What happened? With Sandy and Bobby…?

KIT	"Kit's Video Diary. Chapter 507." How do I get that cover-girl look?
SHEILA	What happened, Kit? What really happened?
	But KIT is intoxicated with her own performance. She dances in to mug for the camera.
KIT	Ooh, Alberto!… Will you put that on TV?
SHEILA	Kit, let's get real…
KIT	I'll release that…. Oooh, Alberto! "Kit's Video Diary, Chapter 507." It's yours.
SHEILA	*Mea culpa.*
KIT	Sheila, can I ask you something?
SHEILA	I come up here. All the way from San Francisco. And I start thinking "feature." I start thinking "PBS."
KIT	Why did you stop? Taping me?
SHEILA	Kit, what we have here…. Let me put this in context for you—
KIT	How come? You aren't taping me?
SHEILA	I want content. I've got context. I want content.
KIT	Sheila, it's a joke, right? Like, "Oooh, Alberto!" Like, who cares about hair?
SHEILA	What we have here, Kit, is a serious situation.
KIT	But it's not our fault.
SHEILA	Why is Sandy in court today, Kit?
KIT	She didn't do it.
SHEILA	Three girls are dead…
KIT	You know what Sandy says? Her judge is diabetic.
SHEILA	Now what?
KIT	It means he'll take a break. In court. About every hour and a half or so, to give himself a chance to pee. That's what she says her lawyer says.
SHEILA	I don't know what you're trying to say.
KIT	It means Tommy should call you, right? If he has time, he should call you, since you both work together so well…. What time is it? Eleven?
	SHEILA looks at her watch.
SHEILA	It's ten forty-five.
KIT	But I like Tommy. Really. I mean, did you see how many calls he took last night? In the bar? On his cellphone? Short guys, right? They really need their cellphones.

SHEILA	Let's forget about Tommy…
KIT	The thing about Tommy, why Sandy doesn't like him, he keeps coming on to her.
SHEILA	That's a joke, right?
	She raps.
KIT	Just another white boy, trying to be bad Just another white boy, trying to be bad…
	SHEILA picks up the video camera.
SHEILA	Who is trying to be bad?
KIT	They're dancing. And he's got one hand on her ass, and her hand's underneath his belt buckle. And he's pasted up against her like they're walls and wallpaper… and her tongue's in his—
	She notices SHEILA and her camera. She breaks off.
	You're taping me.
SHEILA	Keep going.
KIT	Why are you taping me?
SHEILA	Keep going.
KIT	Why are you taping me now?
SHEILA	Go on. You're on a roll.
KIT	No. Tell me. Why, Sheila?
SHEILA	Let's just tape, okay?
KIT	Do you want me to talk about what an asshole Tommy is?
SHEILA	This is not about Tommy.
KIT	What is it about? What is it about? What. Is. It. About.
SHEILA	It's about you, Kit.
KIT	You don't care about me.
SHEILA	Yes. I do. Oddly enough, I do.
KIT	Why, Sheila? Why would care you are about me?
SHEILA	Because you're my show, Kit.
KIT	Yes! I will be your show.
SHEILA	When you sign my release.
KIT	So, what should I say? What do you want me to say?
SHEILA	Say whatever you want.

KIT	No… you know, Sheila. You know what would look good. Do you want me to look smart? Do you want me to look stupid.
SHEILA	Do you want to look stupid?
KIT	Because last night, in the bar, you were taping Sandy telling stupid midget-in-blender jokes. Which you must have heard ten years ago. In San Francisco…
SHEILA	It's not about which midget jokes I know.
KIT	But you got them all. On tape. So when Candida gets Sandy on her show, she'll have all these little cards, she'll say "Sandy, why do you think those midget jokes are funny?" And Sandy will tell one of her midget jokes, and she'll look like an idiot.
SHEILA	Sandy's not an idiot, is she Kit?
KIT	But she acts like one, right?
SHEILA	Why is that?
KIT	And so do I, right?
SHEILA	Yes. You act like your head's full of candy floss. Your head's full of pinball. Your whole head's this bar scene, and there's nobody up there except maybe Megadeth.
KIT	You don't like Megadeth?
SHEILA	What do you think?
KIT	Okay. It isn't Mozart.

> *KIT looks a little lost. SHEILA picks up the camera.*

SHEILA	"Kit's Video Diary. Chapter 508."
KIT	No, Sheila…
SHEILA	Megadeath or Mozart?
KIT	No. No. I don't know what to say.

> *SHEILA passes her the camera.*

SHEILA	Then why don't you tape me?
KIT	Sheila? Wha…?
SHEILA	Go ahead. No, I'll tell you my story.
KIT	You're kidding, right?
SHEILA	I work in TV. I don't think it's art, but I don't think it's cheap. I don't think it has to be cheap. *(looks toward KIT and discovers)* You're not taping me?
KIT	Why should I?
SHEILA	Because I'm telling you my story, Kit.

KIT	But why should I care? Sheila?
SHEILA	You don't care about my story?
KIT	No offence.
SHEILA	Why don't you care about my story?
KIT	Well, shouldn't a story be interesting?
SHEILA	Shouldn't. A story be. Interesting. Isn't that a good question…
KIT	Sheila…?
SHEILA	No one likes a dull story.
KIT	Sheila, are you mad at me?
SHEILA	And I come up here. All the way from San Francisco…
KIT	*(picks up camera)* Are you mad at me? Sheila? I'm sorry… I'll tape you.
SHEILA	I come up here six days ago, and I thought it would be easy. Six days in Canada with two bimbettes…
KIT	*(stops taping)* What do you mean? Bimbettes?
SHEILA	Did I say bimbettes?
KIT	Yes. You did. Two bimbettes.
SHEILA	I just meant you're meant to be easy.
KIT	You don't think I'm easy?
SHEILA	But Sandy, she keeps talking to her lawyer. Or her mother. Or her mother and her lawyer.
KIT	That's why I think I like you.
SHEILA	The trial hasn't even started yet, but she's in pain. She's under so much stress. And we lie around the pool some more… we veg out by the pool some more. I mean, it makes me nervous, vegging out. I think the sunblock makes me nervous.
	I'm going crazy. Because nothing is happening. I have so much tape of nothing happening. But I know there is a story there. A good story.
	And it's all so mindless that it's scary.
KIT	Everyone thinks I'm easy. Except you.
SHEILA	You're not taping me.
KIT	Because I was listening to what you were saying…
SHEILA	Can I tell you something? About getting a story? A good TV story?
KIT	Yes!
SHEILA	Right now. You're listening to what you want to hear.

KIT	I don't know what you mean.
SHEILA	Just let the camera do the work.
KIT	What do you mean?
SHEILA	Let the camera tell you. Not what I'm saying. What it is that I don't want to say. What's going on. Where the story is…
	SHEILA plays the tape again.
KIT	*(on tape)* "Kit's Video Diary. Chapter One." In my opinion. It's all Bobby's fault.
SHEILA	Let's talk about Bobby, Kit. I'll take the camera… *(She picks it up.)* Kit? Let's talk about Bobby…
KIT	How come you won't lie to me?
SHEILA	You think I don't lie to you?
KIT	You don't. You don't even bullshit. And everybody bullshits.
SHEILA	It could be we have different standards.
KIT	I don't know what you mean.
SHEILA	For lying. For bullshit. I mean I've spent six days up here. Six days of sunblock. Six days without a reality check. Six days following you around, from swimming pools to bars in strip malls. Where "How're they hanging?" is a greeting.
KIT	Is this some kind of black thing?
SHEILA	What is wrong with you people?
KIT	Is this a black thing? Calling us "you people"?
SHEILA	You and Sandy. All the guys you pick up. Those who aren't named Derek are named Jason.
KIT	What's wrong with Jason?
SHEILA	Please…
KIT	How come you don't like Jason?
SHEILA	Oh, please…
KIT	How. Come. You. Don't…
SHEILA	How come he doesn't know who Sandy is?
KIT	Because she's famous, right?
SHEILA	She is notorious.
KIT	She was in the paper. Did you see her? This morning?
SHEILA	Jason didn't. He lacks something. Any knowledge at all of the world around him. Except for MTV, of course.

KIT	Is this some kind of black thing?
SHEILA	He quotes Ice-T. He seems to listen to Ice-T. And that's about it for Jason. That's as far as he goes with current affairs.
KIT	Is this because there are no, you know, black guys in our bars?
SHEILA	*(picks up camera)* That's good.
KIT	No guys saying "Yo. Yo, ho. Come ova heah."
SHEILA	You're mad. And you're trying to make me mad. Which will look good on tape.
KIT	I'm kidding.
SHEILA	No. No, you're not, Kit.
KIT	I am kidding. Around.
SHEILA	No. You're starting to see what TV is about.
KIT	TV makes you famous.
SHEILA	No. Maybe you're not.
KIT	Geraldo says I am going to be famous for friendship.
SHEILA	Geraldo? *(like "Antichrist")*
KIT	All these people are calling.
SHEILA	Are you talking to Geraldo?
KIT	Sheila? Can I ask you something?
SHEILA	When did Geraldo call?
KIT	How much should we charge? For exclusive?
SHEILA	About Geraldo, Kit…
KIT	You know what? I don't trust him.
SHEILA	Go with that.
KIT	I mean, that's why we turned on the answering machine. That's why we turned off the phone. I mean, why do you think the phone's not ringing?
	SHEILA's cellphone rings in her briefcase.
KIT	Is that for you?
SHEILA	Probably.
KIT	Who is it?
SHEILA	It could be for me. Since it's my cellphone.
	She finds her briefcase and her cellphone.
KIT	Who is it? Tommy?

SHEILA	(on the phone) Hello…. Yes, hello, Boyd.
KIT	Who's Boyd?
SHEILA	(on the phone) I know. I just heard th… (BOYD is yelling at her.) No, I'm not. No, I'm not. Look, Boyd, please… it is under control.

She hangs up.

KIT	Who's Boyd?
SHEILA	Where's the answering machine?
KIT	Sheila? You know, don't you? I mean, how much "How Much" is? Exclusive?
SHEILA	Where's the answering machine?
KIT	In the family room.
SHEILA	Sure. The family room. In the basement.
KIT	Where the TV was.
SHEILA	The basement. It gives me the creeps.

She exits.

KIT	You just think that because of Skippy. Because that's where they say Bobby—(a crash from offstage) Sheila? Sheila, are you okay? Sheila, did you break something?
SHEILA	(offstage) No.
KIT	Did you knock down the picture of Skippy? (no reply from SHEILA) I hate that picture. Skippy on black velvet, and her eyes follow you. And there you are, you're just trying to watch *Married… with Children.* And there's Sandy's little sister, she keeps watching you.

SHEILA enters with an answering machine, trailing extension cords.

SHEILA	That basement is creepy.
KIT	You broke something, right?
SHEILA	Never mind.
KIT	If it was Skippy's picture, you're in shit.
SHEILA	Skippy's picture's fine.
KIT	But you knocked if it off the wall, right? Because it's got all those lights around it, and you were in a hurry, and they're plugged in with the answering machine.
SHEILA	Do you mind if I play this tape back?
KIT	Is this like mail? Is this like opening Sandy's mail?

SHEILA turns on the tape. Clicks of hang-ups, then.

FEMALE VOICE ONE

They're going to lock you up. And I hope they lock you up with a lot of people who know just what to do with a mop han—

SHEILA hits fast forward.

KIT There's a lot of that. If you like that kind of thing.

SHEILA hits play.

MALE VOICE ONE

You slut, you cu—

SHEILA hits fast forward.

KIT You know what I found out about this? As a thing about life? There's not that much to say…. People don't have much to say…

SHEILA hits play.

MALE VOICE TWO

—true what they say you're inta? Hey, babe, you wanna get together to do a little suck and—

SHEILA hits fast forward.

KIT That's the guy before Geraldo.

SHEILA Geraldo…

She hits play.

FEMALE VOICE TWO

—praying for you, hoping that you'll find the Lord, because no matter…

KIT joins the tape as it continues under.

KIT *(with tape)* …because no matter what you've done there's hope. Our Lord died for you in agony, he had nails through his hands, and when he begged for water, we gave him vinegar.

FEMALE VOICE TWO

(continues under) …but he forgave us. "And I saw another mighty angel come down…"

KIT *(over tape)* We gave him vinegar. We turned the blender on.

SHEILA Kit…

KIT catches up to tape, quoting Revelations:

KIT "…from heaven, clothed with a cloud. And a rainbow was upon his head, and his face was as it were the sun, and his feet as pillars of fire…"

SHEILA Kit, please…. Cut it out.

KIT *(with tape)* "And he had in his hand a little book open…"

> *SHEILA slaps KIT. KIT bursts into tears.*

SHEILA   It's okay, Kit…. It's okay, baby.

> *She hugs her. The tape continues under.*

FEMALE VOICE TWO
"These have the power to shut heaven, that it rain not in the days of their prophecy—"

> *SHEILA breaks away from KIT to turn off the tape.*

SHEILA   She's a nutcase. It's okay. It's over.

KIT   If you want to know who called, if that's so important…. Numero Uno must have been *Geraldo*. Numero Two was *Entertainment Tonight*. Then *Lifestyles of the Rich and Famous*, and then Sandy says, "But I'm not rich…" and they say, "Maybe we can help with that."

SHEILA   It's the money again.

KIT   They say fifteen thousand dollars. For Sandy.

SHEILA   That's not the way it works, Kit.

KIT   That's not the way you work, that's for sure.

> *KIT turns on the tape. It plays.*

FEMALE VOICE THREE
"…that Robin would like to help with that."

> *SHEILA turns off the tape.*

KIT   You just keep trying to buy us drinks. You just keep saying, "Sign the release, Kit."

SHEILA   I don't make promises.

KIT   Fifteen thou. Is that good?

SHEILA   I don't make promises I can't keep.

KIT   Did you see Sandy? In the paper? Last week?

SHEILA   Every day last week.

KIT   But on Wednesday, right?

SHEILA   I'm Sandy's clipping service.

KIT   But on Wednesday, in the paper, she's just on her way to court, that's all, and my little sister is just eating her cornflakes, that's all, and my sister says Sandy looks awful…

SHEILA   On Wednesday, she looked like Tammy Faye Baker.

KIT   That's why I slapped my sister, and my mom screamed at me, and I called her what I called her, and she threw me out of the house.

That's why I'm staying with Sandy, who my mom calls my "trashy and perverted friend."

SHEILA   Is this going somewhere?

KIT   Did you think that Sandy looked awful?

SHEILA   What is this about, Kit?

KIT   I guess you thought that she had too much makeup on. Because Sandy's mom said she had too much makeup on. Her mom said she looked like a tart. She called her slut-face.

SHEILA   She was probably right.

KIT   Sandy's mom made her cry. Which smeared her makeup, of course. I mean, it wasn't her fault. I mean, she did look awful, but is that her fault?

SHEILA   Is it makeup again? Is it shampoo again?

KIT   What about Princess Di? Her thighs? And all those guys drilled holes in walls so they could get new angles.

SHEILA   Sandy's no Princess Di.

KIT   You know how much they paid her? Princess Di? Before she died… they had to pay her. Because they took those pictures.

SHEILA   Kit, I'm not going to pay you.

KIT   Why not?

SHEILA   Those photographers. What they paid was damages.

KIT   Right on.

SHEILA   And damages mean hurt or harm. To reputation, for example.

KIT   But all it was, it was a crotch shot, Sheila.

SHEILA   Trust me on this, you can trust me on this. I don't want to defame you. I don't even want to send you up.

KIT   But you could, right?

SHEILA   If I do, you can sue me.

KIT   Oh, wow!

SHEILA   If anything I use is hurtful… to your reputation.

         Pause.

KIT   What if I wrote a book?

SHEILA   Good idea.

KIT   No, really. Everyone writes books. You could help me. How much would we get?

SHEILA	We'll write this book. And you'll make this tape of you reading this book.
KIT	Let's go for it. The book, the board game, T-shirts. Come on, Sheila. We'll make mucho dineros.
SHEILA	Believe me, Kit. There's more to life than money.
KIT	How much do you get paid?
SHEILA	Let's just say it's a learning experience.
KIT	But you do get paid. For coming up here? All the way from San Francisco? How much do you get? For stories? For telling Boyd about me.
SHEILA	It's not enough.
KIT	I bet you got danger pay, in case you got bored. While talking to bimbettes.
SHEILA	Is that the problem?
KIT	You know what I bet?
SHEILA	All right. I called you a bimbette.
KIT	I bet you thought I wasn't listening.
SHEILA	I called you a bimbette, and now you're holding it against me? Kit… Kit, you give lessons in bimbette.
KIT	But there are things that I can tell you. Things that are worth money. And you have money, don't you? Where are you staying? It's cool. There's a pool. There's a bar in your room, and all those soft-core videos on pay—
SHEILA	Oh, please, believe me, I've got live soft-core.
KIT	You mean me?
SHEILA	What do you think?
KIT	You mean me and Sandy.
SHEILA	I don't lie to you.
KIT	You know what I wish? I wish I had your job. How did you get your job? Sheila?
SHEILA	Is it important?

KIT picks up the camera and aims it at SHEILA.

KIT	Sheila? Did you sleep with Boyd?
SHEILA	Oh, please…
KIT	Is Boyd your boss? Did you sleep with him? Is he white?
SHEILA	Why would you want to know that?

KIT	I bet he is. He's white. And you know the difference between you and me?
SHEILA	Yes. I do.
KIT	It's I know who to sleep with.
SHEILA	Kit? Is that why I like you?
KIT	You should have slept with Boyd. You slept with Tommy.
SHEILA	What?
KIT	Didn't you? I'm right—right? You know how I knew? Aside from the fact that you spent all night grabbing his ass.
SHEILA	I did what?
KIT	Why I know, is Tommy told us. What he bought you.
SHEILA	No. He didn't.
KIT	Well, we made him. I mean, when he had his briefcase open, Sandy found this package, and she opened it, and she found this bra…
SHEILA	She what?
KIT	I mean, it's darling, right? This push-up bra, and it opens in front like it's outta *The Story of O,* do you know what I mean?
SHEILA	You mean that you and Sandy saw…
KIT	So did he wrap it up again? I mean, did the gift wrap look wrinkled…? *(SHEILA doesn't answer.)* Sheila?

SHEILA turns away. KIT follows her with the camera.

KIT	You know, you're right about the camera.
SHEILA	Yes. I know.
KIT	It doesn't matter what you say. It's what you're thinking sometimes, isn't it? Shelia? *(side coaching, seductive)* You're thinking, "No, the gift wrap wasn't wrinkled…" You're thinking, "No. Tommy wrapped it up again… because he felt sleazy. Because Sandy had—"
SHEILA	I think I'll take the camera…

But KIT snatches it away.

KIT	How did he wrap it up again? Was it still Disney? Because the first time it was silly, right? A joke, right? It was Mickey Mouse.
SHEILA	Give me the camera, Kit…

SHEILA pursues KIT. KIT keeps taping.

KIT	You know what I think? I think I'd be good at your job…. Let me interview you. What did you want to be when you grew up?
SHEILA	The camera…

KIT	Sheila, are you crying? Why?
SHEILA	I'm not crying.
KIT	Sheila, Tommy loves you, no, really…
SHEILA	No, Kit…
KIT	No, really, Sheila. I know stuff like that.
SHEILA	You don't know anything.
KIT	Tommy says that you're idealistic.
SHEILA	*(as if it were an insult)* I am not "idealistic."
KIT	Tommy says you are. It's because you're so innocent, right? About television. He says that's why he loves you, because you think you're going to change the world. And we're all going to be reading Great Books, and listening to Mozart, and doing volunteer work. All because of your shows for *The Candida Grey Show*.
SHEILA	Tommy didn't say that.
KIT	Yes, he did.

> *SHEILA turns away from KIT, and KIT does not pursue her.*

SHEILA	Tommy did not talk to you. About me.
KIT	No. Sheila…. No, really, only in the highest terms. Because he admires you. He says he and Boyd will never change the world…
SHEILA	I mean, I know Tommy… he and Boyd—
KIT	He said he and Boyd know. That the world pays you more if you leave it alone.
SHEILA	Are you taping this?

> *She turns to discover the camera.*

KIT	Yes, Sheila, yes. I give good interview, don't I?
SHEILA	Good interview.
KIT	You didn't like it? What I made you say?
SHEILA	You don't get to "make people say," Kit.
KIT	But it worked, Sheila, didn't it? And that means it's good interview, right?
SHEILA	There may be more to life, Kit, than good interview.
KIT	Okay. Okay, *Geraldo*, right? You mean, let's get righteous. Let's get angry… throw the chairs around.

> *KIT throws a lawn chair across the stage. SHEILA sets it right again.*

SHEILA	No, Kit…

KIT	Why not? Come on. We'll trash the place.
	KIT throws another chair.
SHEILA	*(as she sets it straight)* Kit, think….
	She raps.
KIT	You're not gonna know unless you try it Let's be lawless, let's run riot… Come on, Sheila. Let's get this on tape.
	SHEILA picks up KIT's orange juice.
SHEILA	What is in this stuff?
	SHEILA's cellphone rings. KIT picks it up as SHEILA sips her drink.
KIT	*(on the phone)* Hello…
SHEILA	This is almost pure vodka.
KIT	*(on the phone)* Hi, Boyd. Guess what? I'm interviewing Sheila. For TV.
SHEILA	Give me the phone.
	SHEILA pursues KIT around lawn furniture.
KIT	*(on the phone)* No, really. We're talking about her sex life. And black power.
SHEILA	Did you hear me?
KIT	*(on the phone)* And she said I was good. She said you should give me a job. Me and Sandy. We should have our own talk show. Sheila wants to call it *Bimbettes from Canada*.
SHEILA	Give me the phone, Kit.
KIT	*(on the phone)* What do you mean?
SHEILA	The phone…
KIT	*(on the phone)* I don't know what you mean.
SHEILA	This isn't funny.
KIT	*(on the phone)* Why would Sandy be in prison?
SHEILA	Prison?
KIT	*(on the phone)* That isn't true.
SHEILA	Prison…? Sandy?
KIT	*(shrieks into the phone)* That isn't true! Dickhead.
SHEILA	*(takes the phone)* Hello, Boyd…
KIT	He says Sandy's pleading guilty.
SHEILA	*(on the phone)* She's what?

KIT	It isn't true. Please. Why would she plead guilty?
	A flashbulb goes off behind KIT. She turns, angry.
	You're back. Dickheads!
SHEILA	*(on the phone)* Boyd, I'm sorry…
KIT	I didn't hear them sneaking up. I'm losing it.
SHEILA	*(on the phone)* I have to go. She's losing it.
	KIT gives somebody the finger.
KIT	Get out! Out! I'm not the story!
SHEILA	*(on the phone)* Right, Boyd…. Whatever you say…. I'll get tape of her losing it.
	She hangs up.
KIT	Sleazy Weasels. No more pictures. Scum buckets.
	KIT turns as if to moon the photographers. SHEILA stops her as more flashbulbs go off.
SHEILA	Kit…
KIT	They're waiting for Sandy. They think she's going to come out here and plead guilty. Why would Sandy plead guilty?
	SHEILA is rearranging lawn umbrellas. To block the paparazzi.
SHEILA	You will have to tell me, Kit.
KIT	They keep taking pictures.
SHEILA	Her plea was guilty. To three charges of manslaughter. And the prosecution has accepted that.
KIT	Do you believe her?
SHEILA	Why would she lie, Kit? About something like that? Because you know her. Since she's your best friend.
KIT	Well, manslaughter? That means it was an accident, right. That means it was Bobby's fault.
SHEILA	But we all know she's cutting a deal.
KIT	Meaning what?
SHEILA	Meaning it was murder. Sandy murdered three girls. Including her sister.
	Pause.
KIT	Where's your release?
SHEILA	My what?

> *KIT opens SHEILA's briefcase. She rifles through the documents, signing everything in sight.*

KIT   I'll sign your release…. I'm signing your release…

> *SHEILA passes documents, and KIT signs them.*

SHEILA   This is my release. And this is Candida's.

KIT   No problem. No problemo.

SHEILA   Aren't you going to read them?

KIT   She isn't guilty, Sheila. And I have to say that, so I have to go on television, right?

SHEILA   All right, Kit.

KIT   Network, right? If I sign this?

SHEILA   Network. Absolutely.

> *KIT sits in front of the camera and addresses it.*

KIT   Sandy was my best friend…

> *SHEILA realizes the camera is not set up properly.*

SHEILA   Wait a minute…

KIT   No, she is my best friend, okay?

SHEILA   No, wait…

KIT   Since we were kids, eh? Kit and Sandy. Since we were nine years old and all we thought about were Barbie dolls. We stayed up all night together. We cut school together, and the first time I got drunk, it was with her.

> *SHEILA frames her shot.*

SHEILA   Okay. That's fine.

KIT   She told my fortune once. She read my palm, all the lines in my hand, and she knew everything about me. She knew my dreams. How I dreamed I stabbed my mother in the throat…

> *A long pause. SHEILA prods.*

SHEILA   She understood your dreams, Kit…?

KIT   What?

SHEILA   She understood your dreams. Why was that?

KIT   Because she's the one I told… about my father.

SHEILA   About… your father…

> *Is she almost afraid of what she knows is coming next?*

KIT	And she understood because she said, you know, it had happened to her, her father was the same, you know…
SHEILA	The same.
	A hint that SHEILA thinks she's being conned?
KIT	And we made a vow, you know, that our fathers would suffer, and for a long time after that, we would check these stupid kid-stuff witch books out of the library and do spells on them, our fathers, late at night. We'd burn our hair, and curse them so their dicks would rot.
	Which may have happened, actually… because my dad turned off me then.
	But I don't think that was the reason. I think my dad turned off me because I was you know, twelve, and I started my period.
	I think he hates women.
	(to SHEILA) I think some guys hate women, don't you?
SHEILA	Is this true Kit?
KIT	Sometimes I think, some guys, they hate women, is that true?
SHEILA	Oh, Kit…
KIT	*(blithely)* The other thing that happened when we were twelve, we had this teacher for sex education, Ms. Henderson, and she was always hugging us, and telling us about good touching and bad touching and telling us to tell, you know, about touching.
	I liked Ms. Henderson. No, I really liked her. So did Sandy. That's why Sandy told.
	She told Ms. H. about the stuff her father did to her, and she told me about how good it was to tell.
	And she said I should tell.
	And I didn't want to, because my dad was off me, it was over. I just wanted to forget it, but Sandy said remember that we had vowed to make them suffer and what if my dad turned into some sex maniac, violating other women.
	Which I didn't think my dad would do, as it happens, because I thought. It was me. I thought my dad couldn't help it. I thought it was me.
SHEILA	Oh, Kit… it wasn't…
KIT	But Sandy says, "Please, Kit…. What about your sister?" We both had little sisters.
	So I told.

But the weird thing was… it didn't feel good telling.

Because Ms. H. kept saying, "Is that what really happened, Kit?" "Tell me what really happened. Tell me exactly what happened."

And I thought, what's to tell, eh? Except your father tells you you're his princess, and he can make you feel as good as you make him feel, and he touches you, and you know it is definitely bad, even when it feels good, and then he says you can make him feel even better, and he puts his thing in your…

He puts his fucking thing in your…

I mean, how many ways do we have to say it, but Ms. H. keeps looking at me without blinking, which makes her look a little scary.

She looks like an android, and she keeps saying, "Tell me what really happened, Kit. Exactly what happened." She didn't believe me. She said, "Is that true, Kit?

And I say, "He says 'You're my princess. You're my Princess Roxie'"
…which makes me feel sick just to think about it.

And Ms. Henderson looks sick. She looks bug-eyed. What disease is that? When your eyeballs are paralyzed?

SHEILA   Kit, you don't have to do this…

KIT   And Sandy. She is getting counselling. And every week she gets to get off school, and she and her mom get to go to T.O. and talk to this guy. Sandy says that he looks like Willem Dafoe.

And I just keep talking to Ms. Bug-Eyed Henderson…. And I can tell, she doesn't like me. I can tell. She thinks I'm weird.

> *A very long pause. Long enough so SHEILA turns away and begins to pack up, both disappointed and relieved that it seems to be over.*

SHEILA   That's good, okay? No, really, Kit, you did real good.

KIT   I talked to Henderson till Christmas.

> *SHEILA goes back to the camera.*

Because after Christmas, she isn't there, and we hear she's a wing nut, and I can't believe that bug-eyed shit was something serious.

Then Sandy tells me what she told Ms. H.

She told Ms. H. my life.

She said she was Princess Roxie.

And she cries. She says she's sorry. She says she had to tell my story. She says she couldn't tell her story.

She said, "If you knew what my dad did to me, you'd understand why I can't talk about it."

That's what she said. That's what she told me. And I believed her.

SHEILA Why, Kit?

KIT So you see. I gave her something. Which I like to remember, sometimes, because most times, with Sandy, it was what she gave me, most times for sure.

SHEILA Why is Sandy your friend?

KIT I've worn her clothes. I've worn her underwear…

SHEILA Kit?

KIT We were fourteen, eh? And she had this idea we'd trade brains. For a week, we'd be each other. We'd wear each other's clothes for a whole week, we'd trade lunches in the cafeteria, and Walkman tapes, and she'd quit smoking, and I'd start smoking. Wherever we were, we'd try to be the other person.

She got all our friends to call her Kit. They called me Sandy.

It was wicked.

If someone said "Sandy," I'd have to answer. If someone said "Kit," I'd have to say, like, "Why are you calling me Kit, because I'm Sandy."

Because she did my hair like hers, and I did hers like mine, and we did each other's makeup just like we were looking in a mirror. It was better than a mirror. I was looking in a mirror. Seeing Sandy.

Being Sandy…

Sandy. She is so beautiful. And she knows it. And she doesn't care. She would do my eyeliner, I mean, she would do her eyeliner on my eyes, and she'd say, "Sandy, wow, you're gorgeous!" And she'd kiss me.

Pause. SHEILA sees new revelations. She prods, gently.

SHEILA And she'd kiss you…

KIT And we handed in each other's homework, eh? All week.

SHEILA And she'd kiss you, Kit…

KIT But the teachers didn't get it. They thought we were trying to scam something. They didn't see…

They didn't see the possibilities. It was an experiment. A psychological experiment. Like the stuff we were studying. Like 1837. Like Greenpeace. *(She laughs.)*

So we made detention three times that week, easy, but we didn't care. We couldn't stop laughing. It was wicked.

Then we wrote in each other's diaries.

First we read each other's diaries.

And Sandy's diary was all that she wanted this guy, Brad, to do to her, and mine was not. My diary was about my body, mostly. About how I hate my body.

Sometimes how I hate my mother.

And my father.

But mostly my body.

>   *Pause.*

SHEILA   Kit... *(KIT looks blank.)* Kit? You hate your body...

KIT   Do you just want to talk about sex?

SHEILA   Did I say...?

KIT   Sandy's tongue in my mouth? My dad's dick?

SHEILA   I didn't say...

KIT   This is "Kit's Video Diary. Chapter 1312." Can I say what happened? What really happened? Can I say something real?

SHEILA   You can say what you want.

>   *Now SHEILA concentrates on getting good videotape.*

KIT   So Sandy and I traded brains. And every night for the whole week, Sandy would take my diary and write about how she hated how she looked, how she hated her parents, and I'd write about Brad trying to undo my bra. Then we'd read what we wrote to each other, and scream laughing. It was wicked.

It was so wicked.

So we'd waltz into the cafeteria every day at lunch. We used to eat with Brad and Ken, we were all sort of going out, but this week, Monday, Sandy just sat down with Ken, and I sat with Brad, and we didn't say anything, we just were each other.

I felt kind of sorry for Ken, because he's kind of scared of Sandy, but she sits down beside him, and she's doing my stuff that I liked to do with him. I liked to touch him. I like to touch, I don't like getting touched, he understood that—you understand that, don't you.

SHEILA   Keep going, Kit...

KIT   He wore this earring, one earring? I liked to play with it. Sandy's playing with his earring, and I'm telling Brad what a dork he is, which is what Sandy does. She rakes him over.

I say, "Got another hard-on, Brad." And I look at his crotch, which is what Sandy would do.

And the weird thing is, there's this bulge in his jeans.

And the guys are going crazy. Because they don't know what's going on, and when they figure out what's going on, they're still going crazy. Because I am being Sandy and she's me, and we're talking about double dating Friday night, and the guys are wondering, how far is this going to go? You can see that they see it's an experiment.

And Brad's still got a hard-on. Can I say that on TV?

SHEILA   Yes.

KIT   So Sandy and I are laughing. We don't even have to talk about it. We just know we're going to do it.

Friday.

KIT begins to move. SHEILA follows her with the camera.

So I'm in the front seat with Brad, and he reaches for me and he calls me Sandy, and it's like nothing bad has ever happened. I am Sandy. I am floating and nothing can happen, except I'll get exactly what I want. Exactly what I wrote about. Brad will kiss me wherever I want him to. And then he'll jerk himself off, like in the diary.

And he'll know what I want without asking.

But the next thing I know, Ken is swearing at Sandy, and they're punching each other around in the back seat.

And he's saying, you f-word, you c-word, he's saying, "Damn you, bitch. Screw you."

And he says that Sandy's making fun of me. And he says it's not funny.

And he's crying. He's actually crying. And he's trying to get out of the car, which makes everything turn into some stupid cartoon, because it's a two-door, and we're all clowns piling out of the car. And Sandy's saying, "Oh, Ken, puhleeze…" And I'm saying "Please, Ken…"

And Brad is trying to pull his zipper up and say "Be cool, man," all at the same time, and Ken just splits. He takes off.

And Sandy says, "Let him go."

Her eyes were so bright.

But I was crying. I couldn't stop crying.

And she hugged me. And she kissed my hair. She said, "Sandy, you're crying." She said, "Sandy, don't please… I'm the one who cries."

I couldn't stop crying…

SHEILA	Kit…

SHEILA puts down the camera. She hugs KIT. KIT breaks away.

KIT   So Sandy says, "Fuck it. You go find him, then."

So I went.

So the first thing that happened, I slipped in the mud, in the creek, I went down to the creek…

And the second thing that happened was I found him…

He was under the bridge. And someone had left a can of spray paint there, and he was trying to write "Anarchy," he was screaming "Anarchy!"

And I reached for his hand, and he hit me, by accident, he didn't mean to hit me, but he hit me with the spray can, and he said, "God, I'm sorry. I'm so sorry."

And I kissed him until he kissed me back, and it was wonderful. His tongue in my mouth. I was floating. I wanted him. And that wouldn't have happened, except for Sandy.

Where's the camera?

SHEILA has put the camera down. She looks around for it.

SHEILA   What?

KIT   Don't you want this on tape?

SHEILA   Kit…? Are you okay?

KIT   I want this on tape. I want this on TV, so come on, Sheila…

KIT sets herself up in front of the camera.

If it weren't for Sandy, I'd still be eating Mr. Big bars, and throwing up, and kissing people with my mouth closed.

I want to say this on TV. Because she isn't guilty. Even if she says she's guilty.

SHEILA   Are you sure she isn't guilty?

KIT addresses the camera.

KIT   We did stuff like that when we were kids, of course…. That was before she met Bobby…

Very distant sound of thunder.

SHEILA   Forget Bobby…

KIT   Was that thunder?

SHEILA   You and Sandy, Kit…

KIT   That's weird, eh? There's thunder and the sun's still out.

SHEILA   Because no one cares about Bobby. Bobby's history. He's toast. Bobby's
             in jail, and Sandy's made a deal to keep him there.

KIT   You probably think I'm going to say it's all his fault.

             But… I mean, I know him, and I don't like him…. I mean, he wants to
             be a singer, a rap singer, but he's pitiful.

             Thunder.

             She raps.

             Just another white boy trying to be bad
             Just another white boy trying to be bad…

             Thunder. KIT looks up at the sky.

             I mean. He beat her up. He kept beating her up…

SHEILA   Yes. I know he kept beating her up.

KIT   It's going to rain. That's weird, eh?

SHEILA   Let's remember, Kit. Bobby is toast. And let's talk about you…

KIT   Let's play a game.

SHEILA   Bobby's not the story, Kit…. Who cares?

KIT   You know how to play I Never?

SHEILA   Bobby's over. He's the bad guy…. You and Sandy…

KIT   I say, "I've never played strip poker," and then if I have played strip
             poker, then I have to drink. And so do you.

             She drinks. She looks up at SHEILA.

KIT   You never played strip poker?

SHEILA   No.

KIT   Have you got one? I've got another one. I never beat the tax on
             cigarettes. *(She drinks.)* I've never done cocaine. *(She drinks.)* I've never
             researched a TV program called "Mothers Whose Sons Are Gay Bar
             Strippers." So, on that one, you drink and I don't… Sheila?

SHEILA   I don't drink while I'm working.

KIT   Oh. Wow.

SHEILA   And I am working. On your story.

KIT   "Kit's Video Diary."

SHEILA   Yes.

KIT   Let's try to find out who I am.

SHEILA   Go for it.

KIT	"Kit's Video Diary. Chapter 6008." Kit. She's all bimbette and bar games. Are you going to tape this, Sheila?
	SHEILA is camera-ready.
SHEILA	If it's important.
KIT	I never saw Bobby beat Sandy. *(She drinks.)* I never saw Bobby fuck Sandy. *(She drinks.)* I never saw Bobby fuck Skippy. Not even on videotape. *(She drinks.)*
SHEILA	You never saw what?
	KIT shakes her head as if to clear it.
KIT	I shouldn't have drunk that. .
SHEILA	What videotape?
KIT	Because I didn't see it. Not exactly.
SHEILA	You say Bobby…. You saw Skippy…
KIT	No, I told you. Not exactly.
SHEILA	What did you see, Kit?
KIT	You know all those tapes in the basement? The ones the cops gave back?
SHEILA	The basement.
KIT	You should watch those tapes.
SHEILA	Is this true, Kit?
KIT	You should watch those tapes. Carefully. It could be a Sweeps Week thing.
SHEILA	I don't want a Sweeps Week thing.
KIT	Are you sure? Sheila?
SHEILA	I want the story. I want the true, real story.
	KIT takes another drink, which empties her pitcher. She gets up to fill it, staggers, and falls back in her chair.
KIT	The true story is I've gone blind.
SHEILA	No. You haven't
	KIT stands, giggling, pretending to be blind.
KIT	See me… feel me… touch me… heal me…
	Her hands are outstretched. Thunder. The light grows darker. KIT's eyes snap open.
	The true story is, it's starting to rain. That's weird, eh?

The true story is I know... that I've done everything that Sandy's done. That's why I know. She didn't do it.

SHEILA   What have you done, Kit?

KIT   The true story is that she said that she did it.

SHEILA   What have you done, Kit?

KIT   The true story is...

> *Crack of lightning. Blackout.*

ACT TWO

We are in a well-appointed rec room with a wet bar, a TV, a VCR, and a huge library of videotapes. The rec room is in the basement. There are stairs leading to the first floor.

Pot lights over the wet bar illuminate a vodka bottle, KIT's glass, and her yogurt. A TV screen is lit, facing upstage. These are the only lights in the room, except for the lights over the space where a picture once hung. This picture, a large, bad, black velvet painting of a pretty, blond, young girl, leans against the wall underneath the light.

There is a light from offstage, where a clothes dryer is running. There's another door, which leads to a bathroom. Unlit. The whole place smells, not unpleasantly, of fabric softener.

The stage is empty. SHEILA enters down the stairs. She is carrying too much stuff, the stuff from the deck, from Act One. Her briefcase, the camcorder, the tripod, a microphone. Whatever she isn't carrying is already in the room.

Her progress down the stairs is awkward. She is wet and grumpy.

SHEILA   Let's get all this stuff in out of the rain, you say. And I take the TV, and the VCR, and the camcorder, and the tripod, and the answering machine, and your Walkman, and your tapes, and your sunglasses, and your tie-dyed silk robe.

I am lugging your stuff around? Why? *(She mimics KIT.)* "Sheila, can I ask you something? Is this a black thing?" No, Kit, it's an adult thing. It's a responsible thing, it's the way the world works. You clean up your messes. You bring things inside from the rain. What did you bring in?

Your highball glass. Straight to the bar.

She dips a finger in KIT's glass and licks it.

The suburban living room. St. Catharines, 1997, but it looks like 1950. There is vodka straight up on the bar. There's the black velvet painting of Skippy.

SHEILA does not want to meet SKIPPY's eyes.

But there's videotape of course. All this videotape.

And this letter, framed above the bar. It's from *America's Funniest Home Videos,* I see, and it says, "Thank you for your interest." Right.

She might set up her camera so she's ready to tape.

Be careful of your videographer, Kit. Because remember what
Chomsky says… TV doesn't sell information. TV doesn't sell
entertainment. TV sells customers. Try to remember that.

You watch too much TV, Kit. You've spent too much time with
America's Funniest.(waiting to watch Sandy's father's tape) What was
on that tape, Kit? Was it Sandy? Was it Skippy? *(turns back to face
SKIPPY's picture)* Hello, Skippy.

> *KIT enters from the bathroom and creeps up behind SHEILA. She is
> holding something behind her back and trying not to laugh. It seems
> she has a hairdryer, which she turns on and blows on SHEILA's neck.
> SHEILA is startled. She screams.*

KIT	Relax. It's only me.
SHEILA	What is that?
KIT	It's trashy old white-trashy me. And it's only a hairdryer.
SHEILA	Turn if off.
KIT	But your hair's wet.
SHEILA	Yes. I know my hair's wet.
KIT	And your sweater's wet. Look at your sleeve.
SHEILA	My sleeve is fine.
KIT	No. Sheila, you're soaked. No, really. What happened?
SHEILA	Nothing happened.
KIT	Oh, no, I bet I know. I bet you were chasing my release. I bet it blew down into the pool, and you had to fish it out. Did you get it?
SHEILA	You said there were videos.
KIT	I bet you got it.
SHEILA	You wanted me to see a video.
KIT	Because your shoulder's wet, so you went for it, right? You're out there fishing for your papers, and you would have dived in for them, wouldn't you?
SHEILA	Which video?

> *KIT drinks from her vodka smoothie.*

KIT	I want to play I Never.
SHEILA	I want out of here. As soon as possible.
KIT	I never fished in a chlorinated pool in my DKNY sweater. *(She puts down her glass.)* Sheila, you're supposed to drink. *(SHEILA doesn't respond.)* Okay, I know, you're working, so you don't have to drink vodka. Okay. No alcohol, okay? What do you want?

She brings out a blender. She pours milk into it. And yogurt.

This will be a virgin vodka smoothie.

She mixes the yogurt and milk. She pours it into a pitcher.

So we can both play I Never... and we can get to know each other.

I never fished in a chlorinated.... Come on. Don't you want me to trust you?

SHEILA fills her glass. She glares at KIT.

SHEILA	I have never fished in a chlorinated pool in my DKNY sweater. *(She drinks.)* Satisfied?
KIT	Good thing you had a ballpoint pen.
SHEILA	I never remember releases should always be signed in indelible ink. *(She drinks.)*
KIT	You want to change?
SHEILA	No, thanks.
KIT	Sandy won't mind.
SHEILA	I said, no thanks.
KIT	You're shivering.
SHEILA	It's because this place gives me the creeps.
KIT	Me too. Know why? Because of Skippy... *(She indicates the picture.)* And down here. In the basement. This is where she...
SHEILA	Yes, I know.
KIT	That's weird, right?
SHEILA	Yes.
KIT	The picture doesn't look like her.
SHEILA	I'm glad it doesn't look like her.
KIT	And that's weird too. Because it cost mucho dineros.
SHEILA	It looks like she's selling peanut butter.
KIT	Because it could have looked like her. Because there's lots of pictures of her. On videotape. All this videotape... *(KIT rummages through the videotape.)* There's tape of Skippy being born.
SHEILA	Being born.
KIT	That's weird, right? Sandy's dad. He was always a video freak.
SHEILA	Is that the tape you wanted me to see?

SHEILA begins to look through the tapes with some curiosity.

KIT	Would it be good? On *Candida?*

KIT aims the camera at SHEILA. SHELIA pushes it away.

If you showed Skippy…. Maybe being born, down here where she….
I mean where she…

SHEILA   I don't need tape of Skippy being born, Kit. No.

KIT pops in a videotape, which begins playing on a monitor. It's a little kid's birthday party. Very innocent.

KIT   That's her. But she's already born. Would that be better?

SHEILA   *(reads tape labels)* "Skippy's First Christmas." "Skippy Learns to Skate."

KIT   She used to watch those tapes like all the time…

SHEILA   Skippy and Tippy.

KIT   Forget *Snow White*, she'd watch herself on video, you know, over and over again.

SHEILA   Skippy, and Tippy too.

KIT   That's supposed to be bad for kids, right. For babies? To watch TV. Because they don't learn to talk. But Skippy could talk.

SHEILA   Who's Tippy?

KIT   You couldn't shut her up most times.

SHEILA ejects the first tape and pops in another. The pictures show a child with a cocker spaniel.

SHEILA   Tippy is her dog. Of course.

KIT   When she was little, when we'd babysit, that's how we'd shut her up. We'd set up her playpen right in front of the TV, and we'd pop in the tape and we'd say, "Look, Skippy, who's that, Skippy? That's you with Tippy, Skippy…." And she'd laugh.

She'd watch herself.

Not being born.

I mean, we used to watch that tape, but it was kind of gross, and the lighting was bad.

I mean, we'd show Skippy falling down. Eating cake. She didn't care. She'd laugh.

And she never got bored with it.

SHEILA ejects the tape. KIT is worried.

Are you bored with it?

SHEILA   We're playing games, Kit.

KIT	No. No, we're not…. We're just trying to get to know each other… so we can trust each other. Because we have to trust each other.
SHEILA	You are playing games, Kit. Why?
KIT	I never had sex on camera. *(She drinks; SHEILA doesn't.)* You've had sex on camera, Sheila.
SHEILA	No.
KIT	You and Tommy? With all your equipment. It has to be state of the art.
SHEILA	Sorry, no.
KIT	Okay, here's one. I never stripped on camera. *(She drinks, SHEILA doesn't.)* Sheila?
SHEILA	You want a confession. But that's true. I've never stripped on camera.
KIT	You're kidding. Why not? What is video for? How do you spend your time, Sheila? When you're not "not drinking when you're working"? Wait, I know…
	I never taped my boyfriend in the shower. *(She drinks. SHEILA smiles at a fond memory.)* I got you. Right? I got you.
SHEILA	I never taped my boyfriend in the shower. *(She drinks, she remembers.)* And I've never been in love for no good reason. Except he made me laugh, and he was just as smart as I was… and I wanted him… I really wanted him…
	I guess I should drink to that.
	She drinks. She thinks about Tommy.
KIT	Sheila? Are you talking about Tommy?
SHEILA	I have never called my mom a racist. *(She drinks.)*
KIT	Oh, wow, Sheila, don't be sad, it's not your fault…
SHEILA	You sound like my little sister, Kit…
KIT	Do I? Really?
SHEILA	We could call our show that. *Little Sisters.*
KIT	We could work on our show, right, Sheila?
SHEILA	Right. *(She prepares to tape.)*
KIT	I'd never want to watch Sandy's secret sex videos. *(She drinks.)*
	Pause.
	Come on, Sheila? Never? Come on, they're not so bad. It's all consensual sex. And it might give you, you know, insight, right? Like, you might understand Sandy.
SHEILA	I'd never want to watch Sandy's secret sex videos.

Another pause. Then SHEILA drinks. KIT is delighted.

KIT Right. Right on. But I'm sorry. The cops have all the good stuff. And they'll still need it, right? For Bobby's trial.

SHEILA *Mea culpa.*

KIT Sheila? Sheila, are you mad at me?

SHEILA Why would I be mad, Kit?

KIT Because I kind of lied to you. About the tapes…. All just so you would play I Never.

SHEILA And you got me. Didn't you?

KIT I'm sorry.

SHEILA No, I wanted to watch. Why, I wonder?

KIT You just thought it would be good. For *Candida.* Or for our show…

SHEILA But, does that make it right?

KIT What do you mean?

SHEILA But, does that make it right?

KIT Sheila? It's all consensual, Sheila.

SHEILA But, does that make it right? Kit?

KIT You know what happens? Once you do something? Once you have something?

SHEILA Yes. I do. Yes.

KIT You want more.

SHEILA I wanted more. I wanted "Sandy's Secret Sex Videos." True, *mea culpa.*

So, I'm not mad at you, Kit. Because I think… I think you've taught me something. About me. About my work. About how much I wanted this story.

Call Tommy and tell him that I understand. How it's a game. Pro-ball.

And you know what else I think? That calls for a drink.

SHEILA goes for KIT's vodka bottle. Unfortunately, it's almost empty although it may be enough to make a light drinker confused about how much she's drunk. SHEILA dribbles what's left in the bottle into her glass.

KIT Right on.

SHEILA I never drink while I'm working. *(She drinks.)*

KIT I've got an idea for our show. What if I'm watching your tape? And we see me watching "Mothers Whose Sons Are Gay Bar Strippers"…

SHEILA	No, let's just talk, Kit. Let's just try to understand. How did it happen? Why did it happen?
KIT	We're there, watching Troy's mom…
SHEILA	Because your best friend… she's admitted that she killed her sister. Hasn't she? Kit? How do you deal with that?

        Pause.

KIT	Sheila, it's good. We're watching Troy's mom. We're yelling, "Go, Troy! Go, Troy!"
SHEILA	How are you going to deal with that?

        Long pause.

KIT	I have never watched myself on television. (*She drinks, as SHEILA watches in amazement.*) Oh, come on, Sheila. You've watched yourself on television. Please. You work in television, don't you?
SHEILA	Yes.
KIT	And we're playing I Never, aren't we? I have never watched myself on television. (*She drinks.*) Sheila?

        She looks expectantly at SHEILA, until SHEILA picks up her glass again.

SHEILA	I forgot. That we're both playing games. And I guess at this point you may want to tape me.

        SHEILA passes KIT the camera.

KIT	You want me to tape you.
SHEILA	Since I guess at this point we are in this together.
KIT	You want me to tape you, for our show? Sheila, wow!
SHEILA	I have never watched myself on television. (*She drinks.*)
KIT	(*side coaching*) That was great, Sheila.
SHEILA	I never liked it.

        She drinks again. She shakes her head as if to clear it, then waves off KIT's camera, amused by her mistake.

        No, that's true. I don't drink if it's true.

KIT	(*still taping*) No, really. You look good. It's great.
SHEILA	Wait! I know… where we go next…
KIT	Sheila! Yes! You're on a roll! (*gets up, staggers*) What's wrong? I've gone blind!
	Sheila?
SHEILA	Touch me… feel me…

KIT	Sheila? Are you all right?
SHEILA	Me? Never better. Give me the camera, Kit.
KIT	Why?
SHEILA	We'll tape you, the young rock-opera diva. Skippy's picture in the background…
KIT	Sheila, whoa…
SHEILA	Subtext. It's all subtext…
KIT	Sheila, please… don't kid around.
SHEILA	Why did Tommy go blind? I mean, not my Tommy…
KIT	Are you okay? Sheila?
SHEILA	See me… feel me…
KIT	Let's just calm down, okay…? And we'll just play I Never…
	SHEILA is excited, on a roll. The recklessness comes from drunkenness, perhaps
SHEILA	No! No more I Never…. We've done I Never!
KIT	I don't know what you mean.
SHEILA	I Never is good, Kit. I will make you look good in I Never. It's not midget-blender jokes.
KIT	Sheila?
SHEILA	But I Never is denial. We've got lots of denial. We have been there, done that…
KIT	Sheila. Oh, wow…
SHEILA	Let's move on from denial.
	She takes the camera back. Focuses on KIT. KIT looks at the camera, uneasy.
KIT	You mean me, don't you.
SHEILA	Where do you want to start?
KIT	I guess you think it's easy.
SHEILA	You think that it's supposed to be?
KIT	It isn't easy, is it? Making films. I mean making good films.
SHEILA	But, let's try.
KIT	Bobby thought it was easy.
SHEILA	Is Bobby the story?

KIT	All the best films, they were my films. And Bobby never understood. He never really understood.
SHEILA	Let's go for the story.
KIT	Bobby thinks that it's all about him.
SHEILA	But let's get the whole story.
KIT	As long as he was there. In the centre of the frame. And his dick was there. And someone else, calling him "The King." It's all so sad. It's all so bogus.
SHEILA	You know what I'm good at? Getting stories…
KIT	Bobby's fascinated.
SHEILA	Getting people to trust me…
KIT	We're supposed to be so fasc-in-ated. Please. I mean, guys, right?
SHEILA	You trust me.
KIT	Bobby's tapes were so retro. They were just like Sandy's dad's.
SHEILA	I guess I'm like you, Kit. I'm famous for friendship.
KIT	Sandy's dad's tapes.
SHEILA	Kit…
KIT	Sandy's dad's tapes…
SHEILA	Kit, don't trust me.

SHEILA puts down the camera. KIT, pacing frantically, doesn't notice.

KIT	No, I want to tell you. Because we found these tapes, in a shoebox, at the back of her mom's closet. In with a vibrator. And a tube of Vaseline.
	They are making out. On tape. Her mom and dad. We thought that was wicked. So wicked.
	And pitiful too. And pitiful also. What a creep, eh? I mean, who cares, right? Why bother? I mean, we watched it a lot but we were kids, right? Please, it wasn't that interesting.
	I mean, the cops gave it back. You could see it.

She notices that SHEILA isn't taping. She is worried.

	But you don't want to see it, do you?
SHEILA	I don't care about Sandy's mom and dad.
KIT	No. I don't blame you. The lighting is bad, and no one else is there, so they can't move the camera.

KIT So you can guess, right? Where he's focused? Pen-e-tra-tion. Who cares? Not even Sandy's mom. I bet.

SHEILA Kit, where are Bobby's tapes?

KIT Sheila, the cops have them. I mean, the later tapes because they were okay. I mean, after we got lights, which was my idea. And we started moving the camera. And we put in the songs.

SHEILA I think you know something, about Bobby's tapes…

> *KIT is rifling through tapes.*
>
> *She raps.*

KIT Just another white boy, trying to be bad
Just another white boy, trying to be bad…

SHEILA Are there tapes the cops don't know about?

> *KIT picks a tape off of the shelf.*

KIT You'll like this one. Bobby's in this one. And Sandy and me. *Tout le gang.* This is when we went to Mexico.

> *KIT turns on the video. We see her asleep in the back seat of a car. A rap backbeat comes from the car stereo. The refrain "Just another white boy…" repeats under. The camera stays focused on the sleeping KIT.*
>
> *SHEILA picks up the beat, ironically:*

SHEILA Just another white boy, trying to be bad…

KIT Right on.

SHEILA *(almost sings it)* Let's go. To Mexico. With Bobby.

> *The camera switches focus. From the car interior to an interior hotel room.*

KIT Look, this is our hotel.

> *In the hotel room, everyone is jumping up and down in a primitive kind of dance. Some people are jumping on the bed. They are all yelling "NAFTA! NAFTA!" Continues under.*

SHEILA NAFTA?

KIT I don't remember this part.

SHEILA You were worried about free trade?

KIT I don't remember. I was drunk.

SHEILA *(She raps.)* Just a bunch of white kids trying to be bad…

KIT We broke the bed. We had to pay for it.

SHEILA raps to the backbeat. The action on videotape continues under as described. KIT joins her.

SHEILA   They all keep saying it's Free Trade
You know what I think? I think you got laid
You're down there lookin' for a major time

KIT   You talk like that's a major crime

SHEILA   Just major party
Bobby's hope
Was you'd maybe smuggle back

A little cheap dope
Just a bunch of white kids tryin' to be bad
Just a bunch of white kids tryin' to be bad

KIT   You ever been to Mexico?

SHEILA echoes "Mexico!"

It's just like here there, I don't know
Like our hotel's Best Western, right?

SHEILA   And Bobby's drinkin' Miller Lite

KIT   So what's so wrong with what Bobby did?
So there's this poor dude, with his kid
When all we've seen is Denny's cans

SHEILA   Fan-fucking-tastic!

KIT   They were Mexicans
So he shot some video. So, why not?
One small problemo. He forgot
To run it by him. Bobby forgot
To run it by this Mexican guy
And this poor dude, he had an attitude

And Sandy says he lost control
Because he thought we stole his soul
And Bobby's freaking, so's this guy
This poor dude. Can I ask you why?
What's wrong with shooting video?
What's wrong with shooting video?

What's wrong with shooting video?
What's wrong with shooting video?

SHEILA fears KIT might go on forever.

SHEILA   Kit…

KIT interrupts as videotape cuts to BOBBY, at the hotel, his forehead tended to by the girls on the trip.

KIT	There's Bobby. Do you think he's cute?
SHEILA	Cute?
KIT	I think he's cute as shit. And lucky too. And lucky also. Because I bet, up to then, that's the worst thing that ever happened to him. Do you know what I mean? I mean, Bobby's just playing back the tape, like, through the viewfinder. It's for the kids. The kids are cute, and sure, maybe he's a little close, and maybe his hand is, you know…
SHEILA	His hand is…
KIT	But he's just showing the kids what they look like, right, and this dude starts screaming, this dude is apeshit. No one knows what he's saying. I'm like "Excuse me? I'm not Mexican?"
	So, some poor dude in Mexico freaks and throws a rock at Bobby, and he hits him. And I bet he still has the scar, if you look really closely.
	Otherwise you'd think he was perfect, right. He looks like a choir boy, right. He looks like a kid. And maybe that scar, you know, is from some dumb, stupid, street-hockey puck. Who knows?
	SHEILA shakes her head as if to clear it.
SHEILA	His hand is….
KIT	Who'd think it was because he was stealing some kid's soul in Mexico?
SHEILA	*(has not heard this)* Kit, I'm sorry… I feel dizzy…
KIT	We were making a videotape. Of how we went to Mexico. Is something wrong with that? Do we have to get beat up? Oh, please.
SHEILA	Something's wrong.
KIT	Please, do you get beat up? When you come up here for my story?
SHEILA	Kit, I don't know…. I feel…
KIT	Are you stealing my soul?
SHEILA	I feel sick.
	She exists to the bathroom. KIT calls after her.
KIT	No, Sheila, it's okay. You can take my picture. I don't mind. In fact, I kind of like it. There's all this tape of me, sleeping all the way to Mexico, and I never get tired of watching it. I love it.
	SHEILA appears in the bathroom door, looking drawn. KIT smiles at her.
	She raps.
	Somewhere in this book I read This guy named Andy Warhol said

	That someday, everyone would be
	Famous for fifteen minutes on TV
SHEILA	Kit...
KIT	You think Sandy killed her sister? Really?
SHEILA	I feel terrible.
KIT	That would... that would be so wicked.
SHEILA	I'm sorry... I...
KIT	How could she kill her sister?
SHEILA	I don't know.
KIT	You know Skippy's friends, they'd all come over just to be with Sandy.... I mean, even after Skippy...
	And Sandy's mom. She liked it. She said it was like Skippy was still...
	So the kids would come over. They'd sleep over and stay up all night talking, telling ghost stories. They were a hoot.
	And we'd get them off. They liked that. Maybe roll a few joints. Maybe spike their Shirley Temples. They'd get high so fast. They'd get high just thinking about getting high.
	Sandy's mom wasn't there, then.
	But they were so funny. They were off-the-wall. And Sandy would bring out all her makeup and they'd tart each other up.
	But then one night, there's one kid, and she changes the rules. She finds Mr. Symonds's gun.
SHEILA	Mr. Symonds's gun?
KIT	She finds Sandy's dad's gun. Down here. In this drawer. *(KIT produces a gun.)* And we gave her hell for that. Because, please. This is not about guns.
SHEILA	Kit...
KIT	I mean, who did she think she was? Nancy Drew?
SHEILA	Kit, what is it about?
KIT	Then, one night, they're watching that Madonna movie, *Truth or Dare.* And pretty soon, they're daring each other to moon each other. And then it's dance naked. They were so cute. They were out of control. Look, it wasn't dirty. It wasn't about sex. They were just having fun. They enjoyed it. They came back, didn't they?
	They came back for more.
	They were just having fun. I can show you the videotapes.

SHEILA	The videotapes.
	KIT begins sorting through videotapes.
KIT	They made videotapes. Of each other. Why not? It was fun, that's all. Well, maybe some of them were kind of gross.
SHEILA	The videotapes. The gun.
KIT	But, all that other stuff, it didn't happen. I know what happened. I can show you what happened. There's little girls in baby-doll pajamas, maybe just a little high. Maybe pulling down their baby-doll pajamas. There is nothing there you haven't seen Madonna do.
	It's like prime-time television. It's like daytime television.
	Well, almost.
SHEILA	How, almost?
KIT	You want to see, don't you? And it's here, somewhere. Why would they throw it out? It looks like a Calvin Klein ad.
SHEILA	What's on these tapes, Kit? That the cops gave back?
	KIT pours herself a drink.
KIT	I have never found Calvin Klein ads attractive. *(She drinks.)* I have never bought Calvin Klein jeans. *(She drinks.)* I have never watched pre-teen soft-porn video. *(She drinks.)* I've never even wanted to. *(She holds out a tape to SHEILA, who reaches for it.)* But if you want to see it, then you have to play I Never.
SHEILA	I don't want to drink anymore.
KIT	Come on, Sheila. No, it would be good. In your film. Come on. They're cute. They're like bimbettes in training.
	I guess I should hit erase.
SHEILA	Don't hit erase.
KIT	Right on.
	She hands SHEILA a glass. SHEILA looks on it with some distaste.
SHEILA	I'm not going to drink anymore, Kit.
	KIT mixes her a new drink.
KIT	You don't have to. Drink your virgin vodka smoothie. Sheila? It's about Calvin Klein ads. It's "I've never bought Calvin Klein jeans."
SHEILA	I have never bought Calvin Klein jeans.
	KIT pours. SHEILA drinks.
KIT	Okay. I'll show you.

She pops a videotape into the VCR. It is very dark. We can't see what is going on. We hear breathing, rustling, perhaps the very occasional midget-blender-joke laugh.

SHEILA   What's that?

KIT   This is one of Bobby's tapes. It's before we got lights.

SHEILA   I can't see anything.

KIT   But Sandy thinks this tape is awesome. I say, Sandy, please, it's in your mind. It's so dark. There's nothing there. But she plays it. Over and over again.

　　　　　What's going on? Can you see what's going on?

SHEILA   Nothing's going on.

KIT   But Sandy loves this tape. And she laughs, you know, that midget-in-a-blender laugh that chills your blood. And she says, I think we should set up your lights, Kit. And I think we should put this tape in the VCR. And I think you should fuck Bobby while this tape is playing in the background. And I think I should tape you. Fucking Bobby.

　　　　　Which is the tape the cops have. Which is consensual.

　　　　　Which I think it is the worst thing I have ever done.

SHEILA   This tape is completely dark, Kit…

KIT   I hate this tape so much. This tape gives me the creeps so much…. Listen…

SHEILA   I don't know what's going on.

KIT   I keep thinking I know what's happening. On this tape. I know why Sandy's laughing. But that's crazy, right? I mean, do you know? Can you tell what's happening?

　　　　　I mean, the cops gave this tape back. And they would know, wouldn't they? What was happening? Because their equipment, it's state of the art, isn't it? They've enhanced it, I bet, this tape, haven't they? Because the government, the government can take your picture when they're out in space…

　　　　　I keep thinking I know what's on this tape.

　　　　　But I have to be careful what I remember…

　　　　　That's what my therapist says. Because I'm suggestible. I know I'm suggestible. My therapist says, "Are you sure, Kit?" "Are you sure that really happened?" She thinks I have "False Memory Syndrome." She thinks I made it up about my father because I wanted him to…

　　　　　She's a Freudian, right?

　　　　　Sheila?

KIT   Do you have a therapist? Is she Freudian?

             Sheila?

             Sheila?

             Hello? Are you awake?

             SHEILA doesn't seem to be. KIT empties her pitcher of vodka over SHEILA's head. SHEILA sputters and thrashes.

SHEILA   Help me!

KIT   Oh, wow…. Oh, Sheila, please, I'm sorry…. You're all wet. Let me help you.

             She pulls SHEILA's sweater off, which is drenched.

SHEILA   That's so cold.

KIT   That's so cool. That is such a nice bra.

SHEILA   Yes, I know.

KIT   That's a bra that does up in the front, like *The Story of O*. And it's lacy.

SHEILA   Yes, I know about my bra, Kit…

KIT   I got vodka on it.

SHEILA   Yes.

KIT   I just thought you weren't conscious.

SHEILA   It's all right, Kit. I'm conscious.

KIT   I was thinking of Skippy. Because that's how they say it happened with Skippy. Because she was unconscious. Because she was out of her mind.

SHEILA   I'm not out of my mind.

KIT   You might be.

SHEILA   I might be what?

KIT   No, I mean, really. I mean, unless you have a tolerance for horse tranqs.

SHEILA   A what for what?

KIT   Or whatever they are. You can get them in Mexico.

SHEILA   You drugged me.

KIT   I'm sorry.

SHEILA   You drugged me. Why?

KIT   Just like Sandy drugged Skippy. That's so evil, right?

SHEILA   You want Sandy as your role model?

KIT   No, Sheila…

SHEILA	All right. I'm out of here.
KIT	I was trying to be Sandy, that's all. So we could try to understand.
SHEILA	Where's my camera?
KIT	Maybe if I wore her sweatshirt.

She puts on a Disney sweatshirt from the laundry room.

SHEILA	Where's my briefcase?
KIT	Sheila, please.

SHEILA gathers her things together.

SHEILA	Goodbye, Kit.
KIT	Sheila, don't go, please.
SHEILA	You are a very sick puppy.
KIT	Sheila, help me?
SHEILA	Why?
KIT	It's just that Skippy was like you. Please. She wasn't a drinker. I mean, she was drinking eggnog. It was spiked—hey, it was Christmas. And our mom and dad knew, and they thought it was cute. And they knew she'd just act stupid, and then she'd fall asleep.
	But we knew what she wanted. Really. She wanted to get off. Really. She wanted to stay up all night. *(KIT takes out a bottle of pills.)* And so we got her drunk. But we also got her high.
SHEILA	Those pills. That's how you drugged me, I suppose…?
KIT	If you're drinking, they sort of feel like poppers. Except you feel, you know, even wilder, maybe. You feel lawless.
SHEILA	And you love it. Feeling lawless.
KIT	Sometimes they make you paranoid, and sometimes they make you, you know, dippy, like you'll do stupid pet tricks for hours. You'll eat fire.
SHEILA	Or breathe fire.
KIT	Sometimes you get depressed. You get, like, suicidal.
SHEILA	I'm not depressed. I'm angry, Kit…
KIT	I get depressed. Whenever I take these things.
SHEILA	Then I suggest you stop.

KIT takes a pill. She shakes her head as if to clear it.

SHEILA	What are you doing?
KIT	No, that's not right. I'm Sandy. Sandy doesn't get depressed.

SHEILA	What are those things?
KIT	Sheila? Help me?
SHEILA	How many of these did you take?
KIT	I don't like it down here. In this basement, right? It's creepy, it's so creepy.
	You know why? It used to be a bomb shelter. No. No, really. In the fifties when this house was built, and Sandy's dad, I mean our dad, he says this is good…. Because what if there's a moral breakdown, right?
SHEILA	"What if" there's a moral breakdown?
KIT	He's got his baked beans down here. And his guns.
	KIT finds the gun.
SHEILA	Kit, please, put that gun down.
KIT	Do you think it's still raining? Outside?
SHEILA	Kit? The gun?
KIT	It was raining. And the sun was shining.
SHEILA	Put the gun away, Kit.
KIT	And it made me think that everything had started. Six, six, six.
SHEILA	Nothing has started, Kit.
KIT	You keep calling me "Kit." Why?
SHEILA	Kit, you're not Sandy.
KIT	Are you sure?
SHEILA	You don't get to be Sandy by wearing her clothes.
KIT	Do you know that? Really?
SHEILA	I'm cold.
KIT	Do you know that really? Sheila?
SHEILA	I'm so cold, Kit. Can I wear your sweater?
	Pause. KIT pulls off her sweatshirt and gives it to SHEILA, who puts it on.
	So. Do you think I'm Sandy? *(pause)* I'm not Sandy. And neither are you.
KIT	But I think I've done everything Sandy's done, haven't I?
SHEILA	Is that true, Kit?
KIT	Maybe more. Because we used to dare each other, and I've never said "No" to a dare. I mean, you know me, right? I don't know when to stop…

And I should have known, shouldn't I? Maybe I knew. "Kit's Video Diary. Chapter 2001." Where Sandy's taping me and Bobby, and in the background of that tape, we're playing Skippy's tape...

SHEILA   Skippy's tape?

> *SHEILA turns toward the monitor.*

KIT   You can see, can't you? You can see that it's not like they said. *(The tape continues as obscurely as before.)* I mean, it might be kind of gross. But it's not like they said. *(We might hear SANDY's laugh on tape.)* And anyway, she's sorry. Sandy's sorry. She's full of remorse. Really, Sheila. She would be, wouldn't she?

SHEILA   You would be, wouldn't you?

> *KIT nods.*

You know when I knew that I wanted this story? I did the research. I saw you on some stupid *News at Seven*. You were protecting Sandy. You were shielding Sandy from some camera. You were crying, Kit...

KIT   You think it's hard to cry?

SHEILA   Kit? Are you crying?

KIT   You want me to tell you what happened? Everything that happened? Okay. Why not? I'll just look straight at the camera, and I'll tell you.

SHEILA   Give me the gun first.

KIT   No, I think the gun is good. If I'm waving the gun around. If no one knows what I'm going to do. Sheila, it's so lawless. Look, shouldn't you be taping me?

SHEILA   No. I don't think so.

KIT   But you're a journalist, aren't you? A videographer.

SHEILA   Yes. I am. But—

KIT   Say that you were a war correspondent. Say that this was Bosnia.

SHEILA   But would you have that gun, Kit? If I didn't have this camera?

KIT   Sheila? What?

SHEILA   If you try to record the existence of sub-atomic particles, it changes their behaviour. Did you know that?

> *She aims the camera at KIT. KIT is uncomfortable. She puts down the gun.*

KIT   You know what you want when you try something? Something lawless? Something wild?

You want more. That's weird, right? More. It's because you get used to it.

Because it isn't lawless if you're doing it. Because everything you do, you make excuses for.

I mean, you know that, don't you? You do this show, this great show, like "Mothers Whose Sons Are Gay Bar Strippers"... I loved that show, that show was fun, but when it's over, what do you do next? Sheila? Then what do you do?

SHEILA   I don't know.

KIT   Wait! I've got an idea. Sheila? Do you want to hear it?

SHEILA   No. I don't. No.

KIT   "Mothers Whose Sons Are Gay Bar Stripper Killers." It could be awesome. It could be a Sweeps Week thing. Because there's Troy, and maybe he saw this gay bar stripper on TV and, you know, he got aroused, you know, and, you know, he couldn't deal with it, and so, he made up all these canisters of nerve gas...

SHEILA   Kit... no more...

KIT   Too gross, right? And not true? And it has to be true. So you know what could happen? At the end? It would be like TV. It would all be a dream. Like the tape of Skippy dying...

SHEILA   Skippy dying?

She looks at the tape again.

KIT   I hate this tape.

SHEILA   You think Skippy is dying? On that tape?

KIT pushes a button on the VCR.

KIT   Whoops. I hit erase.

SHEILA   Kit...

KIT   No, it's okay, Sheila. You don't want to see it. You don't want it to have happened. You want to start over, don't you? With blank tape. Want to make our own tape? "Kit and Sheila's Video Diary..."

SHEILA   Kit, please...

KIT   *Bimbettes in Canada.* Scene one. Warning. Gunshots.

She shoots out the light over Skippy's picture. She laughs.

KIT   Gunshots. Partial nudity. Strong language and gross jokes about men, right, Sheila.

SHEILA   Give me the gun, Kit...

KIT   Want to play that back?

SHEILA   I want you to give me the gun.

KIT replays a videotape of furniture, which includes an offscreen gunshot.

KIT   This camera wasn't framed right, was it?

SHEILA   The gun, Kit…

KIT   Or maybe it didn't happen.

SHEILA   Kit…

KIT pops videotapes in all available monitors, and they all display white noise.

KIT   You want to see what happened? Nothing happened. It was all a dream.

Black out stage lights. We see video screens filled with white noise.

SHEILA   Kit, please…

Gunshot. A flash in the dark.

Kit, please…. Are you all right?

Blackout screens.

The end.

AFTERWORDS

Afterword

On December 11, 2000, Florence Gibson was at the memorial for Carol Bolt. It was there, she said, "that I began to realize the full extent of Carol's legacy. She was a mentor, a teacher, an educator, an artist who worked in many fields including radio, film, television, and opera. She was a political activist who helped put together a national organization for the benefit of all Canadian playwrights, said the voices, the letters, the memories, the tears. And I didn't know, because I didn't know Carol. I knew the plays." ("Carol Bolt")

When one reflects on Carol's legacy, one can see that most of her plays resonate with the ideal of community, assert its importance, its centrality. She believed in this and she lived what she believed. This applies to the creative process which best suited her: the cooperative, sharing milieu of Toronto Free Theatre (although she proved versatile and able to move from the collective and on-the-spot creativity to the solitude of the word processor). She always said plays were just written by a writer, they were made in the theatre. It also applies to the subjects Bolt chose to write about—the history, issues, perspectives of *this* society—as well as to her focus on leaders and group efforts. She thought collectively. She was one of those people who believed it mattered that we are a society of individuals who share something, and not just an accidental crowd. Is it old-fashioned to believe, as she did, that theatre can help generate positive and life-affirming ties between strangers? She wanted her plays to reflect upon things her audience could relate to, to reflect our common heritage and history, our common goals, and the particular concerns of this community. The sensibility and value system evident in her plays are her own: the values and virtues she theatricalizes, she lived.

Carol Bolt was the kind of creative person who flourished in a group. The group provided a community and a support system; it also offered a repertory of styles and themes. This was certainly the case at the beginning of her career in the seventies when, as Martin Kinch described earlier, so many theatre artists shared a vision, a sense of purpose: to build Canadian cultural awareness, to perform to Canadian audiences who were becoming more interested in their own culture. The group also gave her the confidence to work at the height of her powers. In those early days she was unstoppable. And she thanked the community in her way: she fought for their shared interests like a fierce virago. She had courage and conviction, says Sally Clark, and a hugely generous spirit. "She wasn't just advancing her own career. She treated us like we were all in this together—she was very idealistic about that." Bolt paid her community back, big time. Even when her fortunes at the box office fluctuated, even when she was looking elsewhere and moving into the areas of radio and television (far more isolated and isolating experiences), her commitment to the profession never wavered. No wonder she was so well-loved, as you will read below.

Bolt had a lot of energy; she was a hard worker. Her husband said "driven" might be the more apt expression. She was truly prolific; she always had a dozen projects on the go. Not only are there all the plays and productions listed in the bibliography, there are numerous files with drafts of unproduced works at Library and Archives Canada, works with titles such as *Fidelity Quartet, Star Quality, Survival, Dangerous Patriots, Ghostwriters, Vietnaming,* and many, many others. Writing and revising continuously, she made notes longhand; she never composed on the typewriter. Working with her on *Red Emma,* Martin Kinch commented on how quickly she wrote; how quickly she came to the heart of each scene and how she had a very strong sense of who she was writing for. She could write to the specific strengths of the actor she had in mind. Fast and responsive, she would write her plays on a kind of internal stage… constantly in rehearsal, constantly rewriting in rehearsal; she would literally be upstairs rewriting the next scene! Carol Bolt was a real playwright, he said, one who could derive enormous pleasure from the work.

At the same time, Bolt was giving workshops, teaching playwriting, and mentoring at various institutions. She was a workshop leader for the Algonquin College Summer Institute of Film and Television; an instructor teaching "Writing for the Stage" at Ryerson College and "Playwriting I" at York University. She also taught for the National Theatre School in Ottawa and Playwrights' Workshop Montréal. Her longest association was with Toronto's Ryerson Polytechnic University in Toronto, where she taught from 1990–1998. The course titles would vary, but the nature of the work remained the same. The huge number of files at Library and Archives Canada called Other Peoples Plays (and many of these have multiple drafts) are materials from her mentoring and dramaturgy. At times she was a dramaturge for Toronto Free Theatre, TV Ontario's Youth Year program, Young Peoples Theatre summer school for a decade and, for a very long time, for the Labrador Arts Festival. She loved working with young people. According to Glenda MacFarlane, Bolt was the most popular playwright of all in the "Playwrights in the School" program run by Playwrights Union (now defunct):

> She was the best at doing it, too—kids loved her. I went out to watch her in action several times and she really was marvellous at getting kids to open up and find stories that were their own. Later, when I ended up working with teenagers on collective plays, I often found myself thinking, "What would Carol do?" (I wish I'd told her that…).

Friends and fellow playwrights have spoken of Bolt as a positive force and a force to be reckoned with—brave, determined, opinionated, sometimes intimidating, warm, generous, and often wildly funny. She also had strength and quiet resolve. She held her views passionately, about feminism especially and justice in general, but she was also terrific fun to be with. Glenda MacFarlane laughingly recalled a train ride to a playwrights' event in Quebec City and how they spent the trip drinking and outlining a book that would tell the *real* story of the history of Canuck theatre, "a compendium of scandals and silliness: a list of Passe Muraille sex triangles, a sample rejection letter from Urjo Kareda, that sort of thing." Many will remember the hilarious letter Nancy Beatty read at the memorial. Bolt was responding to someone in the West who accused the Playwrights Co-op of being Toronto-centric. Bolt argued vehemently and at length. Then she signed it, "Fuck you. Love, Carol."

Her most significant contributions are those she made to the theatre community at large. We have concrete evidence of her good works. The results have been enduring. "She was a tremendous pioneering force in Canadian theatre," said artistic director Ken Gass, "both in terms of her own body of work and her tireless advocacy on behalf of playwrights across the country" (Taylor, 2000). That advocacy began in the seventies when a small group of like-minded people wrote the Gaspe Manifesto which launched the challenge that would result in the creation of the Playwrights Co-op (1972), and then the Guild of Canadian Playwrights (1977). These two organizations united to form the Playwrights Union of Canada, and then separated again. Rex Deverell writes a lively account of this critical part of Canadian theatre history:

> These were heady times. It would be a mistake to say that Carol did all this by herself or that she was the first with the vision. The evolving organization was making the decisions and everybody was part of the process—taking turns, often, as chairs, executive members, or council members. But in those early days, of us all, Carol stood out as a galvanizing presence. (See p. 542)

Past President Paul Ledoux also praises Bolt for her tremendous importance to Canadian theatre:

> Canadian plays are distributed, produced, and studied in schools and universities around the world. The Playwrights Union of Canada is an organization to be proud of and there isn't a single aspect of its development that hasn't benefited from the attentions of Carol Bolt. (See p. 550)

She did an impressive amount of work for this organization especially and her energy, organizational skills, and intense dedication were everywhere in evidence. Florence Gibson became a member after things were well underway, and she remarked:

> She offered zeal, enthusiasm, commitment, and amazing talent. I didn't know where it all came from. And I didn't know where she got the nerve.
>
> She was the only woman successfully making her way in a sea of men; nationalistic theatre men hell-bent on rescuing us from the British and American imports that had dominated Canadian stages for decades. As is often the case when politics reach a flashpoint, male bravado puts forward a restraining hand: "Stand back; this is a job for a man." But there was Carol, writing amazing feminist plays like *Red Emma...*, seated at the "round table" of the fledgling Playwrights Co-op, having her say. Getting her way. Being counted, listened to, acknowledged, and *produced*. ("Carol Bolt")

Bolt was always involved with the Playwrights Union in some capacity. Naturally, however, different projects took her attention at different times. For example, in the eighties it was the committee work with the Public Lending Rights Commission and the Toronto Arts Council; in the nineties it was the Union's Women's Caucus and, at various points, it was as board member for Equity Showcase Theatre, CanCopy, Nightwood Theatre, Playwrights' Workshop Montréal, to name a few.

Carol Bolt's tireless engagement with arts advocacy has been publicly acknowledged. Nominated by her colleagues who, in this way, expressed the esteem and appreciation they felt, Bolt received the 1977 Queen's Silver Jubilee Medal. According to David Bolt, their son Alex keeps this medal with him as a talisman whenever he travels. Bolt was dismayed to discover that her pioneering efforts had been overlooked in the first major publication which documented the 1970s rise of alternate theatre. Happily, her memorial service proved a splendid corrective. To honour her further, the Guild of Canadian Playwrights designated the Carol Bolt Reading Room in 2000 and, in 2001, the Canadian Authors Association created the Carol Bolt Award for Excellence in Drama (see p.555). Still, it is not enough.

Reading Carol Bolt has been produced to celebrate the contributions of this cherished artist and advocate, this much-missed buddy. According to Jewish lore, a person lives on in the memories of those left behind. In that spirit I have collected here the writing of four of her fellow playwrights, each with a unique connection, who share my affection, admiration, and respect for that singular woman, CAROL BOLT.

> *Every once in a while I have a flash of her dedicated intensity. I don't know many who joyfully pushed in so many worlds.* (Larry Zacharko)

—Cynthia Zimmerman

"The Adamant Carol Bolt and the Playwrights Co-op: Personal Reminiscences"

One day in 1970 or '71, I received a letter inviting me to discuss the possibility of forming a new organization for playwrights. I was an emerging playwright—or a playwright was emerging from me. I was seeking identity and comfort. So on the indicated night I climbed a rickety stairway up over a garage on Dupont Street in Toronto—an old building next to a recently established theatre, Factory Lab, and around the corner from the new Tarragon Theatre—and found myself in the midst of a raging battle. Leading the forces on one side was a young woman I knew of—but had not met. Her name was Carol Bolt. She was facing down two older established writers who *knew* how to organize. They had been part of a playwrights group within the Alliance of Canadian Cinema, Television and Radio Artists (ACTRA) and felt playwrights needed clout and the way to achieve it would be within ACTRA.

Carol was adamant: "I don't want those guys in ACTRA speaking for me—not when it comes to theatre." She was insisting that we needed to find our own voices as playwrights and we now had an ideal opportunity to do exactly that.

Nineteen-seventy to '72 were pivotal years in Canadian theatre history. In the wake of Canada's Centennial celebrations, there was a powerful concern about national identity. The Canada Council had shown itself willing to make funds available for the development of playwrights. The Council called a few theatre artists together at Stanley House in the Gaspé for a consultation. Carol, Tom Hendry, Jack Gray, and George Ryga were invited as playwrights. The question was: What would it take to develop a truly national theatre, instead of one that, among a surfeit of European and American plays, occasionally produced one written by a Canadian?

The group produced a manifesto calling for radical change. "We believe there is no meaningful Canadian theatre except where our playwrights take a major role in it. That they have not done so to date is a scandal and a disgrace. ...We recommend... that all Canadian grant giving agencies stipulate that no later than the first of January, 1973, any theatre receiving funds will be required to include in its repertoire at least one Canadian work in each two works it produces." The manifesto called for a guaranteed income for senior playwrights, continuing subsidy for others, production grants for new work, and automatic publishing of produced Canadian scripts. [1] The recommendations were hard for producers to swallow—but they became a catalyst for a sea of change in attitude.

Of course, change was already in the air. In Toronto, directors like Bill Glassco and Ken Gass were founding theatres to do only Canadian scripts. George Luscombe's Toronto Workshop Productions had been successfully working with Canadian stories since the early '60s. Paul Thompson was busy dedicating Theatre Passe Muraille toward the same goals.

The Trudeau government initiative "Opportunities for Youth" had unleashed an army of young theatre folk creating good/bad/radical/banal/exciting theatre across the nation. (Many of today's prominent writers and directors got their start in OFY troupes.) And it was precisely this matrix that the Gaspé group said would give birth—finally—to a truly significant Canadian theatre. Out of quantity would come quality.

Forming our own organization was key. As Carol said, this was not the time to marginalize ourselves in a large union like ACTRA. And besides, ACTRA had no jurisdiction in theatre, or an ambiguous one at best. We would stand up as writers for the stage—as playwrights—as artists who could not merely work within a nascent Canadian theatre, but as the creators of that theatre. This was an opportunity to launch a movement!

I was older than Carol, by about a month, but I always felt like a little brother trotting after her, saying "Me, too, Carol" because I had caught her excitement and something of her vision. It was logical. If the traditional diet of our theatre, American plays, British plays, the European classics, was to change, it had to start with the playwrights. Where else? And it was already happening!

---

[1] "A Strange Enterprise: The dilemma of the playwright in Canada*, The Gaspé Manifesto." Published in *Canadian Theatre History: Selected Readings*. Ed. Don Rubin. Toronto: Playwrights Canada Press, 1996, 2004. 292–96.
*Footnote reads "Conclusions and recommendations of a seminar sponsored by the Canadian Council at Stanley House, 19–23 July 1971."

These were heady times. It would be a mistake to say that Carol did all this by herself or that she was the first with the vision. The evolving organization was making the decisions and everybody was part of the process—taking turns, often, as chairs, executive members, or council members. But in those early days, of us all, Carol stood out as a galvanizing presence.

Over the course of a series of meetings, the assembled writers decided that there were three ways in which we could influence the theatre environment: to make our scripts readily available, to lobby government and funding agencies, and to advocate on behalf of our members to producers. To these ends our new organization would be run by playwrights—and we would call ourselves "Playwrights Co-op."

Tom Hendry managed to find us a grant and we hired our first executive director in the person of Daryl Sharp. (He left shortly to become a Jungian analyst—we used to say that we drove him to analysis.)

We didn't see ourselves as a publisher—not at first. But we saw ourselves as a central clearing house for anyone who wanted to stage a Canadian play.

I can still see the "state of the art" mimeograph machine in the middle of the office. For the young gaffers reading this, mimeographing was an inexpensive, labour intensive, low-tech method of producing copies in quantity. One had to type the scripts onto stencils which rotated around an inked drum. Until we hired more help, we would bring in our scripts on stencils, or some of our faster typists would take scripts home to type. I remember Carol volunteering to type stencils. She was that dedicated to making this new enterprise work.

Our original plan was that the criterion for membership was simple acceptance of a script. Members set about vetting submissions. Things were very casual. There was a mattress in the back room for those who preferred reading in a supine position. (One or two of the readers were not very gentle with the feedback they gave to the putative writers—so we decided we had to vet the feedback.) Finally we were able to hire a reader who could offer writers tactful comments on their scripts.

I had become resident playwright at Saskatchewan's Globe Theatre. I was shuttling back and forth between Regina and Saskatchewan—sometimes on the executive, sometimes on the national council. Carol was often on the same council, sometimes in the chair—and she was always available, always on top of the issues, always willing to devote effort and time beyond the call of duty. I remember asking how she managed to find time to write her plays. She said she wrote late into the night—when her family had gone to bed and people had stopped phoning.

The adamance I had noted when we first met was a deeply inherent character trait. It came, not from an arbitrary stubbornness, but from a keen mind, a quick insight, and an uncommon ability to stay focussed on goals. When controversy arose, Carol refused to be mowed down by what others took for granted. When she had said, "I don't want those guys in ACTRA to speak for me," there was a subtext of feminism. She was saying that she would stand for herself—a woman writing plays in a society that privileged male authority.

As time went on, the organization grew—there were more and more writers becoming members. One day we received word from those who oversee co-operatives that we did not meet the legal definition of a co-op and that we had to change our name. We became Playwrights Canada in 1979.

Meanwhile, however, it had become obvious that while the organization was successfully supplying scripts to the public, our other agenda, of being able to set standards about royalty rates and commissioning fees, and building a welcoming environment for writers—was not being met. Nor were we able to speak as a credible national body of professional playwrights to the theatre community. Carol and others began to see the need for another arm that would devote itself to achieving a kind of collective agreement with theatres and to lobby on our behalf with governmental agencies. Even the Canada Council was saying that it would welcome standardization of fees—since it had begun to make grants available for theatres to stage new work.

I remember getting a call in Regina from Carol outlining the strategy. We would have our founding meeting in Calgary—no Toronto-centricity here. Our membership would be composed of those who had a track record of professional productions. By 1977 we were able to launch this militant new arm—the Guild of Canadian Playwrights.

Almost from the beginning we ran into trouble. PACT, the Professional Association of Canadian Theatres, resisted contracts; some of the playwrights preferred their own way of negotiating; there were power plays—and the most serious threat of all, an attempt to pit Playwrights Canada against the new organization. Ultimately we saw we had to bring the two arms back together again—Playwrights Canada became the Playwrights Union of Canada, PUC.

With our united voice we were able to bring PACT to the negotiating table and agreements over contracts. We started by asking for a meeting. PACT said they would attend as long as the threat of a contract wasn't hanging over their heads. Carol, Paul Ledoux, Alf Silver, and I (if I remember correctly) met with them at the Playwrights Union office. Unbeknownst to them, we had fastened a draft of a contract to a light fixture over their heads. We tried to keep a solemn demeanour throughout the discussion.

By 2002, PUC's publications, under the imprint of Playwrights Canada Press had become a major enterprise. It was decided to hive it off as an incorporated publishing house and, to avoid confusion, "PUC" was renamed the Playwrights Guild of Canada.

In 1993, while Carol was president of PUC, there was a federal election and all of us were concerned about cutbacks to funding of the arts. Carol came up with an idea that we would have a telephone line which would give an opportunity for the public to call in and listen to a "rant" by a playwright about arts funding. I thought this was a really stupid idea. Who would call in to listen to that sort of thing? But Carol was adamant and volunteered to organize it. She persuaded a number of prominent writers and playwrights to participate. Margaret Atwood contributed a cartoon—depicting Carol stealing "old ties" from the establishment. The cartoon was published in the *Toronto Star* and "Dial-a-Tirade" was hugely successful, registering more than three hundred callers a day over the course of the campaign. [2]

Over the years, the Bolt family and the Deverell family had become close friends. We didn't know that Carol's time would be cut short so soon. When the diagnosis had been made and the prognosis clear, many of her friends came to visit her in her illness. Various health and healing suggestions were offered. Everyone had advice. She told some of us that she wasn't afraid of death. I thought at first that she was saying she had accepted the business of dying. But on consideration, I have begun to feel she was saying something else. I'm sure it was the adamant Carol who was speaking. She would confront death on her own terms and nobody else's.

—Rex Deverell

"Carol"

Carol had a twilight about her. As our teacher at the National Theatre School, when Carol entered the wintry glare of the classroom in her long sweaters and knit hats and large glasses and beguiled grin, it darkened. She was a different weather. A dose of night, she drew us in.

Carol challenged us to write about real people. I had recently read Rosemary Sullivan's *Shadow Maker* and proposed writing a play about Gwendolyn MacEwen. Carol was immediately ignited. She may have even clapped her hands. She had known Gwendolyn fitfully and circumferentially, but had been present at Gwendolyn's ominous 1987 performance at the Bamboo Club. Carol recalled the words Gwendolyn had hurled at her audience, how she had fallen from her stool, how people wanted to help her but she had ordered them away. It would be Gwendolyn's last public appearance. Carol dared me to dig in and around it.

I wrote my play over the course of five years. Through every draft I used—as I did with every play I have written since—Carol's cue card system. To build her plays, Carol recorded her thoughts and research on coloured cue cards. Each colour signified the various components of the play: blue for a line of dialogue, yellow for a stage direction, pink for a character detail, white for a sound cue. As they accumulated so too did the play. Carol told us to take note of everything; like lived experience, the most random miscellany could prove to be the most formative.

The system seemed so straightforward, so pristine. For us, a languorous brood smoking moodily and drinking cheap draft, draping ourselves across every idea, every argument, it was a respite from the chaos we courted. We had, until that time, believed the creative process to be a feral one, a Russian roulette. Carol offered a method that promised to tame our work without spoiling its wildness. Hers was an invention and we were won over.

---

[2] Mentioned in the *Toronto Star*, "Artists' rants give Dial-A-Tirade callers an earful." Saturday 23 October 1993. By Henry Mietkieiewicz. L1 and L14.

We graduated. After working in bush camps in Northern Ontario as I did every summer, I moved to Toronto with, among other things, two thick stacks of cue cards about Gwendolyn MacEwen. I called Carol. With subdued giddiness, she explained that she lived in the east end, near the fire hall. I had never spoken to her on the telephone. Her tone excited me; in her voice, there was always the glint of mischief.

When she opened the door, there it was again, that exquisite gloom lurking about her. It was not gothic or threatening or doomful. It was intimacy—instantly on offer. She welcomed me with that marvelling grin, those trailing knits and led me through her hallway, the sunken hue of a submarine. She ushered me into a room where she had set out cheeses and olives and meats she had prepared for our meeting. She was elegant.

As Carol spoke about her work and inquired about mine, it was as if she carried a torch and we were not in her home, but in the catacombs. Fire in hand, she would pause whenever we reached the doorstep to a hidden chamber. Hand on the doorknob, Carol would wink back to me. Anything could be waiting there for us: Diane Arbus fishing out a photograph, Red Emma in a sensual stronghold, a bullfighter eating an apple.

Carol and I were both chasing ghosts. As I wrestled with the velvet-clad puzzle that was Gwendolyn MacEwen, I felt burdened by my responsibilities as biographer. Fiction is so untethered; this was its opposite. I was circling an icon, a sister, an aunt, a daughter, a wife. Carol rallied: what makes biographical theatre not only interesting but vital is not your accuracy in rendering the subject—having your facts librarian-straight and lining them up for the stage—but your engagement of the subject; where do your obsessions meet hers? Allow her to be the chatter in your mind. Cut your tomatoes as she did. Love a hulk. Wear heavy bronze earrings. Read everything she read. Speak Arabic and Greek and Hebrew aloud. Live on Toronto Island. Interview everyone who knew her. Walk the same routes, the same alleyways. Be tenacious. Be tireless. Be her. Whatever the risks, Carol was entirely unafraid of discovery.

Carol got very sick very quickly. Writing *The Gwendolyn Poems* became a race against her diagnosis. Foolishly or not, I felt that we had entered into this riddle together—and that the completion of the play might act as a kind of balm against the disease. I trusted that a draft in my hands would be a tangible response to her counsel. Evidence of how it had mattered.

When I finished the first draft, I called Carol instantly. I had used my cue cards and they had resulted in something I felt was much sturdier than anything I had ever written before. My apartment in those days was tiny. You could barely dance in the kitchen. I could hear my neighbours fight and make love through an adjoining wooden door. The floor was splintered. These details linger only because they act as the context for a moment I will not forget. No one answered the telephone. It was evening. I left a message telling Carol that I had completed the draft, the play now existed. Her husband, David, called me back immediately. Carol had died earlier that day.

I thought about how quickly Carol could move between ferocity and jest. How she was a rebel, a queen, a friend, a mentor, a mother, a wife. How knowing her was a kind of enchantment. How when I sat across from her in her home that first visit, and looked at her, those luminous eyes, I saw that she was full of hidden chambers. Hundreds. Thousands. How many did she open for us and how many did she keep locked? How many had she still intended to write?

David and I spoke briefly that night. Hushed and concentrated, we were bent together straining to chase a flickering light.

—Claudia Dey

"Following in Her Footsteps: Big Shoes to Fill"

When Carol Bolt, one of Canada's finest and best-known playwrights, died in 2000, I felt, like many other Canadian women playwrights, something more than the loss to the community and to the Playwrights Union of Canada, now called the Playwrights Guild. Carol had written some of our finest plays, and now there would be no more; she was a founding member of the Union who continued to serve the organization for more than thirty years as president, chairing committees, or establishing policy and procedure with incisive, impressive command. But there I was at her memorial service some weeks after her death, feeling as if I'd been left with a hole in my heart.

After Carol died, I realized I knew very little about her. Born in Winnipeg and growing up in British Columbia, Carol was one of a group of artists who came to Toronto in the early 1970s with the intention of being a playwright of distinctive voice, creating new Canadian plays for the new theatres coming into existence. (Factory Theatre, Tarragon Theatre, and Theatre Passe Muraille)

Equally important for me was the fact that Carol was one of very few women playwrights successfully making her way in a sea of men; men who were rejecting the British and American imports that had dominated Canadian stages for decades.

It was at her memorial that I realized the full extent of Carol's legacy. She was a mentor, a teacher, an educator, an artist who worked in many fields, including radio, film, television, and opera. But there was one question I now wished I'd asked: How did you do it without being labelled with one of the most silencing of adjectives a feminist endures: strident.

Because some fifteen years later, when I came on the scene, the Fraticelli report[3] had come out, putting numbers to something we all knew: roughly 90% of all directors, artistic directors, and playwrights being produced in Canadian theatres were male.

Rattling home on the Bathurst streetcar, that hole in my heart felt even bigger. I ought to do more, to have done more. But more what? More shouting into the wind? We'd entered an era where government funding had been reduced to a trickle, the focus was fiscal, the commissions were for one-person shows. It seemed to me that we'd had our kick at the can during the "feminist years" in Canadian theatre back in the eighties—back when race and colour and sexual orientation divided us. Back when many of us lost sight of the fact that being female might just be the only thing we had in common.

I got home, turned on the light over my desk and thought about Carol's voice. I could hear her intuitively putting the collective first. I could see her entering a room and embracing the warring factions. She spoke like a poet, a dramatist: from her own perspective, from the here and now. There she was, I thought, honouring the unities in every aspect of her life. With her ability to maintain a comprehensive perspective, she could include her most entrenched opposition. She could get the most die-hard opponent to do what needed to be done. She saw no need to separate herself from the fullness of humanity, and that included the men. With this innate ability to be immersed in the collective and yet not lose sight of her individuality, the paradox of Carol Bolt was revealed to me: unique yet integral, Carol was someone who lived to make the whole more than the sum of its parts. It was as if the magic of theatre had been revealed to me in her life; she lived by her work; her work and her life were one.

It then occurred to me that perhaps that hole in my heart, that restless, uneasy feeling, had to do with filling Carol's shoes. Carol had moved on, but she had left a pair of shoes in the middle of the road. A big pair waiting for someone to step into them. And my uneasiness was that they might be too big for me. How does one fill the shoes that someone like Carol leaves? One step at a time, I'm pretty sure she'd say.

---

[3] In her article, Florence Gibson mentions "the Fraticelli report." Its full title is "The Status of Women in Canadian Theatre," by Rina Fraticelli. Published under the auspices of the Status of Women, it covered the years 1978 to 1981 (June 1982). Many of the Union playwrights were dismayed, some were outraged, by Fraticelli's findings: "Ten percent of the plays produced on Canadian stages between 1978 and 1981 were written by women compared to 77% written by men." This statistic is determined by gender alone; nationality is not a factor.

Carol wrote up the results of a follow-up survey conducted by the Women's Caucus of Playwrights Union in 1991. It was published in *CanPlay* (July/August 1996: 6–7) and entitled: "The Zimmerman Report: Canadian Women in the Theatre: A Statistical Survey." There is an apocryphal Carol Bolt story connected to this subject. At an annual general meeting in the '90s, the Women's Caucus representative reported that only one-third of the Canadian plays produced by theatres that year were by women. Carol suggested they do the math again. This time it turned out to be one-third female playwrights, one-third male, and one-third Norm Foster.

A full-scale and intensive follow-up study to the Fraticelli Report was undertaken jointly by Nightwood Theatre, the Playwrights Guild of Canada, and PACT. With research conducted by Rebecca Burton, *Adding it Up: The Status of Women in Canadian Theatre* was published in 2006. To summarize, it concludes that although women have made gains since 1981, in 2006 they were still far from realizing parity with their male colleagues.

Carol's memory is honoured annually through the Carol Bolt Award, a $1,000 prize for the best Canadian script published or produced that year. I would like to see it become a more significant and substantial award, an award whose value and prestige reflects the woman for whom it is named. And I'm working on that, one step at a time.

—Florence Gibson

"A Star in the Firmament of Canadian Theatre" [4]

> Myth is more appealing than fact. It postulates that heroism is possible, that people can be noble and effective and change things. Maybe that's why I'm interested in myth. (Carol Bolt)

Carol Bolt's latest play is called *Lives of the Poets*. It's a comedy about a group of authors gathered together to read at Canadian Lit celebrations in a community called Wendigo Falls. But no one has come to the reading. The writers are trapped in a deserted library in the middle of a blizzard with an avaricious American producer (who once managed the Mountie account for Disney), a half-mad puppeteer (who organized the event), and a Cree busboy who worships their work (and is a would-be poet).

Against a background of self-doubt, sellout, and collapsing personal relationships, the characters struggle with the meaning of their lives as artists and find redemption in the collective howl of a bp Nichol sound poem. The script is funny, touching, and inspiring, but despite her best efforts, Bolt was unable to complete her work before her death this week from cancer.

This particular play remains unfinished, but Bolt has left behind a legacy of inestimable value. She was a pioneer, a multitalented writer who excelled in all the fields of dramatic art. Her work was shaped by an astute political sensibility and even when full of outrage, never lacked for humour. Most of her plays asked questions about heroes and the making of myths.

Her work for children brought to life tales of Canadian heroes and the Chalmers Award-winning *Icetime* made a hero of a contemporary girl trying to join an all-male hockey league. There was a wonderful series of radio dramas about Mary Pickford, Louis B. Mayer, and the other Canadians who ruled Hollywood in its golden era. Her play and the opera *Red Emma* painted an exuberant portrait of anarchist Emma Goldman. In *Famous*, the best friend of a murderer is turned into a celebrity by the perverse mythmaking of our modern media, and in *Gabe*, a Métis kid fresh out of jail looks for the spirit of Louis Riel on the mean city streets of Winnipeg.

Bolt was a leading voice in the struggle for the development of a national theatre. She believed in a Canadian theatre and always stood up for what she believed in. Like

---

[4] Originally published in *The Globe and Mail*, Thursday, November 30, 2000.

the subjects of her plays, she possessed mythic qualities. In the first flowering of Canadian theatre in the seventies, she was a star. While others were struggling to find their voice, Carol was writing hits. *One Night Stand*, a tightly-wound thriller that explored the sexual politics of the era, had even been made into an award-winning film. Her career suggested that not only could one write plays for Canadians but one might also, just possibly, be able to make a living at it.

In the last few weeks of her illness, I spent a lot of time talking to our mutual friends, playwrights, actors, and directors. They remembered Carol as a role model and a source of encouragement. Some spoke of her extraordinary energy field and her commitment to her profession. Everyone commented on her approachability and generosity. She was a complex person, often shy in private, but with a wickedly wry sense of humour, a laugh that bubbled up from deep in her soul, and a willingness to engage fully in the life of her community because so much needed to be done.

One of Carol's greatest gifts to the country was her unfailing thirty-year commitment to the profession of playwriting. The Playwrights Union of Canada is, in a way, a monument to that commitment.

From its earliest days, when the organization then known as the Playwrights Co-op was little more than an idea and a mimeograph machine, Carol was a force to be reckoned with. She could be a fiercely combative advocate of her beliefs and when she got mad, the ground shook. Her irony could be icy, her logic precise, and her eye for detail formidable. She rarely lost an argument, but then again, she was usually right.

Today, PUC distributes a catalogue of more than three thousand scripts, administers rights for hundreds of amateur productions, and negotiates contracts on behalf of roughly four hundred professional playwrights. Canadian plays are distributed, produced, and studied in schools and universities around the world. PUC is an organization to be proud of, and there isn't a single aspect of its development that hasn't benefited from the attentions of Carol Bolt.

She was also an educator: she visited hundreds of public schools in the course of her career; she was a major contributor to Jim Henson's series *Fraggle Rock*; she worked for the Institute of Child Studies at the University of Toronto and taught at Ryerson, Concordia, and the National Theatre School. She also ran workshops at Young People's Theatre, developing collective creations with her students. She taught that writing was something you struggled with and that plays were built with hard work as much as passion. In full flight with a class, she was a sight to behold, and the young people, whether they were in grade three or on the verge of a professional career, loved her.

I think that special power came from the love she knew inside her own family. The love she shared with her husband, David, and her son, Alexander. She never lost her ability to inspire. She has inspired me many times in the past. And in the future, if I'm feeling like one of those storm-stranded writers trapped in Wendigo Falls, I know her memory will pull me through.

—Paul Ledoux

Dear Carol,

I am distressed to learn that you have not been well lately. This unwelcome news puts you at the center of my thoughts.

I remember those Toronto Free Theatre days with great fondness. I guess we were actually going through a renaissance without recognizing it; at least at the time I didn't get it. It all seemed quite normal. I expected things to get better and better, not having the slightest appreciation of what a magnificent time it was—so many muscular ideas, so much passion, such glorious, arrogant idealism. Few art scenes that I've come across have proved half as exciting as the one that we shared for that brief period in the seventies. There is a saying, "Bright things burn quickly." On the other hand, there is another saying, "All old days are good," so maybe my memory is just playing ego tricks. But I don't think so.

In New York my favorite restaurant is called John's and it's been operating since the very beginning of the century under the same name, in the same location. John, the original owner, was from Sicily and was an ardent socialist. He had a cousin in the Cosa Nostra who warned other wise guys to stay away from his crazy bomb-wielding relative. This makes John's the only Italian restaurant in New York without some Mafia affiliation. Emma Goldman frequented the restaurant in the early days and when I'm slurping down my cappelini and hoisting a glass of Chianti, I often think of your wonderful play Red Emma.

Anyway Carol, you were always such a wonderfully frank advisor and good friend, not to mention an excellent house mate, that it's hard to imagine how I've muddled along for so many years without being in touch. I'm wishing you all the best.

Much love,

Des McAnuff

Carol Bolt

(1941–2000)

Chronology of Important Dates

1941   Born Carol Johnson, Winnipeg, Manitoba, 25 August.

1961   Graduated University of British Columbia, Bachelor of Arts.

Lived in London, Israel, Montreal, and finally settled in Toronto.

1969   Canada Council Arts Grant.

Marries actor David Bolt, 19 June.

1970   *Daganawida.* Toronto: Toronto Workshop Productions, 13 January. Dir. George Luscombe. (Theatre for Young Audiences [TYA])

"Something for Olivia's Scrapbook." (David Helwig story adapted for television.) *Theatre Canada: Canadian Short Stories.* CBC TV: October. The first of many works produced for television.

"Guy and Jack." *Saskatchewan Writers.* CBC Radio. The first of many works produced for radio.

1971   *Next Year Country.* (later revised as *Buffalo Jump*) Regina: Globe Theatre, March. Dir. Ken Kramer.

1972   Founding member of Playwright's Co-op, January.

Canada Council Arts Grant.

Buffalo Jump. (Revised and rewritten version of *Next Year Country*) Toronto: Theatre Passe Muraille, May. Dir. Paul Thompson. Excerpt from this production broadcast on CBC Radio: "This Country in the Morning."

My Best Friend is Twelve Feet High. (One act, TYA) Toronto: Young People's Theatre, 27 July. Dir. Ray Whelan. [Toronto: Open Circle Theatre, 2 February. Dir. Ray Whelan.]

Cyclone Jack. Toronto: Young People's Theatre, November. Dir. Timothy Bond. Subsequent YPT tour of Ontario schools 1972–73. Music by Paul Vigna.

1973   28 May, birth of son Alex.

Ontario Arts Council Grant.

Dramaturge for Toronto Free Theatre and for the Labrador Arts Festival.

Gabe. Toronto: Toronto Free Theatre, 6 February. Dir. Robert Handforth.

Pauline. (Based on the poems of Pauline Johnson) Toronto: Theatre Passe Muraille, 22 March. Dir. Paul Thompson. Excerpt broadcast on CBC Radio: "This Country in the Morning."

Tangleflags. (One act, TYA) Toronto: Young People's Theatre, September. Dir. Ray Whelan. Music by Jane Vasey. (Toured Ontario schools, 1974–75 season)

1974   *The Bluebird.* Toronto: St. Lawrence Centre by Black Box Theatre, February. Dir. Mikulas Kravjansky. Joint production by Young People's Theatre. Based on the story *The Bluebird* by Marie d'Aulnoy. Text by Carol Bolt. Narrated by Frances Hyland.

Blue. (One-act, TYA) Toronto: Young People's Theatre. Dir. Timothy Bond. Music by Paul Vigna.

Maurice. (One-act musical for high school) Toronto: Young People's Theatre and Prologue to the Performing Arts, April. Dir. Timothy Bond, toured Ontario schools 1974–75 season. Commission grant from the Ontario Arts Council.

Red Emma: Queen of the Anarchists. Toronto: Toronto Free Theatre, February. Dir. Martin Kinch.

Shelter. Toronto: produced jointly by University Alumnae Dramatic Club and Young People's Theatre, Firehall Theatre: November. Dir. Eric Steiner. First professional production: Toronto: Toronto Arts Productions at the St. Lawrence Centre, October 1975. Dir. Eric Steiner. Part of a double bill with Michel Tremblay's *Surprise! Surprise!* (also directed by Steiner): a co-production with Theatre London: London, Ontario, November.

1975   *Finding Bumble.* (One-act, TYA) Toronto: Young People's Theatre at the Ontario Science Centre, 3 February. Dir. Timothy Bond.

1976   Publication of *Playwrights in Profile: Carol Bolt.* This anthology of plays is the first in the Playwrights Co-op series.

Red Emma. Adapted and broadcast for television, CBC: *Performance,* January. Producer Allan King, dir. Martin Kinch, music by Phillip Schreibman.

Bethune. (Norman Bethune: On Board the S.S. Empress *of Asia.)* Gravenhurst and Port Carling: Muskoka Summer Theatre, summer. Dir. Michael Ayoub.

Okey Doke. Kingston, Ontario: Collective creation commissioned and first produced by Queen's University Drama Department, summer. Dir. Bud Berkom and Gary Wagner. Production toured Ontario the same summer.

1977   Awarded Silver Jubilee Medal.

Ontario Arts Council Grant.

Writer-in-Residence, University of Toronto, 1977–78.

TV Lounge. (One-act) Toronto: Redlight Theatre, February. Dir. Steven Whistance-Smith.

Revised version of *Buffalo Jump.* Ottawa: Great Canadian Theatre Company. Dir. Bill Law. New material added.

One Night Stand. Toronto: Tarragon Theatre, April. Dir. Eric Steiner. Original music by Carol Pope.

Desperados. Toronto: Toronto Free Theatre, October. Dir. Martin Kinch.

Cyclone Jack. Adapted for CBC television's educational programming. Producer Sandy Stewart. Special broadcast, February.

1978   Chalmers Award finalist *(One Night Stand).*

One Night Stand. CBC Radio: *Front Row Centre,* March. Allan King adaptation. Won three Canadian Film Awards in 1978, including Best Television Drama.

1979   Writer-in-residence, University of Connecticut at Storrs, March–April.

Escape Entertainment. Workshopped at Factory Theatre Lab as *Deadline.*

1980   Writer-in-Residence, Australian Playwrights Colony.

1981   Dramatist-in-Residence, the New Drama Centre, Toronto Public Library.

Escape Entertainment. Toronto: Tarragon Theatre, January. Dir. Timothy Bond.

Love of Life. (One-act) Toronto: Solar Stage, July. Revised version of *TV Lounge* (1977).

Love or Money. Blyth, Ontario: Blyth Summer Festival, summer. Dir. Keith Batten.

1983   Dramaturge at Young People's Theatre Summer School (1983–88).

Attended Banff Playwrights' Colony.

Survival. Toronto: Factory Theatre Lab. Workshop production. Dir. Jackie Maxwell.

1984   Writer-in-Residence, Saskatchewan Writers Guild.

1985   Dramaturge for TVOntario Youth Year Program.

1986   Board of Directors, Toronto Arts Council, March, 1986–1988.

Co-chair of Theatre Committee, Toronto Arts Council 1986–1988.

Member of Literary Committee, Toronto Arts Council 1986–1988.

1987	Served on the Public Lending Right Commission 1987–1988.
	Icetime. Toronto: Theatre-on-the-Move, January. Dir. Michel Lefebre. (TYA)
1988	Chalmers Best Play for Children Award (for *Icetime*).
	But the Universe is a Green Dragon. (Adapted from book by Brian Swimme.) Toronto: The Theatre Centre, December. Dirs. Elizabeth Szathmary and Vinetta Strombergs. (TYA)
1989	Attended Norman Jewison's Canadian Centre for Advanced Film Studies.
	Yellow Ribbons wins the Gold Medal for Drama at the New York International Radio Awards.
	Harvest: A Musical. Caravan Stage Company, Ontario Tour: summer. Dir. Paul Kirby. Music by Michael Patterson and Chris Snell.
1989–1995	Labrador Arts Festival, Dramaturge.
1991	Playwright-in-Residence, Playwrights' Workshop Montréal.
	Elected to the 1991–92 Board of Directors of CanCopy.
1992	Teaches creative writing at Concordia University, Montreal (1992–94).
	The Birds. Toronto: Barry Zuckerman Amphitheatre. Dir. Lynda Hill. Workshop production (collective with Lynda Hill, Betty Quan, Marion de Vries, and Carol Bolt as contributing writers).
	Talking to Dolphins. CBC Radio, "Studio Theatre '92." October. Radio adaptation of *Harvest: A Musical.*
1993	*Rosie Learns French* in *YUL—A Theatrical Odyssey.* (Collective.) Montreal: le Centre Interculturel Strathearn, April.
1994	Reading of *Buffalo Jump* by original cast members. Part of the "Over 30" Reading Series, Playwrights Union of Canada.
	Fatso. Montreal: Montreal Youth Theatre. Dir. Michel Lefebre. (TYA)
	Playwrights Union Delegate to the Third International Women Playwrights Conference, Adelaide, Australia: July.
1995	*Red Emma: The Opera.* (Libretto) Toronto: Canadian Opera Company, duMaurier Theatre Centre, 28 November – 3 December. Dir. David William, music by Gary Kulesha.
1997	*Famous.* Toronto: Tarragon Theatre, November 1997. Produced by Carpe Diem Theatre. Dir. Pam Eddenden.
1998	Visiting Artist, Labrador Arts Festival.

Edited collection, *Who Asked Us Anyway?* Published by the Labrador School Board to commemorate the twenty-fifth anniversary of the Labrador Creative Arts Festival.

1999   *Mean to Me.* Workshop production. Kincardine, Ontario: Bluewater Summer Playhouse, August. Toronto: Factory Theatre, SummerWorks late-night cabaret featuring songs from the new musical (14–16 August).

2000   Carol Bolt dies of liver cancer, 28 November.

"A Tribute to Carol Bolt: In Celebration of her Life." Factory Theatre, 11 December. A staged reading of her new play, *Lives of the Poets*, directed by Brian Richmond, was scheduled for this day at Hart House Theatre. The reading was cancelled and replaced by a memorial.

Playwrights Union of Canada designates the Carol Bolt Reading Room.

One Night Stand: Una Aventura. (Revised Version) Victoria: Belfry Theatre. Co-produced with Essential Players. Dir. Michael McLaughlin.

2001   Canadian Authors Association inaugural Carol Bolt Award for best English-language play.

Canadian Authors Association Carol Bolt Award
Winners

2002   Kent Stetson – *The Harps of God*

2003   Daniel Goldfarb – *Adam Baum and the Jew Movie*

2004   Florence Gibson – *Home is My Road*

2005   Mieko Ouchi – *The Red Priest (Eight Ways to Say Goodbye)*

2006   John Mighton – *Half Life*

2007   Stephen Massicotte – *The Oxford Roof Climber's Rebellion*

2008   Colleen Murphy – *The December Man (L'homme de décembre)*

2009   Vern Thiessen – *Vimy*

2010   Michael Nathanson – *Talk*

BIBLIOGRAPHY

Published Stage Plays

I Wish. In *Upstage and Down.* Ed. D.P. McGarity. Toronto: Macmillan, 1968.
First produced under the name of Carol Johnson. (*One Plus One Plus One: Three One Acts.* Toronto: Central Library Theatre, August 1966.)

Buffalo Jump. Toronto: Playwrights Co-op, 1972. Toronto: Theatre Passe Muraille, May 1972.
Also published in *Major Plays of the Canadian Theatre, 1934–1984.* Ed. R. Perkyns. Toronto: Irwin, 1984.
Earlier version entitled *Next Year Country.* Dir. Ken Kramer. Regina: Globe Theatre, March 1971.

Cyclone Jack. Toronto: Playwrights Co-op, 1972.
Also published in *A Collection of Canadian Plays IV.* Ed. R. Kalman. Toronto: Simon & Pierre, 1975.
First produced: Dir. Timothy Bond. Toronto: Young People's Theatre, 1972.

My Best Friend is Twelve Feet High. Toronto: Playwrights Co-op, 1972.
Also published in *Class Acts: Six Plays for Children.* Toronto: Playwrights Canada Press, 1992.
First produced: Dir. Ray Whelan. Toronto: Young People's Theatre, July 1972.

Gabe. Toronto: Playwrights Co-op, 1973.
First produced: Dir. Robert Handforth. Toronto: Toronto Free Theatre, February 1973.

Tangleflags. Toronto: Playwrights Co-op, 1973.
First produced: Dir. Ray Whelan. Toronto: Young People's Theatre, September 1973.

Finding Bumble. Toronto: Playwrights Union of Canada, 1974.
First produced: Dir. Timothy Bond. Toronto: Young People's Theatre at the Ontario Science Centre, February 1975.

Maurice. In *Performing Arts Magazine* (Winter 1974): 42–50.
Also published by Playwrights Co-op, 1975 and in *Cues and Entrances: Canadian One Act Plays.* Ed. H. Beissel. Toronto: Gage, 1977.
First produced: Dir. Timothy Bond. Toronto: Young People's Theatre and Prologue to the Performing Arts, April 1974.

Red Emma. Toronto: Playwright's Co-op, 1974.
First produced: Dir. Martin Kinch. Toronto: Toronto Free Theatre, February 1974.

Shelter. Toronto: Playwrights Co-op, 1975.
First produced: Dir. Eric Steiner. Joint amateur production by University Alumnae Dramatic Club and Young People's Theatre. Toronto: Firehall Theatre,

November 1974.
Subsequently produced: Dir. Eric Steiner. Toronto Arts Productions at the St. Lawrence Centre, October 1975.

Playwrights in Profile: Carol Bolt. (Anthology includes *Buffalo Jump; Gabe; Red Emma*). Introduction by Sandra Souchotte. Toronto: Playwrights Co-op, 1976.

TV Lounge: A Play. Toronto: Playwrights Union of Canada, 1977.
First produced: Dir. Steven Whistance-Smith. Toronto: Redlight Theatre, February 1977.

One Night Stand: A Comedy Thriller. Toronto: Playwrights Co-op, 1977.
First produced: Dir. Eric Steiner. Toronto: Tarragon Theatre, April 1977.
One Night Stand: Una Aventura. Revised version. Toronto: Playwrights Canada Press, Second Scene Editions, 2002.
First produced: Dir. Michael McLaughlin. Victoria: Belfry Theatre, 2000.

Escape Entertainment. Toronto: Playwrights Canada Press, 1981.
First produced: Dir. Timothy Bond. Toronto: Tarragon Theatre, January 1981.

Icetime. Toronto: Nelson Canada, 1993.
First produced: Dir. Michael Lefebre. Theatre-on-the Move, January 1988.

Compañeras. Toronto: Playwrights Guild of Canada, 1993.
Also published in *Adventures for (Big) Girls: Seven Radio Plays.* Ed. Ann Jansen. Winnipeg: Blizzard, 1993: 51–76.
First produced by commission for CBC Radio: "Studio Theatre." 12 March 1993.

Fatso. Toronto: Playwrights Union of Canada, 1994.
First produced: Montreal Youth Theatre, 1994.

Rosie Learns French. Toronto: Playwrights Union of Canada, 1993.
First produced as part of P.O.V. Production's *YUL—A Theatrical Odyssey* Montreal: April 1993.

Famous. Toronto: PUC Play Service, 1997.
First produced: Dir. Pam Eddenden. Toronto: Tarragon Theatre, November 1997.
Earlier version entitled *Waiting for Sandy.* Excerpt in *Taking the Stage: Selections From Plays by Canadian Women.* Ed. C.D. Zimmerman. Toronto: Playwrights Canada Press, 1994: 80–87.

Unpublished Stage Plays

Daganawida. Dir. George Luscombe. Toronto Workshop Productions, January 1970.

Next Year Country. Dir. Ken Kramer. Regina: Globe Theatre, February 1971.

The Bluebird. Dir. Mikulas Kravjansky. Toronto: joint production by Young People's Theatre together with CentreStage at the St. Lawrence Centre, 1974. Based on the story *The Bluebird* by Marie d'Aulnoy. Text by Carol Bolt. Narrated by Frances Hyland.

Pauline. (Based on the poems of Pauline Johnson: a collaboration of writer, director, and actors Ann Anglin, Janet Amos, and Peter Kunder). Dir. Paul Thompson. Toronto: Theatre Passe Muraille, March 1973.

Blue. Dir. Timothy Bond. Toronto: Young People's Theatre, 1974.

Norman Bethune: On Board the S.S. Empress *of Asia.* Dir. Michael Ayoub. Gravenhurst: Muskoka Summer Theatre, summer 1976.

Okey Doke (A collective). Kingston: Queen's University Drama Department, summer 1976.

Desperados. Toronto: Toronto Free Theatre, October 1977.

Love of Life. (A revised version of *TV Lounge*). Toronto: Solar Stage, July 1981.

Love or Money. Blyth: Blyth Summer Festival, summer 1981.

Survival. Workshop production. Dir. Jackie Maxwell. Toronto: Factory Theatre Lab, 1983.

But the Universe is a Green Dragon (Adapted from book by Brian Swimme). Dirs. Elizabeth Szathmary and Vinetta Strombergs. Toronto: The Theatre Centre, December 1988.

Harvest. Dir. Paul Kirby. Ontario Tour: Caravan Stage Company, summer 1989.

Mean to Me. Workshop production. Kincardine, Ontario: Bluewater Summer Playhouse, August 1999.

Television, Film, and Radio
Television

"Something for Olivia's Scrapbook." (David Helwig story adapted for television by Carol Bolt). *Theatre Canada: Canadian Short Stories.* Prod. René Bonnière. CBC TV: October 1970.

"Valerie." *To See Ourselves.* Prod. René Bonnière. CBC TV: 1971.

"A Nice Girl Like You." *The Collaborators.* Prod. René Bonnière. CBC TV: November 1974.

Red Emma: Queen of the Anarchists. Performance. Based on the Toronto Free Theatre production directed by Martin Kinch. Prod. Allan King. CBC TV: Allan King Associates, January 1976.

Cyclone Jack. Adapted for CBC television's educational programming. Prod. Sandy Stewart. CBC TV: February 1977.

One Night Stand. Front Row Centre. CBC TV: Allan King Associates, March 1978.

"The Move." Story credit. *King of Kensington.* CBC TV: 1978.

"In a Far Country." *Klondike Series.* CBC TV: 1981.

"Mayor Charlotte." *The Winners.* Prod. Laura Phillips. CBC TV: February 1982.

"I Don't Care." *Fraggle Rock.* Prod. Lawrence Merkin. CBC TV and Henson Associates: 1983.

"The Delinquent," "The School Show," "The Séance," "Invasion from Outer Space," and "Twinners." *Edison Twins.* CBC TV: 1983.

"Dungeons and Raccoons," and "All the News that Fits" with bp Nichol. *The Raccoons.* Prod. Kevin Gillis. CBC TV: 1984.

"The Common Factor." *Edison Twins.* CBC TV: 1985.

Film

Fidelity. Script credits. Prod. Allan King. Allan King Associates: 1975.

Radio

"Guy and Jack." *Saskatchewan Writers.* CBC Radio: 1970.

"Fast Forward." *CBC Stage.* CBC Radio: 6 November 1976.

"Tinsel on my Stetson." *Morningside.* CBC Radio: 5–9 March 1984.

"United Artists." *Stereo Theatre.* CBC Radio: May 1984.
>   Part One: "Silent Pictures" 13 May 1984. Originally aired, 11 June 1983.
>   Part Two: "Home Movies" 20 May 1984.
>   Part Three: "Film Noir" 27 May 1984.

"Seeing God." *Vanishing Point.* CBC Radio: 24 May 1985.

"Unconscious." *Sunday Matinee.* CBC Radio: 19 January 1986.

"Dancing with Each Other." *Morningside.* CBC Radio: 13–17 April 1987.

"Canadians in Hollywood." *Stereo Theatre.* CBC Radio: June 1987.
>   Part One: "Mayer in Love" 7 June 1987.
>   Part Two: "Huckleberry Capone" 14 June 1987.
>   Part Three: "King Louis" 21 June 1987.

"Yellow Ribbons." *Stereo Theatre.* CBC Radio: 27 December 1987.

"Family Parties." "Canadian Free Theatre" on *Sunday Matinee.* CBC Radio: 01 May 1988.

"Canadians in Hollywood." *Stereo Theatre.* CBC Radio: July/August 1988.
>   Part One: "Two Cowboys and a Lady" 31 July 1988.
>   Part Two: "Monsoon" 7 August 1988.
>   Part Three: "Kemo Sabe" 14 August 1988.

"Baby Machines." *Aircraft.* CBC Radio: 4 December 1988.

"Ninja Secrets." *Sunday Matinee.* CBC Radio: 10 December 1989.

"Talking to Dolphins." *Studio Theatre.* CBC Radio: 16 October 1992.

"Compañeras." *Studio Theatre.* CBC Radio: 12 March 1993.

"Red Emma: The Opera." Libretto by Carol Bolt, music by Gary Kulesha. *Two New Hours.* CBC Radio: 10 March 1996.

Selected Other Writing

"Anger, Tears and History." Unpublished, undated. Available at Library and Archives Canada (Carol Bolt Fonds: MG 31.D89: File 37.8).

"*Daganawida*: the Birth of a Canadian Play." *Canadian Books for Children.* 4.3 (1970): 5–11.

"Making Connections." Rev. of *The Penguin Book of Modern Drama. Books in Canada.* April 1985: 21–22.

Drama in the Classroom. Teachers' Resource Guide: Playwrights on Tour Program. Toronto: Playwrights Union of Canada, 1986.

"Dot Dot Dot… or Some Notes on Notation in Play Scripts." *Open Letter.* (Spring 1987): 51–56.

"Female Leads: Searching for Feminism in the Theatre." *Canadian Forum 67.* (June–July 1987): 37–40.

"Introduction to 'Two Cowboys and a Lady.'" *Studio Theatre.* CBC Radio: 31 July 1988.

"Introduction to 'Monsoon.'" *Studio Theatre.* CBC Radio: 07 August 1988.

"Rotters and Cads." Rev. of *Moo; Toronto, Mississippi/Jewel* and *Memories of You. Books in Canada.* (March 1990): 37–38.

Red Emma: The Opera. Libretto by Carol Bolt and music by Gary Kulesha. Dir. David William. Toronto: Canadian Opera Company at Harbourfront, 28–29 November, 1–3 December 1995.

"One Word at a Time: Playwright Carol Bolt reflects on the art of becoming an opera librettist." *Opera Canada* 37.1 (Spring 1996): 12–13.

"The Zimmerman Report: Canadian Women in the Theatre: A Statistical Survey." *CanPlay.* July/August 1996: 7–8.

Who Asked Us Anyway?: A Collection of Plays Celebrating the First 20 Years of the Labrador Creative Arts Festival. Edited and Introduction by Carol Bolt. Goose Bay: Labrador School Board, 1998.

Interviews

Anon. "University of Toronto's Writer-in-Residence." *The Varsity* 21 November 1977.

Doty, Anne. "Interview with Carol Bolt." *York Theatre Journal* 3.2 (April 1974): 40–46.

Lister, Rota. "An Interview with Carol Bolt." *World Literature Written in English* 17 (1978): 144–53.

Poole, Fiona. "Carol Bolt and *Shelter.*" *The Varsity* 29 November 1974.

Rudakoff, Judith. "Carol Bolt." *Fair Play. Twelve Women Speak: Conversations with Canadian Playwrights.* Ed. Judith Rudakoff and Rita Much. Toronto: Simon & Pierre, 1990. 175–89.

Steinberg, Matt. "Bolt, Upright with *Famous.*" *The Theatre News Pickering* 4.1 (1998): 20–21.

Zimmerman, Cynthia. "Carol Bolt." In *The Work: Conversations with English-Canadian Playwrights.* Ed. Zimmerman and Robert Wallace. Toronto: Coach House Press, 1982. 264–76.

Selected CBC Radio Interviews

"What About Us?" *Tuesday Night.* Panel with Carol Bolt and others. 8 August 1972.

As It Happens. Interview with Carol Bolt. 18 February 1974.

The Entertainment Section. Panel with Carol Bolt, Margaret Atwood, and others. 24 August 1976.

Festive Theatre. Panel Discussion on alternate theatre in Canada with Carol Bolt and others. 13 March 1978.

Authors. Joyce Davidson. Carol Bolt and Tom Hendry. 17 August 1978.

Variety Tonight. Vicky Gabereau. 8 June 1983.

Dayshift. Erika Ritter. 14 January 1986.

Two New Hours. Carol Bolt and Gary Kulesha are interviewed for the radio premiere of *Red Emma.* 10 March 1996.

SECONDARY SOURCES – Selected Articles and Reviews

Anon. "Carol Bolt: Queen of Our Playwrights." *Scene Changes II* 6 (July/August 1974): 13–14.

Anon. "Play Panel at Glendon." *Toronto Star* 23 February 1976.

Anon. "Playwrights Meeting to Talk about Union." *The Globe and Mail* 18 March 1977.

Adilman, Sid. "*One Night Stand* a Movie Project." *Toronto Star* 1 June 1977.

Bemrose, John. "Hymns to Anarchy." *Maclean's* 108:50 (11 December 1995): 71.

Bennett, Susan. "Diversity and Voice: A Celebration of Canadian Women Writing for Performance." *On-Stage and Off-Stage: English Canadian Drama in Discourse.* Ed. Albert-Reiner Glaap and Rolf Althof. St. John's: Breakwater, 1996. 60–73.

Bessai, Diane. "Documentary Theatre in Canada: An Investigation into Questions and Backgrounds." *Canadian Drama* 6.1 (1980): 9–21.

———. "Three Plays by Carol Bolt." *Canadian Drama* 4 (Spring 1978): 64–67.

———. "The Regionalism of Canadian Drama." *Canadian Literature* 85 (1980): 7–20.

———. *Playwrights of Collective Creation.* Toronto: Simon & Pierre, 1992. 56–63.

Brissenden, Connie. Rev. of *Escape Entertainment. Arts National* CBC Radio: 6 January 1981.

Chapman, Geoff. "Carol Bolt's New Play Destined to be *Famous.*" *Toronto Star* 27 November 1997.

Cohen, Nathan. "*Daganawida* Needs Some More Work." *Toronto Star* 14 January 1970.

Conlogue, Ray. "Bolt Film Spoof too Close to Subject." Rev. of *Escape Entertainment. The Globe and Mail* 5 January 1981.

———. "Blyth's Hit also its Worthiest Drama." Review of *Love or Money. The Globe and Mail* 18 July 1981.

———. "Five Playwrights Off to Australia." *The Globe and Mail* 1 May 1980.

———. "Hendry: a Great Pulpit for Letting Loose." *The Globe and Mail* 20 March 1982.

Conolly, L.W, ed. "Carol Bolt: *Buffalo Jump.*" *Canadian Drama and the Critics.* Vancouver: Talonbooks, 1995. 99–106.

Cook, Michael. "Ignored Again." *Canadian Theatre Review* (Spring 1976): 87–91.

Corbeil, Carole. "Carol Bolt Escapes Into Romance." *The Globe and Mail* 3 January 1981.

———. "Six Women Asked for a Work of Passion." *The Globe and Mail* 13 January 1986.

Czarnecki, Mark. "*Escape Entertainment.*" *Maclean's* 23 February 1981.

Desjardins, Lucie. "Canadian Playwright Carol Bolt." *The Archivist* 16.5 (1989): 16.

Entz, Marvin. "Making Movies Canadian Style." *Georgia Straight.* January 1988.

Erdelyi, Joseph. "Canadian Plays Funny." *Ottawa Citizen* 23 October 1975.

Filewod, Allan. *Collective Encounters: Documentary Theatre in English Canada.* Toronto: U of T Press, 1987.

Frankel, Oz. "Whatever Happened to 'Red Emma?' Emma Goldman, from Alien Rebel to American Icon." *Journal of American History* 83.3 (December 1996): 903–43.

Fraser, John. "The Bolt Scenario: Keep Them Coming." *The Globe and Mail.* 14 March 1977.

————. "*One Night Stand:* Better and Better." *The Globe and Mail* 11 April 1977.

————. "Plays a Pair of Winning Caricatures." *The Globe and Mail* 23 October 1975.

————. "Playwrights Unite for More Exposure." *The Globe and Mail* 12 May 1977.

French, William. "Literary Tours Opportunity to Study Word and World." *The Globe and Mail* 24 April 1979.

Garnet, Gale. "Canadian Actors: High Praise and Low Pay." *Toronto Star* 23 November 1971.

Gibson, Florence. "Carol Bolt." http://section15.ca/features/people/2003/10/09/carol_bolt/.

Godfrey, Stephen. "*One Night Stand.*" *The Globe and Mail* 8 March 1978.

Gould, Allan. "Ready When You Are, C.B." *Radio Guide* June 1983: 8–10.

Groberman, Michael. "Outdated Play Berated." *Vancouver Sun* 22–29 January 1988.

Guran, Martha. "Theatre Thrills the Young." *Toronto Star* 9 February 1974.

Hunt, Rosemary. "Reviews/Comptes Rendus: 'Who Asked Us Anyway?: A Collection of Plays Celebrating the First Twenty Years of the Labrador Creative Arts Festival.'" *Theatre Research in Canada* 21:2 (Spring 2000): 67–69.

Hutcheon, Linda, George Elliot Clarke. "Opera in Canada: A Conversation." *Journal of Canadian Studies* 35.3 (Fall 2000): 184–201.

James, Noah. "Close Up: The Queen Bee of Canadian Playwrights." *Miss Chatelaine* January 1978: 16, 17.

Johnson, Brian. "Hard-luck Play Still Subtle Mix of Humour, Terror." Rev. of *One Night Stand. The Globe and Mail* 3 August 1978.

Johnston, Denis. *Up the Mainstream: the Rise of Toronto's Alternative Theatres.* Toronto: U of T Press, 1991.

Kaplan, Jon. "*One Night Stand*: Theatre Preview." *NOW* (March 2001).

Kareda, Urjo. "*Buffalo Jump*: A Play on Depression Misery." *Toronto Star* 19 May 1972.

————. "Canadian Play's Author a Theatrical Nationalist." *Toronto Star* 18 May 1972.

————. "Carol Bolt Play is Delightful." Review of *Finding Bumble. Toronto Star* 3 May 1975.

————. "Free Theatre's *Red Emma* a Wonderful, Disciplined Play." *Toronto Star* 21 February 1974.

————. "Fresh and Attractive Play Tours Schools." Rev. of *Cyclone Jack. Toronto Star* November 1972.

————. "In Review: Toronto." Rev. of *Red Emma. Opera News* 60.12 (March 1996): 43.

————. "New Political Play Hooks Audience." Rev. of *Maurice. Toronto Star* 3 April 1974.

———. "Theatre Conference a Bewildering Misadventure." *Toronto Star* 5 March 1975.

———. "A Truly Canadian Comedy Explodes with Wit." Rev. of *Shelter. Toronto Star* 22 November 1974.

Kirby, Blake. "CBC Shows Skill in Switching Play to Screen." Review of screen version of *Red Emma. The Globe and Mail* 2 January 1976.

Kinch, Martin. "Canadian Theatre: In for the Long Haul." *This Magazine* 10, no. 5–6 (November/December 1976).

Knelman, Martin. "Shooting Games." Rev. of *Escape Entertainment. Saturday Night* 96.3 (March 1981): 57–58.

———. "One Night Standout." *Canadian Magazine* (4 March 1978): 8.

———. "One Night Standout: Alternate Theatre's Carol Bolt Brings a Teasing, Scary Thriller to CBC-TV." *The Canadian* 1 October 1977.

———. "Vocal Gymnastics from GBS." Rev. of *Desparados. Saturday Night* 92.10 (December 1977): 98–99.

Ledoux, Paul. "Appreciation: A Star in the Firmament of Canadian Theatre." *The Globe and Mail* 30 November 2000.

Leggatt, Alexander. "Drama." *University of Toronto Quarterly* 47:4 (Summer 1978): 367–77.

"Letter to the Editor." Signed by Hrant Alianak, Carol Bolt, Alix Dolgoy, Miro Kinch, Des McAnuff, and 25 Others. *The Globe and Mail* 27 March 1982.

Louise Bresky reviews *One Night Stand. Arts National.* CBC Radio: Toronto. 15 January 1979.

———. "Canadian Plays are as Good as Anywhere. Admit It. It Won't Hurt." *The Globe and Mail* 3 December 1977.

Littler, William. "Canadian Opera's *Emma* Blessed with Good Cast." *Toronto Star* 29 November 1995.

Mallet, Gina. "Bethune Play Reduces His Sound and Fury." Rev. of *Bethune. Toronto Star* 1 September 1976.

———. "New Carol Bolt Play Launched Too Soon." Rev. of *Desparados. Toronto Star* 6 October 1977.

———. "Play Demands its Audience Try to Escape." Rev. of *Escape Entertainment. Toronto Star* 8 January 1981.

MacNiven, Elina. "Radio Trilogy is a Labour of Admiration." *The Globe and Mail* 12 May 1984.

McCaughna, David. "Carol Bolt's Wit Undermined." Rev. of *Shelter. Toronto Star* 23 October 1975.

————. "Drama on Student's Wavelength." Rev. of *Cyclone Jack*. *Toronto Star* 5 February 1976.

————. "*Gabe*: a Forceful Portrait of Life Among the Métis." *Toronto Star* 15 February 1973.

McDonald, Larry. "Socialism and the English Canadian Literary Tradition." *Essays on Canadian Writing* 68 (Summer 1999): 213–42.

Messenger, A.P. "*Playwrights in Profile: Carol Bolt*." *Canadian Literature Review* 74 (1977): 90–95.

Mietkiewicz, Henry. "Artists' Rants Give Dial-a-Tirade Callers an Earful." *Toronto Star* 23 October 1993.

Montagnes, A. *Playwrights in Profile: Carol Bolt*. Review in *Performing Arts and Entertainment In Canada* 14:2 (1977): 48–49.

Neil, Boyd. "A Theatre's Growing Pains." *The Globe and Mail* 30 September 1983.

Nett, Emily M. "Protest and Prophecy in Four Canadian Dramas." *Canadian Drama*. 4.1 (1978): 9–19.

Oberst, Paul. "Key Part Missing, Says Fan." *The Globe and Mail* 15 January 1981.

O'Farrell, Lawrence. "Challenging our Assumptions: Playwrights and the Drama Curriculum." *Canadian Journal of Education* 18:3 (Summer 1993): 106.

Osachoff, Margaret Gail. "Riel on Stage." *Canadian Drama* 8.2 (1986): 129–44.

Ouzounian, Richard. "Canadian Theatre's Autumn Season Triggers Déjà-vu." *The Globe and Mail* 28 September 1996.

————. "Comedy-thriller erotic." *Toronto Star* 9 March 2001.

————. "Stage Loses Leading Writer." *Toronto Star* 29 November 2000.

Page, Malcolm. "Confusion and Tedium." Rev. of *Tangleflags* and *My Best Friend is 12 Feet High*. *Canadian Children's Literature* 8 (1977): 142–43.

Poole, Elissa. "*Emma* Falls Prey to Scoring." *The Globe and Mail* 30 November 1995.

————. "Music Review: *Red Emma*." *The Globe and Mail* 20 November 1995.

Pope, Charles. "In Review: *Shelter* and *Surprise, Surprise*." *Scene Changes* 3.11 (November 1975–January 1976): 16–17.

Porter, Mackenzie. "Some Patrons Take Cue from Title to Escape." Rev. of *Escape Entertainment*. *The Sun* 22 January 1981.

Prentice, Bill. "Bolt Heads Off in a New Direction for the Dramatic Series on Mayer." *Broadcast Week* 12:10 (6 June 1987).

Raeburn, Alan. Rev. of *Famous* by Carol Bolt. *Theatre News* 4.1 (1998): 20–21.

Rafelman, Rachel. "Backstage: Canadian Playwrights Come Out of the Warehouse." *Flare Magazine* 32.3 (November 1979).

Rasky, Frank. "Carol Bolt at Redlight: Playwright Shows Pioneer Spirit." *Toronto Star* 14 March 1977.

Redfern, Jon. "The Case for Children's Scripts." *Canadian Theatre Review* (Spring 1976): 36–39.

Renzetti, Elizabeth. "Capitalizing on the Red Feminist." *The Globe and Mail* 25 November 1995.

Rubin, Don. Ed. *Canadian Theatre History.* Toronto: Copp Clark Ltd., 1996.

Sanderson, Vicky. "Four Tries, Four Successes in Marathon Theatre Evening." Rev. of *Love of Life. The Globe and Mail* 13 July 1981.

Sarkar, E. "*Playwrights in Profile: Carol Bolt.*" *World Literature Written in English* 16.2 (1977): 366–67.

Schallenberg, Gary. "*Icetime,* Carol Bolt." Rev. of *Icetime. Canadian Children's Literature* 57–58 (1990): 97–99.

Scott, Shelley. "Critical Hysteria: *Famous* by Carol Bolt." In *The Violent Woman as a New Theatrical Character Type: Cases from Canadian Drama.* Lewiston: Edwin Mellen Press, 2007: 17–39.

Smith, Patricia Keeney. "The Various Talents of Carol Bolt." *The Canadian Forum* 63 (April 1983): 18.

Smith, Stephen. "*Harvest*: a Troubled Work that Hasn't Met Ambitions." *The Kingston Whig-Standard* 29 June 1989.

Souchotte, Sandra. Introduction to *Playwrights in Profile: Carol Bolt.* Toronto, Playwrights Co-op, 1976. 7–13.

Sullivan, Rosemary. "Writing Lives" in *Writing Life: Celebrated Canadian and International Authors on Writing and Life.* Ed. Constance Rooke. Toronto: McClelland and Stewart, 2006, 367–80.

Sumi, Glenn. "*Famous* Walks Exploitation Line." *NOW* 20–26 November 1997.

Taylor, Kate. "Playwright Helped Canadian Theatre Find New Directions." *The Globe and Mail* 29 November 2000.

———. "*Famous* Holds Mirror up to Narcissism and Draws a Blank." *The Globe and Mail* 27 November 1997.

Wagner, Vit. "Something Horrific this Way Comes." Rev. of *Famous. Toronto Star* 20 November 1997.

———. "*Red Emma:* Fiery Passions and Heroic Struggles of Anarchist Visionary Emma Goldman Inspire Intimate Opera that is Right Story for Now." *Toronto Star* 25 November 1995.

———. "Play asks a BIG one." Rev. of *But the Universe is a Green Dragon. Toronto Star* 11 December 1988.

———. "Dragon Adventure Aims at Cosmic Harmony." *Toronto Star* 2 December 1988.

Walkom, Tom. "They're Writing a Musical About Quebec's Maurice Duplessis." *Toronto Star* 23 July 1973.

Wallbanger, Irma. "*Buffalo Jump*: A Vibrant Theatre Experience." *The Ontarian* 18 March 1975.

Wasserman, Jerry. "Books in review: *Checking the Baggage* and *Escape Entertainment*." *Canadian Literature* 101 (Summer 1984): 91–93.

Whittaker, Herbert. "Bolt's *Bethune* Intricate and Full of Insight." *The Globe and Mail* 1 September 1976.

———. "*Daganawida*: Patchwork but Admirable." *The Globe and Mail* 14 January 1970.

———. "An Ingenious *Buffalo Jump*." *The Globe and Mail* 19 May 1972.

———. "Plays for Teens Sound Training for Playwrights." Rev. of *Cyclone Jack*. *The Globe and Mail* 19 March 1973.

———. "*Red Emma* a Bouncy Little Musical." *The Globe and Mail* 25 February 1974.

———. "Rock Musical about Maurice Duplessis Engaging, but Pulls No Punches." *The Globe and Mail* 3 April 1974.

Zimmerman, Cynthia. "Carol Bolt: Making Issues Entertaining." *Playwriting Women: Female Voices in English Canada*. Toronto: Simon & Pierre, 1994. 29–58.

———. Carol Bolt." *The Dictionary of Literary Biography, Volume 60: Canadian Writers since 1960*. Ed. W.H. New. Columbia, S.C. Bruccoli Clark, 1987: 16–19.

About the Editor

Cynthia Zimmerman has been a highly regarded commentator on Canadian playwriting and the voice of women on the Canadian stage over the course of her career at Glendon College, York University, where she is a professor in the English department.

A previous book review editor of the international journal *Modern Drama* and a member of its advisory board, Zimmerman has authored or co-authored a number of books, including *Playwriting Women: Female Voices in English Canada*, and produced many articles, chapters, and public papers. She edited the successful anthology *Taking the Stage*, as well as *The Betty Lambert Reader*, both for Playwrights Canada Press. In 2008 she completed the last of the three volumes of *Sharon Pollock: Collected Works*.

She says that working on the Bolt collection has been a special pleasure: "It has been a privilege to be in such close contact with her writings and to feel, at times, her presence once again. I am honoured to have had the opportunity to celebrate and promote the legacy of this remarkable woman, Carol Bolt."

Carol Bolt
(1941–2000)